Penalties of Empire: Capital Trials in Colonial Hong Kong

'Dr Munn is a distinguished scholar in the legal history of Hong Kong. This impressive work focuses on the administration of justice in capital cases in the context of the conditions of the society at the time. His account of events and people is lively and masterly. His observations and insights are illuminating and perceptive. This outstanding book deserves to be widely read.'

—**The Honourable Andrew Li Kwok Nang**, First Chief Justice of the Hong Kong SAR (1997–2010)

'This book is an extraordinary attempt to approach European colonial culture from a fresh perspective by scrutinising the work that courts did. By excavating the judicial archives, Chris Munn gives us an entirely new account of how colonial justice both worked and failed to achieve its aims.'

—**Timothy Brook**, author of *The Price of Collapse: The Little Ice Age and the Fall of Ming China*

'In this richly detailed exploration of nine capital trials chosen from among the hundreds that took place in Hong Kong between 1844 and 1993, Chris Munn provides a stimulating exploration of British colonial rule. Authoritative and engagingly written, *Penalties of Empire* takes the reader into the heart of some of the most controversial episodes in Hong Kong's modern history.'

—**Robert Bickers**, University of Bristol

'We must have a procedure – if we are going to hang anyone – that is just,' said Chief Justice Sir Francis Piggott in 1909, on discovering that Chinese accused of murder were being denied interpretation in Hong Kong's courts. Due process, no matter how costly or inconvenient, was 'one of the penalties of empire,' he declared.

Penalties of Empire explores how judges, juries, and lawyers strove to deliver justice during the 150 years when the death penalty was in force in Hong Kong. Nine main chapters focus on key capital trials in the first century of British rule. Among the cases are piracies, assassinations, and crimes of passion and desperation. These chapters describe the proceedings in court and the participants involved. They also explore the debates surrounding each case and the exercise or denial of mercy by governors. Two final chapters discuss the decline of the death penalty after World War II, its suspension after 1966, and the controversies leading to its formal abolition in 1993. *Penalties of Empire* traces the evolution of criminal justice at its highest levels. It also offers a prism for understanding some of the broader forces at work in Hong Kong's history.

Penalties of Empire

Penalties of Empire

Capital Trials in Colonial Hong Kong

Christopher Munn

HKU PRESS
香港大學出版社

Hong Kong University Press
The University of Hong Kong
Pok Fu Lam Road
Hong Kong
https://hkupress.hku.hk

ISBN 978-988-8876-88-4 (*Hardback*)

British Library Cataloguing-in-Publication Data
A catalogue record for this book is available from the British Library.

Digitally printed

In memory of my father

Patrick Munn

1935–2020

Contents

Maps and Tables

Abbreviations, Conventions, and Caveats

CBE	Commander of the Order of the British Empire
CM	*China Mail*
CMG	Companion of the Order of St Michael and St George
CO	Colonial Office
ExCo	Executive Council
FCO	Foreign and Commonwealth Office
FOC	*Friend of China*
HKDP	*Hongkong Daily Press*
HKGG	*Hong Kong Government Gazette*
HKH	*Hong Kong Hansard*
HKLJ	*Hong Kong Law Journal*
HKLR	Hong Kong Law Reports
HKPRO	Hong Kong Public Records Office
HKR	*Hongkong Register*
HKRS	Hong Kong Record Series
HKSP	*Hong Kong Sessional Papers*
HKT	*Hongkong Telegraph*
HKWP	*Hongkong Weekly Press*
ICAC	Independent Commission Against Corruption
ICCPR	International Covenant on Civil and Political Rights

JCPC	Judicial Committee of the Privy Council
JP	Justice of the Peace
KC	King's Counsel
KSDN	*Kung Sheung Daily News*
KSEN	*Kung Sheung Evening News*
LN	Legal Notice
MBE	Member of the Order of the British Empire
MC	Military Cross
MP	Member of Parliament
OBE	Officer of the Order of the British Empire
OCM	*Overland China Mail*
OFOC	*Overland Friend of China*
QC	Queen's Counsel
SAR	Special Administrative Region
SCMP	*South China Morning Post*
TNA	The National Archives (Kew, London, UK)
UK	United Kingdom
UKPC	United Kingdom Privy Council
US	United States
WTYP	*Wa Tsz Yat Po*

Notes:

1. All currency is in Hong Kong dollars unless otherwise stated.
2. 'Secretary of State' refers to the Secretary of State for War and the Colonies (up to 1854), the Secretary of State for the Colonies (1854–1966), the Secretary of State for Commonwealth Affairs (1966–1968), or the Secretary of State for Foreign and Commonwealth Affairs (1968–), unless otherwise stated.
3. Except for minor changes in punctuation and capitalization to aid comprehension, variations in spelling and in romanization of Chinese names have been left intact in the quotations.
4. This book contains derogatory and offensive quotations about certain ethnic groups and classes of people. These quotations have been included because they are necessary to an understanding of some of the attitudes that underlay the administration of the law in colonial Hong Kong.
5. The People's Republic of China regards the British administration of Hong Kong, 1841–1997 as an occupation of Chinese sovereign territory resulting from a series of unequal treaties, not as a colony under British sovereignty. The British government, however, treated Hong Kong as a Crown colony, an integral part of its colonial empire. It is almost impossible to discuss Hong Kong's political and legal history under British administration without reference to the words 'colony' 'colonist' or 'colonial'. The terms have therefore been left in where they arise in quotations or where they form a necessary part of the narrative or explanation.

1

Introduction

'Penalties of Empire'

On 22 October 1908 an altercation took place on the Peak Tram, the funicular railway linking urban Hong Kong to the Hill District reserved for Europeans and their servants. Koo Tung (a 'shop coolie') and a friend were on their way to collect a debt. A man in white livery sitting behind them stretched his legs and muddied Koo's clothes. Words were exchanged, and when the tram reached the Peak the man challenged Koo to a fight. Koo declined and he and his friend hurried on their way. Half a mile on, near the Peak Church, they joined some of Koo's clansmen and again encountered the man in white. He called out other men from houses nearby and they beat Koo to death with bamboo poles. Three of them, 'sedan chair coolies' employed by Europeans, were charged with his murder. They were tried a few weeks later by the Chief Justice, Sir Francis Piggott, and a jury of seven Europeans; a Japanese juror with poor English was excused. Two of the accused, Li Shek-pang and Hung Loi, were found guilty of the lesser offence of manslaughter. The third, Kwok Leung, was acquitted.[1]

The verdict was typical enough for a case the newspapers described as a 'clan fight', a 'tribal row', a 'coolie affray'. The accused were Hoklo from north-eastern Guangdong, reputedly a 'rougher, wilder set of men than the Cantonese' and speaking a different dialect.[2] The witnesses against them were Cantonese from nearby Xiangshan County. The jury struggled to make sense of confusing prosecution evidence but took only fourteen minutes to return verdicts of manslaughter. This avoided the risk of sending innocent men to their deaths and

1. *SCMP*, 30 October and 6, 18, 20, and 26 November 1908 and 6–8 January 1909; *HKT*, 23 October 1908; *HKWP*, 9 January 1909.
2. James Dyer Ball, *Things Chinese, or Notes Connected with China* (Hong Kong: Kelly & Walsh Ltd, 1903), 346.

saved time on a case in which they probably had little interest. Murder carried the death penalty and required a unanimous verdict. Manslaughter needed only a majority, and the punishment could be anything from life imprisonment to a fine. It was now the judge's task to hand down sentences.

Just as Chief Justice Piggott was about to sentence Li and Hung, their counsel, Horace Calthrop, rose to apply for a point of law to be referred to the Full Court – a sitting of both judges of the Supreme Court. None of the evidence had been interpreted to the accused, he said. The Hoklo dialect was so different from Cantonese they could barely understand the Chinese witnesses, let alone those who testified in English. No one, said Calthrop, should be convicted without hearing the evidence. The prosecutor, the Attorney General, William Rees-Davies, interjected that in Cyprus (where he had recently served) the courts heard evidence in Greek and Turkish, and it was not interpreted to the accused if he was represented by counsel. A similar practice had taken root in Hong Kong, where those on trial for murder were assisted by a barrister at public expense. Providing an interpreter as well would, said Rees-Davies, be 'opening up a tremendous precedent'. If, for example, 'you have three prisoners all speaking different dialects the evidence of each witness would have to be interpreted into all three dialects'.

That, remarked Piggott, was 'one of the penalties of Empire'.

The Full Court – Piggott and Henry Gompertz, the Puisne (or ordinary) Judge – heard the point of law four weeks later. Calthrop argued that defendants must understand the evidence against them. Otherwise, they could not challenge it or assist counsel in cross-examination. He cited English cases in which judges had ordered the acquittal of deaf defendants unable to follow proceedings. Rees-Davies replied that it was a matter of practice, not law. He produced an affidavit by the interpreter, Li Hong-mi. 'I have read it,' said Piggott. 'Its effect is that in murder cases, the most serious cases, the rule of translation is to be the slightest.' The law required the accused to be present at trial, he said. But if they did not understand the evidence they might as well be absent. Rees-Davies again raised the practice in Cyprus.

> **Piggott** — If we decide against you in this case, I may say that the Courts in the other Colony will follow our practice.
>
> **Rees-Davies** — I doubt it.
>
> **Piggott** — If we have an empire of many nationalities we must have a procedure – if we are going to hang anyone – that is just.[3]

Piggott and Gompertz quashed the convictions. 'In the trial of human beings for crimes, the law of England requires the utmost consideration for the accused, and the most scrupulous exactness in the conduct of the proceedings,' said Piggott: 'time and money

3. *HKDP*, 4 February 1909.

are nothing compared with liberty and life'. The judgment, *R v Kwok Leung*, has since been cited around the world as an authority on the right of the accused to interpretation.[4] Even so, Piggott had to remind the interpreter to tell Li and Hung they were discharged and could leave the court. Against protests by Calthrop, Rees-Davies then announced that he would file fresh indictments for murder against them. They were rearrested on leaving the court and committed for trial the following week. The case was, however, abandoned because material witnesses were absent.[5]

By 'penalties of Empire' Chief Justice Piggott did not mean the punishments imposed by the courts but rather the duty to dispense justice to the millions of people who lived under British imperial rule, whatever inconveniences that might entail. It was part of what Rudyard Kipling described as the 'white man's burden'. Piggott thought he was carrying more than his fair share of that burden. He grumbled about his unbearable workload and the strain of Hong Kong's sultry climate: a day in court left him 'dripping with perspiration and absolutely exhausted'.[6] He upset European businessmen by finding for their Chinese counterparties. He received no thanks for championing the rights of the accused at a time when governors wanted tough justice. His strident criticisms of officials in open court, said one governor, were 'calculated to lower the dignity of the Government in the eyes of the Chinese who do not appreciate our ideas of the mutual relations between the judiciary and the Executive'. Piggott infuriated officials with his incessant complaints. 'The root fact is that the man is a cad and is unable to conceal his nature,' wrote Reginald Stubbs, then a Colonial Office clerk, later a Governor of Hong Kong.[7]

The last straw was Piggott's opposition to reforms to the Full Court intended to rectify the anomaly whereby the Chief Justice, who had a casting vote, effectively decided appeals from his own judgments. The government proposed adding a temporary third judge, the Judge of the British Supreme Court in Shanghai, who would visit Hong Kong twice a year to sit on the court when it heard appeals in civil cases. That, protested Piggott, would do

---

4. *SCMP*, 4 and 26 February 1909; *HKWP*, 1 March 1909; *R v Kwok Leung and Others* (1909) 4 HKLR 161. Anna Koo, 'Truth through Court Interpreters', *International Journal of Evidence and Proof* 13 (2009): 212–224. Celia Brown-Blake, 'Fair Trial, Language and the Right to Interpretation,' *International Journal on Minority and Group Rights* 13 (2006): 391–412.
5. Rees-Davies cited *R v Drury* (1849) 3 Car & K. 193, which held that, if a verdict was reversed because of a procedural error, the accused could not plead autrefois acquit (double jeopardy). Calthrop wrote to Members of Parliament and the Colonial Office objecting to the fresh indictment as 'absolutely illegal'. As a result of an accident in November 1909 Calthrop died near the site of the Peak Murder. After dinner at a friend's house, he set off on foot to his house on Conduit Road after missing the last Peak tram. He tripped into a water channel, falling to his death. He had arrived in Hong Kong in 1904 after practice in the Gold Coast, a British colony in West Africa. Calthrop to Cox, 28 February and 4 March 1909, CO 129/364, 171–178; Lugard to Secretary of State, 25 March 1909, TNA CO 129/355, 428–434; *SCMP*, 8 November 1909.
6. *SCMP*, 7 June 1907; Piggott to Lugard, 14 April 1908, CO 129/347, 167. See Peter Wesley-Smith, 'Sir Francis Piggott: Chief Justice in His Own Cause', *HKLJ*, Vol. 12 (1982): 260–292.
7. Lugard to Crewe, 15 July 1909, CO 129/357, 120–143.

nothing to relieve the Supreme Court's growing caseload, which required a *permanent* third judge. Worse still for him, the Shanghai judge, who had seniority over Piggott, would now preside over the expanded Full Court. Piggott publicly criticized the reforms. In response, the government enacted legislation in 1910 empowering the Governor to require a judge to retire after the age of sixty (Piggott was fifty-eight). When Piggott baulked at being 'discharged like a Chinese coolie' the Governor pulled out an order by the King stating that it was his pleasure that Piggott should cease to hold office on 30 April 1912.[8] Piggott was replaced by Rees-Davies, who proved to be a more compliant Chief Justice.

This book explores how the British authorities struggled to administer justice to the inhabitants of a small colony in a region of political turmoil, widespread poverty, and high crime rates – in short, how they tried to discharge, and occasionally evade, Piggott's 'penalties of Empire'. The book examines nine capital trials in early British Hong Kong, the first in 1857, and the last in 1934. After discussing the decline in capital punishment after World War II, it concludes with an account of the events leading to its abolition in the final years of British rule.

The death penalty in colonial Hong Kong

The death penalty was in force in Hong Kong from 1844 until its formal abolition in 1993. The last execution took place in 1966, a year after the suspension of the death penalty for murder in Great Britain. Some 750 capital cases involving an estimated 1,500 defendants were tried by the civilian courts in the 122 years while the death penalty was in use. During that time the courts pronounced sentence of death on 573.[9] Of these, 375 persons (373 men and 2 women) were executed by hanging: the cases are summarized in **Table 1.** Most of the remaining 198 had their sentences reduced by the Governor in Council to penalties ranging from probation to life imprisonment. In the early years of British rule a further 185 or so men were sentenced to 'death recorded', mostly for non-fatal piracies: this invariably

8. After a spell in Peking as constitutional adviser to Yuan Shikai, Piggott, short of money, returned to Hong Kong in 1913 to practise law: at this time there was no ban on former judges practising at the Bar. In May 1914 a coughing fit drove a blood clot to his brain. His doctor advised him to return to England. He was now so indebted that the government provided £50 out of a charitable fund for his passage. In 1922 he was adjudged bankrupt in England, with debts of £15,000. He died in 1925. Lugard to Harcourt, 4 October and 29 December 1911, CO 129/380, 221–232 and 381, 522–549; Piggott to Crown Agents, 23 March 1912, CO 129/394, 282; *HKH*, 15 April 1912; May to Harcourt, 15 June 1914, CO 129/411, 353–357; Official Receiver to Colonial Office, 3 August 1922, CO 129/478, 141–149.
9. These figures exclude twenty-four men sentenced to death (twenty-one of whom were executed) in War Crimes trials held in Hong Kong in 1946–1949, and the unknown numbers executed during the Japanese occupation in 1941–1945.

Table 1: Death Sentences by the British Hong Kong Civilian Courts, 1841–1966

Years	Death sentences		Hanged	Remarks
	Murder	Other Crimes		
1844–1845	4	4	4	1 murder sentence by the Court of Justice with Criminal and Admiralty Jurisdiction; 1 shooting with intent to murder; 3 robbery with violence
1846–1850	10	30	22	30 aggravated piracy (13 hanged)
1851–1855	15	0	10	
1856–1860	20	4	11	3 aggravated piracy (1 hanged); 1 burglary with violence
1861–1865	52	5	45	5 aggravated piracy (4 hanged); 36 murders were piracies
1866–1870	14	17	21	17 aggravated piracy (11 hanged)
1871–1875	18	0	6	
1876–1880	10	0	7	
1881–1885	2	0	1	
1886–1890	2	0	0	
1891–1895	4	0	4	
1896–1900	16	0	12	
1901–1905	17	0	11	
1906–1910	22	0	9	
1911–1915	10	0	6	
1916–1920	27	0	22	
1921–1925	22	0	16	1 woman hanged (1923)
1926–1930	17	19	33	16 aggravated piracy (16 hanged); 6 murders were piracies
1931–1935	10	0	7	
1936–1940	41	1	24	1 aggravated piracy (1 hanged); 1 woman hanged (1940)
1941	15	0	4	
1946–1950	41	7	36	5 treason (5 hanged); 2 aggravated piracy; 2 (1 treason, 1 murder) convicted by the British Military Administration's General Military Court
1951–1955	34	2	31	2 unlawful use of firearms (2 hanged)
1956–1960	33	0	24	
1961–1965	26	0	8	
1966	2	0	1	
Totals	**484**	**89**	**375**	

Notes:

1. 'Death recorded' judgments (leading to automatic commutation) are not included.
2. Those not hanged fell into four categories: (1) sentence commuted (the majority); (2) free pardon; (3) the 3 men convicted of robbery with violence in 1845 who committed suicide in their cell.
3. The hangings for 1936–1940 exclude a probable hanging for 1 murder conviction in 1940, of Li Hung-fui for the murder of a European during the robbery of a jewellery shop, likely to have taken place in 1941 after an unsuccessful petition to the Privy Council; his hanging cannot be confirmed from sources.
4. The fate of 6 sentenced to death for murder in 1941, one of them a woman, cannot be verified from Executive Council minutes or official statistics, which are no longer extant. It is probable, from the mercy recommendations from juries reported in the press, and from the absence of the usual press reports of hangings, that at least 5 of the sentences, including that of the woman, were commuted.

Sources: ExCo Minutes; annual Supreme Court Statistics and Gaol Returns (*Hong Kong Blue Books*, *HKGG*); newspapers; notebook of capitally convicted prisoners, 1956–1971, HKPRO HKRS519-1.

resulted in commutation. From 1967 to 1993, judges handed down 264 death sentences: all of them were commuted to imprisonment.[10]

Hong Kong largely followed English law on capital crimes. Unlike some British colonies in Asia, including the Straits Settlements and Ceylon, Hong Kong did not adopt the Indian Penal Code of 1860, a simplified codification of English criminal law which differed from English law in its treatment of homicide.[11] Under local enactments, the law of England in effect on 5 April 1843 was in full force in Hong Kong except where 'inapplicable to the local circumstances of the said Colony, or of its inhabitants'.[12] This was the date on which Hong Kong obtained its own legislature. From then on, the Hong Kong government enacted its own laws, known as 'ordinances'. They were passed by a Legislative Council made up of appointed members, most of them officials, and consented to by the Governor. The imperial government could disallow ordinances or legislate for the colony, though it did so rarely.[13] The Governor took advice from an Executive Council, which, from 1896, had a minority of appointed unofficial members. The functions of the councils were set out in Letters Patent and Royal Instructions first issued by the Crown in 1843. These instruments defined the powers of the Governor and required him to review all capital convictions in consultation with his Executive Council ('the Governor in Council').

In the early nineteenth century England was in the process of dismantling the 'Bloody Code', which prescribed capital punishment for some 200 crimes, many of them offences against property. Under this regime, the landed elite maintained authority through a mixture of terror and mercy: more people were sentenced to death in England than in any other European country, but over half of them received pardons and a lesser punishment.[14]

---

10. Mark S. Gaylord and John F. Galliher, 'Death Penalty Politics and Symbolic Law in Hong Kong', *International Journal of the Sociology of Law*, Vol. 22 (1994), Table 3; Commissioner of Correctional Services, *Annual Review* 1993, 14.
11. For example, the Indian Penal Code placed the burden on the prosecution to prove that the accused had intended to kill or inflict serious bodily harm in order for the offence to constitute murder, whereas English law assumed malice aforethought. The doctrine of felony murder, under which in England until 1957 (Hong Kong, 1963) a homicide accidentally committed during the commission of a felony was treated as murder, was not part of the code. The code also allowed a court to impose either death or life transportation (from 1955, life imprisonment) and a fine as a punishment for murder, an option not adopted in the Straits Settlements or Ceylon. Indian Penal Code 1860 s. 300–302. I am indebted to Mitra Sharafi for her guidance on these points.
12. Reformulated by the Application of English Law Ordinance 1966, which, while providing for the common law and the rules of equity to be in force in Hong Kong, 'so far as they may be applicable', specified which pre-1843 English statutes were in force. Ordinances Nos. 15 of 1844, 6 of 1845, 2 of 1846, 12 of 1873, and 2 of 1966.
13. See Norman Miners, 'Disallowance and the Administrative Review of Hong Kong Legislation by the Colonial Office, 1844–1947', *HKLJ*, Vol. 18 (1988): 218–248.
14. See Douglas Hay, 'Property, Authority and the Criminal Law', in Douglas Hay, Peter Linebaugh, John G. Rule, E. P. Thompson, and Cal Winslow, *Albion's Fatal Tree: Crime and Society in Eighteenth-Century England* (Harmondsworth: Penguin Books Ltd, 1977); Simon Devereaux, *Execution, State & Society in England, 1660–1900* (Cambridge University Press, 2023); Leon Radzinowicz, *A History of English Criminal Law and Its Administration from 1750*, Vol. 1, *The Movement for Reform* (London: Stevens & Sons, 1948); House of

By 1843, the number of capital offences had been reduced to about a dozen: murder; attempted murder causing injury; sodomy; bestiality; burglary with violence; robbery with cutting and wounding; piracy with endangering life; arson of houses with people therein or of ships with intent to murder; hanging false lights to cause shipwreck; setting fire to HM ships of war, arsenals, or dockyards; and high treason.[15] By the 1840s usually only murderers were hanged in England; the last hangings for piracy (the first since 1830) took place in 1864 and the last for attempted murder in 1861.

At first, the death penalty was applied widely in Hong Kong. The first three Chinese sentenced to death, in February 1845, were convicted of robbery with violence; they hanged themselves in their cell, to the dismay of some colonists who felt cheated of a chance to teach the Chinese population a 'salutary lesson'.[16] That lesson came three months later with the hanging in July 1845 of Chun Afoon, who was also convicted of a non-fatal crime: cutting and wounding in an attack on the premises of Jardine, Matheson & Co., the Scottish opium merchants. A dozen or so other men were hanged for non-fatal piracy with violence in the 1840s. Most persons convicted of non-fatal capital crimes, however, were spared execution through sentences of 'death recorded' or commutation. This was the outcome of the very first capital sentence imposed by the Hong Kong Supreme Court,[17] in October 1844 on an Irish soldier.[18]

Commons, *Report from the Select Committee on Capital Punishment* (London: His Majesty's Stationery Office, 1931), vii–xv; and Brian P. Block and John Hostettler, *Hanging in the Balance: A History of the Abolition of Capital Punishment in Britain* (Winchester: Waterside Press, 1997).

15. *Report of the Capital Punishment Commission* (London: Eyre and Spottiswoode, 1866), 660.
16. They left inscriptions on their cell wall recording their names and native places, and the hope that Triad Society brethren would avenge their deaths. *FOC*, 26 February 1845; *CM*, 6 March 1845; *HKR*, 4 March 1845.
17. But not the first capital sentence imposed by a British court in Hong Kong. On 4 March 1844 Salvador Lacrase, a seaman on a British ship, was convicted of murdering the ship's mate by the Court of Justice with Criminal and Admiralty Jurisdiction over British subjects in China. The trial was presided over by the Governor, Sir Henry Pottinger, and Lieutenant-Governor, George D'Aguilar, with a twelve-man jury. Established in 1833 in Canton (though never in session there), the court was transferred to Hong Kong in January 1843. Lacrase's sentence was commuted to transportation. The court had earlier been convened on a ship in Hong Kong harbour in 1839 to try five British sailors for offences relating to the killing of a Tsim Sha Tsui villager, Lin Weixi: the alleged murderer was not tried because the grand jury did not find a true bill. Pottinger to Aberdeen, 27 March 1844, CO 129/8, 172–240; *FOC*, 5 and 9 March 1844; *HKR*, 5 March 1844; Elliot to Palmerston, 27 August 1839, in *Correspondence Relating to China* (London: Harrison, 1840), 433; *Chinese Repository* 8, no. 4 (1839–1840): 180–194; *Canton Press*, 17 August 1839.
18. 'The details are such as cannot appear in a public journal,' observed the *Hongkong Register*. John Brennan was convicted of 'bestiality with a bitch'. The jury recommended mercy and Chief Justice Hulme recorded sentence of death, adding that he had no doubt the Governor would commute it to life transportation. Brennan was sent to Van Diemen's Land with nine other convicts. *HKR*, 8 October 1844; ExCo Minutes, 25 October 1844, TNA CO 131/1, 69; Brennan, John, convict record, 1 April 1844–31 January 1846, Archives Office of Tasmania, CON37-1-2, 447.

From 1861, capital punishment in England was restricted to four offences: murder; high treason; piracy with violence; and arson of HM ships, arsenals, or dockyards. This was the last stage in the dismantling of the 'Bloody Code'. Hong Kong followed in 1865 with ordinances limiting the death penalty to the same four offences. The provisions were almost identical to those in the English acts of 1861, except they omitted the power to try murders by British subjects in foreign territories.[19] By coincidence, imperial legislation in 1865 ended Hong Kong's extraterritorial jurisdiction over British subjects in China and Japan by creating a British Supreme Court for China based in Shanghai.[20] Hong Kong's courts nevertheless retained jurisdiction over offences on British ships and piracies on the high seas.

Hong Kong largely continued to follow English reforms on capital punishment, usually with delays. In the troubled conditions of the late 1940s and 1950s the death penalty was also extended to offences against the armed forces under the British Military Administration (1945–1946), and to possession of explosives (1950–1956). The key changes are set out in **Table 2.**

Table 2: Legislation on Capital Punishment in England and Wales and Hong Kong, 1866–1993

Year	England and Wales	Hong Kong	References and Observations
1866		Governor in Council empowered, when commuting a death sentence, to order that the prisoner be publicly flogged.	Suppression of Piracy Ordinances Nos. 9 of 1866 and 1 of 1868: not used; repealed 1901. ***See Chapter 3.***
1868	Abolition of public executions: hangings to take place only within prisons.	From 1893 all hangings take place within Victoria Gaol or, from 1937, Stanley Prison.	Capital Punishment Amendment Act 1868. By administrative measures in Hong Kong until incorporated in the Prisons Ordinance, No. 17 of 1954. ***See Chapter 4.***
1908	Capital punishment of children under 16 years of age prohibited; children convicted of murder to be detained at HM's pleasure.	Adopted in 1909.	Children's Act 1908. Ordinance No. 6 of 1909.

(continued on p. 9)

19. Offences Against the Person Act 1861; Ordinances Nos. 3–10 of 1865.
20. Hong Kong retained extraterritorial jurisdiction over offences committed by British subjects in Macao and, from 1868, offences committed on land by British subjects within six miles of Hong Kong (other than on the mainland of China), extended in 1877 to ten miles. Orders in Council, 9 March 1865, 28 March 1868, and 23 October 1877, *HKGG*, 17 June 1865, 6 June 1868, and 29 December 1877.

Table 2 (continued)

Year	England and Wales	Hong Kong	References and Observations
1922	Infanticide of their new-born babies by mothers with disturbed minds punishable as manslaughter.	Adopted in 1934 on instructions from Secretary of State.	Infanticide Acts 1922, 1938. Ordinances Nos. 37 of 1934 and 2 of 1939.
1931	Capital punishment replaced by life penal servitude for pregnant women convicted of capital offences. (Formerly, sentence of death was arrested until delivery of child.)	Adopted in 1934 on instructions from Secretary of State.	Sentence of Death (Expectant Mothers) Act 1931. Ordinances Nos. 37 of 1934 and 2 of 1939.
1933	Capital punishment of persons under 18 years of age prohibited.	Adopted in 1952.	Children and Young Persons Act 1933. Ordinance No. 29 of 1952.
1947		Death penalty temporarily in force for all participants in armed robberies resulting in death, without the need to prove common intention.	Suppression of Robbery Ordinance, No. 13 of 1947 (not used, expired March 1948). ***See Chapter 11.***
1950		Death penalty for possession of explosives or using arms or explosives without lawful authority, whether or not resulting in death.	Regulation 116-A of the Emergency Regulations, revoked in 1956. ***See Chapter 11.***
1957	Death penalty only for murders in furtherance of theft; by shooting or explosion; to avoid arrest; of police or prison officers, or for repeated murders. New defences of diminished responsibility and loss of self-control under provocation, reducing murder to manslaughter. Killings in furtherance of other offences no longer murder. Suicide pacts reduced from murder to manslaughter.	Partly adopted in 1963, without the restrictions on the use of the death penalty.	Homicide Act 1957. Homicide Ordinance, No. 16 of 1963. ***See Chapter 11.***
1965	Death penalty for murder suspended for five years.		Murder (Abolition of Death Penalty) Act 1965.
1969	Death penalty for murder abolished.		Death penalty abolished in UK for arson in HM dockyards etc. in 1971; for treason and piracy with violence in 1998.
1993		Capital punishment for all offences abolished.	Crimes (Amendment) Ordinance, No. 24 of 1993. ***See Chapter 12.***

The capital trial in Hong Kong

The courts in Hong Kong similarly followed the practice of English courts in existence in 1843, except where inapplicable or modified by legislation.[21] Changing procedures in England were usually adopted in legislation or by reference to rulings by the higher English courts, as in the Peak Murder trial: this came naturally to Hong Kong's judges and lawyers, most of whom had been trained in London. The key legislation, the Criminal Procedure Ordinance 1899, drafted by Chief Justice Sir John Carrington, drew on English practice and the Indictable Offences (Procedure) Ordinance 1891 of British Guiana, which he had also drafted.[22] Hong Kong departed from English practice in some key areas, notably in the composition of juries, the provision of legal aid, and the system of criminal appeals. The courts also relied heavily on interpreters.

Investigations and arrests

If a victim in a capital case was killed and the body found, a post-mortem examination was carried out by a government medical officer, who sent a report to the Coroner. The Coroner, usually a magistrate,[23] decided whether to order an autopsy. If the death was sudden, violent, or suspicious, he had the option of conducting an inquest or 'death enquiry',[24] with or without a jury of three, to find out how the deceased died. If the verdict was death by murder or manslaughter and the suspect was known, the Coroner would issue an arrest warrant; usually, however, such verdicts referred to 'a person or persons unknown'. Where bodies were dumped in the streets or the harbour, the identity of the victim was often also a mystery.

Many culprits escaped justice. Up to the 1950s, people could move freely in and out of Hong Kong by land or sea. The treaties between the UK and China did not provide for the extradition of Chinese fugitives to face trial in Hong Kong.[25] The government got around this by offering rewards or sending gunboats to capture suspects, particularly if the victims were European. In some other cases suspects were tried by Chinese courts for crimes committed in Hong Kong. Within Hong Kong, suspects in domestic homicides or deaths

21. Ordinances Nos. 15 of 1844 s.3, 6 of 1845 s.4, 2 of 1846 s.3, 12 of 1873 s.8, 13 of 1899 s. 10.
22. The British Guiana legislation incorporated existing English statute law and some of the procedural clauses in the Criminal Code (Indictable Offences) Bill in England, which, among other provisions, codified and clarified common law. The bill was not enacted. Report on Ordinance No. 13 of 1899, CO 129/292, 331–336.
23. The separate position of Coroner was abolished in 1888 and restored in 1967. Ordinances Nos. 17 of 1888 and 57 of 1967.
24. The term used for inquests in Hong Kong from 1888 to 1997.
25. The Supplementary Treaty or Treaty of the Bogue 1843, article 9, provided for the rendition of Chinese fugitives from Hong Kong to China, and of British fugitives from China to Hong Kong. Its successor, the Treaty of Tientsin 1858, article 21, provided for the former but was silent on the latter.

from fights were often caught in the act or arrested after a hue and cry: some households and shops kept police whistles for this purpose. In other cases, suspects were found after police investigations, sometimes with the help of rewards and networks of paid informers. The police had wide powers of arrest.[26] Even so, for a variety reasons – intimidation of witnesses, the ease of escape, poor investigative capabilities – detection rates were low up to the 1950s, especially for murders. Through excess zeal, public pressure, corruption, or plain incompetence, the police often got the wrong man. Allegations of fabricated or coerced confessions were common up to the 1970s.

Except for serious offences, or arrests made on a magistrate's warrant, police were required to charge arrested persons and bring them before a magistrate as soon as possible – stipulated as within forty-eight hours in 1890 – or release them on police bail pending their appearance before a magistrate.[27] The period was sometimes extended in times of emergency, for example to fourteen days following the riots of 1956 and 1967.[28] In some cases police made use of longer periods of detention under the Deportation Ordinance to detain suspects. Magistrates had the power to grant bail in murder cases until 1890, although they rarely made use of it.[29]

Committal proceedings

The magistrate conducted a preliminary hearing, also known as committal proceedings, to determine if there was prima facie evidence to commit a person for trial in the Supreme Court. In contrast to the justices of the peace who presided over such proceedings in provincial England, magistrates in Hong Kong were salaried officials. Despite having a wider jurisdiction and greater sentencing powers, early Hong Kong magistrates often lacked the legal qualifications and experience required of stipendiary magistrates in London and other English cities.[30] As in England, they had powers to remand the accused for up to eight days, repeatedly if necessary, to enable witnesses to be produced and time allocated

26. Police in Hong Kong were empowered to arrest without warrant any person charged with any offence, or on reasonable suspicion of guilt of any offence. For the development of these powers, and comparisons with England, see John Rear, 'The Power of Arrest in Hong Kong', *HKLJ*, Vol. 1 (1971): 142–193.
27. The forty-eight-hour limit, adopted from the Summary Jurisdiction Act 1879, was specified in the Magistrates Ordinances Nos. 10 of 1890 s. 27 and 41 of 1932 s. 26, then in Police Force Ordinances Nos. 2 of 1936 s. 2(3) and 41 of 1948 s. 47. See also Ordinances Nos. 12 of 1844 s. 11 and 9 of 1862 s. 18.
28. Emergency (Detention) Regulations 1956, *HKGG*, Supplement No. 2, 14 October 1956; Emergency (Principal) Regulations (Commencement) (No.3) Order 1967, *HKGG*, Legal Supplement No. 2, 28 July 1967.
29. In 1868 the magistrate Charles May granted bail to five men charged with murder during a street fight, after committing them for trial. They were subsequently acquitted. The power to grant bail in cases of murder was, from 1890, restricted to judges. Ordinance No. 10 of 1890 s. 95; *HKDP*, 17 February and 5 March 1868.
30. See May Holdsworth and Christopher Munn, *Crime, Justice and Punishment in Colonial Hong Kong: Central Police Station, Central Magistracy and Victoria Gaol* (Hong Kong: Hong Kong University Press, 2020), Chapter 5.

for committal hearings: these usually took place in the afternoon, after the magistrate had disposed of the day's summary cases.

The prosecutor at this stage was usually the Crown Solicitor or, from the 1920s, an assistant attorney general or Crown counsel. The prosecutor called witnesses, who gave evidence on oath against the accused. The accused or his lawyer (if he had one) could cross-examine them. The magistrate wrote down the evidence and had it read back to each witness for signature. Copies of these statements, known as depositions, were sent to the Attorney General, the accused, and the Supreme Court. They could, at the prosecutor's discretion, be used as evidence at trial: discrepancies between depositions and testimony at trial often played a key part in the defence. After hearing witnesses for the prosecution, the magistrate cautioned the accused that he was not obliged to say anything but that anything he said would be taken down in writing and might be given in evidence against him at trial. The accused could also call witnesses. Often the safer course was to reserve the defence for the trial: some magistrates even advised this.[31] If the magistrate found there was a prima facie case, he committed the accused for trial at the next criminal sessions of the Supreme Court and bound over the witnesses to appear.

Committal proceedings could be long and laborious. Some cases were adjourned week after week while witnesses were found and court time allocated. Proceedings took place in open court, although the magistrate had powers to exclude the public if it served the ends of justice.[32] Concerns sometimes arose about duplication of work by the courts and the possibility that reports of committal proceedings, and discussion of them in clubs and tiffin rooms, might prejudice jurors. Reforms began in 1965, when statements of prosecution witnesses were made admissible in committal proceedings in place of oral evidence.[33] Restrictions on reporting were introduced in 1971.[34] Until then, journalists could report proceedings freely, but editors and printers were liable for contempt of court if anything they published was prejudicial to the trial.

The trial venue

Most capital cases in Hong Kong were tried by the Supreme Court: the exceptions were piracies tried by the Vice-Admiralty Court (1847–1849), cases tried by the General

31. In a trial in 1931 it came out that the magistrate had advised the accused to say nothing and wait for the trial, where he would have counsel. The Chief Justice, Sir Joseph Kemp, censured him for exceeding his duties, saying that similar criticisms had been made from the bench before. The trial resulted in a hung jury. A retrial led to an acquittal after the accused convinced the jury he had taken no part in the murder but had been coerced into helping dispose of the body by his adoptive father, who had absconded. *SCMP*, 24–27 and 30 June and 3 and 7–11 July 1931.
32. Magistrates Ordinances, Nos. 10 of 1890 s. 71, and 41 of 1932 s. 74.
33. Ordinance No. 49 of 1965. The court and the accused still had the right to require a witness to give oral evidence.
34. Ordinance No. 6 of 1971, based on the Criminal Justice Act 1967, enacted after similar concerns in England.

Military Court (1945–1946), and trials of servicemen by courts martial. After initially using temporary premises, from 1848 the Supreme Court sat in the former Exchange Building on Queen's Road, and, from 1912 to 1978, the Law Courts in Statue Square. From 1854, criminal sessions were usually held towards the end of each month, with special sessions for some trials.[35]

Trial procedure

Trials broadly followed the procedure used in England. For murder cases this was roughly as follows:

1. The accused was escorted into the dock by prison officers and called on to plead. If he pleaded not guilty, a jury was empanelled and sworn or affirmed to try the case.
2. The prosecutor opened the case by stating the facts of the alleged crime, the nature of the charge, and the evidence he intended to bring.
3. The prosecution called its witnesses, each in turn, who were sworn or affirmed, examined by the prosecution, and cross-examined by the accused or his counsel. After all prosecution witnesses had given evidence, any statement made by the accused to the committing magistrate might be read out. The case for the prosecution then closed.
4. The defence then had several options:
   (a) It might make a submission of no case to answer. If the judge agreed, he would direct the jury to acquit the accused. If he disagreed, the trial would continue.
   (b) It might decide to call no witnesses, in which case the defence would address the jury and have the final word before the judge summed up.
   (c) It might, after addressing the jury, call and examine witnesses, who would then be cross-examined by the prosecution. The defence would then make its closing address, followed by the prosecution, which would have the last word before the judge's summing up.[36]
5. The judge summed up for the jury by reviewing the evidence and explaining the law, the issues in the case, and the standard of proof required.
6. The jury retired to a private room (or remained in the jury box) to consider their verdict. In murder cases, they might find the accused

35. Up to March 1847 criminal sessions were held four times a year, and then, until 1854, five times. Under legislation in 1971, they became continuous. Davis to Grey, 17 April 1847, CO 129/19, 285–295; *HKGG*, 4 November 1854; *HKH*, 17 November 1971; Ordinance No. 63 of 1971.

36. If the Attorney General himself prosecuted, he had a right of final reply even if the defence called no evidence. From 1972 the defence had the right to make the last speech. Ordinance No. 34 of 1972; *HKH*, 10 May 1972.

(a) guilty of murder, in which case the verdict must be unanimous; they might add to the verdict a recommendation to mercy, with or without reasons;
(b) not guilty of murder, in which case the verdict must be unanimous, except for the period 1851–1887, when it could be by majority;
(c) guilty of manslaughter, in which case a majority verdict was acceptable; or
(d) guilty but insane, in which case the judge ordered that the accused be detained during Her or His Majesty's pleasure, to be signified by the Governor.[37]

If the jury failed to agree on a verdict, the judge ordered a retrial with a fresh jury.

7. If the accused was found not guilty he was discharged. If the verdict was manslaughter the judge imposed a sentence of up to life imprisonment. If the verdict was murder he (usually) asked the accused if he had anything to say why sentence of death should not be passed against him. With or without assuming the ceremonial black cap, the judge then pronounced that 'the sentence of the court is that you will be taken hence to the place from whence you came and thence to the place of execution, and that you will be there hanged by the neck until you be dead, and that your body be buried in such place as His Excellency the Governor shall order. And may the Lord have mercy on your soul!'[38]

The prosecution

In England, responsibility for prosecuting crime gradually shifted from private citizens and local police forces to the Director of Public Prosecutions, who, from 1886, was required to conduct all prosecutions in capital cases.[39] Until 1933, bills of indictment for criminal offences were presented to a grand jury of 12–23 jurors, who were usually justices of the peace. They heard evidence in camera from prosecution witnesses before finding either a 'true bill', which became the indictment, or 'no true bill', in which case the accused was discharged. After the formalization of committal proceedings in England in 1848, grand juries became largely redundant as a safeguard against malicious prosecutions.[40] In Hong Kong, and some other colonies, the functions of a grand jury were exercised by the Attorney General, who decided whether to put the accused on trial.[41] The usual practice was to omit charges relating to any other offence. For murders with more than one victim,

37. Under the Homicide Ordinance, No. 16 of 1963, the defence of diminished responsibility, reducing murder to manslaughter, became available, in addition to the insanity defence.
38. Simplified in 1963 to 'suffer death in the manner authorized by law'. Ordinance No. 16 of 1963 s. 6.
39. Regulations under the Prosecution of Offences Acts 1879 and 1884 made in 1886; D.J. Bentley, *English Criminal Justice in the Nineteenth Century* (London: Hambledon Press, 1998), 83–87.
40. *Halsbury's Laws of England* (London: Butterworth, 1907–1917) Vol. 9 (1909): 345–348; Royal Commission on Delay in the King's Bench Division, Second and Final Report (House of Commons Cd. 7177, 1913), 22.
41. Ordinances Nos. 15 of 1844 s. 92, 8 of 1845 s. 1, 2 of 1869 s. 3, and No. 9 of 1899 s. 16–18. The exception was in the short-lived Vice-Admiralty Court, 1847–1849, which made use of grand juries: see Chapter 3.

the indictment usually contained a single count of murder of only one person. This, as one judge explained, avoided placing a person 'in the embarrassing position of having to answer two charges of such gravity at the same time'.[42] It also simplified the task of prosecution and jury.

Initially the Attorney General prosecuted in most trials. The duty was gradually delegated to other government lawyers, with some prosecutions briefed out to barristers in private practice, following general practice in England. The concentration of power in the executive authorities saved time and resources. It avoided the possibility that grand juries, dominated by Europeans, might block the prosecution of a European accused of a crime against a non-European. One of the disadvantages was the facility it allowed to false accusations, particularly in the early years.[43]

The accused

The great majority of capital defendants were Chinese men. This reflected the demography of Hong Kong, which was about 95 per cent Chinese and, until the 1960s, predominantly male. Their ages ranged from twelve to seventy, with most in their twenties and thirties. In some piracy trials, men were tried in groups of a dozen or more. Deaths from gang robberies sometimes also led to the trial of large groups together: up to 1963, under the doctrine of felony murder developed by English courts, a homicide in furtherance of a felony accompanied by violence was deemed to be murder, whether intentional or not; the doctrine of common design (or joint enterprise) made all participants equally liable, no matter how small their part in the crime. Other than for piracies, the greatest numbers of defendants tried together for a capital crime were in the poisoning case of 1857 (Chapter 2), in which ten men were tried, and the fatal attack in 1888 by chain-gang prisoners on a turnkey, for which ten men were tried for murder and acquitted. For domestic murders, increasingly common in the twentieth century, the number of defendants was usually one or two.

Most defendants, including the small number of non-Chinese tried for murder, were of low status. As transients or sojourners, many had little understanding of trial procedure or of English law. As outsiders with little or no stake in the colony, they were often treated harshly. Until the provision of legal aid for defendants on murder charges from the 1870s, the few who could afford lawyers had some chance of acquittal through procedural errors or discrepancies in evidence: according to colonial wisdom, these were usually the guilty who had profited from crime. Others had to rely on their wits or on help from the judge.

42. *SCMP*, 20 September 1934, in the Keung Tsz-pan case: see Chapter 9. The rule was included in the Criminal Procedure Ordinance 1899 s. 19(1) but repealed in 1919, though it continued as general practice up to the 1960s. It was not always followed: see, for example, the charges against Cheung Ashiu in Chapter 4.

43. See Christopher Munn, *Anglo-China: Chinese People and British Rule in Hong Kong, 1841–1880* (Richmond: Curzon, 2001, repr. Hong Kong: Hong Kong University Press, 2009), 183–187.

Legal representation was, in any case, a novel practice: defence counsel in England had only been permitted to examine witnesses or address the court in felony trials since 1836.

Soon after the opening of the Supreme Court, calls were raised for capital defendants to be given legal aid. In 1845 the Colonial Treasurer, Robert Montgomery Martin, wrote a letter of protest to the Governor about the treatment of the first three Chinese sentenced to death, who committed suicide in their cell. Convinced that they did not know whether they were being tried by English or Chinese laws, he urged that counsel be supplied to all Chinese facing the death penalty or transportation.[44] This was partly achieved some 25 years later by a policy initiated in 1872 whereby the trial judge assigned cases to barristers at public expense to defendants charged with murder. Justified by language barriers, legal aid in murder trials followed the practice in some other colonies. Generally, solicitors were also provided, since, unlike some colonies, Hong Kong had a dual legal profession. This policy was in advance of practice in England, where state-funded legal aid was only extended to defendants in 1903.[45] The provision of lawyers resulted in a marked increase in the rate of acquittals. Except for a brief period in the 1890s, legal assistance was not extended to committal proceedings. The other drawback was that, until the Peak Murder case of 1908–1909, defendants supplied with counsel were usually not also afforded interpretation.

The legal profession in Hong Kong grew from a small number of practitioners, some not even legally qualified, into a tight-knit community of experienced barristers and solicitors from a variety of backgrounds. Most were trained in London.[46] Some had practised in England or in other colonies, or in Shanghai. Given Hong Kong's role as a centre of trade, the most lucrative work was in civil litigation. Except in murder trials, or where they or their friends had funds, few defendants had legal representation. Even as late as the 1950s only about 20 per cent of criminal defendants in the Supreme Court, including many facing possible life imprisonment, were legally represented.[47] The need felt by some counsel to defend their own role implies that representing capital defendants attracted a certain stigma. 'There is sometimes a feeling that lawyers are apt to be very smart, that they want watching and that they are ready for possible trickery that will assist them in obtaining their ends,' said one of Hong Kong's most successful barristers, F.C. Jenkin, on the 'measure of suspicion' with which many regarded the legal profession.[48]

---

44. Robert Montgomery Martin, *Reports, Minutes and Despatches on the British Position and Prospects in China* (London: Harrison, 1846), 132.
45. Poor Prisoners Defence Act 1903. Before this, under the system of 'dock briefs', a defendant could, in court, brief a barrister without the aid of a solicitor for a fee of one guinea. The practice was not adopted in Hong Kong.
46. See Christopher Munn, *A Special Standing in the World: The Faculty of Law at the University of Hong Kong, 1969–2019* (Hong Kong: Hong Kong University Press, 2019), Chapter 1.
47. *Hansard* HC Deb, 31 October 1957 vol 575 cc387–8.
48. *SCMP*, 17 August 1927.

Unrepresented defendants could cross-examine prosecution witnesses and call their own witnesses. Before 1906, however, they were not permitted to give evidence on oath. The rule was designed to prevent self-incrimination under cross-examination. Along with the right to silence, the presumption of innocence, and the judge's duty to assist the accused, this was an example of what one early Chief Justice, John Smale, described as 'the great care which the English law takes to throw round prisoners all the protection it possibly can'.[49] The change in 1906 followed an English reform in 1898, whose proponents argued that excluding testimony by the accused denied to the jury an account from the one person who knew most about the facts – an account that could lead to acquittal of the innocent and more certain conviction of the guilty. It was the latter that the Attorney General, Sir Henry Berkeley, chose to stress when introducing the reform in Hong Kong: a guilty man would now no longer have the 'loophole of escape' by receiving the benefit of the doubt from a jury that was unable to hear him in his own defence.[50] Perhaps for this reason, defence counsel were cautious about putting their clients in the witness box.

Both before and after the 1906 reform, defendants had other opportunities to explain their actions. One was through the written statement taken down in committal proceedings: often this was just a simple denial, but sometimes it could play an important role in exculpating the accused. The accused could also, if unrepresented, address the court in his own defence. A third option was an unsworn statement from the dock, usually at the close of the prosecution's case. Because it was not on oath, and could not be tested by cross-examination, this lacked the value of sworn testimony. Partly for this reason, the option was abolished in 1972.[51] A fourth possibility, available from 1872 to 1912, was for the judge to directly examine the accused and treat his replies as evidence. This power, not available in English courts, drew on practice in India. Judges only rarely made use of it and could not compel defendants to answer.[52]

Finally, if the jury returned a verdict of guilty, the judge asked the accused if he had anything to say why sentence of death should not be passed. This part of the trial, known

---

49. Smale made this point when insisting that an informant called as a witness by the accused in a murder trial be produced in court. The prosecutor, Julian Pauncefote, had objected, arguing that if the prosecution had 'to bring forward every Chinese who gave information to the police, and subject such men to have their throats cut – he had no hesitation in saying so – they would never get any information at all'. *HKDP*, 23, 26, and 29 July 1870.
50. *HKH*, 11 October 1906; Ordinance No. 14 of 1906; Bentley, *English Criminal Justice*, Chapter 17.
51. In 1968, after a magistrate refused to allow an unsworn statement, the Full Court reviewed the practice and recommended it be abolished. In parallel, the government proposed to abolish the option for those charged under new anti-corruption legislation: officials in London initially opposed this, but when they discovered that the UK's Criminal Law Revision Committee was considering general abolition of the unsworn statement they relented, provided abolition was general for all offences. It was abolished in Hong Kong for all trials in 1972, and in England in 1982. *Tseng Ping Yee v The Queen* [1969] HKLR 304; Ordinance No. 34 of 1972. TNA FCO 40/228 and 234.
52. It was repealed after the accused had the right to give sworn evidence. See Chapter 4.

as the 'allocutus', was originally the time for the accused to plead 'benefit of clergy',[53] or that he had received a pardon, or to raise a defect in the indictment, or, in the case of a woman, to claim pregnancy. It was now more usually an opportunity to say something in mitigation: although the judge had no discretion in sentencing if the verdict was guilty of murder, the Governor might take anything said into account when considering whether to exercise mercy. As often as not, however, anything the accused did say at this stage was dismissed by the judge as irrelevant. Legislation in 1921 made it optional for the judge to put the question (see Chapter 7).

The judge

Most capital trials were presided over by a judge with a jury. The judge guided the jury and decided questions of law, including whether evidence should be withheld from the jury. The jury decided factual issues and delivered the verdict. Having heard the evidence and closing submissions in trials that ran their full course, the judge summed up for the jury. After the creation of the Court of Criminal Appeal in 1933, the failure of a judge to properly direct the jury on points of law or arguments put forward by the defence was a common ground for appeal.

The early Supreme Court had only one judge, the Chief Justice. A second Puisne Judge was added in 1873. Temporary additional judges were appointed from the 1930s. But a permanent third judge was not added until 1949, when Hong Kong's population was nearly two million: the wide criminal jurisdiction of magistrates, and the creation of an intermediate District Court in 1953, ensured that only the most serious criminal cases were tried in the Supreme Court by judge and jury. The Supreme Court bench gradually increased to six judges by 1966, when the last hanging took place, and thirty-one by 1993, when the death penalty was abolished.

Before the appointment of a Hong Kong-born Chinese judge in 1971, all Supreme Court judges were men of British or British-colonial origin. In contrast to England, where judges were appointed from the private Bar, most judges in Hong Kong from the 1880s to the 1970s had formerly served as colonial magistrates or attorneys general, some with little or no experience of private practice. In the early twentieth century some of these emerged from the cadet service, an elite cadre of civil servants, after being called to the Bar while serving as administrators or magistrates. Neither long service in the executive branch nor the rise of a 'civil service judiciary' necessarily made a judge 'prosecution-minded', a

53. In England, up to 1827, a defendant claiming benefit of clergy could avoid the death penalty for certain crimes, originally by reciting a passage (the 'neck verse': the first verse of Psalm 51) from the Bible to demonstrate literacy.

criticism levelled at some judges in the later years of British rule.[54] A few, like Chief Justice Rees-Davies, who succeeded Piggott in 1912 after serving for five years as Attorney General, leaned towards the prosecution where colonial interests were at stake. Most, however, quickly adjusted to their new roles. Some were keen to address abuses they had seen as prosecutors. Hong Kong's most fiercely independent judge, Sir John Smale (Chief Justice 1866–1882), had formerly been a zealous attorney general, intent on prosecuting abuses in the coolie trade. Sir Joseph Kemp, responsible while Attorney General for the Emergency Regulations Ordinance 1922 and other draconian laws,[55] had no tolerance for the police blunders that plagued prosecutions during his term as Chief Justice (1930–1934).

Again, in contrast to England, judges in Hong Kong had no formal security of tenure until 1967: in that year the Letters Patent were amended so that, except on retirement (then at sixty-two), Supreme Court judges could only be removed for misbehaviour or inability to discharge their duties, after recommendations to the Privy Council by a tribunal of judges.[56] By then, the independence of colonial judges had been long established as a 'high constitutional principle'.[57] Nevertheless, five of the judges presiding over the trials in this book were the targets of attempts by officials to remove them: the attempts succeeded in the cases of Henry Ball (1873), Sir Henry Berkeley (in Fiji, 1902), and Sir Francis Piggott (1912), but failed for John Hulme (1847) and Sir John Smale (1868 and 1872). The reasons varied, but for three (Smale, Berkeley, and Piggott) displeasure at their approach to criminal justice was a factor.

The jury

Hong Kong's jury system differed markedly from that in England and some other colonies: its development is summarized in **Table 3** (see p. 20). Jury lists were compiled annually by the Sheriff or, from 1882, the Registrar of the Supreme Court. Up to 1929 they were approved by the Legislative Council, usually in closed session, and thereafter by the Governor in Council.[58] Common jurors were required to be males aged between twenty-one and sixty, resident in Hong Kong, of sound mind, and not deaf or blind. In 1947 women became eligible to serve. Various categories, such as civil servants, lawyers, physicians, and clergymen, were exempted. The Governor designated some jurors as special jurors. These were required to be 'an esquire or person of higher degree', usually bankers or merchants. Jurors' names were kept on cards: the Sheriff or Registrar drew by ballot a

---

54. See Eric Barnes, 'The Independence of the Judiciary in Hong Kong', *HKLJ*, Vol. 6 (1976): 7–26 and the editorial in that issue; and de Basto to McPetrie, 7 May 1970, FCO 40/298, encl. 12.
55. See Chapter 8.
56. *HKGG*, 17 November 1967.
57. Kenneth Roberts-Wray, *Commonwealth and Colonial Law* (London: Stevens & Sons, 1966), 492–505.
58. In the 1930s special committees of the Executive Council were tasked with reviewing the lists.

Table 3: Development of the Jury System in Hong Kong, 1844–1960

Year	Jury System	References and Observations
1844	Petty (trial) juries to consist of six men. No grand jury. Jury lists compiled annually by Sheriff. Qualifications: male residents aged twenty-one to sixty, of sound mind, not afflicted with deafness, blindness or other infirmity, holding property to the monthly value of $25 or more or with an annual income of $1,000 or more. Exemptions: government employees, barristers, physicians, attorneys, clergymen, military and naval officers. Special juries, consisting of esquires or persons of higher degree, or bankers or merchants, may be appointed by the court upon application and payment of fees and expenses by plaintiff, prosecutor, or defendant, except in cases of treason or felony. No challenge of jurors by accused except for cause.	England: grand juries of twelve to twenty-three men to find or ignore indictments; petty juries of twelve men; similar qualifications and exemptions; aliens excluded, except on juries *de medietate linguae*. Similar arrangements for special juries. Jury lists compiled annually by churchwardens and other local officials, approved by justices of the peace in petty session, and kept by county sheriffs. Accused allowed up to twenty peremptory challenges. Ordinances Nos. 15 of 1844 and 7 of 1845.
1849	Minimum income qualification reduced to $500.	Ordinance No. 4 of 1849.
1851	Property and income qualifications removed. Persons ignorant of the English language excluded. Majority verdicts allowed, except for guilty verdicts in capital cases. Jury list to be approved by Governor and Legislative Council, who are also required to designate no less than twenty-four special jurors. Special juries not to be used for trying treason or felonies. Special jurors liable to serve on common juries, as in England (this provision repealed in 1860).	England: property qualifications removed in 1974; majority verdicts allowed from 1967. Majority verdicts of not less than five out of seven jurors allowed under the Straits Settlements Criminal Procedure Code (No. 6 of 1873) in all cases, including capital, with the concurrence of the judge. Ordinances Nos. 4 of 1851 and 2 of 1860.
1858	Size of juries increased to seven men.	Ordinance No. 3 of 1858
1872	Special juries made available for trial of felonies at discretion of Attorney General or by order of the judge upon application by the accused, who may, at the discretion of the judge, be required to remunerate jurors according to the scale for civil trials.	Similar arrangements in some other colonies, e.g. Ceylon from 1871. Under the Straits Settlements Criminal Procedure Code (Ordinance No. 6 of 1873), all capital cases required to be tried by special juries: majority verdicts allowed with concurrence of judge.
1882	Position of Sheriff abolished; responsibility for compiling jury lists transferred to Registrar of Supreme Court.	Ordinance No. 24 of 1882.

(continued on p. 21)

Table 3 (continued)

Year	Jury System	References and Observations
1887	Exemptions from jury service extended to employees of foreign governments, editors and staff of daily newspapers, chemists and druggists, masters of steamers, and local pilots. Unanimity now required in not guilty, as well as guilty, verdicts in capital cases.	Ordinance No. 18 of 1887.
1894	Verdicts in non-capital cases now require a majority of at least five jurors.	Ordinance No. 3 of 1894.
1929	Jury lists to be approved by Governor in Council.	Ordinance No. 8 of 1929.
1947	Women eligible to serve as jurors. Judges empowered to order all-male or all-female juries and to exempt a woman by reason of the nature of the evidence.	England: women eligible to serve as jurors from 1919. Ordinance No. 37 of 1947.
1960	Responsibility for compiling jury lists transferred from Registrar of Supreme Court to Commissioner of Registration, who is responsible for issuing identity cards and compiling the electoral registrar for the Urban Council.	Ordinance No. 39 of 1960.

specified number[59] to form a panel at each session. At trial, the cards of those summoned were drawn from a box until a jury was formed. This was repeated for each trial unless, with the consent of both sides, the same jury was used for consecutive trials.

Initially, jurors were required to hold property with a monthly value of at least $25 or to have an annual income of at least $1,000. Early juries consisted of six men – half the size of juries in England.[60] Owing to a shortage of eligible persons, early jury lists were small and unstable. The 1851 jury list had only ninety-five names, less than half the number in 1848, reflecting an exodus of colonists amid doubts about Hong Kong's prospects, despite a reduction of the income requirement to $500.[61] After complaints from jurors about the burdens imposed on them, the government made two further departures from English practice in 1851: property qualifications were removed; and majority verdicts became acceptable in all cases except for guilty verdicts in capital trials (and, from 1887, not guilty verdicts in capital trials). The size of juries was increased to seven in 1858 to make majority

59. Up to 1851 the Sheriff summoned jurors in order of their appearance on the jury list, alphabetically by surname, until it was exhausted. From 1950 the number to be summoned was specified by a judge: Ordinance No. 32 of 1950.
60. The size of juries in other colonies varied and changed over time. In the late nineteenth century, for example, it was seven in the Straits Settlements; between seven and nine in Ceylon; and nine in Mauritius.
61. Correspondence Between the Governor and Justices of the Peace, January–March 1851, CO 129/36, 150.

verdicts easier. Majority verdicts were not admissible in England until 1967. Property qualifications were not removed there until 1972.

There were no nationality requirements.[62] An explicit English-language requirement was introduced in Hong Kong in 1851: this, said one Chief Justice, was 'an elastic definition'.[63] Initially, jury lists were dominated by British names, with all but a few foreigners weeded out.[64] Over the decades, however, the lists came to reflect the multinational composition of Hong Kong society. 'Nowhere are juries more cosmopolitan or names more picturesque,' remarked the *South China Morning Post* in 1924.[65] The 902-strong list for 1900, for example, included a variety of Europeans and members of Hong Kong's Indian, Parsi, Japanese, Eurasian, Baghdadi Jewish, and Portuguese communities. But it had only thirty-six Chinese names, even though the Chinese population at this time included some 140,000 males aged between twenty-one and sixty. Most were temporary residents with little English. Yet the permanent community of Chinese merchants, clerks and professionals numbered far more than thirty-six. Some were no doubt reluctant to come forward. Officials also had difficulty in assessing standards of English. There seems nevertheless to have been an aversion to putting Chinese on juries in Hong Kong's early decades. This may have been simple prejudice, or a reflection of experience in colonies where 'native' jurors were allegedly corruptible or unwilling to convict because of religious scruples or ethnic solidarity. Although, for various reasons, many Hong Kong juries were reluctant to convict capitally, these factors do not appear to have significantly influenced the behaviour of Chinese jurors.[66]

Discussions about Chinese jurors began soon after the creation of the Supreme Court. In his protest in 1845, Montgomery Martin urged that in capital trials juries should be half composed of countrymen of the accused. A similar practice had long existed in England: up to 1870 aliens were entitled to be tried by a jury *de medietate linguae*, half of which was made up of aliens, though not necessarily of the same nationality as the accused.[67] Hong

62. In contrast to England and some other colonies, such as Mauritius, where jurors had to be British subjects.
63. Chief Justice Sir Henry Blackall at the Opening of the Legal Year, *SCMP*, 21 October 1947.
64. In 1852, for example, thirty jurors were taken off the original list posted at the Courthouse, half because of absence from Hong Kong, the rest, all Portuguese, because of inadequate English. *HKR*, 6 January and 16 March 1852.
65. 'We recall a juror who rose at the first syllable, walked the full width of the court and had taken his seat before the clerk had concluded calling his name.' In fact, the Singapore jury lists were far more diverse. *SCMP*, 27 August 1924.
66. See Elizabeth Kolsky, *Colonial Justice in British India* (Cambridge: Cambridge University Press, 2010), 217–221; and John D. Rogers, *Crime, Justice and Society in Colonial Sri Lanka* (London: Curzon Press, 1987), 66–67.
67. This was abolished by the Aliens Act 1870. However, under an inverted form of jury *de medietate linguae*, in India and several other colonies, European defendants had the right to require at least half of the jurors to be Europeans. See Deborah A. Ramirez, The Mixed Jury and the Ancient Custom of Trial by Jury *de Medietate Linguae*: A History and a Proposal for Change', *Boston University Law Review* 74, no. 5 (November 1994): 777–818.

Kong's first Chief Justice, John Hulme, confronted this question when, in 1845, an Indian defendant asked for such a jury. The request was withdrawn, but Hulme reported that he would have refused it anyway as inapplicable to local circumstances.[68] Claiming to reflect colonial opinion, early newspapers were ambivalent about adding Chinese to the jury list. The *Friend of China* said it would be a 'noble step in the right direction' but 'the bulk of our citizens would rather keep Chinese as they are – altogether out of the Jury box.' In 1858 the editor of the *Hong Kong Register* claimed credit for proposing the first Chinese juror, the Christian Wong Shing, but urged 'great care' in 'putting Chinese on the jury on this precedent.' Wong's inclusion, at a time when Britain and China were at war, was so contentious that it was put to the vote in the Legislative Council. It was passed by four votes to three, with Chief Justice Hulme among those opposing.[69]

With the growth of a settled middle class, the proportion of Chinese names on jury lists increased, from the meagre 4 per cent in 1900 to about 16 per cent in 1930, 43 per cent in 1941, and 40 per cent in 1951, when the total number of jurors was over 6,000.[70] Apart from the British, the largest groups were Germans and Portuguese. Germans were removed in 1915, and again in 1940. Portuguese made up a fifth to a quarter of names from the 1870s, falling to about an eighth by 1940. Descended from colonists who had married local women, they originated from Macao, an old Portuguese settlement forty miles from Hong Kong. As Macao's prospects declined, many settled in Hong Kong. Speaking their own dialect, and now largely endogamous, they were, officials observed, colonists in the true sense, 'a European community in the Tropics, thoroughly acclimatized, and apparently not recruited from Europe.' Classified as a distinct 'race' in censuses, they numbered over 3,000 in 1931, a figure exceeded only by Chinese, Indians, and 'British races.'[71]

Portuguese men were generally employed as clerks and assistants, the middling occupations from which common jurors were drawn. Most juries from the 1870s to the 1930s contained at least one Portuguese; some had a majority. Along with the inclusion of other nationalities, this raised concerns about the large number of jurors who, as the *Daily Press* put it in 1874, had 'little acquaintance with English, and no ideas of legal proceedings.' In 1895 the Chief Justice, Sir Fielding Clarke, also complained that some Chinese with no knowledge of English, and some Portuguese with very little, had been added to the jury list; he also noted that many Portuguese jurors had a good understanding of colloquial Chinese, the language of most witnesses.[72] In 1874 the Sheriff attempted, unsuccessfully,

68. Davis to Stanley, 16 July 1845, CO 129/12, 312–313.
69. *FOC*, 16 July 1851; *HKR*, 2 March 1858; Legislative Council minutes, 24 February 1858, CO 131/4, 454–455.
70. Jury lists are to be found either in the *Hong Kong Government Gazette* or the *Hong Kong Sessional Papers*.
71. Census Reports for 1897 and 1931, *HKSP*, 26/1897 and 5/1931.
72. *HKDP*, 18 September 1874; Clarke to Ripon, 23 January 1895, CO 129/270, 261–263.

to remove all but two Portuguese from the jury list.[73] A different solution appeared in 1872 with legislation allowing the use of special juries in criminal trials. The small special jury list was then made up mainly of British elites; in later years it included wealthy Chinese but few Portuguese. Governors placed limits on the numbers of special jurors. Names were scrutinized so that only the most trusted were selected. Special juries tried nearly half the capital cases in the last quarter of the nineteenth century. After that they were used less frequently, typically for complex or politically sensitive trials.

Limited English was not the only concern about Portuguese jurors. Portugal was one of the first countries to abandon the death penalty. No one had been executed there since 1846;[74] the penalty was repealed in 1867, reflecting a general revulsion against capital punishment and pride in the country's progressive policies.[75] Some officials believed that Portuguese in Hong Kong shared these views, and that defence counsel played upon them by stressing the ignominy of hanging.[76] How far such views influenced verdicts is unclear. But they came to the fore in campaigns for mercy for the few Portuguese sentenced to death. One of these was Joao Ozorio, convicted in 1898 of murdering a love rival.[77] For his trial the prosecution had averted the empanelment of Portuguese jurors by ordering a special jury. In some other cases it tried to ensure all-British juries by asking other jurors to 'stand by'. At a murder trial in 1910 no fewer than five Portuguese jurors were asked to stand by. Their exclusion was all the stranger, the *China Mail* observed, since they were born in Hong Kong and understood Chinese, and the jurors replacing them were 'of three or four different races'.[78] In 1934 the Executive Council discussed, but did not pursue, a plan to exclude Portuguese jurors entirely from murder trials.[79] In the early 1960s the government

73. They were restored after complaints that it breached the Jury Ordinance. The Sheriff, Alfred Lister, had earlier, as Coroner, illegally excluded Portuguese from juries by selecting, rather than balloting, jurors. *OCM*, 5 February 1874.
74. In Macao, however, a Brazilian was executed by firing squad in 1847 for murdering a Chinese: *CM* 6 May 1847.
75. Charter of Law of Abolition of the Death Penalty (Portugal), 1867; *Report of the Capital Punishment Commission* (London: Eyre and Spottiswoode, 1866), 516–537.
76. Deane, Captain-Superintendent of Police, to Stewart, 12 May 1886, CO 129/227, 99.
77. A petition from the Portuguese community on his behalf was unsuccessful and Ozorio was hanged. Concerns in Lisbon about capital punishment also prevented the implementation of extradition agreements between Hong Kong and Macao in the 1870s and 1880s. In the Anglo-Portuguese Extradition Treaty 1894, extended to Hong Kong, the Portuguese government stated it would not deliver up any person accused of any crime punishable with death. *HKDP*, 2 July 1898; William Meigh Goodman, *Reminiscences of a Colonial Judge* (London: Kingsgate Press, 1907), 169–170; Pauncefote to Colonial Office, 28 September 1878, CO 129/183, 231–233; *HKGG*, 12 May 1894.
78. The case involved the alleged murder by drowning of a woman near Lamma Island. The defendant was acquitted. The jury consisted of four British, one Dutch, one Italian, and a Hong Kong-born Muslim. *CM*, 26 September 1910.
79. ExCo Minutes, 21 February 1934, CO 131/91, 38.

considered exempting all aliens from jury service but rejected the idea on the ground that 'jurors with a good knowledge of English are already too few'.[80]

Being turned off juries was one of many indignities complained of by Portuguese residents.[81] Jury service was a badge of citizenship, particularly when rate-paying jurors became electors for the Sanitary Board in 1888. By the 1890s, some English-speaking Chinese were keen to attain the status of special juror.[82] Yet jury service was an onerous duty, and heavy demands were made on the small pool of jurors. They were often kept waiting for hours before being called.[83] Interpretation made trials long and tedious. Poor acoustics rendered some proceedings barely audible. The air in the old Courthouse was so oppressive in summer that jurors sometimes fainted; a similar 'atmosphere' prevailed in the new courts. The old Courthouse had no jury room. In the new Law Courts jurors complained that their deliberations, especially in murder cases, were observed by crowds of onlookers staring through the windows of the library (then serving as the jury room) from the veranda outside.[84] Many jurors asked to be excused, claiming urgent business, illness, or insufficient English. Some jurors simply failed to appear when summoned and were reprimanded and fined. Europeans 'dislike serving on common juries,' wrote Chief Justice Sir Fielding Clarke in 1895, 'especially in cases where only Chinese are concerned'. But he rejected claims that juries were prejudiced against Chinese.[85]

Jurors often played an active role in trials, putting questions to witnesses or offering suggestions on interpretation. They were expected to attend carefully to proceedings. For not doing so, David Welsh, a juror in a murder trial in 1872, was fined $50 for contempt of court. He apologized and the fine was remitted. But he was then imprisoned for contempt after writing a letter to the *Daily Press* denying the accusation and claiming that the judge's own inattention had resulted in a miscarriage of justice.[86] Welsh's cocky attitude contrasts

80. Black to Secretary of State, 17 April 1962, CO 1030/1293, 22.
81. For others see José Pedro Braga, *The Rights of Aliens in Hongkong: Being a Record of the Discussion Carried on Through the Medium of the Public Press as to the Employment of Aliens in the Colony* (Hong Kong: Noronha & Co., 1895).
82. J.W. Norton-Kyshe, *The History of the Laws and Courts of Hong Kong from the Earliest Period to 1898* (Hong Kong: Noronha & Co., 1898), Vol. I, 578–579.
83. See, for example, the satirical 'A Juryman's Day', *HKDP*, 19 May 1920, which describes how a juror spends the whole morning and much of the afternoon, 'hot, thirsty; temperature and barometer rising', waiting in court only to find that the case for which he and twenty-nine other jurors have been summoned has to be postponed to the next day because the principal witness is ill. He decides not to turn up the next day, even at risk of being fined $25.
84. The Attorney General undertook to remedy this. *CM*, 22 and 23 September 1925.
85. Claims of prejudice were made by Chinese consulted by James Stewart Lockhart, the Registrar General. Clarke to Ripon, 23 January 1895, CO 129/270, 260–263.
86. The alleged murder arose out of a dispute between men cutting grass in the hills near Wong Nai Chung. After contradictory evidence about whether the accused had a beard at the time of the murder, the Acting Attorney General, at the suggestion of the judge, entered a *nolle prosequi*. Welsh was sent to gaol for fourteen days but was

with the distress of a Chinese juror a century later at the death sentences imposed on three youths in a trial which he and other jurors had struggled to follow: 'I am now feeling guilty conscience due to my meagre understanding during the procedure, and I cannot sleep well.'[87] Such insights into a juror's mind are rare. The secrecy of the jury room was broken only by the occasional dispute about what was agreed.[88] One instance occurred in 1947. After the foreman returned verdicts of guilty of murder against two men, three jurors told the judge in chambers they had not agreed to the verdicts. When the case went to appeal, counsel for the two men, Leo D'Almada KC, asked the court to bear in mind 'the differences in race, temperament and character of those serving as jurors'. A similar situation would never occur in England, he suggested.[89] The court dismissed the appeal, ruling that the jurors should have spoken up when the verdict was announced.[90]

Witnesses

On 17 December 1851 the criminal sessions ended abruptly with most of the cases left untried. A shopkeeper, Looi Acheong, 'after long explanations between him and the interpreter', had pleaded guilty to perjury: he had falsely sworn to the genuineness of a forged opium order in a civil trial. When Chief Justice Hulme sentenced him to a year's imprisonment, jurors asked if he had been properly sworn in the first place. The courts had struggled to find a satisfactory form of oath for Chinese witnesses. In the early magistrate's court, witnesses cut off the head of a live cock, invoking the wrath of heaven if they lied. This way of getting at the truth was allowed by the Supreme Court in some civil cases.[91] But the oath for Chinese witnesses in early criminal trials was to burn sheets of paper inscribed with imprecations, a practice taken from Penang. This 'not only appeared to foreigners absurd, but was laughed at by the Chinese themselves', said jurors in Looi's trial; if the oath was inef-

---

released after three days following a further apology and a petition to the Governor signed by 170 residents. The judge was Henry Ball: see Chapter 3. *HKDP*, 21, 27 and 30 March and 4, 5, 8, and 9 April 1872.

87. This episode was highlighted in a report on juries by the Bar Association. The death sentences were commuted to prison terms of ten to fifteen years. Hong Kong Bar Association, *Annual Statement*, 1971–1972, 38; *SCMP*, 28 April 1971.
88. However, the absence of a statutory prohibition, analogous to the Contempt of Court Act 1981, on disclosing jury deliberations has allowed research that is not possible in some other places. See Peter Duff, Mark Findlay, Carla Howarth, and Chan Tsang-fai, *Juries: A Hong Kong Perspective* (Hong Kong: Hong Kong University Press, 1992).
89. See, however, *R v Ibbtsam Ul Hamid* [2016] EWCA Crim 449, an English case of conspiracy to defraud the Revenue, in which jurors also subsequently informed the judge that the verdicts had not been unanimous.
90. *SCMP*, 18 February 1948.
91. For example, in three disputes in 1918 and 1922, judges allowed litigants to 'undergo the ordeal of the cock's head' at the Man Mo Temple. In one case the plaintiff completed the ritual but the defendant refused. The judge, Rees-Davies, found for the plaintiff. *SCMP*, 13, 17, 24, and 25 September 1918 and 23 March 1922; *Huazi ribao*, 14 September 1918.

fective, he should have been acquitted. Hulme consulted the interpreter, Daniel Caldwell, who advised that Chinese had no belief in a God or future state as Christians understood it and did not consider 'lying in the abstract' to be a sin. He suggested replacing the oath for Chinese witnesses with a warning that they would be severely punished if they gave false evidence.[92] This was embodied in legislation in 1856, which, in turn, was replaced in 1860 by a simple declaration by non-Christian witnesses that they would tell the truth.[93]

'Native mendacity' was a commonplace feature of colonial dogma throughout the British Empire. A supposed propensity to tell lies, particularly to Europeans, became part of the stereotyped 'Chinese character' formed by missionaries and journalists and reinforced by commentary on the courts. 'Lying is one of their most notorious characteristics', remarked the *Chinese Recorder* in 1870; 'there is no oath so sacred that will bind a Chinaman'.[94] Lying among the Chinese, wrote the *Times* journalist George Cooke, was 'as unexceptionable as punning among the English'.[95] Hong Kong did not follow the practice in some other places of restricting evidence from non-Europeans.[96] But 'the bare fact that Chinese testimony is very little relied upon',[97] was axiomatic among colonists in the nineteenth century and beyond. It relied on a dubious premise that Europeans, in contrast, told the truth. It also flew in the face of much evidence to the contrary. Only rarely was it challenged, albeit with reservations. 'I hold the respectable Chinese like respectable Englishmen to be usually the witnesses of truth,' wrote Chief Justice Smale. Customs might differ from place to place, he added, but 'in spite of all these differences human nature is pretty much the same all the world over'.[98]

As experience of criminal justice in Hong Kong accumulated, commentary on Chinese evidence shifted from the moralistic to the practical. During the crisis over oaths in 1851,

---

92. *CM*, 18 December 1851; *HKR*, 23 December 1851; *FOC*, 7 January 1852.
93. Ordinances Nos. 15 of 1856, 7 of 1857, and 2 of 1860. See Munn, *Anglo-China*, 229–233; and Paul R. Katz, *Divine Justice: Religion and the Development of Chinese Legal Culture* (Abingdon: Routledge, 2009), 123–129.
94. 'On Chinese Oaths and Swearing', *The Chinese Recorder and Missionary Journal* 3 (September 1870): 104–105.
95. George Wingrove Cooke, *China: Being "The Times" Special Correspondence from China in the Years 1857–58* (London: Routledge, 1858), x.
96. In 1840 legislation in New South Wales allowing unsworn Aboriginal testimony was disallowed in London after advice from the Law Officers that witnesses had to perceive future moral or religious consequences to giving false testimony. This approach was reversed in 1843 by an act authorizing colonies to enact laws allowing unsworn indigenous testimony. South Australia then enacted a series of such laws, but with restrictions, such as a proviso, in force from 1844 to 1848, that no one could be convicted solely upon it. From 1854 to 1870, Chinese in California were prohibited from giving evidence for or against a white person. Similar restrictions applied in some other US states. Damen Ward, 'Imperial Policy, Colonial Government and Indigenous Testimony in South Australia and New Zealand in the 1840s', in Shaunnagh Dorsett and Ian Hunter, *Law and Politics in British Colonial Thought: Transpositions of Empire* (New York: Palgrave Macmillan, 2010); Gabriel J. Chin, '"A Chinaman's Chance" in Court: Asian Pacific Americans and Racial Rules of Evidence', *UC Irvine Law Review* 3 (2013): 965–990.
97. *HKDP*, 30 October 1873.
98. Smale to Henry Holland, 17 July 1872, CO 129/161, 493–494.

an 'intelligent Chinese' explained to the *Hongkong Register* the low value placed on witness evidence by magistrates in China, who 'only make the people confess the truth by threatenings and tortures, and then compare the confessions together and decide the case; or they would find out the truth by arts and private inquiries without calling for witnesses'.[99] These inquisitorial methods contrasted with the open, adversarial form of trials in Hong Kong, where witnesses were often confused by cross-examination. The problem was aggravated by reliance on interpretation, which introduced further doubts about the quality of Chinese evidence. In particular, the use of different interpreters of varying ability in the Magistracy and the Supreme Court sometimes led to discrepancies between depositions and evidence at trial, which were exploited by counsel. 'A little comment on such differences exaggerates them in the minds of ordinary jurymen into wilful falsehoods,' remarked the Captain-Superintendent of Police, F.H. May, in 1893.[100]

A more serious concern, highlighted by May and others, was a belief that Chinese witnesses were commonly tampered with between committal and trial. Combined with a reluctance to meddle in other people's affairs, fear of the authorities, and a lack of confidence in the courts, this was one reason why many witnesses failed to appear at trial. Much of the crime in and around Hong Kong was organized by gangs, who used the city as a base and were familiar with the courts. A secret committee in 1886 heard that Triad gangs, numbering some 30,000, had gained control of prostitution, gambling, and many other activities legal and illegal. By intimidating or removing witnesses and infiltrating the courts they had allegedly prevented cases from going to trial, including at least nine murders. No one dared complain for fear of being 'murdered and cooked and returned before his own front door', said one witness, a Chinese detective.[101] Where cases did lead to conviction, witnesses risked becoming targets of revenge.[102]

Officials believed that dark forces were also behind the 'cooking' of evidence. Fabricated testimony was rife in the early years. Investigations by missionaries and Chinese merchants exposed several false accusations. By the early twentieth century the Supreme Court's civil business had become clogged with fictitious claims. Allegedly, they were concocted by Li Hong-mi, the interpreter in the Peak Murder trial, now, in retirement, working as a solicitor's clerk.[103] Fears about similar practices loomed over many criminal trials.

99. *HKR*, 30 December 1851.

100. May to Colonial Secretary, 13 June 1893, CO 129/264, 471–472.

101. 'Triad Society: Report and Proceedings on the', 21 May 1886, CO 129/227, 330.

102. Lugard to Harcourt, 26 April 1911, CO 129/376, 529; Munn, *Anglo-China*, 180–191.

103. Following his retirement in 1909, after thirty-six years' service, Li joined various solicitors' firms and allegedly swindled litigants and financed spurious claims through a network of touts and champerters. In 1918, under specially enacted legislation, Governor May attempted to deport him. Li and his lawyers took the case to the Privy Council and defeated the attempt on a technicality. Christopher Munn, 'Margins of Justice in Colonial Hong Kong: Extrajudicial Power, Solicitors' Clerks, and the Case of Li Hong Mi, 1917–1920', *Law and Humanities* 11, no. 1 (2017): 102–120.

These too were exploited by counsel: 'if there is a discrepancy, he urges that the evidence is unreliable', remarked Walter Deane, Captain-Superintendent of Police, in 1886; 'if there is no discrepancy, the evidence fits so well, it is a conspiracy', given 'the natural distrust any juror has to all Asiatic testimony'.[104] In the trial of Leung Wo in 1922 (Chapter 8) both prosecution and judge concluded that the defence witnesses were all joined in a conspiracy to defeat the ends of justice.[105]

The government and the courts adopted various measures to address the problems with witnesses. In the early years some witnesses were detained in the gaol to ensure they appeared at trial. From the 1850s, attempts were made to segregate witnesses waiting to give evidence, though this proved difficult in the overcrowded courthouse. Legislation in 1851 allowed written depositions taken at the committal stage to be received as evidence at trial if the witnesses had disappeared: this measure, an extension of the established practice of accepting dying depositions from murder victims on the point of death, was widely criticized as a breach of the fundamental right of the accused to cross-examine his accusers.[106] By the late nineteenth century police officers were 'shadowing' witnesses they feared were unlikely to appear at trial.[107] The reluctance of witnesses to come forward encouraged the police to rely on rewards, accomplice evidence, and paid informers, most of whom were members of the criminal underworld.

The police themselves contributed to the problems. From the early years up to the 1970s, when the government took determined action, they were notoriously corrupt. The committee in 1886 heard evidence that the Chinese contingent, forming nearly half the force, was almost wholly infiltrated by the Triad Society. Revelations that year about bribes from gambling dens led to the dismissal of fifty-one Chinese constables. Again, in 1897, over a hundred European, Indian, and Chinese officers were dismissed in a similar scandal. Extortion by police was a daily hazard for ordinary people.[108] The force's multinational composition aggravated the generally poor relations with the public. 'How do you expect Cantonese people to understand communicating with the Hongkong Police?' asked Sin Tak-fan, a businessman, formerly a solicitor's clerk, in 1892.[109] 'People of our class are frightened of those people', said a 15-year-old witness, the sole survivor of a piracy of his family's fishing boat in 1926, when asked why he had not gone to the police.[110] To many, the police were just one of several predatory organizations that were best avoided.

---

104. Deane to Stewart, 12 May 1886, CO 129/227, 100.
105. See Chapter 8, and, for other examples, Chapters 2, 3, 4, and 5.
106. Ordinances Nos. 1 of 1851, 7 of 1857, 6 of 1864, and 2 of 1889 s. 29.
107. May to Colonial Secretary, 13 June 1893, CO 129/264, 470.
108. Holdsworth and Munn, *Crime, Justice and Punishment in Colonial Hong Kong*, 164–165.
109. Reports of the Special Committee appointed to investigate the Po Leung Kuk, *HKSP*, 34/1893, 125–126.
110. *SCMP*, 21 September 1926.

Corrupt practices and slipshod procedures resulted in poor performances by police witnesses at trial. Careless procedures, mishandled exhibits, defective identity parades, and a frequently cavalier approach to the facts were easily exposed by counsel. Investigations were handicapped by the ease with which culprits could flee to the Mainland. Well into the twentieth century, rules adopted from England also discouraged interrogation of suspects in custody.[111] For this reason, judges were sceptical of confessions and vigilant in rejecting those obtained without caution or by other improper means.[112] Claims of coerced, induced, or fabricated confessions were common, and often convincing enough to acquit the accused. They were so frequent in the post-war years that by the 1960s the 'voir dire', in which such claims were tested in the absence of the jury, became a routine feature of criminal trials: according to one judge, the reliance of the 'overwhelming preponderance' of cases on 'so-called "voluntary confessions"' placed severe strains on 'the whole fabric of the administration of justice'.[113]

Incompetent policing, combined with porous borders and lack of cooperation from the public, resulted in low rates of arrest and conviction, particularly for murders and other serious crimes. During the thirty years from 1910 to 1939, for example, the five-year moving averages of arrest rates for known murder cases varied between 35 per cent and 50 per cent; the proportion of known murder cases reaching the Supreme Court ranged from 20 per cent to 45 per cent; and conviction rates were between 31 per cent and 73 per cent. Needless to say, these figures were lower than comparable figures for England and Wales.[114] The figures for Hong Kong improved in the twenty years from 1946, with detection rates for murders rising from about 35 per cent in the late 1940s to over 80 per cent in the late 1950s and early 1960s, the result of improved investigation skills, greater cooperation from the public, and, most important, the imposition of immigration and border controls in the early 1950s.

---

111. It was, wrote Lord Brampton in his introduction to Vincent's *Police Code*, 'wrong to question such person touching the crime of which he is accused'. Howard Vincent, *The Police Code* (London: Butterworth & Co., 1912), xv.

112. See *R v Wong Chiu Kwai* (1908) 3 HKLR 89, in which the Full Court (Piggott and Gompertz) quashed the murder conviction of three men on the ground that a confession by one of them, obtained by police during a search without a warrant, was inadmissible. In a case in 1930, Cheung Pak-yau, a New Territories villager, was bludgeoned by his wife and daughter-in-law after having sexually assaulted the latter. He was then buried head downwards by villagers, probably while still alive. The case collapsed when it was revealed that the daughter-in-law had been coerced by threats of imprisonment from a police constable into giving evidence against her mother-in-law at committal proceedings: *SCMP*, 30 September, 2 and 10 October, and 18–21 November 1930.

113. Sir Ivo Rigby in *Wong Ho-ming v The Queen* [1970] HKCA 95, and *Li Kar-wah v The Queen* [1970] HKLR 572.

114. In England in these years the arrest rate (including suicides of suspects) was about 80 per cent; the conviction rate (including, as for Hong Kong, verdicts of insanity) 76 per cent. The detection rate for homicides in modern Hong Kong is close to 100 per cent.

Interpreters

The language of the Hong Kong courts was English. Because most defendants and witnesses were Chinese and understood little, if any, English, the interpreter was an essential element at all stages in criminal justice. As the Peak Murder trial showed, the task of interpretation was complicated by the variety of mutually unintelligible Chinese dialects current in Hong Kong, as well as by the frequent need for interpretation in other languages. Interpretation increased the length of trials and, according to one governor, made cross-examination 'almost useless'.[115] The great differences between Chinese and English sometimes gave rise to arguments in court about correct interpretation. Yet, as with jury deliberations, the process was a mystery to most observers, not least because the interpreter was often the only court official who could understand all the proceedings. Suspicions arose that some interpreters bullied witnesses, or advised them on their answers, or were themselves tangled up in the cases they interpreted. Finding a supply of competent and trustworthy interpreters preoccupied governors in the nineteenth century.

The problem was acute in the early years, when the court relied in part on a stream of temporary interpreters[116] but mainly on Daniel Caldwell, a talented linguist who was also a police officer and Registrar General and Protector of Chinese (1856–1861). During those turbulent times he was the main – practically the only – link between government and people.[117] His scandalous connection with a notorious criminal led to his dismissal. The government then resolved that interpretation in the Supreme Court should be led by men who were not only not Chinese but who, unlike Caldwell, were also 'gentlemen'. Starting in the mid-1850s, governors attempted a series of schemes to deliver on this aim. They fell into two broad categories: the employment of Chinese-speaking Europeans available in Hong Kong – the 'men-on-the-spot' solution; and the training of 'gentlemen interpreters', preferably recruited in Britain – the 'more young men remedy'.[118] From 1860 to 1909 the former method prevailed. The Supreme Court interpreter up to 1880 was Rafael Arcanjo Rozario, a Portuguese from Macao, whose abilities were often called into question. He

---

115. Governor Sir G.W. Des Voeux in the Legislative Council, *HKDP*, 17 May 1889.

116. Among them were several who were to rise to prominence. Thomas Wade, who was interpreter for short periods in the 1840s, was later British Minister in Peking and an originator of the Wade-Giles system of Romanizing Chinese. Wei Akwong, interpreter in 1855, became one of the wealthiest men in Hong Kong. Yung Wing, the first Chinese graduate of Yale University, acted as interpreter in 1855. He also attempted to train as an attorney but was driven out by lawyers who feared that his abilities in English and Chinese would put them out of business. Yung later led the Qing government's Chinese Education Mission to the United States (1872–1881).

117. See Christopher Munn, 'Colonialism "in a Chinese Atmosphere": The Caldwell Affair and the Perils of Collaboration in Early Colonial Hong Kong', in *New Frontiers: Imperialism's New Communities in East Asia, 1842–1953*, ed. Robert Bickers and Christian Henriot (Manchester: Manchester University Press, 2000).

118. *HKDP*, 23 November 1874.

was succeeded by James Dyer Ball, a scholar fluent in several Chinese dialects who had been raised in Canton by missionary parents. Ball was assisted by Li Hong-mi. Both were described as irreplaceable by a committee on interpretation in 1900.[119]

Ball retired in 1909 and was succeeded by Nicholas Nolan, the son of the head turnkey and matron of Victoria Gaol. Nolan was one of only two graduates of a scheme introduced in 1889 to recruit student-interpreters from among local non-Chinese schoolboys. Praised by Gompertz as 'an artist in interpretation', he was fluent in four Chinese dialects, and in Portuguese, Spanish, and Tagalog.[120] His premature death in 1920 left the court in difficulty. Although the government had largely accepted that Chinese should be employed as interpreters in preference to Europeans, it continued to insist that the Chief Interpreter should be a 'gentleman of social position and a European.'[121] The Registrar advertised for this elusive person for many months, but to no avail. In December 1923 the government appointed John Dodd, the son of a tea merchant, who had been educated in Hong Kong. Dodd held the position until 1929, when, after losing money in business speculations, he was adjudicated bankrupt.[122] Finally, in 1934, the government abandoned its insistence on appointing a European and promoted Ng Chak-wing as Chief Interpreter. Ng had been a Supreme Court interpreter since 1917 and had acted as chief in the intervals surrounding Dodd's term. Ng served with distinction until his death in service at the age of sixty in 1951, having been awarded an MBE in 1948.[123]

Judgment and sentence

The interpreter's last task in a trial was to interpret the judgment and sentence to the accused. In passing judgment, the judge might state his agreement with the verdict and comment on the nature of the crime. In manslaughter verdicts the judge might even indicate his disagreement, either directly or by remarking that the verdict was 'lenient', or the crime borderline murder: for reasons ranging from sympathy for the accused to doubts about the evidence, juries allegedly had a tendency to downgrade murder to manslaughter.[124] In

119. Report of a Committee to enquire into the question of interpretation, 13 March 1900, CO 129/298, 333.
120. *CM*, 24 and 26 January 1920. Gompertz was also an accomplished linguist, proficient in three Chinese dialects.
121. Report of a Committee to Enquire into Interpretation in the Public Service, in Blake to Chamberlain, 3 April 1900, CO 129/298, 319–359: see especially pp. 341–343; *SCMP*, 27 May 1920.
122. *SCMP*, 6 June and 6 December 1929.
123. *SCMP*, 4 and 5 April 1951.
124. In the S.S. *Tanda* case in 1930, for example, a Japanese passenger killed a Chinese cook whom he alleged had drugged him and taken gambling winnings from him. After a trial plagued with interpretation problems, the jury returned a verdict of manslaughter. The judge, John Wood, disagreed, saying that, according to the evidence, the proper verdict would have been murder. He sentenced the accused to fourteen years' imprisonment. *HKDP*, 6 and 7 June 1930. For later commentary on the reluctance of juries to return verdicts of murder see *SCMP*, 12 May 1972 and 13 November 1975. For similar views in England see *Royal Commission on Capital Punishment 1949–1953, Report*, 7–8.

such cases the sentence might be severe, even the maximum of life imprisonment. More usually, the punishment for manslaughter was a fixed-term sentence, often as short as two years if provocation was acute. In a case in 1868, the killing of a Chinese by an American with no provocation, it was a fine of $500. Occasionally, a judge disagreed with a verdict of murder. This happened in 1907 when four Sikhs were convicted on accomplice evidence of murdering another Sikh in a robbery, despite Piggott's warnings of the dangers of such evidence. Believing a miscarriage of justice had occurred, Piggott urged pardons. The Governor in Council disagreed but commuted the sentences to life imprisonment because there was doubt over who struck the blows.[125]

Unless the verdict was guilty but insane, the only sentence for murder was death. However, up to 1865 for murder, and longer for other capital felonies, the judge could *record*, rather than *pronounce*, sentence of death if he believed the accused deserved mercy.[126] This invariably resulted in commutation. 'Death recorded' was the standard sentence for non-fatal piracies with violence: its last use appears to have been in 1874.[127] It was also applied to at least fifteen men convicted of murder between 1851 and 1857, in most cases because of problems with evidence. In 1907, when the formula was long forgotten,[128] Piggott applied his version of 'death recorded' in another case where he disagreed with the verdict. A swineherd at Pok Fu Lam admitted killing a colleague and his son after getting blind drunk. Under cross-examination, the sole witness, the deceased's widow, withdrew evidence she had given to the magistrate about a quarrel over the killing of a dog for food. Counsel for the defence, Ho Kai, urged a verdict of manslaughter. When the all-European jury returned a verdict of murder, Piggott refused to pass sentence 'in the ordinary way'. Instead, holding the black cap rather than placing it over his wig, he passed sentence of death 'in the formal manner'. This resulted in commutation because Piggott's comments, reported in the press, 'practically bound the Government to this course'.[129]

---

125. After the commutations by May, Piggott asked the new Governor, Lugard, to reconsider the decision. *HKDP*, 19 and 20 July 1907; Lugard to Piggott, 6 August 1907, HKPRO HKRS102-1, 136–137.

126. Judgment of Death Act 1823, originally applicable to all felonies except murder, was extended to murder in 1837: J.E. Davis, *The Criminal Law Consolidation Statues of the 24 & 25 Victoria, Chapters 94 to 100* (London: Butterworths, 1861), 244–245; Ordinance No. 4 of 1865 s. 2. It ceased to be available for other felonies in Hong Kong in 1966, having been excluded from the Application of English Law Ordinance.

127. Two men received sentences of death recorded, commuted to ten years' penal servitude, for piracy with wounding on a fishing boat off Cape D'Aguilar. *HKDP*, 22 and 23 September 1874; *OCM*, 26 September 1874; ExCo Minutes, 21 October 1874, CO 131/9, 115.

128. So obsolete that the column 'death recorded' in the proforma annual returns of criminal cases was for many years mistakenly used to record actual executions.

129. *SCMP*, 22 and 23 May 1907; ExCo Minutes, 30 May 1907, CO 131/35, 511.

Life or death: Review of capital sentences

Prisoners sentenced to death were held in a condemned cell pending a review of their case. The Royal Instructions required the Governor to review every death sentence at the first convenient opportunity with the aid of a report from the trial judge and advice from the Executive Council. Early hangings followed swiftly upon sentencing and confirmation, sometimes within a few days, usually within two weeks. In the 1890s the interval settled at three or four weeks from sentence, reflecting the practice in England of letting three Sundays pass between sentence and execution. The gap sometimes extended to several months after the creation of the Court of Criminal Appeal in 1933, and with the greater frequency of petitions to the Privy Council from the 1950s. Appeals were almost routine for murders after World War II, even where counsel conceded they could find no grounds. Before the war, the Judicial Committee of the Privy Council agreed to hear only two appeals against capital convictions from Hong Kong: those of Ibrahim (1914) and Chung Chi-cheung (1938).[130] Neither succeeded. From 1947 to 1966, twenty-six men in eighteen murder cases petitioned the Privy Council. Leave to appeal was given in three cases. Only one succeeded.[131]

The Governor, in reviewing capital sentences, was required 'to decide either to extend or to withhold a pardon or reprieve according to your own deliberate judgment'.[132] If he decided against the majority of his council he had to record his reasons. This delegation of the royal prerogative of mercy, common throughout the empire, resembled the practice in the UK where the Home Secretary reviewed murder convictions, in consultation with officials and judges, before deciding whether to advise the sovereign to exercise mercy. The differences were that a colonial governor personally exercised the prerogative and was required to consult his council. The sovereign retained a residual prerogative and exercised it twice in relation to death sentences in Hong Kong on the advice of the Secretary of State: in 1852 and 1973.[133] Generally, however, ministers in London were reluctant to intervene,

130. For Ibrahim see Chapter 8; for Chung see footnote 133 below.

131. The murder conviction against Chan Kau in 1953 was reduced to manslaughter on the ground that the judge had wrongly withdrawn from the jury a defence of provocation. Chan had got caught up in a fight between two groups employed at the Naval Dockyard at Stonecutters Island and had grabbed a knife and stabbed a man in self-defence. The Judicial Committee held that, in the light of recent English judgments, the defence was not required to satisfy the jury that self-defence was necessary. The case was remitted to the Supreme Court, which sentenced Chan to fifteen years' hard labour. *Chan Kau v The Queen* [1954] UKPC 40; *SCMP*, 28 January 1955.

132. Royal Instructions to the Governor of Hong Kong (1843), article 35, CO 385/35. Similar wording was used in later versions of the Royal Instructions until the abolition of the death penalty in 1993.

133. See Chapters 3 and 12. In 1937 Chung Chi-cheung, a cabin boy, was convicted of murdering the British captain of a Chinese customs cruiser in Hong Kong waters. He appealed to the Privy Council on the ground that the Supreme Court had no jurisdiction over the ship. Before the appeal was dismissed, the Attorney General of England suggested commutation of Chung's death sentence because he had already spent fifteen months in the

holding that the delegation was to the Governor personally, and that he alone was responsible for exercising it.

The Royal Instructions stated that the Governor should only exercise mercy if it appeared 'expedient to do so'. How far principles emerged that were comparable to the quasi-jurisprudence developed in the Home Office is difficult to assess: Executive Council minutes rarely recorded discussions of capital cases. Governors varied in their approaches. Some, like Sir John Bowring (1854–1859) and Sir John Pope Hennessy (1877–1882), had reservations about the death penalty and commuted some sentences against the advice of their council. Sir William Peel (1930–1935) and Sir Murray MacLehose (1971–1982) paid heed to public opinion; MacLehose was also constrained by political opinion in England. Others had few qualms. Among those who commuted few sentences were Sir Hercules Robinson (1859–1865), Sir William Robinson (1891–1898), Sir Reginald Stubbs (1919–1925), Sir Cecil Clementi (1925–1930), and Sir Alexander Grantham (1947–1957). Most of these served in times of high crime rates and political instability; they took a more lenient view of purely domestic cases. The exception was Sir William Robinson, who reviewed nine death sentences and confirmed them all,[134] including one, the outcome of a trivial quarrel, in which his council was evenly divided. The spate of hangings during his term ended a twelve-year period with only four capital convictions and one execution.

If the reasoning behind the use of mercy is not usually recorded, some patterns can still be deduced from explanations that survive, or from extrapolation. Crimes directly challenging the authority, security, or economic interests of the colonial state, or resulting in the deaths of colonists, other persons of high status, or police officers, were least likely to attract mercy: justified by the need for deterrent punishments, this was to varying degrees a pattern in other colonies.[135] Armed robberies and kidnappings were also dealt with severely. If these elements were absent, factors generally leading to commutations in the UK came into play: for example, unsafe convictions; suicide pacts with one survivor (treated

condemned cell waiting for the appeal to be heard: the Governor, Sir Geoffry Northcote, duly commuted the sentence to life imprisonment. *Chung Chi Cheung v the King* [1938] UKPC 75; CO 129/562/2 'Privy Council Appeals: Chung Chi Cheung' (1937); CO 129/568/9 'Privy Council Appeals: Chung Chi Cheung' (1938). See also, Norman J. Miners, 'The Governor, The Secretary of State and the Prerogative of Mercy', *HKLJ*, Vol. 17 (1987): 77–89.

134. Two others during his term were confirmed by his deputies Wilsone Black and Sir George O'Brien.

135. See Stacey Hynd, 'Murder and Mercy: Capital Punishment in Colonial Kenya, ca. 1909–1956', *International Journal of African Historical Studies* 45, no. 1 (2012): 81–101, and '"The Extreme Penalty of the Law": Mercy and the Death Penalty as Aspects of State Power in Colonial Nyasaland, c. 1903–47', *Journal of Eastern African Studies* 4, no. 3 (2010): 542–559; William S. Lofquist, 'Identifying the Condemned: Reconstructing and Analyzing the History of Executions in the Bahamas', *International Journal of Bahamian Studies* 16 (2010): 19–34; Alastair McLure, 'Sovereignty, Law, and the Politics of Forgiveness in Colonial India, 1858–1903', *Comparative Studies of South Asia, Africa and the Middle East* 38, no. 3 (2018): 385–401; and Clare Anderson, 'Execution and Its Aftermath in the Nineteenth-Century British Empire', in *A Global History of Execution and the Criminal Corpse*, ed. Richard Ward (London: Palgrave MacMillan, 2015).

as manslaughter from 1963); infanticides of newborn babies by mothers (manslaughter from 1934); crimes by women or young persons; murders with a degree of provocation insufficient for a verdict of manslaughter, especially in cases of adultery or fights; murders committed on a sudden impulse, or from mental imbalance not amounting to insanity; and recommendations to mercy by jury or judge.[136] In murders during gang robberies or piracies the Executive Council sometimes tried to identify the leaders or those who dealt the fatal blow. In the early years the council also acted as a de facto court of appeal when hearing claims of false accusations.

There were many deviations from these patterns, and occasional confusion about what principles should be applied. In a case in 1908, for example, both Chief Justice Piggott and Attorney General Rees-Davies mistakenly advised the Executive Council that it was no longer the practice in England to hang women.[137] The desire for exemplary punishment when violent crime was prevalent might trump all mitigating factors. Decisions in some unexplained cases may be the result of the 'primitive lotteries' and 'caprice' observed in some other jurisdictions.[138]

Apart from rare instances of free pardons, commutation took the form of a pardon conditional on serving a term of transportation (1844–1858), penal servitude (1858-1887),[139] imprisonment (with hard labour from 1887 to 1959), or some other punishment. Prison might be for a period of years or for life. From 1883, following the practice in Ceylon, the Governor in Council reviewed all life sentences after fifteen years (ten for those over sixty). In 1938 the maximum for a life sentence was fixed at fifteen years for a well-conducted

136. See Leon Radzinowicz and Roger Hood, *A History of English Criminal Law and its Administration from 1750*, Vol. 5, *The Emergence of Penal Policy* (Oxford: Clarendon Press, 1990), 677–681; and Sir Edward Troup, *The Home Office* (London: Putnam's Sons Ltd, 1925), 62–71.

137. Lam Kiu poisoned her partner Cheung Fuk after a violent quarrel over her relations with another man. She then took the poison but survived. The Executive Council was evenly split, and, after hearing from Piggott and Rees-Davies, Lugard commuted her death sentence to penal servitude for life. He reported this to the Secretary of State, who replied that many women had been hanged in England in recent years and asked for an explanation. This gave rise to another 'tiresome' dispute with Piggott, who denied having given the advice in such categorical terms. Lam Kiu was released in 1923. *HKDP*, 21 January 1908; ExCo Minutes, 4 February and 22 June 1908, CO 131/35, 637 and 674, and 11 January 1923, CO 131/60, 488; Lugard to Crewe, 10 February 1908, CO 129/346, 147–154, and 11 and 25 June 1908, CO 129/347, 478–482 and 563–565.

138. See, for example, Carolyn Strange (on Canada), 'The Lottery of Death: Capital Punishment, 1867–1976', *Manitoba Law Journal* 23, no. 3 (1996): 594–619; and Ian O'Donnell, *Justice, Mercy, and Caprice: Clemency and the Death Penalty in Ireland* (Oxford: Oxford University Press, 2017).

139. Penal servitude, introduced in England to replace transportation, began with total isolation; then work in association and separate confinement at night; and, finally, release under police supervision. In the crowded Victoria Gaol distinctions between penal servitude and hard labour had ceased to exist by the time penal servitude was abolished in 1887, when police supervision was also introduced. However, for many years after abolition Executive Council minutes continued to use the term 'penal servitude'. Ordinances Nos. 10 of 1858 and 10 and 11 of 1887.

prisoner.[140] In 1920, reviews after seven, ten, fifteen, and twenty years were extended to all prisoners serving over ten years.[141] From 1952, under a policy adopted from Nigeria, if the Governor commuted a death sentence he imposed a fixed term rather than life, taking advice from the trial judge: the reasons were, first, that life was disproportionately harsh for young offenders, and, secondly, that it was better to take advice from those familiar with the case than to await reviews many years later.[142] The policy broke down in the early 1970s, when life became the standard term for commuted death sentences.

Death by judicial hanging

Prisoners condemned to death were confined separately from other prisoners and kept under twenty-four-hour observation. They were allowed visits from relatives, friends, lawyers, and priests, and received a special diet at the discretion of the gaol authorities. Sometimes the Sheriff or some other official spent time with the prisoner in an attempt to elicit a confession or information about accomplices. In some notorious early piracy cases, colonists eager for a sight of the prisoners were also admitted. All executions in British Hong Kong took the form of hanging by the neck.

The first hanging took place shortly after 6 a.m. on 5 November 1844 at a place close to the Chinese quarter: a promontory at West Point, above a bend on Queen's Road, next to 'Edger's Bungalow'.[143] The condemned man was Costa Persey, an Indian camp-follower of the 98th Regiment. He had been convicted of murdering a Sergeant Crosby after being punished for drunkenness. Persey had embraced Christianity through the efforts of Catholic priests, who had spent the night with him. Escorted on foot from the gaol, over a mile away, he walked firmly up the steps to the gallows. The first attempt to hang him failed when the noose gave way. Kissing his crucifix, Persey calmly waited for it to be fixed. The second attempt worked, and 'after a few struggles he ceased to exist'. Many curious Chinese watched the execution.[144]

Hangings continued at West Point until 1856. Condemned men were marched from the gaol under a large military guard. Sometimes other convicts were led out in procession to witness the spectacle. The place of execution was then moved to the Magistracy compound high above Arbuthnot Road. The site was visible from the neighbouring streets

140. ExCo Minutes, 9 May 1883 and 12 January 1938, CO 131/12, 335–336 and CO 131/98, 83.
141. *HKGG*, 12 March 1920. From 1959 a Board of Review advised on early releases on special grounds.
142. In a few exceptions, life, rather than a fixed term, was imposed. Some fifty persons, found insane or under the age of eighteen, were also detained at Her Majesty's pleasure in the period 1952–1974 – not all in cases of murder. HKRS146-13-5 'Prisoners' (1946–1974); CO 1030/1265 'Review of Long Term Prison Sentences – Hong Kong' (1960–1962).
143. The site is now occupied by the Tsan Yuk Hospital, a maternity hospital. ExCo Minutes, 11 October 1844, CO 131/1, 64–65.
144. *HKR*, 5 November 1844; FOC, 6 November 1844.

and houses. It was closer to Victoria Gaol and more tightly controlled amid fears of rescue attempts. The move allowed the military escort to be halved, from a hundred to fifty.[145] The Magistracy compound continued to be used until 1879, when executions, still held in public, were moved to a yard near the gaol. From 1893, after an eleven-year pause in hangings, all executions were carried out in private within Victoria Gaol in the presence of gaol staff, a medical officer, a priest, an interpreter, and the hangman.[146] From 1937, hangings took place in a special 'execution suite' in Stanley Prison.

From 1844 to 1849, the government employed as hangman Mogul Jaun (or 'Moggle-John'), an Indian Muslim who also acted as a police constable.[147] In 1849 he was sentenced to ten years' transportation for stealing plate and cutlery from a dwelling house.[148] The position was then abolished. For the next three decades executioners were hired ad hoc, sometimes from among the gaol turnkeys, or prisoners promised early release for performing the task. In a case in 1849, the executions of six men convicted of piracy with violence were carried out by an American whose brother had been killed by pirates.[149] In another, in 1879, two Siamese and a Javanese convicted of murdering the captain of a British ship were hanged by a European sailor accommodated in the gaol as a destitute.[150] The last public hanging, of the Indian soldier Tika Ram in 1882, was carried out by another European sailor under sentence of eighteen months' imprisonment for robbing another sailor.[151] After hangings resumed in the 1890s, more systematic arrangements were adopted. At first an official hangman, like the peripatetic hangman in England, received a fee for each neck.[152] Then volunteers from among the warders carried out executions: in the early 1960s the two warders who performed the duty received $75 for each execution.[153] In 1990, long after executions had ceased, an unedifying dispute took place between two retired prison officers over who exactly had been the last hangman.[154]

---

145. Two hangings in the early months of 1857 were held within the Gaol compound. ExCo Minutes, 17 March 1856, CO 131/3, 57–58; *FOC*, 26 March 1856 and 11 April 1857; *HKR*, 1 April 1856; *CM*, 19 February 1857; Bowring to Labouchere, 7 April 1856, CO 129/55, 72–73.
146. *CM*, 8 August 1893.
147. The government originally had in mind a Chinese candidate. Some accounts of early hangings refer to a Chinese hangman, perhaps mistakenly, since his face was veiled. *Hong Kong Blue Book* 1848, 112; *HKR*, 8 July 1845.
148. Mogul Jaun was transported to Penang. He is described as aged thirty-four and carrying out the trade of 'doctor' in the transport list. *CM*, 19 July 1849; Transport List, 5 November 1849, CO 129/30, 305.
149. *FOC*, 9 June 1849.
150. *CM*, 28 May 1879.
151. He received $25 for carrying out the hanging. *HKDP*, 6 July 1882.
152. One of them was named as 'J. Elma', who, for a fee of $12.50 for each neck, carried out hangings in the 1900s, including those of Smith, Nason and Hogmann in 1905: see Chapter 6. *SCMP*, 23 March 1910.
153. Answers to enquiries by the *Hong Kong Standard*, 25 November 1964, HKPRO HKRS70-2-180.
154. John Fleming, then running a car-hire firm on Lantau, claimed that he was the last hangman in a newspaper interview in 1986, and again in a television documentary in 1990. The claim was disputed by another former

Because they were carried out by untrained men on portable gallows, many early executions were bungled. Some prisoners were kept waiting for long periods with the noose around their neck while workmen hammered loose the rusted bolt to release the trap. In a double hanging in 1853, those in attendance were 'nearly fainting from the horror' of seeing the prisoners left half-strangled by their nooses when the trap dropped only a short distance. In a triple hanging in 1850, two of the prisoners fainted; the third kept shouting 'Fidee, fidee!' – 'Hurry, hurry!' 'A most aufuller Sight I never saw,' wrote one horrified witness; it was 'a Piece of Brutality', a 'Disgrace to Englishmen'.[155] Where proceedings did not break down the attitude of prisoners varied from quiet resignation, even sullen indifference, to fearful trembling. Some were fortified with alcohol or drugged with opium. Others, particularly those who had been recently baptized, made speeches repenting their crimes and exhorting the crowd to convert to Christianity. Some expressed regret at leaving their mothers without support. A few took the opportunity to protest their innocence and name the real culprits.[156] At the last public hanging, in 1882, the condemned man, the Indian soldier, Tika Ram, asked for all the men of his company to be present, and for the government to pay for the wood for his cremation.[157]

When, from the 1890s, hangings took place in private, the process became more efficient, aided by new apparatus based on designs from England and experience gained by the prison officers designated as hangmen. For a while, reporters were allowed to witness the private executions. Procedures were then tightened. Only occasionally did details emerge about the final days of condemned prisoners: for example, the request by Ho Fat in 1922 to be interred beside his victim, his wife,[158] or the report in 1923 that the first woman to be hanged, Chan Pak, 'went to her death singing a Chinese song': she was sharply rebuked for doing so by her male accomplice, who had helped her drown her elderly husband, and who was hanged with her.[159]

Hangings took place at 5 a.m. or 6 a.m., signalled by the tolling of a bell in the gaol. The bodies were left to hang for half an hour. A medical officer then certified death. Inquests into the deaths of executed prisoners were not usually held until 1888, when legislation required the magistrate serving as coroner to hold an inquest with a jury of three within

---

prison officer, Richard Brimmicombe-Wood, then working as a health and safety advisor at a holiday camp in the UK, who said he had participated in over thirty hangings in the 1950s and 1960s and that Fleming had not been present at any of them. *SCMP*, 8 November 1986, 15 March 1990, and 7 October 1991.

155. Letter from 'Signature illegible', *CM*, 2 May 1850; *FOC*, 25 May 1850; *CM*, 22 May 1856; *HKR*, 4 January 1853.

156. For detailed accounts see, for example, *CM*, 21 January and 29 April 1847, 28 December 1848, 3 November 1868, 25 October 1869, 19 December 1878, and 28 May and 2 September 1879; and HKR, 4 May 1852.

157. It appears that these requests were not granted. *HKT*, 1 July 1882.

158. Ho admitted to murdering her when she ignored his advice to give up prostitution. *SCMP*, 17 August 1922.

159. *HKDP*, 30 November 1923.

twenty-four hours.[160] Some verdicts gave the cause of death: fracture of the neck if the hanging was quick, strangulation if it was botched. From the 1930s the cause, if reported, was usually simply 'death by judicial hanging'. The place of burial was decided by the Governor.[161] In a few cases, relatives or friends were allowed to take away the body for burial.[162] More usually, bodies were buried in a designated place. Governor Davis decided in 1847 this should be within the gaol precincts: 'their prevalent superstition', he believed, would make 'the lowest of the population' less ready to commit crimes merely to obtain shelter there.[163] This continued until the late 1850s. Bodies were then buried in cemeteries at Mount Davis at the western end of Hong Kong Island, and, later, at the Coffee Plantation at Caroline Hill near So Kon Po.[164] From 1937, the bodies were buried in the cemetery at Stanley Prison.[165]

The significance of capital punishment

Capital punishment is intended to prevent criminals from reoffending, deter others from crime, and provide retributive justice for society and victims' families. How far it achieves these aims has long been the subject of debate. Opponents argue that the punishment is barbaric, that it is irrevocable if the condemned person is later found to be innocent, that it has no deterrent effect, and that the state has no right to take away a person's life. Aspects of this debate erupted in Hong Kong in the 1930s, when some voices called for abolition, and again in the 1970s, when political leaders demanded the resumption of hangings at a time of rising crime.

In a colonial setting, capital punishment was part of the apparatus of state violence designed to maintain the authority of an alien dominant elite – an apparatus which, for much of Hong Kong's history, officials deemed necessary to discipline an unruly population. Violent punishments persisted in Hong Kong long after they became obsolete elsewhere. Hangings, like floggings, were carried out by non-Chinese. The great majority of

160. Ordinance No. 17 of 1888 s. 7, modelled on the Capital Punishment Act 1868 s. 5.
161. Ordinance No. 4 of 1865 (repealed in 1963) required the court so to direct when pronouncing sentence; Ordinance No. 17 of 1954 stated that it should be in a prison cemetery designated by the Governor in Council.
162. In 1873 the Imam requested the body of Ahmed, a Malay sailor convicted of murdering another Malay on a British ship near Guam, to have it interred according to Muslim rites 'on the ground that freedom of Religion is tolerated under British Rule'. The Governor, Sir Arthur Kennedy, acceded, but not on the ground stated, and not as a precedent. The family of Chiu Yuk-fai, convicted of the Charcoal Murder in 1937 (see Chapter 10) was also allowed to take away his body for burial. ExCo Minutes, 31 July 1873, CO 131/8, 300; *SCMP*, 12 June 1937.
163. ExCo Minutes, 22 April 1847; CM, 4 February 1858.
164. So called after attempts to grow coffee there in the 1850s.
165. Samson Chan, 'Colonial Penality: A Case Study of Hong Kong's Penal Policy and Programmes under British Administration (1945–1997) (PhD Thesis, University of Hull, 2012), 167–168.

those hanged were Chinese. In proportion to population, far more people were hanged in Hong Kong than in England: in 1852, 1865, 1866, 1927, and 1956–1959 the actual numbers exceeded the totals in the whole of England and Wales.[166] Yet, by colonial standards, the numbers were not high. In the Straits Settlements, the nearest British colony to Hong Kong, with a comparable albeit larger population, 304 persons were executed in the fifty years from 1889 to 1938, compared with 128 in Hong Kong.[167]

Hangings in colonial Hong Kong were the end-result of a system of justice presided over by British judges and officials, in which, as one Attorney General put it, 'nineteen-twentieths of the prisoners and witnesses are Chinese and the majority of the jurors are foreigners'.[168] This was hardly the intention of early British officials, who envisaged the criminal courts mainly as tools to control their own people. Shortly after the British occupation of Hong Kong Island, British and Chinese officials set about negotiating a form of divided jurisdiction whereby Chinese offenders would be tried under Chinese law by Chinese officials, either on the Mainland or in Hong Kong. In 1843, while these negotiations were in progress, Hong Kong's Chief Magistrate investigated a murder at Chai Wan, at the eastern end of Hong Kong Island, with this in mind. The proposals, mirroring the extraterritoriality allowed to the British in the treaty ports, broke down when the British government, seeing practical difficulties, asserted absolute sovereignty over Hong Kong and its rapidly growing Chinese population.[169]

No Chinese government fully recognized British sovereignty. But the large number of convicted Chinese criminals in the Hong Kong gaol, claimed Governor Davis in 1844, 'proved' that Chinese officials tacitly accepted British jurisdiction.[170] A year later he reported that the execution of Chun Afoon, 'the first instance of the kind under British Law in China', established 'the once disputed British jurisdiction over Chinese in capital cases' and 'the sovereignty of Her Majesty in this Colony'. Davis also claimed that the hanging of

166. The 369 men and women hanged in Hong Kong during 1844–1966 compare with approximately 1,500 persons hanged in the same period in England and Wales, a jurisdiction with a population over 160 times that of Hong Kong in the 1860s and about 15 times in the 1960s.

167. Reports on Gaols and Prisoners and Judicial Returns, *Straits Settlements Blue Books* 1889–1938 (Singapore, Penang, Malacca). The total excludes forty-seven Indian soldiers tried by court martial and executed after the 1915 mutiny. The population of the Straits Settlements was about twice that of Hong Kong at the start of this period, and about 25 per cent higher at the end. The high incidence of homicides and other crimes in the Straits has been attributed to high rates of immigration, clashes between secret societies, and gang robberies: Nordin Hussin and Shakimah Che Hasbullah, 'Crimes in the Straits Settlements before World War II', *Pertanika Journal of Social Sciences & Humanities*, Vol. 20(1) (March 2012): 121–136. It also appears that, compared with Hong Kong, a larger proportion of reported murders in the Straits resulted in trial and conviction.

168. 'Report by the Attorney General [William Goodman] on the jurisdiction of Magistrates to inflict sentences of 12 months' imprisonment under section 80 of 10 of 1890', 8 December 1894, CO 129/264, 469.

169. See Ivan Lee, *Extradition and Empire: Sovereignty and Subjecthood in Hong Kong* (Cambridge: Cambridge University Press, 2025), Chapter 1.

170. Davis to Stanley, 5 July 1844, CO 129/6, 361.

Chun, 'at the same time, and on the same drop', with an Englishman convicted of murder 'demonstrated to Her Majesty's Chinese subjects at Hongkong the perfect equality of British Law'.[171] The death penalty thus had a political significance far beyond its function as a punishment for serious crime.

The suspects in the 1843 Chai Wan murder were not handed over to Chinese officials. Reviewing the case, the Governor, Sir Henry Pottinger, was struck by what it revealed about 'the extraordinary (and, according to our notions repugnant) system of Chinese Jurisprudence'. The accuser, in reporting the case to the magistrate in Xin'an County, had signed a bond consenting to punishment if he failed to establish the accusation. He had also, 'as a matter of course', asked that the accused be examined by torture.[172] Revulsion at the harshness of Qing justice was a running theme among British officials. They were nevertheless willing to hand over offenders to the Chinese courts knowing that guarantees against torture or *lingchi* (death by slicing) had little value. Colonial officials and their Chinese advisors also cited the severity of Qing justice when advocating flogging for Chinese offenders. Yet neither floggings nor conditions in Victoria Gaol, bad as they were, could match the harshness with which the Qing authorities treated offenders.

In arguing for the surrender on request of non-resident Chinese wanted by the Qing authorities for crimes committed on the Mainland, Governor Sir William Des Voeux played down differences by referring to executions in England in which men were left hanging alive for up to twenty minutes before they died. He might as easily have cited the dismal record of botched hangings in early Hong Kong.[173] Some observers believed that transportation to other colonies, the main secondary punishment in Hong Kong's early years, was as fearful to Chinese as death itself, if not worse. 'Chinese call transportation *death*,' observed the *Friend of China*, 'as they say they will never see the transportees again – they will never return to China – in fact they are *done for*.'[174] Yet hangings and transportation were weak deterrents in comparison to the beheadings imposed in China on rebels and pirates, or the *lingchi* inflicted on their leaders, which destroyed the somatic integrity necessary, according to Chinese beliefs, for repose in the afterlife.[175]

171. A dubious claim. Chun was convicted of a cutting and wounding an Indian guard and English blacksmith with intent to murder in a seaborne attack on Jardine Matheson's premises. The Englishman, Charles Ingwood, a sailor from HMS *Driver*, was convicted under the Supreme Court's extraterritorial jurisdiction of the murder of another Englishman by tying him up and drowning him after a drunken quarrel at Whampoa. Davis to Stanley, 4 July 1845, CO 129/12, 263; Davis to Aberdeen, 25 July 1845, TNA FO 17/100, 194–195; *HKR*, 1 and 8 July 1845; FOC, 5 July 1845.
172. Pottinger to Stanley, 9 December 1843, CO 129/2, 381–384.
173. *HKDP*, 28 May 1889.
174. *FOC*, 5 March 1856, explaining why a gang of men who had murdered a man in revenge for giving evidence leading to sentences of transportation against two of their comrades had accused him of causing their deaths.
175. Hangings were comparable to strangulation, the lightest form of capital punishment in the Qing Code: see Chaloner Alabaster, *Notes and Commentaries on Chinese Criminal Law* (London: Luzac & Co., 1899),

In the light of the Chai Wan case, Pottinger proposed assimilating justice for Chinese in Hong Kong to that of China: a magistrate or judge would dispense summary justice; sentences above a certain level would be confirmed by the Governor.[176] 'The utter inapplicability of any form resembling "Trial by Jury" to Her Majesty's Chinese Subjects' was, in his view, 'too obvious to require any comment'. Trial by jury was, however, established in Hong Kong and used widely in the early years. Officials soon came to regret this. 'The unfitness of our criminal procedure to the circumstances of this Colony has long since passed almost into a proverb,' remarked a commission of enquiry in 1872.[177] With 'its myths allied to the jury system', British justice 'is seen by the untutored masses as essentially a gamble, with the cards dealt in favour of the most persuasive liar and/or the cleverest attorney or advocate', wrote a senior official a hundred years later.[178] The history of criminal justice in Hong Kong is in part a series of attempts to shift trials away from juries into the summary courts. This process did not, however, affect capital offences, all of which were tried by juries or, in 1945–1946, by a panel of judges. Combined with the protections given to defendants and scrupulous observance of procedural rules, reliance on juries reflected the 'considerable anxiety' that such cases gave to judges and prosecutors.[179] For this reason, capital trials tended to be recorded and discussed in detail in official reports and the press. They therefore offer opportunities to examine the workings of justice at the highest levels.

The organization and themes of this book

The next nine chapters of this book examine capital cases from the first hundred years of British rule. Two final chapters trace the events leading to the suspension of the death penalty in 1966 and its formal abolition in 1993. Each of the main chapters presents one key trial, or a cluster of related trials, setting it in historical context and explaining its significance in the development of criminal justice. Other comparable cases are briefly described. The cases are mostly murders but also include a mass poisoning and several piracies. The murders arose variously from jealousy, revenge, political acts, and killings incidental to other offences. The discussion highlights the colonial relationship, ranging from attempts to accommodate Chinese custom to outright confrontations between government and people. Particular attention is given to proceedings after trial, where governors and their

---

57–63, and Timothy Brook, Jérôme Bourgon, and Gregory Blue, *Death by a Thousand Cuts* (Cambridge, Massachusetts: Harvard University Press, 2008), Chapters 1 and 2. Some bodies in Hong Kong may not have been left intact: a report in 1868 refers to a collection of heads from executed bodies kept at the Civil Hospital, probably for craniological research: *HKDP*, 3 November 1868.

176. Pottinger briefly implemented a system along these lines: see Christopher Munn, '"Scratching with a Rattan": William Caine and the Hong Kong Magistracy, 1841–1844', *HKLJ*, Vol. 25 (1995): 213–238.

177. Report of the Police Commission, 27 June 1872, CO 129/158, 302.

178. A.T. Clark to Secretary for Home Affairs, 22 December 1971, HKPRO HKRS260-1-22, encl. 25.

179. Goodman, *Reminiscences*, 168.

councils determined the fate of those convicted, often amid public controversy. The cases have been chosen partly for the availability of sources able to throw light from different perspectives. Some also illustrate turning points in the administration of justice, such as the provision of legal aid in murder trials or the creation of the Court of Criminal Appeal. They are therefore not a scientific sample. Nor are they representative of the majority of capital trials in colonial Hong Kong: if they were, the book would consist mainly of murders resulting from robberies or quarrels over resources. Few of the cases here set legal precedents or raised difficult questions of law. They are nevertheless important for what they say about relations between courts, people, and government in Hong Kong's history.

Chapter 2 explores Hong Kong's most famous early case: the mass poisoning of colonists by agents of the Qing government in 1857, shortly after the outbreak of the Second Opium War. The ten men were tried by an all-British jury at a time when many colonists, including the Attorney General, were demanding their summary execution.

Chapter 3 examines piracy trials, taking as examples three connected trials resulting in no fewer than eleven executions in 1866. Piracy trials presented special difficulties with evidence, giving rise both to miscarriages of justice and to suspicions that well-resourced defendants were evading justice by manipulating witnesses. The chapter examines attempts to reduce reliance on the Supreme Court in such cases by more summary forms of justice and by channelling cases to the Chinese courts, where punishment was harsher and more certain.

Chapter 4 describes the part played by a murder in 1878 in the movement to provide lawyers at public expense for defendants in murder trials. The case brings into focus the approaches to justice by two progressive yet controversial figures in nineteenth-century Hong Kong: the Governor, Sir John Hennessy, and the Chief Justice, Sir John Smale. An examination of other murder cases from the late nineteenth century suggests that the introduction of legal aid markedly improved chances of acquittal. At the same time, the dearth of capital convictions prompted concerns that murderers were not being brought to justice.

Chapter 5 deals with the cross-border legal consequences of the assassination in Hong Kong of the revolutionary Yeung Ku-wan by agents of the Qing government in 1900, after attempts to have him extradited for trial in China proved unsuccessful. The chapter focuses on attempts by the Governor, Sir Henry Blake, to secure justice. It also examines the evolution of extradition policy and Hong Kong's precarious role as a refuge and base for revolutionaries.

Chapter 6 discusses the murder in 1903 of a boatwoman and her daughter by three unemployed European sailors in a reckless plan to sail to Singapore in search of work. This highly charged case was a rare instance of Europeans tried for the murder of Chinese, and an illustration of how social status was sometimes as important as ethnicity in the treatment of offenders. The case prompted new policies to deal with the growing number of destitute Europeans, who were a practical problem and an embarrassment to the colonial community.

Chapter 7 recounts the murder of two warders during an escape from Victoria Gaol by four prisoners in 1919. All four were captured and brought to trial. Two of them used their trials to raise grievances about the treatment of prisoners, which then became the subject of an official enquiry. The chapter discusses the evolution of penal policies in the light of this case and other confrontations in Victoria Gaol during the early twentieth century.

Chapter 8 focuses on the assassination of the manager of a firm bringing in blackleg crews from northern ports during the seamen's strike of 1922, one of a series of disputes between workers and employers that prompted draconian responses from the government. The trial of the alleged assassin, conducted in an atmosphere of extreme animosity between people and government, raises questions about the quality of justice in political cases.

Chapter 9 recounts the sensational trial in 1932 of a son of one of Hong Kong's wealthiest families for the murder of a rival in love. The trial broke all records in Hong Kong for its length and for the enormous resources devoted to the defence. After conviction, the family launched an intensive campaign for mercy. The chapter explores male jealousy as a motive for murder, and as a justification for leniency in the context of Qing law and Chinese custom.

Chapter 10 explores the trial and retrial of an unemployed Chinese man convicted of murdering a European child in 1934, allegedly for political motives. The case led to the first murder appeal heard in Hong Kong. It also raised concerns about racial prejudice in the administration of justice and fed into an emerging debate on the death penalty. This case gave rise to another large-scale campaign for mercy.

Chapter 11 examines the surge in capital crimes and capital punishment in the decade after World War II and the decline in capital convictions and hangings in the early 1960s. The decline, the chapter suggests, was attributable to declining crime rates, more effective policing and detection, changes in the law, and a growing disinclination among juries to convict capitally.

Chapter 12 discusses the debates and controversies leading to de facto abolition of capital punishment in Hong Kong in 1975 and its formal abolition in 1993.

The trials in this book underline themes and patterns uncovered by research into criminal justice in other colonies: the sudden, large-scale imposition of laws, legal institutions and legal culture by one society on another; the emphasis on control and protection of trade and property; the reliance on violent punishments; the difficulties with trial by jury in a mixed population; and the privileging of respectable Europeans and persons of wealth and high status.[180] They illustrate the uses, and sometimes abuses, of the courts by what might loosely be described as the colonized population – loosely, because for the first hundred years of British rule Hong Kong was a city mainly of sojourners whose roots and allegiances lay elsewhere. The narratives and controversies described here also highlight the tensions between those – mostly judges and lawyers – who insisted on equality before the law and due process and those – mostly officials – who advocated different treatment for Chinese, particularly in Hong Kong's early decades.

Five connected themes stand out in the special case of Hong Kong. The **first** is the crucial importance of language, the essence of any legal system but particularly of the common law practised in Hong Kong. The gulf in understanding between those who controlled the courts and the majority who appeared before them took many decades to bridge. The **second** is the rapidly growing, yet largely mobile, population, which deepened this gulf. The **third** is the continual pattern of war, rebellion, and banditry in the neighbouring region, which brought weapons and violence into Hong Kong. Connected with these is a **fourth** theme: the complex question of cross-border justice, involving the handling of demands for extradition by the Chinese authorities, the trial of some suspects by Chinese courts for crimes committed within Hong Kong's jurisdiction, and the seizure in Chinese territory of Chinese suspects wanted by the Hong Kong authorities in the absence of a reciprocal extradition agreement. A **fifth** theme is the role of public opinion in shaping criminal justice through petitions and other direct action, or mediated through the press, politics, and religion: at first, this reflected mainly the views of colonists and to a lesser extent the Chinese elite; over the years it became more broadly based and could not be ignored by governors.

Above all, the trials highlight the variety of legal processes and outcomes within the British Empire, where every jurisdiction had its own unique set of circumstances and responded in different ways.[181] Hong Kong adopted some changes in English law, borrowed selectively from other colonies, and developed its own practices and traditions. The complex configuration of judges, juries, lawyers, witnesses, and defendants in any given trial often produced unexpected outcomes, even for crimes that struck at the very heart of British rule. Perhaps no trial anywhere in the British Empire demonstrates this more strongly than the first case in this book: the attempt to extirpate the British presence in Hong Kong by poisoning the colonists' breakfast.

---

180. See Sally Engle Merry's seminal essay 'Law and Colonialism', *Law and Society Review* Vol. 25, No. 4 (1991): 889–922.

181. See Martin J. Wiener, *An Empire on Trial: Race, Murder, and Justice under British Rule, 1870–1935* (Cambridge University Press, 2009), 230.

2

'A Diabolical Plot'

The Poisoning of the European Community, 1857

The mail for India on Thursday 15 January 1857 carried the news that Hong Kong 'had been poisoned by a Chinese, and half the colony was dead and the other half dying'.[1] That morning, hundreds of people, including the Governor, the Chief Justice, and the Attorney General, had breakfasted on bread baked with rat poison from the Esing Bakery. Its owner, Cheong Alum (張亞霖), and his family had left suddenly for Macao on the *Shamrock*, a scheduled steamer. Stealing a march on the police, William Robinet, an American entrepreneur, chartered a steamship and reached Macao that evening. He found Cheong still on the *Shamrock*: its return to Hong Kong had been delayed because the crew had eaten the bread. Robinet bundled Cheong off to a guardhouse to await the arrival of the Hong Kong police. Cheong's first question was 'Anybody have die at Hong Kong?' To which Robinet replied, 'No; but you have poisoned almost everybody with arsenic.'[2] Cheong and his family were taken back to Hong Kong the next morning. By evening, fifty-one other men had been arrested in connection with the poisoning.

Some 400 people – a quarter of the civilian European population, as well as Parsis, Muslims, and Chinese servants – had eaten the bread. Rumours emerged that the poisoning was to be followed by an uprising of the Chinese population, then numbering some 75,000. A huge quantity of arsenic, estimated at ten pounds, had been mixed into the dough. 'The cry of "poisoned loaves" ran like an electric shock from house to house', recalled the Governor, Sir John Bowring.[3] Physicians sent notices warning European

1. Augustine Heard, 'The Poisoning in Hong Kong – An Episode of Life in China Forty Years Ago' (*c.* 1894), Baker Library, Harvard Business School, Heard I/Box: GQ-1 GQ-2, Folder GQ-2-1.
2. *CM* (Extra), 7 February 1857.
3. Lewin B. Bowring, ed., *Autobiographical Recollections of Sir John Bowring* (London: King & Co., 1877), 95.

households not to eat the bread and recommending emetics of mustard and raw eggs. Most people had already vomited up the bread, so great was the amount of arsenic. No one died immediately, but many endured fevers and headaches. Some lost hair and teeth. Those who ate least suffered most. Months later, the deaths of three people, including Lady Bowring, the Governor's wife, were traced to the poison's lingering effects.[4]

Hong Kong in the Second Opium War

Hong Kong was in a state of siege. War between Britain and China had broken out a second time. On 8 October 1856, police in Canton had boarded the *Arrow*, a Chinese-owned lorcha, and arrested twelve of its crew on suspicion of piracy. The *Arrow* had been registered under an ordinance that extended protection under the British flag to ships owned by Chinese with property in Hong Kong. Although its registration had expired, its Irish captain claimed that police had torn down the British ensign, an act denied by the Chinese authorities. Led on by Harry Parkes, the headstrong British Consul in Canton, Bowring demanded a public restoration of the crew and an apology from the Imperial Commissioner, Ye Mingchen. If satisfaction was not received within forty-eight hours it would be exacted by the Royal Navy. Some days later the crew were delivered to the British Consulate, but not publicly, nor with an apology. On 23 October British ships captured forts along the Canton River and started bombarding Canton, setting off fires and killing people 'in untold numbers'.[5] On a trifling pretext Bowring had instigated what became known as the Second Opium War (1856–1860). The British now intended to punish the Cantonese and extend the treaty rights imposed on China after the first Opium War (1839–1842).

Now in his sixty-fifth year, Bowring had been a leading member of the Peace Society, a proponent of free trade, and an intimate of Jeremy Bentham. As a radical Member of Parliament in the 1840s he spoke against the death penalty, the opium trade, and the flogging of Chinese in Hong Kong. Failure in business forced him to take paid work. In 1848 he was appointed British Consul in Canton. In 1854 he was promoted Governor of Hong Kong and Plenipotentiary to China. As Britain's chief diplomat in the Far East he had opportunities for promoting peace and commerce in a vast region. But the outbreak of war curtailed his diplomacy and made Hong Kong a target for terrorism. The Palmerston government endorsed his actions, but appointed Lord Elgin to lead an expeditionary force

4. One of the others was the American merchant Sandwith Drinker, a witness in the trial. E.J. Eitel, *Europe in China: The History of Hongkong from the Beginning to the Year 1882* (Hong Kong: Kelly & Walsh, 1895), 311.
5. Correspondence between Sir John Bowring, HBM Plenipotentiary, and Yeh, Imperial Commissioner, *HKGG*, 28 November 1856; J.Y. Wong, 'The "Arrow" Incident: A Reappraisal', *Modern Asian Studies* 8, no. 3 (1974): 373–389. 'Address of the Inhabitants of the whole City to his Excellency the Plenipotentiary of Great Britain', in House of Commons, *Papers Relating to the Proceedings of Her Majesty's Naval Forces at Canton* (London: Harrison, 1857), 67.

to China and replace Bowring as Plenipotentiary. The force was delayed for many months, first, by parliamentary opposition to Palmerston's aggressive stance, which triggered a general election, then by diversion of the troops to help put down rebellion in India. In response to the continuing bombardment of Canton, Ye Mingchen ordered all Chinese to leave Hong Kong and offered a reward of $30 for every British head brought to him.[6] Gentry in neighbouring counties recruited militia, plotted incendiary attacks, and offered $10,000 for the destruction of the British colony.[7] On 30 December 1856, two weeks before the poisoning, militiamen disguised as passengers had taken over the steamer *Thistle* in the Canton River, killing the eleven foreigners on board and carrying off their heads in handkerchiefs.[8]

The hostilities added another layer to the upheavals in the region. The Taiping Rebellion (1850–1864), a large-scale revolt against the Qing dynasty, had spurred uprisings by secret societies as it swept through the southern provinces. The response by the Qing government was ruthless. Later, while a prisoner of the British, Ye Mingchen claimed he had sentenced to death over 100,000 rebels and bandits. That number, he boasted, must be quadrupled if the villages destroyed on his orders were taken into account.[9] Nominally neutral, Hong Kong became a base for rebels, a refuge for fleeing Qing officials, and a safe haven for Chinese merchants. After the outbreak of war in 1856, Western merchants in Canton moved to Hong Kong, reinforcing its role as a haven – albeit a precarious one.

The *Arrow* affair coincided with troubles within Hong Kong. Bowring had hoped to turn the colony into a model city, and to 'remove that repugnance which has hitherto prevented a single Chinaman of wealth or reputation from making the island his place of abode'.[10] But his policies aroused opposition. On 16 October 1856 a public meeting – the largest yet held in the colony – condemned recent legislation and called for a committee of ratepayers to negotiate with the government. 'General misgovernment' was driving Chinese from the colony, said one participant. The public were particularly aggrieved by a Buildings and Nuisances Ordinance enacted in April 1856 with retrospective provisions to address the dire state of sanitation in the overcrowded city. Actions against jerry-built 'coolie houses' had upset European and Chinese speculators alike. Another new law,

6. Proclamation by Yeh, 28 October 1856, in House of Commons, *Papers Relating to the Proceedings of Her Majesty's Naval Forces at Canton*, 40.
7. Proclamation by the Committee of Co-operation, 25 November 1856, in House of Commons, *Papers Relating to the Proceedings of Her Majesty's Naval Forces at Canton*, 129; Wade to Bowring, 30 December 1856, in House of Commons, *Further Papers Relating to the Proceedings of Her Majesty's Naval Forces at Canton*, 18.
8. Bowring to Clarendon, 31 December 1856, in House of Commons, *Further Papers Relating to the Proceedings of Her Majesty's Naval Forces at Canton*, 17; *FOC*, 3 January 1857; *CM*, 8 January 1857.
9. Cooke, *China*, 397.
10. Bowring to Grey, 24 January 1855, CO 129/49, 60.

aimed at Chinese residents, prescribed flogging for cutting trees or urinating in the streets. Chinese at the meeting complained bitterly about the 'total inefficiency' of the police.[11]

In November the government launched a vigorous campaign against street hawkers and illegal structures, resulting in heavy fines. Chinese shops closed in protest. A procession on Queen's Road numbered over 40,000 at one point, when the Lieutenant-Governor, William Caine, was confronted by a mob shouting '*ta fankweilo*!' ('beat the foreign devils!'). The army was brought out. Leaders of the Chinese community met at the Man Mo Temple to frame a petition. They asked that the government remit fines in nuisance cases. They also urged that policemen should only beat those they saw stealing, and not 'strike every one they take into custody'. Caine blamed the protest on the *Arrow* dispute. Ye Mingchen's agents were working on people's fears, he reported. 'The vilest of Chinese of all classes' were flooding into Hong Kong to plunder the wealth of merchants seeking refuge from the troubles in Canton.[12] The government reinforced defences with the aid of American and French sailors and formed a 'gaol brigade' of European convicts. It imposed a curfew on Chinese residents and drafted laws to tighten controls.

The architect of the Buildings Ordinance was the new Attorney General, Thomas Chisholm Anstey. The son of a Tasmania landowner, he was a graduate of London University and a member of Middle Temple. He had the faculty of 'impressing persons of ability and learning with his own profound research and intellectual vigour'. Yet he was also 'quick, irritable, and decisive' and 'exceedingly impatient of contradiction'.[13] A convert to Catholicism, he wrote pamphlets on the legal position of Catholics. As the Member of Parliament for the Irish constituency of Youghal (1847–1852), he urged repeal of the union not only with Ireland but also with Scotland. He was 'a malcontent of the highest bore-power',[14] a reputation crowned by his five-hour speech denouncing Palmerston's foreign policy. In October 1855 Anstey was appointed Attorney General of Hong Kong through the patronage of Sir William Molesworth, Secretary of State for the Colonies in Palmerston's government.

Anstey's friends regretted that so brilliant a legal mind should be sent to 'that pestilential dog-hole'.[15] Some saw it as Palmerston's revenge: Anstey 'was so indefatigable in worrying everybody that the Government made him Attorney-General at Hong Kong', wrote the barrister William Ballantine.[16] Anstey claimed he was never even told of his appointment

11. *CM*, 16 and 30 October 1856; Ordinances Nos. 8 and 12 of 1856.
12. Caine to Labouchere, 22 November 1856, CO 129/59, 199–207.
13. Obituary, *Law Times*, 6 September 1873.
14. Sidney Lee (rev. K.D. Reynolds), 'Anstey, Thomas Chisholm', *Oxford Dictionary of National Biography*.
15. *Morning Advertiser*, 16 October 1856.
16. Ballantine added that Anstey 'celebrated the night before that fixed for his departure by breaking the heads of a couple of policemen, and thus nearly lost his appointment'. Ballantine helped settle the matter. William Ballantine, *Some Experiences of a Barrister's Life*, 6th edition (New York: J.M. Stoddart, 1883), 468.

until after it was gazetted. Though reportedly happy with 'the great pay' (£1,000 a year), he left 'in a diabolic frame of mind', claiming to be 'the victim of all kinds of machinations to get rid of him'.[17] Within months of arriving he accused the outgoing Chief Magistrate of incompetence and his successor, W.H. Mitchell, of taking bribes from prisoners sentenced to death. The Executive Council advised there was insufficient evidence. Anstey prosecuted anyway and Mitchell was acquitted.[18] He then accused Mitchell (a property owner) of packing the bench with justices of the peace to defeat the Buildings and Nuisances Ordinance. When Anstey secured a mandamus from the Supreme Court ordering them to convict in one notorious case, the justices protested against encroachment on judicial freedom. Anstey urged their wholesale dismissal.[19] Mitchell sued Anstey for slander. Before the case was tried, Anstey swore an affidavit that he had no faith in Hong Kong's special jurors because he had incurred so much ill will. The special jury hearing the case nevertheless found for Anstey.[20]

Anstey then spread it around that the Chief Justice had been 'drunk as drunk could be' at an official dinner. This was perilous ground. Nine years earlier the same Chief Justice, John Hulme, had been suspended after being found guilty by the Executive Council of drunkenness at a party for Chinese officials. The Secretary of State had reinstated Hulme and had expressed his dismay at the vindictiveness with which the Governor, Sir John Davis, had pursued the charge. Anstey now demanded a similar enquiry. He produced a report alleging that Hulme had mismanaged the Supreme Court; that he was lazy and prone to procrastination – allegations which, though well founded, were rejected in petitions from lawyers and jurors. Staff in the Colonial Office knew of Hulme's tendency to 'transgress the limits'. But they were appalled by Anstey's tone – 'so bitter and malignant, so full of coarse and yet studied insolence'. The Secretary of State ordered him to make a 'public expression of regret' and threatened to suspend him if he did not. Anstey grudgingly complied. But Hulme refused to accept anything short of an apology and demanded Anstey's recall.[21]

The main casualty in Anstey's feuds was Governor Bowring himself. Try as he might to avoid taking sides, he had been drawn ineluctably into the attacks on the Chief Justice, officials, justices, and jurors. The efficiency of government and his own reputation had suffered as a result. The Colonial Office believed his bumbling attempts to restore harmony

17. *Liverpool Albion*, 21 January 1856.
18. Bowring to Labouchere, 7 June and 8 July 1856, CO 129/56, 240–270 and CO 129/57, 83–134; *FOC*, 2 April and 28 June 1856.
19. Bowring to Labouchere, 9 September and 7, 10, and 14 October 1856, CO 129/58, 181–228, 260–271, 278–289, and 378–408.
20. Norton-Kyshe, *History*, Vol. I, 392–405.
21. Bowring to Labouchere, 3 June, and 11 and 13 November 1856, CO 129/56, 9–158, CO 129/59, 79–98 and 175–183.

had made matters worse. Anstey even smeared Bowring himself, declaring in his trial for slander that he would never have accepted an appointment under such a person if he had had the choice.[22] By the end of 1856 Bowring was avoiding his Attorney General, preferring, out of self-respect, to communicate in writing.

The rush to trial

Such was the state of government when, at a meeting of his Executive Council on 19 January 1857, Bowring received advice on what to do with Cheong Alum and his men. Claiming to reflect public opinion, the Colonial Secretary, William Mercer, urged that they be 'brought to capital and immediate punishment' under martial law. 'The Law of civilized nations may well be put aside in dealing with the treacherous and reckless barbarians by whom we are surrounded in swarms, and on whom in the social and domestic relations of daily life we are necessarily dependent.' Lieutenant-Governor Caine supported a court martial. The Officer Commanding the Troops opposed it. Anstey believed he had enough evidence to convict but could not decide if they should be tried by court martial or by a jury. Consulted separately, the Chief Justice warned that the agitated public mood was a reason for delaying the trial, not hurrying it on. Bowring declared he would not proclaim '*expostfacto*'[23] martial law to try Cheong. 'In a state of public excitement it is the bounden Duty of the Government, while pursuing and punishing the guilty, to take special precaution for the protection of the innocent,' he said. In any case, he added, the Attorney General had said he had enough evidence to convict.[24]

The next morning Anstey told Bowring he would be failing in his duty if he did not allow 'a mode of proceeding by which *at all events* Alum should be put to death.' Many colonists were threatening to kill him 'with their own hands.' He expected a failure of justice if they were tried in the Supreme Court. Several jurors, he said, were in debt to their Chinese compradors, who were under Cheong's influence. Placards had been posted around town, and some compradors were going to European houses 'asserting violently his innocence, and the duty of the Court to set him free.' Anyone so influenced, if selected as a juror, could block a conviction. Bowring stuck to his decision. He would be ashamed if threats of the 'Law of Lynch' were to influence him, he wrote to the Secretary of State. 'I heartily wish I had a more temperate adviser at my elbow in moments like these.'[25] When his despatch reached them two months later, officials in London assumed he was covering his back:

22. *OFOC* (Supplement), 19 September 1856.
23. *Ex post facto* because Ordinance No. 2 of 1857, an emergency law enacted nine days before the poisoning, prohibited the trial of civilians by court martial.
24. ExCo Minutes, 19 January 1857, CO 131/4, 13–21.
25. Bowring to Labouchere, 20 January 1857, CO 129/62, 108–115.

newspapers had reported, erroneously, that Cheong and three others had been condemned to death by a military tribunal and shot.[26]

Cheong Alum, his father Cheong Wye-kong, and eight other men were committed for trial. On Anstey's advice, the committal took place not before the new Chief Magistrate, Henry Davies, who was deemed to lack 'local knowledge', but, instead, before Charles May (the Sheriff, Assistant Magistrate, and police chief) and William Mercer (the Colonial Secretary), both of whom were justices of the peace. Details of the proceedings are unclear. But they elicited a statement by Cheong that was to play a key part in his trial. Cheong and his co-defendants were held in Victoria Gaol. The forty-two other detained men were kept in a room measuring fifteen feet square in a police station at the junction of Queen's Road and Wellington Street. This 'Black Hole of Hong Kong' prompted questions in Parliament. May claimed they suffered no hardship. In any case, the gaol was already packed with hundreds of 'suspicious characters' seized in the streets.[27]

The bakery men and other suspicious characters were detained under an ordinance 'for better securing the Peace of the Colony'. Enacted nine days before the poisoning, this law prescribed fines, imprisonment, flogging, and the stocks for Chinese out at night without a pass. It authorized sentries to shoot any Chinese refusing to answer a challenge at night and empowered justices of the peace to detain enemy agents, pirates, and 'Chinamen disaffected to Her Majesty's Government, or otherwise dangerous to the peace and good order of this Colony'. Those detained were liable to deportation. The ordinance had retrospective effect. Actions done under it could not be questioned in any court. The armed forces were to act as if martial law had been proclaimed, though no civilian was amenable to court martial. The Secretary of State observed that it would have been better simply to have proclaimed martial law. He ordered Bowring to suspend the ordinance and re-enact it without the more draconian provisions. Because of time lags in correspondence with London, this was not done until July. The new ordinance retained the curfew and power of deportation, which became long-standing tools for policing Chinese inhabitants. Anstey had drafted the original ordinance. Years later, he disingenuously cited it as an example of how Hong Kong 'may perhaps claim the dubious distinction of having – during its brief existence – furnished nearly as many examples of vitious legislation and administration as the whole body of British colonies'.[28]

---

26. *Evening Standard*, 17 March 1857; *Morning Post*, 17 March 1857.
27. *FOC*, 21 January 1857; *HKR*, 3 February 1857; May to Bridges, 27 July 1857, in House of Commons, *Confinement of Chinese Prisoners at Hong Kong* (1858), 1–3.
28. Ordinances Nos. 2 and 9 of 1857; Bowring to Labouchere, 13 January and 15 July 1857, CO 129/62, 59–78 and CO 129/63, 437–460; Anstey, 'On the Competence of Colonial Legislatures to Enact Laws in Derogation of Common Liability or Common Right', *Papers Read Before The Juridical Society*, Vol. 3 (1868), 447.

R v Cheong Achew, Cheong Aheep, Cheong Achok, Lum Asow, Tam Aleen, Fong Angee, Cheong Amun, Fong Achut, Cheong Alum, and Cheong Wye-kong
Administering poison with intent to commit murder, 2–5 February 1857

The trial took place at the end of the Supreme Court's regular criminal sessions starting in late January. The calendar listed nine other cases, including piracy and murder, slave dealing, and rape. None of the accused in these cases had benefit of counsel. Three cases were abandoned because of contradictory evidence or absent witnesses.[29]

Cheong engaged two of the colony's five barristers, William Bridges and John Day. Bridges reportedly foisted himself on Cheong, taking instructions without a solicitor – a breach of etiquette later criticized by the Chief Justice. Some claimed he had gained access through masonic connections with a gaoler, and had demanded as much as £500 for his fee.[30] Bridges said he had been asked to take on the defence by Cheong's friends: Cheong Assow, an overseer in the Land Office and a cousin of Alum, and the building contractor Tam Achoy, leading figures in the Chinese community, both later confirmed this. Assow put up $1,000 for the defence.[31] To safeguard his fee, Bridges applied to the Supreme Court for money seized in Cheong's shop – $1,225 in total – to be handed over for his defence. Anstey, as Attorney General, successfully opposed the application, saying it was the court's duty to protect Cheong's assets from 'plunder'. Bridges then sought a ruling that a recent ordinance limiting fees and costs did not apply to criminal cases. Otherwise, 'what was to compensate him for the obloquy incurred in undertaking the defence?' Anstey retorted that the court had discretion to decide the fee payable for a brief, which 'ought to content the expectation of Mr Bridges, however exorbitant'.[32]

Since arriving in Hong Kong in 1851, Bridges had made a fortune. For several years he was the *only* barrister, other than the Attorney General, Paul Sterling. This gave him 'the entire lead of all the legal business' in Hong Kong and an annual income of over £3,000.[33] While Sterling was on leave or sitting in for the Chief Justice, Bridges acted for long periods as Attorney General. He refused to act as Chief Justice because the position, unlike that of Attorney General, did not allow private practice. Bowring was concerned about Bridges's business activities, particularly his loans to Chinese at high interest: his house was said

---

29. *CM*, 5 February 1857.
30. £500 (about $2,222) was equivalent to half the Attorney General's annual salary. Murrow to Harrowby, 2 August 1857, CO 129/66, 472–473.
31. *CM*, 3 September 1857 (in which Cheong Assow is erroneously referred to as Le-Assow).
32. *FOC*, 31 January 1857; Ordinance No. 14 of 1856.
33. Bridges to Stanley, June 1858, CO 129/68, 75.

to be full of opium held as collateral.[34] Bridges had expected to succeed Sterling when he became a judge in Ceylon in 1855. The news that Anstey was to be Attorney General instead came as a shock. Bridges protested that Anstey could not match his own hard-won 'knowledge of the Chinese character' – a claim endorsed by officials, merchants, and several Chinese firms.[35] The two became bitter enemies. While in England in 1856 Bridges obtained an honorary Doctor of Civil Law from Oxford[36] and cultivated connections with the Colonial Office. It was a mark of confidence in him, and of misgivings about Anstey, that the government tried to retain him to prosecute the poisoning case.[37] But it was too late. Bridges had already obtained the lucrative brief for the defence. The prosecution was left to Anstey, assisted by the solicitor George Cooper Turner, who, in expectation of an official position, gave his services gratis.[38]

The poisoning trial began on Monday, 2 February 1857.[39] Lasting five days, it was the colony's longest criminal trial so far, and the longest capital trial for decades to come. Each day the accused were marched in manacles and leg irons through the busy streets from gaol to courthouse under escort of the gaol brigade. The court sat in a long room on the upper floor of the courthouse, the former Exchange Building on Queen's Road, constructed by the contractor Tam Achoy. The judicial bench was on a platform at one end. A railed area was reserved for the registrar, clerk, lawyers, and reporters. The jury sat in a box on one side. Prisoners stood in the dock opposite. Witnesses occupied a stand, with an interpreter close by. The trial drew large numbers of spectators: Europeans sat on chairs on two sides of the courtroom; Chinese sat on benches.

Cheong Alum and his nine co-defendants were charged with administering poison with intent to murder, then a capital felony.[40] Although hundreds had been poisoned, the practice at this time was to name only one victim in the indictment. The person chosen was Dr John Carroll Dempster, the Colonial Surgeon. The trial was held before Chief Justice Hulme and a six-man jury, one 'far superior to the ordinary character of juries' in Hong

34. Bowring to Lytton, 9 August 1858, CO 129/68, 231–233; Evidence by Anstey at the first Caldwell enquiry, 1 July 1858, CO 129/68, 485.
35. Bridges to Labouchere, March 1856, CO 129/61, 202–217.
36. This was translated on a large signboard outside Bridges's premises on Queen's Road as *yingguo jinshi* (英國進士), a reference to a Chinese official degree that blurred the separation between his public and private functions. *FOC*, 27 October 1858.
37. ExCo Minutes, 19 January 1857, CO 131/4, 20–21.
38. He was gazetted Crown Solicitor on 6 February 1857, the last day of the trial. His predecessor had resigned on day one of the trial after two months in office, complaining about an inadequate salary and Anstey's 'irritating and dictatorial demeanour'. Hickson to Mercer, 31 January 1857, CO 129/62, 195–201.
39. This account of the trial relies on four main sources: *OFOC* (Supplement), 15 February 1857; *CM* (Extra), 7 February 1857; *HKR* (Extra), 12 February 1857; and *FOC*, 7, 11, and 14 February 1857.
40. Offences Against the Person Act 1837. Later, under the Offences Against the Person Ordinance, No. 4 of 1865, reduced to a maximum penalty of life penal servitude.

Kong or England, Bowring reported.[41] It consisted of Malcolm Macleod (foreman),[42] George Lyall, William Bowra, Edward Duncanson, William Sutton, and John Lemon – all British, and all affected by the poison. Between them, they had served in thirty-seven criminal trials.[43] Sutton was a sailmaker and Lemon a bookbinder, members of the class Anstey believed to be vulnerable to pressure. The others were merchants. Lyall, of Lyall, Still & Co., and Macleod, a partner in Jardine Matheson & Co., were special jurors. Lyall was also a justice of the peace, soon to be appointed to the Legislative Council.[44] He had led the justices in their dispute with Anstey and had chaired the public meeting in October. He had also accompanied leaders of the Chinese community to present their grievances after the protests. Bowra had helped Lyall draft the memorial demanding repeal of Anstey's legislation. All four merchants had defended Hulme against Anstey's allegations. These animosities were to have some influence on the jury's attitude to the trial, and on Anstey's response to its outcome.

The prosecution's case

The trial opened at noon with Anstey's speech for the prosecution. English law had never contemplated such a crime as this, he said. To destroy a whole community by poison was possible only in a place like Hong Kong. He hoped the legislature would make it high treason, but for the time being he had to treat it as an isolated attempt on the life of a single man. Direct proof could not be produced. The jury would therefore have to rely entirely on circumstantial evidence. And in so secret a crime 'there should be allowed a greater latitude, and the mercy of the law should be restrained, not relaxed'. Anstey cited the Overbury case of 1616, in which Sir Francis Bacon had described poisoning as second only to high treason, a crime 'so secret, as that if, in all cases of impoisonment, you should require testimony, you were as good proclaim impunity'.[45]

Anstey then read out other cases from Britain and the United States where, in the absence of direct evidence, poisoners had been convicted on presumed motives, suspicious

41. Bowring to Labouchere, 25 February 1857, CO 129/62, 326–332.
42. Juries did not select a foreman at this time. The juror whose name was first called sat nearest to the Chief Justice and became, by custom, the medium of communication with the court.
43. Only Lyall appears never to sat on a Hong Kong criminal jury before. Among the others, Bowra had been a juror in ten trials, Duncanson in one, Macleod in four, Sutton in six, and Lemon in sixteen.
44. Special jurors were liable to serve on common juries from 1851 to 1860; justices of the peace up to 1984.
45. Basil Montagu, ed., *The Works of Francis Bacon, Lord Chancellor of England* (Philadelphia: Carey and Hart, 1844), Vol. 2, 321–322. The Earl of Somerset, King James I's favourite, and others were convicted of murder by poisoning of a rival courtier, Sir Thomas Overbury, then a prisoner in the Tower of London, in a complex intrigue at the court of King James I. The death was at first ascribed to natural causes. Bacon was Attorney General at the time.

behaviour, and circumstantial evidence.[46] The magistrates had investigated the case, he said, 'and found them guilty'. He too, 'upon a calm deliberate reflection, had found the bill which put them on their trial'. If the jury agreed, 'they would have but one duty to perform, and that duty would be to convict of the capital felony'. If the men were acquitted, if 'technicalities of British law procured their release', the Chinese would be emboldened to repeat 'their diabolical attempt'. The British community would be 'looked upon with contempt'. He would prove that Cheong's motives were 'prejudice against us barbarians, and the hope of reward from his Government and fellow-countrymen; and everyone knew that a Chinaman was never at a loss for a witness'.

This snide non sequitur was designed to undermine defence evidence by playing on suspicions about the reliability of Chinese evidence. In 1856, in the light of Caldwell's advice some years earlier, Anstey had introduced legislation replacing the oath for Chinese witnesses with a warning that they would be severely punished if they gave false evidence, even if it was not material to the case.[47] The legislation was disallowed in 1857 and replaced in 1860 by a simple declaration for non-Christian witnesses. But meanwhile, in the poisoning trial, European witnesses were sworn while Chinese witnesses were warned.[48] Caldwell was the interpreter. He was now also Registrar General and Protector of Chinese, one of the most powerful men in Hong Kong.

The case for the prosecution took up three days. Anstey called thirty-two witnesses, starting with Dr Dempster, who described how he and his family had been poisoned. Various servants – Atai, Acheong, Ahing, Aloi (colonists usually knew Chinese only by their given names) – told how the bread was delivered from Esing Bakery. They confirmed that the bakery was owned by Cheong, and that a sample of the same bread was taken to Dempster's colleague, Dr Aurelius Harland, for analysis. Harland testified that the bread contained large amounts of arsenic, but that samples of flour, pastry, and yeast from the bakery did not. The conclusion was that the arsenic was added to the dough at the bakery. Charles May and his assistant, Alexander Grandpré, described the police investigations. The evidence of the remaining prosecution witnesses was intended mainly to prove that Cheong had behaved suspiciously before and after the poisoning.

---

46. The cases were *R v Nairn and Ogilvie* (Scotland, 1765) – arsenic in a cup of tea; *R v Donellan* (England, 1781) – cyanide in a purging draught; *The People v Kesler* (New York State, 1817) – arsenic in a cup of herbal tea; *Pennsylvania v Lucretia Chapman* and *Pennsylvania v Espos y Mina* (Pennsylvania, 1832) – arsenic in soup.
47. *CM*, 18 December 1851; *FOC*, 7 January 1852.
48. The Law Officers in London described Anstey's ordinance as 'repugnant to reason and justice'. It was disallowed on the advice of ministers and replaced with a new ordinance in September 1857 omitting this provision. Owing to time lags in communication, the disallowance was not proclaimed in Hong Kong until May 1857. Ordinances 15 of 1856, 7 of 1856, and 2 of 1860; Bowring to Labouchere, 9 September 1856, CO 129/58, 150–180; Law Officers to Labouchere, 10 March 1857, CO 129/66, 20–22.

William Tarrant, editor of the *Friend of China*, testified that one of the accused, Cheong Aheep, had been on the *Thistle* during the attack on 30 December 1856. Aheep was one of the men who delivered bread from the Esing Bakery. Tarrant had not liked the 'suspicious unwillingness' with which Aheep had given evidence at the inquest on the *Thistle*. When he saw him deliver bread to his house on 15 January he told his comprador not to order any more bread from Esing for fear it might be poisoned. Tarrant's premonition came too late. The rest of his evidence described how he had eaten the bread, vomited over a servant, and continued to vomit all day. He pointed out that Cheong Alum had been charterer of the *Thistle* at the time of the attack. Andrew Dixson, editor of the *China Mail* and a juror at the *Thistle* inquest, also testified to Aheep's suspicious behaviour. Dixson said he had asked Alum about rumours in the Chinese community that he had received a mandarin's button and $9,000 for the *Thistle* affair. Cheong had replied that, on the contrary, Chinese officials had offered $5,000 for his capture; he had been thinking of moving to Singapore to avoid trouble.

Other European prosecution witnesses addressed the question of whether Cheong had been planning to leave. Cheong had seemed undecided on the point. His business had been thriving. He had large contracts to supply ships and the army commissariat, as well as a retail business in a separate shop: the bakery was in Spring Garden Lane, the shop was on Queen's Road East. According to George Duddell, an entrepreneur who had helped him set up the bakery, Cheong had only just installed new machines. Cheong had explained to him that he had told people he was planning to leave, but he was not really going away. Duddell estimated the bakery to be worth $6,000. Some business associates spoke of money owed by Cheong. Others said they owed him money. The evidence that came closest to linking Cheong to the poisoned dough came from the American merchant Sandwith Drinker, who had ordered a large quantity of ship's biscuit from Cheong. He had refused to believe Cheong's story that a notice outside his shop about his departure had been put up only to deceive the mandarins. On 14 January he insisted on going with Cheong to the bakery. There he saw the biscuit drying in a loft and was satisfied. He also saw men mixing dough. When he offered to take Cheong back to the shop in his boat, Cheong said he had business to attend to and would walk home.

All of this was tenuous and inconclusive, illustrative simply of the transactions between Cheong and his colonial clients. As Bridges pointed out, the prosecution evidence tended 'more to acquit them of this awful crime than convict them'. This applied even more strongly to the evidence about Cheong's departure for Macao on the day of the poisoning. William Robinet, who had gone in pursuit of Cheong, testified that Cheong had stayed on board the *Shamrock* after his children and the crew had fallen sick. Under cross-examination, he said that Cheong had offered $50 to the captain, then $100 to the *Shamrock*'s agent, to take him back at once, which was refused. The captain, steward and chief officer confirmed this. Cheong was anxious to return to Hong Kong to 'make inquiries about the poisoned bread because he supplied the Government and troops', said the captain. He added, under cross-examination, that Cheong had not known of his intention to detain him and had stayed on the ship voluntarily.

Problems with jurors

Two episodes in the trial seemed to bear out Anstey's concerns about jurors. At the start of day two, Anstey rose to say that one of the jurors, William Bowra, had been discussing the case with friends the evening before: juries at this time were usually not sequestered overnight in the rare trials that lasted over a day. He had 'expressed himself in rather strong language' about Anstey's harsh treatment of the accused. Anstey produced a witness. Bowra admitted to having 'passed a remark', but it was 'false to say he had gone to so great a length'. Another juror, John Lemon, then rose to say that, on the contrary, 'it was the opinion of Mr Bowra that the prisoners were guilty'. Despite their oath to give a true verdict according to the evidence, it was not uncommon for jurors to make up their minds before hearing the defence.[49] Bowra said he hoped his explanation was sufficient but would be 'only too happy to give up his place as a juror if the Attorney General wished it'. Hulme accepted the explanation. Bowra remained on the jury.

The second episode seemed even more to confirm Anstey's concerns. When the court resumed on day three, another juror, William Sutton, revealed that his servant had said that a cousin of Cheong Alum was willing to pay $100 to any juror who would help acquit Cheong. Sutton had replied he would do no such thing, as it was not the English custom. The Chief Justice then barred Chinese from leaving the court and ordered the arrest of the servant and his cousin, who were brought before the court that afternoon. The 'cousin', Wong Akeen, a bookbinder, said he was only a friend of Alum. He had heard that Sutton was in court 'pressing the matter of Ahlum's business' and had said he would sell his shop and give him $100 if Sutton did not press the matter. The offer was entirely his own initiative. He had not spoken to any of Alum's relations since the poisoning, or to any foreigners. Hulme sentenced him to six months' imprisonment for contempt of court.

Cheong Alum's statement

The centrepiece of the trial was the voluntary statement made by Cheong Alum in committal proceedings. At Anstey's request, this was read out by the Registrar towards the end of the first day of the trial. It began with a simple denial: 'He never had any idea of doing such a thing.' On 2 December 1856, he said, the authorities in his native county of Xiangshan,

---

49. 'All matters coming before the Court are discussed out of doors, and the minds of Jurymen, if not made up, much biased before they hear the Evidence.' Bonham to Grey, 10 September 1851, CO 129/37, 269.

near Macao, had put up notices ordering all persons in Hong Kong to return. If they did not, they would be punished as traitors. On 5 January soldiers went to his grandmother's house to extort money because he had not returned. On 10 January she wrote to Cheong's father in Hong Kong, asking him to return with all the family except Cheong: officials had offered a reward of $5,000 for his arrest. The family consisted of Cheong's wife and two small sons. Cheong and his father agreed they should go home on 15 January, the deadline set by officials for all Chinese to leave Hong Kong.[50] Cheong would take them as far as Macao and then return to Hong Kong. On 14 January, he ordered his bakers to make a few small loaves for the journey. Before boarding the *Shamrock* the next morning, Cheong heard that the staff at the bakery had fallen sick from soup taken at supper. During the voyage he ate some of the bread and gave some to his children, his wife, his father, two servants, and another passenger. All of them fell ill. By the time they reached Macao at 1 p.m. it was clear that something was wrong. Cheong decided he should immediately return to Hong Kong. 'If he were killed 500 times it would not compensate for the number of lives that would be lost by his customers.' When he heard the *Shamrock* would not leave at two as scheduled, he offered $50 to the captain, and then $100 to its agent, A.G. Agabeg, to leave that night. At 7 p.m. Robinet appeared and Cheong went ashore with him. When the police arrived he was taken back to the *Shamrock* to await his return to Hong Kong the next day.

Cheong said that if he intended to poison his customers and flee he would not have gone to such expense in buying new machinery. Nor would he have spent $1,400 only a day or two before his departure on large quantities of flour which had not yet been delivered. He had left over $1,000 in cash in his shop, where he had been living upstairs for several weeks. He rarely visited the bakery, where his family lived, because he did not wish to be seen on the streets. He confirmed his visit to the bakery on 14 January with Sandwith Drinker. He did not return with him but instead walked to the Commissariat to deal with a large order. During the protest in November 'he did not join with the people, but continued to make his bread as usual, and when he sent it out it was seized upon, and they threatened to seize his house and property'. In view of the reward offered for him, he believed he had enemies who may have bribed his bakers to poison the bread. 'Knowing that the Europeans patronize him so extensively, he hopes, if it be proved that he is guilty, that not only he but his whole family may be beheaded.'

The defence

Nothing in Cheong's statement was contradicted by the evidence for the prosecution. His account was also corroborated by the witnesses called by the defence. Their appearance on

50. Letter from 'Vigilans', 4 January 1857, in *OFOC* (Supplement), 15 January 1857.

the fourth day of the trial was preceded by a scathing address by Cheong's counsel, Bridges. He demanded to know why the accused had been committed for trial in such an irregular way. He asked why so many other men from the bakery were still being detained 'in a filthy place, unfit for any human being to live in'. Every difficulty had been placed in the prisoners' way to prevent a fair and impartial trial, he said. The Attorney General had done all he could to aggravate the crime in the minds of the jury by quoting 'some of the worst cases ever tried in the British dominions'. Yet he had so failed to attach the crime to the prisoners that, even if they had not been defended, it would have been impossible to find them guilty. The evidence against Cheong was 'hardly worth noticing'; that against the other prisoners was 'contemptible'.

Bridges called fourteen witnesses. Some confirmed large contracts with Cheong for the Commissariat and the US Navy. They would willingly have entered into further contracts with him. However, one associate, William Pustau, admitted under cross-examination that Cheong owed him $15,000 for flour and hire of steamers, including the *Thistle*. Other witnesses confirmed Cheong's account of events on the *Shamrock*. Its agent, Agabeg, denied anything had been said about detaining Cheong, who could have easily disembarked when the ship reached Macao. Ho Achai, nurse to Cheong's boys, had heard the bakers vomiting after supper on 14 January. She described how the family had fallen sick after eating the bread. She confirmed Cheong's plan to return as soon as he had landed his family in Macao. Her evidence was so similar to Cheong's statement that, pressed by Anstey, she denied having had any contact with him while under detention in the police station, or that she was his concubine. Her husband was in California, she said; she was not related to Cheong. She had been urged to give evidence at the trial by several Chinese, including Cheong Assow, Alum's cousin, who had put up the money for his defence. Assow's clerk, Cheong Afoo, had, with his wife, been in the same cabin as Alum on the *Shamrock*. Both gave evidence that they and Cheong's family had fallen sick from the bread. Afoo also confirmed Alum's eagerness to return to Hong Kong.

The verdict

The last day of the trial was taken up by Anstey's closing speech. About a third of it was devoted to attacking Bridges's lapse in etiquette in taking instructions without a solicitor, and to explaining the irregular committal proceedings before May and Mercer. Anstey said it was he who advised the government to follow this course. Had the investigation been left to the magistrate, Henry Davies (a barrister), the technicalities of British law would have led to repeated postponements, which would have been 'most deleterious to the ends of justice'. The crime 'deserved the fate of a drum-head court-martial', not a trial by jury, said Anstey. 'Would anyone have disapproved if a different course had been pursued towards the prisoners, and instead of allowing them a trial, which such monsters do not deserve, they had been dealt with in a summary manner, and had suffered those short and sharp pangs of death which they had intended we should suffer?'

Anstey then went over the evidence. He began with the facts that about ten pounds of arsenic had been mixed into the dough at the Esing Bakery, and that Cheong and his father had been at the bakery when the dough was mixed. 'Can you suppose they knew nothing about the poison?' he asked. Cheong had not fired Aheep after his performance at the *Thistle* inquest. On the contrary, he had retained him to deliver the poisoned bread. Anstey weighed Cheong's claims that his business was flourishing against his debts and his plans to leave Hong Kong. The fact that he owed so much to Pustau – an admission extorted 'by main force' – had made the reward of $9,000 offered by the mandarins irresistible. At this point Bridges objected that no evidence had been given about a reward; it was mere rumour, alluded to by Dixson. True, said Anstey, 'but the jury and the court could draw inferences when these were salient from the evidence, and inferred from the mass of incoherent perjuries that had been given in the defence'.

As for Cheong's statement, was it not remarkable, asked Anstey, that it combined 'the ingenuity and ability of the European with the low cunning of the Chinese?' His departure for Macao on the day of the crime was hardly the conduct of 'an innocent and unconscious man'. The claim that he and his family had eaten the bread was a fabrication: 'Chinamen do not eat bread, you know!' Anstey had attempted to prove this by calling a gaoler to testify that Cheong had never eaten bread while awaiting trial. The claim that Cheong and his family fell sick was a lie, or at most it was seasickness, since the symptoms were slight. The first question by Cheong on his arrest by Robinet – 'Any man have die Hong Kong side?' – was a clear betrayal of his guilt. 'Who told him that there was mortality in the case?' The whole of his statement, 'although well got up', was in fact 'a tissue of perjury'. The prisoners' guilt was established by their own defence.

Anstey concluded with a warning to the jury. An acquittal would be 'a great, an unappreciable calamity in this small community!' It would be a precedent. 'Let it once be seen that the law is powerless, – let it be established in the Chinese mind that this Court has not the power to check deeds like these, unless they are convicted, and carried into execution in the street or the market place, – then no longer is the life of an European safe in the colony.' Unable, even in his peroration, to resist a swipe against Bridges, he spoke of an impression current in the colony that justice was corrupt, 'that the laws of England have no terror in their threats for men wealthy and wise enough to submit to the exactions of their practitioners, and that a judicious prodigality in the matter of fees and costs will always purchase immunity'. It was the jury's duty to disabuse people of this error, he said. He then resumed his seat, to the stamping of feet in approval in the public gallery.

After a short adjournment Hulme summed up. The evidence against nine of the prisoners was slight, he said, amounting only to their connection with the bakery. But Cheong himself had been shown to have been at the bakery on 14 January while the dough was being mixed. If the jury thought he had mixed the poison, or ordered it to be mixed, or had any knowledge of it, they must find him guilty. He read over the evidence and Cheong's statement, noting that Cheong's own family had fallen sick from the bread and that Cheong had offered $50 and $100 to return to Hong Kong. These were prima facie proofs of his innocence, 'but the jury might consider them merely as clever ruses on the part of a guilty man in dread of suspicion'. The *Hongkong Register* remarked that Hulme 'summed up decidedly against Ahlum as an accessory before the fact'. Anstey later observed that he had 'summed up with impartiality', and had 'strongly approved' of his 'exposition of the law of evidence applicable to that case of secret crime'. However, from 'one or two expressions which seemed to escape from his lips unawares, the impression generally entertained is that his Lordship inclined to the belief in Alum's guilt'.[51]

The jury retired for about fifty minutes and returned with a verdict of not guilty by a majority of five to one. This was received with hisses from the public gallery.

> The Judge looked at the Attorney General, and the Attorney looked at the Judge, but as the prisoners were acquitted be discharged they must. Before they left the hall, however, they were again arrested, and taken to gaol as suspicious characters.[52]

According to one report, the ten acquitted men 'were huddled like swine out of the dock, under the impression that they were being taken to a place of execution'. They were 'pushed in bewilderment into the street, and there roughly seized by their tails by the ruffians of the Jail Brigade', while the Attorney General 'stood, balked of his prey, laughing in derision at them on the steps of the Court House!!'[53]

The real culprits?

Even if they accepted that the prosecution failed through lack of proof, many colonists continued to refer to Cheong as 'the poisoner'. Opinion among Chinese is less easy to gauge. Respectable Chinese were 'quite disposed to believe that Alum had not personally taken an active part in the crime, might not even have been cognizant of it', recalled the American merchant Augustine Heard. But they also thought that, under Chinese law, 'he as head and owner of the establishment was responsible for the acts of his workmen, and merited all the punishment – even unto death – which might belong to them'. The acquittal, said

---

51. Norton-Kyshe quotes Hulme as saying 'I, in common with the Attorney-General, am desirous that justice should be done on the perpetrator of this crime, but hanging the wrong man will not further the ends of justice.' This does not appear in any of the newspaper accounts. Like his summary of Anstey's closing speech as 'Better to hang the wrong man than confess that British sagacity and activity have failed to discover the real criminals', this much-quoted remark may have been an embellishment. *HKR*, 10 February 1857; Anstey's Report, CO 129/62, 231; Norton-Kyshe, *History*, Vol. I, 417–418.
52. *OFOC* (Supplement), 15 February 1857.
53. Murrow to the Earl of Harrowby, 2 August 1857, CO 129/66, 472.

Heard, caused a 'great change' by eroding the personal responsibility Chinese compradors assumed for crimes by servants they engaged for foreign employers.[54]

If Cheong had no part in the poisoning, who then was the culprit? The evidence of Chinese official involvement is inconclusive. Replying to protests from American and French diplomats, Imperial Commissioner Ye Mingchen vaguely suggested that natives of the districts near Hong Kong had taken this way of avenging the 'unnumbered evils which have been inflicted upon the Chinese by the English'. Later, in 1858, while in transit in Hong Kong as a prisoner of war, he denied all knowledge of the poisoning.[55] Letters seized by British forces between leaders of the 'anti-barbarian agitation' committee in Xinan, the county next to Hong Kong, refer only in passing to the poisoning, whereas they describe in some detail various other plots initiated by the committee.[56] The historian J.Y. Wong plausibly suggests that the poisoner was an aggrieved son whose parents were killed in a devastating fire ignited in Canton on 12 January by British naval bombardment.[57] Another explanation was that the poisoning was an accident. Cheong's first thought was that it was something in the water.[58] A biography from 1904 simply records that 'one day, through carelessness, a worker dropped some odd things (雜物) into the flour'.[59] In his speech for the defence, Bridges questioned the assumption that the Chinese authorities had instigated the poisoning. He suggested a jealous business rival or an aggrieved employee may have been behind it. Some in England suggested no poisoning had occurred at all, or that Bowring had exaggerated it for political reasons.[60]

Two further names were linked to the poisoning. In his statement, Cheong Alum mentioned certain staff, including Alun, one of his foremen. Alun fled on the day of the poisoning along with a man named Atsoi, who is described elsewhere as a foreman at the bakery. The government offered rewards of $1,000 for their 'apprehension and conviction'. In his summing up, the Chief Justice assumed it was Alun and Atsoi who had mixed the arsenic with the dough. The two men were never traced. How far they were culpable, and what their motives may have been, can only be guessed at.[61]

---

54. Heard, 'The Poisoning in Hong Kong'.
55. Ye to Parker and Ye to the Count de Courcy, 3 February 1857, in House of Commons, *Further Papers Relating to the Proceedings of Her Majesty's Naval Forces at Canton*, 17 and 349; Cooke, *China*, 429.
56. Wade to Bowring, 14 April 1857, CO 129/65, 406–411.
57. J.Y. Wong, *Deadly Dreams: Opium and the Arrow War (1856–1860) in China* (Cambridge: Cambridge University Press, 1998), 26.
58. Evidence by Alexander Maclebean, steward on the *Shamrock*, *CM*, (Extra), 7 February 1857; *OFOC*, Supplement, 15 February 1857.
59. Biography of Cheong Alum by Chen Zhaochang (陳昭常), translated by Choi Chi-cheung, *Journal of the Royal Asiatic Society Hong Kong Branch*, Vol. 24 (1984): 283.
60. See Kate Lowe and Eugene McLaughlin, '"Caution! The Bread is Poisoned,": The Hong Kong Mass Poisoning of January 1857', *Journal of Imperial and Commonwealth History*, Vol. 4, No. 2 (2015): 202–203.
61. *OFOC*, Supplement, 15 February 1857; *CM*, (Extra), 7 February 1857; *HKGG*, 31 January 1857; ExCo Minutes, 19 January 1857, CO 131/4, 21.

Anstey's antics

Anstey professed to be at a loss to explain the verdict. He probed the motives of jurors. The sole juror who dissented from the acquittal, he discovered, was the foreman, Malcolm Macleod. Another juror, John Lemon, added his signature to a memorial 'deeply regretting the recent verdict'. Anstey now claimed that not only Bowra but also Lyall had expressed a belief in Cheong's innocence before the trial took place and had said he would do 'everything to get him off'. Pressed for evidence, Anstey said he had heard that Bowra had 'declared in general terms that he would never concur, if he could help it, in any verdict for the side on which I acted as Counsel, should it fall to his lot to be a juror'. He accused Bridges of making 'repeated signals' towards the jury box, suggesting that an understanding existed between him and one of the jurors. He probably meant Lyall, who had Bridges on retainer. Bridges brushed all this aside, saying he did not think Anstey 'to be at times perfectly sane'. Herman Merivale, Permanent Undersecretary in the Colonial Office, formed a similar view. When Anstey persisted, Bridges asked for the matter to be referred to the Chief Justice, the jury, and the Bar, which Bowring refused to allow. Anstey also alleged that some witnesses had, by testifying for Cheong, made 'discreditable attempts' to secure their claims against his assets, which would have been forfeited to the Crown had he been convicted.[62]

Still convinced of the guilt of the defendants, Anstey proposed *repeated* prosecutions on the same charges, pointing out they had so far been tried only for poisoning Dr Dempster. There were at least 200 other victims whose names could be put on fresh indictments, he said.[63] He drafted a bill making it a treasonable felony for anyone to mix poison into food or drink 'with intent to destroy Her Majesty's subjects or any class of Her Majesty's subjects'. The United Kingdom could not be destroyed by a single blow, he explained. 'It has more than one neck. But *our* community has not that advantage.' The bill would make it easier to secure convictions: an option of a Scottish verdict of 'not proven' would allow repeated prosecutions on the same charges.[64]

Bowring described these proposals as 'somewhat deranged'.[65] He wearily sent them to the Secretary of State, who rejected the draft ordinance but was prepared to allow a fresh prosecution if new evidence 'of the strongest, as well as clearest, character' was discovered.

62. Bowring to Labouchere, 11 February 1857, CO 129/62, 217–244; Anstey to Bridges, 21 February 1857, CO 129/62, 447–448.
63. Anstey to Mercer, 9 February 1857, CO 129/62, 233–234.
64. In 1858, in a draft bill, Anstey tried to introduce the verdict of 'not proven' more generally for criminal trials. This was rejected by Bowring. The ordinance as enacted increased the size of juries from six to seven, making it easier for juries to come to a majority verdict. A further proposal by Anstey, to allow majority verdicts in capital trials, was defeated in council. Bowring to Labouchere, 12 February 1857 & 25 March 1858, CO 129/62, 253–272 and CO 129/67, 312–319; *HKGG*, 27 March 1858; Ordinance No. 3 of 1858.
65. Bowring to Labouchere, 9 August 1858, CO 129/68, 223.

No such evidence was found. Anstey's treason proposal arrived in the Colonial Office on 8 April 1857, along with news of the acquittal. This was too late to have any impact on the general election, which took place in late March and resulted in a large majority for Palmerston. The poisoning and other alleged atrocities by the Chinese had featured in his election addresses, boosting support for his campaign. False news that the culprits had been summarily tried and shot added to the sensation. At the height of the campaign, some newspapers carried a detailed confession of the crime by Cheong Alum given to a mysterious 'Captain Adams'.[66]

When reports of the trial reached the British press in April, the tide of opinion turned to sympathy for Cheong and his men. They had faced all kinds of obstacles and prejudices, remarked *Bell's Weekly Messenger*. They were tried for an atrocious crime during a war against their own nation. Government power was arrayed against them 'in every way and form that a colonial court of justice will allow'. And yet, 'despite of all this, A-lum was acquitted! Rotten indeed must have been the evidence against him.'[67] There was no positive proof of guilt, said the *Morning Post*, and the circumstantial evidence was far from satisfactory. Anstey had tried too hard, 'and possibly somewhat too pertinaciously', for a conviction. Nothing more disgusted a jury than 'over-professional zeal'.[68]

Criminal justice in the 1850s

In attempting to explain his failure in the poisoning case, the *Morning Post* suggested that Anstey was 'nearly wholly without legal experience', and that this was 'probably the first prosecution he ever conducted'. Anstey had, in fact, prosecuted no fewer than sixty criminal cases in the twelve months since his arrival in Hong Kong in early 1856, resulting in convictions of 109 of the 152 defendants. This was a high conviction rate, particularly since eight cases, involving twenty-four defendants, were abandoned when witnesses retracted evidence they had given in committal proceedings: two of them feared that, like a witness in a previous case, they would be murdered for identifying the accused.[69] Only thirty defendants were defended by counsel: twenty-four of these were acquitted or discharged. Justice in Hong Kong continued along a well-worn path of rushed prosecutions, unrepresented defendants, unreliable witnesses, and juries only too willing to return verdicts of guilty, sometimes without waiting to hear the defence. In contrast to the care taken over

66. *The Times*, 21 and 28 March 1857; *The Globe*, 24 March 1857; Wong, *Deadly Dreams*, 226–228.
67. Cheong was invariably referred to as 'A-lum' or 'Alum', to the amusement of the satirical magazine *Punch*. Alum was a substance commonly used to adulterate flour. It was 'surely a mythical name', suggested one official in London on first reading of the trial. *Bell's Weekly*, 11 April 1857; marginal annotation in Bowring to Labouchere, 15 January 1857, CO 129/62, 95.
68. *Morning Post*, 10 April 1857.
69. They were each sentenced to six months' imprisonment for perjury. *HKR*, 20 May 1856.

the poisoning case, the trial immediately before it was a travesty of justice. Unrepresented by counsel, the defendant, Wong Awah, could not even understand proceedings. When he tried to call witnesses the interpreter told him it was too late. He did not even know the trial was over, or that he had been sentenced to death for piracy and murder, until three days later. With the help of missionaries, Wong petitioned to be allowed to find friends to give evidence, but the petition was rejected. He was hanged on 19 February 1857.[70]

'The comfort is,' wrote Bowring in 1858, that 'in no part of China is there *so much* Justice or *so little* venality as here and we do far better than would be expected with the instruments at our Command.'[71] This self-satisfied claim hardly stands up to scrutiny. Some of the many false accusations and miscarriages of justice of these years were clearly exposed when the Executive Council was forced to step in. On various occasions, when considering petitions for mercy, the council served as a de facto court of appeal, allowing lawyers to present new evidence and overturning some convictions. No other effective appellate remedies in criminal cases existed at this time.[72]

In the first such 'appeal', in March 1856, seven men were sentenced to death for the murder of an Indian guard during a robbery of a silversmith's shop at So Kon Po, near the Jardine Matheson establishment at East Point. Shortly after the trial, a rash of placards alleged that the silversmith had falsely accused men who had refused to pay him blackmail. When the case reached the Executive Council, Bowring decided to hold what amounted to a retrial, with prisoners and witnesses present in the council chamber. After a three-day hearing, one prisoner received a free pardon; the sentences on the others were commuted to life transportation. The matter did not end there. The missionary James Legge sent a Chinese preacher to Fung Shu Shan, a village near Mirs Bay, to investigate an alibi claimed by another prisoner, Lee Assow. Several people confirmed his alibi. Some told of how he had sold his wife to pay the blackmail and had been robbed of the proceeds by a middleman. One villager railed against the state of justice in Hong Kong:

> If one is apprehended there by another, who says he is a thief, he is held to be a thief. If that other wishes him to live, he lives; if he wishes him to die, he dies. There is no regard to

70. *CM*, 5 February 1857; ExCo minutes, 9 and 16 February 1856; Davies to Caine, 9 April 1857, CO 129/64, 348.
71. The comment appeared in a despatch on yet another squabble involving Anstey. While Attorney General he had, in his private capacity, appeared for Teep Ching-leu, a plaintiff in the Sheriff's court claiming damages for false imprisonment: the defendant, Lum Ah-kun, had accused Teep of theft, but the magistrate had discharged him. The jury found for Teep but awarded minimal damages. Anstey then had Lum arrested on a charge of perjury for giving contradictory evidence. The jury sent him a public letter of protest, objecting to this, and placing the blame on poor interpretation. Anstey withdrew the charge. Bowring to Labouchere, 13 February 1858, CO 129/67, 167–190; Norton-Kyshe, *History* Vol I, 462–464.
72. Petitions to the Privy Council were theoretically possible but impractical in such cases. Similar limitations also applied in England: see Bentley, *English Criminal Justice in the Nineteenth Century*, Chapter 25.

> Heavenly principles. If one man witness against him, though many men stand security for him, he cannot get out.[73]

Bowring consulted the Secretary of State, only to be reminded that the exercise of mercy lay with the Governor alone. In October Bowring granted Lee a free pardon.[74] The Colonial Office thought the episode 'a very strange proceeding', particularly since the council could not take evidence on oath: Merivale put it down to 'the uncertainty of justice administered under such circumstances of language, etc.' Anstey, the prosecutor in the case, described the hearing as 'an absurd second trial' before 'an incompetent Executive Council' against the will of every member except Bowring himself. 'If this is to go on, we might as well not pass sentence at all,' remarked Chief Justice Hulme on a similar rehearing of another case.[75] Bowring's intervention nevertheless exposed grave problems in the administration of justice and saved innocent men from the gallows.

Set against such cases, the trial of Cheong Alum was a remarkable feat of justice at a time of great peril. It took place when even those 'most kind to the Chinese loathed the whole race', recalled Bridges.[76] The clamour for lynching and the calls for trial by court martial suggest the outcome could have been different. The very official who should have championed the rule of law – the Attorney General – tried to subvert justice at every stage of proceedings. The insistence by the Governor and Chief Justice on a proper trial saved Cheong and his men from summary execution. Witnesses, defence counsel, judge, and jurors played their parts to ensure that justice was done. The trial and the verdict avoided the kind of savage responses to risings in India, Jamaica, and other parts of the Empire in the mid-nineteenth century. What the reaction might have been if the poison had succeeded can only be a matter for speculation.

---

73. Report of Lae A-sze (April 1856), CO 129/55, 192.
74. It was a letter from Lee that prompted Anstey's prosecution of the Sheriff and Acting Chief Magistrate, W.H. Mitchell, for malversation of office. While awaiting execution, the prisoners were allowed extra rations. Taking advantage of this, they induced Mitchell's servant to send out daily to a cookhouse for the best food, not realizing they would be charged for it. When Mitchell received the bill for the staggering sum of $227.50, he questioned the prisoners through his servant and advised them to find the money from their friends. Conflating this with the investigations then in progress into the claims of false accusations, Lee wrote to a friend saying that Mitchell had asked for 'victual money', on payment of which they would be pardoned by the Governor on the Queen's birthday. The letter found its way to an employee of the *China Mail*, who passed it to Anstey. At Mitchell's trial, both Lee and another prisoner insisted they had understood the possibility of a pardon to be dependent on the payment of the 'victual money'. *CM*, 3 January and 13 March 1856; Bowring to Labouchere, 7 and 24 April, 7 June 1856, and 7 October 1856, CO 129/55, 73–101 and 180–194, CO 129/56, 240–270, and CO 129/58, 258–259.
75. Evidence by Anstey and Wohang at the first Caldwell enquiry, 1 July 1858, CO 129/68, 485, 492, and 493; Minute by Merivale, 11 June 1856, CO 129/55, 75; *HKR*, 2 March, 6 April and 15 July 1858.
76. Memorandum by Bridges, 27 July 1857, in House of Commons, *Confinement of Chinese Prisoners at Hong Kong* (1858) 4.

Historians have celebrated the acquittal of Cheong and his men as a vindication of the rule of law. It was, wrote J.W. Norton-Kyshe, the first chronicler of Hong Kong's courts, 'to the honour of the British name' that they 'were not only tried at the place where their crime was committed, but tried by a judge who had himself suffered from that crime, assisted by a jury all equally victims of the atrocious crime'.[77] By this case 'the reputation of British justice had been established', observes a more recent historian, Kwasi Kwarteng.[78] Few colonists saw it in this way. Whatever their views on Anstey's conduct, many continued to regret the outcome. 'The verdict of the jury,' remarked the *Hongkong Register*, 'in effect opens the stomach of every man in the colony to poison, without fear or danger of detection to the poisoner.'[79]

The acquittals marked no turning point in justice. Supreme Court trials continued to be rushed, with conviction rates at about 70 per cent in 1857. Only twenty-five of the 231 men put on trial that year, including the ten in the poisoning case, are recorded as having had the benefit of counsel. No fewer than fifty-one men were sentenced to death in 1857. However, all but six received 'death recorded' sentences, which were commuted to transportation as a matter of routine: most were for crimes not resulting in loss of life, such as piracy or robbery with violence. Only three of the six on whom sentence of death was pronounced were executed. One was Wong Awah. The other two were convicted of crimes against British nationals connected with the hostilities between Britain and China.

One of these was the leader of a rising in March among a 432-strong 'cargo of coolies' (as the captain described them) on the *Gulnare*, a British ship bound for Havana, shortly after its departure from Swatow. The ship's interpreter warned the captain of the rising, and the crew suppressed it: nine coolies were shot dead, three jumped overboard, and thirty were wounded. Eighteen others were convicted of piracy with violence. Fifteen received sentences of death recorded, commuted to life transportation. Sentence of death was pronounced on the other three. Against advice from his Executive Council that all three should hang, Bowring confirmed the death sentence on only one, Ng King-seang. He said that, while none of them had committed murder, Ng was clearly the ringleader, and 'of a superior station in life' (the *Friend of China* describes him as a 'mandarin agent'). Ng was hanged in the gaol on 9 April 1857. The *Gulnare* resumed its journey with 326 'emigrants', fifty-eight of whom died on the voyage. Those who reached Havana alive entered a system in which indentured labourers were treated worse than slaves. The seventeen transported for life, to the British colony of Labuan, almost certainly had better prospects.[80]

---

77. Norton-Kyshe, *History*, Vol. I, 418.
78. Kwasi Kwarteng, *Ghosts of Empire: Britain's Legacies in the Modern World* (New York: Public Affairs, 2013), 333.
79. *HKR*, 12 February 1857.
80. *FOC*, 1 and 11 April 1857; *CM* (Supplement), 2 April 1857; ExCo Minutes, 6 April 1857, CO 131/4, 72–73; Bowring to Labouchere, 10 April 1857, CO 129/63, 5–11; E.R. Mitchell, Emigration Officer, Hong Kong, to Carnarvon, 23 July 1858, CO 129/72, 334–335.

The third man to be executed in 1857 was Ho Apo, a servant of the elderly auctioneer Charles Markwick. On the night of 1 April, Ho strangled him in his bed and fled when the curfew was lifted in the morning. At first, it seemed that Ho had disturbed Markwick while stealing from his room. Worried about Chinese government plots 'against English life and property', Bowring took extreme measures to capture Ho. He announced a reward of $500. He then sent Daniel Caldwell with a contingent of men on a steamer to Ho's native village of Im-tin, on the north coast of Mirs Bay. Caldwell took back two village elders and held them hostage in the gaol until Ho was found. A few days later Ho was found in Im-tin and brought to Hong Kong; a request from his mother for the $500 reward was refused. He was tried for murder on 4 May. The jury instantly returned a verdict of guilty. Ho was hanged on 13 May, shortly after confessing.[81]

Intelligence received by Caldwell suggested that Markwick's murder was more than just a robbery. Valuables stolen from him were traced to the house of Chun Ah-cheen, the headman of the town of Stanley, on the south of Hong Kong Island. The search uncovered a letter from Chen Guiji, head of the committee appointed by Ye Mingchen to plan attacks on Hong Kong. Chen had offered Chun a $50,000 reward and official rank for the heads of 'the only two in Hong Kong who know all about the Chinese': Caldwell and Lieutenant-Governor Caine. Chun and two others were tried for high treason on 2 May 1857, the first treason case in Hong Kong. Anstey prosecuted. The barrister John Day appeared for Chun, arguing to no avail that he was not a British subject and could not be tried for treason, and that the hostilities were piracies, not a national war. Witnesses from Stanley told how Chun had asked them to help with the assassination, and how Chinese officials had often visited his house. Chun was sentenced to 'death recorded'.[82] His co-defendants were acquitted. According to the *Daily Press*, the main prosecution witness and his family were murdered later in the year.[83]

High treason was an extraordinary charge for a half-baked conspiracy to murder two colonial officials. In this, and in the other political convictions, there is a sense that the colony was straining to compensate for other attacks on Europeans in which the culprits got away. The *Friend of China* suggested as much when it criticized Bowring for allowing the hanging of the 'mandarin agent', Ng King-seang, to be carried out within the walls of the gaol, with only a few spectators present. Better, said the *Friend*, to hang him in the most public place as a warning to other agents, 'of whom there are no doubt plenty amongst

81. The incursion into Chinese territory was referred to the Law Officers in London, who, while noting the hostilities between Britain and China at the time, advised that it set a dangerous precedent that should not be followed in future. *CM*, 7 and 14 May 1857; Bowring to Labouchere, 23 April and 14 May 1857, CO 129/63, 17–24 and 113–114; Hammond, Foreign Office, to Merivale, 9 July 1857, CO 129/65, 413–416.

82. *FOC*, 6 May 1857; *CM*, 23 April and 7 May 1857; Bowring to Labouchere, 14 and 23 April 1857, CO 129/63, 15–53.

83. Bowring to Labouchere, 14 November 1857, CO 129/65, 17–31.

us'. It would 'show that our legal tribunals are not the simple burlesque shows which the Chinese are beginning to imagine them'.[84] The next hanging, of Markwick's murderer Ho Apo, took place at one of the most visible sites in the city, on a scaffold erected above Arbuthnot Road outside the Magistracy. Shortly before Ho's execution, on 13 May, residents of Stanley gathered outside the Magistracy, complaining of a 'breach of faith'. They had wrongly believed that the man to be hanged was their headman, Chun Ah-cheen, convicted of treason earlier in the month. They had paid a large sum of money to the police informer, Ma-chow Wong, who had promised to intercede to reduce the sentence to transportation.[85] But Chun's sentence of 'death recorded' was commuted to transportation as a matter of routine. He was shipped to Labuan later that year.

The fate of Cheong Alum

Most defendants in criminal trials in early colonial Hong Kong were of lowly status. They are generally described as coolies, boatmen, fishermen, hawkers, cooks, or stonecutters. A few, of the middling sort, were shopkeepers, moneychangers, artisans, and ships' masters. Cheong Alum, in contrast, was from the elite class of compradors, contractors, merchants, and interpreters who had close connections with Europeans. His trial revealed a dense network of contacts with European clients, founded on trust and goodwill. The missionary James Legge described him as 'a tall, imposing-looking man for a Chinese', and well educated. Cheong, he recalled, 'quite took me under his patronage, had the books ready, and maintained perfect order' among all who attended services in the gaol. 'The respect and deference shown to him by all the prisoners were wonderful.'[86]

Cheong Pui-lam (張霈霖), to use his full name, was twenty-eight at the time of the poisoning. He was a native of Yagang, a village eight miles north of Macao. His father was a teacher of some repute. Alum was the eldest of three sons. He showed promise as a scholar but had to give up his studies at the age of thirteen because the family was poor. He followed an uncle to Macao, where he learned how to do business with foreigners. In 1846 he moved to Hong Kong. He became comprador to various firms, including Murrow, Stephenson & Co., which pioneered steamship services to San Francisco.[87] Having acquired capital and connections, Cheong branched out on his own. He helped establish steamship services between Hong Kong and Macao. In the early 1850s he founded the Esing Bakery with the help of George Duddell, and in 1856 opened a branch in Canton. By now the bakery was the largest purveyor of bread in Hong Kong. According to his cousin Assow, Cheong Alum

84. *FOC*, 11 April 1857.

85. *CM*, 14 May 1857, 78; Anstey to Bridges, 8 July 1857, CO 129/68, 352–361.

86. Legge, 'The Colony of Hong Kong', 171.

87. Biography of Cheong Alum by Chen Zhaochang.

was worth about $30,000.[88] The poisoning trial ruined him financially. On 1 February 1857, at the government's request, George Duddell took over the Esing Bakery, replacing all of its flour at great expense. In March his warehouses were destroyed by a fire started by one of Chen Guiji's spies, causing losses of $17,000.[89]

Cheong's co-defendants were released two weeks after the trial: all but two, born in Hong Kong, were deported to China. Cheong was held in prison pending instructions from London, the Chief Justice having told the Governor he would rule against any attempt to release him by habeas corpus. The government received five petitions with advice on how Cheong should be dealt with. The first was from sixteen European merchants and justices of the peace, including Lyall, Duncanson, jurors in Cheong's trial, and Bridges, his counsel. They argued that further detention was 'calculated to throw discredit on our system of administering justice in the eyes of the Chinese population, who have been led to understand that a man cannot be twice called in question for the same offence'. They proposed 'voluntary banishment' with one or two months' grace for Cheong to settle his affairs. Another petition, signed by fifty European residents, deeply regretted the verdict and proposed deportation 'to some place in the Island of Formosa'. A third, from thirty-eight Europeans and Parsis, described Cheong as a dangerous spy and urged indefinite detention. Two petitions were presented by Tam Achoy and sixty Chinese residents. They advised that, after settling his debts, Cheong should be allowed to leave Hong Kong, with security taken against his return.[90]

The Secretary of State directed that the best course of action was the one recommended in the petitions from Tam Achoy.[91] This decision did not reach Hong Kong until early July. Even then, Cheong continued to be detained in Victoria Gaol for another three weeks, this time as a debtor, even though no formal claims had been made against him. Since 14 February Bridges had been acting as Colonial Secretary during Mercer's absence on sick leave. This gave him control over the timing of Cheong's release. At the same time, he insisted on maintaining his private practice as a condition of taking up the acting position. In June, the editor of the *Friend of China*, William Tarrant, sued Cheong for having sold bread fraudulently warranted to be wholesome and fit food. A special jury awarded him damages of $1,010 with costs. But Bridges, as Cheong's counsel, raised a point of law, and the Chief Justice held the award in abeyance. Cheong was released on 1 August and immediately left the colony before Tarrant was able to obtain his damages. Tarrant accused Bridges of releasing Cheong to avoid an 'exposé', in any future bankruptcy proceedings, of his 'astounding extortion in the shape of lawyers' fees'. Bridges prosecuted

88. *CM*, 3 September 1857.

89. *FOC*, 7 March 1857; Memorial of George Duddell, in House of Commons, *Correspondence Relating to the Chinese Indemnity Fund* (1873), 2.

90. ExCo Minutes, 9 and 16 February 1857, CO 131/4, 45–51 and 54–55.

91. Labouchere to Bowring, 8 May 1857, CO 129/62, 227–229.

Tarrant for criminal libel. During the trial Bridges revealed he had received $1,150 in fees from Cheong and had no reason to dread any exposé. Tarrant was fined £100, which was paid out of a subscription by sympathizers.[92]

Tarrant's trial heralded a round of scandals that convulsed the colony. Anstey, Tarrant, and other journalists launched a campaign against corruption, targeting, first, Bridges's conflicts of interest. In 1858 the press revealed that he had been legal adviser to a group of Chinese merchants who had been awarded the monopoly on the sale of retail opium, even though, as Colonial Secretary, he had played a key part in assessing the bids. Egged on by Anstey, the *Hongkong Register* urged Bridges to resign. Bridges demanded an enquiry. A committee chaired by the Chief Magistrate, Henry Davies, found that, though blameworthy in his conduct, his honesty and honour remained 'quite unimpeached'.[93]

Bowring did not ask Bridges to resign. On the contrary, he begged him to stay on. While the opium enquiry was in progress Anstey launched an attack on the Registrar General, Daniel Caldwell, who had been the interpreter in the poisoning and many other trials. Anstey called Caldwell a brothel-keeper, and his Chinese wife a 'harlot'. He accused him of consorting with pirates, and being in league with his informant, Ma-chow Wong, who had been transported to Labuan in September 1857 for piracy. Bowring appointed a commission under the Surveyor General, Charles Cleverly, a friend of Caldwell and a fellow freemason. It cleared Caldwell of most of the charges but confirmed his relationship with Wong, and his practice of arresting persons at Wong's behest. Caldwell remained in office until a more vigorous enquiry in 1861 found him unfit to continue in public service.[94] His accuser, Anstey, had been suspended in August 1858, shortly after the first Caldwell enquiry: Bowring had finally had enough of his 'uncontrollable, restless and turbulent temper'.[95] Anstey returned to England to pursue his campaign against misgovernment in Hong Kong. He then joined the Bombay Bar. Bridges resigned in the same month as Anstey. He finally left Hong Kong in 1861 to avoid entanglement in the second Caldwell enquiry. He retired to Devon, where he sat as a magistrate and wrote *A Handy Book for Justices of the Peace.*

Cheong Alum's banishment from Hong Kong was for a term of only five years. But he did not return. He went first to Macao, where he opened a store selling Western goods. 'He lived as if nothing had happened.' In 1860 he arranged the construction of Chinese junks for the French government, which in 1862 invited him to settle in its expanding territories in Indochina. Starting with brick kilns, he established several new businesses there and became a leader of the Chinese community, helping people in their dealings with the

92. *CM*, 3 September 1857.

93. 'Report and Proceedings of the Committee of the Legislative Council to Inquire into Certain Statements Involving the Integrity of the Acting Colonial Secretary', *HKGG*, 19 June 1858.

94. Robinson to Newcastle, 16 September 1861, CO 129/82, 539–540.

95. Bowring to Labouchere, 4 June 1858, CO 129/68, 70.

French government. By the 1880s he was chief manager in Saigon of the China Merchants Steam Navigation Company, and its contractor for importing rice from Vietnam to China. He had three wives, four concubines, three daughters, and ten sons, two of whom passed the Qing official examinations and achieved the rank of *juren*. Cheong purchased official rank for himself, his father, and his grandfather. The French government also awarded him honours and distinctions. By the time of his death in 1900 at the age of seventy-three he was one of the wealthiest and most respected men in Vietnam.[96]

In contrast, William Robinet, the man who had arrested Cheong in Macao, saw his reputation ruined in a bizarre fraud. In December 1857 he brokered a shipment of silk from Hong Kong to Valparaiso, insured it heavily, and accompanied it as supercargo. On the voyage the ship mysteriously caught fire. After putting it out, the crew opened the cargo to reveal, not bales of silk, but bundles of old sacking. Before reaching Valparaiso they found a note in his cabin saying he had thrown himself overboard. But three days later he emerged out of hiding and told the captain that, on seeing sharks in the water, he had changed his mind. He told creditors in Valparaiso he was the victim of the 'vengeance of the Chinese' for having captured 'the Baker of Hongkong'. He returned to Hong Kong, where he was arrested by creditors. Insolvency hearings in 1858 exposed a business built on overtrading, sharp practice, and probable fraud. For his general misconduct, the Supreme Court committed him to the debtors' gaol for eighteen months.[97]

96. Biography of Cheong Alum by Chen Zhaochang.

97. *CM*, 26 August, 21 October, and 4, 11, 18, 25, and 27 November 1858; *HKR*, 16, 23, and 30 November 1858. Robinet described himself as 'a native of Peru, son of a native of Calcutta, and an American citizen', having lived in the US and South America and served in the Peruvian navy. While in China and Hong Kong he was at various times Consul for Peru, Chile, and Ecuador. He was also involved in a scheme for annexing Taiwan to the US. Harold D. Langley, 'Gideon Nye and the Formosa Annexation Scheme', *Pacific Historical Review*, Vol. 34, No. 4 (November 1965): 397–420; Elizabeth Sinn, *Pacific Crossing: California Gold, Chinese Migration, and the Making of Hong Kong* (Hong Kong: Hong Kong University Press, 2013), 150–153.

3

'The Great Colonial Disgrace'

The Carl *and* Caesar *Piracies, 1866*

On Friday 15 June 1866, in the space of a few hours, a gang of Chinese pirates attacked and plundered two European sailing ships, the *Carl* and the *Caesar*, near Hong Kong. They killed the captain of the *Carl*. The Hong Kong authorities tracked down eighteen of the gang and tried seventeen of them over the summer: fifteen were convicted of piracy with endangering life and eleven were hanged – enough, remarked the Governor, Sir Richard MacDonnell, 'to make a striking example'.[1] Seven were hanged on a single day in one of the colony's largest mass executions. More people were hanged in Hong Kong in the 1860s than in any other decade, nearly all for piracy. Piracy, said MacDonnell, was 'the great Colonial disgrace'.[2] It disrupted trade and embarrassed the authorities in Hong Kong, where pirates planned their attacks and – colonists claimed – manipulated the law to avoid punishment. A determination to eradicate the problem became a defining feature of MacDonnell's governorship. The trials of the *Carl* and *Caesar* pirates, and more especially their executions, formed the dramatic centrepiece of his campaign.

Driven by poverty and opportunity, piracy was an age-old problem in the seas and waterways of China's maritime provinces. Pirates were part of a flourishing shadow economy, trading their booty at friendly ports. Early in the nineteenth century a massive pirate fleet, with hundreds of ships, dominated the South China Sea. Its leader, Cheung Po-tsai, surrendered to Qing forces in 1810. He was pardoned and sent to suppress other

1. The eighteenth committed suicide before trial. MacDonnell to Cardwell, 11 August 1866, CO 129/114, 258–260.
2. Legislative Council Proceedings, *Hongkong Mercury*, 26 July 1866, CO 129/114, 189.

pirate fleets.[3] In the mid-nineteenth century, as war and rebellion weakened the Chinese state, piracy waxed again. The opening of Hong Kong and the treaty ports offered fresh opportunities. Qing officials 'could not comprehend the freedom with which Piratical Vessels could fit out at Hongkong', reported the British Consul in Canton.[4] 'No matter what they want, whether to buy, sell, victual, or refit, here they are welcome; no papers are asked or given,' said the *China Mail*.[5] Spies gleaned intelligence about the movements of ships. Plots were hatched under the noses of the authorities. Pawnbrokers, opium shops, and silversmiths disposed of pillaged cargoes. By the 1840s large pirate fleets had again emerged in the South China Sea. Some were now aiming their guns at foreign ships.

Measures against piracy ranged from schemes of prevention to attempts at suppression by naval action. Among preventive measures contemplated in Hong Kong were monitoring ships through registration and disarming Chinese vessels – especially of stinkpots, the smoking missiles launched by pirates to spread fire and confusion. From time to time merchants organized convoys: some were barely distinguishable from the pirate ventures they sought to deter. Occasionally the Royal Navy provided escorts and patrolled pirate haunts. But the navy was thinly spread, and the islands and inlets of the China coast were ideal hiding places. Because pirates took refuge on land or in Chinese waters, prevention required cooperation between governments. The Qing authorities were weakened by war and preoccupied with internal rebellion. It was, remarked the *China Mail*, too much to expect Britain on its own to undertake 'a task so hopelessly chivalrous as the suppression of Chinese piracy'.[6]

In the absence of strong government, traders made peace with pirates by paying protection money. The Qing tradition of co-opting their leaders to keep piracy at bay continued well into the nineteenth century. Echoing this, officials in Hong Kong favoured certain criminals with immunity in return for intelligence about pirates: the most flagrant example was the alliance between Ma-chow Wong and Daniel Caldwell, who served as guide in naval expeditions against pirates. The largest were the campaigns in 1849 against the fleets of Shap-ng-tsai and Chui Apo. Both had bases in Hong Kong. Shap-ng-tsai left after the Qing authorities sought his rendition.[7] Chui Apo's base was at Wong Ma Kok on the Stanley Peninsula. He fled in early 1849 after taking part in the killing of two British army officers who had molested women in the village. Later that year naval steamships destroyed twenty-three of Chui's ships, killing some 400 men. Chui escaped with over a thousand others, some of whom took refuge in Hong Kong. In October, working with Qing officials,

3. Dian H. Murray, *Pirates of the South China Coast 1790–1810* (Stanford, California: Stanford University Press, 1987).
4. Robertson to Hammond, 28 May 1866, FO 17/802, 260.
5. *OCM*, 14 March 1863.
6. Robertson to Mercer, 22 May 1866, FO 17/803, 41–48; *CM*, 12 March 1863.
7. John C. Dalrymple Hay, *The Suppression of Piracy in the China Sea* (London: Edward Stanford, 1889), 27.

the Royal Navy destroyed fifty-eight of Shap-ng-tsai's fleet near Hainan, killing some 1,700 people.[8] Shap-ng-tsai escaped with the rump of his fleet and was co-opted by the Qing authorities.[9] Chui was captured in Canton in 1851, taken to Hong Kong on a British gunboat, and convicted of manslaughter. Before his sentence of transportation could be carried out, he hanged himself.[10]

These displays of British naval power pleased merchants in Hong Kong, who feted officers with dinners and presents of silver plate. But the wholesale massacres that accompanied them made no distinction between pirates and their hostages, among whom were women and children. Official rewards paid in head money for each pirate killed or captured caused controversy. Those for the campaign against Shap-ng-tsai totalled £42,425, shared among 363 officers and men. Politicians in London were appalled by the staggering cost and the slaughter of so many people. In 1850 the head money system was reformed on less generous lines.[11]

Prisoners from an earlier expedition against Shap-ng-tsai's fleet reportedly told their captors that his advisors had proposed jettisoning their weapons, declaring themselves to be fishermen, and allowing the foreigners to board. Even if arrested they faced no danger, 'as Hongkong Law required absolute proof of their having committed acts of Piracy before it could even detain them, and this proof the foreigners were not in a position to make good!' Shap-ng-tsai decided, however, to make his escape. The *Hongkong Register*'s outraged report of his flight was followed by a comment on a 'pet pirate' who had been so astonished at his acquittal on a flawed indictment that he appeared in court the next day as a spectator, keen to learn more about 'the eccentric functions of a law which pronounced him "not guilty" of a crime that had only a moment before been thoroughly substantiated against him.'[12]

Piracy and the Hong Kong courts

The 'pet pirate', Leong Yun-tau, was acquitted by Hong Kong's Vice-Admiralty Court, which tried piracy cases from 1847 to 1849. Its criminal jurisdiction was absorbed by the Supreme Court in 1850. The Vice-Admiralty Court was notorious for its 'lumbering machinery', which, unlike that of the Supreme Court, had not been adjusted to meet Hong

8. Bonham to Grey, 3 November 1849, CO 129/30, 255–302; Beresford Scott, *An Account of the Destruction of the Fleets of the Celebrated Pirate Chieftains Chui-apoo and Shap-ng-tsai* (London: Savill and Edwards, 1851).
9. Grace Fox, *British Admirals and Chinese Pirates, 1832–1869* (London: Kegan Paul, 1940), 107–109; Scott, *An Account of the Destruction of the Fleets of the Celebrated Pirate Chieftains*, 102; Bonham to Palmerston, 12 September 1849, CO 129/30, 257–260.
10. Munn, *Anglo-China*, 204–207.
11. 'Pirates' Head Money' (House of Commons, 27 June 1851); Piracy Act 1850.
12. The flaw, wrongly stating who owned the pirated property, was noticed by Chief Justice Hulme. *HKR*, 4 December 1849 (italics in the original); *CM*, 22 November 1849.

Kong's meagre resources. Criminal sessions required three judges and scores of jurors to supply a grand jury of up to twenty-three men and trial juries of twelve.[13] Grand juries determined whether a case should go to trial. Some had no scruples about blocking prosecutions of Europeans.[14] Long delays between arrest and convening the court offered opportunities for pirate gangs to tamper with witnesses. The sessions in November 1849 which acquitted Leong Yun-tau heard seven other cases: four were thrown out by the grand jury; one, a charge of piracy against thirteen Chinese, collapsed because witnesses could not identify them; two, a revolt on one British ship and larceny on another, resulted in prison sentences for ten men, all of them British.

If legal loopholes and unreliable evidence allegedly led to acquittals of guilty pirates, those without means faced formidable obstacles. Few understood English procedure. Interpretation was inadequate. It was often impossible to produce alibi witnesses. Prosecutions relied mainly on identification, a fragile basis for conviction when victims found it 'difficult to identify a Chinaman only seen once and that under circumstances of excitement'.[15] These defects worked to the advantage of false accusers. In 1847, Too Apo, a participant in an attack on British opium ships, turned Queen's evidence in return for a pardon. Caldwell took him on as an informant. Too Apo then set about blackmailing people, telling them he 'was in the service of the English' and it was up to him whether they should live or die. It later came out that four men convicted on his evidence were innocent. Too Apo was convicted of extortion. The men were pardoned.[16]

Doubtful evidence and legal technicalities kept conviction rates below 50 per cent in the Vice-Admiralty Court. Even so, in the three years in which it tried piracies the court condemned twenty-five men to death, eleven of whom were hanged. When the Supreme Court took over in 1850, conviction rates in piracy cases were at first even lower. They then rose to an average of over 70 per cent in the decade or so from 1855 – a result partly

---

13. Cases were tried by three out of a panel of commissioners comprising the Governor, Chief Justice, Commander of British Forces, Colonial Secretary, Chief Magistrate, and Flag Officers of naval ships.
14. For example, in 1848, Captain Cole of the *Spec*, a convoy ship engaged for protection by fishermen off Ningbo, was charged with piracy and murder after giving orders to fire on a suspected pirate junk and then allowing his crew to plunder it. A Royal Navy ship caught Cole in the act and took him to Hong Kong for trial. The British community raised money for his defence. A key prosecution witness was allegedly abducted from the police station in which he was being held by Cole's supporters. The grand jury refused to find a true bill of indictment and Cole was freed without trial. The Admiralty found it 'difficult to imagine a grosser case of outrage and piracy' and were troubled by the connivance of Cole's friends. Chief Justice Hulme's biased directions, observed Merivale in the Colonial Office, were 'almost equivalent to a direction to the grand jury not to find a true bill'. *HKR*, 10 October 1848; Bonham to Palmerston, 17 October 1848, CO 129/26, 132–156; Admiralty to Merivale, 30 December 1848, CO 129/27, 19.
15. *CM*, 5 June 1862.
16. Munn, *Anglo-China*, 184.

of simplified procedures and the acceptance of majority verdicts in non-capital cases,[17] but also of hardening attitudes in the face of rising crime: 'it was no unusual thing' in a piracy case, remarked the *China Mail*, 'to hear grave men say that if they should be on this jury, they would hang them all'.[18] Still, governors complained that fewer than a quarter of those charged before the magistrates, 'of whose guilt there can be little moral doubt', were eventually convicted.[19]

According to an old legal definition, piracy is 'a sea term for robbery'.[20] Under international law, piracy on the high seas – 'piracy *jure gentium*' – is a crime against all nations, triable anywhere, no matter by whom, or against whom it is committed. The Piracy Act 1837, applied to Hong Kong through the reception of English law in 1843, prescribed transportation of at least fifteen years for simple piracy[21] and death for wounding or otherwise endangering life. Courts in Hong Kong could try any case of piracy on the high seas and any crime committed on a British ship. The crime of piracy also embraced the numerous revolts by 'coolies' on ships bound for the Americas, many of whom were kidnapped or duped into signing contracts. Pirates and coolies came from the same class of 'bare sticks' – 'the too abundant population of reckless and needy men' denied a settled life by poverty.[22] Imperial economics put a similar price on them: £20 in head money for every pirate killed in Royal Navy expeditions; £15 to £38 for Chinese coolies 'resold' as slaves in Cuba.[23]

---

17. Ordinance No. 1 of 1850 allowed changes to indictments during trial to address problems in tracing ownership of property and accommodate 'the frequent Discrepancies in Chinese Testimony'. Ordinance No. 1 of 1851 (repealed in 1856) allowed the reading of depositions at trial in the absence of witnesses, addressing fears that witnesses were being removed 'by force or bribery'. Ordinance No. 4 of 1852 reduced notice of trial from ten to five days and simplified indictments for murder and piracy. Ordinances Nos. 6 of 1856, 1 of 1857, and 3 of 1865 further simplified indictments and restricted grounds for objections on technicalities. Majority verdicts in non-capital cases were allowed from 1851 and were made easier by increasing the size of juries from six to seven in 1858: Ordinances Nos. 4 of 1851 and 3 of 1858. Some of the changes relating to indictments (but not depositions or juries) drew on reforms in England.
18. The comment came after the acquittal of seventeen men charged with piracy of the British ship *Eagle* and the murder of its captain. The jury foreman had allegedly said that 'he would never join in a verdict that would take away a human life'. The men were remanded in gaol while the Attorney General considered whether to indict them for the murder of one of the crew, which he appears not to have done. *CM*, 5 June 1862.
19. Robinson to Cardwell, 9 August 1864, CO 129/99, 333; MacDonnell to Alcock, 16 May 1866, CO 129/113, 181.
20. *R v Dawson* (1696), 13 State Tr. 454. This definition, endorsed by the Judicial Committee of the Privy Council in *Attorney General v Kwok-a-Sing (Hong Kong)* [1873] UKPC 58, proved problematic: see Chapter 9.
21. Or up to three years' imprisonment in lesser cases.
22. Thomas Sutherland to the Board of Directors of the P. &. O. Company, 15 November 1865, FO 17/802, 51; Jung-fang Tsai, *Hong Kong in Chinese History: Community and Social Unrest in the British Colony, 1842–1913* (New York: Columbia University Press, 1993), 19–26; Robert J. Antony, *Unruly People: Crime, Community, and State in Late Imperial South China* (Hong Kong: Hong Kong University Press, 2016), 127–132.
23. *The Cuba Commission Report* (1876, repr. Baltimore, Maryland: Johns Hopkins University Press, 1993), 89.

About a third of all defendants before the Supreme Court in the 1850s and 1860s were charged with one or other category of piracy. Convictions for piracies and murders on the high seas accounted for over half of the 410 men transported from Hong Kong to penal establishments in Penang, Singapore, and Labuan in the eleven years from 1848. Most were sentenced to 'death recorded' for piracy with violence: the death penalty was then commuted as a matter of course, usually to transportation for life. From 1858, colonies refused to take prisoners from Hong Kong. Transportation was replaced by penal servitude in the increasingly overcrowded Victoria Gaol.

While most seaborne crimes tried in Hong Kong occurred in the sea lanes off the China coast, some occurred hundreds of miles away. Six of the eight men executed in 1852 were Filipino and Portuguese crewmembers of the British ship *Herald* who had mutinied in the Sunda Strait – 2,000 miles from Hong Kong – and murdered the captain and his wife and four crew. The case was transferred from Singapore because witnesses were in Hong Kong. Ten defendants received death sentences, four of which were commuted to transportation. The crime was brutal, and the leader confessed before execution. But newspapers were appalled by the hanging of so many men, all on the same day, and disgusted by visits to the condemned cell by colonists 'elbowing' the Catholic priests to get a view of the prisoners.[24] Hangings on such a scale were, according to the Governor, Sir George Bonham, 'contrary to the spirit of the present age'.[25]

Piracy and the Chinese courts

Bonham and the Chief Justice, John Hulme, were on leave when the *Herald* trial took place. But they were already embroiled in a dispute about the death penalty. In 1850 Bonham had commuted death sentences pronounced by Hulme against nine Chinese convicted of piracy with stabbing on a Chinese junk off Hainan. Hulme had objected to this because the prisoners had also confessed to 'wholesale murders' in another piracy, for which they were not tried. The nine had been arrested in Hong Kong on information given to Caldwell. So powerful were they believed to be that Hulme was given military protection after the trial amid rumours of an assassination plot. There were few capital convictions over the next eighteen months, but in all of them, instead of *pronouncing* the death penalty, Hulme merely *recorded* sentence of death, which effectively meant commutation. The press saw this as a protest against Bonham's commutations in the case of the nine Chinese pirates.[26]

The dispute came to a head in February 1852, when Hulme *recorded* sentence of death against two Javanese convicted of murdering the English chief mate on the British ship

24. Jervois to Grey, 5 May 1852, CO 129/40, 26–57; *HKR*, 27 April and 4 and 11 May 1852; *CM*, 29 April 1852.
25. Hulme to Grey, paraphrasing Bonham's views, 8 July 1852, CO 129/41, 206.
26. *FOC*, 30 October 1850.

Corcyra near Taiwan. In passing sentence, he said he would not have hesitated to *pronounce* sentence of death had it not been for the commutations in the case of the nine pirates. Incensed by Hulme's attitude, and uncertain of his powers, Bonham referred the case to London.[27] Asked for an explanation, Hulme argued that to condemn the Javanese would have given 'a very dangerous impression and one striking at the root of justice itself, that there was one law for avenging the murder of a Chinaman and another law for avenging the murder of an Englishman'. The Secretary of State rebuked Hulme for having been guided 'not by the merits of the case before him, or by the law which bears upon it, but by his own speculations as to the manner in which the Prerogative of Mercy may be exercised by the Executive Authorities'. After consulting Bonham (who was again in London), the Secretary of State, in a rare intervention, used the Queen's residual prerogative to instruct Bonham's deputy to commute the sentences to transportation.[28]

Bonham had had doubts about the trial of the nine pirates. They claimed that they themselves been seized by pirates but could not prove it, for they had no witnesses. It was impossible to assess the guilt of each prisoner from Hulme's sparse notes, the only official record. Bonham considered hanging only the first three named on the indictment, but when he found they were just eighteen, nineteen, and twenty-one years old, he decided that all nine should be spared. More important to Bonham was the matter of policy. The crime had occurred 300 miles away, by and against Chinese who had no link with Hong Kong. Hanging these men would create 'a most inconvenient precedent', since action would be expected against piracies anywhere along the China coast or off Japan – even, Bonham added, the coast of California: 'we may have, at some time or other, one hundred convicts under sentence of death.' Had the nine men been hanged, there would be no reason 'why execution, under like circumstances, should not be done on ten times as many'.[29]

Although it had also taken place far away, the murder on the *Corcyra* was, for Bonham, a different matter. The *Corcyra* was a British ship, the victim a British subject. The culprits, born in Java under the Dutch flag, had shipped at Singapore. In Bonham's view, the case clearly affected British interests. Moreover, crimes on British ships were becoming too common: the *Herald* case was about to come to trial; there were reports of a murderous revolt on a British coolie ship off Cambodia. These were proper cases for the Hong Kong courts, said Bonham. But the courts were 'ill-adapted' to try cases in which victims and

27. Complicating matters, the Attorney General had advised that the sentence might be unsafe because the Judgment of Death Act 1823 required the court, before *recording* sentence of death, to be of opinion that the prisoners were 'fit and proper subjects to be recommended for the Royal Mercy'. Hulme had made it clear at the trial that they were not fit for mercy. Note by Sterling, 26 February 1852, CO 129/39, 108–109.

28. *CM*, 18 July 1850; Bonham to Grey, 6 August 1850, CO 129/33, 169–187, and 26 February and 8 July 1852, CO 129/39, 86–113 and 229–233; Hulme to Grey, 8 July 1852, CO 129/41, 204–217; Journal of John Fortunatus Evelyn Wright, HKPRO HKMS143-1, 2 August 1850.

29. Bonham to Grey, 6 August 1850, CO 129/33, 169–187.

defendants were 'all Chinese and unconnected with this or any other British Colony'. He proposed sending such cases to the Chinese authorities.[30]

Despite concerns by the Foreign Secretary, Lord Palmerston, Royal Navy ships already routinely handed over men captured at sea to the Chinese authorities – some 300 in 1847 alone, and over 100 in 1864.[31] Some alleged pirates were handed over after their discharge by courts in Hong Kong: the *Hongkong Register* called this 'giving justice a second chance'.[32] In 1850, under the treaties between Britain and China, Bonham enacted procedures for handing over fugitive Chinese subjects, even without requests from the Chinese authorities.[33] From 1849 to 1856, 144 persons were surrendered, mostly for piracy.[34] In 1857 Governor Bowring sent to the Kowloon authorities seventy-three alleged pirates captured near the harbour: the system of justice in piracy cases was defective, he said; it was impossible to hang so many men, or transport them, or keep them in prison. The press condemned him for this. The Secretary of State also rejected the idea that courts were 'inadequate to the duty of trying Chinese offenders', and told Bowring that trying piracy was 'one of the most important purposes for which the Supreme Court at Hong Kong is established'.[35] Renditions nevertheless continued.[36]

Qing justice had many attractions for governors who were distrustful of their own courts, squeamish about hangings, and alarmed by the growing number of prisoners in Victoria Gaol. Trials of pirates in China took place with none of the delays or procedural pitfalls of justice in Hong Kong. The punishment was decapitation and exposure of the head near the scene of the crime; the leaders were liable to *lingchi* – death by slicing. In the troubled state of China, officials were ordered to try and execute rebels, bandits, and pirates without the usual careful process of review all the way up to the Emperor.[37] Of fifty-eight

30. Bonham to Grey, 6 August 1850, CO 129/33, 173.
31. Palmerston proposed that Chinese courts should be asked to sentence such pirates to hard labour and hand them back to the British for transportation. Addington to Hawes, 11 August 1849, CO 129/31, 45–47.
32. Munn, *Anglo-China*, 247–250; *HKR*, 20 November 1849.
33. Article IX of the Supplementary Treaty 1843 specified two forms of rendition: (a) rendition of fugitive Chinese discovered in Hong Kong at the initiative of the British authorities; and (b) rendition of fugitive Chinese on requisition from the Chinese authorities *on proof or admission of their guilt*. Ordinance No. 2 of 1850 set out a system of extradition requiring a hearing by a magistrate and a final decision by the Governor. But instead of proof of guilt it only required a finding of 'probable cause for believing' the fugitive had committed a crime. The Treaty of Tientsin (1858) required a requisition from the Chinese authorities: sometimes Hong Kong officials got round this by 'suggesting' requisitions to their Chinese counterparts.
34. 'Approximate Return of Chinese handed over to their own authorities', CO 129/63, 480.
35. Bowring to Labouchere, 28 February and 14 October 1857, CO 129/62, 338–347 and CO 129/63, 472–480.
36. MacDonnell gave a total of seventy-three extraditions connected with piracy during 1860–1866: MacDonnell to Alcock, 16 May 1866, CO 129/113, 175–182. For a more detailed discussion see Ivan Lee, *Extradition and Empire*.
37. In 1853 *wangming* (王命: 'royal order') or summary executions were extended to all provinces; formerly they applied to certain regions, such as Guangdong, where banditry was rife. Weiting Guo, 'The Speed of Justice:

pirates handed over by HMS *Grasshopper* at Namoa in October 1864, for example, thirty were beheaded within a few days; the rest, reported the Governor, Sir Hercules Robinson, were awaiting trial and had little chance of escaping punishment.[38]

Robinson and his deputy, William Mercer, attempted to consolidate Bonham's distinction between British and non-British interests. An ordinance of 1865 empowered the Governor to hand over to the Chinese authorities Chinese charged with piracies not committed in colonial waters, or against British subjects or Hong Kong residents.[39] This was frustrated by concerns in London about China's 'semi-barbaric' system of justice, which required confession of guilt, extracted if necessary by torture. British diplomats and naval captains sought guarantees against torture or *lingchi* in such cases. Yet these were worth little. The ordinance also came at a time of controversy in Parliament over the surrender and subsequent execution by *lingchi* of a Taiping rebel leader, a political rendition violating the right to asylum.[40] The Law Officers objected that it was 'unprecedented' for a nation to surrender persons for offences over which its own courts had jurisdiction. The ordinance was disallowed on the advice of the Secretary of State.[41] Although naval captains continued to hand over pirates captured at sea in flagrante delicto, those arrested in Hong Kong could now only be tried by the Hong Kong courts.

The crisis of the 1860s

By the 1860s Hong Kong was thus increasingly unable to offload piracy cases to the Chinese courts. At the same time, pirates were becoming ever more daring. They were no longer targeting only 'helpless native craft' but were making 'murderous attacks' on European ships almost within sight of Hong Kong. European and American renegades were now advising some of them on weaponry and the relative power of naval ships.[42] The whole of China's

Summary Execution and Legal Culture in Qing Dynasty China, 1644–1912' (University of British Columbia PhD dissertation, 2016), 2–3 and 217–227; Robertson to Robinson, CO 129/99, 351–352.

38. Some pirates reportedly found substitutes to undergo punishment on their behalf. In a case in 1865, two of nineteen pirates handed over by HMS *Grasshopper* at Amoy were released when a friend bribed the judge in open court with a handkerchief full of Mexican dollars. The report estimated that, for similar reasons, only fourteen out of fifty pirates handed over by British gunboats at Amoy were executed. Robinson to Cardwell, 27 December 1864, CO 129/101, 181–183; *London and China Telegraph*, 27 February 1866.
39. Robinson to Cardwell, 9 August 1864, CO 129/99, 332–342; Mercer to Cardwell, 10 July 1865, CO 129/105, 449–456; Ordinance No. 13 of 1865.
40. Officials claimed he was merely a common criminal. But recent research suggests that they were aware he was a Taiping leader. Jenny Huangfu Day, 'The Enigma of a Taiping Fugitive: The Illusion of Justice and the "Political Offence Exception" in Extradition from Hong Kong', *Law and History Review*, Vol. 39, No. 3 (2021).
41. Law Officers to Cardwell, 13 January 1866, CO 129/118, 24–28; Cardwell to Mercer, 26 January 1866, CO 129/117, 235–236.
42. Remarks by Captain Nolloth, April 1866, CO 129/108, 29; Nolloth to Robinson, 25 February 1864, CO 129/97, 265–267.

foreign trade, estimated at £100 million per annum, was at risk.[43] Despite the supposed defects of British justice, Victoria Gaol was filling up with pirates and other violent criminals, who could no longer be transported. In 1862 the average gaol population was 520, twice that of 1858. Robinson commissioned a second prison on Stonecutters Island, off Kowloon. A hulk anchored nearby housed the 200–300 convicts tasked with building it: 144 died in this process, 38 when a boat capsized; another hundred escaped on a single day in 1864. In 1866 the new prison was abandoned before it was finished, having cost over $90,000. This wasteful project, along with an increased military contribution of $94,000 per annum and the new Hong Kong Mint (closed in 1868 with a loss of over $500,000), turned a healthy surplus into a gaping deficit.

'Death recorded' sentences declined and clemency was applied more sparingly. From 1862 to 1866 a total of sixty-nine men were sentenced to death and fifty-three were hanged – the same number as in the whole of the preceding eighteen years, and more than two-thirds the number in all of England and Wales in these five years.[44] Forty-five of the fifty-three were convicted of piracy with murder or violence, in about half the cases against European ships. All but five of those hanged were Chinese. The exceptions, a Spaniard and four Portuguese, were hanged on 8 August 1865 against objections from the Governor of Macao, the Spanish Consul, and a Portuguese juror, F.H. de Azevedo, who said he had agreed to the verdict only on the understanding that there would be a recommendation to mercy, which was not forthcoming.[45] Large-scale executions became a feature of Hong Kong justice in the 1860s. They culminated in the hanging of eleven men from the same pirate gang in the space of five weeks in 1866 for attacks on the *Carl* and the *Caesar*.

The *Carl* and *Caesar* piracies

'As a general rule,' wrote the new Governor, Sir Richard MacDonnell, in June 1866, 'Chinese Pirates are not unnecessarily cruel.' When resistance ceased they turned to plunder, locking up the crew and disabling the ship to prevent an early report of the crime. There were many exceptions. In the same despatch MacDonnell reported a piracy on a junk in which the crew of thirty-eight were all murdered, and another in which three pirate junks fought with the crew of a passage boat near Macao for two hours. When the pirates boarded they killed

43. Foreign Office to Admiralty, 9 January 1866, FO 17/802, 53.

44. Hong Kong's population at this time was under 125,000; that of England and Wales over 21 million.

45. Acting Governor Mercer doubted Azevedo's story, attributing it to pressure after the trial. The prisoners were not represented at trial, but the barrister Edward Pollard appeared for them before the Executive Council, arguing that Azevedo's claim destroyed the unanimity necessary for a capital verdict. Mercer to Cardwell, 8 August 1865, CO 129/106, 14–34; *HKDP*, 28 and 31 July and 8 August 1865.

fifteen of the crew. The many cases known to the police were probably only a fifth of the piracies occurring near Hong Kong, MacDonnell estimated.[46]

The piracies of the *Carl* and *Caesar* on 15 June 1866 followed the general rule. The ships were small, lightly armed, low in the water, and powered by sail: this made them vulnerable in calms or light winds to pirate junks, which could be powered by long oars as well as sails.[47] Resistance in both cases was slight. The *Carl*, a Danish schooner under Captain Hasenberg, left Hong Kong on 14 June with a crew of six Europeans and two Chinese, bound for North China with a cargo of gin, tobacco, and cotton. The ship was armed with two small cannons, twelve rifles, and two revolvers. On departing, the crew saw three junks following at a distance. At noon the next day they were near Single Island (Qingzhou), thirty miles east of Hong Kong. Suddenly a pirate junk began to approach at speed, firing a cannon. As they got closer, the pirates fired guns and catapulted stinkpots onto the deck. Some forty pirates then boarded. The crew offered no resistance. Some climbed up to the foretop, a platform part way up the front mast. The captain remained on the quarterdeck, sprawled over a rail and bleeding from a bullet wound. Shouting in English, the pirate leaders ordered the crew down and demanded opium and money. When told there was none, they ransacked the ship, taking the crew's clothes and food, a gold ring from the ship's mate Johan Schacht, cases of gin, and a barometer. Before leaving they ordered the crew into the hold and nailed down the hatches. All that remained of Captain Hasenberg was a pool of blood on the quarterdeck. Nearby, his dog lay bleeding from wounds inflicted when it had set upon the pirates.[48]

The pirates then turned their sights on the *Caesar*, a British barque with a crew of fourteen, mostly Malays, armed with two cannons, ten muskets, a rifle, and a revolver. The captain was a German, Hermann Schück, whose pregnant wife, Minna, was also on board. The *Caesar* had left Hong Kong in the early hours of 14 June, shortly before the *Carl*, bound for Amoy with a cargo of rice. It too was shadowed by a junk, which stayed close when the *Caesar* anchored for the night in Mirs Bay – so close that the crew fired warning shots, and heard shots fired in return. The junk was nowhere to be seen the next morning. By late afternoon the *Caesar* was near Pedro Blanco, two pinnacle rocks twenty-five miles east of Single Island. Suddenly the junk reappeared and started firing, keeping up fire until it came alongside. The *Caesar* returned fire but, seeing resistance was useless, Schück took some men up to the foretop, where Minna had sought refuge. The rest of the crew went below with the mate, Paul Rosino, who had injured his foot when firing a six-pounder gun. Throwing stinkpots and grappling hooks, and armed with muskets, revolvers, and halberds, some forty-five pirates then boarded.

46. MacDonnell to Cardwell, 27 June 1866, CO 129/113, 526–560.

47. I am indebted to Stephen Davies for his advice on this.

48. Statement of Johann Schacht, 20 June 1866, CO 129/113, 546–548; *CM*, 21 June 1866. The accounts here are from *HKDP*, 9, 11, 27, and 28 July and 9, 10, 11, and 21 August 1866; and *CM*, 5 July 1866.

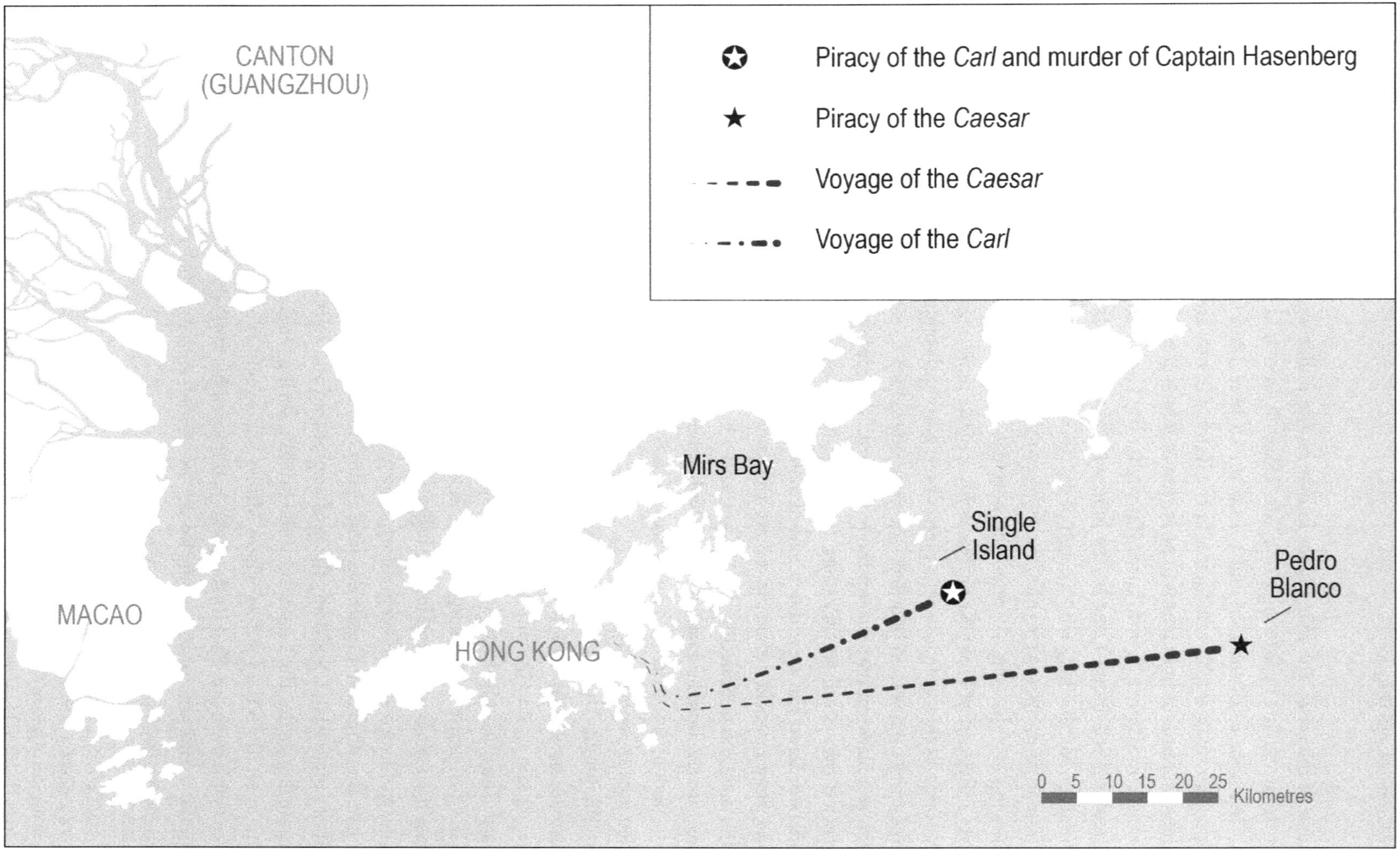

Map 1: The *Carl* and *Caesar* Piracies, 1866

As the pirates began looting, Schück called from the foretop to ask who was in charge. The leader, Cheang Tsat-tai, stepped out from the crowd and declared 'my belong captain'. He told Schück and the others to come down. Schück refused and the pirates started firing, narrowly missing his head. Two of them then climbed up the rigging. Schück kicked one of them down and pointed a revolver at the other. Eventually, Schück and the other crewmen climbed down, leaving the gun with Minna, who stayed on the foretop. When Schück reached the deck, Cheang struck him on the arm with the back of his sword and asked 'what for flog me with your big gun?' The pirates stripped Schück of his clothes and examined his body. Again, the demand was for money and opium. But Schück told them there was only rice on board. The sight of a distant steamer interrupted the pillaging. Cheang sent half his men back to the junk, which sailed out of sight while it passed. Most of the *Caesar*'s crew were put below deck. Schück was locked in a cabin. A little later he heard screams from Minna, who was still on the foretop. Cheang had climbed up the rigging, seized hold of her, and taken her revolver, wedding ring, and earrings. Schück squeezed through the cabin window and climbed up the rigging to rescue her just as Cheang was climbing down the other side.

Schück and his wife were kept under guard in their quarters while the crew were made to transfer hundreds of bags of rice onto the pirate junk. The pirates stripped the crew and took the ship's instruments, guns, charts, and signalling flags. Cheang, now wearing Schück's trousers, joined the Schücks and asked for tea and food. At Schück's request, Cheang gave back Minna's wedding ring in return for another ring: however, it was not her ring, but the ring taken earlier from the mate of the *Carl*; hers was later returned by another pirate. Cheang told them to sail to Amoy, threatening to kill them all if they returned to Hong Kong. Schück replied that if they were to go anywhere Cheang must return his instruments and charts. Cheang did so. When Schück pointed out that the barometer was not his, Cheang replied that he had taken three ships that day: 'you belong number three.' Fatigued from his exploits, Cheang sat chatting with Minna on a sofa in her cabin. At midnight he bade farewell, shook hands, and said 'chin chin'. The Schücks emerged to find the deck strewn with broken glass, the rigging cut, and the boats stove in. Helped by a passing ship, the *Caesar* made its way back to Hong Kong, where Minna was fêted as the bravest woman in the East.[49]

Investigations and arrests

When entering Hong Kong harbour on 19 June, Schück believed he saw the very junk that had attacked the *Caesar*. But information obtained by the police suggested the pirates had

49. Michael Schück Montemayor, *Captain Hermann Leopold Schück: The Saga of a German Sea Captain in 19th Century Sulu-Sulawesi Seas* (Manila: University of the Philippines Press, 2005), 19.

gone to Canton. With the help of the British Consul, Governor MacDonnell arranged for Schück and his steward, Chun Aching, to go there. He advised the consul that if they found the pirates the consul should decide whether to hand them to the Chinese authorities or send them to Hong Kong.[50] They failed to find the pirates. Meanwhile, the *Carl* returned to Hong Kong. Two of its crew made searches in the harbour and at Macao, which also yielded nothing. A week later, acting on new information and accompanied by Schück, the police searched houses and boats at East Point, where they found plates, spoons, and other items from the *Carl* and *Caesar*. They arrested nine men and a woman. After identity parades at the police station and hearings in the Magistracy, the magistrate, James Whyte, committed five of the men for trial.

MacDonnell then took control. He had arrived in Hong Kong in March 1866. This was his last position before retirement. An abrasive, overbearing man, he stirred controversy everywhere. His aggressive policies in The Gambia had drawn opposition from Black inhabitants. His resistance to reform in South Australia and Nova Scotia had also made him unpopular. Yet he was decisive and energetic – qualities welcomed by colonists in Hong Kong. After Robinson's profligate governorship and Mercer's torpid administration 'the cry was for a Caesar' who had Hong Kong's real interests at heart.[51] MacDonnell was a barrister and a former Chief Justice of The Gambia. He now applied his forensic skills to the *Carl* and *Caesar* piracies. This was necessary, he said, because the police had no detective capabilities and were unlikely to acquire any under their inept chief, Captain William Quin. They knew nothing of the haunts of pirates, or of those who equipped them or disposed of their booty. They were, said MacDonnell, the most useless force he had ever come across. They were only roused into action now because he had got rid of several 'worthless and corrupt characters' and taken personal charge of the case.[52]

The technique used by MacDonnell was to encourage one or more of the prisoners to give information against their accomplices in the hope of lenient treatment.[53] He claimed the method had never been used in Hong Kong: in fact, it had been used on several occasions, including the Too Apo fiasco in 1847. MacDonnell was dismayed to learn that all five prisoners in the *Carl* and *Caesar* case had been kept in the same cell while awaiting trial. No attempt had been made to obtain information from them about accomplices or receivers. With the aid of Francis Douglas, the Gaol Superintendent, MacDonnell now tried to admit one or more of them to Queen's evidence. One prisoner, Cheong Sing-fat, was inclined to help, but only if another prisoner, Tai Num-tuk, was allowed to do likewise. Tai directed the police to another house near East Point, where a shopkeeper had bought rice looted from the *Caesar*. They seized the shop's books, which showed that the purchase was from

50. MacDonnell to Cardwell, 27 June 1866, CO 129/113, 526–531.
51. Eitel, *Europe in China*, 411.
52. MacDonnell to Cardwell, 26 July 1866, CO 129/114, 122–132.
53. ExCo Minutes, 14 July 1866, CO 131/5, 218.

the pirate chief Cheang Tsat-tai, now believed to be in Macao. Information from Tai and Cheong enabled the police to track down several more suspects. In early July, twelve more men were committed for trial.

R v Low Ayee, Tai Num-tuk, Cheong Sing-fat, Lum Tiu-tuk and Lo Wun-chik Piracy and murder, piracy and endangering life, 10 July 1866

The first five men were tried in the Supreme Court on 10 July 1866 for piracy and murder in the first of three trials arising from the *Carl* and *Caesar* piracies. The judge was the Acting Chief Justice, Henry Ball. The prosecutor was the Acting Attorney General, Julian Pauncefote. Both men had been acting in these positions for over a year: the Chief Justice, Henry Adams, went home on sick leave in May 1865 and died in August. Pauncefote, a London barrister, had moved to Hong Kong in 1862 after losing heavily in a bank collapse. Ball was Judge of the Court of Summary Jurisdiction (1862–1873), another of Robinson's white elephants. His court had so little business that he was called upon to act as Chief Justice, Attorney General, Colonial Secretary, or Magistrate while the incumbents were on leave. At Ball's urging, in 1865 the Supreme Court was empowered to order public floggings with the cat-o'-nine-tails for males convicted of violent crimes. Ball made great use of this punishment, declaring that short prison sentences with public whippings were far more salutary than many years of penal servitude.[54] In the six months after the ordinance came into effect Ball sentenced forty-eight men, including ten pirates, to a total of 4,956 lashes. He alarmed colonists by ordering floggings for Europeans, though they were not carried out. Although a harsh sentencer and an irritable personality, Ball was a diligent and fair-minded judge – as far as conditions at this time allowed.

The first trial was brief.[55] The accused had no counsel. The jury consisted of a milliner, a storekeeper, an accountant, an engineer, an assistant in a merchant house, a broker, and one whose identity is unclear.[56] The interpreter was Rafael Rozario, a Portuguese from Macao who spoke English, Cantonese, Hakka, Malay, and Hindustani, though not all with equal facility. The prosecution focused only on the *Carl* piracy: Schück had for the time being taken the *Caesar* to Amoy. Johan Schacht, the mate of the *Carl* who had reported the

54. Ordinance No. 12 of 1865, based on the English 'Garotters' Act of 1863, which prescribed flogging as an additional punishment for robberies involving personal violence; *HKDP*, 24 November 1865.

55. The only detailed account is in *HKDP*, 11 July 1866, supplemented by a report on the committal proceedings in *CM*, 5 July 1866.

56. George Stokes (foreman), assistant at Lyall, Still & Co.; W. Antey, superintendent fitter, Hongkong Gas Co.; Samuel Baker, owner of the Millinery Store in Queen's Road; James Taylor, accountant, Commercial Bank; Frederick Blackhead, storekeeper, Blackhead & Co.; C.D. Bottomley, a broker; and one 'P.M. Bance', a name not on the Jury List, possibly a talesman picked from bystanders.

piracy, gave his account. Two sailors, John Schnedil and H. Hasenberg (probably a relative of the captain), and the ship's cook, Chun Ating, described how the pirates had overrun the ship. Schnedil was the last to see the dying Captain Hasenberg.

With most piracy trials the first hurdle was to identify the culprits. Confusion over names and faces was a chronic problem for the early Hong Kong courts. In piracy cases, observed the *China Mail* of an earlier trial, large numbers of men were 'squeezed together' in the dock 'like sheep in a Smithfield pen, and scarcely more distinguishable in their appearance'.[57] Chinese men arraigned before the courts generally wore the same drab clothing and had queues, or 'tails' – long plaits of hair at the back of a half-shaven crown. Many gave false names, or identified themselves by their number in the fraternal ranking: Ayee, Asam, Asay (亞二, 亞三, 亞四), and so on. The confusion could be potentially fatal. In 1862, two men were sentenced to death for murder. The sentence on one was commuted to penal servitude. However, the missionary James Legge, in a visit to the gaol, discovered that the warrant of commutation bore the name of the other man: the mistake was eventually corrected and the right man was hanged.[58]

For the *Carl* and *Caesar* piracies, the police went to great lengths to ensure correct identification. Captain Quin explained how the witnesses had picked out the first five defendants in his presence from thirty men in identity parades at the gaol; there could have been no collusion because the witnesses attended separately and entered and left by different doors. Schacht, who had identified all five accused, was, however, challenged in cross-examination: he replied that he recognized only the first, Low Ayee, by his face. Schnedil identified the second and fourth defendants, and Hasenberg the second only. Chun Ating, the cook, identified only the fourth, Lum Tiu-tuk. Challenged by Lum, Chun said he remembered him because he had taken his best suit of clothes. Asked if they had anything to say, the five accused all denied involvement in the crime. Only two, Lum Tiu-tuk and Lo Wun-chik, called witnesses, though who they were and what they said is not recorded: 'their evidence,' remarked the *Daily Press*, 'was of such a description as to need no comment being of the usual character brought forward in such cases.'

After the case for the defence, Pauncefote withdrew the charge of murder, leaving only piracy with violence, still a capital offence. Judge Ball summed up carefully, 'pointing out to the jury how strong, and in what degree, the evidence produced before the Court affected the prisoners individually'. After a few minutes' discussion, without leaving the box, the jury returned a unanimous verdict of 'Guilty, of piracy, with intent to murder' against all five men. This was explained to the prisoners by Rozario. Ball put on the black cap and pronounced sentence of death, telling them he held out no hope of any remission of their

57. *CM*, 27 January 1848.
58. Hannah Legge to Frank Islip, 16 June 1862; ExCo Minutes, 24 and 26 March 1862, CO 131/5, 37–40; *CM*, 20 March 1862.

sentence. He was reportedly 'much affected' by this ritual. The prisoners, in contrast, 'received their sentence with perfect indifference'.

MacDonnell spared Tai Num-tuk and Cheong Sing-fat in return for the information they had given: their sentences were commuted to penal servitude.[59] The three others – Low Ayee, Lum Tiu-tuk and Lo Wun-chik – were hanged together outside the Magistracy on Arbuthnot Road at 6 a.m. on Friday 20 July 1866. The day before, one of them (it is not clear who) had confessed to being present during the piracies. Inmates from the gaol were lined up to 'take a lesson' from the execution. A large turnout of spectators, consisting of more Europeans than Chinese, gathered in the street below. The Gaol Superintendent Francis Douglas, the Sheriff Malcolm Tonnochy, and the missionary James Legge were in attendance. Attired in a convict's jacket and a gauze visor, the hangman mounted the scaffold to check the equipment: he was probably Andrew Johnson, a turnkey who served as hangman in the mid-1860s.[60] The prisoners followed, looking 'cowed, sullen, obstinate, and revengeful', each attended by a Catholic priest. One was so nervous that he had to be helped up the ladder. Nooses were put around their necks. On a signal from the Sheriff, the lever was pulled, the trap opened, and the men were left swinging. Two died without a struggle. The third had convulsions for some time, 'and must have suffered considerably before life was entirely extinct'.

Even this was not enough for some observers. 'To the Chinamen,' wrote the editor of the *Daily Press*, Alfred Sinnett, on the day of the execution,

> death by hanging is a small matter. They are careless of life, it is said, and we make a mistake in *only* hanging them. We ought to cut off their heads or hands, mutilate the bodies in some way, so as to play upon the national superstition, and enhance the horror of death, with the horror of a mutilated existence after death.[61]

Sinnett then discussed how unsuited were 'the forms and ceremonies' of English courts to Chinese, whose only ideas of justice were 'revenge, cruelty, oppression as the case may be'. Justice would be better served if they were not defended by counsel, but rather 'examined more in accordance with the forms of oriental tribunals'. This would avoid weakening 'the great lesson which has been taught this morning' when, in the next trial, 'some prisoner

59. For Cheong, seven years. For Tai, the term is not clear. However, MacDonnell planned to pardon him and 'enable him to go to some place of safety beyond the vengeance of his old piratical associates'. A year after his trial, Cheong, now in Victoria Gaol, gave evidence in committal proceedings against another man alleged to have taken part in the *Carl* and *Caesar* piracies. The case does not appear to have gone to trial. ExCo Minutes, 14 July and 25 August 1866, CO 131/5, 215–221 and 232–233; *HKDP*, 2, 4, and 11 July 1867.

60. *HKDP*, 29 October 1868.

61. *HKDP*, 20 July 1866. Alfred Sinnett (1840–1921) edited the *Hongkong Daily Press* during 1865–1868, having briefly worked for the *Daily Telegraph* in London. He was later a leading light in the Theosophical movement. Mercer reported that his arrival, and that of the new editor of the *China Mail*, the former consular official N.B. Dennys, heralded 'a change in the direction' in Hong Kong's newspapers, meaning they were less hostile than earlier editors towards officials. Mercer to Cardwell, 9 February 1866, CO 129/111, 335–336.

about whose guilt probably Chinese lookers on will be troubled with very little doubt, will be represented by an ingenious barrister or attorney fertile in expedients for "getting off" an accused person'. All this for a trial in which no defence counsel appeared and all five accused were found guilty.

R v Wong Mee-sing, Ng Ashu, Lee Akow, Lum Asing, Cheang Ayik, Chun Ayee, Mak Yow-ping, Leong Akee, Tang Afook, Tsang Afat and Yeep Afoo Piracy and endangering life, 26–27 July 1866

The second trial lasted two days. Crowds of spectators descended on the courthouse, 'rendering the atmosphere of the Court almost suffocating'.[62] Early in the morning on the first day, one of the accused, Fok Akwan, hanged himself. He tied his queue round his neck and attached it to a hook used to prop open a window high up in his cell, which he had reached using an upturned slop bucket. Six witnesses had identified Fok at the Magistracy. 'Thus,' observed the *China Mail*, 'has the poor wretch cheated the gallows, to which in all likelihood he was most justly entitled.'[63] There were now eleven defendants. The judge, again, was Ball. The prosecutor was Pauncefote.[64] The accused were unrepresented. The jury consisted of Jeliangee Pestonjee, a Parsi merchant, Lourenço Gutierrez, a Portuguese assistant in an English firm, and five Englishmen.[65]

Captain Schück was now back in Hong Kong, and the centre of attention in this trial was the *Caesar*. Schück began his evidence with an account of the attack. He pointed out three of the accused, whom he had seen plundering the ship or guarding the crew. Inspector da Silva and Gaol Superintendent Douglas described how, on information received (from Tai Num-tuk), the accused had been arrested at East Point and Wan Chai on 26 June and 5 July. Douglas revealed that seven identity parades had been held, in which thirty to forty men had been mixed with the accused. Pauncefote then examined the crew. The task was complicated by the fact that three of the Malays bore the same name, variously Romanized as Ahmud, Ahmet, and Ahmed, and their depositions had got mixed up. Judge Ball also noticed that two sets of depositions had been put in evidence. This, said Pauncefote, was because the defendants had been charged before the magistrate on different occasions and in different groups. Exasperated, Ball considered striking out the depositions altogether. The case 'was the most difficult one to understand he had ever heard'. It would have been better to have tried the men in batches, he said.

---

62. The account that follows is taken mainly from *HKDP*, 27 and 28 July 1866.
63. MacDonnell to Cardwell, 11 August 1866, CO 129/114, 258–260; *CM*, 26 July 1866.
64. Now holding the substantive position of Attorney General.
65. John F.A. Sander, merchant; Thomas Smith, clerk with the P. & O.; W.S. Riddell, accountant at the Asiatic Bank; T.W. Barrington, clerk; and William Punchard, superintendent of the Sailors' Home.

Ball allowed the depositions by the three Malays to be altered to conform with their evidence at trial. The other crewmembers then testified. Between them, they identified all eleven accused. Some of the accused challenged the evidence of the Chinese and Malay witnesses, pointing to inconsistencies in the identity parades at the gaol. Douglas and Quin were called to explain. Both stressed the special measures taken to prevent contact between witnesses. This ended the case for the prosecution. One of the accused, Tang Afook, then asked that a discharge certificate from the ship *Eugenie*, which had been taken from him in gaol, be put in as evidence. Ball asked if anything was known about this. Douglas confirmed it had been found and Ball ordered it to be produced.

Then, at about 6 p.m., just as Ball was about to adjourn, the foreman of the jury intervened. He said that 'if the prisoners had no exculpatory evidence to bring forward, they had made up their minds as to their Verdict'. Ball was furious. He was surprised that 'any body of respectable persons sitting in that box should have made such a remark before hearing what any one of the eleven prisoners had to say to the charge brought against them'. Another juror repeated the remark, saying they were quite unanimous. 'I dare say you are,' retorted Ball. He then ordered the jury to be taken away by a court officer to the Oriental Hotel, where they were to be kept for the night.[66]

In contrast to the simple denials in the first trial, all eleven accused gave accounts of their whereabouts on 15 June, the day of the piracies. In support of their alibis, nine called a dozen witnesses, six of them women. Mid-June was a memorable time: the Dragon Boat Festival took place on the 17th, a point stressed by one witness when pressed by Pauncefote. Two of the accused, Ng Ashu and Lum Asing, claimed to be fruit hawkers at East Point: they called neighbours who had seen them there in mid-June. Another four, Cheang Ayik, Chun Ayee, Mak Yow-ping, and Leong Akee, claimed to be connected with a shop known as the Wo Lee: two witnesses merely averred that Cheang had returned from his native place on the 14th and that Chun was an honest man.

Three defendants were also able to produce documents in support of their alibis. Wong Mee-sing claimed to be a seaman on the *On-hing* passage boat plying between Hong Kong and Macao. He called the master of the *On-hing*, who produced a logbook to show he had employed Wong from 8 May to 26 June. Lee Akow, a stonecutter, called Lee Sa-moon, who produced a wage book showing that Lee had been working on the new Hong Kong Mint at East Point throughout June. He also said that workers there were given passes. Lee said the police had taken his pass. Ball called for the inspector who had directed the searches of

66. This may have been the first case of overnight sequestration of a jury. Sequestration ordered in a later trial, in 1868, caused controversy. The case (wounding with murderous intent, a non-capital offence from 1865) lasted two days. The Jury Ordinance allowed discretion, but the Chief Justice, John Smale, held that sequestration was obligatory in criminal trials. After this case, the law was amended to make sequestration obligatory only for capital felonies. In 1872 the law was again amended so that sequestration in all cases was at the judge's discretion. *HKDP*, 27 February 1868; Ordinances Nos. 7 of 1868 and 8 of 1872.

the accused, only to find it impossible to determine 'who really searched them, who took charge of the articles found on them, or whether the prisoners had been searched at all'. The discharge from the *Eugenie* requested by Tang Afook was, however, produced. Tang also called a shipmate, who testified that he had been discharged on 1 July. Immediately after this, Tsang Afat tried a similar defence, saying his discharge had also been taken from him. The judge remarked several times on the laxity of the police in keeping the chain of evidence: as an example, he referred to a penknife stolen from Rosino, the mate of the *Caesar*, and found on one of the accused, which was now missing.

Pauncefote sought to discredit the defence witnesses in cross-examination. He asked them how they came to be called as witnesses. He asked those in charge of boats if they had licences, and if some of the women were married to the men for whom they gave evidence. He asked one witness whether he had ever been in prison, to which the reply was 'no'. After the last defendant, Yeep Afoo, had called a neighbour to testify that he had been sick at home since 13 May, Pauncefote made his closing speech. Ball then read out a petition on behalf of the stonecutter, Lee Akow, before summing up. He noted the 'clear and satisfactory' manner in which Schück had given his evidence. He warned the jury not to be influenced by the suicide of Fok Akwan. He drew attention to the 'slight nature' of the evidence against some of the accused. He then read over the whole of the evidence. Finally, Ball said that the management of the case by the police 'reflected disgrace on all concerned in the matter'. He suggested that something 'ought to be done to reduce that department to a state of order and discipline'. Pauncefote agreed.

Now less eager to rush to judgment, the jury took a full forty-five minutes to reach their verdict. They found all the accused guilty of piracy with violence except two: Ng Ashu, the fruit hawker, and Tang Afook, the seaman from the *Eugenie*. Ng and Tang had been identified only by the *Caesar's* carpenter, Chun Asun; under cross-examination by these two defendants and Ball, Chun had admitted that he had failed to pick out Ng in the first of two identity parades, and that it was dusk when he claimed to have seen Tang on the *Caesar*. One juror recommended two other prisoners, Wong Mee-sing and Lee Akow, to mercy. Ball then put on his black cap and pronounced sentence of death on the nine prisoners, holding out no hope for a remission of their sentence.

The condemned men were, as usual, asked about their spiritual needs. Three asked to see a minister of the Church of England. Three asked to see a Catholic priest. The other three asked to see James Legge. Colonial observers tended to sneer at such requests: it was doubtful, said the *China Mail*, 'whether sufficient time will be afforded these criminals to derive such instruction as may benefit their souls greatly, previous to their final exit'.[67] Yet, apart from any spiritual comfort they might receive, prisoners had good reasons for making these requests. Priests could help them contact family and friends and arrange support for

67. *CM*, 2 August 1866.

dependants. Catholic priests offered clothes and coffins to prisoners who agreed to be baptized.[68] Gaol Regulations enjoined the Anglican Colonial Chaplain, who had a government salary, to 'specially tender his assistance' to all condemned prisoners.[69] Those who were not Anglicans were allowed their own priests. In practice, Anglican ministers at this time 'couldn't be bothered' with prisoners. Catholic priests, in contrast, would sometimes 'grind away all night on one poor pirate'.[70]

In a few cases, missionaries used their networks of converts to seek justice for men with unsafe convictions. The expert in this was the protestant missionary, James Legge, who held weekly services in the gaol, and whose command of Chinese enabled him to speak with prisoners. 'We ought to do what we can to see that they leave our jails, not only with the fear of man upon them, but taught their duty also to fear God,' he said in a speech at Government House in 1865 on being presented with a silver tea set for his public services.[71] Legge was a towering figure in this Lilliputian place. During his thirty years in Hong Kong he founded the Union Church, trained Chinese preachers, helped plan the education system, and produced the first English translation of the Confucian classics. In the 1860s he helped train a body of student interpreters – graduates from Britain who were taught Chinese with the aim of supplying reliable interpretation in the courts. The 'cadets' who emerged from this did not, in the end, interpret in the courts, though some became magistrates and judges. Instead, the cadet officers formed Hong Kong's administrative service, a cadre of officials serving at the highest levels of government.

Legge described his visits to pirates under sentence of death as 'the most wretched experience' of his time in Hong Kong. Except for a few who were caught red-handed, he could recall only one case in which the prisoner confessed his guilt.[72] 'You see,' explained his wife Hannah, 'neither the Judge, lawyers, magistrates or jury know anything of Chinese so the prisoners, poor fellows, are at the mercy of Portuguese and Chinese interpreters, who are too ready to take bribes and interpret accordingly.'[73] There were, observed the *Friend of China*, many impositions on Legge's good nature, and he was reluctant 'to interfere between the law and its victim'.[74] But in this case, the Gaol Superintendent, Douglas, asked him for help. Legge became convinced that Wong Mee-sing, one of the accused recommended to mercy, was innocent. He persuaded the Colonial Secretary, W.H. Rennie,

68. Hannah Legge to Frank Islip, 16 June 1862, in Letters of James and Hannah Legge 1859–1897, School of Oriental and African Studies Library, London, MS 380476/15.
69. From 1884 a salary was also paid to a Catholic chaplain. Regulations for the Government of the Gaol, *HKGG*, 12 March 1859; Bowen to Derby, 25 August 1884, CO 129/217, 209–215.
70. James Legge, quoted in Marilyn Laura Bowman, *James Legge and the Chinese Classics: A Brilliant Scot in the Turmoil of Colonial Hong Kong* (Victoria, British Columbia, Canada: FriesenPress, 2016), 437–438.
71. Helen Edith Legge, *James Legge, Missionary and Scholar* (London: Religious Tract Society, 1905), 158.
72. Legge, 'The Colony of Hongkong', 168.
73. Hannah Legge to Frank Islip, 16 June 1862.
74. *FOC*, 10 November 1860.

that the logbook of the *On-hing*, accepted as evidence in the trial, clearly showed that Wong had been on the boat on the day of the piracies. The sole witness who identified him – one of the Ahmeds – had been mistaken.[75]

MacDonnell and his council – Rennie, Pauncefote, and Major-General Guy (Commandant of the Garrison) – considered the death sentences on the nine men on 3 August, with Ball and Douglas in attendance. MacDonnell produced a letter from Legge setting out the evidence in favour of Wong Mee-sing. No one had any doubt that all eleven had taken part in the piracies and were accessories to the murder of Captain Hasenberg, said MacDonnell. But, after discussing the case for several hours, the council concluded that not only Wong Mee-sing but also Lee Akow, the stonecutter also recommended to mercy, should be reprieved. MacDonnell commuted their sentences to penal servitude.[76]

The seven other men were executed early in the morning on 8 August 1866. The day before, another prisoner, Wong Qui-fook, had been hanged for the murder of a German woman and her child in a robbery on a ship in the harbour. Large crowds, mostly of Europeans, had gathered outside the Magistracy to watch as the hangman, 'hideously attired in a black mask and long blue Chinese coat', despatched Wong. Accompanied by two priests, Wong had confessed his crime on the scaffold, naming an accomplice and repeating the name over and over until the bolt was drawn. In contrast, the seven pirates sobbed and cried from the moment they mounted the scaffold. One of them fainted. Catholic priests had converted three of them six days earlier and had been with them almost continuously since then. Legge attended to one of the others. The crowds were smaller than the day before and there were few Chinese: possibly they were deterred by reports of placards threatening to burn down the city if the men were executed.[77] The seven men were hanged in two batches of four and three. This matched the record set a year earlier for the largest number of hangings in a single day in Hong Kong: the seven men executed in 1865 were convicted of the piracy of a junk just outside Hong Kong harbour in which some eighty people were reportedly killed.[78]

R v Cheang Tsat-tai
Piracy and endangering life, 18 and 20 August 1866

Following investigations by Gaol Superintendent Douglas and Inspector Dennis Daly, Cheang Tsat-tai, the pirate leader, was captured in Macao in late July and taken to Hong

75. Bowman, *James Legge*, 438; Legge, *James Legge*, 159.
76. ExCo Minutes, 3 and 25 August 1866, CO 131/5, 226–229 and 231–232; MacDonnell to Cardwell, 11 August 1866, CO 129/114, 258–260.
77. *CM*, 2 August 1866.
78. W.F. Mayers and N.B. Dennys, *The Treaty Ports of China and Japan: A Complete Guide to the Open Ports of those Countries* (Hong Kong: Shortrede and Co., 1867), 108; *HKDP*, 6 June 1865.

Kong. At committal proceedings he was assisted by a lawyer, or rather by the articled clerk, J.J. Francis, who appeared on behalf of his principal, William Gaskell, to cross-examine witnesses.[79] Cheang was identified by Hermann and Minna Schück and two of the *Caesar's* crew. While giving evidence, one of the crew, Aloong, a Malay Chinese, suddenly pointed to a man in the gallery, saying 'that is another of the pirates'. The man was arrested and held overnight. The next day two men came forward to vouch for him. He was a regular spectator, well known to court staff. Aloong withdrew the allegation.[80]

Cheang had reportedly been arraigned in the Hong Kong courts twice before for piracy but had been discharged both times on 'legal quibbles'.[81] His appearance before the Supreme Court on 18 August was brief. He pleaded not guilty and requested a lawyer, saying he had no money to pay for one. He also asked for more time to collect his witnesses. Henry Ball, still acting as Chief Justice, said it was not his practice to request any 'gentleman of the bar' to assist a prisoner. The Attorney General, Julian Pauncefote, said the request was 'a mere subterfuge'; it was not for lack of funds that Cheang was unable to find a lawyer or secure his witnesses. Pauncefote urged against delay, since the key witnesses, the Schücks, intended to go to Amoy on a ship due to leave at 2 p.m. on Monday. Cheang said his witnesses would arrive on Monday and would prove he was a fisherman at Macao. Ball adjourned the case to 11:30 a.m. on Monday.[82]

By Monday Cheang had found a lawyer, the barrister Frederick Barnard. Recently qualified in London, Barnard had been in Hong Kong for only three months. During that time he had appeared in the Summary Jurisdiction Court and had represented the failing Agra and Masterman's Bank in its dispute with the Hongkong and Shanghai Bank.[83] His criminal practice had begun well with a piracy case on 26 May in which Ball had directed the jury to acquit seven of the eight defendants. There was no instructing solicitor in Cheang's case: J.J. Francis had withdrawn after a dispute over his fee. The jury consisted of two Portuguese and five British: except for one who was an engineer, all were clerks or

79. Born in Dublin in 1839, Francis served in the Second Opium War as a non-commissioned officer and bought himself out of the army to article with solicitors in Hong Kong. He sold his practice in 1873 to fund preparation for the Bar at Gray's Inn and London University. He was admitted as a barrister in Hong Kong in 1877 and became a Queen's Counsel in 1886. Walter Greenwood, 'John Joseph Francis, Citizen of Hong Kong, A Biographical Note', *Journal of the Hong Kong Branch of the Royal Asiatic Society* 26 (1986): 17–45.
80. *HKDP*, 10 and 11 August 1866.
81. *London and China Telegraph*, 29 September 1866.
82. *HKDP*, 20 August 1866.
83. The Agra and Masterman's Bank was one of several banks caught up in a financial panic sparked by the failure of Overend, Gurney and Co. Its suspension in June, along with that of the Commercial Bank, prompted a general run on banks in Hong Kong and a panic sell-off by Chinese holders of banknotes at discounts of as much as 80 per cent. *London and China Telegraph*, 20 and 27 August and 15 September 1866.

assistants in foreign firms; one, F.H. de Azevedo, was the juror in the trial of the Spanish and Portuguese pirates in 1865 who had objected to their execution.[84]

The first witness, Captain Schück, described the attack on the *Caesar*. This was the fourth time he had given evidence in court, and fatigue was setting in. His cross-examination was described as 'decidedly cross'. It elicited much laughter, mostly at Barnard's expense. It was no laughing matter for his client, said Barnard. To which Shück replied, 'Yes, and it was no laughing matter when he fired at me.' Barnard asked Shück to describe the stinkpots hurled at the *Caesar*. Schück refused. Barnard asked why he put his wife in the foretop when the pirates were firing at the rigging. 'I put her there because I wished to do so,' said Schück. Pressed on this, he retorted, 'It is none of your business why I did so. What is it to you where I put my wife?'

Barnard — Was the prisoner dressed the same as now when he was on your ship?

Schück — No.

Barnard — Then how do you recognize him, how do you know it is the same man?

Schück — I know him by his countenance and appearance generally.

Barnard — But have you not noticed a great similarity between all Chinamen.

Schück — They all have tails [i.e. pigtails, or queues].[85]

In fact, Cheang had an unforgettable face. In her evidence, Minna Schück said she had seen a great deal of Cheang while he was on the *Caesar*. He had sat chatting with her on a sofa for over two hours. She had picked him out of some twenty-five men lined up in the gaol and had no doubt at all that he was the leader. Cross-examined by Barnard, she said she noticed 'he had very small eyes, and had a peculiar manner of shutting them'. The same habit 'was very conspicuous while the prisoner was in the dock', observed the *China Mail*.

The court then adjourned for tiffin, in time for the Schücks to catch their ship to Amoy. Proceedings resumed at 2 p.m., and the prosecution continued its case. One of the crewmembers named Ahmed described the attack and his conversations with Cheang, over cups of tea, about the *Caesar*'s cargo. Cross-examined by Barnard, Ahmed described Cheang's dress – a jacket and black silk trousers (taken from Schück) and a red belt, which matched the description by Minna Schück. He recalled that Cheang had a black spot on his cheek: an examination of Cheang at this point revealed a mole on his face. Then it was the turn of Aloong, the Malay-Chinese crewmember. Refusing to give evidence in Chinese, 'as the prisoner would understand all he said', he spoke in Malay. Rozario, the interpreter,

84. F.H. de Azevedo, clerk, Jardine, Matheson & Co.; J.G. Hodgson, assistant cashier, Comptoir d'Escompte; A.F. dos Remedios, clerk, Lapraik's; W.W. Plaisted, assistant, Birley & Co.; W.K. Hughes, assistant, Wilkinson & Co.; J.M. Matson, assistant, Oriental Bank; Charles Speechley, engineer. Accounts of the trial appear in *CM*, 23 August 1866 and *HKDP*, 20 and 21 August 1866.

85. *CM*, 23 August 1866.

had struggled with Ahmed's evidence, also in Malay. He now had even more difficulty with Aloong, who could not understand the questions put to him. The evidence, as far as it was comprehensible, nevertheless corroborated that of the Schücks and Ahmed. To Barnard's question about his misidentification of the spectator in the magistrate's court, Aloong simply said he had made a mistake.

Douglas and Daly gave evidence of how the prosecution witnesses had been segregated from each other during the identity parades. Douglas recounted how Schück walked past all twenty-five men, inmates of the gaol in plain clothes, and then 'ran at the prisoner and knocked his head against the stone pillar, saying, this is the man'. Inspector William Jones, described how he had gone to Macao, received Cheang from the commandant there, and brought him back to Hong Kong. There were no extradition arrangements between the two places at this time, but cooperation of this kind was common practice.

Barnard had intended to ask for a further remand: the witnesses sent for by Cheang had not yet arrived. But he realized that 'in a case of this kind it was out of the question'. Why this should be so was not explained. Perhaps he knew Cheang's claim to have witnesses was simply a delaying tactic. Barnard did his best in the circumstances. He tried 'to shake the evidence as to the identity' of the pirate chief. He drew attention to discrepancies in evidence: Schück had testified that Cheang fired at him twice with a musket, while two other witnesses had sworn that he fired only once with a pistol. He also asked the jury to remember that the Schücks were man and wife, 'and if you think that nothing occurred between them from the 7th to the 8th, that as man and wife, no conversation took place between them as to what Captain Schück did at the gaol, you must think very differently from what I do and from what the generality of men do.'

Ball then summed up. He noted 'several considerable discrepancies' but said the main facts were the same throughout. Schück's encounters with Cheang gave him ample opportunity for identification. His evidence alone was enough to guarantee a guilty verdict, said Ball. But in a case of life and death it was not usual to give a verdict on the evidence of one person alone. In this case no such difficulty arose since there were three other witnesses. Although 'no case of identity could be much more thorough', Ball urged the jury to give every consideration to the 'very able speech' by counsel for the defence, and to 'abide solely by the evidence'. The jury retired at 5:55 p.m. and returned after four minutes with a verdict of '"Guilty" of piracy and endangering of the lives of Hermann Schück and other of H.M. subjects on board the barque *Cæsar*'. Ball pronounced sentence of death, telling Cheang he must hope for no remission.

Cheang had been silent throughout the trial. According to the *China Mail,* he 'did not in the least alter his sullen demeanour on the sentence being interpreted to him'. The Governor in Council confirmed the death sentence. While awaiting execution, Cheang admitted to gaolers that he had been present at the *Caesar* piracy but insisted this was the first time he had ever taken part in anything of the kind. He had been forced to do so under threats of denunciation as a pirate. A man named Akoo was the leader, he insisted. Cheang told Legge that he planned to make a speech on the scaffold. Some speculated he would implicate others. The execution at 6 a.m. on Wednesday 29 August 1866 attracted few, mostly European, spectators. Cheang mounted the scaffold with a Catholic priest, maintaining 'his indifference of demeanour to the last moment'. Warned by the Sheriff not to make false statements, Cheang merely said he had told the truth, and since he was going to die in a few minutes it was no use telling lies. When the hangman pulled the bolt, the drop fell only a few inches. A second, more forceful pull caused the drop to give way. Cheang struggled violently for several minutes. Then his body went still.[86]

Large numbers of police were present at the *Carl* and *Caesar* executions. This standard precaution was particularly necessary after threats to burn down the city. Revenge of a different kind came a few weeks later. On 22 September 1866 the American schooner *Lubra* left Hong Kong for Japan with a European crew and a cargo of rifles and gunpowder. At dusk the next day it was attacked near Pedro Blanco. The attack followed a familiar pattern. The pirate junk pulled alongside. The pirates threw stinkpots and fired at the crew, killing one and wounding others, before boarding. Their leader, Leong Sun-kit, said he knew there was opium and gold on board. The captain, Benjamin Howes, insisted there was none. The pirates then looted the ship. At about midnight one of them went up to Howes, who was sitting on a sofa in his cabin with his wife and two children. He shot Howes in the head. Before leaving, the pirates smashed open a barrel of gunpowder and lit a trail of powder. The fuse failed and the ship returned to Hong Kong. The American community offered a $1,000 reward. Assisted by agents, the police tracked Leong through the neighbouring districts before capturing him in Hong Kong. He was hanged on 8 December with another pirate, Lum Kum-pow, who had murdered a family on a fishing junk. Leong and his men were said to be part of Cheang Tsat-tai's gang. They had sworn to avenge their comrades' deaths. 'You kill Chinaman we makee kill you,' one of them had said when asked by a crew-member why they had continued shooting even after taking control of the *Lubra*.[87]

An end to piracy?

The executions of Leong and Lum brought the number of hangings in 1866 to fourteen – two more than in all of England and Wales that year. In 1867, five men were hanged in Hong Kong – four for piracy and murder. Then, over the next decade, only nine hangings took place, only two of which were for piracy and murder. Four years after the *Carl* and *Caesar* trials, MacDonnell confidently reported that piracies known to the police had declined

86. *CM*, 30 August 1866; *HKDP*, 29 August 1866.

87. *HKDP*, 25 September, 26 November and 8 December 1866; *CM*, 27 September 1866; *London and China Telegraph*, 12 November 1866; MacDonnell to Carnarvon, 14 December 1866, CO 129/116, 312–321.

from fifty in 1865, committed by over 3,000 pirates, to five in 1869, committed by fewer than a hundred.[88] There were still 'thousands now pirates at heart as much as they were before'. But piracy had become 'a bad speculation'. Hong Kong 'had got rid of the questionable honour of being the depot of pirates'. At the close of the criminal sessions in March 1870 the Chief Justice, John Smale, congratulated MacDonnell on the decline in piracy and other crimes. Two years later, in a public lecture, James Legge spoke of piracy almost as a feature of the remote past. Bad men, he said, were now 'kept habitually obedient to the law by the form of justice armed with power in their mind's eye more than by outbursts of indignation occasionally aroused against them, and from which they always hope to escape'.[89]

Larger processes at work in the region contributed to this new state of affairs. Sailing vessels were gradually replaced by steamships able to outdistance pirate junks. After defeating the Taiping Rebellion in 1864, the Qing government turned its attention to putting down piracy, using steam-driven gunboats and taking part in actions with the Royal Navy. The Chinese Imperial Maritime Customs Service, created in 1854 under British management, offered an incentive for action, since trade lost to piracy damaged revenue at a time when taxes on trade were a growing source of income for the Qing government.[90] In a separate initiative from 1867 known as the 'Customs Blockade', gunboats of the Canton Customs intercepted Chinese vessels in the waters near Hong Kong to enforce taxes on opium, salt, and other goods. Although described by MacDonnell as a 'piratical squeeze', and resented by merchants as a ploy to snuff out Hong Kong's native trade, these activities also had a deterrent effect on piracy.[91]

MacDonnell disparaged suggestions that the Chinese authorities had any role in the decline in piracy. The explanation, he claimed, was to be found in the stringent measures taken by him in Hong Kong.[92] Piracy – 'the great Colonial disgrace' – was one of the main determinants of policy in the early part of his administration. Before leaving for Hong Kong he had made a study of the problem. He arrived with a battery of proposals, some based on earlier schemes, others strikingly original. 'What is wanted is action,' he wrote in a report on a naval expedition undertaken while the *Carl* and *Caesar* trials were in progress: the expedition destroyed twenty-two pirate junks, killing about eighty pirates.[93] Throughout that summer MacDonnell and Pauncefote were hard at work drafting legislation with such 'unusual provisions' and 'of so important and wide application as to amount almost to a

88. Summary of Returns of Piracy and Robbery 1 January 1864 to 14 August 1869, CO 129/143, 176.
89. *CM*, 31 March 1870; *HKDP*, 21 March 1870; Legge, 'The Colony of Hongkong', 168.
90. Jonathan Chappell, 'Maritime Raiding, International Law and the Suppression of Piracy on the South China Coast', *International History Review* (2017).
91. Eitel, *Europe in China*, 415–419; MacDonnell to Buckingham, 7 April 1868, CO 129/130, 33–45.
92. MacDonnell to Granville, 10 January 1870, CO 129/143, 164–169.
93. MacDonnell to Cardwell, 27 July 1866, CO 129/152–157.

social revolution of our relations towards the Chinese population.'[94] The aim was to prevent piracies and other crimes through surveillance and harsher treatment of criminals.

The Harbour and Coasts Ordinance required all Chinese junks in Hong Kong waters to be licensed, to berth in designated anchorages, and to report to the Harbour Master's Office on arrival. The Victoria Registration Ordinance required Chinese households and servants to register, and householders to report details of their tenants.[95] Earlier attempts at registration and control had been dead letters. MacDonnell resolved to enforce his measures with draconian powers of search, inquisition, and punishment. He rejected complaints of discrimination by Chinese leaders. European ships were already required to register, he told them in a hectoring rebuke. 'You yourselves must have seen that great pains are taken to administer the Law with strict Justice, and that, if it were not for Chinese Thieves, Pirates, and other bad characters, this Government would not have the expense of such a numerous Police, and such extensive Prisons.'[96]

Taxes to fund these measures aroused opposition from Chinese and colonists alike. MacDonnell imposed stamp duties on business transactions and introduced a scheme of licensed gaming houses. He brushed aside objections, arguing that regulation would reduce police corruption and enable bad characters to be monitored. Restricted to Chinese punters, the licensed gaming houses lasted for five years: they were abolished in 1872 after a campaign by Chief Justice Smale, missionaries, and Chinese leaders. Smale estimated that over $20 million had been lost at the gaming tables, to the detriment of the city's trade. The windfall to the government was over $200,000 per annum, equal to a quarter of regular revenue. Held in a special fund, it was used to augment the police, equip steam launches, and support schools for Chinese, 'whose unfortunate propensities make them the sole contributors to the fund'. A grant was also made towards the new Tung Wah Hospital, which quickly became a centre of Chinese political power.[97]

At the request of legislators and barristers, MacDonnell rehabilitated Daniel Caldwell and put him in charge of a 'secret police' of Chinese detectives, with provision for rewards for informants. The gaming licensees hired Caldwell at huge expense to monitor suspicious characters and protect their franchise. To reduce pressure on the gaol, MacDonnell introduced a 'voluntary' scheme of early release for prisoners. This was conditional on their receiving a tattoo of an arrow on the ear, or a circle on the neck, and being deported on pain of flogging and further imprisonment if they returned. The policy of restoring to the neighbouring province 'the scum and crime of the worst criminal population of China'

94. MacDonnell to Buckingham, 29 October 1867, CO 129/125, 104.
95. Ordinances Nos. 6, 7, and 8 of 1866.
96. Reply of His Excellency Sir Richard Graves MacDonnell, C.B., October 1866, CO 129/115, 221–223.
97. MacDonnell to Granville, 15 September 1869, 281; Munn, *Anglo-China*, 345–346; Elizabeth Sinn, *Power and Charity: A Chinese Merchant Elite in Colonial Hong Kong* (Hong Kong: Hong Kong University Press, 2003)

brought the prison population down from a peak of nearly 1,000 in 1865 to a daily average of 525 in 1872, the last year of MacDonnell's term.[98]

MacDonnell's attempts at judicial reform were less productive. Legislation in 1866–1868 provided for a High Court for the Suppression of Piracy. This was intended to address claims that piracy was encouraged by problems in obtaining convictions in the Supreme Court – criticisms which, after the *Carl* and *Caesar* trials, even MacDonnell had to agree were baseless. The new court was to consist of the Chief Justice, the Judge of the Court of Summary Jurisdiction, the Admiral or Senior Naval Officer, and two members appointed by the Governor, with a quorum of three, at least one of whom was to be a judge. Juries were to be dispensed with. Lawyers were permitted to appear. The court could be convened quickly to prevent tampering with witnesses. In addition to the existing death penalty for piracy with murder and piracy with violence, the court was initially given discretionary powers to impose the death penalty on persons convicted of setting forth, aiding, maintaining, or advising pirates in cases resulting in murder.[99] The legislation also created several reverse-onus offences: for example, being found with pirated goods without giving a satisfactory account; or 'being seen within twenty-one Days on board a Junk, &c. proved to have taken part in Piracy and unable to satisfy the Court as to non-complicity', which carried a penalty of up to fourteen years' penal servitude. The Governor in Council could order floggings for prisoners whose death sentences, whether pronounced by the new court or the Supreme Court, were commuted. However, concerns arose in Hong Kong and among the Law Officers in London about whether Hong Kong's legislature had the power to confer on courts jurisdiction beyond the limits of the colony, or to dispense with trial by jury in the Supreme Court in piracy cases. The Admiralty also objected to the appointment of naval officers to the court. Despite amendments to address these concerns, the piracy court never sat. The reverse-onus offences were, however, retained: legislation in 1867 now placed them within the jurisdiction of the Supreme Court.[100]

The number of piracy cases before the Supreme Court declined dramatically, to one or two cases per annum in 1871–1890, then to a mere half dozen in the thirty years from 1891 to 1920. Many of these prosecutions were not for piracy per se but for the reverse-onus offences created by MacDonnell's ordinances. Piracy re-emerged in the 1920s and 1930s as China was once again convulsed by civil war and foreign invasion. Thirty men were hanged for piracy with violence or murder during these years; no one condemned to death was

98. Munn, *Anglo-China*, 341–366.

99. This was excluded from the 1868 legislation.

100. Ordinances Nos. 9 of 1866, 12 of 1867, and 1 of 1868. The flogging provision was repealed by Ordinance No. 3 of 1881. The court itself was finally abolished by Ordinance No. 29 of 1901. MacDonnell to Carnarvon, 28 and 29 August 1866, CO 129/114, 503–515; Law Officers to Carnarvon, 29 November 1866, CO 129/118, 41–54; MacDonnell to Buckingham, 19 September and 12 October 1867, CO 129/124, 363–369 and CO 129/125, 5–14.

shown mercy. In 1927, executions again exceeded the number in England and Wales: eight men were hanged for the piracy of the S.S. *Sunning* near Amoy, and another seven for the piracy of the S.S. *Irene* in Bias Bay. The hangman, Bert Plumb, bought a motorcycle out of his fee of $50 per neck.[101]

In the meantime, the worst piracies on British ships in the late nineteenth century were dealt with by the Chinese authorities. Only two such cases even touched the Hong Kong courts. The first occurred in 1874, when some seventy pirates disguised as passengers seized the S.S. *Spark* on the Canton River, killing its American captain and a European passenger. Having occurred on a British ship in Chinese waters, the crime was triable in both British and Chinese courts. One of the pirates was arrested, tried, and hanged in Hong Kong. Eight others captured by the Chinese authorities were tried and beheaded in Canton; the corpse of a ninth man, who had died from wounds, was also beheaded. The Governor, Sir Arthur Kennedy, thanked the Acting Viceroy, Zhang Zhaodong, for this energetic response. Kennedy was concerned that piracy would revive now that the Royal Navy had wound down its patrols, and the end of the coolie trade had deprived 'thirty thousands of the ruffians of China' of a means of subsistence. But Sino-British cooperation soured when the magistrate, Charles May, refused a request for the extradition to Canton of two other alleged *Spark* pirates arrested in Hong Kong on information from Chinese officials. Instead, he committed them for trial in the Supreme Court. Zhang refused to send over key witnesses and the two men were discharged.[102]

The second piracy occurred on 10 December 1890 off Mendoza Island (Xiaoxing Shan), not far from where the *Carl* and *Caesar* were attacked nearly twenty-five years earlier. Forty or fifty pirates, heavily armed and disguised as passengers, seized the S.S. *Namoa*, a ship plying between Hong Kong and Swatow. They killed the British captain, the Filipino quartermaster, and a European passenger, and robbed some 200 Chinese passengers, many of whom were returning from San Francisco with their savings. While colonists were complaining about the poor precautions on the *Namoa* and the dilatory response of the Royal Navy, the Chinese Navy tracked down dozens of suspects. Nineteen men were beheaded in two mass executions in April and May 1891 on the beach outside Kowloon City, just across the border from British Kowloon. Parties of colonists went to see the executions. Photographs of the beheadings circulated widely. The site became a tourist attraction. In contrast, seven suspects arrested in Hong Kong were released for lack of evidence – two

101. Reminiscence by Leo D'Almada, *SCMP*, 25 January 1976.

102. May mistakenly understood the crime to be piracy *jure gentium*, which bound him to commit the men for trial in Hong Kong. Despite legislation in Hong Kong and instructions from London that 'proof of guilt' in the Treaty of Tientsin should be taken to mean 'probable cause', he also held that the evidence was too unreliable for rendition but was sufficient to try the case by jury in Hong Kong. Zhang's displeasure was aggravated by May's decision to commit some witnesses sent from Canton to prison for perjury. Kennedy to Carnarvon, 26 August 1874 and 8 February 1875, CO 129/167, 672–683 and CO 129/170, 83–135.

just as their trial was about to start.[103] This was one of several maiden sessions in the late nineteenth century, where the absence of cases was marked by the presentation of a pair of white gloves to the Chief Justice.

103. Fleming to Knutsford, 16 December 1890, CO 129/247, 588–605; Police Report for 1890, *HKSP*, 9/91; *HKDP*, 12–19, 25, 27, and 29 December 1890, and 18 April 1891; *HKT*, 23, 27, and 29 December 1890, 18 April 1891, and 17–18 September 1895; Goodman, *Reminiscences of a Colonial Judge*, 111–113.

4

'A Hanging Would Do Good to the Colony'

The Shek O Murder, 1878

Poring over a map of the China coast in 1842, the artist Robert Grindlay noticed a 'ridiculous' resemblance between Hong Kong Island and the much larger island of Great Britain. The new colony was 'a perfect miniature' of our 'right little, tight little island', he declared. The discovery delighted those who saw Hong Kong as 'the future capital of Anglo-China', a 'miniature representative of Great Britain, its laws, its manners, its institutions'.[1] But the idea is not as far-fetched as it may seem. The map in question, Wyld's *Map to Illustrate the War in China* (1842), shows China's coastline on an east-west axis, with north to the right. Rotated ninety degrees clockwise in this way, the shape of Hong Kong Island does indeed resemble that of Great Britain – or at least England and Wales. If Norfolk is represented by North Point, then Hong Kong's Land's End is Cape D'Aguilar, a rocky promontory at the end of the mountainous D'Aguilar Peninsula.

The two largest villages on the D'Aguilar Peninsula are Hok Tsui and Shek O. So remote were they from colonial activities that they were left out of the earliest British survey purporting to list all the places on Hong Kong Island.[2] Villagers grudgingly paid land rent to the new regime but continued as before to manage their own affairs: the granite watchtower at Hok Tsui, built for security against pirates, still stands today. When, in 1847, police landed at Shek O to investigate the wreck of a junk, they were greeted by villagers lined up on the beach 'with long bamboo pikes as if to fight'. The police found property from the wreck

1. *London Atlas*, quoted in *FOC*, 12 May 1842; T.C. Anstey, speaking (sarcastically) at a public meeting in Newcastle, June 1859, *Newcastle Chronicle*, 25 June 1859, CO 129/75, 228.
2. 'Names of Villages and Hamlets on the Island of Hongkong', *Canton Register*, 1 June 1841.

in the villagers' homes. The headman and two other men were convicted of plundering, sentenced to fifteen years' transportation, and shipped to Penang.[3]

Apart from police patrols, the earliest symbol of the colonial presence in this remote place was Hong Kong's first lighthouse, opened at Cape D'Aguilar in 1875. On 9 March 1878 it was the scene of an alleged crime. Lo Ping-kiu, a thirty-three-year-old widow from Hok Tsui, was taking clothes to her brothers-in-law who worked there. She alleged that the light keeper, Archibald Baird, dragged her into his room, locked the door, threw her on the floor, and raped her. Before letting her out he offered money, which she refused. She told her brothers-in-law she had had sex with a foreigner and must kill herself. A relative in government employ helped her report the matter. The committal proceedings were an ordeal: 'you are all taking the European's part,' she said when questioned by Baird's solicitor, Henry Caldwell.[4] The trial, before the Acting Chief Justice, Francis Snowden, and a special jury, was no easier. Baird's counsel, J.J. Francis, insinuated that Lo's youngest child was conceived *after* her husband's death. The 'trifling resistance' she offered, he said, was just the 'mock modesty' of a common prostitute. When the jury acquitted Baird, Snowden assured Lo that 'no blame attached to her at all', adding that 'he understood the Chinese attached great value to the chastity of their widows'. That, interjected the interpreter, Rafael Rozario, 'was another class of widows'.[5]

The chastity of another young widow from the D'Aguilar Peninsula was at the centre of what became known as the Shek O murder, which occurred just a few weeks after the rape trial. Chan Amui, a Hakka woman born in Shek O, supported herself and her two sons by working in the fields, cutting grass, and selling vegetables in the city. Her husband, a fisherman, had died the previous October. Since then, she had formed an intimate friendship with another fisherman, Cheung Ashiu, a native of Nantou, who had lived in Shek O for twenty-five years. Cheung gave her small amounts of money for her children and sometimes stayed with her overnight. They kept the liaison secret. In January 1878 he invited her to move into his own house, but she refused. On 28 May, during a visit to the village, her married elder sister, Chan Ngau-mui, who lived in Kowloon City, invited her to go there with her the next day, saying she would give her a present of rice. They left before sunrise, taking the path over the hills towards Shau Kei Wan, on the north side of the island. Amui's

3. *HKR*, 2 November 1847; Transport List, 6 November 1847, CO 129/21, 122–124.
4. Daniel Caldwell's brother. He was formerly Registrar of the Singapore Recorder's Court but fled after embezzling money. He was admitted to practise in Hong Kong in 1866. Norton-Kyshe, *History*, Vol. I, 590.
5. Baird was removed to the Green Island Lighthouse, which was attacked by armed men on 10 June 1878. Some believed this was connected with the alleged rape. He then returned to Cape D'Aguilar, where, despite further disputes with villagers, he remained until his retirement in 1896. *HKDP*, 16 and 18 March and 12 and 13 April 1878; *CM*, 26 June 1878; ExCo Minutes, 15 August 1878, CO 131/10, 77.

younger son, the three-year-old Li Amuk, was strapped to Ngau-mui's back. The eldest, ten-year-old Li Achung, was left to look after the house.[6]

Cheung Ashiu usually kept out of the way during Chan Ngau-mui's visits to Shek O. He knew she had told Amui to have nothing to do with him. On the eve of their departure he said to Amui, 'your sister is coming to take you away to get a living'. When he heard they had left he grabbed a chopper and ran after them. He found them on a bend in the path on the hillside above Big Wave Bay, close to Shek O Gap.[7] He grabbed hold of Ngau-mui, demanding to know where they were going and insisting that Amui repay the money he had given her. Then, according to his account at the inquest, Amui went at him with a sickle, cutting him on the forehead, rendering him 'partly insensible'. He took the chopper from under his jacket and gave her two cuts on the head. The sisters then hit him on the head with a stone. He could not remember the rest of the fight. But according to Amui, Cheung grabbed Ngau-mui by the wrist and chopped at the boy, still strapped to her back. Ngau-mui pushed away Cheung, who then chopped her on the neck, chest, and arms. When Amui went to help her, Cheung cut her on the neck and head. Amui eventually got hold of the chopper and threw it to the ground. According to her, there was no sickle: the cut on Cheung's forehead came from his own chopper.

Seeing a farmer working in a field below, Amui cried out 'save life! (救命!)'. The farmer was Chan Amo, a fifty-seven-year-old clansman of hers. It took him half an hour to reach her. He found Cheung sitting on the ground, with Amui holding his queue and Ngau-mui pressing him down. Cheung had blood on his face and clothes, and a cut on his forehead. The sisters and the child were also covered in blood. Amo took hold of Cheung and asked why he had attacked them. Cheung only replied that he was prepared to die. After binding Ngau-mui's neck with herbs and rags, Amo started to lead the group back to Shek O. But Ngau-mui was too badly injured to walk. Seeing a foreigner approaching in the distance, Amo left the sisters with Cheung while he went to Shek O to get help.

The foreigner was Pio D'Almeida, the Portuguese assistant light keeper from Cape D'Aguilar, who happened to be on his way to Victoria. When he reached the scene he worked out what had happened and took Cheung on foot to the police station at Shau Kei Wan. Amo returned later with two Sikh constables, who took the sisters and the boy by boat to Shau Kei Wan. From there they were taken to the Civil Hospital in Victoria. The cut on Cheung's forehead was superficial. The injuries to the women and boy were grave. Ngau-mui's windpipe was severed and she was unable to speak. She died the next morning. Seven hours had elapsed before her arrival at the hospital. Had she been treated earlier she

6. The account is taken from the judge's notes, coroner's report, Executive Council minutes, and other documents in Hennessy to Hicks Beach, 31 July 1878, CO 129/181, 316–384; *HKDP*, 30 and 31 May and 4, 6, and 20 June; and *CM*, 30 May and 5, 19, and 20 June.
7. Now a wooded area within the Shek O Country Park, in the 1870s it was mostly grassland.

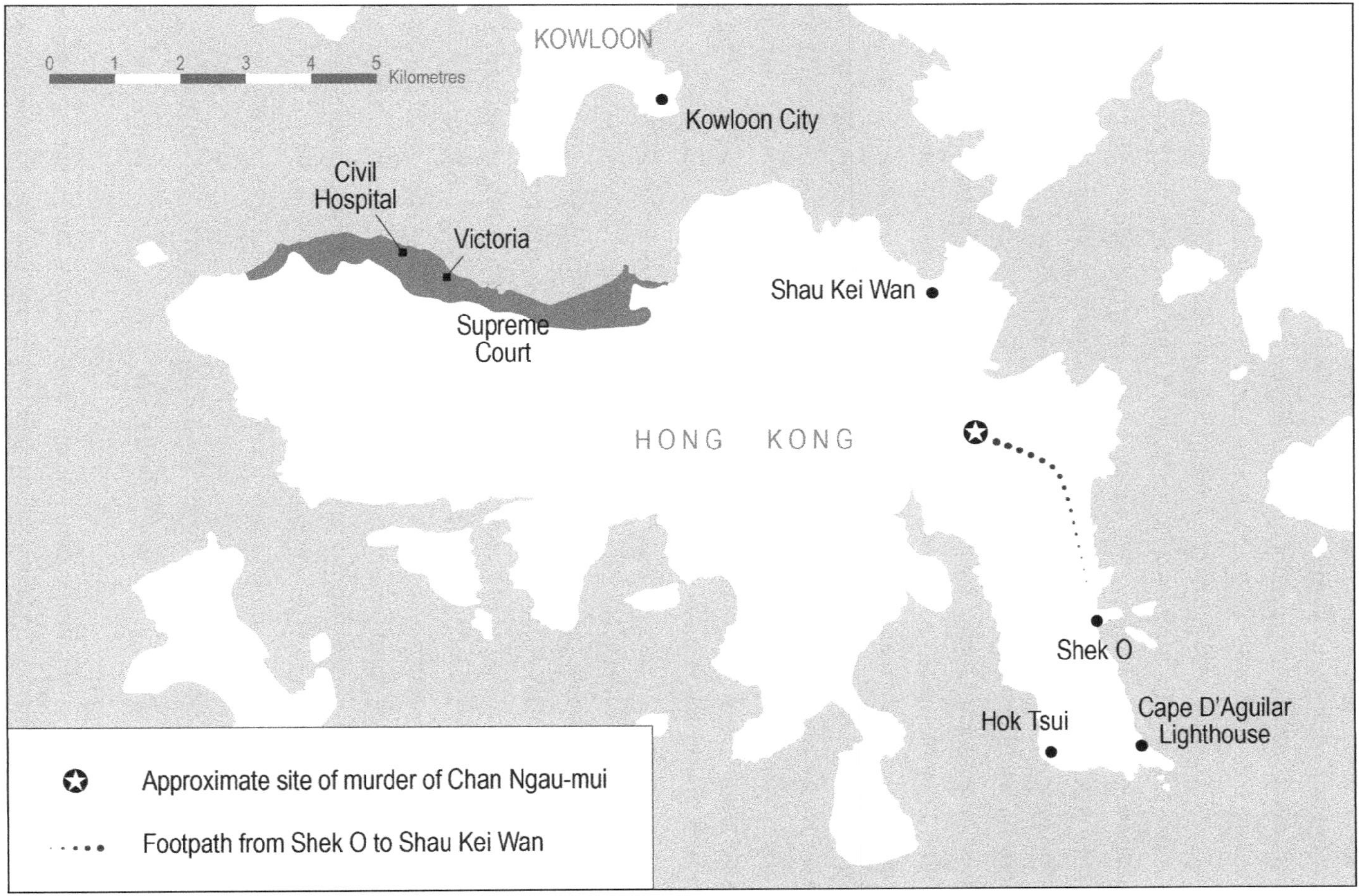

Map 2: The Shek O Murder, 1878

would probably have recovered, the physician in charge, Dr Alexander von der Horck, later testified. Amui and her son recovered after five days in hospital.

R v Cheung Ashiu
Murder, and wounding with intent to murder, 19 June 1878

An inquest by the Coroner, Charles Creagh, and a jury of three men returned a verdict of wilful murder against Cheung Ashiu. On 5 June, in a joint sitting, the magistrates Charles May and James Russell committed him for trial for the murder of Chan Ngau-mui and for wounding Li Amuk and Chan Amui with intent to murder. The trial took place on 19 June before Acting Chief Justice Snowden and a jury of seven: four British, two Germans, and a Portuguese.[8] The Attorney General, George Phillippo, prosecuted. Thomas Hayllar QC defended Cheung under a recently introduced policy of providing counsel at public expense to defendants in murder trials. There were five prosecution witnesses: Chan Amui, Dr von der Horck, Chan Amo, Pio D'Almeida, and Inspector J.C. Swanson, who had received Cheung and the sisters at Shau Kei Wan. The defence called no witnesses, but Cheung's statement at the inquest was put before the jury.

Chan Amui, the only eyewitness competent to testify, was first to give evidence. Villagers had talked to her since the inquest and committal proceedings. Now, in the Supreme Court, before another group of foreign men, she changed her story. Having spoken earlier of her intimacy with Cheung, she now denied it. Cheung had asked her to cook for him and had sometimes left money for her son. But he never came to her house, she now said, and had never slept there at night. In another departure from her pre-trial statements, she now said that Cheung had tried to tear a bangle from Ngau-mui's wrist, implying the motive was robbery. When, at Hayllar's request, her statements were read over, she admitted her relationship with Cheung. Her explanation threw yet more doubt on her credibility. 'The mind of a woman you must make allowance for, one time it is one way, one time another,' she said. She admitted that a villager had come to see her and had 'said how things happened'. But she denied she had threatened to get a clansman to beat Cheung after he had become angry on the eve of the murder. She insisted that she had no sickle with her on the journey, and that Cheung had struck first.

There was no doubt that Cheung had killed Chan Ngau-mui, said Hayllar for the defence. Chan Amui's evidence was amply corroborated. But 'to save her reputation and the reputation of her village – for the Chinese place great value on the purity of their widows', she had altered her story to supply a motive of robbery. When challenged, her

8. John Grant Smith, storekeeper, McEwen Frickel & Co.; Julius Seier, assistant, Meyer & Co.; Julius Hartmann, assistant, Pustau & Co.; Henry Crawford, assistant, Lane Crawford & Co.; William Howes Percival, assistant, North-China Insurance Co.; Henrique Hyndman, assistant, China Sugar Refinery; and John Inglis, shipwright.

answer had been 'a very clever one, that they must not expect too much from the mind of a woman on these things'. The truth, said Hayllar, was that Ngau-mui had heard 'that all things were not straight' and had decided to take her sister away. Cheung had surmised she was going to marry her sister to someone else, and he was going to lose both his mistress and the money he had given her. After a quarrel, he went after them 'with his blood greatly heated'. There was no excuse for the chopper, said Hayllar, but Cheung must have believed the women would have their sickles. No sickle had been found, but nor had any proper search been made. If Amui had struck first with a sickle, there was enough provocation to reduce the crime to manslaughter. 'Women of this kind are neither nice in the use of their tongues nor nice in the use of their hands,' said Hayllar. Since the jury could not trust Chan Amui's evidence implicitly, he asked them to take a merciful view and to suppose she had struck Cheung first.

Snowden re-called Chan Amui and asked if she had been carrying a sickle. She replied that neither she nor her sister had a sickle. She also denied they had struck Cheung on the head with a stone. In his summing up Snowden noted the variations in Chan Amui's evidence but made some allowance for this 'as he understood that Chinese of all classes attached a great deal of importance to the virtue of their widows'. Otherwise, her testimony 'bore the stamp of truth'. Looking at the medical testimony, 'he could not imagine a more savage attack'. The jury might charitably believe the injury to the child was accidental. But there was little doubt the prisoner wilfully assaulted Chan Amui. If Cheung was struck first, as he claimed, and retaliated in a passion, then the jury might find a verdict of manslaughter. But if they believed that Cheung, 'actuated by malice, went out with this chopper, waylaid the women, and wounded them in the manner which led to the death of the deceased they must find him guilty of murder'.

The jury retired at 3 p.m. and returned after a few minutes with a verdict of murder. Asked why sentence of death should not be passed on him, Cheung said that Chan Amui fell in love with him after the death of her husband and begged him to take pity on the two children. He gave her money for their support. Her elder sister wished to take her away, and when they left the house he followed and tried to stop them. 'The sister turned round and struck him on the forehead with a grass hook, and he did what he could in his defence.' After assuming the black cap, Snowden said that everyone would have been glad if the circumstances had allowed the jury to convict Cheung of an offence that would not have cost him his life. But they could not have done less than find him guilty of murder. He then passed sentence of death on Cheung.

Governor Hennessy and capital punishment

The evidence, reported Snowden to the Governor, showed that 'a very savage murder was committed with very great premeditation – and without the least provocation on the part of the murdered woman'. There was reason to think that Cheung Ashiu's intention was 'to murder both women, and that he would have succeeded but for the vigorous resistance they made'. The Governor and his Executive Council discussed Cheung's case on 28 June and 1 July with Snowden in attendance. The council had four members: the Officer in Command of the Troops, Major-General Edward Donovan; the acting Colonial Secretary, John Price; the Attorney General, George Phillippo; and the Colonial Treasurer and Registrar General, Cecil Clementi Smith. Only Price recommended mercy. The Governor agreed with Price and commuted the death sentence to life penal servitude. This was only the second time a Hong Kong governor commuted a death sentence against the advice of his council. The first was the *Gulnare* piracy in 1857, where the difference was over whether one or three of the ringleaders should hang.[9]

The Governor was John Pope Hennessy (1877–1882). A barrister and former Conservative Member of Parliament, Hennessy was also an Irish Catholic with a Eurasian wife. He was vain, quarrelsome, and vindictive, especially towards subordinates. But he held humane and progressive views. During a long colonial career, he made genuine attempts to advance the interests of native peoples. The policy throughout the British Empire was 'perfect fair play and justice to all', he told leaders of Hong Kong's Chinese community, with 'no distinction between any class, or creed, or nationality'.[10] To educate people about the law he published bilingual summaries of trials in the *Government Gazette*. He held that the accused should be tried by his peers, and that 'the jury should therefore be of the same race as the person who was tried'.[11] This prompted modest increases in the number of Chinese jurors from seven in 1880 (in a list of 480 names) to twenty-three in 1881, and thirty-two in 1882. He appointed Hong Kong's first Chinese barrister, Ng Choy, to both the Magistracy and Legislative Council, and granted British nationality to wealthy Chinese residents. Hong Kong, he said, had the potential to become a 'flourishing Anglo-Chinese community'.[12]

Hennessy's 'chinomania' unnerved colonists, not least because it was a recognition of rising Chinese economic power. Even more unsettling was his attack on penal policies in force since the 1860s. These included ample use of the cat-o'-nine-tails and early release of Chinese prisoners, who were then deported to the Mainland with arrows tattooed on their earlobes or circles on their necks. Flogging as a judicial punishment was already on the

9. ExCo Minutes, 28 June and 1 July 1878, CO 131/10, 51–69. For the *Gulnare* case see Chapter 2.
10. *HKGG*, 16 February 1878.
11. A rare instance in which the Legislative Council's scrutiny of the jury list was open to the press. Hennessy acknowledged that one of the reasons was the English-language requirement. *CM*, 28 February and 1 March 1881.
12. See James Pope-Hennessy, *Verandah: Some Episodes in the Crown Colonies 1867–1889* (London: G. Allen and Unwin, 1964); and P. Kevin MacKeown, *A Stormy Petrel: The Life and Times of John Pope Hennessy* (Hong Kong: City University of Hong Kong Press, 2020).

decline: the Supreme Court had sentenced only fifty-five men to public floggings in the five years before 1877. The main abuses were in the gaol, where nearly 2,000 floggings had been inflicted in the decade ending in 1876. Hennessy abolished public floggings and replaced whipping on the back with caning on the buttocks, which posed less risk to vital organs.[13] Against opposition from colonists, he ended the early-release scheme and curtailed the scope of corporal punishment. Prisoners now generally served their full sentences, with remission of up to a third for good conduct. During Hennessy's five-year term the gaol population doubled, from 332 to 678. Plans were discussed for re-commissioning the abandoned gaol on Stonecutters Island, and for a new gaol on Pokfulam Road.[14]

Cheung Ashiu was the first person to be sentenced to death since Hennessy's arrival in April 1877. Hennessy's decision to commute the sentence now prompted speculation about whether, in addition to his other reformist views, he was conscientiously opposed to capital punishment. The commutation produced no fewer than six editorials and five letters in the two main newspapers.[15] Writing to the *China Mail*, 'A Juror' divulged that the jury had decided its verdict even before retiring and had only left the jury box to avoid seeming too hasty. He could hardly have imagined that such a 'cold-blooded and atrocious killing' would take up so much of the Executive Council's time. He would never again 'acquiesce in a verdict of guilty against a native'. Sharing this outrage, the *Mail* accused Hennessy of using his power of clemency 'for the purpose of annulling the most important law of the Empire, because he may not happen to have confidence in its principle'. In his 'excessive humanity', said the *Mail*, he 'was inclined to treat the question of capital punishment in the same way as he has dealt with that of the next severest penalty, namely, flogging.' After his decision in this 'exceptionally brutal' case, said the *Daily Press*, 'Mr Hennessy can never consent to any execution taking place in this Colony.'

Not everyone agreed. In two letters to the *China Mail*, 'Fidus Achates' urged commentators not to speculate about Hennessy's views on capital punishment. The crime, he argued, was 'entirely unpremeditated'. Cheung had 'no animosity or ill feeling whatever to the wretched woman who became a victim to his insensate fury'. A writer calling himself 'Rattle the Bones' asked, 'how would the man have been treated, had he been an Englishman?' He would, said 'Rattle the Bones', have been given an attorney weeks before trial to prepare his defence. Every flaw in the prosecution evidence 'would have been brought forward in

---

13. Kate Lowe and Eugene McLaughlin, 'An "El Dorado of Riches and a Place of Unpunished Crime": The Politics of Penal Reform in Hong Kong, 1877–1882', *Criminal Justice History*, Vol. 14 (1993): 57–89; and 'Sir John Pope Hennessy and the "Native Race Craze": Colonial Government in Hong Kong, 1877–1882', *Journal of Imperial and Commonwealth History* 20, no. 2 (1992): 223–247.
14. The plans came to nothing. The site on Pokfulam Road is now occupied by the University of Hong Kong. Hennessy to Hicks Beach, 31 May 1879, CO 129/184, 583–590; Price to Colonial Office, 5 March 1882, CO 129/206, 441–449.
15. *CM*, 1–6, 8, and 15 July 1878; *HKDP*, 3, 8 13, and 15 July 1878.

the strongest possible manner to discredit the value of her whole evidence'. Cheung, in contrast, was dragged out of gaol:

> the jacket in which he was arrested, still soaked in blood, is thrown over him, the preliminaries of the trial begin, and whilst the Barrister appointed for his defence is robing he has just five minutes to explain through an Interpreter what the Barrister happens to ask him in order to get up something like a defence.[16]

No search was made for a sickle. No questions were asked about Chan Amui's claim she was merely going to Kowloon to get some rice, or about her 'personalia' generally. Had enquiry been made, 'Rattle the Bones' dramatically revealed, it would have shown that 'she was going to be married to a man in Third Street, Sai-ying-poon, that the wretched prisoner, mad with love and jealousy, did not know what he was doing'. That was why Cheung made no attempt to escape. Had he been an Englishman, the letter concluded, he would have been judged temporarily insane and found guilty of manslaughter.

This prompted a fifth and final letter, from the foreman of the jury.[17] Answering the question put by 'Rattle the Bones', he said that, as far as the jury were concerned, if the defendant had been an Englishman 'he would have had the same justice neither more nor less, than he had as a Chinaman'. The public endorsed the verdict, he said. Cheung was ably defended, yet not a single extenuating point could be found in his favour. The jury had no choice but to find him guilty. Even so, the foreman concluded, 'Rattle the Bones' ought to have conveyed his knowledge about Amui's marriage to the court; '"had he been an Englishman" he would have tried to put wrong right, where he saw need.'

Concerns that Hennessy was trying to abolish the death penalty spread to the Chinese community when he hesitated over a second death sentence that summer.[18] Tam Atai was convicted of murdering his lover Chun Ayew. Tam had paid $120 to redeem her from a brothel in Macao and had taken her to live with him in Kowloon. But she joined a brothel on Hollywood Road. His attempts to get her back led to a row. He then bought a knife, returned to the brothel, and stabbed her. He did not deny the killing. His counsel, J.J. Francis, urged a manslaughter verdict. Tam, 'a man of small intelligence', had been under great provocation. 'The Government do not acquaint the Chinese of the penalties they incur until they are imprisoned or hanged,' he said.[19] Awaiting news in gaol, Tam was, according to a Protestant missionary, much 'taken up with the idea of his being reprieved,

16. *CM*, 14 July 1878.
17. Probably John Grant Smith, whose name appears first in the reports of the trial.
18. 'If he commutes the sentence of those condemned to be hung and imprisons for life and also does away with flogging on the back then his benevolence may possibly be somewhat excessive', read a Chinese placard dated 6 October 1878, issued by 'all the shops of this port'. The placard was nevertheless largely supportive of Hennessy's criminal justice reforms. *HKDP*, 10 October 1878.
19. *HKDP*, 16 and 19 July, and 29 August 1878; *CM*, 18–20 July and 28 August 1878.

as in his own country he would not have been put to death for murdering a person who stood in such relation to him as the unfortunate woman'.[20]

Hennessy sympathized with this view. Tam's cohabitation with Chun and her refusal to leave the brothel would surely have been mitigating factors under Chinese custom, he suggested when the Executive Council considered the case. The council disagreed. The trial judge, Snowden, and the Attorney General, Phillippo, urged that it was of 'the utmost importance that the Chinese population should know that they were as much bound by the law of the land as the English and other residents were'. Hennessy confirmed the death sentence. After learning of his fate, Tam sent away the Protestant missionary and converted to Catholicism, probably, said one cynic, after being promised burial in a new suit of clothes in the Catholic Cemetery. He was hanged outside the Magistracy on 30 September 1878. The executioner, a European undergoing a two-year sentence, was promised a pardon for the service. Among the prisoners brought out to witness this event was the Shek O murderer, Cheung Ashiu.[21]

Six more men – an American, a Siamese, two Javanese, and two Chinese – were sentenced to death during the remainder of Hennessy's term in Hong Kong. Following the advice of his Executive Council, Hennessy confirmed five of these sentences and commuted one, the only case in which jury and judge recommended mercy.[22] Some years earlier, while Governor of Barbados, Hennessy had 'mentioned his horror and disapproval of capital punishment' to his deputy on the island of St Lucia, G. W. Des Voeux (later, Governor of Hong Kong 1887–1891). He had asked to see the papers on any death sentence before they went to Des Voeux's Executive Council. In a particularly hideous case of child-murder in 1876, Des Voeux was determined to have the culprit hanged. He decided not to consult Hennessy, fearing he would advise commutation. When he later forwarded a report on the execution, Hennessy did not bother to reply.[23]

Capital punishment was a burning topic when Hennessy was a Member of Parliament in the 1860s. A Royal Commission on the question was appointed in 1864. Four of its twelve members advised abolition. But the only reform to result was the ending of public executions in 1868.[24] This measure was not adopted in Hong Kong. Despite having pioneered the abolition of public hangings while Governor of South Australia (1855–1861), MacDonnell advised that any element of secrecy was 'inadvisable amongst so suspicious

20. Letter from Bishop Burdon, *HKDP*, 2 October 1878.
21. *CM*, 3 October 1878; ExCo Minutes, 13 September 1878, CO 131/10, 109–111; *HKDP*, 1 October 1878.
22. A man fatally stabbed another in the leg for beating him the night before. *CM*, 23 March 1881.
23. G. William Des Voeux, *My Colonial Service in British Guiana, St Lucia, Trinidad, Fiji, Australia, Newfoundland, and Hong Kong, with Interludes* (London: John Murray, 1903), Vol. I, 273–275.
24. Block and Hostettler, *Hanging in the Balance*, Chapters 5 and 6; Devereaux, *Execution, State & Society in England*, Chapter 9.

a race as the Chinese'.[25] Hennessy reopened the question in 1878. With support from the judges and the Executive Council, he proposed legislation requiring executions to be held in private. No legislation was enacted, but in 1879 hangings were moved from the Magistracy compound to a yard near the gaol, though they were still held in public.[26] Hennessy was also slow to address the cruellest aspect of capital punishment: the chronically defective state of the gallows, which caused Tam Atai and others to struggle for several minutes after the lever was pulled because the drop was too short.[27]

How do we explain this falling off of interest, given Hennessy's horror of capital punishment? Why, despite predictions that he would say 'a great deal on that hackneyed theme', did he avoid the subject in a much-anticipated speech on crime after his return to England in 1882?[28] Quite simply, among his many causes, the topic did not sustain his attention. Like most colonial governors, Hennessy reformulated his principles from place to place, according to differing political conditions, and was selective in his campaigns.[29] He did not, for example, interfere with Hong Kong's 'light and pass' system (a curfew on Chinese residents in force until 1897), despite describing it as a 'monstrous injustice'.[30] The Colonial Office supported his penal reforms because they reflected policy at home. But tinkering with capital punishment was a different matter altogether. Concerned that Hennessy was going too far in Cheung's case, the Secretary of State stressed that it was not his duty to comment on a governor's exercise of mercy. But he warned Hennessy that 'very strong grounds' were needed to justify going against his council and the trial judge.[31]

Hennessy clearly took this to heart. In any case, he was more interested in procedural details than principles. After the aborted business of private hangings he pursued other procedural issues, such as the form in which the Governor should sign the execution warrant, and whether the judge should specify the time and place.[32] His reason for sparing

---

25. MacDonnell even claimed credit for influencing the change in the UK. After his abolition of public hangings in South Australia he attended several public executions in England and was so struck by the 'horrors' surrounding them that he suggested to the Home Secretary a similar reform in the UK. MacDonnell to Buckingham, 15 September 1868, CO 129/132, 324–326.
26. ExCo Minutes, 15 August 1878, CO 131/10, 73–74; *CM*, 28 May and 2 September 1879.
27. The Gaol Superintendent, Malcolm Tonnochy, claimed the gallows used in Hong Kong was simpler and less likely to get out of order than the one at Newgate. New apparatus was finally constructed in 1882 on the basis of diagrams from England, with a drop of eight feet and a brass ring instead of a slipknot. Hennessy to Kimberley, 12 April 1881, CO 129/192, 489–492; *CM*, 4 and 5 July 1882.
28. *Sheffield Independent*, 24 August 1882; *Transactions of the National Association for the Promotion of Social Science: Nottingham Meeting, 1882* (London: Longmans, Green, and Co. 1883), 212–220.
29. David Lambert and Philip Howell, 'John Pope Hennessy and the Translation of "Slavery" between late nineteenth-century Barbados and Hong Kong', *History Workshop Journal*, Vol. 55 Issue 1, 1–24.
30. *CM*, 5 October 1878.
31. Hicks Beach to Hennessy, 30 September 1878, CO 129/181, 383–384.
32. ExCo Minutes, 13 September and 9 October 1878 and 22 May 1879, CO 131/10, 111–112, 115–116 and 182–183.

Cheung was also, in essence, a matter of procedural justice. The court had assigned counsel at a standard fee of $25, fixed in 1872 for murder trials and paid from public funds. But it had failed to follow the advice of the Chief Justice, Sir John Smale, and provide a solicitor as well. 'The elucidation of innocence,' said Smale, could only be obtained by assigning *both* counsel *and* attorney, paid a proper fee. 'All grounds of defence require to be ferreted out. They are often unknown or unthought of even by the accused,' he advised. 'A defence, not to be a delusion, must be thoroughly got up.'[33]

Smale's advice came in a letter in September 1877 following a dispute over fees for the solicitor and barrister he had assigned in a murder trial. Two Italian sailors were tried by Smale and a special jury for the murder of a Chilean sailor after a night in the bars and brothels of Sheung Wan. Witnesses of nine different nationalities gave evidence in five languages.[34] The interpretation, by Rozario, was challenged by counsel, jurors, and witnesses. A Portuguese witness claimed she could not even follow his Portuguese. 'If he was incompetent, the Governor was responsible for it,' said Smale, after a juror observed that the remark 'you shall not *leave* tomorrow', attributed to one of the accused, was rendered by Rozario as 'you shall not *live* tomorrow'. After a three-day trial, the jury returned a verdict of manslaughter. In mitigation, J.J. Francis, counsel for the accused, pleaded that the men were mad drunk and, being southern Europeans, easily provoked. Smale imposed sentences of two and three years' penal servitude.[35] When the government refused to allow fees of $50 to Francis and $25 to Henry Dennys, the solicitor, Hennessy intervened and approved the payments.[36]

There were no murder trials from then until Cheung Ashiu's trial in June 1878. In March, Smale went on leave. His letter on legal representation was not shown to Acting Chief Justice Snowden, or to the Attorney General. Only Hennessy remembered it. He read it out when the Executive Council reviewed Cheung's case, saying the failure to assign a solicitor had worked against Cheung. No attempt had been made to verify his claim that the women had attacked him first – a claim supported by D'Almeida's evidence and by a separate statement from the Colonial Surgeon that Cheung had a scalp wound. Hennessy queried Snowden's 'entire credence' to Chan Amui when she had tried to hide her 'improper intimacy' with Cheung. It had since come to light that she had given a false name[37] and had

33. Smale to Colonial Secretary, 12 September 1877, *HKGG*, 6 July 1878.
34. Irish, Portuguese, Baghdadi Jewish, German, English, Chinese, Muslim Indian, 'coloured' (possibly West Indian or American), and a native of the French colony of Réunion. The languages were English, Portuguese, Spanish, Hindustani, and Chinese. A separate Italian interpreter was provided for the accused.
35. *OCM*, 11 August 1877.
36. Snowden to Price, 12 July 1878, CO 129/181, 399.
37. The Chinese characters are not given in the reports, but 'Chan Amui' most likely meant 'Younger Sister Chan' (陳亞妹), which was probably the name by which she was known in her village.

falsely described herself as a widow: in fact, she had 'got married with much ceremony in the interval between her leaving Shek O and the trial'.

The 'native prisoner', Hennessy told his council, knew nothing of the procedure of the courts; judge, jury, and counsel knew nothing of the language of the prisoner or witnesses. The accused, after having been brought into the court,

> was there and then asked through an Interpreter by the learned Counsel assigned to him what was his case. A few hurried words were whispered, whilst the Counsel was putting on his gown, and then the trial proceeded. The ablest Counsel in the world could not have made a real defence or elicited all the material facts from the witnesses under such circumstances.[38]

And yet he was bound to assume, when a capital case was submitted to him for his decision, that 'all the evidence which could be adduced in favour of the accused had been so adduced before sentence was passed'. That it was not so in this case was because 'the strongly expressed opinion of the Chief Justice of the Colony was set aside'.[39]

To ensure Smale's advice was not ignored in future, Hennessy published his letter in the *Gazette*, with a note that he concurred in Smale's opinion, which, however, was not acted upon in Cheung's case. This barbed remark mortified Snowden. He protested that it led to 'the unavoidable inference' that a miscarriage of justice had occurred, which he denied. There was no rule requiring a judge to assign a solicitor in a capital trial, he said. The leading barrister, Hayllar, had done all that 'skill and prudence could suggest' for Cheung. He had interviewed him before trial with the interpreter, E.J. Eitel, and had not asked for a solicitor, probably because Cheung had been caught red-handed and the only hope was to reduce the crime to manslaughter by cross-examination.[40]

A month after Snowden's protest the Deputy Registrar of the Supreme Court, Frederick Huffam, absconded to Macao with some $50,000 held by him as trustee of estates in bankruptcy. He was brought back to Hong Kong, convicted, and sentenced by Snowden to fourteen years' penal servitude, reduced to seven by the Full Court.[41] Officials blamed Snowden for having known earlier of Huffam's misdeeds. Snowden blamed Hennessy, who, he alleged, had heard about Huffam's intended flight the night before. Rumours spread that

38. Minute by Hennessy, CO 129/181, 372. The similarities between this and the letter to the *China Mail* from 'Rattle the Bones' suggest that Hennessy was the instigator, if not the author, of that letter.
39. ExCo Minutes, 28 June and 1 July 1878, and minute by Hennessy, CO 129/181, 346–373.
40. Snowden to Price, 12 July 1878, CO 129/181, 394–407.
41. Huffam's counsel, J.J. Francis, persuaded the Full Court that the money embezzled was not public money but money held in trust, which carried a lesser sentence. Hennessy to Hicks Beach, 31 August 1878, CO 129/181, 591–634; *CM*, 26 October and 2, 8, and 11 November 1878; Ordinances Nos. 13 of 1870 and 1 of 1881; *HKGG*, 12 May 1894.

Hennessy was about to suspend Snowden as Acting Chief Justice. Eventually, the Secretary of State ordered him to make a public apology to Hennessy.[42]

Chief Justice Smale and the elucidation of innocence

Sir John Smale returned from leave at the end of 1878. He had been Chief Justice since 1866, and before that Attorney General since 1861. He was now seventy-three and in poor health. Many had expected – indeed hoped – he would not return. But, despite being 'most anxious to get rid of him', Colonial Office staff were loath to raise the matter: he was 'a "philanthropist"', they observed; any pressure would 'only produce a violent explosion', they feared.[43] To them he was 'a byword and a scandal', an 'inefficient old man who never was good for much.'[44] Problems started shortly after his appointment as Chief Justice, when, during heated exchanges in court, he fined and suspended Edward Pollard, Hong Kong's first Queen's Counsel, for contempt; the decision was quashed by the Privy Council.[45] They culminated, shortly before his departure in 1882, in a public quarrel with the Supreme Court Registrar, Henry Gibbons, resulting in the latter's suspension and resignation.[46] By then Smale's court was said to resemble a bear garden.

Smale's 'outbursts of intemperance'[47] sealed his reputation as an erratic and cantankerous judge. They are a running theme in the *History of the Laws and Courts of Hong Kong* (1898) by James Norton-Kyshe, a later Supreme Court Registrar, which largely overlooks Smale's efforts to improve the quality of criminal justice. Born in Exeter, Smale was educated at Manchester College, York, a dissenting academy with a tradition of supporting humane causes, such as the abolition of slavery. He studied at Inner Temple in 1828 and became a solicitor before being called to the Bar in 1842. For a while he was part-owner of the liberal *Exeter Weekly Times* and an author of law reports. As Attorney General of Hong Kong 1861–1866, he secured capital convictions of over forty men, most of whom were hanged. He shared a common view that, because of its wide use in China, flogging of Chinese for violent crimes was 'almost a necessity here.'[48]

42. *CM*, 10 October 1878 and 31 May 1879; Hennessy to Hicks Beach, 31 August 1878, CO 129/181, 595–634; Snowden to Herbert, 14 and 25 July 1879, CO 129/186, 467 and 470–479.
43. Minutes by Robert Herbert and Lord Kimberley, 18 September 1880, CO 129/192, 466–467.
44. Minutes by Robert Meade, 17 May 1881, and Herbert, 18 September 1881, CO 129/192, 455 and 466.
45. The incident was triggered by difficulty in understanding a witness, 'a difficulty increased by some confusion or ignorance on the part of the interpreter [Rozario]'; petition of E.H. Pollard and affidavit of J.C. Whyte, in *Petition for the Reversal of the Sentence Passed on Mr Pollard QC by The Honorable Mr Smale, Chief-Justice of Hongkong* (Hong Kong: Daily Press, 1867), 4 and 13; Norton-Kyshe, *History*, Vol. II, Chapter 48.
46. Norton-Kyshe, *History*, Vol. II, 304–324.
47. *HKDP*, 27 July 1880.
48. Smale to Alexander, 7 January 1864, CO 129/97, 56.

As Chief Justice, Smale showed a new independence. He took pains to ensure that defendants benefited from the protections of English law. Juries found an unaccustomed thoroughness in his guidance at trials. Convicted criminals heard lectures on the reasoning behind their sentences. Some received sympathy: 'it has often passed my mind that if I had been tempted by their surroundings I might have done as they did,' said Smale of those driven to crime by 'hunger or sickness or distress'.[49] As judge and legislator,[50] he attacked Governor MacDonnell's policy of licensed gambling, sparing no opportunity to condemn it as a cause of crime. He campaigned against corruption, the coolie trade, and trafficking in women and children. He was, in effect, the leading voice of dissent in Hong Kong. Whereas MacDonnell defended discriminatory policies as necessary for the 'self-preservation' of Europeans, Smale espoused a crude doctrine of equality. 'That the Chinese come within our definition of the "white man" is clear, not only from their colour, but from their culture as a nation,' he said.[51] Perhaps inevitably, disputes soon arose over his handling of murders of Europeans by Chinese.

The first clash occurred in 1868, when two Chinese men were tried for the murder of William Yancey, an American dockyard supervisor, in a raid on his house in Kowloon. They were handed over to the Hong Kong police by Chinese officials with their written confessions. The police advised them they need not say anything, but omitted to mention that any statements they made might be used against them. Their statements to the police were the only evidence produced in court. When their counsel, Hayllar, showed they had not been properly cautioned, Smale ruled the evidence inadmissible and they were acquitted. MacDonnell criticized this as a 'failure of justice'. It was incredible 'under the circumstances in which this Colony is placed' that the Chief Justice should have rejected key evidence on such grounds, he said. These views were conveyed to Smale with a request for explanations for the guidance of the police. Smale saw this as interference in his judicial functions and demanded that the correspondence be sent to London. MacDonnell forwarded it with his own account of the episode, taking the opportunity, in another despatch in the same mail, to denigrate Smale as 'not quite *compos mentis*'. The Secretary of State warned MacDonnell that he had gone too far.[52]

---

49. *HKDP*, 11 July 1876.
50. Up to 1888 the Chief Justice was an *ex officio* member of the Legislative Council.
51. *HKDP*, 3 April 1871.
52. In another case tried earlier on the same day as the Yancey murder, Henry Shatswell, first mate of the American ship *Sooloo*, was charged with murder. While the *Sooloo* was in harbour he had thrown a large stone over the side in an attempt to sink a Chinese 'rum-boat', whose occupants were selling alcohol. The stone hit the boatman and killed him. Without waiting to hear the facts, the all-European jury returned a verdict of manslaughter with a recommendation to mercy. Smale rebuked them for basing their verdict on what they had heard outside court. During arguments by Pollard QC on Shatswell's behalf, Smale made the point that 'it was a Chinaman who was killed'. Pollard replied that 'it was well known that the value or estimate put upon human life by the Chinese was not that which existed among the Western Nations'. Smale fined Shatswell $500, adding that he feared this

Of equal concern to MacDonnell and his officials was Smale's treatment of murders of Europeans arising from the coolie trade. Since the exposure of abuses in the 1850s, the government had tried to deter kidnapping and improve conditions on coolie ships by regulation and, from 1870, by confining the trade to British colonies. As a result, the trade moved to Macao, where, according to MacDonnell, it amounted to 'a renewal of the slave trade'.[53] Hong Kong firms continued to profit by fitting out coolie ships. In 1867 Smale called for a ban on all emigration of Chinese labourers from Hong Kong. He lobbied the Colonial Office about the 'lifetime of exile and slavery' faced by men forced into contracts with no real sense of what they were doing.[54] From the bench he likened the coolie trade to the slave trade and said the Portuguese had learned it from the British.

The authorities in Hong Kong were as eager as Smale to stamp out abuses. But they were also intent on punishing leaders of murderous revolts on coolie ships. In October 1870 the French ship *Nouvelle Pénélope* set sail from Macao for Peru with 300 coolies under locked hatches. Four days into the voyage the coolies mutinied, killed the captain and eight crewmembers, and beached the ship. Seventy-two of them reappeared in Macao and were handed over to Chinese officials: thirty-one were beheaded. Others took refuge in Hong Kong. One of these was Kwok Asing, the alleged leader of the mutiny, who was arrested in Hong Kong in January 1871. Smale urged lawyers to take up his case, even suggesting grounds on which they should seek his release.[55] J.J. Francis took on the case and Smale granted a writ of *habeas corpus*. He declared the *Nouvelle Pénélope* to be a slave ship, its captain a pirate, and its passengers slaves. Kwok had 'a right to take life to free himself from such constraint on his personal liberty'. His actions were not only lawful but laudable, said Smale, adding that he would have done the same in his position.[56]

Kwok was rearrested after a request for extradition by the French Consul. When the consul withdrew the request, Kwok was committed for trial on a charge of piracy *jure gentium*. On 22 May Smale issued another writ of habeas corpus on the ground that Kwok had been committed for the same offence for which he had already been released by writ.[57]

---

leniency 'might be construed into disregard of human life'. The dead man's mother, who relied on him as her only support, was awarded an allowance of $5 per month, paid out of the fine. *CM*, 19 November 1868; *HKDP*, 20 November 1868; MacDonnell to Granville, 3 and 5 April 1869, CO 129/137, 22–67 and 84–90; ExCo Minutes, 2 December 1868, CO 131/7, 108.

53. MacDonnell to Buckingham, 28 June 1867, CO 129/122, 313.
54. What was 'most fearful', he added, was that sending 'Asiatic men being such as they are without women on long sea voyages' converted 'each Coolie Ship into a floating Sodom'. Memorial from Smale and Whittall, 27 June 1867, CO 129/122, 319–320; Smale to Rogers, 6 October 1869, CO 129/142, 338–339.
55. *Correspondence Respecting the Emigration of Chinese Coolies from Macao* (London: Harrison and Sons, 1871), 7–9; Smale to Pauncefote, 14 January 1871, CO 129/153, 171–174; ExCo Minutes, 24 February 1871, CO 131/7, 302; Peter Wesley-Smith, 'Kwok A-Sing, Sir John Smale, and the Macao Coolie Trade', *Law Lectures for Practitioners* (Hong Kong: Hong Kong Law Journal Ltd, 1993), 124–134.
56. *HKDP*, 30 March and 1 and 3 April 1871.
57. *HKDP*, 19 April, and 23 and 26 May 1871.

The Attorney General, Pauncefote, tried to browbeat him into reversing this decision, even producing telegrams from London with the Law Officers' opinion that Kwok *could* be tried for piracy.[58] While this was going on, news arrived of a revolt on another coolie ship, the *Don Juan*, shortly after its departure from Macao: the ship was set on fire; over 500 men, locked below deck, perished.[59] In July, with the help of J.J. Francis (guided, allegedly, by Smale),[60] Kwok took action against Pauncefote under the Habeas Corpus Act, which prescribed a fine of £500 for anyone detaining on the same offence a person who had already been released by habeas corpus. Despite pressure from Smale to convict Pauncefote, a special jury acquitted him by a majority of four to three.[61] The government appealed to the Privy Council. Two years later the Judicial Committee upheld Smale's refusal to allow Kwok to be surrendered to the Chinese government, since the crime took place on a French ship on the high seas. But it ruled there *was* enough evidence to justify his trial in Hong Kong for piracy, a crime justiciable everywhere.[62] MacDonnell again tried unsuccessfully to have Smale removed, claiming he was suffering from a hopeless 'disease of the brain'.[63]

The Kwok Asing case reverberated around the world. Smale was praised in Parliament as an 'honour to his country'. His judgments were also printed for the US Congress: 'some such startling decision', remarked the US Consul in Hong Kong, was needed 'to arouse Western civilization to a sense of its duty concerning this new and infamous slave trade'.[64] In Hong Kong, legislation in 1873 made it illegal to fit out coolie ships or assist the Macao coolie trade. The Chinese authorities blockaded Macao to prevent the trade. Finally, at the end of 1873, the Governor of Macao proclaimed that Chinese emigration from Macao must end within three months. As the *China Mail* later recalled, Smale's actions sounded

---

58. This was one of the first uses of the submarine cable to Hong Kong, opened a few days earlier. Smale held that the Law Officers had been misled by the telegram from Hong Kong, which read 'May Chief Justice be ordered home on leave, and the Pirate brought to Trial?' He suggested that if they thought Kwok was triable for piracy he might be sent to the Old Bailey, since he could not receive a fair trial in Hong Kong, where 'almost every person' had an interest in the Macao coolie trade. Whitfield to Kimberley, 24 June 1871, and Decision re Kwok-a-Sing, 21 June 1871, CO 129/150, 399–402 and 419–435.
59. *HKDP*, 23–26 May 1871; Whitfield to Kimberley, 24 May 1871, CO 129/150, 88–190; HC Deb (23 May 1873) vol. 216 col. 376.
60. Whitfield to Kimberley, 6 and 20 July 1871 and 5 December 1871, CO 129/151, 34–44 and 133–153 and CO 129/153, 153–188.
61. The dissenting jurors were Germans, who, said Pauncefote, 'no doubt thought it safer to obey the directions of the Bench'. *HKDP*, 18–22 July 1871; Pauncefote to Whitfield, 18 July 1871, CO 129/151, 139.
62. *Attorney General v Kwok-a-Sing* [1873] UKPC 58.
63. MacDonnell to Kimberley, 9 January 1872, CO 129/156, 26–62; Wesley-Smith, 'Kwok A-Sing', 129–131.
64. HC Deb (16 February 1872) vol. 209 col. 531; *The Executive Documents Printed by Order of the House of Representatives During the Second Session of the Forty-Second Congress, 1871–'72* (Washington, DC: Government Printing Office, 1872), 194–207 and 215–219.

'the death-knell of the Macao Coolie Traffic'.[65] But it was another case that left a deeper impression on Smale himself: a miscarriage of justice in 1869, in which four innocent men narrowly escaped hanging. The case was still on his mind in 1877, when he referred to it in his letter on legal representation: had the four men been properly defended, he remarked, the full facts would have become clear at once.

In the early hours of Sunday 19 April 1869, a gang of some forty men, armed with spears, landed from a junk near Shau Kei Wan with the aim of plundering shops. Police intercepted them and a fight ensued. Two Indian constables were wounded and an Irish sergeant, James Mahoney, was killed. The government offered a reward of $500 for information. In October Shek Aluk, the master of a junk, and three of his crew were tried for murder before Pauncefote, acting as Chief Justice while Smale was on leave. Hayllar volunteered as defence counsel. The main prosecution witness was a member of the gang, possibly its leader. Two other witnesses claimed to have been on the junk. All three had shared in the reward and, by giving information, avoided prosecution. Despite warnings by Hayllar about the risks of accomplice evidence, much of it contradictory in this case, the jury convicted the four men. Pauncefote condemned them to death. As they were removed they 'set up a most terrible howling, which they kept up after leaving the court building'.[66]

Preoccupied with festivities for a visit by Prince Alfred, Duke of Edinburgh, the Executive Council waited a month before reviewing the death sentences. During that time leaders of the Chinese community petitioned that the men had been falsely accused. The Governor in Council commuted their death sentences to life penal servitude on the ground that it was not known who actually killed Mahoney. Not satisfied with this, the merchant Li Tak-cheong made enquiries and found that the men had been nowhere near the scene of the crime. In January 1870, 'at the request of the Chinese community', Li took the unusual step of engaging Hayllar to prosecute the three witnesses for perjury and conspiracy, along with an ex-policeman who had suborned them. Now back in Hong Kong, Smale sentenced them to prison, praised Li for his efforts, and reproved the investigating officer, Inspector Dennis Daly, for 'extreme carelessness or stupidity' in having so readily believed his informants; Daly later resigned. Shek Aluk and his men were brought from gaol to attend the sentencing of their accusers. They were 'not only not guilty, but innocent – absolutely innocent and peaceable sailors', Smale told them. MacDonnell granted free pardons.[67] He ordered an enquiry by the magistrates and the Registrar General. They con-

65. Ordinances Nos. 3, 5, and 6 of 1873; *CM*, 6 October 1879; Sinn, *Power and Charity*, 103–105; Robert L. Irick, *Ch'ing Policy Toward the Coolie Trade, 1847–1878* (Taipei: Chinese Materials Center, 1982), Chapter 5; Watt Stewart, *Chinese Bondage in Peru: A History of the Chinese Coolie in Peru, 1849–1874* (Westport, Connecticut: Greenwood Press, 1970), Chapter 2.

66. *CM*, 22 and 23 October 1869; *HKDP*, 23 October 1869.

67. *HKDP*, 23 October 1869, 3–10 and 17–18 January 1870; ExCo Minutes, 27 November 1869 and 20 January 1870, CO 131/7, 144–145 and 165–166.

cluded that official rewards and police ineptitude had encouraged false accusations not only in this case but also in another case of murder of a European, in which a suspect was repeatedly remanded for a total of nine months before the Supreme Court discharged him. MacDonnell suppressed the report as 'offensive'.[68]

Smale conducted his own review in an attempt to understand what security there was for innocent men sentenced to 'the irrevocable penalty of death'. He confessed to having 'shuddered' when confronted with this question. He noted that sixty-seven men had been hanged in Hong Kong in the decade since 1860, a figure, he estimated, equal to over half the number in England in the same period.[69] Whereas fifteen judges imposed death sentences in England, Hong Kong had just one criminal judge, who bore 'a responsibility greater I believe than weighs on any other Judge administering English Criminal Law'. Yet there was 'no just ground for alarm'. The Gaol Superintendent, Francis Douglas, had assured him that in nearly every case ending in execution since 1861, the year of Smale's arrival, the criminal had confessed his crime after trial.[70] Still, Smale concluded, the criminal calendar showed such great errors by the police that a searching enquiry was required.[71]

Judicial reform in the 1870s

A commission of enquiry into police and crime, chaired by Thomas Hayllar, reported in 1872. The papers on the Shau Kei Wan murder were among the documents submitted. The commission recommended employing more Chinese police and greater use of the lash, the stocks, and tattooing. It observed that 'the unfitness of our criminal procedure to the circumstances of this Colony' had 'long since passed almost into a proverb'.

> Clumsy, and often wholly illogical in itself, its useful application is only possible among the people to whom it owes its origin. A love of truth and fair play is essential to any race before they can be successfully subjected to it; whilst its formal, rigid rules seem specially framed to favour the escape of guilt among a people famed for subtlety and dissimulation, and to foster grievous conspiracies against the innocent.[72]

In particular, remarked the commission, the English law against examination of the accused aroused among Chinese 'a contempt which often finds expression in the bringing of carefully supported false charges to avenge private quarrels or piques'.

This prompted two changes to criminal procedure. The first was an ordinance to allow judges and magistrates to orally examine the accused and to treat the answers as evidence;

68. Whitfield to Kimberley, 6 March 1871, CO 129/149, 234–297.
69. The actual figure for England was 139.
70. This should be compared with the observation in 1872 by James Legge that he could recall only one pirate under sentence of death who confessed his guilt: see Chapter 3.
71. *HKDP*, 18 and 19 January 1870.
72. Report of the Police Commission, 27 June 1872, CO 129/158, 302.

the accused was not obliged to answer. This drew on the Indian Code of Criminal Procedure (1861) and was urged by Hayllar (who had practised in Bombay) while acting as Attorney General. It was necessary, he said, owing to the 'general untrustworthiness of Chinese witnesses', who regarded perjury 'rather in the light of a duty than as a moral offence'.[73] Examination of the accused was prohibited in English courts at this time. Some American states allowed examination and cross-examination of the accused on oath, but similar reforms were not enacted in England until 1898 (1906 in Hong Kong).[74] Smale opposed Hayllar's measure because it departed from English practice and used terms such as 'interrogate', which implied a form of 'Star Chamber questioning'. He also rejected Hayllar's assertions about the untrustworthiness of Chinese witnesses. The Secretary of State, however, endorsed the provision, believing it would provide a direct method of arriving at the truth, especially for the innocent.[75]

The second change reorganized the jurisdiction of magistrates. Although most magistrates in early colonial Hong Kong had no legal qualifications, they had greater powers than those exercised by stipendiary magistrates in England. From 1862 a Hong Kong magistrate could summarily try any offence punishable by imprisonment, fine or whipping (but not penal servitude, which was usually for a minimum of three years), and could impose up to six months' imprisonment, a fine of $50, and, for males, two canings of up to thirty-six blows each. Defendants had no right to opt for trial by jury, but the magistrate could commit them to the Supreme Court if an indictable offence required a heavier sentence.[76]

In 1875 the discovery of defects in the legislation prompted the drafting of a new magistrates ordinance. The government proposed to allow magistrates to try summarily any indictable offence not punishable by death or life penal servitude; their sentencing powers were to stay the same, and they were to continue to be able to send cases to the Supreme Court. The Attorney General cited problems with Chinese evidence and the hardships of transients and poorer people who had to wait about the Supreme Court for trial. Since magistrates were closely watched, any 'serious want of discretion' would be corrected. The judges, Smale and Snowden, opposed this sweeping change. A compromise was reached in the form of a list of offences reserved for trial in the Supreme Court: this included offences

73. Hayllar, report on Ordinance No. 3 of 1872, 8 April 1872, CO 129/157, 361–366.

74. Bentley, *English Criminal Justice in the Nineteenth Century*, Chapter 16.

75. Re-enacted in 1873 to bring it more into line with the Indian Code, it was not widely used. In a private prosecution for criminal libel in 1889, J.J. Francis objected to its use by Acting Chief Justice Fielding Clarke, saying it had never been used before; Clarke overruled him. Clarke used the provision again in 1895 to examine a boatman and his wife accused of murdering a Norwegian sailor; defended by Ho Kai, the two were acquitted. The provision was repealed in 1912 as being inconsistent with the 1906 legislation allowing the accused to testify. Ordinances Nos. 3 of 1872 and 18 of 1873; MacDonnell to Kimberley, 11 April 1872, and Kennedy to Kimberley, 26 April 1872, 420–437, CO 129/157, 353–372; Smale to Holland, CO 129/161, 488–495; *HKDP*, 10 December 1873 and 21 November 1895; *CM*, 21 October 1889.

76. Ordinance No. 6 of 1862.

punishable by death or life penal servitude (except burglary), perjury, defamation, bigamy, blasphemy, bribery, arson, and forgery. The long-term effect was a large decline in the Supreme Court's criminal caseload.[77]

The Supreme Court itself saw important changes during this decade. In 1873 the Court of Summary Jurisdiction was abolished and a judge added to the Supreme Court, which now consisted of the Chief Justice and a Puisne Judge. The Judge of the Court of Summary Jurisdiction, Henry Ball (who had presided over the piracy trials in Chapter 2), laid claim to the new position. However, he suffered epileptic fits on the bench. A memorial from colonists objected to his sitting in the Supreme Court and he was pensioned off under protest. Pauncefote became Puisne Judge instead.[78] Almost immediately, he was promoted to Chief Justice of the Leeward Islands[79] and was succeeded by Francis Snowden, who arrived in May 1874. Sitting together as the 'Full Court', the two judges could hear appeals from any decision by one judge in civil cases. Although there was no right of appeal in criminal cases, a judge could reserve a question of law in a criminal trial for the Full Court.[80] The second judge also enabled two courts to operate in parallel in the monthly criminal sessions.

A further reform was the use of special juries in some criminal trials. As in England, a minority of jurors, usually leading merchants, were designated 'special jurors' by virtue of their status and knowledge. Juries made up entirely of special jurors were used in civil trials in England involving commercial issues or matters of honour. But, although special jurors were individually liable to serve on common juries, special juries were not used in criminal trials. In early colonial Hong Kong, except for the decade 1851–1860, special jurors were

77. The change had no immediate impact on the Supreme Court's criminal caseload, which increased in the late 1870s after Hennessy's insistence that prisoners should receive sentences proportionate to their crimes rather than be given short sentences in the Magistracy, then tattooed and deported. However, two later changes contributed to a decline in criminal defendants before the Supreme Court, from over 200 in 1879 to an average of 134 in 1886–1890, and 44 in 1891–1895, despite an increase in population from 139,144 in 1876 to 253,514 in 1895. The first was a policy from the mid-1880s of prosecuting repeat offenders under the Larceny Ordinance in the Magistracy, where they received short prison sentences, followed by deportation, instead of committing them to the Supreme Court with the prospect of a heavier sentence. The second was an increase in magistrates' sentencing powers in 1890 to a maximum of twelve months' imprisonment and a $200 fine: this was reduced to six months and $100 in 1895 after objections from the Chief Justice. Kennedy to Carnarvon, 29 November 1875, CO 129/171, 582–593; *HKGG*, 20 November 1875; *HKDP*, 24 November 1875; Ordinance No. 16 of 1875; Order by the Governor, 6 June 1885, and Acting Colonial Secretary to Wodehouse, Police Magistrate, 22 August 1885, Correspondence Relative to the Magistrates Court, Police and Prisons, January–December 1885, HKPRO HKRS101-1-4-7, 69, 181; Ordinances Nos. 10 of 1890 and 12 of 1895.
78. Kennedy to Kimberley, 3 July 1873, CO 129/164, 19–26 and 73–87.
79. He went on to an outstanding official career, ending it as Britain's first Ambassador to the US.
80. One early instance arose out of the *Spark* piracy case of 1874 (see Chapter 3). Counsel for the accused, Alfred Handley, objected that the piracy and murder with which his client was charged had taken place in waters under Chinese jurisdiction. Smale asked Snowden to join him for a hearing before the Full Court. They overruled the objection on the ground that murder on a British ship came within the jurisdiction of the Supreme Court. *HKDP*, 30 September 1874.

exempted from serving on common juries.[81] As a result, they were rarely called for jury service at all.[82] Legislation in 1872 allowed any criminal case to be tried by a special jury at the request of the Attorney General, the accused, or the judge. A similar option existed in Ceylon and, for capital trials of 'European British subjects', in British India.[83] Again, the impetus came from Hayllar. His reason was striking:

> In the mixed European Community of this Colony, it not infrequently happens that out of the Common Jury placed in the box not more than one or two understand the English language sufficiently to follow the evidence, the arguments of Counsel and the summing up of the Judge, otherwise than imperfectly, and I have more than once known the whole Jury to consist of foreigners, Portuguese, Germans and so forth.[84]

In 'ordinary unimportant trials' such juries were generally able to catch the meaning of the judge and be guided by him. But they were 'trials by Judge and *Jury* only in name'. From time to time it was 'absolutely essential to the ends of Justice that the Crown or the Prisoner should have the privilege of resort to a more intelligent and independent tribunal', particularly in cases of life and death. Following this reform, special juries tried over a third of the sixty capital cases from 1872 to 1900, often where the accused or victim was non-Chinese.

The special jury lists at this time had a proportionately greater number of Chinese compared with common jury lists. In the 1880s Chinese jurors began to appear on some special juries in murder trials. The first was Fung Tang, comprador of the Oriental Bank, who served on a special jury in 1884 that acquitted two men accused on flimsy evidence. The others were Chau Ping, manager of the Yuen Fat Hong, a large trading firm, and Fung Wa-chuen, comprador of the National Bank of China. The first Chinese to serve on a common jury in a murder trial was Chow Dart-tong, a merchant, in 1889: that jury found the chair coolie Choi Akow guilty of the manslaughter of another chair coolie during a fight in Shelley Street, a verdict described as 'lenient' by the judge, Fielding Clarke: Choi had walked away from the fight and returned with a knife.[85]

Legal aid in murder trials

The first criminal trials by special jury, in November 1872, also led to the provision of legal aid in murder trials. In the first, a soldier, Edward Jones, was charged with the murder of another soldier. Jones pleaded guilty, but when William Drummond, a young barrister, offered to defend him gratis, he changed his plea to not guilty. A solicitor, William Brereton, volunteered to assist him. The Acting Chief Justice, Pauncefote, gave them several days

81. Bonham to Grey, 10 September 1851, CO 129/37, 267–277; Ordinances Nos. 4 of 1851 and 2 of 1860.
82. Special juries were used in two or three civil trials per annum at this time.
83. Ordinance No. 8 of 1872; Ordinance No. 20 of 1871 (Ceylon); Act No. XIII of 1865 (India) s. 11.
84. Report by Hayllar on Ordinance No. 8 of 1872, 2 August 1872, CO 129/158, 413–414.
85. Clarke sentenced Choi to ten years' imprisonment with hard labour. *CM*, 19 October 1889.

to prepare. Drummond conducted a detailed defence, calling other soldiers, physicians, and gaol staff to show that Jones was of unsound mind. After a three-day trial, the special jury found Jones not guilty by reason of insanity. Pauncefote ordered that he be detained pending Her Majesty's pleasure.[86]

The second trial, also by a special jury, took place the next day. Lee Alai, a 'street coolie', was accused of stabbing to death his lover, Lum Sui-wan, after quarrelling with her outside the house where he lodged. Again, Drummond offered to defend gratis. But this time no solicitor came forward. The prosecution relied on a dying declaration from Lum, accusing one 'Achun' (Lee's alias), and on evidence from Lee's landlady, who had seen the fight but not the stabbing. Unable to confer with Lee, and with no solicitor to find evidence, Drummond could only point out defects in the prosecution's case: the lack of proof of the weapon used, the identification of Lee by only one witness, and the assumption that 'Achun' was the same man as Lee. Seeing that two jurors had served in the last case, he asked what chance Jones would have stood had he been similarly handicapped. He now had 'to defend the man's life before them absolutely without a fragment of paper, or anything to go upon more than the prosecution itself'. The jury convicted Lee of murder. Asked if he had anything to say before sentence, Lee 'was understood to say that if he had defended himself the result would have been different'.[87]

Drummond's efforts did not go unnoticed. The Governor, Sir Arthur Kennedy, recalled that it was the custom in colonies where he had served for the government to pay a fee of five guineas to counsel assigned by judges to defend prisoners in capital cases. Similar ideas had been mooted in Hong Kong as early as 1845. In the *Herald* case of 1852 Governor Bonham had engaged the attorney, William Gaskell, to defend two Javanese in their trial for the murder of a British ship's mate.[88] Kennedy and his council now resolved that counsel should be assigned to the accused in all murder cases and that the government should pay a fixed fee of $25 for the service.[89]

After returning from leave in November 1872, Smale stretched this policy to include solicitors as well as barristers.[90] This produced mixed results for some defendants. In July

86. Jones was shipped to England and held in Broadmoor. *HKDP*, 5–7 November 1872.

87. The *Mail* gave a different version of Lee's allocutus: 'he would not die happy, not being satisfied with the verdict, as the woman was his mistress, and if he did not kill her, she would have killed him.' Lee was hanged on 17 November. *HKDP*, 8 November 1872, *OCM*, 14 November 1872.

88. See Chapter 3.

89. Roughly equivalent to five guineas. ExCo Minutes, 30 November 1872, CO 131/8, 189. Kennedy had served in The Gambia, Sierra Leone, Western Australia, and Vancouver Island.

90. In 1873 some legislators called for fusion of the legal profession, following the practice in many other colonies and attempted in Hong Kong from 1858 to 1864. The Governor, Kennedy, refused to allow complete fusion but legislation was enacted to permit barristers to hold consultations and take fees from clients without the intervention of a solicitor, and to appear in criminal (but not civil) trials without the assistance of a solicitor. The provision was repealed in 1925. *HKDP*, 21 August 1873; Kennedy to Kimberley, 14 October 1873, CO

1873 Ahmet, a Malay seaman, was tried for the murder of a Malay boatswain on a British ship some 1,000 miles east of the Philippines. The barrister Henry Kingsmill appeared in court to defend him, but Smale objected to his acting without a solicitor. Smale felt so strongly that he paid for a solicitor himself and adjourned the case. Ahmet then confessed to the murder to the solicitor, Matthew Stephens. His confession, the only clear evidence against him, was read out in court. He was convicted and hanged.[91] In 1875, six men and two women were tried for piracy and murder of the wife and sons of the master of a junk near Aberdeen. The women, defended by Alfred Handley, instructed by Henry Dennys, were acquitted. The men were defended by Kingsmill, instructed by the firm Caldwell and Brereton. Three were convicted. When the Executive Council reviewed the case it learned that two had alibis not raised at trial: their solicitors had never bothered to ask them. The police confirmed the alibis and the men were pardoned.[92] The Full Court censured Brereton for a 'technical' contempt of court.[93]

Fees were fixed in 1879 at $50 to counsel and $25 to the solicitor for defending, at public expense, persons tried for murder in the Supreme Court. For a few years, solicitors were also paid a fee for representing defendants on murder charges in committal proceedings before a magistrate.[94] Conviction rates were, of course, affected by other factors than a 'well got up' defence. But, along with a shift in the nature of capital crimes from piracies to street quarrels and domestic disputes, the change resulted in palpable improvements to justice. Prosecutions were more carefully prepared. Defences consisted not just of picking away at the prosecution's case but also of alibis and other evidence by witnesses for the defence. The conviction rate for the seventy-four persons tried for murder in the twenty years from 1878 was 31 per cent (42 per cent including manslaughter verdicts), compared with conviction rates of over 70 per cent in the decade 1868–1877, and over 60 per cent in 1858–1867.

In late 1897, possibly for financial reasons, the courts reverted to the original scheme of 1872, with payment of $25 to counsel only. For the next seven years counsel in murder trials usually appeared without solicitors. The conviction rate for those years rose to 87 per cent. From 1905, the practice of assigning a solicitor as well as counsel was largely resumed, probably on the initiative of the new Chief Justice, Sir Francis Piggott.[95] During his seven-year term the conviction rate for murder fell to 40 per cent: six of the thirty-eight acquittals

---

129/165, 170–177; Ordinance No. 15 of 1873; Peter Wesley-Smith, 'Nineteenth-Century Fusion of the Legal Profession in Hong Kong', *HKLJ*, Vol. 22 (1992): 257–268.

91. *HKDP*, 23 and 25 July 1873; Snowden to Price, 12 July 1878, CO 129/181, 405; ExCo Minutes, 31 July 1873, CO 131/8, 299.
92. *HKDP*, 22, 25, and 26 October 1875; ExCo Minutes, 14 and 27 November 1875, CO 131/9, 209–214 and 217–220.
93. *HKDP*, 16 and 25 November 1875; *OCM*, 25 November 1875.
94. Norton-Kyshe, *History*, Vol. II, 271.
95. The power to grant legal aid in capital trials was formalized by rules 32–34 of the Criminal Appeal Rules, 1933.

were the result of appeals on legal points to the Full Court. The swings in conviction rates underline the importance of full legal representation. While no doubt some defendants with legal aid were acquitted on technicalities, the swings also suggest that police were bringing many innocent people to trial, while the culprits evaded justice.

Better representation was made possible by the growth of the legal profession. In the last thirty years of the nineteenth century over seventy-five solicitors and barristers were admitted in Hong Kong. Most qualified in England and were abreast of the latest practices in the London courts.[96] Several barristers had university degrees. Some moved to richer pickings in the British Supreme Court in Shanghai, which took over the extraterritorial functions of Hong Kong's Supreme Court in 1865: William Drummond, the barrister who helped initiate legal aid in Hong Kong, moved there in 1874 and became the counsel of choice for wealthy Chinese.[97] Other barristers, such as J.J. Francis, Marcus Slade, and Ernest Sharp, forged successful careers in Hong Kong.

The late nineteenth century saw the admission of three Chinese barristers. The first, Ng Choy, admitted in 1877, left in 1882 for a career in the Qing government.[98] His brother-in-law, Ho Kai, represented fifty-one defendants in twenty-one murder trials during the thirty years following his admission in 1882: thirty-one were acquitted; five were convicted of manslaughter. Ho was Hong Kong born and British educated, a physician, a barrister, and a Legislative Councillor. His forensic technique relied on detailed cross-examination of witnesses, credible alibis, and dogged pursuit of legal points, resulting in the first murder convictions to be quashed by the Full Court, in 1908.[99] His demolition of prosecution evidence was sometimes so complete that juries declared they wished to acquit without hearing the defence – a contrast to the rush to convict by some earlier juries.[100]

Ho Kai's fluency in English and Chinese enabled him to surmount language barriers. For others, the appointment of the Chinese scholar James Dyer Ball as assistant interpreter in 1878 and interpreter in 1881 raised hopes that the Supreme Court would 'become

96. Five solicitors did their articles and examinations in Hong Kong.

97. Andrew Hillier and Christopher Munn, 'China's Able Advocate: The Controversial Career of William Venn Drummond', *Journal of the Royal Asiatic Society Hong Kong*, Vol. 61 (2021): 122–149.

98. Ng Choy (Wu Tingfang) defended four men in two murder trials: Chung Awing, accused in 1878 of murdering his wife and found unfit to plead on the ground of insanity; and three sailors convicted of the *Kate Waters* murder (1879). The third Chinese barrister, Wei Pui, son of the comprador Wei Akwong and brother of the Legislative Councillor Wei Yuk, was admitted in 1888 but was not active in the courts.

99. Three men, on accomplice evidence and a confession obtained during the course of a search without warrant, were convicted of murdering two men and a boy in a robbery near Sha Tin. They were defended by Ho Kai and Marcus Slade. Against warnings by the Attorney General, Rees-Davis, about interfering with a verdict properly arrived at by a jury, the Full Court (Piggott and Gompertz) ruled the confession inadmissible. *R v Wong Chiu Kwai* (1908) 3 HKLR 89; *HKWP*, 25 and 30 May and 8, 13 and 27 June 1908.

100. Ho Kai also frequently took on prosecution briefs for non-capital crimes, with similar success.

something more than "a Babel of tongues".'[101] His promotion followed the death of Rafael Rozario, whose failings had long caused concern. Snowden observed that he could neither write English correctly nor read Chinese properly: 'it was often necessary for the judge almost to conjecture the meaning of the English into which he transferred the evidence of a Chinese witness'. Complaints in 1869 about his 'inattention to Chinese suitors' led to a reprimand. In 1880 Eitel discovered that Rozario had been incorrectly interpreting legal terms, for example by telling prisoners sentenced to penal servitude they had been sentenced to deportation. There were other great complaints, recalled Snowden, 'but he did his best; and his retirement was looked forward to as the only remedy'.[102] In contrast, Dyer Ball, master of half a dozen Chinese dialects, was described as indispensable. He served as interpreter until his retirement in 1909.

The virtual abolition of capital punishment

Low conviction rates led to a pause in hangings. Only one person was executed between 1880 and 1892: Tika Ram, an Indian soldier, hanged in 1882 for the murder of Lachmi, an eleven-year-old girl whose family had refused him permission to marry her.[103] Hangings resumed in August 1893 with the execution of Li Ayau for the murder of another eleven-year-old girl, Chan Chun, after her mother, his lover, had left him. The Governor, Sir William Robinson, attributed the long hiatus to a decline in crime.[104] This is doubtful. In 1883–1892 the police arrested over fifty persons for murder. The Supreme Court tried thirty-five. Three were convicted of murder and four of manslaughter. The death sentences on the three convicted men divided the Executive Council. The first two, for a fatal robbery in 1888, were commuted to life imprisonment by Frederick Stewart, Acting Governor, against objections from two of the six members. His reasons were that it was not known who fired the fatal shot and that identification relied solely on evidence from a twelve-year-old boy.[105] The third was commuted in 1891 to twenty years' imprisonment by Governor Des Voeux against majority advice, following a petition that the motive was revenge against a man who had seduced the prisoner's wife. Des Voeux said he knew of 'no special danger likely to accrue to the people of Hong Kong from the commutation'.[106]

Some did not share these sanguine attitudes. The idea that 'a hanging would do good to the colony' gained currency. The *China Mail* was appalled by the commutations in 1888.

---

101. *CM*, 11 February 1879.
102. Snowden to Stewart, 9 June 1881, CO 129/193, 271–276; ExCo Minutes, 13 January and 21 October 1869, CO 131/7, 134–135 and 141; *HKGG*, 17 July 1880; *OCM*, 9 and 23 June 1881.
103. *CM*, 22 June and 5 July 1882 and 21 and 22 July and 8 August 1893.
104. *HKH*, 4 December 1893.
105. Stewart to Knutsford, 17 December 1888, CO 129/239, 420–447.
106. ExCo Minutes, 3 January 1891, CO 131/20, 4–5; *CM*, 23 December 1890.

They could have only one result: 'the encouragement of robbery and murder'. And since 'life' meant only ten or twelve years, the men, brutalized by their treatment in gaol, 'will be thrown out on the world ready to recommence their career of crime'. The *Hongkong Telegraph*, founded in 1881 by Robert Fraser-Smith, a supporter of Hennessy, ridiculed the *Mail* for its dismay at being deprived of a 'hanging match'. Although, as partners in a felony, the men were guilty of murder, it was now usual practice in England to hang only those who actually did the killing, it said.[107] As for the commutation in 1891, the *Mail* could only assume it was because 1891 was Hong Kong's jubilee year.[108] When executions resumed in 1893, the *Mail* complained that the condemned man, Li Ayau, should have been hanged in the Chinese Recreation Ground in Taipingshan, not in the gaol, with only officials and reporters present. This was Hong Kong's first private execution. The hangman, Emin Deen, an Indian turnkey, had himself been acquitted of murder only a year before.[109]

Various explanations were put forward for the low conviction rates and the failure to do justice for victims. The police blamed the reluctance of Chinese witnesses to come forward. In 1886 the Chief Justice, Sir George Phillippo, echoed this criticism after an acquittal for murder, the eleventh in a succession of acquittals or manslaughter verdicts: 'If the friends or neighbours are not satisfied they must learn that it is their fault.'[110] Those who did come forward were often treated with distrust. Earlier in 1886 a juror in a perjury trial had declared that 'he had no confidence in Chinese evidence and consequently he would hold it as of no value whatever'. All those dealing with Chinese witnesses had to take that into account, said Phillippo, and 'must just do their best'.[111] Some said that inconsistencies were to be expected, given that different interpreters translated the same evidence at the Coroner's, Magistrate's, and Supreme Courts.[112] Others pointed to false accusations, witness tampering (especially by the Triad Society), a tendency to embellish the truth, and different ideas of reality and time. 'If you ask a witness whether he is certain of such and such a thing, he may reply that he is seven-tenths certain,' recalled Sir William Goodman, Attorney General 1889–1902, and Chief Justice 1902–1905. 'A counsel in England,' he wrote 'would be surprised to receive such an answer as "the time it would take to drink a cup of tea."'[113]

107. *CM*, 10 December 1888; *HKT*, 10 December 1888.

108. *OCM*, 8 January 1891.

109. The victim was Ram Sammy, an Indian watchman at the China Sugar Refinery. Emin Deen was tried by a special jury and defended by J.J. Francis. *OCM*, 17 August 1893; *CM*, 2–5 August 1892 and 8 August 1893.

110. *OCM*, 28 December 1886.

111. The juror was David Knox Griffiths, a photographer whose scenes of Chinese life were widely circulated. *CM*, 23 August 1886.

112. This was the view of Smale and of two Captain-Superintendents of Police. *OCM*, 7 December 1876; Deane to Stewart, 12 May 1886, CO 129/227, 100; Report by May, 13 June 1893, CO 129/264, 471.

113. Goodman, *Reminiscences*, 98–99.

Poor comprehension of English among jurors continued to be a problem. Few understood Chinese either, 'and if they do sit too far off to hear all the witnesses say,' said the Captain-Superintendent of Police, F.H. May.[114] Added to this were suspicions by officials that some jurors, especially Portuguese jurors, were opposed to capital punishment. Other reasons were more curious. Some early jurors, trying several cases in the same sessions, were unwilling to have the death of more than one defendant on their consciences.[115] In a trial in 1898 of a man whose wife's body was found in a trunk in a boarding house, Goodman, who had prosecuted the case, shared the 'blank astonishment of everyone, including the prisoner' at the verdict of not guilty. He learned later that two special jurors in the case had been tried for manslaughter years before: 'the anxiety they had undergone had made them unwilling to find a fellow creature guilty of murder.'[116]

With concerns about miscarriages of justice, and misgivings about the death penalty among some jurors, the easiest course was acquittal, which from 1887 required unanimity in capital cases, or a verdict of manslaughter, which did not. In an editorial in 1889 entitled 'The Virtual Abolition of Capital Punishment', the *Mail* criticized 'an unfortunate tendency' by juries to look on 'the murdering of one coolie by another as a trivial matter':

> We can never teach Chinese coolies the sacredness of human life, on which the very foundation of human society is laid, until we show our own regard for it in the acts of our Courts of justice. If we adopt the Chinese standard and look upon the life of a coolie as something for which a $50 note is equivalent, we cannot expect the coolie himself to have a much higher notion of human life, and he may quite as readily show his estimation thereof by murdering a European on slight provocation as by murdering one of his own class.[117]

A case the previous year prompted comparable comments in a petition claiming to be from 'the Chinese community of Hong Kong'. A man was killed in a gang fight in Tank Lane over non-payment of hush money by a gambling den to an informer, leading to a police raid. Three of the informer's gang were tried and acquitted of his murder by a special jury. The

---

114. Report by May, 13 June 1893, CO 129/264, 470–473.

115. Protest by John Smale, Attorney General, 28 May 1863, against the confirmation (later reversed) of the death sentence on Charles Adams, a sailor convicted of the murder of John Adams, chief mate of the *Beatrice*, despite a recommendation to mercy by the jury. ExCo Minutes, 3 June 1863, CO 131/5, 79–83.

116. One of them was David Gillies, a British employee of the Hongkong and Whampoa Dock Company. One evening in 1876, during the undocking of a rubbish boat at Aberdeen Docks, he slapped some of the coolies for not working fast enough. One of them, Low Aleong, fell down. Gillies kicked him twice in the abdomen, rupturing his spleen. Four coolies gave consistent evidence at the inquest, committal, and trial. But counsel for Gillies, Alfred Handley, argued that they must have concocted the evidence, since 'no Englishman would do such a thing'. Smale said he 'trembled for the cause of justice in this colony' if after four witnesses had given testimony 'beyond all power of impeachment', nothing had been adduced. The special jury acquitted Gillies. Goodman, *Reminiscences*, 170–171; *OCM*, 7 December 1876.

117. *OCM*, 30 October 1889.

petitioners complained that counsel for the defence, J.J. Francis, had 'deferred the grievance of the people to his own pocket'. The judge had connived at this and set the murderer free, they said. If such a crime went unpunished, Hong Kong, with its myriad Chinese residents, would 'descend into chaos'. The petition asked for the culprit to be rearrested and executed 'to secure peace to Hong Kong'.[118]

Female adultery and male jealousy

Cheung Ashiu, the Shek O murderer, was released from his life sentence in 1888 following a petition from villagers. He was placed under police supervision for five years under the Prevention of Crimes Ordinance.[119] Enacted in 1887, the ordinance was one of several measures designed to ease pressure on prison accommodation. Among the others were an increase in offences punishable by flogging, greater use of deportation, and a new policy of reviewing life sentences after fifteen years (ten for those over sixty).[120]

As Cheung's and other cases in this chapter show, many murder victims in the late nineteenth century were women, or children, or male love rivals. This shift towards domestic murders reflected a growth in family life. It also aligned homicide patterns more closely with those in settled communities. Hong Kong offered opportunities for enterprising women.[121] But for many it was a place of danger and exploitation. As a port city where men far outnumbered women, Hong Kong had a thriving sex industry. It also served as an entrepôt for women and girls trafficked into prostitution overseas. A system of licensed brothels and compulsory inspections, aimed at protecting the health of British servicemen, was enacted in 1857 and reinforced by MacDonnell's Contagious Diseases Ordinance of 1867: an enquiry in 1877 exposed shameful abuses.[122] Some self-styled 'experts', such as J.J. Francis (quoting the magistrate Charles May and a Chinese doctor) believed that five-sixths of all Chinese women in Hong Kong 'come under the denomination of prostitutes to whom money being offered they would consent to sexual intercourse'.[123] Such attitudes

118. The judge, Acting Chief Justice Russell, had, in fact, rebuked the jury for insisting they had made up their minds to acquit all three of murder before the defence opened. Petition on the Tank Lane Murder Case, June 1888: Correspondence Relative to the Magistrates Court, Police and Prisons, April–December 1888, HKPRO, HKRS101-1-4-10, 465–475; *CM*, 21–23 June 1888; *HKDP*, 22 and 23 June 1888.
119. Ordinance No. 11 of 1887, modelled on English acts.
120. ExCo Minutes, 16 November 1888, CO 131/20, 78.
121. See Carl T. Smith, 'Ng Akew, One of Hong Kong's "Protected Women"', *Chung Chi Bulletin*, Vol. 46 (1969): 13–27; and Elizabeth Sinn, 'Women at Work: Chinese Brothel Keepers in Nineteenth-Century Hong Kong', *Journal of Women's History*, Vol. 19, No. 3 (Fall 2007): 87–111.
122. *Report of the Commissioners to Enquire into the Working of the Contagious Diseases Ordinance, 1867* (Hong Kong: Noronha & Sons, 1879).
123. J.J. Francis, Memorandum on the subject of Slavery in Hong Kong, *Correspondence Respecting the Alleged Existence of Chinese Slavery in Hong Kong* (London: Eyre and Spottiswoode, 1882), 102.

help explain the alleged behaviour of Baird, the defence adopted by Francis, and the interjection by Rozario in the rape case which opened this chapter.

Francis's assertion came in a debate triggered by Chief Justice Smale over the status of *mui tsai* – Chinese girls sold by poor families to wealthy families, to be brought up as adopted daughters and married off when they came of age. In China this was sometimes an alternative to infanticide. In Hong Kong it degenerated into trafficking, kidnapping, and other abuses. In a kidnapping case in 1879, Smale ruled that the *mui tsai* system, even in its most benign forms, was slavery and thus illegal. He attempted to *direct* the Attorney General to prosecute two other persons who had purchased the kidnapped girl some years earlier. Smale's campaign, with its echoes of his earlier crusade against the coolie trade, brought him accolades in Britain. But this time his attempt to force change from the bench was less successful. The Chinese elite mounted a vigorous counter-campaign. They opposed any attempt to abolish the *mui tsai* system and proposed the formation of a Chinese-run society to combat kidnapping and other evils. The society – the Po Leung Kuk – was established in 1880 with legal assistance from Francis. The *mui tsai* system continued to be tolerated until its abolition in the twentieth century.[124]

Officials also took a lenient approach towards patriarchal responses to adultery. In Chinese law, if a man killed both his wife and her paramour *in flagrante delicto* he was immune from punishment.[125] In the villages of Guangdong Province adulterous women and their paramours were traditionally trussed up in pig cages and drowned. In English law, loss of control on discovery of infidelity might reduce a murder to manslaughter.[126] Some men in Hong Kong saw it as their right to kill unfaithful or deserting partners. Police found that witnesses were even more reluctant than usual to assist in such cases. In 1893, for example, Chim Pui, a villager from Ma Tau Wai, slit his wife's throat after accusing her of adultery. He escaped to Chinese territory, where the authorities released him after a flogging. 'As a matter of fact,' the Hong Kong police report observed, 'the wife having been notoriously unfaithful, the sympathies of her countrymen were with her murderer.'[127]

Ma Tau Wai, on the fringes of British Kowloon, appears to have been a hotspot for adultery. In 1874, four men from the village were convicted of murdering a man during a fight. A special jury recommended mercy because there had been no apparent premeditation. When Smale sentenced them to death the prisoners went down on their knees crying

---

124. John M. Carroll, 'A National Custom: Debating Female Servitude in Late Nineteenth-Century Hong Kong', *Modern Asian Studies*, Vol. 43, No. 6 (2009): 1463–1493.
125. William C. Jones, trans., *The Great Qing Code*, article 285 (Oxford: Clarendon Press, 1994), 271; Marinus Johan Meijer, *Murder and Adultery in Late Imperial China: A Study of Law and Morality* (Leiden: Brill, 1991).
126. The defence originally applied only if a husband killed the male paramour. In the nineteenth century it was extended to the killing of an adulterous wife: see K.J. Kesselring, 'No Greater Provocation? Adultery and the Mitigation of Murder in English Law', *Law and History Review*, Vol. 34, No. 1 (2016): 199–225.
127. Report of the Captain Superintendent of Police for 1893, *HKSP*, 2/94.

for mercy and clinging to the rails of the dock. Spectators took up the cry, and the court was in uproar. Later that month a fifth man, the village headman, was convicted of taking part in the same murder, again with a recommendation to mercy. During his trial it came out that the victim had been seeing a woman in the village whose husband was away in Siam. Governor Kennedy commuted all five death sentences to life penal servitude. Then, just before his departure in 1877, he pardoned the men after consulting Smale. They were brought before the court to receive a homily from Smale. 'Their conduct had been actuated probably not by wickedness, but by a wish to protect the morals of their village,' he said. The Governor had therefore been merciful. He hoped they would return to their village and that 'now all things would go right with them'.[128]

But things did not go right. Within a few months, four more Ma Tau Wai villagers were tried for false imprisonment and assault, having seized and beaten another man they accused of adultery with a village woman whose husband was in California. They tied up the two lovers and demanded money as reparation. After they were found guilty their counsel, J.J. Francis, addressed the court in mitigation. They had acted strictly according to Chinese custom, he said. Knowing nothing of English law, they had supposed that their customs had been allowed to continue after Kowloon was ceded to Britain seventeen years earlier. He cited Elliot's 1841 proclamation promising Chinese residents full protection of their customs. He even argued there was 'sufficiently grave doubt' over whether the custom they had followed had ever been forbidden by Hong Kong law.

Smale would hear none of this. Such practices 'must be put down, and put down with a strong hand, or we had better close the courts of justice, better have no police but let the strongest do as he will'. He pointed to another custom, the custom for men 'to leave their wives for years and to go and get wives elsewhere, and leave the poor wretches here half starving in miserable plight, in a state which is contrary to their contract, and then come down upon them with the penalty of death if they on their part sink to the immorality of their husbands'. It had been 'mistaken leniency' to have pardoned the Ma Tau Wai murderers, he said, and folly on his part to have advised it. He sentenced the villagers to three years' penal servitude. On their removal from the dock 'a loud lamentation was set up by several women, apparently the prisoners' wives'.[129]

In 1873, and again in 1883, the Committee of the Tung Wah Hospital requested a law to prohibit adultery, pointing out that the British had passed such laws in India. Behaving 'as if they were a bench of magistrates', the committee often handled marital disputes. When Governor Kennedy demurred, they reminded him that the Bible also prohibited adultery. It was 'almost intolerable' that the Chinese should lecture the Governor 'upon the

128. *HKDP*, 1, 4 and 24 April 1874 and 17 March 1877.
129. *CM*, 23 July 1877; *HKDP*, 24 and 25 July 1877.

inferiority of himself and the nation he represents,' said the *Daily Press*.[130] But in 1903 the government made it illegal to knowingly receive or harbour any Chinese woman who had left her husband. The law was expanded in the form of the 'Chinese Marriage Preservation Ordinance 1912', which prescribed fines of up to \$500 for adultery (or six months' imprisonment in default) for the wife and her paramour, who was also liable to pay up to \$500 in reparation. The change of mind was prompted by the addition of the New Territories to Hong Kong. Rural leaders there complained that wives were now deserting their husbands upon their 'newly discovered immunity from the consequences which under Chinese rule would have followed such action'. The adultery law was applied to urban as well as rural Hong Kong. Over the next fifty years it was used by husbands against wives pursuing clandestine affairs in boarding houses and cinemas. Fines were often at the maximum limit. A few offenders went to prison.[131]

Sexual jealousy was not confined to Chinese men. In September 1879 Governor Hennessy discovered Thomas Hayllar and Lady Hennessy going through 'indecent prints' of classical statues in her boudoir at Mountain Lodge, the Governor's house on the Peak. The two men had been friends and allies: Hennessy had appointed Hayllar to the Legislative Council and to chair the enquiry into the contagious diseases ordinance; he had even recommended him to succeed Smale as Chief Justice. Now Hayllar and his wife were banished from Government House. Later, in a chance meeting near Mountain Lodge in 1881, Hennessy allegedly set about Hayllar with an umbrella in an 'insane and violent' attack. When rumours spread about the incident, Hennessy instructed his private secretary, E.J. Eitel, to show a dossier on the dispute to any Legislative Councillor who was interested. Eitel went about this with too much enthusiasm. Hayllar took out an action for slander, which he eventually withdrew after letters of apology from Eitel and Hennessy. The quarrel was probably the cause of Hayllar's departure in 1882. It also contributed to the home government's decision to withdraw Hennessy from Hong Kong later that year.[132]

---

130. *HKDP*, 9 January and 15 and 19 May 1873; Marsh to Kimberley, 20 June 1882 and Bowen to Derby, 6 August 1883, CO 129/201, 359–384 and CO 129/201, 62-77; Sinn, *Power and Charity*, 91–92.

131. The penalties for desertion by a wife under Qing law ranged from a hundred blows to strangulation, usually reduced to penal servitude. The penal provisions in Hong Kong were repealed in 1939, but the right to damages was retained. Proceedings could only be instituted at the instance of the aggrieved husband. A few prosecutions were brought under the ordinance in the 1950s, usually without success. As late as 1965 the Heung Yee Kuk, the representative body of New Territories villagers, called for the limit on damages to be raised from \$500 to \$50,000. The law was repealed in 1970. Ordinances Nos. 19 of 1903, 28 of 1910, and 42 of 1912. May to Lyttelton, 27 November 1903, CO 129/320, 100–106; May to Lyttelton, 30 January 1905, CO 129/328, 110–112; *HKH*, 1 September 1939; *SCMP*, 18 August 1965.

132. Pope-Hennessy, *Verandah*, 213–228; MacKeown, *Stormy Petrel*, 238–241, 262–264.

5

Death of a Reformer

The Assassination of Yeung Ku-wan, 1901

In the early hours of Sunday 28 October 1900, ten packets of dynamite were denotated under a house next to the Viceroy's yamen[1] in Canton. The explosion destroyed neighbouring dwellings and part of the yamen wall, crushing to death several men, women, and children. The police arrested Shi Jianru, a tenant of the house. From an old gentry family, Shi was a student at the Canton Christian College. He was also a member of Sun Yat-sen's Revive China Society, dedicated to overthrowing the Qing dynasty. He was taken before the Nanhai District Magistrate, who, faced with denials, ordered torture. First, Shi was beaten with bamboo rods. Next, he was pinioned to an upended bench with his arms tied to its legs. Then he was made to kneel and a rod was placed horizontally on his calves and pressed down by men standing on each end. After days of torture, Shi seemed 'more dead than alive'. Eventually he confessed to plotting the explosion with a servant, Song Xiaodong, who had since fled. Shi was executed on 9 November. His severed head was displayed in a cage near the site of the explosion.[2]

The explosion was planned to coincide with an uprising in Huizhou – an armed revolt in districts east of Canton organized by the Revive China Society with the help of the Triad Society and other bandit gangs. The aim was to draw government forces and prepare the ground for an attack on Canton itself. The uprising took advantage of the weakened state of Qing rule after the defeat of the anti-foreign Boxer Rebellion and the occupation of

---

1. A yamen (衙門) is an office or residence of a senior Chinese official.
2. Blake to Chamberlain, 31 May 1901, CO 129/305, 194–259; *OCM*, 19 November 1900; Harold Z. Schiffrin, *Sun Yat-sen and the Origins of the Chinese Revolution* (Oakland, California: University of California Press, 1968), 248–251; Edward J.M. Rhoads, *China's Republican Revolution: The Case of Kwangtung, 1895–1913* (Cambridge Massachusetts: Harvard University Press, 1975), 43–46.

Peking by an eight-nation alliance. However, by the time of Shi's explosion, Qing forces had already put down the uprising. Shi's target was Deshou, Acting Viceroy of Guangdong and Guangxi, and a reactionary sympathetic to the Boxers. The explosion merely jolted him out of bed and broke some of the yamen's crockery.[3]

According to Shi's confession, the instigator of the explosion was Yeung Ku-wan, one of the leaders of the Revive China Society, then resident in Hong Kong. A few weeks before the explosion, at a meeting in Hong Kong, Yeung had appointed Shi director of operations in Canton, with Song Xiaodong as his deputy. Yeung had then sent funds to Shi through the Hongkong and Shanghai Bank. Another of Yeung's confederates, the physician Yang Xiangfu, under interrogation by the Canton police, revealed that Yeung had organized the smuggling of dynamite from Macao to Canton. Explosions were to have gone off not only at the Viceroy's yamen but also at other locations, including gunpowder magazines and the treasury. Officials would be assassinated and the city would descend into chaos. But for some reason – probably, said Yang, swindling by the agents employed – nothing happened at the other places. Armed with the confessions of Shi and Yang, Deshou requested the extradition of Yeung Ku-wan, 'this murderous wretch, this virulent ruffian', to face trial in Canton.[4]

Yeung Ku-wan was the son of a Penang-born interpreter who had accompanied British forces during their occupation of Canton in 1858–1861. In 1875, at the age of fourteen, he entered into an apprenticeship at the Naval Dockyard in Hong Kong but was forced to end it when a machine accident severed three fingers on his right hand. He attended St Paul's College and taught at St Joseph's College. He then joined the China Merchants Steam Navigation Company and later worked for David Sassoon & Co., a shipping firm. He converted to Christianity. In 1891 he co-founded the *Furen Wenshe*, ostensibly a study group but in fact an anti-dynastic society. In 1895 it merged with Sun Yat-sen's Revive China Society. From Hong Kong, Yeung directed the society's first attempt at an uprising in Canton, in October 1895, shortly after China's defeat in the Sino-Japanese War. The Hong Kong authorities discovered the plot and tipped off the Canton government. The uprising collapsed without a shot fired. Yeung fled and spent the next few years overseas before returning to Hong Kong in June 1900. He opened an evening school at No. 52 Gage Street, placing an inordinate amount of faith in the safety of Hong Kong. He reassured Triad allies who were planning a looting spree in Hong Kong after the Huizhou Uprising that the Hong Kong authorities would not bother them if their offence was political, and that lawyers had been retained to 'help us if we got into trouble.' To warnings that Chinese

3. Schiffrin, *Sun Yat-sen*, Chapter 8.
4. Yeung Ku-wan (楊衢雲: Yang Quyun in pinyin) is also romanized as 'Yeung Kui-wan' or 'Yeung Kue-wan' in some reports. Acting Viceroy to Consul-General Scott, 26 December 1900, CO 129/305, 224–233.

officials had offered rewards for his assassination he replied, 'there was no danger in Hong Kong, everybody's place in Hong Kong was safe.'[5]

Sun Yat-sen and Yeung Ku-wan moved in Westernized circles. They depended on funds from overseas Chinese. Their allies in Hong Kong included the Australian-born Tse Tsan-tai and the barrister and legislator Ho Kai. Ho drew up manifestos and cultivated support from the *China Mail* and *Hongkong Telegraph*, assuring readers that, in contrast to the Boxers in the north, the revolutionaries were no threat to foreigners. In 1900 Ho was an intermediary in negotiations for an independent government in the south between the Governor, Sir Henry Blake, the outgoing Viceroy, Li Hongzhang, and Sun Yat-sen. Blake's diplomatic intrigues were aimed at preventing a power vacuum in a region with large British interests. But the negotiations came to nothing: Li bluntly told him that the main danger to peace was Hong Kong itself.[6] Two years earlier, in 1898, partly with the aim of improving the security of Hong Kong, Britain had leased from the Qing government the New Territories, the rural hinterland north of Kowloon, for a term of ninety-nine years. Attempts to enforce British rule there came up against armed resistance by villagers. British troops brutally suppressed the rebellion, killing some 500 insurgents.[7] Five of the rebels were convicted of murder.[8] For years to come the New Territories and the region beyond were plagued by banditry and lawlessness.

The New Territories massacre was a stain on Blake's otherwise progressive administration (1898–1903). He was particularly sympathetic towards the reform movement. The 'whole Chinese population above the coolie class' supported reform in China, but not rebellion, which harmed business, he said in response to claims by the Chinese Minister in London that Hong Kong was a base for anti-Qing agitation.[9] The minister, Luo Fenglu,

---

5. Robinson to Chamberlain, 11 March 1896, CO 129/271, 437–448; Statements by Kong Kung-hi and Wong Ping, 6 and 8 February 1901, CO 129/305, 520–522; Statement by Kung A-i (Kong Kung-hi), 7 November 1900, CO 129/301, 522–523; Schiffrin, *Sun Yat-sen*, Chapter 4; Chan Lau Kit-ching, *China, Britain and Hong Kong, 1895–1945* (Hong Kong: Chinese University Press, 1990), 45–57.
6. Blake to Chamberlain, 13, 17, and 19 July 1900, CO 129/300, 89–93, 115–121, and 142–159; Schiffrin, *Sun Yat-sen*, Chapter 7; Chan Lau, *China, Britain and Hong Kong*, 45–57; Statement by Wong Ping, 8 February 1901, CO 129/305, 522.
7. Patrick H. Hase, *The Six-Day War of 1899: Hong Kong in the Age of Imperialism* (Hong Kong: Hong Kong University Press, 2008), 116–117.
8. Two men were hanged for murdering a man employed to post proclamations on the British takeover. In another case, a leader of the revolt, Ng Kei-cheung, his nephew, and another villager were convicted of a similar murder. The death sentences on Ng and the villager were commuted to life and ten years' imprisonment. The nephew was granted a free pardon. Ng later also received a free pardon. *CM*, 29 and 30 June and 1, 3, and 5 July 1899; *HKWP*, 12 August 1899; ExCo Minutes, 17 July and 17 August 1899, CO 131/26, 453 and 462; Blake to Chamberlain, 10 July 1899, CO 120/292, 263–270; Hase, *The Six-Day War*, 100–101 and 147–148; Peter Wesley-Smith, *Unequal Treaty: China, Great Britain and Hong Kong's New Territories* (Hong Kong: Oxford University Press, 1980), 70–71.
9. Blake to Chamberlain, 12 and 23 March 1901, CO 129/304, 88 and 380–385; Luo to Lansdowne, 12 January 1901, CO 129/308, 208–209.

was urging action against Kang Youwei, an advocate of constitutional monarchy at odds with the revolutionary republicanism of Sun Yat-sen and Yeung Ku-wan. Blake gave Kang police protection and only persuaded him to leave for Singapore in early 1901 after an imperial edict offered rewards for his assassination. Such people could not 'be interfered with except by violating all the principles of liberty of thought upon which our Empire has been built,' said Blake.[10]

Asylum, banishment, and extradition

Blake, Robinson, and other governors had to steer a narrow course between cooperating with the Qing authorities and upholding Britain's policy of asylum for political refugees. They did not wish Hong Kong to become a base for subversion. Yet they were appalled by the Qing government's treatment of its opponents and anxious to avoid controversies in Parliament. They also had to consider the possibility that anti-Qing rebels might one day hold the reins of government. Governors used various tools to keep Hong Kong out of China's problems. Proclamations enforced neutrality and forbade arms exports during the anti-dynastic Taiping Rebellion (1850–1864), the Sino-French War (1884–1885), and the Sino-Japanese War (1894–1895). The Foreign Enlistment Act was deployed to prevent the raising of rebel troops. A Peace Preservation Ordinance, enacted during the Sino-French War, enabled swift action to be taken against protests. The most efficient tool, however, was the power of the Governor in Council to deport practically anyone on pain of imprisonment. A secret, extrajudicial process, deportation was used against 'dangerous characters' ranging from discharged convicts to refugees deemed to have abused the city's hospitality. It was, said Blake's chief of police, 'our best trump card'.[11]

Another method of dealing with undesirables was extradition: the surrender, on request, of fugitives to the Chinese authorities under the treaties between Britain and China.[12] In contrast to deportation, extradition was a slow and cumbersome process. It began with a request from the Chinese authorities for the surrender of a wanted person.[13] The alleged fugitive was then arrested. After hearings in open court, a magistrate decided if a prima facie case existed; if it did, he committed the fugitive to gaol. The Governor then

10. Blake to Chamberlain, 12 March 1901, CO 129/304, 380–385; Chan Lau, *China, Britain and Hong Kong*, 39–41.
11. Christopher Munn, '"Our Best Trump Card": A Brief History of Deportation in Hong Kong, 1857–1955', in *Civil Unrest and Governance in Hong Kong: Law and Order from Historical and Cultural Perspectives*, ed. Michael H.K. Ng and John D. Wong (Abingdon: Routledge, 2017), 26–45.
12. For the extradition provisions in the treaties see Chapter 3.
13. Ordinance No. 2 of 1850, in force until 1889, also empowered the Governor to extradite persons suspected of crimes against the government of China even without a request from the Chinese authorities. Governors would sometimes also 'invite' the Chinese authorities to request the extradition of suspicious persons known to be in the colony.

decided whether to hand over the fugitive or release him. The treaties stipulated 'proof of their guilt', a higher standard than for other countries. The Secretary of State had advised in 1863 that this should be interpreted simply as evidence sufficient to commit a person for trial. But some magistrates, sceptical of evidence given by witnesses from China, insisted on searching investigations. British officials suspected that some extradition requests were concocted to disguise political motives or levy blackmail. They were also concerned about the use of torture in Chinese courts to extract confessions, which were deemed necessary for convictions in serious cases.[14] The British authorities required undertakings that those surrendered would not be tortured or tried for other crimes. Yet, as diplomats pointed out, such undertakings were generally worthless. Since many of the crimes for which fugitives were sought were capital crimes, a decision in an extradition case, remarked one Attorney General, was 'really a decision involving the consequences of a verdict of guilty or not guilty in a capital case'.[15] For this reason, some prisoners awaiting extradition preferred to hang themselves in Victoria Gaol.

Increasingly, laborious extradition procedures led to failures of justice. In what was by no means an isolated case, thirteen men wanted for murder in a clan dispute in a village in Guangdong were held for a year in Victoria Gaol in 1880–1881 while a sceptical Governor Hennessy investigated guarantees by Chinese officials that they would not be tortured: a similar guarantee for a group of fugitives surrendered in 1879 had been ignored. Having allegedly killed three members of the same family, the men were liable to death by *lingchi* – death by slicing. All thirteen were released on a writ of habeas corpus in November 1881 on the ground that the proceedings before the magistrate had been irregular. However, most were rearrested along with other alleged accomplices in 1883 after fresh requests from the Canton authorities. They were then held for eleven months as lawyers argued their fate. By now they had also converted to Catholicism, and the Bishop, John Raimondi, had taken up their cause. From information gathered by missionaries, Raimondi claimed that the men were victims of false accusations by a powerful branch of their clan which had been trying to squeeze money out of them. Far from being murdered, the alleged victim, the head man of the village, was 'the terror of all the district': he had tortured some of his opponents to death; even the Prefect was afraid of him. The Viceroy had acquiesced because he was 'trembling with fear lest the populace will rise up' in the aftermath of the Logan case, in which a British court in Canton had sentenced a British national to a mere seven years'

14. Some forms of judicial torture, such as beating with bamboo rods, finger and ankle presses, and kneeling on chains, were allowed within specified limits, which were often exceeded. Hewlett, 'Description of Chinese Criminal Procedure at Canton', 22 January 1883, CO 129/207, 215–220; Derk Bodde and Clarence Morris, *Law in Imperial China* (Cambridge, Massachusetts: Harvard University Press, 1967), 97–98; Nancy Park, 'Imperial Chinese Justice and the Law of Torture', *Late Imperial China*, Vol. 29, No. 2 (December 2008): 37–67.
15. Memorandum by Edward O'Malley, 14 May 1884, CO 129/216, 217.

imprisonment for deliberately killing a Chinese boy.[16] The Church lobbied the British government. The Chinese Minister in London countered that Britain was failing to observe its treaty obligations. The men were finally released in October 1884 on instructions from the British government.[17]

The 'accumulating experience of the local lawyers' was making extradition more and more difficult, complained Governor Des Voeux in 1888. Witnesses brought from China were prone to break down under cross-examination. Magistrates could not be relied upon to exercise sound judgment and preferred to commit prisoners even where they doubted the evidence, thus throwing all responsibility on the Governor. Excessive precautions against surrendering innocent people had created a dangerous community of resident criminals, said Des Voeux. Chinese officials were equally frustrated by the failure of so many extradition requests. The Hong Kong courts refused to accept depositions, and instead required eyewitnesses to be interrogated on every detail, complained Viceroy Zhang Zhidong in 1887: 'if their statements contain an occasional inconsistency, the defendant's lawyers will get them absolved.' Zhang also complained about the thousands of dollars spent by the Canton authorities on hiring lawyers – 'and yet renditions often fail, contrary to what the treaties say'.[18] By now some Chinese officials were bypassing extradition altogether by offering rewards for fugitives seized in Hong Kong, or, mirroring British practices, sending soldiers to make arrests in British territory.[19]

Aware of Chinese grievances, British officials floated proposals for a full extradition treaty, which would also allow extradition of Chinese criminals fleeing from Hong Kong to mainland China – something not covered by existing treaties. This proposal came to

16. For the Logan case see Chapter 6.
17. Hennessy to Kimberley, 28 July and 14 December 1881, CO 129/193, 536–582 and CO 129/195, 351–544; Bowen to Derby, 31 December 1883 and 17 May 1884, CO 129/213, 278–341 and CO 129/216, 125–226; Foreign Office to Colonial Office, 30 September and 9 October 1884, CO 129/219, 234–240 and 264–268; Marsh to Derby, 14 October 1884, CO 129/217, 500–502. For an analysis of the diplomacy in this case see Jenny Huangfu Day, 'Mediating Sovereignty: The Qing legation in London and its diplomatic representation of China, 1876–1901', *Modern Asian Studies* (2020).
18. Zhang, a proponent of China's Self-Strengthening Movement, was later a leading advocate of judicial reform in China. Des Voeux to Holland, 22 December 1887, CO 129/234, 630; 王彥威 [Wang Yanwei], ed., 清季外交史料 [Late Qing Historical Diplomatic Materials], Vol. 3, 1504: I am indebted to Jenny Huangfu Day for this and other materials on extradition.
19. A physician resident in Kowloon for over twenty years, alleged by Qing officials to be a Triad leader, was seized on a ferry in colonial waters in 1886 and beheaded in Kowloon City; his head and body were later delivered to his relatives in Hong Kong. Two alleged robbers arrested by Chinese soldiers in the then border village of Sham Shui Po in 1889 were returned after diplomatic protests just before they were due to be executed. Extradition proceedings were then commenced, but they were released because of insufficient evidence. Marsh to Stanhope, 1 November and 4 December 1886, CO 129/229, 3–49 and 175–209; Des Voeux to Knutsford, 28 August and 14 October 1889, CO 129/242, 122–209 and 386–393.

nothing.[20] So too did a proposal to have judges, rather than magistrates, investigate extradition requests: the judges objected that this might require them to hear habeas corpus applications against their own decisions. Des Voeux then proposed a radically simplified system, allowing extraditions to be processed through written depositions, and restricting the presumption of innocence in such cases to Chinese resident in Hong Kong for two years or more: members of 'the moveable portion of the population' would be surrendered on demand, without enquiry. Officials in London rejected this 'lazy and unjustifiable proposal' as 'repugnant to British feeling'. The Secretary of State instructed Des Voeux to revive an earlier bill proposed in 1875 in the light of the Kwok Asing case, but since forgotten: modelled on the latest UK legislation governing extradition to European and other states, the bill contained many safeguards but also permitted depositions to be received as evidence in extradition proceedings.[21]

The bill prompted an acrimonious debate in the Legislative Council. Unofficial members argued that reliance on depositions would make persecution and extortion even easier. Des Voeux confessed to having 'had previously no idea of the terror of the Mandarins which pervades all classes of Chinese in this colony'. The bill was narrowly passed, but with concessions. Des Voeux backed down on depositions and further agreed that requests for extraditing anyone resident in Hong Kong for over a year would be considered by the Governor in Council with the aid of the Chief Justice. The resulting Chinese Extradition Ordinance 1889 included for the first time a list of extraditable offences based on Britain's treaties with European states. It explicitly forbade extradition for political offences and specified a fifteen-day period after committal by a magistrate to allow for habeas corpus proceedings. The general effect, as Des Voeux put it, was to lessen the responsibility of magistrates and increase that of the Governor in Council.[22]

The 1889 ordinance was no more satisfactory to Chinese officials. They continued to complain about a general unwillingness of the Hong Kong government to give up fugitives.[23] In 1896, following the 1895 Canton Uprising, the Viceroy asked for sedition to be made an extraditable offence. Seizing on this, Governor Robinson proposed amendments to allow dissidents such as Sun Yat-sen and Yeung Ku-wan to be surrendered in return for the cession of Chinese territory north of Kowloon – the future New Territories. The Secretary of State, Joseph Chamberlain, replied that he would rather go to war to gain

---

20. Foreign Office to Colonial Office, 23 August 1887, Chinese Legation to Salisbury, 10 October 1887, CO 129/235, 398–401 and 430–431.
21. Des Voeux to Knutsford, 8 August 1888, CO 129/238, 462–515; Opinion of E.J. Ackroyd, Acting Attorney General in the case of Ching Sam, 6 September 1887, CO 129/234, 286–292; Foreign Office to Colonial Office, 26 October 1888 and 25 January 1889, CO 129/240, 192–201 and CO 129/243, 232–240; Law Officers to Lord Knutsford, 15 December 1888, CO 129/240, 84–91.
22. Des Voeux to Knutsford, 29 July 1889, CO 129/241, 828–837; Ordinance No. 26 of 1889; *HKDP*, 17 and 28 May and 19 and 26 June 1889; Des Voeux, *My Colonial Service*, II, 256–267.
23. Luo Fenglu to Salisbury, 2 August 1899, CO 129/295, 481–482.

territory than hand over political prisoners to be cut into pieces.[24] In 1897 the Viceroy again requested reforms, including joint investigations by the Hong Kong and Chinese authorities, the banning of lawyers from proceedings, and notification of persons banished from Hong Kong. The British and Hong Kong governments rejected these proposals but conceded on one point: the ordinance was amended to allow magistrates to receive depositions taken by Chinese courts in requests for non-Hong Kong residents in homicide, piracy, and robbery cases.[25]

When Acting Viceroy Deshou requested Yeung Ku-wan's surrender on 23 November 1900, discussions about extradition had reached an impasse. In late 1898 a Hong Kong magistrate had discharged Chung Sui-yeung, an alleged Triad leader, said to be an ally of Sun Yat-sen, who was wanted for burglary and extortion in Xin'an County. Chinese officials alleged that Chung was also the 'arch-ringleader' of resistance to the British occupation of the New Territories. The magistrate had released him because of lack of evidence. The Chinese Minister in London, Luo Fenglu, protested that the Hong Kong government's policies breached treaty obligations, which did not distinguish between political and non-political offences.[26] In early 1900 Blake refused to extradite two alleged pirates after he learned that sailors arrested in Canton in a similar case had confessed under torture. Later that year he refused to hand over another fugitive without an undertaking from the Chinese authorities that a British consular official would be allowed to attend the trial to ensure no torture took place. The Consul-General informed him that such safeguards were useless, since torture was legal in Chinese courts: if the judge believed the accused to be guilty, the trial would not be complete until he confessed or died; to insist on having a consular official at the trial would only lead to the deaths of surrendered fugitives in prison before they could be tried. Cecil Clementi, later Governor of Hong Kong, then a cadet officer tasked with drafting Blake's letters, privately agreed: it was 'ridiculous, mad, idiotic' that, 'at this momentous period in the history of China', the only subject that interested Blake was the 'torture question'.[27]

Correspondence on Yeung Ku-wan's surrender took several weeks as the British Consul-General in Canton, Benjamin Scott, responded to requests from Hong Kong for more information. Scott forwarded letters from Deshou detailing Yeung's role in the explosion at the Viceroy's yamen, with copies of the confessions of Shi Jianru and Yang Xiangfu. On 8 January 1901 the Hong Kong government informed Scott that Blake intended to

24. Robinson to Chamberlain, 7 July 1896, CO 129/272, 300–313.
25. Ordinance No. 23 of 1897; Robinson to Chamberlain, 5 May 1897, CO 129/275, 495–529.
26. *OCM*, 5, 12, 19, and 26 November 1898; Luo Fenglu to Salisbury, 2 August 1899, CO 129/295, 481–482; Blake to Chamberlain, 8 and 10 November 1899, CO 129/294, 276–282 and 316–323.
27. Blake to Chamberlain, 31 May 1901, CO 129/305, 194–216; Cecil Clementi, Diaries 1901–1905, Oxford, Bodleian Libraries MSS Brit. Emp. S.600/26, 12 February 1901: I am indebted to Graham Hutchings for this and other materials on Clementi.

deal with the request according to the provisions added to the Chinese Extradition Ordinance in 1897, which allowed requests to be dealt with by written depositions sent over by the Chinese authorities if the fugitive had lived in Hong Kong for less than six out of the previous twelve months. Yeung had, in fact, returned to Hong Kong in June, but depositions would not have worked anyway: the 1897 provisions required them to be taken down in the presence of a British consular official to certify that no coercion had been used. Shi Jianru had been executed after confessing under torture. Neither Shi Jianru's confession nor that of Yang Xiangfu had been taken down in the presence of a consular official. Moreover, the only detail of Shi Jianru's confession that could be verified in Hong Kong – the remittance of funds to him by Yeung through the Hongkong Bank – was found to be false. A request based upon such a confession could not be granted, Blake concluded. Putting up a further obstacle, he asked that a Hong Kong official should be present if Yeung was tried in Canton – a rejoinder to Scott's earlier insistence that it was futile for consular officials to attend such trials.[28]

The assassination

Before Blake's response was conveyed to the Acting Viceroy the case took a dramatic turn. On the evening of Thursday 10 January 1901 Yeung Ku-wan was teaching English to a class of five young men in a room on the first floor of No. 52 Gage Street. The house was situated at the corner of Aberdeen Street, a steep thoroughfare leading from Caine Road down to the waterfront. His wife, Yeung Pun-shi, and their son and two daughters were resting in cubicles behind the room. The first floor was accessible by steps leading from Aberdeen Street into a rear alley, then known as Sam Kwai Lane.[29] At about 6:30 p.m., while Yeung was reading to the class, a man entered from the lane and walked up to Yeung's desk. Without saying a word he took out a revolver and fired four shots. One bullet hit Yeung's head. The others entered his left shoulder, chest, and abdomen. Along with three other men who had stood guard outside, the assassin then walked down Aberdeen Street, apparently unnoticed by crowds of hawkers and pedestrians. At the waterfront three of the gang boarded a sampan; the fourth disappeared into the crowds.[30]

Hearing the shots, Yeung Pun-shi rushed into the schoolroom. She found her husband slumped on his desk, his head in his hands. The book he had been reading from was lying

28. Correspondence between Lockhart, Colonial Secretary, and Scott, Consul-General, 26 November 1900 – 8 January 1901, CO 129/305, 217–234; Blake to Chamberlain, 12 March 1901, CO 129/304, 382.
29. Probably named after Daniel Caldwell (see Chapter 2), whose Chinese name was 'Sam Kwai' (三貴). Caldwell and his family once had a house on Hollywood Road near the junction with Aberdeen Street. The name is now Sam Ka (三家) Lane.
30. *CM*, 11 January 1901; *HKDP*, 12 January 1901; *HKT*, 20 May 1903; *R v Lui Chiu alias Li Kwai Fan*, May 1903: Notes of the Acting Chief Justice, FO 17/1718, 568–578.

on the desk, pierced by a bullet. The students had run away. Pun-shi and her elder daughter helped Yeung to a bed and put a handkerchief to his head. Still conscious, he told her he had been shot at the instigation of the Chinese government. She sent a servant to the Alice Memorial Hospital next door but the doctor refused to come. The servant then fetched a district watchman. A police sergeant, Hau Hang,[31] on duty nearby, heard a police whistle and also went to the scene. He had Yeung moved to the Civil Hospital in Sai Ying Pun. The surgeon, John Bell, found it impossible to operate on Yeung. At 9 p.m. he took down a dying declaration. Yeung said he did not know the assassin but knew the Chinese government had sent him from Canton: 'I hope the British Government will do me a justice. That is all.' Shortly after this, Chief Detective Inspector John Hanson arrived. He elicited from Yeung the names of those who had warned him of the plot, and of some of those involved in it.[32]

Yeung died in the early hours on Friday 11 January 1901. His funeral took place at the Happy Valley Cemetery on the afternoon of the 12th. The hearse was followed by a long procession of friends and supporters. A priest read the Christian burial service. Police were present in case an attempt was made on the lives of some of the mourners.[33] The large monument erected by his friends was left uninscribed for fear it would be desecrated.[34] From his exile in Japan, Sun Yat-sen raised money for Yeung's family and circulated a letter of condolence. Tse Tsan-tai described Yeung as 'one of the noblest of China's patriots, who suffered martyrdom in the cause of Freedom and Independence'.[35]

Investigations and discoveries

The assassination shocked the city. Noting that a shopkeeper in Yau Ma Tei had been chopped to death by an employee only a day before, the *Hongkong Telegraph* concluded that life and property were no more secure than in the neighbouring Chinese territory, which was rapidly descending into lawlessness. Escaping capture by boat, criminals were able 'to laugh at our police system'. That such a savage attack should take place in the heart

31. Hau Hang joined the force in 1886. He was one of seventy-five police officers – European, Indian, and Chinese – dismissed in 1897, and in one case convicted, for taking bribes in the Wa Lane gambling house scandal. He was re-employed in 1898 on the urging of F.H. May, who pointed out that Hau was one of only four Chinese officers to have confessed their guilt, while others, known to have taken bribes, stayed in the force; that he had identified other culprits; that it was impossible, for the salaries offered, to get 'absolutely honest' Chinese policemen; and that it was better to keep them than see them use their knowledge for nefarious purposes. Much commended for meritorious service, Hau was the first Chinese officer to be promoted to inspector, in 1920. Black to Chamberlain, 30 September 1898, CO 129/285, 299–311.
32. Dying Declaration, 10 January 1901, FO 17/1718, 577; Minute by May, 14 June 1901, CO 129/305, 536.
33. *HKT*, 14 January 1901; *HKDP*, 14 January 1901.
34. In 2011 the Hong Kong government erected a plaque at the grave with a biography of Yeung.
35. Tse Tsan-tai, 'The Chinese Republic', *SCMP*, 24 November 1924.

of the city, a few streets away from the police headquarters, was 'not only monstrous in itself' but 'astounding in its possibilities', declared the *China Mail.* Some early reports blamed the murder on rival reformers disappointed with the failed Huizhou Uprising. But most assumed that the Qing authorities were behind it. 'If everyone who denounces the rottenness of the Chinese Government, and who hopes and prays for a radical reform in its methods, is to be done to death upon British soil, who can be said to be safe?' asked the *China Mail.* An anonymous correspondent said that Acting Viceroy Deshou had offered a large reward for Yeung dead or alive, that Hong Kong was full of spies, and that assassins were awaiting other opportunities. He urged the British government to hold Deshou responsible for the murder of Yeung, 'a hero and a patriot' who was a British subject, and to demand the immediate production of the murderers.[36] This, in essence, was the course pursued by Governor Blake in the weeks and months following the assassination.

Blake offered a reward of $500 and a pardon for anyone giving information leading to a conviction. The police made urgent enquiries. Their Captain-Superintendent, F.H. May – later, as Governor, also the target of an assassin's bullet[37] – had, since assuming the position in 1893, tried to improve the force's detective capabilities. He now personally led the investigation and, together with Chief Inspector Hanson, interrogated informants, witnesses, and likely accomplices. Chief among them was Ng Sui-shang (alias Ng Lo-sam), who had been helping the police identify 'bad characters' for several years. May sent for Ng on the night of the murder and told him that Yeung had named him on his deathbed. Ng denied all knowledge but helped search for two of his associates who had also been implicated. They, along with others who knew of the plot, had already left Hong Kong. But over the next few months some were induced to return with the help of an increased reward of $2,000. One, Kong Ngau-ying, was fetched in a steam launch from a village near Nantou by a party led by Hanson, who 'practically had to bribe the man's family and the elders of the village to let him come away'.[38]

36. *HKT*, 12 January 1901; *CM*, 14, 15 and 16 January 1901; *HKDP*, 17 January 1901; Swettenham to Chamberlain, 23 January 1901, FO 17/1718, 497.
37. May – now Sir Henry May – was appointed Governor of Hong Kong in 1912 after a short term as Governor of Fiji. On the day of his return, while he and his wife and daughters were being carried in sedan chairs to the City Hall, a young man, Li Hon-hung, broke through the crowd and held a revolver to May's head. A swift intervention by Indian constables saved him. Li pleaded guilty to attempted murder and was sentenced to life imprisonment. His motives were anger over May's ill treatment of Chinese and the ban on the circulation of coins minted in Canton. May pardoned Li in 1918 in a ceremony at Government House. 'You made a great mistake when you tried to kill me,' he said. 'I am the representative of the great King of England and no man can kill me.' Norman Miners, 'The Attempt to Assassinate the Governor in 1912', *Journal of the Hong Kong Branch of the Royal Asiatic Society*, Vol. 22 (1982): 279–285; Phoebe Whitworth, *View from the Peak: An Autobiography* (Cambridge: T.G. Whitworth, 2001), 128–131.
38. Minute by May, 14 June 1901, CO 129/305, 536–538.

Kong Ngau-ying and his brother had taken part in the Huizhou Uprising but had since defected to the Qing government. They pointed the finger back at Ng Sui-shang, who, they said, had been deeply involved in the murder plot as an emissary between Qing officials and the assassins. Kong Ngau-ying, a forty-four-year-old brothelkeeper long resident in Yau Ma Tei, had been engaged by Ng as a police informer in 1899. Both men had been present at the Battle of Tai Po in April that year, when villagers resisted the British takeover of the New Territories. In September 1900 Ng asked Kong to track down refugee rebels in Hong Kong. In October he asked him to recruit men to kill Yeung. Over the next few months Kong attended meetings in Hong Kong and Canton with Ng, various Canton officials, and a succession of candidates for the role of assassin. The officials promised a reward of $20,000 and official rank for those who killed Yeung. Kong was present in Aberdeen Street on 10 January, the day of the murder. In February he went to Canton to ask for his share of the reward but was told that the affair had nothing to do with him. He then sent someone to Ng Sui-shang, who denied all knowledge of him and stopped paying his monthly retainer as an informer.[39]

Snubbed by his co-conspirators, Kong now gave the names of three men he had seen leaving the alley behind Yeung's house:

Tung Cheung, an unemployed policeman from Huzhou (Guangxi province)

Chan Lam-tsai, an informer and policeman in Canton

Tsui Fuk, an unemployed yamen runner.

Kong also named Li Ka-cheuk as the Canton official who had co-ordinated the murder and disbursed the rewards. Li was commander of the Canton city guard. He had played a key role in pursuing those involved in the aborted Canton Uprising in 1895.[40]

The Acting Attorney General, Henry Pollock KC, and Hong Kong's leading barrister, J.J. Francis KC, considered whether to prosecute Ng Sui-shang for conspiracy to murder. They advised that the only witnesses against him were Kong Ngau-ying, an accomplice, and Kong's brother, who had attended some of the meetings with Canton officials. The chances of a conviction were slender. Since the case was political, failure would 'certainly cause the Hong Kong Government to "lose face" vis-à-vis the Chinese Government'. Instead, Pollock and Francis agreed with a proposal by May to banish Ng. He had undoubtedly been of assistance in tracing bad characters, said May, but his complicity in the murder now made him a 'dangerous person to have in the colony'.[41]

---

39. Statements by Kong Kung-hi and Kong Ying, 6 February and 6 April 1901, CO 129/305, 520–521 and 525–528.
40. Schiffrin, *Sun Yat-sen*, 83–84 and 95.
41. Pollock to May, 26 June 1901, and May to Lockhart, 28 June 1901, CO 129/305, 530–533.

Governor Blake accepted this advice but wished to take the matter further. The evidence showed that the Canton authorities had ordered the assassination, he concluded. He proposed that the British government should demand from the Chinese government reparation of $20,000 for Yeung's widow. This proposal, based on 'very nebulous evidence', seemed to officials in London to 'border on the ridiculous'. The Consul General in Canton advised it should not be pursued.[42] Blake agreed to let the matter drop. However, the police enquiries had inadvertently set in motion events pointing more clearly to complicity by the Canton authorities. In September 1901 Chan Lam-tsai, one of the three men named by Kong as having taken part in the murder, was executed in Canton for conspiring against Chinese officials. His widow and brother later visited Hong Kong and told friends of Yeung Ku-wan that the real reason for Chan's execution was that a letter from May had been found on him asking him to come to Hong Kong to give evidence against Ng Sui-shang. They also showed official letters appointing Chan to minor official rank, allegedly for his part in the murder. The Hong Kong police believed that Ng had instigated Chan's arrest. They also believed Ng to have been behind a request by the Chinese authorities in June 1902 for the extradition of Wong Mang-tsap for robbery. Wong had helped the police bring Kong Ngau-ying back to Hong Kong to give evidence against Ng. He had a clear alibi and was discharged by the magistrate.[43]

At first, the Hong Kong police had thought that Chan was merely an accomplice; they now believed he was the man who fired the shots that killed Yeung Ku-wan. Since Chan was now dead, the matter might have ended there. However, on 5 April 1903, acting on information, the police arrested a thirty-six-year-old man in Hong Kong and charged him with Yeung's murder. The man was not one of those named by Kong Ngau-ying. He was the least memorable of the four assassins. In reports he is named variously as Lui Chiu, Lui Chui, Liu Chui, Liu Chu, Lau Chui, and Lau Cheu. Some knew him as 'Hakka Tsai' ('Hakka Boy'), others by the nickname 'Sow' (哨), meaning 'protruding teeth'. Most sources agree that he had an alias (or possibly a principal name) of Li Kwai-fan.[44]

R v Lui Chiu (alias Li Kwai-fan) Murder, 20 and 21 May 1903

The committal proceedings against Li Kwai-fan took place on 28 April 1903 before Francis Hazeland. Rare for magistrates at this time, Hazeland was *both* legally qualified *and* fluent in Cantonese. The son of a Portuguese mother and an English father, he was the first

---

42. Foreign Office to Colonial Office, 23 January 1902, CO 129/314, 180–185.
43. Gascoigne to Chamberlain, 12 August 1902, CO 129/312, 174–176; *OCM*, 14 July 1902.
44. The Chinese-language press was no clearer: the *Wa Tsz Yat Po* refers to him on different dates as 'Liu Chu' (廖珠) and 'Lui Chiu' (呂超). *WTYP*, 21 May and 18 June 1903; Blake to Chamberlain, 19 June 1903, CO 129/317, 492–523.

magistrate to have been born and educated in Hong Kong.[45] At the request of the prosecutor, the Crown Solicitor Francis Bowley, Hazeland held the hearing in camera. This unusual arrangement was linked to the case's 'political significance'.[46] No doubt one of the aims was to protect witnesses, who were even more reluctant than usual to come forward. Hazeland committed Li for trial.

Li's trial was held in the May criminal sessions of the Supreme Court. The sessions also tried two manslaughters, an arson case, and a robbery. The Chief Justice, Sir William Goodman, was on holiday in Japan. His place was filled by the Attorney General, Sir Henry Berkeley, who presided over Li's trial. Ernest Sharp KC, JP, a barrister now acting as Attorney General, prosecuted.[47] The *China Mail* asked why a short absence by the Chief Justice should produce such 'a flutter in the legal dovecote', since the Puisne Judge, Alfred Wise, had often acted as Chief Justice. The likely explanation was that Berkeley was being groomed as Goodman's successor. Berkeley was Chief Justice of Fiji (1889–1902) but was removed after displeasing the Fiji government by granting writs of habeas corpus for two chiefs who had been confined without trial under a draconian 'Disaffected Natives Ordinance'.[48] Berkeley acquiesced in a transfer to Hong Kong as Attorney General in expectation of the chief justiceship when Goodman retired. However, owing to the Fiji episode, and because staff in the Colonial Office considered him 'absolutely useless' as an Attorney General, he was to be disappointed. Instead, in 1905, despite a recommendation by the Governor in favour of Berkeley, the position went to Sir Francis Piggott, a decision the Colonial Office came to regret. Berkeley resigned as Attorney General in 1906 and took up private practice in Hong Kong.[49]

The court assigned a barrister to defend Li Kwai-fan: at this time the practice of providing capital defendants with *both* a barrister *and* a solicitor at government expense was

45. Francis Arthur Hazeland (1861–1931) was the son of Francis Innes Hazeland, the Crown Solicitor, and Maria da Silva. Educated at the Government Central School, he was appointed a judge's clerk in 1878 and held various positions in the Supreme Court before being called to the Bar by Inner Temple in 1900. He was a magistrate from 1901 until his retirement in 1916.

46. *HKT*, 28 April 1903.

47. Sharp was admitted to practise in Hong Kong in 1894. A leading freemason, he was also active in Shanghai, where he joined W.V. Drummond's practice. He served the government in various capacities, and was an Executive Councillor from 1916 until his death in 1922. *HKDP*, 10 February 1922.

48. The chiefs, one of whom was a magistrate, had led a movement for federation with New Zealand, which the Fiji government was determined to suppress. The case became controversial through the involvement of Berkeley's brother, Humphrey, a campaigner for federation, and a 'very bad character' in the eyes of the Colonial Office: a solicitor, he had applied for the writs of habeas corpus. *CM*, 15 April 1903; Robert Nicole, *Disturbing History: Resistance in Early Colonial Fiji* (Honolulu: University of Hawaii Press, 2011), Chapter 3.

49. Officials also cited a rule against promoting someone from attorney general to chief justice in the same colony, a rule usually ignored in Hong Kong. Nathan to Lyttelton, 2 December 1904, CO 129/324, 430–438; Minute by Reginald Stubbs, Colonial Office, 17 October 1909, CO 129/358, 106.

in abeyance.[50] The barrister, Thomas Phillips, was a partner in W.V. Drummond's firm in Shanghai.[51] He was in Hong Kong from December 1901 to November 1903, appearing mainly in civil trials. Three months before Li's trial, he had been assigned to defend nineteen Chinese labourers charged with murdering an Indian watchman in an affray set off when the watchman hit a woman he accused of stealing some wood. The trial was about to begin when the prosecutor, Berkeley, entered a *nolle prosequi* on the murder charge. Phillips, who had so far hardly said a word, chose not to stay on to defend the men on a lesser charge of riot. 'You seem to have been very successful,' joked Chief Justice Goodman as Phillips left the court.[52] Two days before Li's trial, Phillips had prosecuted a manslaughter case in the May sessions.[53] Apart from a robbery case in 1902, this seems to have been the extent of his experience of criminal trials in Hong Kong.

The common jury balloted for Li's trial consisted of four employees of commercial firms, a broker, a spinner, and an employee at the Sailor's Home.[54] Rare for the time, this was an all-British jury.[55] Peter Dow, an employee of Jardine Matheson and a leading light in the Philharmonic Society, was elected foreman. The trial lasted two days. When the court rose at 3:30 p.m. on the first day, Berkeley directed that the jury be locked up for the night in the Hongkong Hotel, a measure so unusual that it prompted the *Daily Press* to look for precedents. It found one in a recently published history by J.W. Norton-Kyshe, the Registrar of the Supreme Court.[56] Frustrated in his many requests for promotion, Norton-Kyshe had been behind an article in the *Hongkong Telegraph* criticizing Sharp's appointment as Acting Attorney General and suggesting that he himself would have been a better

---

50. The main sources for this trial are R v Lui Chiu alias Li Kwai Fan: Notes of the Acting Chief Justice, 20 May 1903, FO 17/1718, 568–578; *HKWP*, 23 May 1903; and *CM* and *HKT*, 20–22 May 1903.
51. The legal profession serving the British Supreme Court in Shanghai was a fused one, with no distinction in practice between barristers and solicitors.
52. Had the murder charge proceeded, the trial would have set the record for the number of defendants in a murder trial in Hong Kong. A special dock was constructed for the nineteen men, each of whom had a numbered plate hanging from his neck. *OCM*, 23 February 1903; *HKT*, 20 February 1903.
53. This arose out of a 'coolie fight' at Jardine Matheson & Co.'s wharf at West Point. The victim suffered a ruptured spleen. Four men, undefended, were found guilty. Berkeley described them as 'silly in allowing temper to get the better of them', but, since they had already been in prison for six weeks, discharged them when the court rose. *OCM*, 23 May 1903.
54. Peter Dow, assistant, Jardine Matheson & Co.; William Nicholls, clerk, Hong Kong and Whampoa Dock Co. Ltd; Robert Saxon, spinner, Hong Kong Cotton Spinning, Weaving and Dyeing Co. Ltd; Joseph William Crouch, assistant, Butterfield and Swire; Percy Hardman, assistant, Sailor's Home; John Archibald Temple Plummer, assistant Bradley Co.; Alec Stuart Anton, broker, Benjamin Kelly & Potts.
55. The sources do not say if the prosecution had asked jurors of other nationalities to 'stand by'.
56. Norton-Kyshe records a case from 1868 as the first instance of overnight sequestration. There is an earlier precedent in one of the piracy trials of 1866: see Chapter 3. *HKDP*, 21 May 1903.

choice. Norton-Kyshe's disputes with judges were soon to erupt into a series of confrontations leading to his dismissal and mental breakdown.[57]

Two themes stood out in Sharp's opening speech for the prosecution: clear evidence that senior officials in Canton, including Acting Viceroy Deshou, were behind the murder; and a conspiracy of silence among the many people who knew of the plot, took no part in it, but did nothing to prevent it. The silence, said Sharp, arose from fear of the Qing authorities and 'the innate characteristic of the race to avoid taking action in anything which does not directly concern them'. Sharp's claim that Chinese officials had paid rewards was so shocking that the judge, Berkeley, interrupted to tell him he must produce evidence of this 'very serious allegation'. Sharp assured him he would do so. Sending emissaries to murder a person 'under the protection of our flag' was an intolerable breach of international rights, he said. It was possible that the officials had patriotic motives. But this could not be said of Li Kwai-fan and his gang: on the contrary, they were driven 'by the meanest and most sordid motives of money to be gained'.

Sharp reminded the jury of the doctrine of common design, under which all members of a gang were equally guilty even though some may only have kept watch while a felony was committed. As a lookout, Li Kwai-fan fell into this category. But Sharp also intended to show that he was more than a stooge: he was, in fact, the local anchorman in the plot, the 'principal leader' of the gang whose failure to recruit men in Hong Kong had, however, prompted Canton officials to send down their own assassins.

The first of Sharp's fourteen witnesses testified to the events on the evening of 10 January 1901. Among these were Yeung's widow, Yeung Pun-shi, and his eldest daughter, Yeung Kam-ha, now nineteen years old; two students, one present in the classroom when the gunman shot Yeung, the other who, late for class, saw 'two strange men' walking down Sam Kwai Lane and Aberdeen Street towards Queen's Road; Sergeant Hau Hang, who responded to the calls for help; and Dr Bell from the Civil Hospital, who produced Yeung's dying declaration. None of those present at or near the scene of the crime was able to identify any of the murderers. After they had given their evidence in chief, Phillips put questions only to the students. One of them, Lam San-yau, now twenty years old, confirmed that the gunman was the only stranger in the classroom but was unable to say if the accused was the man who fired the shot. The other, Li Ngai-man, now twenty-one, said that the accused was not one of the two men he saw emerging from Sam Kwai Lane.

Sharp then called five witnesses to testify to Li Kwai-fan's participation in the murder plot and the involvement of Chinese officials. The first was Tam Chung, a fisherman. Tam got to know Li through his uncle, who owned a 'marriage boat' (a floating restaurant) at

57. *HKT*, 16 April 1903. Norton-Kyshe was allegedly also behind the *China Mail* article of 15 April questioning the appointment of Berkeley as Acting Chief Justice. Peter Wesley-Smith, 'James William Norton-Kyshe', *HKLJ*, Vol. 2, No. 3 (1972): 278–293.

Yau Ma Tei. Li took Tam on as a cook at $3 a month in a house near Hollywood Road. Tam attended meetings where Li and others discussed the plot with emissaries of Li Ka-cheuk, the commander of the Canton City Guard. Li Kwai-fan asked Tam if he would help him 'beat' Yeung ('*ta*', 打, which Tam said meant 'shoot'), but Tam refused. He then distanced himself from Li and returned to his uncle in Yau Ma Tei. However, at 8 p.m. on the night of the murder Li turned up in a sampan at the uncle's boat asking to stay the night, saying he had just killed Yeung Ku-wan. The uncle refused to help him. The next time Tam saw Li was nearly a year later, on the Canton River on board the *Kin Yui*, a man-of-war under Captain Yeung Tsing-kai, one of Li Ka-cheuk's emissaries. Over dinner, Li Kwai-fan boasted to Tam that he had received several hundred dollars and a crystal button denoting fifth official rank. 'You are a coward,' said Li, 'otherwise you would have plenty of money to spend and a button to wear.'

Phillips cross-examined Tam at length. He ascertained that Li had owed Tam money and asked if this was the reason he was giving evidence against him:

> **Tam** — No; I have had no quarrel with Prisoner, no ill-feeling against him.
>
> **Phillips** — You were afraid to give information when asked to shoot Yeung Kui wan?
>
> **Tam** — Yes.
>
> **Phillips** — When did you give information to the Police?
>
> **Tam** — I have never given information to the Police.
>
> **Phillips** — When did the Police come to you?
>
> **Tam** — They came to look for me about 10th or 11th April last (1903). When Police came I was bound to tell what I knew.
>
> **Phillips** — Did you then think you were safe in telling?
>
> **Tam** — Yes, because the Police seemed already to know about the matter. I was under their protection.
>
> **Phillips** — Why not put yourself under their protection in January 1901, and then disclose the plot to murder?
>
> **Tam** — Well, you see I was then afraid to report, as some dark night I might be attacked.
>
> **Phillips** — Are you afraid to go out now?
>
> **Tam** — Yes.[58]

Far from shaking Tam's evidence, Phillips's questions elicited more details about the meetings with Chinese officials. He asked Tam to repeat in Chinese 'without stopping' what Li Ka-cheuk's emissary had said to Li Kwai-fan about the reward. This was rendered by the interpreter, Li Hong-mi, as 'Ah Fan, there is a man named Yeung Kui-wan in Hongkong, there is a reward of about 10,000 dollars and several "buttons."'

58. Notes of the Acting Chief Justice, 20 May 1903, FO 17/1718, 572.

Sharp's next witness was Chan Wan, a cook on the *Zafiro*, a ship plying between Hong Kong and Manila. Chan was the younger brother of Chan Lam-tsai, whom he described as 'a soldier when times were busy and a gambler when they were slack'. He had attended meetings with his brother and other conspirators in Li Ka-cheuk's barracks in Canton before the assassination. He confirmed that Li Ka-cheuk had specially instructed his brother to shoot Yeung, and that his brother had been executed in Canton after Li had found on him letters from F.H. May. Chan Wan had been present at meetings at the barracks in the days after the assassination. It was here that he had seen Li Kwai-fan for the first time, bickering with others over 'which of the gang was the most courageous'. Li had boasted that he had encountered Yeung several times in the streets in Hong Kong and would have 'done the job' then, had there not been policemen nearby. Chan Lam-tsai had retorted that if it hadn't been for him and Tung Cheung, 'your plan would not have been carried out. The thing had been in your hands a very long time, but you had not been able to put it through.' During these quarrels Chan learned that his brother, Chan Lam-tsai, had been the one who had shot Yeung. Tung Cheung had followed behind. Li Kwai-fan and Tsui Fuk had stayed outside as lookouts.

From the discussions in the barracks, Chan Wan also learned about the distribution of rewards. Li Kwai-fan, Chan Lam-tsai, and Tung Cheung had each received $2,000 and a crystal button: about twenty such buttons were given out, but Chan Wan did not know what the other conspirators had received. He produced a certificate of merit, signed by Li Ka-cheuk, and a patent bearing the seal of Acting Viceroy Deshou conferring official rank on Chan Lam-tsai. The certificate praised him for the 'arrest of the leader of the Kolao Society', an anti-dynastic society allied with the Revive China Society: Chan pointed out that the Chinese term for this leader, 'Tsing Lung Tau' (正龍頭), referred to Yeung Ku-wan. After the murder, Chan continued to see Li Kwai-fan, now sporting his crystal button, on a junk commanded by his brother Chan Lam-tsai. Phillips's questions sought to exploit discrepancies between Chan's deposition taken down by the magistrate and his evidence in court, alleging that his memory had been 'refreshed' by someone during the interval between the two. The discrepancies were minor and Chan had no difficulty in explaining them. 'I replied to what I was asked,' he said when asked why he had not told the magistrate the details of the discussions in the barracks after the assassination.

Sharp then called Kong Ngau-ying, the brothelkeeper and former rebel who had given information to the police about the plot in 1901. Kong now described himself as a fishmonger. He had not mentioned Li Kwai-fan by name in his statement of 1901 but had instead named the ex-police informant Ng Sui-shang (alias Ng Lo-sam) as the intermediary between the Hong Kong conspirators and Canton officials. Kong now added Li to the three assassins – Lam, Tung, and Tsui – he had earlier named to the police. He described the meetings with Yeung Tsing-kai and other emissaries of Li Ka-cheuk at Ng's house. Li Kwai-fan was the leader who had taken them to Ng's house on the day of the murder, and thence to Yeung's house. Kong then described the deployment of the gang around the house. He had been at the corner of Gough Street and Aberdeen Street – almost opposite the house – and had seen Li and Tsui standing guard while Chan and Tung entered the house by Sam Kwai Lane at the rear: it was dark, but a streetlamp illuminated the scene. He had then heard shots from the house and seen Lam and Tung emerge from the lane and walk down Aberdeen Street, followed by Li and Tsui. He had followed them to the waterfront and seen three of them board a sampan.

The cross-examination by Phillips again focused on why Kong had not reported the meetings with Chinese officials to the police.

> **Kong** — Well, they were acting under orders of the Chinese Government. If I had informed the Hongkong Police, I would have got into trouble.
>
> **Phillips** — Is that your explanation?
>
> **Kong** — Yes.
>
> **Phillips** — Did you give this explanation to the Magistrate: "The deceased was nothing to me and not a friend" — Is that what you said?
>
> **Kong** — Yes.
>
> **Kong** [in response to further questions] — Yes, I stood on that street knowing that the men I followed were going into deceased's house to shoot him.... I did nothing to save deceased because I know nothing of your local customs and laws.
>
> **Phillips** — You know the Police, you kept a brothel for twenty years?
>
> **Kong** — Well, yes; but it was too late for me to report to the Police.
>
> **Phillips** — Why not report after leaving Ng Lo Sam's house instead of waiting outside in Aberdeen Street?
>
> **Kong** — Where was the time? There was no time to do so.
>
> **Phillips** — Why not say to the passers-by "there is going to be a murder done in that house?"
>
> **Kong** — Because I did not know whether they would really carry out their plan of murder.[59]

Asked why he did not go to the police straight after the murder, Kong said he did not see any policemen. Despite the information he had given in 1901, he said his first contact with the police was a month or two before Li's trial, when he was taken to identify him.

Two further witnesses, Wong Sing and Chan Cheung, fishermen from Yau Ma Tei, gave evidence about how Li Kwai-fan had tried to recruit them to kill Yeung. After the murder they had seen him in Canton gloating about the reward. 'Some time ago I asked you to do a certain thing and you were afraid to do it,' Li had said to Chan Cheung. 'Look at me now, I am a Mandarin now and have money to spend.' Phillips again asked why they

59. Notes of the Acting Chief Justice, 20 May 1903, FO 17/1718, 575.

had not gone to the police earlier and again received the reply that they were afraid because Li was acting under orders from the Chinese authorities. Phillips tried to connect Chan to a recent piracy, which Chan simply denied.

The prosecution closed its case at 3:30 p.m. on the second day of the trial. Phillips called no witnesses for the defence and, in a short speech, reviewed the evidence against Li. He had 'never in his life heard such weak testimony in a murder case. It was false, it was perjured, and the witnesses from whom it was obtained were irresponsible persons, most of whom were following the occupation of fishermen.' It was impossible to convict on the evidence of men of such low character, he said. It had been 'conclusively proved' that the actual murderer was Chan Lam-tsai, whose brother had testified that Li had run away when the shots were fired. It had been proved that Li was not the instigator of the murder. Was he now to be 'the scapegoat of others in great position?' The real instigators, said Phillips, were Acting Viceroy Deshou and Li Ka-cheuk. 'He did not know whether any diplomatic steps had been taken to punish any of these people, but these were the persons who were guilty of the murder of Yeung Kue Wan – not this wretched coolie who was before the jury now.'

In his closing speech for the prosecution, Sharp observed that Phillips had asked every witness why he did not tell the police about the plot. Each had answered that he was afraid of the Chinese Government. This was only natural, since the city was full of spies, and most of the families of the witnesses lived in Canton. 'And were they not safe under the protection of the Hongkong police?' he asked:

> This case was an answer in itself. Yeung Kue Wan was not safe under the protection of the Hongkong police. It was questionable whether even now the lives of the witnesses who had given evidence were safe; it was a matter which it was better perhaps not to go into.[60]

Sharp said it was remarkable how the stories of the various witnesses fitted into each other, considering that the evidence had been collected piecemeal by the police. It was also noteworthy that the prisoner had called no witnesses. 'Supposing him innocent, surely he could have produced evidence to meet some of the many statements of the prosecution. For example, if the official rank was conferred on him for some proper reason he could prove it, and if it was not conferred on him at all he could prove that.'

Berkeley then summed up. The defence's case, he said, rested on the idea that, if the prosecution evidence was true, 'the witnesses would have gone to the police or ought to have gone to the police and so saved the man Yeung Kue Wan.' It was for the jury to say whether or not their failure to do so destroyed the value of their testimony. The defence had called no witnesses, he said. The jury might accept that Li could not call witnesses to prove he was not in Hong Kong at the time of the murder; but it was no defence to say that the Canton officials behind the plot were not now standing before them in the dock.

---

60. *HKWP*, 23 May 1903.

Finally, as a possible explanation of the long silence of the prosecution witnesses, Berkeley pointed out that the actual assassin, Chan Lam-tsai, had been beheaded in Canton for being in possession of a letter from the head of the Hong Kong police. It was 'not unnatural to suppose that the deceased man's brother in coming forward to give evidence might be actuated by the strongest of all passions, revenge'.

The jury retired at 4:50 p.m. and returned at 5 p.m with a unanimous verdict of guilty of murder. Berkeley asked Li if he had anything to say why sentence should not be passed on him. Li replied that 'he did not do it; he had nothing more to say'. Berkeley explained to him in some detail the law on common design, as it applied to this case, and then pronounced sentence of death without following the usual custom of donning the black cap. As Li was removed from the dock he shouted, 'It is a false accusation.'

While awaiting execution Li Kwai-fan admitted his complicity in Yeung's murder.[61] He was hanged at 5 a.m. on 17 June 1903 in Victoria Gaol.

Blake demands satisfaction

The evidence at Li Kwai-fan's trial implicated others, including Chinese officials. Governor Blake asked the Acting Attorney General, Sharp, to advise whether action could be taken against them. The Crown Solicitor, Francis Bowley, took further sworn statements from Kong Ngau-ying, Chan Wan, and Tam Chung before the magistrate, Hazeland. On the basis of their statements and their evidence at trial, Sharp advised there were now strong grounds to charge three other men with conspiracy to murder: the informant Ng Sui-shang (deported from Hong Kong two years earlier), the gang member Tung Cheung, and Li Ka-cheuk's principal emissary Yeung Tsing-kai. One of the two other gang members, Chan Lam-tsai, had been executed; the evidence against Tsui Fuk was weak since Chan Wan, one of the two witnesses against him, now denied any knowledge of him. The evidence against Li Ka-cheuk, Commander of the Canton City Guard, Acting Viceroy Deshou, and other officials was less conclusive. However, Sharp did not doubt that they were fully aware of the details of the crime.[62]

Blake now proposed to the Secretary of State that Ng Sui-shang, Tung Cheung, and Yeung Tsing-kai should be extradited to stand trial in Hong Kong. He also proposed that the British government should require the Chinese government to dismiss the officials behind the murder and pay compensation to Yeung Ku-wan's widow. Such demands were problematic. As Blake was aware, the Treaty of Tientsin and the Chinese Extradition Ordinance applied only to the extradition of Chinese nationals from Hong Kong to China. The provisions were not reciprocal, and Blake admitted that the Chinese government was

61. Blake to Chamberlain, 19 June 1903, CO 129/317, 494.
62. Opinion of E.H. Sharp, 6 June 1903, CO 129/317, 503–504.

unlikely to extradite its own nationals to Hong Kong. The usual practice, he said, was for fugitive Chinese from Hong Kong to be tried by Chinese courts, with witnesses sent from Hong Kong to give evidence; there were, he claimed, many cases where persons accused of murder in Hong Kong were brought to justice and executed in China. It would, though, be hopeless to expect the Chinese authorities to deal with Ng, Tung, and Yeung in this way. Blake therefore asked for the 'strongest possible pressure' to be put on the Chinese government to extradite them to Hong Kong.[63] The Foreign Office decided this was out of the question. It also ruled out a secondary proposal to urge the Chinese government to try the men in a Chinese court.[64]

Foreign Office officials could not see the logic behind Blake's demands for dismissals and compensation for Yeung's widow and family – now, inexplicably, raised from \$20,000 to \$50,000. If the evidence against Deshou and Li Ka-cheuk was insufficient to justify prosecution, it seemed unreasonable to expect dismissals or compensation simply on the basis of suspicion.[65] In any case, the demands were rapidly overtaken by events. Tung Cheung, one of the gang of assassins, was executed in Canton in 1904 for some unspecified crime. Only one member of the gang, Tsui Fuk, was now still alive. The only witness against him, the brothelkeeper Kong Ngau-ying, died in early 1904 at the age of forty-five. Kong and his two brothers were also witnesses against the banished informer Ng Sui-shang. A request from the Canton authorities in 1904 for the extradition of Kong's two brothers on charges of robbery (which was refused) suggested it would be impossible to have Ng tried in a Chinese court. The 'weak and useless'[66] Deshou retired in August 1903 and died soon after. Blake found the new Viceroy, Cen Chunxuan, to be 'frank, alert and full of energy'.[67] Cen banished the alleged instigator of the conspiracy, Li Ka-cheuk, to Mongolia in April 1904 for some other offence.

---

63. Blake to Chamberlain, 19 June 1903, CO 129/317, 493–499.
64. British policy was not to request extradition from countries with which Britain had no extradition treaty. The Burmah-Yunnan Frontier Convention of 1894 provided for a reciprocal arrangement for extradition in the border area between China and British Burma. However, neither side was bound to surrender its own nationals – a principle which the Foreign Office believed would be insisted upon by the Chinese government in any negotiations for a comprehensive extradition treaty. In addition, the British government had recently refused to surrender two Chinese nationals from the International Settlement in Shanghai after they had published seditious articles against the Qing government in the *Subao*, a newspaper. In the light of this, the reply of the Chinese government to any request for the extradition to Hong Kong of Chinese nationals 'would be obvious, and . . . unanswerable'. The two *Subao* men, Shang Binglin and Zou Rong, were eventually tried by a Chinese magistrate with a British assessor in the Shanghai Mixed Court in December 1903. They were convicted of seditious libel and sentenced to prison terms of two and three years. Hardinge to Colonial office, 19 August 1903, CO 129/321, 263–267; Schiffrin, *Sun Yat-sen*, 267–274.
65. Satow to the Officer Administering the Government, Hong Kong, 10 May 1904, CO 129/326, 360.
66. Foreign Office minute (author's name illegible), 28 August 1903, FO 17/1718, 606b.
67. Blake to Chamberlain, 17 June 1903, CO 129/317, 410.

The grim fate of so many of those involved was 'not encouraging to the perpetration under the sanction of the Chinese Government of crimes of violence in this Colony,' observed Blake's successor, Sir Matthew Nathan. He agreed that nothing could be gained beyond conveying the serious view taken of any attempt by Chinese officials to violate British territory. The British Minister in Peking, Sir Ernest Satow, declined to do even that.[68] Sympathy with Yeung was now wearing thin. The Hong Kong press had routinely referred to him as a 'reformer'. Yet 'Yeung Kui Wan the "Reformer" was notoriously engaged in fomenting rebellion and planning dynamite outrages,' remarked one Colonial Office clerk. 'He deserved his fate and the only point to complain of was the violation of British territory. In the circ[umstance]s I think that was almost excusable.'[69] The clerk was Reginald Stubbs, a future Governor of Hong Kong.

The Hung Tsun-fuk case, 1903–1904

If Blake failed in his efforts to obtain satisfaction from the Chinese authorities in Yeung Ku-wan's case, he had more success in bringing to account the culprits in a still more flagrant murder, perpetrated in March 1903 with the connivance of Chinese officials.

On 25 January 1903 Hong Kong police raided a tea shop in D'Aguilar Street and arrested four men. They seized documents, flags, maps, uniforms, large quantities of money, and woodcuts of proclamations – all in preparation for an attack on Canton three days later, on Chinese New Year's Eve, by thousands of Triad recruits. Blake seemed almost relieved when the men, charged under the Foreign Enlistment Act, were released by the magistrate for lack of evidence. The police had been 'rather precipitous' in making the arrests, he reported. Presumed at first to be merely the work of Triads, the scheme, was, he claimed, 'a reform movement pure and simple' – a description which one Colonial Office clerk dismissed as 'childish'.[70] The seized woodcuts proclaimed 'a new world', with China 'imitating the Constitutional Government of Europe' under a restored Ming dynasty. The organizer was Hung Tsun-fuk, a sixty-eight-year-old nephew of Hong Xiuquan, the leader of the Taiping Rebellion 1850–1864. Hung, a Christian, had been running a herbalist's shop in Hong Kong while keeping up links with the Triad Society. After the failed Huizhou Uprising, Tse Tsan-tai persuaded him to organize this third attempt at an attack on Canton. It was funded with half a million dollars from another revolutionary, Li Chi-tang, exhausting the inheritance from his father, the great Hong Kong merchant Li Sing. Tipped off by

68. Nathan to Lyttelton, 17 November 1904, CO 129/324, 351–370; Satow to Landsdowne, 7 December 1904, FO 17/1718, 701–702; Campbell to Colonial Office, 18 February 1905, CO 129/330, 362–369.
69. Minute by Stubbs, 23 December 1904, CO 129/324, 351.
70. Blake to Lucas, 31 January 1903, and Blake to the Secretary of State, 29 January 1903, CO 129/316, 116–154; Fiddian to Lucas, 2 March 1903, CO 129/316, 115.

the Hong Kong government, the Canton police arrested Hung's agents. The rebellion collapsed before it had even started.[71]

On 30 March 1903 Chinese newspapers in Hong Kong reported that Hung Tsun-fuk had been captured in Hong Kong and killed, and that his dead body had arrived in Canton on 26 March. The reports added that the capture had been arranged by agents of Admiral Ho Zhangqing, and that a reward of $20,000 had been paid: Admiral Ho had led Qing forces in the defeat of the Huizhou Uprising three years earlier. The Hong Kong police made enquiries and found the reports to be true in all details except the identity of the victim. Hung was, in fact, alive, and left for Singapore on 31 March. The body was that of Ng Luk, a sixty-year-old keeper of an opium divan in Canton, who had been lured to Hong Kong through promises of employment by a man named Cheung Cho-ting. Ng bore a resemblance to Hung. On 16 March he arrived in Hong Kong, where he was met by Cheung and taken to a flat in Sai Ying Pun. Cheung entertained him with wine, food, and prostitutes. Just over a week later Ng's dead body, black and with the mouth oozing foam, was conveyed by boat to Taiping, on the Canton River, where Admiral Ho had his headquarters. Ho reported to the Viceroy that his agents had drugged Hung at a house in Hong Kong, but that while they were taking him by boat he had woken up and started making a noise. Fearing he would give the plot away, they had bound his neck, accidentally strangling him.[72]

Through 'a trustworthy source', the Hong Kong authorities obtained copies of documents connecting Cheung Cho-ting with Admiral Ho and his staff: among them were Cheung's account of events, and a bond verifying that the body sent to Taiping was Hung Tsun-fuk's. An accompanying report from Ho to the Viceroy mentioned a reward offered by the Provincial Treasurer for Hung's capture ($30,000 if alive, $20,000 if dead) and confirmed that Hung had been captured on Ho's instructions. At Blake's request, the British Consul-General, James Scott, made enquiries in Canton and reported that officials there believed themselves to be in possession of Hung's body. Scott spoke to the Viceroy's private secretary, who insisted the Viceroy had nothing to do with the plot. Shocked to learn that the dead man was not Hung, the secretary asked for the real Hung to be handed over 'to enable the Viceroy to denounce the Admiral and his subordinates'. Scott replied that, after what had occurred, he was sure the Hong Kong government would refuse; it was also likely that the Governor would not let the matter rest.[73]

Cheung Cho-ting had fled. Blake proposed that he be extradited to stand trial in Hong Kong. This was 'an exceptional case of such vital importance to the security of the many thousands of Chinese living under the protection of the British Flag' that his extradition

71. Schiffrin, *Sun Yat-sen*, 305–306; Chan Lau, *China, Britain and Hong Kong*, 60–64.

72. Blake to Chamberlain, 18 June 1903 and Blake to Satow 21 August 1903, CO 129/317, 450–453 and CO 129/318, 254–281. James Scott succeeded Benjamin Scott as Consul-General in April 1902.

73. Blake to Satow, 21 August 1903, CO 129/318, 256–281.

should be insisted upon, he said. To expedite matters he sent an arrest warrant direct to Sir Ernest Satow, the British Minister in Peking. Satow demurred. His request to the Chinese authorities was simply for 'the arrest and trial of the perpetrators and instigators'. At the suggestion of Joseph Chamberlain, Secretary of State for the Colonies, a further demand called for the punishment of Admiral Ho and other officials implicated in the crime. In October 1903 Satow conveyed this demand to Prince Qing, the head of the Foreign Affairs Ministry: it was not the identity of the dead man that mattered, he said, 'but the fact that he was murdered in British territory at the instigation of Chinese officials'. Prince Qing ordered an investigation.[74]

The initial results of this investigation did not reassure the British government. The Viceroy at Canton, Cen Chunxuan, ordered Admiral Ho to arrest and interrogate Cheung Cho-ting and the officials concerned in the murder. Further pressure by Satow in Peking and the Acting British Consul-General in Canton, C.W. Campbell, resulted in the trial of Cheung Cho-ting in Canton in February 1904. Cen appointed a judicial commission to investigate the case, consisting of the Provincial Treasurer, the Provincial Judge, the Salt Commissioner, the Grain Intendant, and the Viceroy's Foreign Secretary. Cheung's servants, the coffin-carriers, and Ng Luk's widow (now living in Hong Kong) were taken to Canton to give evidence by Edwin Hallifax, a cadet officer serving as assistant superintendent of police. A team of Hong Kong policemen guarded them during their stay.

British consular officials not only watched over the trial but tried to influence its procedures and outcome.[75] A curious discussion about protocol took place before the trial began – an echo almost of the disputes about the kowtow that had vexed the earliest British diplomatic missions to China. Viceroy Cen asked that, in accordance with custom, witnesses should kneel before the court while giving evidence. Campbell objected that, since the examinations would be lengthy, this would be 'little short of cruelty'. Although the witnesses were Chinese subjects, 'they were British witnesses who could not have come to Canton but for the assurance of protection from the British authorities'. Cen countered that in a Chinese court a Chinese subject was expected to behave as if in the presence of the Emperor: kneeling was equivalent to the oath administered to witnesses in British courts; it 'reminded them of the solemnity of the occasion'. A compromise was reached whereby the witnesses from Hong Kong, on being called, prostrated themselves before the court, but were then allowed to stand for the rest of their examination.

After six days of hearings the court established the guilt of the murderer, Cheung Cho-ting. But evidence of Admiral Ho's complicity was inconclusive. Campbell badgered Viceroy Cen into taking action: 'I told him personally that he must do the best he could

---

74. Blake to Satow, 21 August 1903, CO 129/318, 257; Cox to Foreign Office, 5 October 1903, and Satow to Lansdowne, 8 October 1903, FO 17/1718, 615–625; Satow to Blake, CO 129/323, 173.

75. Satow to Lansdowne, 30 December 1903 and Campbell to Satow, 15 April 1904, FO 17/1718, 633–640.

with the evidence before him,' he reported. 'I pointed out that His Majesty's Government had been patient, and that I should have to object strongly to further delay.' Caught between British demands and the manoeuvrings of Admiral Ho's influential friends, Cen proposed a settlement: Ho would be removed from office by means of a memorial to the Emperor; minor officials complicit in the affair would be dismissed; the murderer Cheung would be executed in the presence of a British consular official; the Viceroy would write to the Hong Kong government apologizing for the violation of territory and thanking it for its assistance in detecting the crime. These measures were endorsed by F.H. May, now administering the government in the hiatus between Blake's departure and Nathan's arrival, and agreed by the British government. Cheung was beheaded on 4 May 1904 after being identified by consular officials present at his trial. Correspondence on the affair was laid before the Hong Kong Legislative Council.[76]

At some point in 1904 Hung Tsun-fuk returned secretly to Hong Kong to regroup his men for another attempt on Canton. He fell ill and died on 5 December. His body was carried in a magnificent hearse to the Colonial Cemetery and buried in a grave not far from that of Yeung Ku-wan. A large contingent of police officers escorted the cortege. The revolutionaries stayed away, fearing spies from Canton.[77] The instigator of Hung's aborted uprising, Tse Tsan-tai, had now withdrawn from revolutionary politics and was devoting his energies to the *South China Morning Post*, which he had co-founded in 1903 with Alfred Cunningham, the former manager of the *Daily Press*.

From extradition to deportation

The intervention in Cheung Cho-ting's trial in Canton came when British power in China was at its zenith. To the surprise of some of his own officials, Governor Blake was also successful in his earlier demand that British officials should be present at the trials of prisoners extradited from Hong Kong to ensure they were not tortured into confessing. Diplomats had long maintained a position articulated by Sir Rutherford Alcock, the British Minister in Peking in the 1860s, that confessions of guilt were an essential feature of Chinese justice, and that such an arrangement would result in fugitives escaping punishment altogether if they refused to confess; it would, said Alcock, 'be equivalent to a Foreign Power insisting that we should dispense with all evidence on oath'.[78] But when Blake raised the matter

76. May to Lyttelton, 28 June 1904, CO 129/323, 169–180; Foreign Office to Colonial Office, 7 July 1904, CO 129/326, 339–347.
77. *OCM*, 19 December 1903.
78. This was in response to suggestions from the Admiralty that consular officials should attend trials of alleged pirates handed over by British naval ships. The position was reaffirmed by the Foreign Secretary, Lord Granville, in 1882, when reports that torture was being used in trials of fugitives surrendered from Hong Kong prompted suggestions that the government should repudiate the rendition clause (Article 21) of the Treaty of Tientsin:

in 1901, the British Minister, Satow, was more amenable. Satow instructed the Consul-General in Canton to raise the matter with the Viceroy, Tao Mo, who, like his successor Cen Chunxian, held progressive views. Tao immediately agreed. The attendance of consular officials at trials in Canton of persons extradited from Hong Kong became standard practice in the remaining ten years of the Qing dynasty.[79]

Blake described this achievement as the 'one thing' he would always look back on with the 'keenest pleasure'. He had observed a 'distinct progress of public opinion' on this question 'even in China'.[80] In the wake of the Boxer Rebellion, the Qing government appointed commissions to propose reforms in all areas of government, including law and justice. One of the members of the Law Revision Commission, Ng Choy (Wu Tingfang), formerly a barrister and magistrate in Hong Kong, proposed a system based on English practices, including the use of juries and adversarial procedure.[81] In the event, however, the criminal code promulgated in 1910 drew on continental European models, via Japan. Memorials to the throne by the commissioners resulted in a series of imperial edicts from 1905 abolishing cruel punishments and judicial torture.[82] In parallel, a Movement for the Abolition of Torture in China was launched by Eugenio Volpicelli, the Italian Consul-General in Hong Kong, Canton, and Macao. The Hong Kong Attorney General, Sir Henry Berkeley, was a member of the committee. Volpicelli translated into Chinese the chapter against judicial torture in Cesare Beccaria's *Dei delitti e delle pene* (*On Crimes and Punishments*), an eighteenth-century treatise influential in continental Europe, where confessions under torture had also been a feature of criminal justice. The translation was circulated in pamphlet form and published in Chinese newspapers in Hong Kong and Canton, where reform-minded officials were said to be strongly supportive of its ideas.[83]

Requests for extraditions increased in the 1900s, a pattern attributed by Hong Kong officials to greater energy by the Chinese authorities in suppressing robberies. Proceedings

---

Granville directed that officials should insist on strict fulfilment of the guarantee against *lingchi* but should merely be satisfied with the Viceroy's assurances that torture would not be applied during trial. Alcock to Stanley, 18 May 1868, 18 May 1868, FO 17/615, 129–139; Pauncefote to Law Officers, 14 June 1882 and Granville to Grosvenor, 6 September 1882, FO 17/1078, 82–84 and 108–111.

79. Consular officials also attended the executions of some extradited criminals. Blake to Chamberlain, 31 May 1901, CO 129/305, 198; Blake to Chamberlain, 1 June 1901, Chamberlain to Blake, 26 July 1901, and Scott to Lansdowne, 2 December 1901, FO 17/1591, 3–4, 14, and 20–30.
80. *SCMP*, 23 November 1903; Blake to Chamberlain, 1 June 1901, FO 17/1591, 4.
81. See Bernard H.K. Luk, 'A Hong Kong Barrister in late-Ch'ing Law Reform', *HKLJ*, Vol. 11 (1981): 339–355; Xu Xiaqun, *Heaven Has Eyes: A History of Chinese Law* (Oxford: Oxford University Press, 2020), Chapter 4. The Draft Criminal and Procedural Law, 1906, is in 大清新法令 (1901–1911) [Qing Law Reforms (1901–1911)] (Shanghai: The Commercial Press, 2010), Vol. 1, 418–456: I am indebted to Professor Chen Xinyu of the School of Law, Tsinghua University for this reference.
82. The frequent reissue of the edict reflected continuing use of torture by some officials.
83. The *Wa Tsz Yat Po*, one of Hong Kong's leading Chinese-language papers, serialized the chapter on 21, 23, and 24 January 1905. *OCM*, 28 January, 20 May, and 25 July 1905.

in Hong Kong became still more complicated after the arrival of Chief Justice Sir Francis Piggott (1905–1912). An expert on extradition, Piggott was more attentive to procedure and individual rights than his predecessor, Goodman, had been. As for 'being a reformer', Goodman had observed when dismissing one habeas corpus application, 'all these people said that when they sought to evade extradition'.[84] Piggott, in contrast, refused to accept 'that any procedure will do so long as the fugitive is caught, and so long as some regular step is taken during the proceedings at some time or other'.[85] He ended the practice in which Hong Kong lawyers acted for the Chinese government in extradition cases.[86] He also opposed the arrangement by which the Chief Justice assisted the Governor in Council in cases involving Hong Kong residents, arguing that it would place him in an embarrassing situation in any subsequent habeas corpus proceedings.[87]

Piggott and other judges granted writs of habeas corpus on political and technical grounds in several extradition cases in the early twentieth century. Officials, in contrast, wished to simplify the system. Revolutionaries in China were turning their sights on foreign imperialists. Hong Kong was now not only a place of asylum but also a theatre of protest against actions by other powers, ranging from the US Chinese exclusion acts to Japanese aggressions on Chinese soil. Increasingly, protests targeted the British presence in China. As a key possession of the strongest global power, Hong Kong was both a product of aggressive Western imperialism and a stark example of the capitalist exploitation that revolutionaries sought to abolish. After the collapse of Qing rule, anti-foreign outbursts evolved into generalized movements against imperialism, culminating, in Hong Kong, in the Seamen's Strike of 1922 and the General Strike-Boycott 1925–1926.

In these turbulent times, governors and diplomats sought cooperation with other colonial regimes – the French in Indochina, the Dutch in the East Indies, the Americans in the Philippines – and with whichever among the competing regimes in southern China seemed able to provide stability. In 1916, when the Supreme Court granted a writ of habeas corpus for a political fugitive wanted by the Canton government, the Governor, Sir Henry May, proposed adopting the 'French system', which would turn extradition to China into

84. *OCM*, 22 November 1902.

85. This came in a judgment by the Full Court in 1908 on an appeal against a failed application for *habeas corpus* by Iu Ki Shing, a rebel wanted by the Canton authorities for robbery. The court ordered Iu's release on the ground that the magistrate had not followed procedures in the ordinance. *In the Matter of Iu Ki Shing* (1908) 3 HKLR 20; *HKDP*, 26 February 1908; Chan Lau, *China, Britain and Hong Kong*, 73–74.

86. The Chinese government had for some time been engaging lawyers to take over extradition cases from the police, while also complaining about the huge expense. In a case in 1905 Piggott ruled that the Chinese government had no *locus standi* in such cases. This function was then taken over by an Assistant Crown Solicitor on behalf of the Hong Kong government, although the Chinese government continued to pay fees. May to Crewe, 9 August and 10 October 1910, CO 129/368, 134–138 and CO 129/369, 143–155.

87. The Chinese Extradition Ordinance was amended to reflect this: Ordinance No. 37 of 1909.

a purely executive process.[88] Nothing came of this. But, after the collapse of the Strike-Boycott in 1926, the staunchly anti-communist Governor, Sir Cecil Clementi, worked with a new hardline regime in Canton to eradicate communists, who had moved their headquarters to Hong Kong to avoid purges in mainland cities. With the help of detectives from Canton, police arrested hundreds of alleged communists. Most were deported. Some, handed over direct to the Canton authorities, faced execution.[89]

In 1929, British diplomats in Canton, objecting to the protection given in Hong Kong to rivals of Chiang Kai-shek, proposed summary deportation of any political refugee whose presence was objectionable to the Chinese government. This would have ended Hong Kong's role as a place of asylum. The Hong Kong government rejected the idea. However, in 1931–1932, under Foreign Office pressure, it tried to adopt the method in the celebrated case of Ho Chi Minh, then resident in Hong Kong. The Governor, Sir William Peel, issued orders for him to be deported to Indochina, where he was wanted by the French authorities for political crimes. Ho's counsel, Francis Jenkin KC, described the manoeuvre as a 'sham under cloak of deportation' aimed at avoiding extradition proceedings in the courts.[90] But the deportation regime was now so impervious that judges felt unable to interfere. The case went to the Privy Council. It was settled after the first day of hearings by an arrangement under which Ho, instead of being sent to Saigon, was deported to his chosen destination, Moscow, via Shanghai and Vladivostok.[91]

---

88. After his discharge by the court, the fugitive, Hung Shiu-lun, was rearrested and deported to Japan, to join Sun Yat-sen. *In re Hung Siu Lun* (1915) 10 HKLR 114; *HKDP*, 25 December 1915; May to Bonar Law, 12 January 1916, CO 129/431, 112–114; ExCo Minutes, 16 March 1916, CO 131/49, 576–577.
89. Chan Lau Kit-ching, *From Nothing to Nothing: The Chinese Communist Movement and Hong Kong, 1921–1936* (Hong Kong: Hong Kong University Press, 1999), 176–189.
90. *HKDP*, 25 August 1931.
91. See Geoffrey C. Gunn, *Ho Chi Minh in Hong Kong: Anti-Colonial Networks, Extradition and the Rule of Law* (Cambridge: Cambridge University Press, 2021).

6

By Sampan to Singapore

The Harbour Murders, 1904

The title of the lecture at the European YMCA on Sunday 4 December 1904 was 'The Moral influence of the European in the Far East'. The speaker was James Dyer Ball, Chief Interpreter to the Supreme Court and Hong Kong's leading sinologist. Born to American missionaries, he had grown up in Canton speaking perfect 'West End' Cantonese before attending universities in London and Liverpool. He was the author of guides to half a dozen Chinese dialects, an *English-Chinese Cookery Book,* and the encyclopaedia *Things Chinese.*[1] His lecture drew a large audience. But those expecting to hear a positive account of European influence were to be disappointed. Although Dyer Ball spoke of the beneficial impact of missionaries and some businessmen, his focus was on the harm done to China. There was the opium trade, of course. Another 'dark question' was the violent behaviour of certain Europeans. Sometimes, for almost no reason, they knocked down or beat Chinese, who refrained from retaliating because they were a peace-loving people. 'There were continually cases of Chinese who happened to have enlarged spleens or other maladies succumbing to kicks from Englishmen,' he told his audience.[2]

Dyer Ball tactfully confined his comments to European behaviour in and around the treaty ports. He reached back nearly sixty years for an example: the Huangzhuqi 'massacre'

1. See Peter Hamilton, 'An American Family's Mission in East Asia, 1838 to 1936: A Commitment to God, Academia and Empire', *Journal of the Royal Asiatic Society Hong Kong Branch,* Vol. 49 (2009): 229–265. 'West End' Cantonese (西關話), spoken in the affluent district of Canton, was regarded by Dyer Ball and later linguists as 'the correct pronunciation of pure Cantonese'. May Bo Ching, 'Itinerant Singers: Triangulating the Canton–Hong Kong–Macau Soundscape', in *Asia Inside Out: Itinerant People,* ed. Eric Tagliacozzo, Helen F. Siu, and Peter C. Perdue (Cambridge, Massachusetts: Harvard University Press, 2019), 244–270.
2. *HKWP,* 12 December 1904.

of 1847, in which six young Englishmen, out hunting birds, had entered a village near Canton, got into a fight, and fatally shot two villagers before being killed themselves.[3] There were recent cases closer to home. One was unfolding on the very day of the lecture. That Sunday morning three young men were arrested by police on a remote beach near Ping Shan in the New Territories. On the Friday and Saturday police had recovered from the harbour the decomposing bodies of a forty-year-old woman and a four-year-old girl. Kwok Tai-chan, identified them as his wife, Chan Yee, and daughter, Kwok Tit, missing since 27 November. The Kwok family, members of the boat-dwelling or 'Tanka' community, lived on a sampan, one of many boats used to ferry passengers to and from ships in the harbour. On Monday 5 December the three men were charged with the murder of Chan Yee and Kwok Tit on the family's sampan on 27 November. Two of the men were Americans. The third was described variously as a Swede, a Finn, a Pole, a Russian Jew. Their nationalities hardly mattered. Most early reports referred to them as 'the three Europeans'. Colonial classifications, from the census to the gaol, bracketed Europeans and Americans together. Chinese witnesses in what became known as the 'Harbour Murders' assumed the three were 'Englishmen'. To colonists they were simply 'beachcombers' – members of a class which, according to the Acting Attorney General, 'was becoming a curse to the community'.[4]

The beachcomber class

The three men were Charles Smith (aged twenty), William Nason (seventeen), both Americans, and Erik Hogmann (twenty-two), a Swedish-speaking Finn. They were unemployed sailors who had been in Hong Kong for several months. Smith had arrived on a ship from Manila. Some weeks before the alleged murders he had met up with Nason, who had probably also been in Manila: the US had recently colonized the Philippines, a former Spanish colony. Hogmann had joined Smith and Nason only on the day of the murders. They were nearly destitute. The police found on Smith $1.60, a razor, a cap, and a stick; on Hogmann five Chinese coins, a safety pin, five cigarettes, a book, a mirror, a bed cover, twelve boxes of matches, a cap, and a stick; and on Nason thirty cents, a bottle of toothache tincture, a knife, a comb, a folding mirror, fishing hooks, and some clothes. All three men had spent time in the House of Detention at Victoria Gaol.[5] Under the Vagrancy Ordinance, police officers could take before a magistrate any person found in the streets

---

3. Insisting that the 'murders' were unprovoked, the British Plenipotentiary and Governor, Sir John Francis Davis, demanded punishment, threatening war. The Imperial Commissioner, Qiying, ordered the execution of four villagers outside their ancestral hall in the presence of British officials and soldiers. Li Chen, *Chinese Law in Imperial Eyes: Sovereignty, Justice and Transcultural Politics* (New York: Columbia University Press, 2016), 193–194.
4. *HKWP*, 26 December 1904.
5. *CM*, 14 December 1904; *OCM*, 13 December 1904.

begging or without visible means of support. The magistrate could then declare him to be a vagrant and commit him to the House of Detention. Inmates there received the same treatment as prisoners on remand, except they were allowed out at certain times to search for work. The magistrate was required to assist any vagrant appearing before him to find work. Lists of seamen-vagrants were sent weekly to the Harbour Master, who was also enjoined to use his best efforts to find them work. If they refused work or escaped from detention they were liable to imprisonment for up to three months.[6]

The Vagrancy Ordinance applied only to non-Chinese persons. Chinese beggars were dealt with by deportation or summary expulsion. In addition, thousands of Chinese destitutes saved from shipwrecks, returning from emigration, or otherwise stranded, were assisted with repatriation by the Tung Wah Hospital.[7] Europeans could only be repatriated at great expense. The government allocated a small amount of money every year for this purpose.[8] The Merchant Shipping Act provided for repatriation of distressed seamen left behind by British ships.[9] The Vagrancy Ordinance imposed liabilities on shipowners and captains for discharging men without the means of subsistence. But these provisions were loosely enforced and easily evaded. Some vagrants could not remember their ships, or were deserters or stowaways. Other 'wandering Europeans' worked their passages from port to port. Their numbers were small but increasing: twenty-nine were committed to the House of Detention in 1898, rising to 113 in 1904: the increase was due partly to the practice by some shipping firms of discharging European crews in Hong Kong and replacing them with Chinese.[10] European destitutes were not just a nuisance but an embarrassment to colonists, who did not wish Chinese to see white people reduced to such a wretched state. 'We don't want Europeans lying about the streets of the Colony,' said the magistrate Henry Gompertz in June 1904 when sending a sailor to the House of Detention. The sailor had

6. Ordinance No. 25 of 1897, a re-enactment of Ordinance No. 12 of 1888 with minor modifications. Modelled on the European Vagrancy Act 1874 of India, the 1888 ordinance formalized existing practices. Marsh to the Secretary of State for the Colonies, 24 July 1886, CO 129/228, 88–103. See Christopher Roberts, 'The Significance and Endurance of Vagrancy and Vagrancy-type Laws in England, the British Empire, and the British Colonial World', *Duke Journal of Comparative & International Law*, Vol. 33 (2023): 181–251.
7. Brewin to May, 26 January 1910, CO 129/365, 424–425.
8. It was from this fund that Governor May provided £50 for a passage to England for the former Chief Justice, Sir Francis Piggott, in 1914: see Chapter 1.
9. The Merchant Shipping Act 1894 empowered colonial governors to compel a British ship to provide a passage home for any distressed seaman, to be paid out of the Mercantile Marine Fund, and recovered, in cases of contravention of the act, from the master or owner of the ship that had discharged the seaman.
10. Particularly, Governor Nathan reported, on ships taking Chinese coolie labourers from Hong Kong to work in the mines in the Transvaal, a practice that was soon to cause controversy in Britain over the harsh conditions in which they worked. Nathan to Lucas, 30 December 1904, Nathan Papers, Oxford, Bodleian Libraries, MS Nathan 328, 68–69; Peter Richardson, 'The Recruiting of Chinese Indentured Labour for the South African Gold-Mines, 1903–1908', *Journal of African History*, Vol. 18, No. 1 (1977): 85–108.

been found lying drunk at the tram terminus with only six cents to his name – enough, he claimed, to live on for one day.[11]

Colonists called such men 'beachcombers', 'loafers', 'bummers', and 'deadbeats'. By the late nineteenth century, newspapers were referring to a 'beachcomber class', a growing population of unemployed sailors who pestered shopkeepers and passers-by for money, and even invaded private offices and homes. Some took to petty crime. A few were dangerous. In 1867 a military deserter, Thomas Banbury, the 'Wild Man of the Hills', lived a 'Robinson Crusoe' life, terrorizing villagers in the Stanley and Aberdeen neighbourhoods, stealing livestock and attacking women while they were out cutting grass, until he was eventually caught and convicted of indecent assault.[12] Some beachcombers found work on ships or in Hong Kong: several were recruited into the police force, and in 1879 a destitute sailor housed in the gaol was employed to carry out a triple hanging.[13] But in a place where Chinese labour was plentiful and cheap, there was little work for the unskilled white man. Outside the House of Detention welfare support was minimal. The Sailors' Home was open only to those who could pay their way. The Missions to Seamen offered only spiritual support. The Hongkong Benevolent Society, formed in 1890, was managed by wives of officials, judges, and other members of the colonial elite. It gave financial support, found work, and paid for passages home for indigent Europeans, including discharged prisoners. But it was careful to distinguish 'cases of real, *bona fide* distress' from what its chairman, Chief Justice Sir William Goodman, described as 'the loafing, plausible beachcomber, who does not deserve the slightest assistance'.[14] Such men, said the *China Mail,* had 'a constitutional antipathy to labour of any kind' and would soon absorb the Society's funds 'in the convenient form of beer'.[15] The most abandoned among them got blind drunk for days on end on *samshu,* a liquor bought from grog-shops or brothels, or at a place known as 'Samshu Corner'.[16]

11. *OCM,* 2 July 1904.
12. He pleaded guilty and was sentenced by Chief Justice Smale to two years' imprisonment. *OCM,* 15 March and 1 November 1867; *HKDP,* 29 November 1867.
13. *CM,* 28 May 1879.
14. *OCM,* 30 January 1904. Stephen Davies, *Strong to Save: Maritime Mission in Hong Kong from Whampoa Reach to the Mariners' Club* (Hong Kong: City University of Hong Kong Press, 2017), Chapter 6.
15. *OCM,* 28 December 1892.
16. Samshu (三燒) was distilled from rice. It was less strong but much cheaper than whisky and was popular among sailors and soldiers. Drunk in large quantities, it was believed to cause violent frenzy. Samshu Corner was on Upper Lascar Row, a street near Hollywood Road. *Report of the Commission on Alcoholic Liquors* (Hong Kong: Noronha & Co., 1898), 20–22, Appendix 7, xxxvi, and Appendix 12.

The Harbour Murders

Charles Smith, William Nason, and Erik Hogmann were not the hardened beachcombers described by Goodman. They were not drunkards, they had a little money, and they wanted work. According to their own accounts, on the day of the murder Nason and Smith went for a bathe in a stream on Bowen Road, just above the city. Smith proposed a plan to get them out of Hong Kong. In the afternoon they wandered back and forth along Queen's Road. They encountered Hogmann some time after 5 p.m. near the Stag Hotel in Central and explained the plan. He agreed to join them. Smith and Nason went to a restaurant to eat while Hogmann bought a few cents worth of bananas and bread for his supper. The three then reassembled at the Sailors' Home at West Point. The plan was to hire a sampan, tie up the Chinese on board, and put them ashore on some island. The three would then sail south to Singapore, where they hoped to find work.[17]

As it got dark the three men walked along the Praya (or seafront) looking for a suitable boat. They got into one sampan, which had five people in it: after realizing that they would 'have to kill somebody if we went off with that number', they made excuses and went ashore. At 8:45 p.m. they reached Pottinger Wharf, about two miles from the Sailors' Home. There, Kwok Tai-chan, asked if they wanted a boat. After haggling in pidgin English, Smith and Kwok agreed on a fare of seventy cents for Kwok's sampan to take them to 'the American boat with two funnels' anchored off Kowloon. Smith climbed down into the sampan by its mast. Hogmann and Nason jumped into it. Smith told Kwok he need not join them, so he stayed on the Praya. His wife, Chan Yee, steered from the stern. Their eldest son, sixteen-year-old Kwok So, rowed the sampan at the bow. Three other members of the family were also in the sampan: two daughters, thirteen-year-old Kwok Nui (or Kwok Tai) and four-year-old Kwok Tit, sat with their mother; another son, nine-year-old Kwok Sai-lo, was asleep in the hold under a tarpaulin shelter.[18] The three passengers sat with Chan Yee and her daughters near the stern.

As Kwok Tai-chan watched the boat disappear he saw one of the men hoist sail. Shortly after this, in the middle of the harbour, the three men began to carry out their plan. Smith pushed the thirteen-year-old Kwok Nui down into the hold, where she knocked her head and lost consciousness. He told Hogmann, the strongest among them, to tackle the mother, Chan Yee, and tie her up. Hogmann caught hold of her and put his hand over her mouth,

17. The sources for this and the following sections are the reports on the arrests and committal proceedings in *CM*, 5–7 and 13–15 December 1904; *HKWP*, 17 December 1904; *HKT*, 14, 15, and 17 December 1904; and *SCMP*, 6, 17, and 14–16 December 1904.

18. The Chinese characters in the reports in the *WTYP*, 7 and 14 December 1904, are 陳二 and 陳意 (Chan Yee), and 郭娣 (Kwok Tai), 郭秩 (Kwok Tit) and 郭蘇 (Kwok So). Kwok Nui (in some reports, Kwok Lui-tsai) is probably 'daughter Kwok' (郭女 or 郭女仔). The father is called Kwok Li-cheong (郭理昌) in some early reports. However, at the trial he is called Kwok Tai-chan.

while Smith took hold of the child, Kwok Tit. Chan Yee resisted and made such a noise that Smith let go of the child, pulled out the tiller, and hit Chan Yee twice over the head with it. The child began to cry and Smith threw her overboard. While this was going on, Nason moved forward to the bow to tackle the boy, Kwok So. The two were close in age: Nason was seventeen; Kwok was sixteen by traditional Chinese reckoning, fifteen according to the Western system. Both were strong, and the struggle was fierce and prolonged. Nason grabbed Kwok by the neck and bit him on the side of his head. Kwok kicked him back. They fought for several minutes. Then Nason took out a knife, hit Kwok over the head with it, and slashed his calf while trying to tie up his legs. The fight continued until they were both half overboard. Nason then let go of Kwok, or pushed him, and Kwok fell into the water. Nason returned to the stern and helped Hogmann subdue Chan Yee, cramming a handkerchief into her mouth, and smashing a lantern, the only source of light. In the darkness he heard a splash and Hogmann say, 'The woman has gone overboard.' The three men then sailed the sampan westwards, past Green Island and Cheung Chau, into open sea.

They landed about eighteen miles away on Cheung Sha, a beach on the south side of Lantau, the largest of the islands of the New Territories. For the next four days they walked around Lantau. After having almost completed a circuit of the whole island, they reached Sham Shui Kok, a hamlet on the northeast coast. There, on the afternoon of Thursday 1 December, the men encountered the fisherman Wong Luk in his shed. Holding up a cigarette paper, they gestured for tobacco. He gave them enough for a cigarette each. He also offered them rice, which they declined. They held up some money, signalling they wished to hire his boat. When Wong refused they stole another boat. Its owner, Chow Fat, and Wong gave chase and persuaded them to change into another boat. Chow then took them across to Castle Peak, at the far west of the mainland New Territories. Smith, Nason, and Hogmann carried on walking along the coast for another three days until they were spotted by Sergeant Kerr on a beach near Mong Tseng, a village overlooking Deep Bay, close to the Chinese border. With his team of Indian policemen, Kerr followed them for a while, then arrested the men and took them to Ping Shan Police Station. Later that day they were taken by police launch to Central Police Station. During the whole of their weeklong trek through the wilder reaches of the New Territories the three men believed they were walking in the direction of Singapore.

Meanwhile, at Cheung Sha, the girl, Kwok Nui, and her younger brother emerged from the wrecked sampan the day after it was beached. Finding themselves alone, and unaware of what had happened to the rest of their family, they walked along the beach until they came across two villagers picking cockles. The villagers looked after them for four days before taking them to the nearest police station, at Cheung Chau, a small but populous island about six miles from Cheung Sha. Their elder brother, Kwok So, had also survived the ordeal. After going overboard on the Sunday night, he had swum to another sampan. Its skipper, Fung Chat-sing, gave him dry clothes and took him back to Pottinger Wharf,

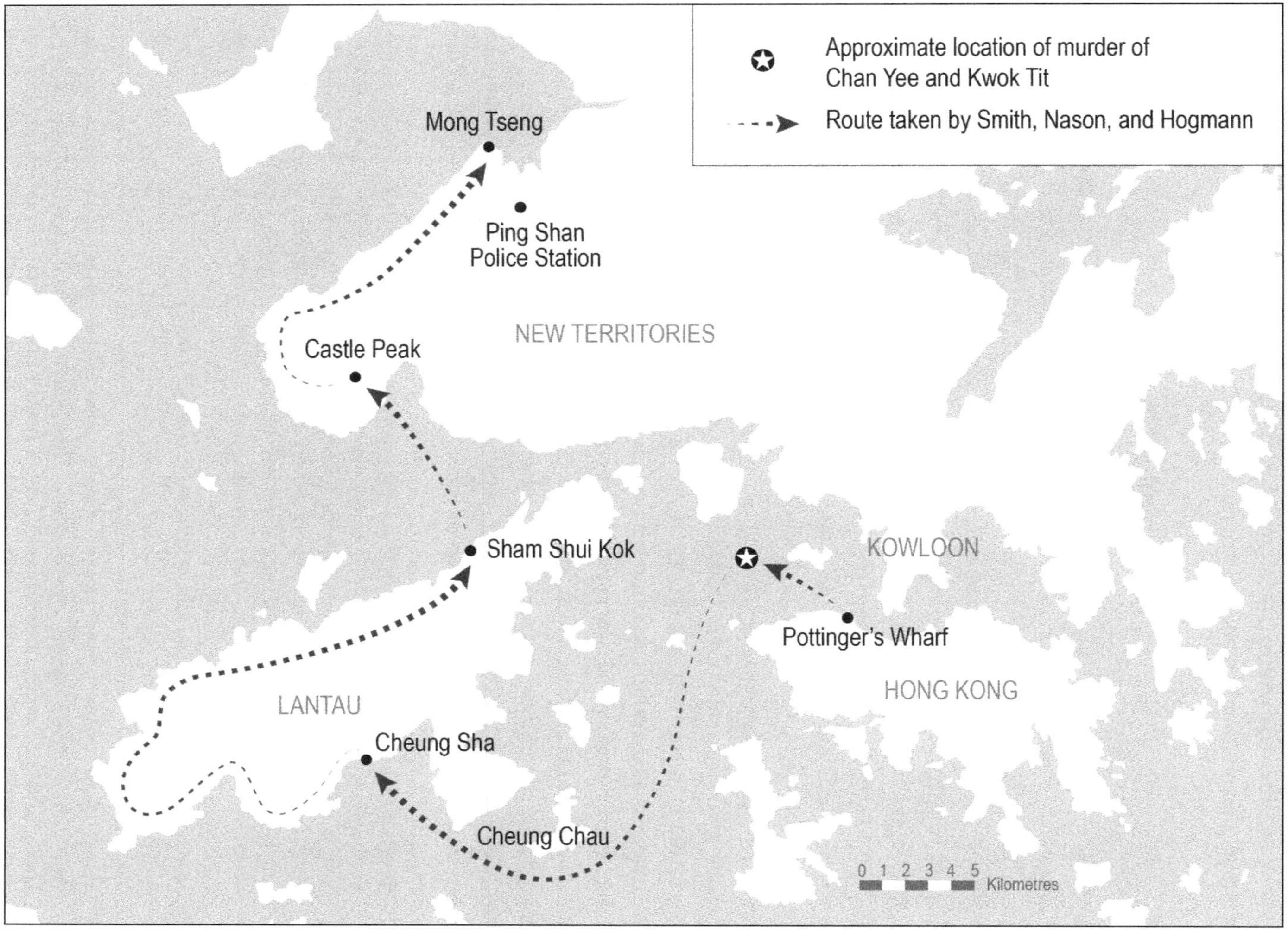

Map 3: The Harbour Murders, 1904

where his father was waiting. They then walked the short distance up Pottinger Street to Central Police Station to report the crime.

The committal hearings

Over the course of three afternoons on 13–15 December the magistrate, Henry Gompertz,[19] heard evidence to determine whether to commit 'the three Englishmen' (as Chinese witnesses persisted in calling them) for trial. The Captain-Superintendent of Police, Francis Badeley, conducted the prosecution. Gompertz heard from the police, the Lantau villagers, and surviving members of the Kwok family. But many of the important details of the case came from statements by the accused themselves. Under English procedures followed in Hong Kong, once all prosecution witnesses had been examined, the magistrate read out their depositions and asked the accused if they had anything to say in answer to the charges; at the same time he cautioned them that they were not obliged to say anything, but that whatever they did say would be taken down in writing and might be given in evidence against them at trial. Whether or not they made a statement, the accused then had the opportunity to call their own witnesses.[20] Many defendants, especially those with lawyers, said nothing and reserved their defence for the trial. Hong Kong magistrates rarely, if ever, made use of the special power given to them in 1872 to question defendants.[21] Nor did they place much weight on confessions to the police, even if made willingly and under caution: judges in England at this time discouraged police interrogation; although practices varied from force to force, some prohibited their officers from putting questions to a person charged with an offence.[22] These restraints fell away by the middle of

19. Originally recruited as a cadet for the Straits Settlements government in 1890, Henry Hessy Johnston Gompertz was fluent in several Chinese dialects. He was a magistrate in Penang in the 1890s, and, after his transfer to Hong Kong in 1897, took a year's leave to study law in England, where he was called to the Bar by Lincoln's Inn in 1899. He presided over the New Territories Land Court from 1902 to 1904 and acted as police magistrate and occasionally as Attorney General and judge until his appointment as Puisne Judge in 1909. He was Chief Justice of the Federated Malay States 1925–1929 and was knighted in 1926. His wife was secretary and later president of the Hong Kong Benevolent Society.
20. Magistrates Ordinance, No. 10 of 1890 (1901 edition), sections 73 and 74.
21. See Chapter 4.
22. The reasons were (1) the common law principle against self-incrimination; (2) the idea that police were 'citizens in uniform', with minimal powers, responsible for maintaining order and making arrests but not, until later in the century, for investigating and detecting crime – this was to counter fears that police forces established in England in the early nineteenth century would become 'continental'-style tools of despotism; (3) the repeal of the power of magistrates in England in 1848 to question the accused, and it was deemed improper that policemen should be allowed to do so; (4) the risk of unfairness to the accused if answers were misrepresented or distorted, or if a confession was obtained through inducement or coercion, or invented; and (5) the incompetence of the accused, until 1899, to give evidence on oath, which originated as a protection against self-incrimination. See Bentley, *English Criminal Justice in the Nineteenth Century*, Chapter 21. In twentieth-century Hong Kong, judges were increasingly sceptical of confessions obtained through police interviews. In some cases in the

the twentieth century as detective methods developed and judicial disapproval of police interrogation declined.[23]

Whatever the inhibitions imposed on the police, Smith, Hogmann, and Nason said a great deal prior to their trial. On 5 December, the day after their arrest, all three made statements under caution to the police – two in the form of confessions. On their first appearance before the magistrate on the 6th, Smith and Nason pleaded not guilty to the three charges: the murder of Chan Yee and Kwok Tit and the attempted murder of Kwok So. Hogmann could not understand the charges. When a Swedish interpreter, Robert Lindblom, was found, Hogmann pleaded guilty to only one of the charges, the murder, in consort with the others, of Chan Yee, adding that he had not touched the girl or the boy. After prosecution witnesses had given evidence during a three-day hearing a week later, Chief Detective Inspector John Hanson read out statements made by the accused on 5 December. Smith's simply denied going on any boat on 27 November and said he had left Kowloon on the 25th to walk to Canton with Hogmann and Nason, whom he had met only on that day. Nason, in contrast, gave a detailed account of the plot to steal a sampan and of his fight with Kwok So, insisting that the plan was merely to tie up the people on board, implying that Kwok So and Chan Yee had fallen or jumped overboard, and stating that Smith had told him he had thrown the young girl, Kwok Tit, into the sea. Hogmann recounted the plot as well as Smith's idea that Hogmann, being the strongest, should tackle the mother, Chan Yee, which he reluctantly agreed to do; in the event, both he and Smith had fought with her, and Nason had helped throw her body overboard.

On the last day of the hearing, the magistrate, Gompertz, said he proposed to commit the three accused for trial. After administering cautions, he asked if they had any statements to make. Smith now changed the story he had given to the police. He admitted that the plot to take a boat was his idea, and said he 'went for the children' and had difficulty keeping them quiet. He put the older one, Kwok Tit, down in the hold, and then 'started back for the other one, the small one. She took fright and jumped overboard. I tried to grab her, but it was too late.' Hogmann stated that he had tried to heave Chan Yee overboard, 'but she either jumped or fell overboard herself'. He asked for Nason's statement to the police, read out the day before, to be translated to him. Nason then amended what he had said about Smith to the police, and said that, after his fight with Kwok So, he had gone to the back of the sampan and had seen Smith chasing 'the small "kid." It had got up on the stern – right at the back, as far as it could get, Smith had just made a grab for it when it jumped overboard.' He also said that Chan Yee had jumped overboard after fighting with Hogmann.

1930s, and especially in the 1960s and 1970s, the question of whether a confession was obtained by coercion or inducement came to dominate many criminal trials.

23. Mike McConville and Luke Marsh, *The Myth of Judicial Independence* (Oxford: Oxford University Press, 2020), Chapters 3 and 4; *Report of the Royal Commission on Police Powers and Procedure* (Cmd 3297, 1929), 60–61.

Nason, the youngest of the three, was the most talkative. His statements were long, detailed, and inconsistent. He also cross-examined witnesses at the committal hearing. Yet his attempt to finesse the story into a hijack resulting in inadvertent deaths was no defence. Any loss of life caused by an act of felony was murder in English law. Under the doctrine of common design, every participant in the felony was equally guilty, whether or not he directly caused the death. There was no reason why Nason or his co-defendants should have known about this: the short-lived practice of assigning solicitors to defendants on capital charges in committal proceedings had ended in 1897.

R v Charles Smith, Erik Hogmann, and William Nason Murder and attempted murder, 22 and 23 December 1904

On Thursday 22 December Smith, Hogmann and Nason, manacled together, were escorted by Sikh and Chinese police with bayonetted rifles from Victoria Gaol down Wyndham Street to the Courthouse on Queen's Road to stand trial in the Supreme Court. There was complete silence as they entered the courtroom, collarless and unkempt, showing, said the *South China Morning Post*, 'signs of the anxious time of the past few days'.[24] Theirs was the only murder case tried in Hong Kong in 1904.[25] Serious crimes reported to the police had fallen by 27 per cent compared with 1905. The forty-nine criminal cases tried in 1904 marked the start of a decline from seventy-eight in 1903 to twenty-six in 1908, after which the caseload increased. In November 1904 the court held a maiden sessions – the eighth, at least, in Hong Kong's history. The Registrar, Arathoon Seth, presented white gloves to the Acting Chief Justice, Sir Henry Berkeley, 'in token of the spotless innocence of the whole population'. Berkeley observed how remarkable this was in a place like Hong Kong, with its 'vast moving criminal population'. He attributed it to the practice of 'dealing with criminals' by deportation.[26] In the December sessions the court tried two armed robberies; a

24. The *Telegraph*, in contrast, reported that none of them 'appeared to realise the terrible seriousness of the situation'. The sources for the trial are *OCM*, 27 December 1904; *HKWP*, 26 December 1904; *SCMP*, 21, 23, and 24 December 1904; *HKT*, 20, 22, and 23 December 1904; and *WTYP*, 24 December 1904.
25. Three other murders were mentioned in the annual police report. In one, an Indian soldier on sentry on Stonecutters Island 'ran amok' and killed two other Indian soldiers before shooting himself. In another, a man killed a woman in a house in Peel Street and then killed himself. In the third, during a robbery at a house at Yuen Leng near Tai Po, a robber standing guard outside shot a woman as she rushed out to raise the alarm. The report noted with satisfaction another trial in 1904 for a murder committed in Hong Kong: that of Cheung Cho-ting, tried and executed in Canton for the murder of Hung Tsun-fuk (see Chapter 5). In another murder, noted in the press but not in the police report, the mutilated body of a servant employed by the Diocesan Girls' School, was found in a lane near West Point. *OCM*, 22 March 1904.
26. Previous maiden sessions were in August 1873, January 1877, February and August 1891, January and November 1892, and January 1893. Further maiden sessions took place in February 1907, June 1914, March and December 1928, August and September 1930, and (probably the last) August 1960. *HKDP*, 19 November 1904; *CM*, 18 November 1892.

'piracy' by a Triad leader who had been levying blackmail in the remote village of Tai O on Lantau Island (tried as demanding money with menaces, riot, and unlawful assembly); and a sexual assault on a European girl: in total seven defendants. All were convicted and sentenced to prison terms ranging from two years to life (for the sexual assault), with twenty-four strokes of the birch for two of the robbers and the Triad leader.[27]

A few days before the trial Smith, Hogmann, and Nason had engaged a solicitor, Oswald Thomson. It is not clear if the government or sympathetic colonists paid for this, or if Thomson gave his services gratis: certainly, none of the accused had means to pay, and the US Consul General does not appear to have interested himself in the case.[28] The three accused were assigned separate counsel, each of them instructed by Thomson. This was a departure from the usual arrangement of providing only one state-funded barrister for any number of defendants in a single murder trial: possibly, it was because they were Europeans. The privilege was all the more remarkable since there were only six barristers in private practice in Hong Kong at this time. The senior barrister, Ernest Sharp KC, was acting as Attorney General while the substantive Attorney General, Sir Henry Berkeley, acted as Chief Justice in the interval between the departure of Goodman in August 1904 and the arrival of his successor, Piggott, in May 1905. Sharp, instructed by the Crown Solicitor Francis Bowley, prosecuted. Berkeley presided as judge. Hogmann was represented by Norman Ferrers, who had joined the Hong Kong Bar in 1902 after practising in the Straits Settlements. This was his second murder trial in Hong Kong.[29] Nason was defended by Horace Calthrop, who had arrived in Hong Kong only in October 1904 after several years in the Gold Coast.[30] Smith's barrister was Hong Kong's leading Chinese

27. *OCM* (supplement), 27 December 1904.

28. The US Consulate was at this time mired in allegations of bribe-taking in the issuing of permits to Chinese not of the 'coolie class' for entry into the US under the Chinese Exclusion Acts. The Consul General, Edward S. Bragg, was a veteran of the Civil War and a former congressman. He was nearly eighty years old. According to Wilbur T. Gracey, the official sent in to investigate, he spent a good deal of his time in the gambling houses of Macao. He was in any case 'too blind, bigoted or prejudiced' to see the corruption going on among his staff. Gracey described the consulate as a 'public scandal', a 'disgrace', and a 'laughing stock', particularly among Chinese. Gracey to Department of State, 24 December 1905, United States Department of State, Despatches from United States Consuls in Hong Kong, 1844–1906.

29. In the first, in January 1903, Ferrers defended Chirutaro Matsumoto, whose wife had run away from him in Taiwan (then a Japanese colony) and had joined a brothel in Hong Kong. Matsumoto followed her and gave her money to pay off her debts and leave the brothel. But she spent the money and refused to leave. He then beat her to death. Ferrers argued there had been provocation and spoke of 'the excitability of the Oriental temperament' and 'the certain amount of authority that was allowed the husband among Eastern peoples'. The judge, Chief Justice Goodman, reminded the court that they were administering English law, which no longer allowed a husband to beat his wife. The jury (three British, two Chinese, a Portuguese, and a Swede), however, were swayed by Ferrers's argument and convicted Matsumoto only of manslaughter, for which he received ten years' imprisonment. *OCM* and *HKWP*, 26 January 1903.

30. In 1906 Calthrop defended the first murder case in which the accused – an ex-employee of a pork shop accused of murdering its accountant – gave testimony on his own behalf. Calthrop objected that he had only been told

resident, the Honourable Ho Kai CMG – legislator, barrister, and physician – now appearing in his eleventh murder case and representing a non-Asian defendant for the first time. Robert Lindblom was sworn in as interpreter for Hogmann. James Dyer Ball interpreted the evidence of the Chinese witnesses.

The prosecutor, Ernest Sharp, asked no fewer than eight of the jurors drawn for the trial to 'stand by'. No reasons were required or given: his aim may have been to obtain, from the assortment of jurors balloted for this sessions, a jury that could fully comprehend the proceedings in English.[31] Most, if not all, of the seven jurors were British subjects, and most were from the class of assistants and engineers from which many common jurors were drawn.[32] Two are of special interest. Solomon Jacob Michael, from a family of brokers and land speculators, was part of the diaspora of Baghdadi Jews who had migrated to Hong Kong and the treaty ports via British India. The more prosperous members of this community identified closely with British interests. The other, the Australian-born Charles Herbert Whiteley Kew, was a clerk with the Hongkong and Kowloon Wharf and Godown Company. A protégé of the banker and legislator, Thomas Whitehead, Kew was to become one of the largest metal traders in the Far East. Under the pseudonym 'Town Dweller' he was a regular writer of letters to newspapers, some of which had a staunchly patriotic tone: for example, during the Canton–Hong Kong Strike-Boycott of 1925–1926 he was one of several correspondents urging a British occupation of Canton. His father, William Ah Kew (Wong Kiu), was a Chinese who had gone to Australia, married Sarah Whiteley, a woman from Yorkshire, and returned with his family to Hong Kong, where he got a job as a police interpreter. Charles Kew and his brothers were educated at the Central Government School and grew up speaking Cantonese as well as English. Probably because of his forceful personality and long experience as a juror, Kew was selected as foreman for this trial.[33]

---

the previous evening that he was to appear for the defendant, even though the defendant had been committed for trial three weeks earlier. 'Such, gentlemen, is how the law is administered here,' he exclaimed when the judge, A.G. Wise, refused to adjourn. The defendant was convicted and hanged. *SCMP*, 19 December 1906 and 8 November 1909; *CM*, 18 December 1908.

31. Of the twenty-four identifiable jurors in this sessions, eleven or twelve were British, eight were German, two were Parsi, and two were Portuguese. Technically, the Attorney General did not challenge jurors, but asked them to 'stand by' until the panel was exhausted, at which point he had to show cause. The accused could only challenge for cause: peremptory challenges by the accused were allowed in Hong Kong only from 1971.

32. The other jurors were Thomas Banks, Chief Engineer, China Sugar Refinery Co.; Charles Mackie, assistant, Gibb Livingston & Co.; Robert King, engineer with Punchard Lowther & Co.; George Smith, assistant, Dodwell & Co.; and J. (John or possibly James) Johnstone, who was one of three Johnstones on the jury list with the same initials – an assistant with Jardine Matheson & Co., an engineer with the Green Island Cement Co. Ltd, and an employee of the Taikoo Sugar Refinery.

33. The Kew family resisted the traditional definition of 'Eurasian', which was only just emerging as a category in the census, cemetery provision, and the segregationist educational and residential policies promoted by the Colonial Secretary, F.H. May. Only forty-two persons identified themselves as Eurasians in the 1911 census, and it was not until the establishment of the Welfare League in 1929 that members of this group asserted their

Although the accused faced two charges of murder and one of attempted murder, the trial, following the rule at the time, was for one charge of murder only: that of the woman, Chan Yee. The three accused pleaded not guilty. During the two-day trial the court was crowded with spectators, European and Chinese. After Sharp gave his opening speech, the prosecution witnesses repeated the evidence they had given at committal proceedings, with some variations. In an attempt to find a more credible motive than a voyage to Singapore, Sharp asked Kwok Tai-chan if there had been money on board the sampan: Kwok replied there was none. The son, Kwok So, now also said Nason had tried to sexually assault him before throwing him overboard. He stuck firmly to his evidence under cross-examination, saying he had been too ashamed to mention it before. As the only survivor conscious throughout the attack, he was cross-examined on other details. The defence focused on the failure of any one of the key witnesses to identify all three defendants, mainly because the night was so dark: Kwok Tai-chan could identify only Smith; Kwok So only Nason. There was none of the bullying of Chinese witnesses common in cross-examination at this time: the tone was subdued and untheatrical.

The main contention came when, towards the end of the prosecution's case, Chief Detective Inspector Hanson began to read out the statements made by the three accused at the police station and before the magistrate. Quoting from *Russell on Crime*,[34] Ho Kai and Ferrers asked for a ruling that only the portions of the statements made by each defendant relating to his own actions should be admitted; the parts implicating other defendants should not go before the jury, since the statement of one defendant was not evidence against another who might be tried with him. Berkeley declined, saying that 'every single thing that a man says should go before the jury', which would then decide on the value to be placed on each statement. Ferrers also objected to Hogmann's statement's being admitted as evidence because it had not been taken down in Swedish but had been translated from Swedish and then taken down in English: 'in the courts at Hongkong there was great carelessness regarding interpretations,' said Ferrers. Berkeley overruled this, but allowed the Swedish interpreter, Robert Lindblom, to be placed in the witness box and examined as to his competence. A prominent freemason, Lindblom was employed as an overseer by the Hong Kong Land Investment Company and Agency Ltd, a company that was then

---

identity as a distinct community: the definition of 'Eurasian' used by the League was offspring or descendants of a union between a Chinese mother and an Occidental father – the reverse of the Kew-Whiteley marriage. Emma Teng, 'Hong Kong's Eurasian "Web" Viewed through the Lens of Inter-Asian Studies: Comments on Engseng Ho's Inter-Asian Concepts for Mobile Societies', *Journal of Asian Studies*, Vol. 76, No. 4 (November 2017): 945; Emma Jinhua Teng, *Eurasian: Mixed Identities in the United States, China, and Hong Kong, 1842–1943* (Oakland: University of California Press, 2013), 243–244.

34. Sir William Oldnall Russell, *A Treatise on Crimes and Misdemeanours* (6th edition, ed. Horace Smith and A.P. Perceval Keep: London: Stevens and Sons, 1896), Vol. III, 526.

transforming Central with large-scale reclamation and grand buildings. Ferrers was satisfied with Lindblom's ability, and the trial continued.

Lindblom's examination took place at the start of the second day of the trial. At the request of the foreman, Berkeley had not ordered the sequestering of jurors overnight, but had simply told them not to discuss the case. The prosecution had concluded its case the day before. The defence called no witnesses. The morning was taken up with speeches by defence counsel, the prosecution's reply, and the judge's summing up. There was little doubt the three defendants had caused the deaths of Chan Yee and her youngest child. The aim of the defence was to persuade the jury that the deaths were unintentional, and the crime manslaughter, not murder. The three barristers struggled to find the right tone to describe the tragedy and to explain the motives of the three young men. Ho Kai said that the prosecution had merely shown that, in stealing a boat to go to Singapore, they were 'guilty of carrying out the maddest prank that has ever been conceived', and that in the execution of 'this absurd plan unfortunately two accidental deaths took place'. The prosecution's efforts to prove a motive of robbery, by asking Kwok Tai-chan if there was money on board, had failed, he said. Its attempt to find another motive – indecent assault of the son, Kwok So – was 'not worthy of consideration' since it came so late. The fact that Nason, the stronger of the two, had fought with Kwok So for so long and had not attacked his vital organs also suggested that Kwok had gone overboard accidentally. Ho criticized a parallel drawn by Sharp in his opening speech between the present case and that of Charles Peace, a notorious burglar in England who had killed and wounded policemen in the course of his crimes.

Ferrers then rose to say that neither of the key witnesses, Kwok Tai-chan and Kwok So, had identified his client, Hogmann. The evidence against him was 'absolutely nothing, and if he had said nothing, and not deliberately thrown the whole case away, he would have been perfectly safe'. Policemen, he said, were only human beings, and naturally took the opportunity to give friendly hints to prisoners.

> Now, how was a man brought to blurt out when he had only got to sit tight to hold his life? It was that he must have gone through an experience that had been so serious to him that his mind became cicatrised and not responsive to the ordinary emotions and passions. Hogmann's mind, he thought, had been so affected. The more he (counsel) thought of this case the more convinced was he that it was a fearful thing for a white man to be 'on the beach' in Hongkong. While you are in want of food the Chinese coolie goes about with rice in plenty, and you, who belong to a class superior, cannot get a friendly word from anyone, but are threatened with starvation, exposed to mental and physical agony.[35]

Ferrers devoted the remainder of his speech to developing this idea that the accused were victims of society. They were not members of the criminal class, he said. Nor were they beachcombers. They were 'nothing but boys', on the threshold of life and only too anxious

35. *SCMP*, 24 December 1904.

to work. The plan to steal a boat, he said, was not a prank but an act of utmost desperation. They were 'absolutely destitute in Hongkong' and determined to get away.

> Let them [the jury] imagine what that meant to those who intended it not as a joke – in the open sea, without provisions, water, preparations, nothing between them and death but a boat, and surrounded with every imaginable horror. How was it that people reduced themselves to that state?[36]

The blame lay with the government, he said. It 'had a duty to the white inhabitants of this place'. It had not discharged that duty, and it had 'no right now to ask the jury to find the prisoners guilty of murder'. If the money paid for their defence had been spent in 'getting them out of the Colony into a White Man's colony, where they could have got a broom to sweep a crossing, they would have done better'. Instead, the unemployed white man was treated worse than a rat, for at least the Sanitary Board gave rats a painless death: this was a reference to the campaigns against bubonic plague, which visited Hong Kong almost annually from 1894 to 1929. Ferrers asked for a verdict of manslaughter and concluded with an appeal for mercy during the Christmas season of goodwill to men.

Calthrop's defence of Nason was no less sentimental. After citing an English case in which a man had been convicted only of manslaughter for unintentionally causing a death during a felony, he asked the jury to extend the same mercy to 'these three young, unfortunate boys'. He criticized Sharp's description of them as a curse to the community. The question was whether they were guilty of murder, not of being beachcombers. He asked if the jury were agreed that Kwok So had told the truth, especially after he brought up indecent assault at the last moment, 'an absolute fabrication to make the case blacker'. As for the confessions, the accused had been half starved for months: 'their horror being so great their confessions were made under such circumstances that they did not know exactly what they were saying.' He asked the jury to think of Nason's parents 'thousands of miles away in America, waiting and hoping against hope that perhaps he may join them again in this festive season of the year; and never dreaming that whether or not he would ever meet them again, depended on the verdict of a British jury'.

These 'ingenious arguments' and emotional appeals cut no ice with the prosecution. In his closing speech, Sharp again described how the accused had set out with a common purpose of stealing a boat and had admitted that they planned to carry it out 'at all hazards and cost'. They had thrown Chan Yee overboard after a long struggle. Referring to evidence about the naked state of her body when it was discovered, 'he could not say that the clothing was stripped off her in the struggle', but 'it was difficult to say how she lost it'. Even if she had jumped or fallen overboard out of fear, they would still be guilty of murder. Had she fallen, they could have tried to rescue her, or might have put forward that plea, but they did not do so. Smith was clearly the leader, but all three were implicated in a crime 'of

36. *SCMP*, 24 December 1904.

an exceptionally callous nature'. The 'one relieving feature in this sad case was the struggle which the boy put up against his assailants'.

Summing up, Berkeley began by dismissing as 'altogether beside the issue' the fact that the accused were beachcombers ('if it be a fact') and the fact ('if it be a fact') that the government did nothing to relieve the needs of this 'floating population'. Their age was 'absolutely immaterial' because they were above the minimum age of criminal responsibility (seven)[37] and were old enough to know right from wrong. It was 'entirely a side issue' that the jury were trying the case at Christmas time. 'You, gentlemen, are sworn to deliver your verdict according to the evidence and not according to the season of the year,' he told them. The fact that Nason ('if it is a fact') had parents thousands of miles away waiting for him should not have been put to the jury at all. It would have been equally improper for the prosecution to remind them that Kwok Tai-chan had stood on the Praya waiting for the return of the sampan and his family. 'It would be appealing to the emotions, and emotions have no place in the trial of this case.'

Berkeley endorsed Sharp's explanation of the 'law of England' – that when several persons joined together for an unlawful purpose, intending to resist by force all who opposed them, if death ensued as the result of that force it was murder and not manslaughter. 'Any other view of the law would be a direct incentive to the perpetration of acts of violence' and would 'put a premium on crime, and render life absolutely insecure'. It was immaterial whether the accused threw the woman and the child overboard. 'The question was why they went overboard? Was it the result of the prisoners' violence?' The jury had been asked to reduce the crime to manslaughter, but that suggestion 'disappeared instantly' when the jury remembered that the accused had made no attempt to rescue those who went overboard. 'The woman whose death they were dealing with undoubtedly came into the water as the result of the illegal acts of the prisoners, who sailed away, after she got into the water, and left her to her fate.'

The jury retired at 1:15 p.m. and returned five minutes later. When asked for the verdict, the foreman, Charles Kew, 'answered in a low tone that all the men had been found guilty, but that they were recommended to mercy'. The accused had nothing to say when asked why sentence of death should not be passed. Before pronouncing sentence Berkeley described the case as 'one of the most outrageous crimes that has ever been perpetrated

---

37. Under the common law rule of *doli incapax*, a child over seven but under fourteen was presumed to be incapable of committing a crime, but this presumption could be rebutted by the prosecution on proof beyond reasonable doubt that, at the time of the offence, the child was well aware that the offence was seriously wrong and not merely naughty. The minimum age, below which a child is absolutely excused from criminal responsibility, was raised in Hong Kong from seven to ten in 2003, having been raised in the UK to eight in 1933 and ten in 1963. The Hong Kong government first proposed to raise the age to ten in 1973 but withdrew the proposal when legislators argued that children between seven and ten were still old enough to carry packets of drugs for drug traffickers. *HKH*, 14 February 1973.

in the annals of the Colony'. He told the prisoners they were a disgrace to their countries, 'but he would not make their situation more painful by saying anything further'. After pronouncing sentence – without wearing the black cap – he said he would forward the jury's recommendation to mercy to the Governor, but he held out no hope. According to the *Hongkong Telegraph*, the condemned men 'betrayed absolutely no emotion or feeling throughout the terrible closing scenes, and appeared, as at the start, quite callous and indifferent to their awful fate'. They were led out of the courthouse by a back entrance to avoid the crowds waiting on Queen's Road to catch a sight of them.

On Friday 30 December 1904 the Governor in Council confirmed the death sentences pronounced on Smith, Hogmann, and Nason on the unanimous advice of members. It was a 'deplorable' case, the Governor, Sir Matthew Nathan, later observed.[38] The date of execution was set for Wednesday 11 January 1905. 'No reasonable person acquainted with the history and details of the crime could have reasonably expected His Excellency to have come to any other decision,' said the *Hongkong Telegraph*: the paper had recently been acquired by a Chinese syndicate and was run by a Portuguese editor, J.P. Braga.[39] 'Unfortunately,' echoed the *Daily Press*, 'some duties, however disagreeable, have to be faced.'[40] One anonymous correspondent nevertheless urged the committee of the Tung Wah Hospital to petition the Governor to commute the sentence on the youngest of the three, the 'boy prisoner' Nason. 'For obvious reasons,' he said, Europeans could not do this: it was a chance for 'our Chinese friends' to 'show that they are capable of kindly feeling, and are not vindictive owing to more or less recent cases of evasion of justice in other ports'.[41] One Chinese newspaper in Hong Kong reported on this call for intercession. But it was

38. ExCo Minutes, 30 December 1904, CO 131/35, 54; Nathan to Lyttelton, 28 June 1905, CO 129/328, 722.
39. The syndicate included Lau Chu-pak, Ho Fook, Ho Tung, and Chau Siu-ki – all leading figures in the Chinese community. Braga was later the representative of the Portuguese community on the Legislative Council, 1929–1937. Frank H.H. King (editor) and Prescott Clarke, *A Research Guide to China-Coast Newspapers, 1822–1911* (East Asian Research Center, Harvard University, 1965), 71.
40. *HKT*, 3 January 1905; *HKDP*, 5 January 1905.
41. The reference was to a case in September 1904 in which sailors from the USS *Helena* at Canton, had pushed Ho Tsoi-yin, the comprador of Butterfield and Swire, off a bridge into the mud below, where he had drowned. Unable to identify the culprits, the US Consul General had offered $3,000 to Ho's relatives. Occurring shortly after killings of Chinese by Americans employed on the Canton-Hankow Railway, the incident produced 'a very strong feeling of resentment among the populace', which was fanned by calls in the Hong Kong press for the trial of the sailors. The resentment festered as the US government hesitated over the compensation, which was finally paid in June 1905. *OCM*, 8 and 22 October 1904 and 13 June 1905; Cheshire to Loomis, 7 and 20 October 1904, and Lay to Department of State, 29 April 1905, United States Department of State, Despatches from United States Consuls in Canton, 1844–1906, Vols. 18 and 19.

not taken up.[42] A last-minute petition from the European community on behalf of all three men attracted a thousand signatures.[43]

The three condemned men reportedly displayed indifference to their predicament, buoyed by a belief that they would be reprieved. When told that this was not to be the case, Smith and Nason broke down and wept, while Hogmann 'took the intimation in the most callous manner possible'.[44] The executions took place shortly after 5 a.m. on 11 January on a scaffold erected just inside the main entrance to the gaol – a place which, as the *Telegraph* noted, was in normal times 'a peaceful flower walk'. No outsiders were admitted, but the press reconstructed events with information from gaol staff. The condemned men were accompanied by the Reverends John France, chaplain of St Peter's Church, and William Bridie of the Wesleyan Chapel. Both were involved with the Missions to Seamen and Sailors' Home and had attended the prisoners since the trial. The hangings took barely more than a minute, while the prison bell tolled. Smith and Hogmann mounted the scaffold but Nason, who seemed 'insensible, and quite oblivious of his position and surroundings', had to be supported. Smith exclaimed, 'Lord have mercy on my soul; may God bless you all', while Hogmann repeated over and over 'My God, My God!' Bridie, the minister, broke down and wept. In the afternoon reporters were allowed in to view the bodies. By then, observed the *Telegraph*, 'the flower pots had been returned to their usual positions, and nothing was left to indicate that only a few hours previously an awful tragedy had been enacted on the spot'.

The coffins containing the bodies were carried by labourers in the dead of night along Caine Road for burial on the outskirts of town.[45] Clearly, the authorities wished to get this distasteful matter over with as quietly as possible. Shortly after the trial the *Telegraph* had declared that 'the majesty of the law and the supreme justice of the British Courts' had been 'vindicated and proved', since it had been shown 'that the life of a Chinese woman, even although she be a sampan coolie, eking out a precarious livelihood as best she can, is as sacred under the British Crown as that of the highest in the land'.[46] There was, however, remarkably little bombast of this kind, and almost no editorial comment on the hangings. The newspapers had moved on to another sensational harbour murder, among members of

42. The report was simply a paraphrase of a report in the *Daily Press* rejecting an argument attributed to the anonymous colonist (which he later denied having made) that since two persons had been murdered only two of the culprits should be hanged. The call was echoed in a letter from 'Have Mercy' to the *China Mail*, 10 January 1905, regretting the failure of 'the better class of our Chinese community' to 'rise to the occasion and show that they also possess some feeling in common with their European fellow citizens'. *HKDP*, 5, 6, and 9 January 1905; *WTYP*, 6 January 1905.
43. *SCMP*, 10 January 1905.
44. *SCMP*, 9 January 1905; *HKT*, 9 January 1905.
45. *HKT*, 11 January 1905; *HKWP*, 14 January 1905; *OCM*, 14 January 1905; *SCMP*, 12 January 1905; *WTYP*, 11 January 1905.
46. *HKT*, 23 December 1904.

a party of Igorot people on board the S.S. *Tremont* on 5 January 1905: they were returning home via Hong Kong after appearing at the St Louis World Fair in a human zoo designed to show Americans how 'savages' lived.[47]

On 18 September 1906, Hong Kong's boat-dwelling communities were devastated by a typhoon, when thousands of people were drowned. Whether the remaining members of the Kwok family were among the casualties is not recorded.[48]

Vagrancy and charity

The Harbour Murders focused attention on the problem of Hong Kong's other floating population. The presence of 'wandering Europeans' in colonies 'populated principally by people of the black or yellow races cannot but have a bad effect on the estimation in which all Europeans are held,' said Governor Nathan. The effect, he added, was 'particularly pernicious in a place where the bulk of the population are Chinese who regard the best Europeans as belonging to a lower civilization than their own and at the same time are easily made the victims of imposture by the worst'. Some of these drifters, he added, were living on the charity of Chinese.[49] Others were turning to crime. In December 1904, while the Harbour Murders case was moving through the courts, vagrants on day-release from the House of Detention went on a violent rampage in Yau Ma Tei. A few weeks later, unemployed Americans posing as detectives held up a Chinese club in Sheung Wan. The large influx of non-Chinese 'male destitutes' was becoming a 'nuisance, danger and expense'.[50] Nathan was determined to take action.

It was a principle at this time to separate the deserving poor from professional beggars. The former could be helped on their way by charity. The latter, colonists believed, needed to be treated severely if Hong Kong was to avoid becoming a magnet for beachcombers.

---

47. The Igorots are a people of northern Luzon in the Philippines. One of the group, Paguin, killed another, Apowan, through jealousy over a woman. Paguin then swam to shore, where he also killed a rickshaw puller. In the court proceedings Nicholas Nolan, interpreter to the Magistracy, interpreted from English into Spanish to the leader of the Igorots, Lazaro Bebit, who then interpreted from Spanish into Ilocano. When the charge of murder was read out, Paguin replied, 'It is true.' The judge, Berkeley, told him to plead not guilty, 'so that we may try him and see what amount of culpability attaches to him'. Paguin was convicted of murder. His death sentence was commuted to life imprisonment. He died in Victoria Gaol in 1913 at the age of forty-five. *SCMP*, 20 January 1905 and 11 June 1913; *OCM*, 14 and 24 January 1905.
48. This was one of the most destructive typhoons in Hong Kong's history. For its impact see Justin Chun-Yin Cheng, 'Everyday Colonialism: The 1906 Typhoon and Governance in Early Twentieth-Century Hong Kong' (Master's Thesis, University of British Columbia, 2021).
49. Nathan to Elgin, 31 January 1906, CO 129/333, 116–117.
50. In the first case, five men entered a house and violently demanded 'chow'. They were sentenced by the magistrate, Gompertz, to fines or imprisonment in default. In the second, three Americans and a European were convicted in the Supreme Court of assault and robbery and sentenced to three years' imprisonment. *HKT*, 16 December 1904; *OCM*, 25 February 1905; Nathan to Lyttelton, 28 June 1905, CO 129/328, 722.

Newspapers floated schemes ranging from agricultural camps in the New Territories to a policy, like that enforced in Manila, of prohibiting indigent sailors from landing.[51] The authorities had long resisted introducing this American-style scheme of immigration control on the grounds that Hong Kong was a free port. In any case, it lacked the resources to enforce it.[52] But the inadequacy of existing legislation was shown when Nathan resolved, in the aftermath of the Harbour Murders, to enforce the Vagrancy Ordinance against ships bringing in destitutes. To do this it was necessary for the destitutes landed by these ships to be declared vagrants by a magistrate. The immediate result was the committal to the House of Detention of two respectable, teetotal, skilled workmen: they had been engaged from England by the Manila Railroad Company but had landed penniless in Hong Kong after having been prevented from working after their arrival in Manila. Their plight was sensationally reported in the English newspapers, some with the headline 'Caged With Coolies'. 'The worst of it all is that he was vaccinated entirely against his wish,' complained the mother of one of them; 'if you could see the scar you might think that he had been vaccinated by means of a pickaxe!'[53]

This episode prompted Nathan to revise the Vagrancy Ordinance. From June 1905, ships' captains bringing in persons who became vagrants within two months of arrival were now required to repay all costs incurred by the government unless they could prove that the person in question possessed $50 or more at the time of arrival. The ordinance also introduced greater rigour to the House of Detention. Instead of being treated like prisoners on remand, vagrants were now fed a reduced diet and were subjected to the same penal labour required of convicted prisoners.[54] Nathan's legislation was credited with having 'a most salutary effect' in reducing the dumping of destitutes in Hong Kong.[55] The number of vagrants sent to the House of Detention declined from 113 in 1904 to an average of about twenty-five per annum over the next twenty years.

---

51. *CM*, 9 and 10 December 1904 and 11 January 1905; *HKDP*, 12 December 1904; *SCMP*, 23 December 1904 and 3, 4, and 15 February 1905.
52. Black to Chamberlain, 26 July 1898, CO 129/284, 203–213; Board of Trade to Colonial Office, 16 November 1905, CO 129/332, 71.
53. The men were platelayers engaged at an annual salary of £300. When they arrived in Manila they were told that the company was not allowed under American law to employ foreigners. They landed in Hong Kong on 15 January 1905, applied to the government for assistance, and were sent to the Sailors' Home. The government decided that Butterfield and Swire, the agents of the ship that brought them to Hong Kong, should refund the expenses incurred by the colony on behalf of the men: this required their committal to the House of Detention as vagrants. After negotiations, Butterfield and Swire undertook to ship the men to England. Smallpox vaccinations, then compulsory for children in Hong Kong, were routinely administered to gaol inmates, for whom it was required by law from 1923. *SCMP*, 1 June 1905; Nathan to Lyttelton, 28 April 1905, CO 129/328, 443–450; Ordinance No. 12 of 1923.
54. Nathan to Lyttelton, 28 June 1905, CO 129/328, 717–727; Ordinance No. 2 of 1905.
55. Stubbs to Milner, 20 April 1920, CO 129/460, 402.

In parallel, the Reverend John France of the Missions to Seamen raised funds to provide meals for unemployed Europeans. When he was criticized by the *China Mail* for holding out 'a sort of premium to thriftless derelicts in other ports' he pointed out that he had found temporary work for several of them and had helped others ship to places where work was available.[56] At its annual meeting in February 1905 the Hongkong Benevolent Society discussed what its chairman, Acting Chief Justice Berkeley, described as 'the all-absorbing topic' – 'the "beachcomber question"'. The meeting agreed to adopt a 'guarantee scheme' proposed by Nathan for deserving cases, in which subscribers would cover the $60 deposit required for admission to the Sailors' Home. Under this 'paradise scheme' (as some newspapers described it), Nathan arranged that, before any destitute was sent to the House of Detention as a vagrant, he would have his case investigated by the chaplain to the Sailors' Home, John France, to determine if he was a seaman and deserving of assistance. Such cases were 'comparatively rare,' Nathan acknowledged.[57] Over the next few years a few dozen men were helped in this way. The Benevolent Society then turned to other topical matters, such as the discouragement of 'mixed marriages' and the establishment of a hostel for single European women.[58]

European violence and European prestige

The trial of Smith, Hogmann, and Nason showed that Europeans who murdered Chinese could be brought to justice. The press observed that they might not have been executed for such a crime had they been tried in Manila, where Smith and Nason had come from.[59] The seventeen-year-old Nason was one of the youngest criminals, possibly *the* youngest, to have been hanged in Hong Kong.[60] Their crime was deliberate and planned. Their victims were a defenceless woman and her children. They showed no remorse until it was too late. Like most other Europeans tried for crimes of violence in Hong Kong, they were of low status. In fact, as outcasts from society, they had no status at all.

---

56. *CM*, 11 and 12 January 1905.
57. *SCMP*, 1 and 8 February 1905; Nathan to Lyttelton, 28 June 1905, CO 129/328, 724–725.
58. These two related questions were close to the heart of the Colonial Secretary and later Governor, Sir Henry May, and his wife, Helena. A hostel for women, funded mainly by donations from the Jewish businessman and philanthropist Sir Ellis Kadoorie and Chinese merchant Ho Kom-tong, was opened in 1916 and named after the president of the Benevolent Society, Helena May. *SCMP*, 13 September 1916.
59. In an appeal in the Philippines Supreme Court (G.R. No. 1287 January 5, 1905 – *US v. Pedro Baguiao et al.*) the convictions of two men of murders committed in a robbery were reduced to homicide and the death sentences commuted to imprisonment on the ground that the facts did not satisfy any of the definitions of murder under the Spanish Penal Code then still in force. *SCMP*, 11 January 1905.
60. It is difficult to be certain of this, since the sources for the early years rarely give the ages of convicts. However, as early as 1850, in a piracy and stabbing case (see Chapter 3), Bonham gave the youth of the three ringleaders, aged eighteen, nineteen, and twenty-one, as a reason for commuting their death sentences.

Seven Westerners[61] – three Englishmen, an Irishman, a Dutchman, and two Americans – were hanged in Hong Kong prior to the executions of Smith, Hogmann, and Nason in 1904. Five were sailors. In the seventh and most recent case, the American Charles Newman, an unemployed watchman, was hanged in 1878 for murdering a Portuguese friend in a jealous rage over a girlfriend.[62] Colonists were only vaguely aware of these precedents. Shortly after the 1904 trial, the *South China Morning Post* declared that 'never before has the Supreme Court been called upon to pass capital sentence upon a European'.[63] Soon, however, a correspondent to the *China Mail* recalled an execution in the 1850s in which three Americans were hanged for the murder of a Chinese boy. 'I saw the ghastly sight from the roof of Douglas Lapraik's old housetop,' he wrote.[64] In fact, only two men, Robert Gibbons and John Jones, were hanged, and they were British, not American; the death sentence passed on the third, Charles Williams (alias Gachet), a Frenchman, was commuted to life penal servitude.[65] This was, nevertheless, the precedent that most resembled the 1904 Harbour Murders. It was the only other case in Hong Kong's colonial period in which Europeans were hanged for murdering Chinese.[66] In a bilingual proclamation in the *Gazette*, the Governor, Sir John Bowring, capitalized on their execution by declaring that it demonstrated that 'under the Authority of British Law, equal justice is dealt to all

61. This compares with only four recorded executions of European civilians in the whole of post-1860 British India: Elizabeth Kolsky, *Colonial Justice in British India* (Cambridge: Cambridge University Press, 2010), 12. Among other non-Chinese executed before 1904, the six men hanged in Hong Kong in the *Herald* case in 1852 (see Chapter 3) were described as Spanish-Filipino and Portuguese (probably of Mestizo descent). João de Matta Ozorio, hanged in 1898 for murdering a love rival, was a Hong Kong-born Portuguese of Macanese descent.
62. Newman feigned madness while awaiting trial, stripping himself naked and smearing the walls of his cell with faeces. He gave up the pretence only a few days before his trial, declaring 'he'd sooner die than live fifteen or twenty years in Gaol after all'. His counsel, Thomas Hayllar, attempted a defence of temporary insanity, but the special jury took only three minutes to convict Newman of murder. *CM*, 3 and 19 December 1878; Colonial Surgeon's Report for 1878, *HKGG*, 9 July 1879.
63. Despite the fact that five of the previous six executions were recorded in Norton-Kyshe's *History of the Laws and Courts of Hong Kong*, published only a few years earlier. *SCMP*, 27 December 1904.
64. Lapraik was an early Hong Kong shipowner and entrepreneur. *CM*, 10 January 1905.
65. The men were sailors on an American ship. They murdered a thirteen-year-old Chinese cabin boy, taking money which he had stolen from the captain's cabin, and threw his body into the harbour, weighted with an iron bar. But the body reappeared, as if, said counsel for the prosecution, W.T. Bridges, 'to demand justice against its murderers'. At the end of a two-day trial, in which the accused were represented by the barrister Henry Kingsmill, the all-British jury took fifteen minutes to find them guilty. *CM*, 3 March 1859.
66. In a case in 1955, James Becker, a locally enlisted driver for the British Army, hanged for the murder of his former girlfriend, Evelyn Fung, was described in press reports as a 'Eurasian'. The only other case in which Europeans were convicted of murdering Chinese was that of George Douthwaite and Douglas Dalton, two servicemen sentenced to death for the murder of a Chinese woman in the New Territories. Their sentences were commuted to twenty and twelve years' imprisonment respectively by the Officer Administering the Government, Robert Black, on the unanimous advice of the Executive Council. *SCMP*, 12 July, 23 and 24 August, and 21 September 1955; Davies, *Strong to Save*, 268–269; 'Trial of British Soldiers Douthwaite & Dalton in Hong Kong (1953)', CO 1023/237.

Persons without regard to Nation, Blood, or to any accidental Circumstances whatever'. More than 2,000 people, including the Chinese military commander at Kowloon, turned out to watch the hangings, on 7 March 1859.[67]

Despite Bowring's claim, some juries in Hong Kong protected Europeans from punishment for killing non-Europeans, especially in the early decades of British rule. Barely a year before the vaunted 1859 executions, Denis Griffin, a carpenter on another American ship, was acquitted of murder *and* manslaughter after he had cut the rope supporting a platform on which ten men were repairing the side of the ship, causing one of them to drown: it was just a 'harmless joke', said his counsel.[68] In another case, tried shortly before the 1904 Harbour Murders, Thomas Hynes, a New Zealander employed as an overseer by Butterfield and Swire, was acquitted of the manslaughter of a Chinese labourer after striking him for not working fast enough. The cause of death was rupture of an enlarged spleen.[69] The case was no doubt on the mind of James Dyer Ball when he referred to Chinese 'continually' succumbing to kicks from Englishmen in this way; in another case earlier in the year a Chinese driver had been kicked by a European constable and had subsequently died of a ruptured spleen.[70] Despite government-led campaigns to eradicate mosquitoes, malaria was endemic, causing enlarged, diseased spleens in severe infections. Ruptured spleens were a factor in about a third of all manslaughter cases in the early 1900s. Most resulted from quarrels and 'coolie fights' among Chinese. Where convictions resulted, the sentences were usually lenient.[71]

Prosecutors often remarked on the readiness with which Chinese resorted to violence over seemingly trivial disputes, and on the deaths of victims weakened by disease in fights with bamboo poles or other tools. Some Europeans also held that violence was necessary for maintaining their prestige in China. Respect, observed the journalist George Cooke in 1858, 'was never attained except while the coolie's ears are hot with the recent application of an Anglo-Saxon palm'.[72] At another of Dyer Ball's talks, the Colonial Secretary, F.H. May, admitted, or rather boasted, that in his early years in China 'he never allowed

67. *HKGG*, 12 March 1859; Bowring to Lytton, 12 March 1859, CO 129/73, 261–262.
68. *CM*, 5 November 1857.
69. Hynes's barrister, Henry Pollock, said that the 'coolies' who claimed they had seen Hynes strike the man twice possibly 'thought that if they made out a strong case against the accused, money might be paid'. The judge (Berkeley) observed that it was just as probable that the victim died from jolts in the rickshaw in which he was carried to hospital. Hynes had earlier served in the Boer War and in the Transvaal police. Immediately after his acquittal he was recruited into the Hong Kong police. He retired in 1936 as Superintendent of Mails at the Post Office and was killed in an air raid in 1941 in Kensington, London, where he was an air raid precautions warden. *OCM*, 22 October 1904; *SCMP*, 16 May 1941.
70. The constable was not identified. Police Report for 1904.
71. Police Reports for 1901–1910, supplemented by newspaper reports.
72. Cooke, *China*, 360.

an opportunity of punching a Chinaman to go past'.[73] Whatever his own misgivings, Dyer Ball's *Cantonese Made Easy* abounds in examples of people beating other people.[74] Violence and the shielding of European perpetrators of violence were features of colonialism everywhere. The worst abuses were in remote outposts, and in India, where, under the Indian Penal Code, murder could more easily be reduced to manslaughter, and manslaughter to 'causing hurt'.[75] Similar outcomes in the volatile region of southern China sometimes risked destabilizing British rule in Hong Kong. A verdict of manslaughter by a British court in Canton in 1883 for the deliberate shooting of a twelve-year-old Chinese boy by James Logan, an employee of the Chinese Imperial Maritime Customs, caused such outrage that rumours spread of 'an intended rising of the Chinese' in Hong Kong. Anti-foreign rioting, triggered by the Logan case, had already broken out in Canton. Hong Kong officials at the time were worried that 'an unprovoked assault on a Chinese by one of the drunken beachcombers who infest this port, or by some European of the same class, might at the present moment cause a violent, though unpremeditated, outburst of feeling amongst the lower classes'.[76]

An 'outburst of feeling' occurred a year after the Logan case, in 1884, when a boycott of French ships during the Sino-French War spiralled into general anti-foreign riots. Beachcombers were not the cause of this, any more than the 1904 Harbour Murders were the cause of a boycott of American goods in 1905. This was a nationalistic protest against

73. May was telling an anecdote about how, when he was riding in China some years earlier, a man startled his pony. May got down and gave him 'a good thrashing'. The two then fell into conversation and the man took May to his house and showed him the nearby graves of his male ancestors going back eighteen generations. This impressed May, whose snobbery got the better of his bigotry. He gave the man a dollar, concluding 'that he was a representative of one of the oldest county families he had ever met'. *OCM*, 29 November 1904.

74. 'Afterwards give him twenty blows with a rattan.' 'Only let him go when he has been beaten.' 'Strike him once', etc. James Dyer Ball, *Cantonese Made Easy* (2nd edition, Hong Kong: China Mail, 1888).

75. Jordanna Bailkin, 'The Boot and the Spleen: When Was Murder Possible in British India?', *Comparative Studies in Society and History*, Vol. 48, No. 2 (April 2006): 462–493; Wiener, *An Empire on Trial.*

76. Logan had been a sergeant in the Hong Kong police 1868–1873. He lived in a neighbourhood outside the European quarter at Shameen and was on bad terms with his Chinese neighbours. He had been drinking with friends through the night. On his return home with two friends at about 6 a.m. he started randomly striking labourers waiting for work in the street. When one of them objected Logan became excited, fetched a pistol from his house, and shot a woman in the shoulder. Uproar ensued, crowds gathered, and Logan fetched another gun and walked to a bridge, where he took aim and shot the boy and another man in the back. He was tried for murder by the British Supreme Court in China sitting in Canton. Dyer Ball was loaned from Hong Kong as interpreter, and Logan was defended by A.G. Wise, a Hong Kong barrister, later a judge. He was convicted of manslaughter and sentenced to seven years' penal servitude, which he served in Hong Kong. Both the Chinese government and the Law Officers in London considered the verdict and the sentence to be inadequate. In a subsequent petition, Logan claimed that the prosecutor had privately assured him he would be released after twelve or eighteen months, 'as my severe sentence was to keep the Chinese quiet'. Marsh to Derby, 3 October 1883, CO 129/212, 7–31; Foreign Office to Colonial Office, 28 October 1885, CO 129/224, 389–404. Douglas Clark, *Gunboat Justice, British and American Law Courts in China and Japan (1842–1943)* (Hong Kong: Earnshaw Books, 2015), Vol. I, 263–272.

the US Chinese Exclusion Acts, led by Chinese merchants and triggered by the suicide in front of the American consulate in Shanghai of Feng Xiawei, a Cantonese man who had been denied entry into the US. The boycott spread through the treaty ports and overseas Chinese communities. It was at its most intense in Canton and Hong Kong, where shops refused to stock American goods and memorial services were held for the martyr Feng Xiawei. Some also attributed the vehemence of anti-American sentiment to the murder of the comprador Ho Tsoi-yin by American sailors in Canton in 1904. 'In the past,' wrote a Chinese correspondent to the *China Mail* in 1905, 'when a Chinaman murdered a foreigner, battleships were sent over, soldiers landed, territories annexed, great indemnities paid, the murderer punished; but when a Chinaman was murdered by an American, $3,000 was deemed sufficient to settle the whole matter.'[77] Amid the outrage over these cases, the more recent murder of a humble boatwoman and her daughter by Americans in Hong Kong appears to have been quickly and utterly forgotten.

77. See page 183, footnote 41. *OCM*, 22 August 1905. See also *SCMP*, 11 November 1905. For the 1884 and 1905 boycotts see Tsai, *Hong Kong in Chinese History*, Chapters 5 and 7.

7

'I Will Smile Even When I Am Hanged'

The Victoria Gaol Murders, 1919

Victoria Gaol loomed above Hong Kong on a steeply sloping site, which it had occupied since the 1840s. As the muster of inmates grew from a few dozen to over 800 in the early twentieth century, new buildings were put up and old ones enlarged, always on the same crowded site. From the 1870s, on repeated directions from London, governors drew up plans for a new gaol in Sai Ying Pun, Causeway Bay, or Kowloon Tong, or considered rebuilding the old, abandoned gaol on Stonecutters Island. Experts urged modernization so that new policies from Britain could be applied. Among these, the 'separate system' was designed to reduce contact among prisoners by keeping them in single cells. But action was delayed by lack of funds and opposition from legislators. The only sure deterrents for Chinese criminals were flogging and deportation, they argued. The gaol was neither overcrowded nor unhealthy; on the contrary, inmates were 'better fed and better housed than outside'.[1] Hong Kong had more pressing needs when the poor were reduced to lifting the covers of sewers to get at the fresh water trickling into them.[2] In 1892 all five unofficial legislators threatened to resign if officials forced through plans to rebuild Victoria Gaol: the

1. Report of the Commission on Insufficient Accommodation in Victoria Gaol, *HKSP*, 34/1886, 147. The death rate among prisoners was much lower in Victoria Gaol than in the more modern prison in Singapore, which was organized mainly on the separate system: 216 deaths (excluding executions and murders) in the years 1901–1920, compared with 687 in Singapore. The average daily number of prisoners in Singapore was higher than in Hong Kong during these years by a range of between 23 per cent and 80 per cent. For the history of Victoria Gaol see May Holdsworth and Christopher Munn, *Crime, Justice and Punishment in Colonial Hong Kong: Central Police Station, Central Magistracy and Victoria Gaol* (Hong Kong: Hong Kong University Press, 2020).
2. Marsh to Granville, 26 June 1886, CO 129/227, 540.

Chinese community had never been so united in its opposition, said the Registrar General.[3] The Legislative Council grudgingly agreed to fund two new halls on a site opposite the gaol, linked by a tunnel under Old Bailey Street. Another new hall was built within the gaol compound in 1915, making the site even more congested.

Opponents of new facilities pointed out that most prisoners were admitted for a few weeks for 'revenue' or 'non-criminal' offences. Tried by magistrates, these offences ranged from illegal hawking to breaches of the retail opium monopoly, a rich source of government income. Over half of admissions to gaol were for non-payment of fines, which, said some, followed too closely the English scales and were too high for Hong Kong's impoverished working population.[4] Varying enforcement policies against these minor offenders were also the reason for large fluctuations in admissions – and for official inertia, since it was hard to justify separate cells for short-term prisoners, whose numbers varied so much. Instead, these prisoners were held in 'association wards', or crammed in threes or fours into single cells, or put up in storerooms and corridors. Many were released early. From 1903, when plague spread to the gaol, short-sentence prisoners were housed in a branch prison at a new reformatory in Causeway Bay, built with a donation from Emanuel Raphael Belilios, a Jewish merchant, and originally intended for boy offenders. The branch prison was closed in 1908, when gaol admissions fell by 20 per cent.[5]

The 'convicts' – prisoners with sentences of two years or more – formed less than a third of the gaol population. Their numbers, however, were growing, from an average of 192 in the first decade of the century to 231 in the second. Criticizing the short sentences meted out for violent crimes, Governor Lugard believed that only sentences of seven years or more would give convicts time to learn a trade and stop them carrying out threats of revenge against witnesses. He considered introducing minimum sentences but was dissuaded by Chief Justice Piggott. Nevertheless, a belief in reformation had by now replaced the old view that, because most convicts came from China, 'the reform of the criminal is no part of our duty'.[6] Officials now wanted to teach them trades that were in demand. After

---

3. Robinson to Ripon, 13 December 1892 and 20 January 1893, CO 129/256, 543–568 and CO 129/258, 220–241.
4. The point, made by legislators during their opposition to rebuilding in 1892, received some sympathy in the Colonial Office. Criticisms of heavy fines were made by the retiring Acting Chief Justice, E.J. Ackroyd, in a speech in 1895. Ripon to Robinson, 24 March 1893, CO 129/258, 240–241; *HKT*, 19 January 1895.
5. Due mainly to a decline in prosecutions for opium and other regulatory offences. Opened in 1900, with specialist teachers from England, the reformatory only ever had one inmate. Magistrates preferred to impose short prison sentences on boy offenders, usually with a caning. After the branch prison closed, the building was leased to the Anglican Church as a refuge for Chinese girls. By 1919 it was reportedly being used as a laundry by the nearby French Convent. Statement Regarding Belilios Reformatory, *HKSP*, 9/1902; Lugard to Crewe, 5 August 1909, CO 129/357, 285–295; *CM* 21 August 1919.
6. Lugard to Harcourt, 26 April 1911, CO 129/376, 528–532.

an obligatory period of shot drill, crank turning, and stone carrying, well-behaved convicts were put to productive work, such as carpentry, tailoring, or printing.

On Sunday 14 December 1919 the gaol had 791 inmates, all but seven of whom were Chinese: admissions that year were 46 per cent higher than in 1918, the result of increased crime and stricter enforcement against petty offenders.[7] After an early supper of rice and fish, the prisoners were locked up until breakfast, a meal almost identical to supper.[8] Each of the 250 or so convicts was housed separately, locked up for eleven or twelve hours at night 'alone with the devils and ghosts his imagination might evolve', as one former gaoler put it.[9] The cells had no artificial light. Prisoners slept on the floor. Defying regulations, some passed the hours talking with others through gaps under the cell doors. Others made model ships out of live cockroaches, gluing on them masts and funnels made of toilet paper and rice paste; occasionally these creatures, with their weird superstructures, were seen scurrying along the corridors, which were dimly lit by gas lamps placed far apart.[10] Warders patrolled with electric lamps in felt-soled slippers, the better to detect prisoners talking to each other.

That Sunday night two men were in the condemned cell, having been sentenced to death for murdering a woman and her daughter.[11] Their cell was on the ground floor of B Wing, a four-storey block mainly housing convicts. They were under constant watch. The guard outside their cell was Assistant Warder Harnam Singh, one of the Indians who made up two-thirds of the gaol's disciplined staff. An Indian guard, Ayub Khan, was patrolling the corridors. Also on the ground floor was James Speed, the warder in charge, who was doing paperwork in the Chief Warder's office, a converted cell. Speed had swapped shifts to allow a colleague to attend a Masonic meeting. He was the only European on duty, and the

7. There were 5,212 admissions in 1919, compared with 3,577 in 1918. The daily average number of prisoners for 1919 was 756, compared with 601 in 1918 – an increase of 26 per cent. In early November, shortly after the number peaked at 866, over 70 prisoners were released early. *SCMP*, 7 and 8 November 1919.
8. European convicts had a more varied diet of bread, suet pudding, potatoes, meat, and soup. Short-sentence prisoners were fed only on rice and water for the first seven days.
9. N.G. Mitchell-Innes, Acting Registrar General, in a debate in the Legislative Council's Finance Committee in 1890 on funding for a gaol extension. The proposal was defeated by unofficial members. Mitchell-Innes, a cadet officer, had acted as Superintendent of the Gaol in 1887. He left Hong Kong in 1895 after being held responsible for thefts from the Treasury, of which he was the head, by its accountant, A.F. Alves. He then embarked on a career in the English prison service. *CM*, 5 December 1890.
10. Kenneth W. Andrew, *Diary of an Ex-Hong Kong Cop* (St Ives: United Writers Publications, 1979), 26–27.
11. In a case that bore similarities to the Harbour Murder (Chapter 6), Cheng Loi and Cheung San-loi, hired a sampan at Tai O on Lantau Island to go fishing. They threw overboard the crew – a woman and her daughter and son. The mother and daughter drowned. The thirteen-year-old son swam to shore, and was the main witness at the trial. The men were hanged on 31 December 1919. *HKDP*, 12 and 13 November 1919.

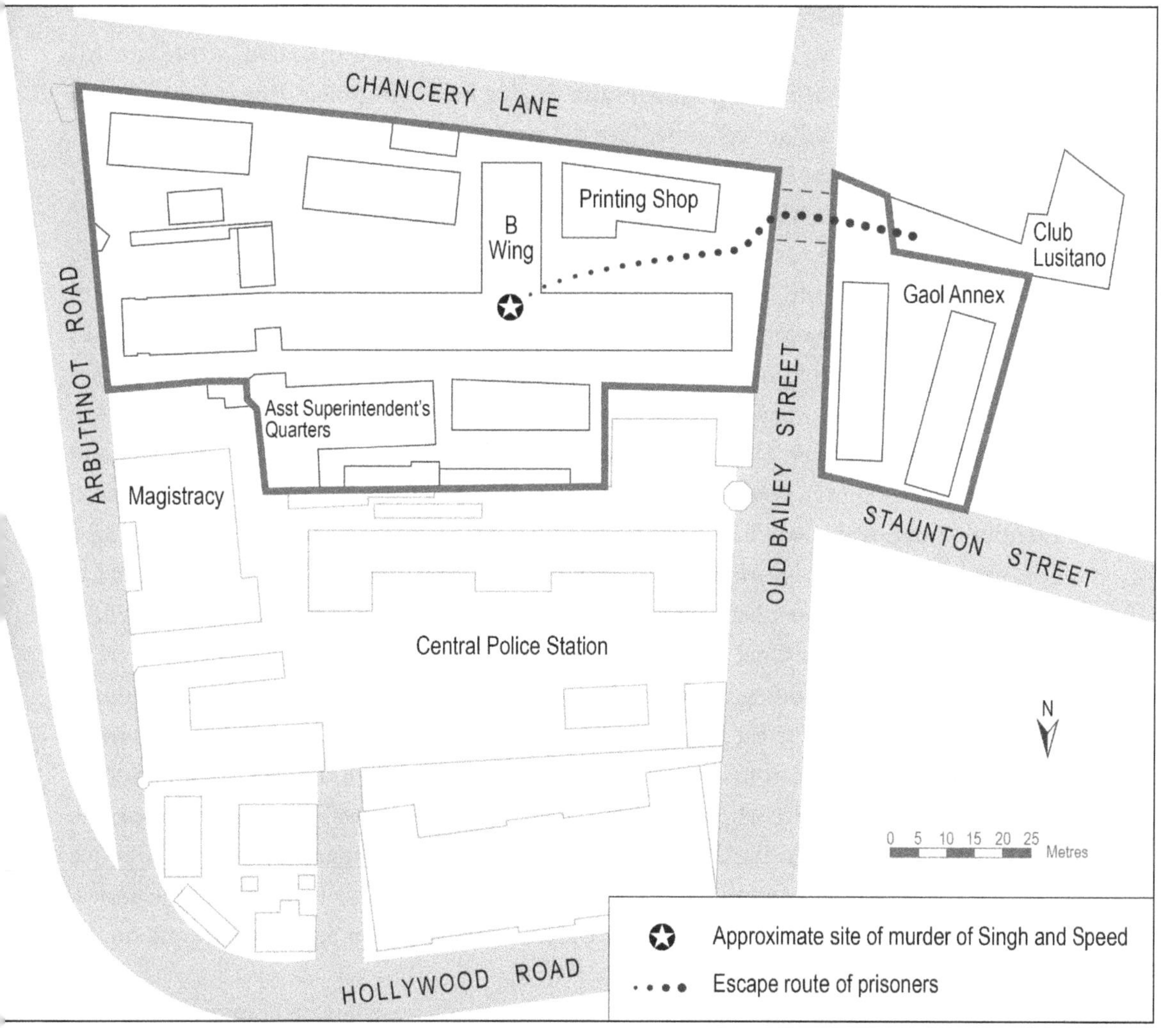

Map 4: The Victoria Gaol Murders, 1919

only officer with a revolver.[12] Ten other Indian staff and four Chinese guards were on duty elsewhere in the gaol.

At about 4 a.m. Ayub Khan noticed two Chinese men, dressed in dark clothes, walking swiftly along the corridor towards Speed's office. Khan followed them but was attacked from behind by two other men. One slashed at him with a dagger, cutting his hand. The other went to the condemned cell and set upon Singh. While fending off his attacker, Khan saw the first two men emerge from the office, pushed by Speed, who then collapsed.

12. The account here draws mainly on reports of the escape and inquest in *HKDP*, *CM*, *SCMP*, *HKT*, and *WTYP*, 15–20 December 1919; and Stubbs to Milner, 31 December 1919, CO 129/456, 478–483.

After further struggles with Khan, Singh, and another guard, Sher Shah, the four men let themselves out into a yard, taking Speed's revolver. Khan rang the alarm. Other guards then reached the scene, blowing whistles and ringing bells. The police, from Central Police Station next door, could not get in because the gate was locked.

In his quarters next to the gaol, John Franks, the Assistant Superintendent in charge, was awakened by the whistles and bells. Accompanied by other European officers, he opened the gate with his keys. Inside he found a scene of confusion. Khan was lying wounded, his turban and broken lamp on the ground nearby. Several guards armed with bamboo sticks, hardly visible in the semi-darkness, were now present. From what Franks could make out, Khan said he had been attacked by a man in plain clothes; he repeated over and over that the man was a policeman. Franks found Speed lying in the corridor, alive but unable to speak. He had been stabbed twenty-seven times on his face, neck, and body. Franks had him moved to the gaol hospital. He died before he could receive medical attention. Singh, still alive, had been carried into a guardroom, where he was lying on a bed, his face slashed open. He was also moved to the gaol hospital. Franks heard him say 'something like "Prisoner 24 attacked me, or cell 24th."' Singh died later that morning while being operated on at the Civil Hospital.

After leaving the building the four prisoners ran across the yard and through the tunnel under Old Bailey Street to the annex on the other side of the street. They climbed the wall with a rope thrown over from outside. One landed on the roof of the servants' quarters of the Club Lusitano – the Portuguese club – which abutted the wall of the gaol annex. He burst into the quarters, woke the club's billiard marker, and demanded tobacco. A police search early on Monday found a blood-stained knife in a lane near the wall of the annex. Other knives fashioned from tools used in the gaol were found in Speed's office and on the roof of the servants' quarters.

On Monday afternoon, escorted by warders and police officers, the bodies of Harnam Singh and James Speed were carried by hearse from Victoria Gaol along Queen's Road to Happy Valley. The cortege halted at the Sikh Temple, where Indian warders removed Singh's coffin. At the nearby Monument – an obelisk erected in 1847 – Speed's coffin, draped with the Union Jack, his cap and belt on top, was placed on a gun carriage drawn by policemen. A firing party from the Hong Kong Defence Corps, of which Speed was a member, led the procession to the Catholic Cemetery, followed by the band of the Wiltshire Regiment playing Chopin's Funeral March. The priest, Father Augustine, spoke of how the army, navy, police, and prison staff were not always 'looked upon with great favour, yet everybody knew that they were absolutely necessary for the safety of the Colony'. A volley was then fired and the 'Last Post' was sounded.[13]

---

13. *SCMP*, *HKT*, and HKDP, 16 December 1919. The Monument, a gathering point for funeral processions at the junction of Morrison Gap Road and Morrison Hill Road, was to men of HMS *Vestal* killed in a battle with Syarif Osman, Raja of Marudu, a rival of James Brooke. It was moved to the Colonial Cemetery in 1968.

In Speed the colonial community found a tragic hero. Some said that by putting up a gallant fight he had given his life that others might live.[14] James Leslie Speed had enlisted in the Royal Garrison Artillery at the age of twenty in 1909 and shipped to Hong Kong in 1910. He bought his discharge in 1912 and signed on as a warder. In late 1915, with a small group of other warders and policemen, he returned to England to serve in the war. While training in Ireland he injured his knees in a throw from a horse and was discharged as medically unfit. After convalescence he served on the front before going down with fever. He returned to the trenches in early 1918 but was gassed. After more time in hospital, he was compulsorily transferred to the Chinese Labour Corps, a common fate for men who were no longer fit to fight.[15] While in Ireland, Speed met Annie Nolan. They married in 1917 and Annie gave birth to a boy in November 1919. Mother and child were about to leave for Hong Kong when news of the murders was telegraphed to London. Her widow's pension of over £74 per annum was supplemented by £600 raised in Hong Kong through benefit football matches, variety concerts, and private donations.[16]

Speed's gravestone was erected by his colleagues more than a year after his murder 'as a permanent mark of appreciation of his courage and devotion to duty'. It also records the death of Harnam Singh and the wounding of Ayub Khan and Sher Shah. The inscription states that Speed met his death at the hands of four escaping convicts and that, in forcing his way through his assailants and giving the general alarm, he averted 'according to the statements of the murderers, all subsequently recaptured and executed, what was intended to be a general outbreak'. It is a rare example of a gravestone that explicitly records the deaths of prisoners condemned to hang.

The inquest, 16–19 December 1919

The inquest (or 'death enquiry') into the deaths of Singh and Speed was held by the magistrate, John Wood, with a jury of three.[17] They heard that the escaped prisoners were

> *Mok Sing* (莫勝) alias *Cheng Pong*, aged twenty-three, prisoner no. 24 from cell 50. A boilermaker originating from Huizhou but claiming Hong Kong birth. Employed in the gaol tinsmith's shop. Sentenced in October 1918 to seven years' hard labour and eighteen strokes of the birch after pleading guilty to kidnapping an eight-year-old boy, a crime described by the Chief Justice, Sir William Rees-Davies, as 'very cowardly'.

14. *SCMP*, 20 December 1919.
15. I am indebted to Patricia O'Sullivan for sharing her research into James Speed's life.
16. In 1922 Annie remarried and the pension was transferred to her son until he came of age. Speed's annual salary was £180. Stubbs to Milner, 20 December 1919, CO 129/456, 436–439, and 21 May and 28 June 1920, CO 129/461, 104–107 and 340–341; *SCMP*, 24 December 1919 and 19 March 1920.
17. Charles Francis Starkey, mining engineer; Francis Arthur Wells, assistant at Butterfield & Swire; and José Julita dos Remedios, clerk at the Hongkong and Shanghai Bank.

Li Hoi-shing (李海勝) alias *Li Chung*, aged twenty-five, prisoner no. 791 from cell 63. From Huizhou, Guangdong. Employed in the gaol shoemaker's shop. Sentenced in April 1915 to ten years' hard labour and twelve strokes of the cat-o'-nine-tails after pleading guilty to robbery with violence of a clerk employed by Watson's Aerated Water Factory.

Wong Kwong (黃廣), aged thirty-one, prisoner no. 850 from cell 62. From Shunde, Guangdong. Employed in the gaol printing shop. Sentenced in April 1916 to ten years' hard labour after pleading guilty to burglariously entering a house in Causeway Bay. He disturbed the occupants, who chased him through several streets until he jumped into the harbour. A Chinese constable rescued him and was awarded $10 for 'an exceptional arrest'. Denying a further charge that he had shot at the constable, Wong told the Chief Justice that if he would not be lenient he could 'have him shot or do anything he liked with him'.

Yeung Po (楊保) alias *Yeung Hop-yin* and *Yeung Yin*, age unknown, prisoner no. 1785 from cell 48, which he shared with three other prisoners. Employed as a painter in the gaol. Sentenced in March 1919 to twelve months' hard labour for returning to Hong Kong before expiry of a term of banishment.[18]

Their cases illustrate some of the measures used at this time to address high rates of violent and predatory crime: long prison sentences, banishment, and the cat, which was reinstated in 1911 after its abolition by Governor Hennessy in 1881.

Evidence from gaol staff suggested that the escape had begun in cell 63, where Li Hoi-shing had cut away a wooden panel covering the back of the lock. He had then removed the back plate and turned the lock with his fingers. Warders later found in Li's cell a chisel blade, a stone, a brush-pen, and two sheets of paper painted green, which he had used to cover up his handiwork. Green was the colour of the gaol's fixtures after a recent repaint. They also found chapati, candied ginger, and a bag of sugar. With a single key, probably made in the gaol's tinsmith's shop, Li unlocked three nearby cells on the same floor, releasing Mok, Wong, and Yeung, but not the three other prisoners sharing Yeung's cell. The key was later found in one of these cells, along with a bottle of green paint, wire, knives, and other tools. The escapees changed into suits of dark flannel made in the gaol's tailor's shop, carefully arranging their discarded prison clothes to make it appear they were sleeping. They then armed themselves with daggers made in the gaol workshops – one a sharpened file, another formed from a shoemaker's knife. They crept down to the ground floor, fought with the warders and guards, opened the gate with another key, and made their escape, shouting threats and obscenities to any guards they met on their way.

The verdict at the inquest was that Speed and Singh had died from injuries inflicted on them by Mok Sing, Li Hoi-shing, and Wong Kwong during their escape. The jury could not determine whether the fourth prisoner, Yeung Po, was in possession of a dagger. Wood

---

18. *SCMP*, 20 April 1915 and 22 October 1918; *HKDP*, 19 April 1916 and 22 October 1918; Report of the Captain Superintendent of Police for 1916.

added it was a mystery why, almost at the end of his twelve-month sentence, Yeung should have joined long-term prisoners in such an undertaking.

In some cases from these years, coroners' juries were encouraged to make findings on more than just the cause of death. In February 1918 fire had swept through bamboo grandstands at the Racecourse, killing over 600 people. Legislation was urgently enacted to allow a special jury to sit at the inquest. The jurors were invited to criticize any officials concerned, and the Coroner put to them twenty-three specific questions. After a twenty-one-day hearing, the jury found that the Director of Public Works and Captain Superintendent of Police (as head of the Fire Brigade) had failed in their duties.[19] The jury enquiring into the deaths of Singh and Speed was a common jury, but it too made recommendations. The same coroner, John Wood, presided over both the racecourse and the gaol inquests.[20]

The jury remarked on 'the unsatisfactory state of affairs at the gaol at the time of the escape'. They recommended improvements to the alarms and the installation of a system capable of flooding the corridors with electric light in an emergency. They observed that some of the gaol buildings were too close to the outer walls, and that a grille fixed to one of the buildings in the gaol annex to prevent scaling of the wall had actually helped the prisoners escape. They also noted that Speed, Singh, and Khan had probably been stabbed with knives made in the gaol itself. They had much to say about the state of discipline and supervision among the gaol staff. They heard, for example, that in April 1919 an Indian warder had lost a master key to the gaol. He had not reported this, and it was only much later that the loss was noticed. The key was never found, and no alterations were made to the locks. The jury concluded that all evidence pointed to collusion between staff and the escaped prisoners. Without this, it could not have been possible for prisoners to have so many tools and clothes in their cells, or for them to have been missed by routine searches of the cells on the Saturday and Sunday.

The jury ascribed these problems to insufficient European staff. They advised that at least two European warders should be on duty at night – a policy that had been suspended in 1915 because of staff shortages. Assistant Superintendent Franks had informed the inquest that the entire disciplined gaol staff at the time of the escape consisted of 90 men – 18 below its approved establishment of 108. Manpower at Victoria Gaol was further reduced by the absence of two European warders on long leave and two others in hospital, and by the need to deploy sixteen staff to a temporary branch prison at the Infectious Diseases Hospital in Kennedy Town, where 172 prisoners were admitted with beriberi in October and November 1919. A worldwide rice crisis, caused by wartime dislocation of trade, poor harvests, and speculation, had caused shortages and price rises. The

19. May to Long, 16 May 1918, CO 129/448, 288–300; Ordinance No. 1 of 1918.
20. A Cantonese-speaking cadet officer, Wood had joined the Hong Kong civil service in 1899. He had been a magistrate since 1908 and was called to the Bar by Lincoln's Inn in 1919; an avuncular figure, he was known by lawyers as 'Pa Wood': Obituary, *SCMP*, 3 October 1953.

government had intervened to purchase rice from Saigon and elsewhere, but this came too late to prevent riots over the summer. Unable to obtain the usual supply of unhulled red rice, the gaol authorities had, from July, fed the prisoners polished rice, which had caused the outbreak of beriberi.[21]

Global upheavals were also partly behind the shortage of staff. Five European warders had gone to fight in the Great War. Three had returned.[22] The war had constricted two main sources of recruits: the armed forces, and the British prison services. Turnover was high. Four unusually long-serving European warders, with an average of twenty years' service, had resigned in 1918–1919. Seven of the twenty-eight European warder posts were now vacant. This, claimed Franks, was the reason why the escape had succeeded: 'It was impossible to get the Indian staff to work with zeal and energy without European supervision.' The Indian staff too were depleted, with eleven of eighty posts vacant.[23] Their turnover was also high. A quarter of them were engaged on temporary terms: Harnam Singh was probably one of this group. To help out, the police had lent the gaol twelve Chinese guards, a departure from a long-standing policy against employing Chinese as gaolers.[24] Most Indian warders spoke Chinese and English and received special language allowances. In contrast, only two European warders were receiving Chinese language allowances.[25] Years before, one superintendent had compiled 'a small book containing the more ordinary expressions in use in the Gaol in low class Cantonese'.[26] Usually, however, Europeans relied on Indian staff or Chinese clerks for any but the most basic communications. Where words failed, some resorted to blows.[27]

Noting in 1912 that over fifty European warders had resigned, deserted, or been sacked in the previous decade, the *South China Morning Post* reflected on the degrading life of the 'underpaid and overworked warder'. Shifts were often over twelve hours at a stretch. Most

21. Preliminary Report on the Purchase and Sale of Rice by the Government of Hongkong During the Year 1919, *HKSP*, 1/1920; Medical and Sanitary Reports for the Year 1919, 48–49.
22. One of the five, Walter May, was killed in action in December 1914. Another, James Miller, decided not to return. The other three – James Speed, Harry Johnson, and Albert Didsbury – returned to Hong Kong in July 1919. A sixth warder, George Gipson, transferred to the Sanitary Department in January 1917, shortly before being seconded for military service.
23. The European staff at full strength consisted of a chief warder, four principal warders, and twenty-two warders; the Indian staff eighteen warders, thirty-six assistant warders, and twenty-six guards.
24. In a reversal of this policy, in 1877 Hennessy appointed four Chinese policemen to replace European turnkeys fired for drunkenness and beating inmates. Two resigned immediately when inmates they had helped convict made threats against their lives. Three, including the two replacements, served until 1884. The fourth absconded in 1890 with $315 deposited by inmates on admission to gaol. The rank of 'Chinese turnkey' was then abolished. Hennessy to Carnarvon, 1 August 1877, CO 129/178, 485–512; Fleming to Knutsford, 17 May 1890, CO 129/245, 158–161; *HKDP*, 27 August 1877; *OCM*, 9 October 1890.
25. One of whom, Sydney Shirvington, resigned in 1920.
26. The book was prepared by N.G. Mitchell-Innes: Report of the Superintendent of Victoria Gaol for 1887.
27. See, for example, letters from 'A Britisher' and 'L.R.', *SCMP*, 8 March 1913 and 27 March 1914.

warders were required to live in quarters next to the gaol in case of emergencies. Among their 'disgusting duties' were searching the 'filthy bodies' of new prisoners and overseeing 'the removal of some hundreds of uncovered night soil buckets from the cells'. Discipline, 'with a big capital D', was enforced more against warders than prisoners, claimed one of the *Post's* sources: a particular grievance was their liability to fines, demotion, and prosecution for breaches of rules. The Indian, mostly Sikh, staff were equally discontented. They complained in 1902, and again in 1910 and 1915, that their pay was barely enough to live on, let alone bring their families to Hong Kong. They were continually comparing their conditions with those of the European warders and Indian police, demanding the same favourable exchange rates for remittances home: in 1910 the guards, the lowest-paid staff, resigned en masse over this issue.[28] At a time of rising nationalism the government was anxious about the loyalty of Indians and suspected that some, including a few police and gaol staff, were spreading sedition.[29]

Questions of trust pervaded relations between the government and its non-European staff. Chinese and other Asians were increasingly employed in positions formerly reserved for Europeans because they were less expensive and more available. At the same time, official suspicion of 'native employees' was fed by frequent reports of embezzlement and bribery, driven, some said, by low pay, lack of supervision, and expensive lifestyles.[30] The government was therefore cautious about placing non-Europeans in sensitive positions. Among the European civil servants, discontent was not confined to the gaol warders. Those still paid in Hong Kong dollars were struggling to maintain a decent standard of living. Some had their careers cut short by disease, alcoholism, or suicide. In the militarized conditions of the region, they also faced the threat of armed violence. In 1918 five policemen were shot dead and six were wounded in a fight with robbers in a house in Gresson Street, the most shocking in a series of police deaths at the hands of criminals.[31] Discontent came to a head in December 1919 when most of a batch of new constables from England decided to return home when they were denied the pay rises they had been led to expect. One, Denis

28. Black to Chamberlain, 25 March 1898, CO 129/282, 148–159; Blake to Chamberlain, 22 March 1899, CO 129/290, 355–362; Gascoigne to Chamberlain, 24 March 1902, CO 129/310, 417–424; May to Lyttelton, 7 June 1904, CO 129/323, 56–61; May to Crewe, 23 March 1910, CO 129/365, 564–571; May to Harcourt, 4 February 1915, CO 129/420, 255–260; Stubbs to Churchill, 24 August 1921, CO 129/468, 600–602.
29. In March 1914 the Sikh Temple, suspected of being a centre of seditious propaganda, was placed out of bounds to soldiers and police. The government also tried to prevent the local press from reporting the mutiny among Indian Muslim troops in Singapore in February 1915. May to Harcourt, 12 March 1915, CO 129/421, 108–113; May to Bonar Law, 486–503, 13 August 1915, CO 129/423, 486–503.
30. See Christopher Munn, 'Carvalho Yeo and the 1928 Hong Kong Treasury Swindle', in *Meeting Place: Encounters across Cultures in Hong Kong, 1841–1984*, ed. Elizabeth Sinn and Christopher Munn (Hong Kong: Hong Kong University Press, 2017).
31. See Patricia O'Sullivan, *Policing Hong Kong: An Irish History: Irishmen in the Hong Kong Police Force, 1864–1950* (Hong Kong: Blacksmith Books, 2018), Chapter 10.

Lavender, sentenced to a month's imprisonment for refusing duty, complained to the press about being 'enticed to this Colony under false pretences to face dangers almost equal to those of the late war, for a salary which is only about half that of the Police at Home'.[32]

Threats of violence also lay behind the monotonous routine of Victoria Gaol. Usually it took the form of fighting among prisoners, but occasionally staff were the targets. On 27 June 1885 the new Superintendent, General Alexander Gordon, was bludgeoned by a prisoner who had been promised a reward by some fifty other prisoners angry about cuts in diet and the severity of his regime. In another conspiracy eighteen months later a group of long-sentence prisoners, assisted by Triads outside, planned to burn down the gaol on Christmas night by leaving a slow fuse under a pile of clothes in the tailor's shop. The day was chosen because the turnkeys were likely to be absent or drunk. The prisoners believed the fire would 'so frighten the Superintendent that he would never come back to Hong Kong' and be replaced by a 'more kind Superintendent'. The plot was discovered by James Logan, then serving his seven-year sentence for killing a boy in Canton (see Chapter 6).[33] A month later, on 31 January 1887, while Gordon was on leave, a general 'mutiny' broke out. Some 160 prisoners, squatting in one of the yards after breakfast, refused to get up and work. European inmates were turned out to remove them to their cells. Sixty-nine of the more defiant protestors were flogged.[34]

Attacks on staff were nevertheless rare. The last fatal one was in 1888, when an assistant turnkey, Cornelius Pereira, was killed during an escape by twelve prisoners from a chain gang working on excavations in Kennedy Town. All of them were recaptured. Ten, placed in the dock in fetters, were tried for murder and acquitted. After pleading guilty to escape, they complained about beatings, inadequate food, lack of sleep, and being forced to work while ill.[35] Chain gangs were suspended after this incident. The last attempted murder was in 1901, when three long-sentence convicts stabbed the Assistant Superintendent, Robert Craig, and a Sikh warder with knives smuggled into the gaol. At their trial the prisoners cross-examined Craig about how their complaints of short rations had been answered with floggings and punishment diets. One asked to 'be deported to the uttermost parts of the

32. Stubbs to Milner, 7 January 1920, CO 129/460, 6–11; *CM*, 24 January 1920; *HKT*, 24 December 1919.

33. Evidence by Logan, 29 December 1886, in Marsh to Stanhope, 31 December 1886, in CO 129/421–434.

34. Marsh to Secretary of State, 1 and 12 February 1887, CO 129/231, 101–107 and 122–161.

35. The escapees commandeered a nearby coal junk. Pereira followed them on board. Two of the prisoners attacked him and he fell overboard and drowned. Ten escapees were captured by police, who happened to be passing in a launch, with the assistance of gaol guards on shore; the eleventh was captured soon after, but the twelfth was not found until 1891. In their trial the ten prisoners were defended by Ho Kai, who stressed the many discrepancies in the evidence given by the guards. Their sentences for escaping ranged from two to five years' imprisonment. *OCM*, 27 September and 21 November 1888; *HKDP*, 24 November 1888.

earth, or sentenced to death, rather than be sent back under Mr Craig'.[36] Instead, the prisoners received additional terms of imprisonment.

The trials in 1920 of Wong Kwong and Mok Sing for the murder of James Speed were to produce even more detailed complaints about conditions in Victoria Gaol.

R v *Wong Kwong*
Murder, 19 and 20 January 1920

The police despatched search parties, offered a reward of $500, and circulated photographs and descriptions of the escaped prisoners to the authorities in Canton, Macao, and other ports. The first to be arrested was Wong Kwong, two days after the escape, on the evening of Tuesday 17 December. The police heard from an informer that he was hiding on the hillside behind Tai Hang Village. Pretending to help him escape from Hong Kong, the informer lured Wong down to the tram terminus at Causeway Bay. Plain-clothes policemen then arrested him. Wong was unarmed and gave no resistance. The next morning police took him to the roof of the Club Lusitano, where he found the knife he had used in the escape. In the afternoon, the third day of the inquest, he was brought before John Wood but declined to make a statement.[37]

Wong was more forthcoming at committal proceedings, held on 8 January 1920. Wood, now sitting as magistrate, heard much the same evidence for the prosecution as had been given at the inquest. Under the usual caution, Wong then made a dramatic statement. He blamed the murder of Speed and Singh on his fellow escapees and declared that his own intention had been to kill the Assistant Superintendent, the Chief Warder, and the visiting Justices of the Peace. They were responsible for short rations given to prisoners, he said, and for their general neglect and ill treatment. He asked for his statement to be submitted to the Governor. The statement was to become a focal point in his trial. Like those of the defendants in the Harbour Murder (Chapter 6), it was, as the judge later observed, to make a difficult defence even more difficult.

The committal proceedings took place in the new Magistracy, opened in 1915 on the site of the old one next to Victoria Gaol. In 1912 the Supreme Court too had moved into new premises, a magnificent building on the new reclamation in Central. Designed by the leading English architect Sir Aston Webb, the new Law Courts had granite façades and a dome modelled on that of St Paul's Cathedral. Construction had taken more than a decade

36. The Superintendent, F.H. May, explained that in 1899 the diet for men on hard labour had been cut; he had translated the new diets into Chinese for the benefit of inmates. *HKT*, 19 and 20 April 1901.

37. *HKDP*, 15, 18, and 19 December 1919; *HKT*, 17 December 1919; Stubbs to Milner, 31 December 1919, CO 129/456, 479.

because of problems with foundations, changes to plans, a shortage of granite, and disputes between the government and the contractor. The delays and cost overruns had become a standing joke. Legislators were unhappy that the design had gone to a London firm: the result was 'very ordinary, yea – common', said one, comparing it 'most unfavourably' with nearby buildings by local architects; it seemed 'sunk right down, apparently by its own weight, until it stands knee deep in mud,' said another. Chief Justice Piggott remarked that 'no one who has familiarity with the conduct of business in the Supreme Court could have approved' the plans. The acoustics in the great central court were so poor that his speech at the opening ceremony was barely audible.[38]

Piggott sat in his new court for only a few months until his dismissal in April 1912. His successor was the Attorney General, William Rees-Davies. From a family of lawyers, Rees-Davies was called to the Bar in 1887. He prosecuted on the South Wales circuit before being elected the Liberal Member of Parliament for Pembrokeshire on his father's retirement. He served as private secretary to the Chancellor of the Exchequer, Sir William Harcourt, in 1893–1895. In 1898, through the patronage of Joseph Chamberlain, he was appointed Attorney General of the Bahamas. From 1902 he served as King's Advocate in Cyprus until his transfer to Hong Kong in 1907. Despite a policy against promoting an attorney general to chief justice in the same colony, he was the fourth Hong Kong Chief Justice to follow this path. Knighted in 1913, he now presided over Wong's trial.

Wong's was the first of six cases to be tried in the January sessions. The others were two cases of assault with intent to rob, a robbery, a forgery, and a 'motor bandit' case, in which three men were convicted and hanged for murdering a Chinese constable while robbing a money-changer's shop on Des Voeux Road West. In a tactic new to Hong Kong, they had escaped in a car after exchanging shots with an Indian constable. Hardly a day passed without a report of some armed robbery by 'desperadoes' from Canton, complained the *Hongkong Telegraph*. It pointed out that Europeans had had to carry passports to enter or leave Hong Kong during the war. Yet the 'ever-changing mass' of Chinese, with their 'very big sprinkling of deep-dyed criminals', came and went as they pleased. It urged the introduction of passports to keep out 'the scum of Canton'.[39]

Charged with murdering James Speed, Wong answered, 'I did not do it.' The jury balloted to try him consisted of Duarte Cezar Baptista, Joaquim Telles D'Almada e Castro, and Francisco Valeriano Vandenberg (all Portuguese); Un Chun-fai (Chinese); Herbert Griffin and Alan Balean (both of British origin); and Frederick Ellis (of Baghdadi Jewish

38. Whitehead to Chamberlain, 1 December 1899, CO 129/296, 486; *HKH*, 9 November 1911; Piggott, quoted in F.H. May to Piggott and Wise, 18 December 1906, in HKPRO HKRS102: Letters from Governor to Chief Justice; *HKDP*, 22 January 1912.
39. *HKT*, 18 December 1919.

descent). All except Ellis, a broker, were assistants in Western firms. Un Chun-fai appears in jurors lists as an assistant or translator in the Asiatic Petroleum Company.[40] Chinese jurors were now appearing more often in criminal trials, particularly after the removal of over a hundred Germans from the jury lists during the war.[41]

The barrister assigned to defend Wong was Raphael Emanuel Belilios, the son of Emanuel Belilios, who had funded the reformatory. Born in Hong Kong in 1880 and educated in England, Belilios junior studied law in Hong Kong with J.J. Francis before attending Middle Temple, where he was called to the Bar in 1903. He began practice in Hong Kong in 1906 but spent much of the next decade in England moving in high society. He was defeated as a Conservative candidate in the two general elections in 1910. In Hong Kong he continued his father's philanthropy and devoted much time to leisure: his yacht 'Dwyn Wen' was soon to make a difficult first voyage from Southampton to Hong Kong. Despite his long absences, Belilios had so far defended thirteen men on capital charges in Hong Kong: eleven were convicted (one of manslaughter), and six hanged.

The prosecutor was the Attorney General, Joseph Kemp KC. Born in Ireland, the son of a businessman, Kemp was educated at the University of Cape Town after his family moved to South Africa. He went to Hong Kong as a cadet in 1898 and served as magistrate and Registrar of the Supreme Court while studying law. Called to the Bar in 1911, he became Crown Solicitor in the same year, and Attorney General in 1915. Kemp opened the trial by asking the jury 'to think of the horror of the time, the darkness, the fear of sudden death they were all in, and the fact that they were all fighting for their lives'. For these reasons, 'one could not expect a clear-cut story'. After handing plans of the gaol to the jury, he described the events on 15 December. It was impossible to prove what part Wong Kwong had taken. Wong had said that he had attacked Ayub Khan: probably, said Kemp, he thought his guilt was less because Khan was the only one of the men attacked who was still alive. If, however, the jury were satisfied that the four convicts set out with the common design of wounding or killing anyone – or if they set out merely to escape but in the process attacked the warders, even if they had no plan to do so – then all four were equally guilty of Speed's murder. There was, said Kemp, 'an abundance of proof' that all four escapees had a common design.

40. Griffin was an assistant in Butterfield & Swire, Balean in the Hongkong and Shanghai Bank, Baptista in Floquet & Knoth, D'Almada e Castro in the International Banking Corporation, and Vandenberg in Reiss & Co., a British firm. The main sources for this trial are *CM* and *HKT*, 19–21 January 1920; and *HKDP*, *SCMP*, and *WTYP*, 20 and 21 January 1920.

41. The 1,286-strong Jury List for 1919 (effective until March 1920) contained about 50 Chinese names and over 280 Portuguese names. The 100 or so Germans on the 1914 list were removed in 1915. A further 115, mostly British, names on the 1919 list were exempted from jury service by virtue of service in the Hong Kong Defence Force. Portuguese therefore accounted for about 25 per cent of active jurors.

Kemp then read out a translation of Wong's statement to the magistrate.[42] This was a mixture of wild braggadocio and specific grievances. It began with an admission that he had once committed a crime and deserved to be in gaol. If he had murdered someone it was also right he should pay the penalty. The government had set out the rations for prisoners, but they were barely enough to make them 30 per cent full. The fish and vegetables were fit only for dogs and pigs. Of course, they did not expect fine cuisine. But European inmates were given oil and sugar, while Chinese prisoners were not. Many had died of starvation as a result, Wong claimed. Seeing so many die, the acting medical officer (a Captain Archer) – praised by all inmates as 'a good doctor' – had allowed extra rations of beef congee, beans, and oil. But prisoners had received only 30 per cent of what he prescribed. Condemned prisoners were entitled to rations to the value of a dollar a day, but the food given to them cost twenty cents or less. Gaol officials tolerated these embezzlements of public money, yet the money gained would not even pay for a single dinner in Shek Tong Tsui. There was laughter at this among the many spectators in court: Shek Tong Tsui, in the western part of the city, was the Chinese nightlife district.

Wong alleged that Indian warders often brought in cigarettes and tobacco, which they gave to good-looking Chinese prisoners with whom they wished to commit 'illegal acts' (his description of these acts, reported the *Wa Tsz Yat Po*, was too obscene to be described in pen and ink). He added that in the previous year Principal Warder No. 32, a European, had been dismissed for a sexual assault on an Indian. Smoking in the gaol was illegal. Bringing in tobacco was a serious offence incurring at least twenty days' hard labour, said Wong. Why had the gaol officials not discovered these abuses? The warders beat prisoners for no reason. But their complaints were only attended to if they had bruises or other marks. And when they complained only the guards were permitted to speak.

Wong said that seventy-six prisoners had taken an oath to use any amount of force to escape, even to the point of death, because they did not have enough food or clothing. They would rather hang than die of starvation. The four escapees had not set out to murder the two warders. It was the others, not he, who had killed them. His plan had been to kill Assistant Superintendent Franks and Alfred Passmore, the Chief Warder, who cheated prisoners out of their food, and also the Chinese justices of the peace, who knew of this but took no notice. He urged the court to investigate the prisoners' grievances and see they were supplied with more rice and sugar. If not, the deaths would be uncountable.

42. There are five versions of this, in *CM*, *SCMP*, *HKT*, and *WTYP*, 9 January 1920; and *HKDP*, 20 January 1920. They vary in length and are not entirely consistent. For example, the *CM* and *SCMP* report Wong as having confessed to the murder, when it seems from the *WTYP* and *HKDP* that he was merely acknowledging that he had been in gaol for a crime previously committed. The English reports also play down the racial distinctions apparent in the report in the *WTYP*. The discussion here relies mainly on the accounts in the *WTYP* and *HKDP*: from the date and internal evidence the former is a direct, if incomplete, report of what Wong said; the latter reports an official translation read out at trial.

> I, Wong Kwong, have committed crimes and deserve worse than death. If my death helps the other prisoners drag out their lives, then I will rest happy in my grave. After death, a man leaves behind his reputation, as a tiger leaves his skin, for hundreds and thousands of years. That is enough to satisfy my wish. I have been a hero for eighteen years and have enjoyed the pleasures of whoring, gambling, and drinking. Among the Chinese in the gaol there are heroes, and also men who look for trouble. The European warders treat us Chinese like ants. Of course, I have no opinion on this. But I do not know why the Chinese justices of the peace who come to visit the gaol show no concern.[43]

He did not care if he was sentenced to death. 'I will laugh when the time for my execution comes,' he said. Then, after singling out one warder, James McLeod, as the only one who was not bad, Wong's statement repeated the demand for an investigation.

Kemp then called a dozen witnesses for the prosecution. Among them were police and medical officers and staff of the gaol, including Ayub Khan, McLeod, and the two singled out by Wong as the men he had wished to kill: Passmore and Franks. Giving evidence on the second day, McLeod said that he had been first on the scene and had found the tools in Li Hoi-shing's cell. Under cross-examination, he said there was no apparent familiarity between the four escapees, and it was unlikely they had had long conversations. He confirmed that neither of the two Indian guards who had survived the attack, Ayub Khan and Sher Shah, had mentioned Wong as one of the attackers.

Franks was the last witness called. The beef congee, he confirmed, had been fed to prisoners after the outbreak of beriberi. He denied that prisoners had been deprived of rations, or that any prisoner had died of starvation. Belilios's cross-examination followed two lines of questioning. First, he asked Franks if Wong had made complaints about the food. Franks said that in April 1918 he had complained he was not getting enough. Franks had told him he was receiving the proper amount and had heard no more complaints. Under re-examination by Kemp, however, he added that Wong had also complained of short rations as recently as 29 November 1919; the shortage had immediately been made good. He could not say if Wong had complained to any justices of the peace because complaints were not recorded. He accepted that tobacco and other items could have been trafficked into the gaol from outside, possibly from prisoners' friends. The chapati and ginger in Li Hoi-shing's cell had probably been given to him by an Indian officer. 'These things happened because of the shortage of staff in the gaol.' In reply to the Chief Justice, he said he had never heard of warders giving presents to prisoners for immoral purposes. Chinese prisoners had, however, complained that Indian warders had made immoral overtures to them. He rejected Wong's claim that a European warder had been fired for making sexual advances to an Indian.

43. *WTYP*, 9 January 1920 (author's translation).

Secondly, Belilios asked if Wong had ever been in the gaol hospital. Franks said that Wong had been treated for syphilis. After Franks had been re-examined, the Chief Justice said, 'I take it, Mr Belilios, that you are going to ask the Jury to believe that owing to the lack of food and attention, this man was not responsible for his actions.' Belilios replied, 'Yes, my Lord. His mind was depraved as a result.'

The case for the defence opened in the afternoon of the second day. Belilios called no witnesses. He began by saying there was not one eyewitness who saw Wong attack anyone. No matter how carefully arranged the plans, Wong was no active partner but a mere 'cat's paw' controlled by men stronger than himself. He doubted if Wong had been taken into the confidence of the other three; it was even probable that he had not known about the plan until shortly before being let out of his cell. As for his 'rambling statement', Belilios asked the jury to consider what state of mind he was in at the time.

> The prisoner thought that a grievous wrong had been done to him. He had given facts and figures of the food supplies; how he got them Counsel did not know. Mr Franks had emphatically denied the prisoner's statement but he could only deny it because his subordinates had not informed him of the things alleged. If the jury believed that the prisoner was actually suffering a real wrong in the neglect of his bodily comforts, through insufficiency of food, and that the suffering had an effect on his mind, it was their duty to bring in a verdict of insanity.[44]

Belilios pointed to Wong's behaviour in the dock, saying he understood Chinese enough to know that the remarks Wong had made were 'nothing more or less than foolish'. If the jury could not find Wong insane, he asked for a recommendation to mercy.

Kemp then concluded for the prosecution. He asked the jury if they could imagine that three desperate men who set out on a desperate venture would ask a fourth to join them merely as a cat's paw. All four prisoners had suits ready for their escape. Wong had a knife and had joined in the attack. He had said that they were prepared to go to any length. His only defence was insanity – 'always the last resort of a man who had no defence'. The defence had argued that Wong suffered from delusions, caused by bad treatment and insufficient food. But he got the same food as others and had made only two complaints in nearly four years. He had alleged immoral practices but had not said that any warders had made overtures to him. Kemp said that to establish a plea of insanity it must be proved that, at the time he committed the crime, the accused did not know what he was doing, or did not know he was doing wrong. Yet the 'whole facts of the case showed that the preparations had been made by clever, sane minds – criminal, desperate minds of cool determined men. Would the others take a madman with them?'

44. *HKDP*, 21 January 1920.

Summing up, Rees-Davies praised Belilios for having 'conducted a difficult case – made more difficult by the statement of the prisoner – with tact and ability'. Franks, he said, had given a general denial to Wong's allegations 'in his very straightforward evidence'. This had not been challenged. Instead, the defence had argued that Wong had laboured under a delusion – that, owing to a disease, his mind was unbalanced. Yet it had been proved that a murder had been committed, that Wong was one of the four men, that preparations had been made, and that an attack had been made on two warders in the outcome of a common design. 'Could the jury – seven men with common sense – on the strength of the plea put forward, say that the prisoner was suffering from such defect of reason at the time of the murder that he did not understand what he was doing or did not understand the nature of the crime?' If the jury found no proof of this, they must find him guilty of murder. If they found his mind was so unhinged that he lacked reason, their verdict must be 'Guilty, but insane'. There were only two possible verdicts.

After an absence of ten minutes the jury returned with a verdict of guilty of murder. At this point in the trial, in accordance with established practice, Rees-Davies asked Wong if he had anything to say why sentence should not be passed on him. Wong then launched into a long harangue, repeating what he had said to the magistrate and insisting that there was proof that prisoners were being underfed and that 'unnatural crime' had been committed in the gaol: he would give the Chief Justice the name of the Indian warder responsible. He begged the Chief Justice to punish those who had cheated the prisoners: 'If your Lordship will investigate the matter, I will smile even when I am hanged.' It was not easy to escape, he said. 'There you are, your Lordship, we succeeded in escaping. How able we are!' Rees-Davies interrupted several times, saying he was not going to stop him, but what he was saying could have no effect on the sentence.

At length, Belilios also interrupted, asking if 'in view of the wild statement of the prisoner', the Chief Justice would defer sentence until enquiry had been made into the state of Wong's mind. Rees-Davies refused. 'You have been convicted practically on your own confession,' he said to Wong. 'The state of affairs as alleged by you to exist in the prison, even if true, cannot excuse your crime.' He then passed sentence of death. Wong resumed his tirade, asking the judge to order that he be given sufficient food during the three weeks he would spend in gaol before execution. The court had already risen, and Rees-Davies, who was partially deaf, did not hear him. Wong was hanged in the gaol on 18 February 1920. The verdict at the inquest was 'death due to strangulation'.[45]

45. *CM*, 18 February 1920.

R v Mok Sing
Murder, 22 March 1920

Belilios had played up the 'wild' and 'rambling' nature of Wong's allegations in an attempt to persuade the jury he was insane. The prosecution had laboured hard to show their falsity – convincingly in the view of the judge. Others were not so sure. 'One could imagine that condemned man with anger in his heart, using all the picturesque language of the Oriental, as he made charge after charge against warders and keepers,' said the *China Mail*. 'Starvation, immorality, bribery and corruption were some of the items.' Then came 'the words of the martyr, ready to die, because he had been a bad man, but anxious to live a good life in his next existence and to leave behind a record of having helped his fellow creatures'. And yet, continued the *Mail*, although his statements were denied, 'they left a nasty conviction behind them that something might be wrong'.[46]

The trial of the next escapee added substance to this suspicion.[47] Mok Sing was captured in Canton in early March and brought to Hong Kong: there was no agreement for Chinese fugitives to be extradited to Hong Kong, but such arrangements were now common. Mok said nothing at committal hearings. When the indictment for the murder of Speed was read to him in the Supreme Court he replied, 'I did it.' The judge, Henry Gompertz, acting as Chief Justice, consulted the Attorney General, Joseph Kemp:

> **Gompertz** — I take it that you will assume that the prisoner has pleaded not guilty and proceed with the case?
>
> **Mok Sing** — It is no good calling for the jurors. I have nothing more to say. The reason why I went to gaol was on account of poverty. I had to go and rob.
>
> **Gompertz** (to the interpreter) — Tell him this is not the time to make a statement. There will be jurors called, and if he wishes to object to any individual the prisoner can say so.[48]

The jury consisted of two Portuguese, three of British origin, and two Chinese, one of whom, Wong Kam-fuk, was a justice of the peace – a member of the group berated by Wong Kwong in his trial. Wong Kam-fuk was comprador to the Kowloon Wharf and Godown Company. Another juror, Martin Maas, an assistant in the Asiatic Petroleum Company, asked for exemption, saying it was a busy time and he was the only European in his department.[49] Gompertz refused. In the event, the jury had little to do. Mok's counsel, Francis Jenkin, cross-examined Chief Detective Inspector William Murison, in charge

46. *CM*, 24 January 1920.
47. Reported in *HKDP*, *SCMP*, *CM*, and *HKT*, 23 March 1920.
48. *SCMP*, 23 March 1920.
49. Maas had made the same argument to get exemption from conscription: this was finally denied him on 1 November 1918, ten days before the end of the war: *SCMP*, 9 August and 2 November 1918. The other jurors were B. Vieira (either Bernadino Senna Vieira, assistant with Thomas W. Symons & Co. or Bomfilho Maria de Vieira, bookkeeper with Kelly & Walsh Ltd); Jorge Maria Ozorio dos Remedios, clerk at the Mercantile Bank of

of the case, in an attempt to elicit whether Mok's confession had been genuine. Murison simply agreed that '"bogus confessions are not infrequent, especially in murder cases."'[50] Jenkin concluded 'there was nothing he could fittingly say on behalf of the prisoner. He had drawn out from the witness what little he wanted, and he did not think he could advantageously say more.' Without retiring, the jury returned a verdict of guilty.

Gompertz asked Mok if he had anything to say why sentence should not be passed against him. Mok made a long statement, echoing claims made by Wong. But, in contrast to Wong, he was calm and coherent. He had been put in prison because he had committed a crime, he said. 'The Government, in doing that, did not intend to kill them, but to put them there to live.' Inmates were given rotten fish and uncooked rice, and less than their entitlement. When they asked for the rice to be cooked they were beaten. When they asked for their food to be weighed they were scolded. The rules said they should have a woollen singlet and jacket, but the clothing given to them (produced in court) was too thin for cold weather. Condemned prisoners received enough food only on the two or three days before their execution. 'Prisoners of all nations in the gaol at Hongkong were supplied with sufficient clothing and shoes except Chinese. He could not see why the Chinese should be so badly treated.' Mok singled out one warder, William Robertson, for praise, but said that the man in charge, Franks, 'did not look after things properly'. Tobacco was smuggled in. Prisoners were fed only rice and water even if they had done nothing wrong. '"Affairs" now in the gaol were very confused.'

Gompertz interrupted, saying the defence had not asked about this when Franks was in the witness box. But Mok coolly replied that he was now making the statement he had been told he would be allowed to make: 'if His Lordship wanted it, he would stop saying anything more against Mr Franks'. Gompertz said he did not want to stop him from saying anything he wanted; 'if that implicated others, that could not be helped'. Mok then gave his version of the crime. He admitted having made the key, but only at Li Hoi-shing's request. He had tried to dissuade Li, but Li had said he was being so badly treated that he would rather be killed while escaping than die in gaol. On the night of the escape Wong Kwong came to his cell door with a watch, $30 in banknotes, and daggers, one of which he handed to Mok, saying, 'Be off'. When Mok hesitated, Wong said he would stab him if did not go. Li unlocked the door and told Mok to stop anyone from pressing the alarms. Li and the fourth escapee, Yeung Po, went into the Chief Warder's office and killed Speed. 'When they came out, the Indian who had been stabbed was making a noise, so they both jumped on the Indian and stabbed him to death.' Ayub Khan grabbed Mok, who cut Khan's hand when he tried to take the dagger.

India; David Macrae, engineer at the Tai Koo Dockyard; Herbert Edward Maslin, manager of Getz Bros & Co.; and Lam Chi-lok, assistant with Donnelly & Whyte.

50. A quotation from Vincent's, *Police Code,* which stressed the need for confessions to be entirely voluntary.

Finally, Mok urged the jury and 'the committee who visited the gaol' to see that prisoners had enough food and clothing. Gompertz said his statement would be sent to the Governor. Mok replied he would rather be dead than serve even one year in Victoria Gaol. As sentence was passed, he exclaimed 'It's all right for me, now I am to be hanged. But as regards the food to be supplied to the other Chinese prisoners, what about it?'

The Pollock Committee

During the three weeks before his execution on 14 April 1920 Mok was interviewed by the committee he mentioned in court. This committee had been appointed in February by the Governor, Sir Reginald Stubbs, to investigate the murders and the claims by Wong Kwong. It consisted of three Legislative Councillors: Henry Pollock KC, JP; Robert Hutchison MBE, JP; and Ho Fook JP. Of Dutch-Chinese parentage, Ho had succeeded his brother, Ho Tung, as chief comprador to Jardine, Matheson & Co. A justice of the peace, and one of the two Chinese representatives on the Legislative Council, he was a director of several companies, including the *Hongkong Telegraph*. Hutchinson was a cadet officer who, as Superintendent of Imports and Exports, had overseen the government's takeover of the retail opium monopoly and the wartime controls on trade.[51] The chairman, Henry Pollock, was from a family of English lawyers: his grandfather had been Attorney General in Peel's administrations; a cousin was Professor of Jurisprudence at Oxford; another was soon to be appointed Master of the Rolls. Nicknamed 'Briefless' by his friends, Pollock was said to be 'prolix to no purpose', and had, as a result, lost his practice.[52] As a politician, he pursued causes ranging from better housing to constitutional reform. He had already raised several questions in the council about conditions in the gaol.

The committee made four visits to the gaol, including one at night. They rejected Wong Kwong's claims about insufficient food: on average, they noted, prisoners gained weight by the time of their discharge, the long-sentence prisoners more so.[53] They found substance in his claims about tobacco being brought into the gaol, and recommended new rules for searches, 'under European supervision', of officers below a certain rank. As for Wong's claims about 'unnatural offences', it was impossible to find adequate evidence. But they deprecated the search of cells by Indian warders only – a system which, in their view, gave opportunities for abuses. They were satisfied there had been no misconduct by Principal

51. He also acted as Colonial Treasurer up to 21 March and then as a magistrate. In September, while on a shooting trip, he was lost at sea, presumed dead, after he fell from a launch in a storm near Castle Peak. He was thirty-nine years old. Stubbs to Milner, 4 October 1920, CO 129/462, 431–435; *SCMP*, 14 September 1920.

52. Unpublished album of photographs with captions, entitled 'Hong Kong – Photographs – 1891'. I am indebted to Cathy Lilburne for this reference. Gompertz to May, 21 September 1917, CO 129/447, 156.

53. Report of the Committee Appointed to Investigate Certain Matters Connected with the Administration of the Victoria Gaol, *HKSP*, 4/1920.

Warder No. 32. They found no evidence that prisoners had been 'ill-used'. But they drew attention to the outbreak of beriberi, caused by the substitution of white rice for red, and the removal of prisoners to hospital, which worsened staff shortages in the main gaol. An attempt to mix bran with the rice to make up the lack of thiamine failed because inmates 'absolutely refused' to eat it. That, said the committee, showed that inmates were by no means as powerless to voice their grievances as Wong claimed.

Although not strictly within their terms of reference, the committee decided to interview Mok Sing because his remarks in court were 'far more connected and coherent' than those of Wong Kwong, who in any case was now dead. They found some truth in Mok's complaints about rotten fish and uncooked rice. In summer the fish had occasionally been bad, though, on complaint, it had been changed for fresh or salt fish by the supplier. The rice during 'the white rice period' in 1919 had been broken and difficult to cook. But they rejected Mok's claims about insufficient food, and his allegations that prisoners were prevented from complaining, though they noted that any prisoner who made three unfounded complaints was punished with rice and water for a day. They did, however, find substance in Mok's complaints about insufficient blankets and clothing. This was owing to wartime shortages of thick flannel. They noted that flannel had now arrived from England, and they recommended a larger reserve of extra blankets.

Wong Kwong and Mok Sing achieved their aim of having their grievances of prisoners investigated. The committee took their complaints seriously but accepted the explanations from Franks of insufficient European staff, unreliable Indian subordinates, and interruptions in the supply of food and equipment. Two Indian warders had already been dismissed for negligence since the discovery of tools and chapati in cell 63. In future, the committee advised, Indian warders should be recruited from India instead of locally. The loss of a key should also lead to instant dismissal. The committee endorsed recommendations by the Coroner's jury for electric lighting in the yards and corridors, improvements to the alarm system, changes to cell-door locks to prevent inmates from dismantling them, and having two European warders on duty at night – measures which were already in train. They recommended proper ledgers to register complaints and permitting justices of the peace to minute in Chinese if they wished. To improve accountability, they recommended removing ultimate responsibility for the gaol from the Captain Superintendent of Police. Shocked by the 'extraordinary lack of supervision' in the tinsmith's shop, where, during one of their visits, they observed a prisoner mending a lock, they recommended closing it down. This was the only point objected to by Franks, who pointed to its usefulness for minor repairs. The tinsmith's shop stayed open.

Although Stubbs concluded that 'matters were by no means so bad' as the inquest suggested, the report of Pollock's committee was a stimulus to reform. The disciplined gaol staff was increased by 45 per cent in 1920. After a recruitment drive among ex-servicemen, European warders increased from twenty-two in early 1920 to forty-eight in 1921. Warders received large pay rises under a general revision of salaries in the face of the decline of the Hong Kong dollar.[54] Prisoners also benefited. The 'antiquated and useless' forms of hard labour – shot drill, the crank, and so on – were replaced by productive work. The rice-and-water diet for short-sentence inmates in their first week was abolished. The cost of prisoners' food grew by 68 per cent in 1920. The average annual cost per prisoner rose threefold, from $88 to $254, most of it for staff costs.[55] On his return from nine months' leave at the end of 1920, after receiving a 52 per cent increase in salary that year, John Franks was appointed Superintendent of Prisons, a position he held until his retirement in 1937.

Gaol murders and mutinies were rife in East Asia in the early decades of the twentieth century. In one of two dozen 'major episodes' in prisons in French Indochina between 1900 and 1930, seventy-two prisoners and three staff were killed in an uprising at Poulo Condore Prison in 1918. In 1930, thirty-four prisoners were killed in a revolt in Rangoon Gaol; tensions between the mainly Burmese inmates and their Indian gaolers during this year of race riots and rebellion were a factor in the revolt.[56] Such events sometimes led to reform. A mass escape by some 200 inmates of the notorious Caohejing Model Prison in Shanghai in March 1920, in which several warders and prisoners were shot dead, was followed by efforts to upgrade prison staff.[57] A revolt in the Singapore Criminal Prison in 1875, resulting in the death of the superintendent and nineteen prisoners, and the hanging of another nine, led to the recruitment of trained warders from England and sped up the building of a modern gaol on the separate system, the envy of Hong Kong officials.[58]

R v Li Hoi-shing
Murder, 18 May 1920

R v Yeung Po
Murder, 18 April 1921

The two other escapees were tried after Pollock's committee had submitted its report. Li Hoi-shing was captured in Swatow, where he had enlisted as a soldier. He was 'extradited'

54. European warders benefited most, with some receiving increases of up to 33 per cent.
55. Reports of the Superintendent of Prisons, 1919–1921; *HKGG*, 26 August 1921 and 31 December 1920.
56. Peter Zinoman, *The Colonial Bastille: A History of Imprisonment in Vietnam, 1862–1940* (Berkeley: University of California Press, 2001), Chapter 5; James Warren, 'The Rangoon Jail Riot of 1930 and the Prison Administration of British Burma', *South East Asia Research*, Vol. 10, No. 1 (2002): 5–29.
57. *SCMP*, 27 March and 8 April 1920; Intelligence Reports of HM's Consular Officers in China for Quarter ended June 30, 1920, CO 129/470, 401.
58. 'Singapore Criminal Prison breakout', *Singapore Infopedia* (online); Anoma Pieris, *Hidden Hands and Divided Landscapes: A Penal History of Singapore's Plural Society* (Honolulu: University of Hawaii Press, 2009), 200–205; Report of the Superintendent of Victoria Gaol for 1885, para. 27.

to Hong Kong in April 1920 and tried on 18 May.[59] Assigned to defend him, Raphael Belilios merely repeated Li's claim at committal proceedings that he knew nothing of the murder but had taken the opportunity to escape when he found tools under the door of his cell. The ringleader, he said, was Yeung Po. Li was silent during his trial, held before Acting Chief Justice Gompertz. The jury quickly found him guilty. He was hanged on 23 June.[60]

Acting on information, detectives from Hong Kong and Canton found Yeung Po in February 1921 playing with children in his village near Fatshan. A reward of $500 had been offered for his arrest, and he too was 'extradited' to Hong Kong. He was tried by Gompertz and a jury of four British, two Portuguese, and one Chinese.[61] Said by some to have organized the escape, Yeung had downplayed his role in statements to the police and the magistrate, which were read out at trial. 'These two persons were not killed by me,' Yeung said. 'I would have been discharged in another three months' time. "Big number prisoners" opened the door and asked me.' One of them took him downstairs, gave him a knife, and told him to keep watch. The prosecution, however, produced a blood-stained sheet of paper found in Speed's office bearing footprints that matched Yeung's feet. Defending Yeung, Francis Jenkin played down his own role as counsel assigned to defend an 'impoverished prisoner': his duty, as he saw it, was 'merely to place before the jury the facts in such a light as they were most favourable to the prisoner'. From Yeung's statements he attempted to show that he shared no common purpose with the others. But Gompertz, in summing up, pointed to the extensive preparations for the escape, indicating common purpose, and the footprints, suggesting that Yeung had taken part in the attack on Speed.

Without retiring, the jury found Yeung guilty of murder. Asked if he had anything to say why sentence of death should not be passed, Yeung shouted that he would leave the matter entirely in the judge's hands. As he was removed from the dock Yeung said, 'To die is nothing, but I first must have some good food.' He was hanged on 11 May 1921. The verdict at the inquest was 'death due to strangulation'.[62]

Procedural reform: The allocutus

The statements by Wong Kwong and Mok Sing between verdict and sentence embarrassed the prosecution, which was unable to respond. Known as the 'allocutus', such a statement

59. *SCMP*, 6 May 1920.

60. The jury consisted of four Portuguese and three British; it would have been five Portuguese but Gompertz directed one juror, F.C. de Souza, to stand down because his uncle, J.F. de Souza, was also on the jury. This was Belilios's last murder trial. He died from heart failure while in England in October 1922 at the age of forty-two. *HKDP* and *SCMP*, 19 May 1920 and 19 October 1922; *HKT*, 23 June 1920.

61. A second Chinese juror, the comprador Lo Cheung-wing, was told to stand down when he said he did not understand English sufficiently. *SCMP*, 1 March 1921; *SCMP*, *HKDP*, and *CM*, 19 April 1921.

62. *SCMP*, 12 May 1921.

could only be made by the accused, some of whom tried to use it as an opportunity to re-open their case. In June 1921 the Attorney General, Kemp, proposed changes to the Criminal Procedure Ordinance to make it optional for a judge to ask the accused if he or she had anything to say before sentence. It was 'a useless privilege,'' said Kemp, since counsel would raise any technical issues during trial, and an undefended prisoner was unlikely to discover them. It was also 'often very distressing to juries who have just found a man guilty to hear him reopen their case.'[63]

Kemp told the Legislative Council that defendants usually said nothing. This may have been true generally, but most of the thirty-eight men convicted of murder in the decade before Kemp's reform did take the opportunity to speak. Some tearfully asserted their innocence, or pleaded they had family to support. Fung Tim, convicted in 1918 of murder during a gang robbery, wept when the jury gave its verdict, saying the gang had forced him to help and had given him no share of the loot: 'My father is old and my wife is young and if I die the whole of my family will be extinct.' Some tried to excuse their crimes. After his conviction in 1916 the seventy-year-old Tsoi Hing-tai, from a village near Yuen Long, explained that actions by a nearby village had harmed the *fung shui* of his own village and brought calamity on its inhabitants, who were dying; his attempts to resolve the dispute had led to an altercation, and he had shot dead an elder from the other village.[64] Some were resigned to their fate: 'If the jury says I'm guilty, I'm guilty, and there's nothing more to it,' said one of the Lantau murderers in 1919.[65] In the Charcoal Murder trial of 1937 (described in Chapter 10) the accused started questioning the jury, until the judge stopped him.[66] Few were as defiant as Wong Kwong and Mok Sing. Even the judges felt powerless to stop them. Although many judges continued to put the question, Kemp's reform now gave the courts control at this fraught stage in a criminal trial.[67]

A new prison

The events of 1919–1921 revived plans to move the gaol out of the city, where, quite apart from the frequent escapes, the noise at night and smoke from the kitchens were a nuisance to nearby residents. Days before the gaol murders, Governor Stubbs, newly arrived in Hong Kong, pointed to the need to replace the old, overcrowded gaol.[68] In 1920 he announced that a site had been acquired from the Kai Tak Land Investment Company at Ngau Chi

63. *HKH*, 23 June 1921.
64. The jury found Tsoi guilty of murder but recommended mercy on account of his advanced age. The Governor in Council commuted his death sentence to life imprisonment. *SCMP*, 21 and 22 September 1916.
65. *SCMP*, 9 February 1918; HKDP, 13 November 1919.
66. *SCMP*, 1 May 1937.
67. Ordinance No. 10 of 1921.
68. Stubbs to Milner, 11 December 1919, CO 129/456, 376.

Wan, near Kowloon City, and that $40,000 had been allocated to start work on a prison and police training school there.[69] Work was suspended after the Strike-Boycott in 1925–1926 deepened the government's deficit. The project was then abandoned when the Air Ministry decided it needed the site for developing the Kai Tak aerodrome; by then nearly $400,000 had been spent on resumption and foundations.[70]

The daily average of prisoners grew from under 800 in 1920 to 1,175 in 1930. Overcrowding was partly relieved by periodic early releases and the opening of an overflow prison at Lai Chi Kok in 1920. Short-sentence prisoners were accommodated there in association in former quarantine sheds; one shed housed juvenile offenders. By the late 1920s Lai Chi Kok had over 300 inmates. But, reported Stubbs, Victoria Gaol continued to be 'terribly crowded, and the outbreak of a serious epidemic would entail consequences of which I do not care to think'. The scrapping of the Ngau Chi Wan project prompted long-overdue improvements to Victoria Gaol, including repairs to cell blocks and a rebuilding of the hospital. The need to decant prisoners into other blocks while these works were in progress worsened the overcrowding.[71]

Escapes and attacks on warders continued. In 1927, hours before they were due to be hanged, four of the men condemned to death in the *Sunning* piracy overpowered warders in their cell, grabbed their revolvers, and shot three of them in the legs; the escape was foiled by locked grilles blocking the corridor.[72] Later that year four other prisoners climbed over the wall by means of scaffolding put up for repairs; they sent a letter from their hideout in Canton to the Chinese General Chamber of Commerce declaring that they had been so badly treated that they felt compelled to escape.[73] In 1929 a prisoner was found attempting such an ingenious yet simple way of escaping that the magistrate opted to try him in camera lest the method became widely known.[74]

The crisis came in 1930. On 22 October, the gaol's 'executioner and flagellator', Bert Plumb, was holding the morning 'sick and punishment parade' when he was stabbed in the back with a sharpened file by Chui Sui-chung. Chui was serving twelve months for larceny.

---

69. Named after its founders, the barrister-politician Sir Kai Ho Kai (who had died in 1914) and his son-in-law, Au Tak, the company planned to reclaim land for housing. Work on the reclamation was slow. The company ran into difficulties in 1923 and the government took over the project. *HKH*, 28 October 1920 and 4 November 1923; May to Bonar Law, 18 November 1915, CO 129/425, 254–267.
70. *HKH* 15 October 1926; Southorn to Amery, 2 November 1928, CO 129/508/8, 28.
71. Reports of the Superintendent of Prisons, 1920–1930; *SCMP*, 10 January and 22 March 1920 and 22 August 1925; Stubbs to Amery, 5 March 1925, CO 129/488, 170–171.
72. *SCMP*, 2 March 1927. For the *Sunning* piracy see Chapter 3.
73. The letter gave enough clues about their whereabouts for the Canton police to recapture three of the escapees; the fourth, who had 'turned "red"' and taken part in several robberies, had already been executed in Canton. *SCMP*, 2 March 1927 and 17 January 1928; *HKDP*, 7 January 1928.
74. Quizzed by reporters after sentencing the prisoner to an additional four months, the magistrate, E.W. Hamilton, suggested that newspapers should hold a competition for the best solution. *CM*, 10 August 1929.

He had, among other infractions, worn out the battery of an alarm button in his cell by continuously pressing it and was waiting to be passed fit for a flogging. Plumb's injuries were so bad that the magistrate rushed to his bedside to take a dying deposition. He nevertheless recovered and testified at Chui's trial for malicious wounding. In a statement from the dock Chui complained that Plumb had repeatedly beaten him. John Wood, now a judge, sentenced Chui to seven years' hard labour.[75] Some linked the case to a gaol strike that began on 16 December and lasted the rest of the month. About 300 mostly long-sentence prisoners refused to work. Eight ringleaders were flogged. For several nights inmates in the annex across Old Bailey Street kept up a litany of organized shouting: a soloist called out 'the gaol-keeper is starving us'; the chorus responded with 'save life!' (救命!). Crowds gathered outside to listen. The editors of four Chinese newspapers were prosecuted for ignoring censors' directions not to report the protest.[76]

Officials blamed this protest on communist agitators, who, they claimed, were communicating with convicts through short-sentence men who were continually in and out of gaol: some were opting for prison over fines for that purpose. But the government was forced to admit that discontent had long been brewing over the quantity and quality of food. In fact, it had already appointed a committee to examine the matter. In early December the committee recommended large increases in rations. Believing these were 'on too generous a scale altogether', the Executive Council asked for more justification, and approved only small, temporary increases suggested by Superintendent Franks. The speed with which inmates got to know about these decisions, and protest against them, was taken as proof of outside influence. Officials insisted that existing diets had served the gaol well for twenty-five years. But legislators asked why the cost of food had been much lower than in previous years. The Governor himself felt it necessary to make a statement denying there had been any reduction in the quantity or quality of diets.[77] Finally, in May 1931, the government announced new scales of diet, doubling the amount of fresh vegetables for Chinese prisoners, increasing the rice ration, and adding beef to the menu twice a week.[78]

Meanwhile, a Retrenchment Commission was considering economies in the face of growing budget deficits, including the replacement of some European employees with recruits from elsewhere. It found the Prison Department to be vastly overstaffed compared with Singapore and Shanghai, especially in its complement of European officers.[79] It

75. *SCMP*, 23 and 24 October and 25 November 1930 and 13 January 1931.

76. *SCMP, HKT, HKDP, CM*, 17–25 December 1930; *SCMP*, 24 January 1931; *CM*, 23 and 29 January 1931.

77. Another committee of Chinese justices of the peace was investigating the protests: its report has not survived, but it seems to have focused on staff discipline. ExCo Minutes, 4 December 1930 and 15 January 1931, CO 131/81, 244–245 and CO 131/84, 22–23; *SCMP*, 23 and 30 December 1930.

78. The comparison is for Class 2 Chinese prisoners (sentenced to two years or more with hard labour) after the first six months, though all classes saw increases. *HKGG*, 19 June 1925 and 15 May 1931.

79. Hong Kong had 1 warder to every 4 prisoners, compared with 1:11 in Singapore and Shanghai; and 1 European warder to every 15 prisoners, compared with 1:32 in Singapore and 1:101 in Shanghai.

recommended reducing the seventy-odd European warders by ten and increasing the number of Indian guards from fifty-four to seventy-four.[80] It rejected the usual objections from Franks that Indians were unreliable. Echoing Pollock's committee, it advised recruitment direct from India rather than from among the unemployed in Hong Kong.

The crux of the problem, however, was not staff, but the gaol itself. Franks told the commission that if he had a properly laid-out prison he could look after three times the number of inmates with the same staff. Since the withdrawal of the Ngau Chi Wan option a third committee had been examining sites for a prison. The strike forced a decision. On 29 December 1930 the Executive Council agreed on a site at Wong Ma Kok, at the tip of the Stanley Peninsula on Hong Kong Island. Plans were drawn up, and Franks was sent to study prisons in Singapore and Shanghai. But in late 1932 the government rejected the site and chose another further up the peninsula.[81] By now, in a reversal of the position in the 1890s, legislators were demanding action while the Colonial Office was hesitating in the light of Hong Kong's worsening finances. The Secretary of State reluctantly sanctioned a public works loan of $25 million for airport development, waterworks, and a prison.[82] Completed in 1937 at a cost of $4 million, the 'Hong Kong Prison at Stanley' occupied a site eleven times the size of Victoria Gaol and could house 1,500 prisoners in single cells. It was one of the best-equipped prisons in the Empire, with spacious cells, modern workshops, vegetable gardens, and an indoor execution suite. Its high walls and single entrance were said to make it escape-proof.[83]

In 1937 all male prisoners were transferred to Stanley. The government had hoped to boost revenue by selling the prime site of Victoria Gaol.[84] But by November the number of inmates at Stanley had reached 2,757, with many prisoners accommodated three to a cell. A committee investigating the increase in numbers noted that, as a result of an 'abnormal excess of petty prosecutions', over half the inmates were illegal hawkers sentenced for a few days. It concluded that prisoners in Hong Kong were overfed and underworked.[85]

80. The lowest pay of a European warder was nine times that of an Indian guard. In addition to the guards, the department employed 140 Indian warders and assistant warders. The total establishment in 1930 was 328.

81. The reasons for rejecting Wong Ma Kok were not recorded, but construction of what became known as Stanley Battery began there in the mid-1930s. ExCo Minutes, 29 December 1930 and 27 October and 8 December 1932, CO 131/81, 264 and CO 131/87, 209 and 236–237; *SCMP*, 3 September and 2 October 1931 and 28 September 1933; Kwong Chi Man and Tsoi Yiu Lun, *Eastern Fortress: A Military History of Hong Kong, 1840–1970* (Hong Kong: Hong Kong University Press, 2014), 111.

82. The correspondence is in CO 129/526/3, 531/14, 534/6, 536/1, 539/12, and 543/12.

83. *HKDP*, 10 September 1936; *SCMP*, *CM*, *HKT*, and *HKDP*, 19 January 1937.

84. A women's prison was opened at the Lai Chi Kok site in 1932. It was intended to be temporary, pending the completion of Stanley Prison, but was retained, and expanded in 1939.

85. The committee found that hard labour was non-existent, that short-term prisoners had no ability or interest in industrial work, and that the same contractor had been supplying food for twenty years at the cost of $13 per prisoner per month – twice the cost of feeding free labourers and police constables. Report of the Committee to Consider the Recent Increase in the Number of Prisoners, *HKSP*, 7/1937.

In mid-1940, when hundreds of thousands of people had sought refuge in Hong Kong from the advancing Japanese army, the daily average of prisoners peaked at 3,495. By then Victoria Gaol had been reopened for remand prisoners, deportees, vagrants, and debtors. In 1941 part of the gaol became a juvenile remand home. Bombed during the war, Victoria Prison, as it was now usually known, was rehabilitated after liberation and used for various custodial purposes until its final decommissioning in 2005.

8

'Running for Nothing'

The Praya Murder, 1922

In early 1922 Hong Kong was preparing for the visit of Edward, Prince of Wales, heir to the British throne. The centrepiece was a pavilion erected on what was known as 'the finest site' – a plot of land on the Praya, or seafront, next to the Hong Kong Club and the Law Courts. Capable of accommodating 3,000 people, this 'monstrosity of lath and plaster'[1] was to be used for the Prince's reception, a Masonic ceremony, a university congregation, and a stone-laying ceremony for St Stephen's Girls' College.[2] Hong Kong was the penultimate stop on the Prince's eight-month Eastern Tour. Aimed at strengthening links between Crown and Empire, the tour encountered protests in India. Over fifty people were killed in riots in Bombay on the day of the Prince's arrival. Disruption also threatened his visit to Hong Kong, scheduled for 6 April. In January, Chinese seamen went on strike when shipowners rejected demands for wage increases.[3] Mediation failed, and thousands of strikers left for Canton. By the end of February some 120,000 other workers had joined in sympathy. Insisting that the strike was directed by 'Bolshevist' agitators in Canton and enforced by fear, the Governor, Sir Reginald Stubbs, outlawed the Chinese Seamen's Union and other unions. On 28 February, using unrepealed wartime powers, he banned Chinese from

1. Letter from 'A Stranger Within the Gate', *HKDP*, 11 February 1922.
2. The Prince pulled a cord and, through an 'ingenious little electrical arrangement', the foundation stone slipped into place in the wall of the building two miles away, on Park Road. *SCMP*, 10 April 1922.
3. Ming Kou Chan, 'Labor and Empire: The Chinese Labor Movement in the Canton Delta, 1895–1927' (PhD thesis, Stanford University, 1975), Chapter 10; and Chan Wai Kwan, *The Making of Hong Kong Society: Three Studies of Class Formation in Early Hong Kong* (Oxford: Oxford University Press, 1991), 166–191.

leaving Hong Kong without a pass.[4] On the same day, the Legislative Council passed the Emergency Regulations Ordinance, enabling the Governor in Council to make 'any regulations whatsoever' in times of emergency without reference to the Legislative Council.[5]

Although the strike was largely peaceful, two violent episodes influenced the course of events. The first occurred on Friday 24 February. Shortly before midday, outside the scaffold-clad Prince's Pavilion, Leung Yuk-tong was shot dead while travelling in his rickshaw to the offices of Butterfield & Swire nearby. Leung was an assistant manager in Jack A Tai & Co., a stevedore shop on the Praya. The shop had been the target of protests by strikers. Leung was supplying crews from northern ports to ships belonging to Butterfield & Swire, as well as labourers for their sugar refinery. He had received threatening letters but had taken no special precautions. He was thirty-nine years old and left a wife and seven children. The suspected assassin ran past the pavilion, through Statue Square, across Des Voeux Road into Wardley Street (now Bank Street), pursued by a crowd shouting 'Chase him! Catch him!' As he turned into Queen's Road, a bank clerk, Francis Pereira, punched him in the face and knocked him down. A passer-by, Vicente Yvanovich, got out of a rickshaw and helped hold the man down. A constable on duty nearby then took him to Central Police Station. The alleged murderer was Leung Wo (梁和), a twenty-four-year-old ship's cook from Shun Tak county near Canton.[6]

The strike escalated. Bakers, cooks, waiters, market coolies, and servants joined in, some in response to threats. The second incident occurred a week after the murder, four days after the government restricted Chinese from leaving. Early on 3 March over 2,000 strikers gathered in Kowloon with the aim of walking over the hills to the border, a journey of about twenty-five miles. Trains had been closed to passengers without exit passes. Police had already turned back other groups. With the help of the army, they planned to round up this group and escort it back under bayonet. But the buses carrying men from the 102nd Grenadiers, an Indian regiment, broke down. Only a few, led by their captain, Hugh Bloxham, were able to catch up with the party of police tracking the procession along Tai Po Road. 'We will not go back,' the strikers said. 'We have no work in Hong Kong. We have no food in Hong Kong.' Moving among the crowds, Thomas King, the Deputy Police Superintendent in charge, saw his own cook and 'boy', whom he had earlier warned not to leave. When some in the procession 'began to get "nasty"', police fired warning shots. The crowds broke through a police barrier near the waterworks at Shek Lei Pui. By then, Bloxham and his Indian soldiers had set up another barrier further on, in a cutting near the

4. The ban brought 'persons of Chinese race' within the ambit of the Travellers Restrictions Ordinance (No. 19 of 1915), which previously applied only to 'all persons of non-Asiatic race or nationality and all Indians'. *HKGG*, 28 February 1922.
5. Ordinance No. 5 of 1922.
6. *WTYP*, 27 February 1922; *SCMP* and *HKDP*, 25 February 1922; Minute of Committal Proceedings, 22 February–3 March 1922, CO 129/475, 45–63.

seventh milestone. King warned he would order the soldiers to fire if the crowd did not turn back, only to be told: 'We will go; we must go; we will die here.' King ordered Bloxham to fire one round low, at the feet. The soldiers fired a volley. The bullets ricocheted around the cutting, hitting twelve men, four of whom died.[7]

The shootings on 3 March provoked an angry response. Printers, bank clerks, engineers, tram conductors, railway staff, and rickshaw pullers now came out in sympathy. On Saturday 4 March the guilds notified the government that, unless the seamen's strike was settled within forty-eight hours, a general strike would be declared. The next day, the shipowners, the Seamen's Union, and officials reached a settlement. The shipowners agreed wage increases of 15–30 per cent – close to the union's original demands. Stubbs rescinded the ban on the union and the restrictions on Chinese departing. The union celebrated with parades as workers returned. The outcome was a humiliation for Stubbs, who now had to defend himself against accusations that he had forced the shipowners to surrender. Stubbs stuck firm to his belief that the strike was instigated by Sun Yat-sen's government in Canton. The 'ignorant coolie class', he reported, were terrorized into joining it and deserved 'some sympathy and pity'. But, in 'lamentable contrast' to the 'self-reliance shewn by the non-Chinese communities', the educated Chinese were 'of no assistance whatever'. The only possible feeling towards them was 'one of the profoundest contempt', he wrote. 'The only possible argument in such circumstances is force.'[8]

Among the terms agreed in the settlement was a promise from the government that a public judicial enquiry would be held into the Tai Po Road shootings. This took the form of a coroner's inquest (or 'death enquiry') into the death of one of the victims, Tam Shui-piu, held by the magistrate John Wood on 9–20 March 1922 with three European special jurors.[9] The Crown Solicitor, George Wakeman, began with a promise that no action would be taken against any witnesses who came forward. Among those who did were wounded men brought from hospital at Wood's request. The solicitor for the police officers, William Shenton, treated them like criminals. 'Do you expect us to believe that you did not know you were breaking the law,' he demanded of Lau Kam-fat, a houseboy. Lau said he had heard none of the police warnings when, standing ten rows behind the front line, he was hit by a bullet. Tse Chan, the 'boy' employed by Deputy Superintendent King, said he 'did not know in what way I was committing an offence'. Police witnesses testified that,

7. Report of inquest, 9–20 March 1922, CO 129/474, 430a–553, *HKDP*, 10–22 March 1922.
8. Stubbs to Churchill, 18 March 1922, CO 129/474, 390–401.
9. F.C. Hall, assistant, Jardine Matheson & Co.; A.K. Ferguson, sub-manager, Chartered Bank; and W.L. Leask, civil engineer, Leigh & Orange. Another special juror, Chau Siu-ki, was balloted for the jury but was excused after informing the Coroner that he had taken part in the negotiations between the shipowners and the Chinese Seamen's Union. A leading member of the Chinese community, Chau was manager of an insurance company and a director of shipping companies. Report of inquest, 9–20 March 1922, CO 129/474, 430a–553; *HKDP*, 10–22 March 1922.

outnumbered by a 'contemptuous' and 'sarcastic' mob, they had feared an assault. Shenton argued that the city had been 'on a war footing'. The crowd's disregard for the law 'stabbed at the vital principles of civilization'. Captain Bloxham, he said, had 'been through the Indian riots and therefore knows what a riot is'.

Wood tried to provide some balance to these histrionic claims, which he dismissed as 'mere rhetoric'. Jurors also requested that Shenton stop asking witnesses if they knew they were breaking the law. The verdict, nevertheless, was 'justifiable homicide'. The jury commended King and his men 'for their conduct and patience under most trying circumstances; and for their personal courage'. They added that the evidence of the Chinese witnesses was 'highly contradictory'. Wood endorsed the verdict as 'the only possible one'. In London, the Colonial Office brushed the matter aside: it was 'not at all a pleasant thing that an emergency order issued by a colonial government should result in the shooting of Chinese,' wrote one official, but it seemed 'to have attained the maximum of effect for the minimum of casualties'.[10] By imperial standards the death count was low. Three years earlier, nearly 400 peaceful protestors had been shot dead by British troops at Amritsar. Four days after the Tai Po Road incident, British troops fired on a mass protest against land tax in Gujarat, killing hundreds of villagers.[11]

The Hong Kong government gave $1,000 to each of the families of the men killed on Tai Po Road and paid the medical expenses of those injured.[12] Labour unions in Canton called on Chinese in Hong Kong to follow the Indian example and boycott the Prince of Wales if the 'unjust' finding of the inquest was not reversed. The Governor of Guangdong, Chen Jiongming, lodged a protest against the Hong Kong government's prevention, 'in times of peace, by force of arms', of 'free men anxious to return to their homes in China'. His successor, Wu Tingfang (Ng Choy, formerly a barrister in Hong Kong), called for King to be punished, 'seeing that his action was contrary, I fear, even to British law'.[13] The inquest, said one Canton newspaper, was 'merely a case of the principal criminal sitting in judgment on the accessory criminals'.[14] In Hong Kong, the Peak Residents' Association debated whether they should pay their servants for the days lost to the strike and worried they would strike again during the Prince's visit.[15]

Such were the relations between British and Chinese when, on the last day of the inquest, the trial of the alleged assassin of Leung Yuk-tong commenced.

---

10. Minute (author's name illegible), 7 June 1922, CO 129/474, 387.
11. David Hardiman, *Gandhi in His Time and Ours: The Global Legacy of His Ideas* (London: Hurst & Co., 2003), 139–142.
12. *HKDP*, 22 March 1922; Stubbs to Churchill, 12 April 1922, CO 129/474, 386–389.
13. King remained in the force and was its head 1933–1940. Jamieson to Alston, 11 March 1922, FO 371/8030, 118; Wu Tingfang to Jamieson, 7 June 1922, CO 129/475, 457–459.
14. *Ta T'ung Pao*, 28 March 1922, CO 129/477, 212.
15. *SCMP*, 28 and 29 March and 18 April 1922.

R v *Leung Wo*
Murder, 20–23 March 1922

Leung Wo made a simple statement when charged at the Central Police Station: 'I was passing the Hong Kong and Shanghai Bank. I do not know what was the matter.' He gave as his address the Hong Kong and Wuchow Steamer Employees Guild Club on Connaught Road. The river city of Wuchow (Wuzhou), a treaty port on the Guangdong–Guangxi border, was a source of food imports to Hong Kong. It had suffered both from the strike and from civil war between the Guangdong and Guangxi armies. Leung's guild had joined the strike but, although the police had raided its premises, it had not yet been banned. The police regarded it as 'the chief resort of the criminal classes', with 'an evil reputation'. For this reason it was declared an unlawful society in October 1922.[16]

Leung was charged before the magistrate, Roger Lindsell, on 25 February, the day after the murder. Committal hearings took place on 2 and 3 March, with Wakeman, the Crown Solicitor, prosecuting. Leung was represented by George Hall Brutton, a solicitor in Hong Kong since 1897. Two other solicitors were present for interested parties: Daniel Lewis for Butterfield & Swire, and F.X. D'Almada for the family of the deceased. Nineteen witnesses gave evidence for the prosecution. Brutton did not cross-examine them or call any witnesses for the defence. Leung remained silent throughout. The *Wa Tsz Yat Po* described him as wearing a tight-fitting shirt, a satin jacket, black trousers, and martial-arts shoes, adding that some of the regulars at the Magistracy said his face looked familiar. Lindsell committed him for trial in the Supreme Court.[17]

The Supreme Court was having problems of its own at this time. Its reputation had suffered from a series of scandals in which certain solicitors' clerks had concocted false claims and 'speculative' lawsuits at the expense of Chinese ignorant of English law. Alerted by Chinese legislators, Governor May had secretly investigated the problem. Lawyers told him the scandals were partly due to the 'weakness of the Bench', which was made up of 'men who either have never been in private practice or have been unsuccessful therein'. They lacked the ability to detect bogus cases, and trials dragged on because they were unable to control their courts. The judges in turn blamed the lawyers for their prolixity, saying that to cut them short would risk injustice or induce nervous breakdowns. May concluded that abuses were rife, and enacted special legislation to deport one alleged culprit, Li Hong-mi, a retired Supreme Court interpreter. Li took the case to the Privy Council, which, in 1920, ruled in his favour on a technicality. Cases of doubtful validity, however, continued to clog the workings of the Supreme Court.[18]

---

16. Police Report for 1922; *HKGG*, 13 October 1922.
17. *WTYP*, 27 February 1922; Minutes by Lindsell, 25 February–3 March 1922, CO 129/475, 44–63.
18. Munn, 'Margins of justice in colonial Hong Kong'.

One of these was the 'Penang Millionaire Will Suit' 1921–1923, which awaited the Chief Justice, Sir William Rees-Davies, on his return from nineteen months' leave in late 1921. The plaintiff, Cheang Thye Gan, claimed to be a son named in the will of Chung Keng Quee, the richest man in Malaya, who had died in 1901. The respondent, Chung's widow, now living in Hong Kong, pleaded that the son in question was dead. The case infuriated Rees-Davies. It 'ought never to have been brought in this Court,' he exclaimed during a wrangle between counsel one hot morning. 'It may be all right for the lawyers, but it is not to the advantage of the Court or of the administration of justice in Hong Kong.'[19] During the trial Cheang's barrister, Ernest Sharp KC, died. His junior, C.G. Alabaster, broke down, leaving only three barristers in private practice, two of whom were acting for the defence.[20] In March 1922 the government enacted emergency legislation to allow Cheang's solicitor, George Hall Brutton, to appear as counsel.[21] In a letter to a friend in the Colonial Office, Rees-Davies said he wished the 'cursed will' had stayed in Penang:

> The testator had ten wives and concubines and numerous progeny natural and adopted. It has involved stacks of expert evidence as to the mode of recognition of the alleged son (the plaintiff), worshipping of ancestors, mourning at funerals by him etc. Of course all the lying usual in Chinese cases is present. It has been quite impossible to stop it.[22]

Rees-Davies tried the case on his own to avoid inflicting 'a serious hardship on a jury of business men were they constrained to sit in such cases'. He eventually found for the respondent.[23] He was to make similar remarks about Chinese witnesses while presiding over the trial of Leung Wo four weeks after writing this letter.

Leung's case was one of three tried in the March criminal sessions. In the other two cases five men were convicted of robbery and sentenced to flogging and prison terms of between three and seven years. Leung's counsel was Francis Jenkin, instructed by Brutton. Since arriving in Hong Kong in 1912, Jenkin had defended nineteen men on murder charges: eleven were convicted, of whom ten were hanged; three were found guilty of manslaughter; one was guilty but insane; and four were acquitted. Acting for the Crown, Jenkin had also prosecuted three men on murder charges, two of whom were convicted. Trained as a soldier in England before joining the Bar, he had organized the Special Police Reserve in Hong Kong during the war, for which he was given a CBE. A journalist recalled him at this time as 'a very handsome, intelligent, clean-cut young man who adorned the wig he

---

19. *HKDP*, 4 May 1922.
20. The third, Henry Pollock KC, on leave for much of 1922, was by now devoting his time to politics.
21. *HKDP*, 24 February 1922; *HKH*, 16 and 23 March 1922; Ordinance, No. 7 of 1922.
22. Rees-Davies to Risley, 23 February 1922, CO 129/474, 310–312.
23. *HKDP*, 2 November 1922.

wore'.[24] During his twenty-five years' practice Jenkin was to gain a reputation as 'one of the most brilliant pleaders ever to have practised in the Colony'.[25]

Jenkin had a flair for the dramatic. In his latest murder trial, in September 1921, he defended a man accused of shooting an actor during a show at the Woping Theatre. To prove that a detective chasing the culprit could not possibly have had an uninterrupted view of him, Jenkin arranged for a bamboo fence, over which the accused had allegedly escaped, to be erected in the courtroom. He had one of the actors re-enact the shooting, and asked policemen to show act out how they had searched his client's clothes, where they had belatedly found (or planted) a theatre ticket. The prosecution's casual tendering of this and other evidence late in the trial would never have been allowed had the accused been a European, said Jenkin. After his demolition of the prosecution over several days of cross-examination, the jury returned a verdict of not guilty.[26]

The prosecutor in the Praya Murder trial was the Attorney General, Joseph Kemp CBE, KC, instructed by the Crown Solicitor, George Wakeman. A special jury was empanelled, the first use of a special jury in a murder case since 1915. The reason seems to have been to prevent outside influence – at least from supporters of the strike – by forming a jury from among the colonial elite: a Chinese common juror at the sessions had received a threatening letter. Two Chinese special jurors drawn for this trial were exempted, one because he had attended the strike negotiations.[27] The jury consisted of

Herbert William Bird JP (foreman), partner in the architectural firm Palmer and Turner, soon to be appointed a Legislative Councillor.

Aaron Sassoon Gubbay, Hong Kong of E.D. Sassoon & Co., and, until recently, a director of the Hongkong & Shanghai Bank.

William Bradley Walker, an American, general manager of Standard Oil.

Walter Sinclair, manager of Reiss & Co. a British firm, director of the Amateur Dramatic Club, later to work as a theatre director in North America.

Harold Sidney Bennett, manager of the China & Japan Telephone & Electric Co.

John Arnold, secretary, Hong Kong, Canton & Macao Steamboat Co. Ltd, a firm directly affected by the seamen's strike.

Albert Edward Crapnell JP, partner in Lane Crawford & Co.

24. Wilfred V. Pennell, *A Lifetime with the Chinese* (Hong Kong: South China Morning Post Ltd, 1974), 13.
25. *HKDP*, 5 March 1936.
26. *HKDP* and *SCMP*, 6–14 September 1921.
27. Stubbs to Churchill, 3 May 1922, CO 129/475, 12.

These men held senior positions in large firms and mixed in the highest social circles. Most lived on the Peak, the residential district reserved for Europeans. Although the trial lasted four days, the jury was not sequestered overnight.[28]

The prosecution's case

In contrast to the inquest into the Tai Po Road shootings, the trial was attended by many Chinese spectators. They were searched by Indian police before entering the courtroom. Kemp called twenty-two witnesses, who fell into six categories. First, government doctors described the cause of Leung Yuk-tong's death (haemorrhage by a bullet entering a large artery), and his brothers confirmed the identity of his body. Next, an overseer from the Public Works Department produced a plan of the scene of the murder. The third category consisted of Pereira, Yvanovich, and policemen involved in Leung Wo's arrest. Those in the fourth, staff of the Hongkong Bank and police officers, dealt with the discovery of a revolver in a flowerbed, which matched the bullet in Leung Yuk-tong's body. The fifth group, employees of Butterfield & Swire, testified that Leung Yuk-tong had supplied men for their ships and sugar refinery during the strike.

The sixth group was the most important, and the most problematic. This comprised witnesses present at the time of the shooting and the assassin's flight through Statue Square. The square was the city's civic centre. On its north side was Connaught Road and the Praya. To the south was Des Voeux Road, along which ran the tramline. Facing the square on Des Voeux Road were the Hongkong and Shanghai Bank and the old City Hall. To the east sat the Law Courts and the Prince's Pavilion. To the west stood the Prince's Building and the Queen's Building. At the centre of the square was a bronze statue of Queen Victoria on a raised island at the intersection of Chater Road and Wardley Street. The gardens in the square were planted with trees and shrubs. The section of Wardley Street passing through Statue Square was lined with railings and ceremonial pillars put up for the royal visit: still being plastered, the pillars were clad in bamboo scaffolding and protected from the rain by mat canopies. The Prince's Pavilion was also surrounded with scaffolding. So too was an extension to the Hongkong Bank under construction near the southwest corner of the square. The forest of pillars, plants, and bamboo poles, and the piles of building materials, were to prove a challenge for those who claimed to have seen Leung Wo flee the scene of the crime.

No witness saw the shooting. The main witness for the prosecution was the sixty-three-year-old Captain David Morgan, master of the S.S. *Kwong Ying*, a steamer plying between Hong Kong and Wuchow – coincidentally, the route worked by members of Leung Wo's

28. The trial is reported in *CM*, 20–24 March 1922; *SCMP* and *HKT*, 21–24 March 1922; *HKWP*, 25 March 1922; and *WTYP*, 21–25 March 1922. The judge's report and notes, a partial transcript, photographs, a plan and other correspondence are in Stubbs to Churchill, 3 May 1922, CO 129/475, 9–123.

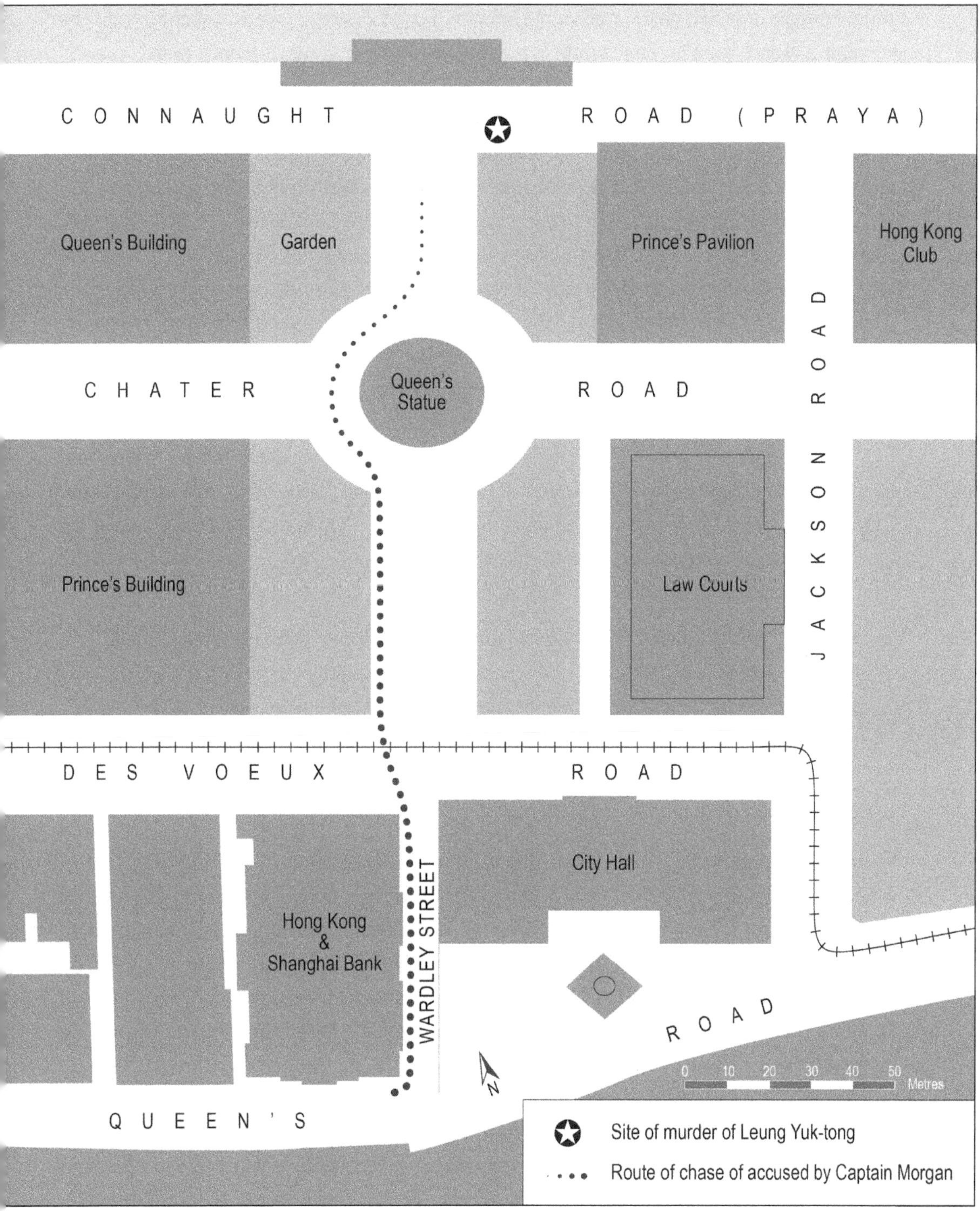

Map 5: The Praya Murder, 1922

guild. Morgan testified that, at about 11:45 a.m. on 24 February, he was standing on the Praya, looking at the Queen's statue 'in a brown study', when he suddenly heard 'a crack'. He saw a rickshaw puller drop the shafts of his rickshaw near the Prince's Pavilion and smoke rising from a man a few yards behind the rickshaw. The man then ran into the square. Morgan chased him past the statue and, after leaping over a heap of bamboo poles, across Des Voeux Road. From there the man ran into Wardley Street between the bank and the City Hall to Queen's Road. Shouting and waving, Morgan was by now losing steam. He momentarily lost sight of the man as he jumped over the poles. He saw a tall European near the City Hall try to grab the man: Morgan identified him in court as Harold Green, Superintendent of the Botanical and Forestry Department. Morgan then found two other Europeans holding the man down at the corner of Wardley Street and Queen's Road. Throughout the chase he had been about twenty yards behind the man – eight yards at the closest point. He had seen no one else running with or after the fleeing man.

Jenkin began his cross-examination of Captain Morgan by declaring that he would establish 'out of the mouths of a number of Crown witnesses' that there were several other Chinese men running through the square at the same time. He first asked Morgan what his 'brown study' had been about. 'Was he, like the rest of us, wrapped in contemplation of the temporary beauties which now adorned Statue Square?'

> **Morgan** — No, I believe I was wondering whether I had won any money in the sweeps—(Laughter).
>
> **Jenkin** — Are you prepared to swear that you did not lose sight of this man on more than one occasion before he turned into Wardley Street?
>
> **Morgan** — You are cutting it too fine.
>
> **Jenkin** — We do in murder cases as a rule.[29]

Morgan admitted he might also have lost sight of the man when one of the pillars intervened. He did not see him throw a gun into the flowerbeds in Statue Square. He did not see his face. Nor did he recall if he was wearing a hat. His description of the man's clothing differed from Leung's clothes produced in court: 'If you don't know for sure, then say you don't know,' the judge, Rees-Davies, advised him. But Morgan was sure that the man captured at the top of Wardley Street was the man he had chased through the square. He insisted he had seen no one else running with or after the accused.

In the afternoon Harold Green gave evidence that placed him in a different position from that recalled by Captain Morgan. In view of this and other contradictions, on day two of the trial, judge and jury, with Morgan and other prosecution witnesses, made a visit to the scene of the crime, just outside the court where the trial was being held. The effect,

29. *CM*, 20 March 1922.

Rees-Davies later reported, was 'greatly to strengthen the case for the prosecution'.[30] The visit caused Morgan to rethink some of his evidence. At Jenkin's request he was recalled for further cross-examination. He now said that the man he had seen near the City Hall was not Green but someone else. He agreed that if the fleeing man had disposed of the revolver in the garden he would have had to throw it over the railings, an act which would have been plainly visible. But he did not see him do this. Asked whether the pillars in the square could have blocked his sight, Morgan replied that the pillars had not yet been erected at the time of the murder. Jenkin then produced photographs commissioned by Brutton a few days after the murder showing the pillars. Morgan replied that not all the pillars had been there on the day of the murder.

Morgan's claim that he and the accused were the only two persons running clashed with the evidence of other prosecution witnesses. Leung Yuk-tong's rickshaw puller, Ng Sz, saw many people running on the Praya right after the shooting. Wong Fat-kwong, the constable on duty on Des Voeux Road, saw three or four men chasing the fleeing man. Fung Chi, coxswain on a fire float moored alongside the Praya, heard a shot and cries of 'save life' ('救命'), and rushed ashore with a crewmate. He saw seven or eight people running towards the Queen's statue. He and his crewmate ran after them. He did not recognize Morgan but remembered passing a man in European clothes. Four of the running men separated in different directions on Des Voeux Road, Fung said under cross-examination. Another three entered Wardley Street: among them, some distance behind the other two, was the accused. At this point, Kemp wished to put to Fung a statement he had made to the police.[31] But Rees-Davies ruled that Fung was not a hostile witness: the prosecution could only re-examine him on the basis of his deposition at committal proceedings. When Kemp declined to do this, Rees-Davies decided to question Fung himself – at great length. Confused by the judge's questions, Fung, through the interpreter, had some difficulty making himself clear but stuck to his account. In his report to the Governor, Rees-Davies said he 'entirely disbelieved this witness'.

The defence

After other witnesses gave evidence about the revolver, Leung's guild, and other matters, the Crown closed its case on the morning of day two. Jenkin then opened by saying that his witnesses would establish beyond doubt that this was a case of mistaken identity. But first he lectured the jury on their duty. 'Living as he did in that circle in the Colony from which the special jurymen were drawn,' he knew that public opinion was such that 'sound-thinking

30. Rees-Davies to Stubbs, 28 March 1922, CO 129/475, 79.
31. Fung's statement to the police on the day of the murder (at CO 129/475, 75), made no mention of running men except the accused and Fung's crewmate (who was not called to give evidence). His evidence at the committal proceedings on 2 March, however, was consistent with that at the trial.

men in the heat of the moment thought that the right mode of treatment was immediate public execution on the spot where the murder took place'. He reminded jurors of their oath to judge the accused 'entirely and solely on the evidence'. He had himself been 'freely and harshly condemned for associating himself with this man'. Such a view was 'subversive of justice as practised in British Courts'. He pointed out that he had been retained by the accused through his solicitor, Brutton, not assigned by the court at public expense (the fee was probably paid by Leung's guild). He would, however, have fought the case just as strenuously had he been assigned. He had made similar remarks in the Theatre Murder trial, where the accused had also paid for his own defence.

Jenkin said that the prosecution stood or fell on the evidence of Captain Morgan. Yet Morgan could not even identify the man by his face or clothes and had been driven into admitting he had lost sight of him no fewer than three times. Witnesses for the defence, said Jenkin, would show that, as the rickshaw moved along the Praya, three men came out from among the pillars in the square. One of them, 'a big man in grey clothes', went up to the rickshaw, lifted the flap, and fired. The men then ran through the square, followed by others who had been standing on the Praya. As they ran they were joined by the accused, who had been standing near the pillars. Two of the men took the lead, followed at some distance by the others. One took a revolver from a hat he was holding, flung it into the garden, and turned right on Des Voeux Road. Some of the other running men also turned right; some turned left; others, including 'the little man' (the accused), went up Wardley Street to Queen's Road. 'You may say,' said Jenkin to the jury,

> 'It's all very well calling all these Chinese workers and building men; but we know what Chinese witnesses are like.' The general condemnation of their evidence is that it is uncertain and unworthy. You may be able to take that view in some cases; you cannot in this case unless you give the same treatment to the witnesses called on behalf of the Crown. If it is possible to find a collection of witnesses who so diametrically contradict each other, are opposed in practically every essential detail in regard to this occurrence, I should be very much surprised indeed.[32]

He submitted that the evidence obtained by the defence, 'through sending round to the various contractors to find out what they knew', would establish his client's innocence.

Jenkin's first witness was the accused himself. From 1906, defendants in criminal trials in Hong Kong were allowed, if they wished, to give evidence on oath from the witness box. This was a double-edged sword, since, unlike an unsworn statement from the dock (then still an option),[33] it exposed them to cross-examination. In reply to Jenkin, Leung Wo said he was a ship's cook and coolie. He left his last ship, the *Kwangchow*, a steamer belonging

32. *SCMP*, 22 March 1922.
33. In 1968, after a magistrate had refused to allow an unsworn statement, the Full Court reviewed the practice and recommended that the Legislature abolish it, which it did in 1972. *Tseng Ping Yee v The Queen* [1969] HKLR 304; Ordinance No. 34 of 1972.

to Butterfield & Swire, at the start of the strike in January, and had stayed at the guild's clubhouse until early February. He then returned to his village until 22 February, when he went to Canton. The next day he took a train to Hong Kong, where he hoped to find work. After spending the night at the clubhouse, he had an early lunch on the 24th in Stanley Street before going down to the Praya. He then walked towards the Naval Yard, just beyond Statue Square, where a man named Ah Cheung, employed there as a coolie, had promised to help him find work. On the way, his attention was drawn by the Queen's statue, which he had never seen before. Near the statue, with his back to the seafront, he watched workmen plastering the ceremonial pillars.

Suddenly, said Leung, he heard a bang like a firecracker and saw two men run past him through the square. Another seven or eight men then came running from the seafront, splitting into two groups as they ran on either side of the statue towards the tramline on Des Voeux Road. Leung ran with them and saw them disperse as they reached Des Voeux Road. He did not notice any foreigners. He ran across Des Voeux Road and up the section of Wardley Street between the bank and the City Hall before being knocked and pressed down by a man in European clothes. At this point he was dazed and had dust in his eyes, but he noticed three other men running behind him: two turned right towards Central Market, one towards Wan Chai.

Jenkin asked Leung to cross the courtroom so the jury could see clearly his protruding front teeth, which, said Jenkin, would help people identify him. Jenkin then asked him to take off his long coat, revealing a black coat underneath – 'not the ordinary Chinese coat', said Jenkin. He then asked for the revolver to be handed to Leung, and told him to put it in his coat pocket: the pocket was so shallow that the gun nearly reached the opening. His trousers had no pocket. Finally, Jenkin asked Leung 'Did you shoot anybody with the revolver or any revolver that day?' Leung replied, 'I did not.' After asking Leung his age (twenty-four), Rees-Davies adjourned the hearing until the next day.

New prosecution evidence

When the trial resumed at 10:30 a.m. on day three, the Attorney General, Kemp, rose to say that 'a rather unusual thing' had happened. A man had visited him that morning with important information about the crime. Kemp had told Jenkin about this. He now asked leave to call this man as a witness. This took Rees-Davies by surprise. In all his 'considerable experience' he had never heard of new evidence being tendered after the committal of the accused, except at the request of the court; the reason, he said, was to give the defence time and opportunity to answer the evidence. In Hong Kong, said Jenkin (perhaps recalling the

Theatre Murder), it was not unusual for new evidence to be served in the course of a trial, but never *after* the prosecution had closed its case.[34]

Rees-Davies suggested an adjournment for the defence to consider the statement of the new witness. Jenkin said this was unnecessary; he could cross-examine at once. His objection was that it was against established practice to call a new prosecution witness at this stage in the trial. He asked for the question to be decided after the trial by the Full Court (the Chief Justice and Puisne Judge): the validity of any conviction would then depend on its ruling. Rees-Davies refused. He had 'great doubts' about whether he ought to allow the evidence and proposed to convene the Full Court straight away. As he was informing the jury of this, Jenkin interrupted. Although he believed the evidence to be inadmissible, the jury, which had heard the discussion, might suspect that important evidence was being withheld on a technicality. He was therefore willing to withdraw his objection so as not to harm his client's case. Rees-Davies left the court to confer with the Puisne Judge, Gompertz. He returned after a few minutes to extract from Jenkin a clear indication that he no longer objected. Kemp then called his surprise witness.

The witness was Douglas Molyneux Larkins, whose office on the top floor of the four-storey Queen's Building overlooked Statue Square. He had read about the case in the papers. His evidence largely corroborated that given two days earlier by Captain Morgan. At about 11:45 a.m., he said, he was sitting at his desk next to the window. He heard a bang and a cry and thought a firecracker had been let off. Someone then shouted that a man had been shot. Larkins went to the verandah and saw three 'scenes' or 'pictures'. First, he saw a European with a stick running from the Praya towards the Queen's statue; two Chinese firemen were running behind him. Then he looked towards the Prince's Pavilion and saw a body lying on the shafts of a rickshaw. Finally, he saw 'a man who looked like a coolie' running towards the bank. He watched him cross Des Voeux Road and disappear into Wardley Street. He then went back inside to telephone for an ambulance. During the chase, he said, there were half a dozen or more Chinese behind the European, but no one in front except for the man who was running. Kemp asked if Larkins had made any previous communication to the authorities on the case. He replied that, apart from calling for an ambulance, he had not.

Under cross-examination, Larkins insisted that 'at the time I saw this coolie running, he was absolutely alone'. Asked about the revolver, he said it was a sunny day and he did not see the man throw it over the railings. Jenkin then pointed out that Larkins was employed in the office of Reiss & Co., and that one of the jurors, Walter Sinclair, worked in the same office; in fact, he was Larkins's boss. He asked if Larkins had discussed the case with Sinclair.

34. The authorities referred to by the lawyers were not helpful: the only precedent that came close was *R v Haynes* (1859) 175 E.R. 898, where the court ruled that the prosecution could not call a new witness after the cases for *both* the prosecution *and* the defence had closed.

Larkins said he had mentioned it to him that morning. In reply to Rees-Davies, he said that he had gone in to see Sinclair 'with my hat and coat on' to tell him he was thinking of going to the Attorney General. Sinclair had said he could not discuss the question but if Larkins had seen anything it was only right he should go. 'That was all that passed.' Rees-Davies said he 'did not think the slightest objection could be taken to that'. The foreman of the jury, Herbert Bird, asked how Sinclair had been able to see how the 'coolie' was clothed. Larkins replied that he had seen him through a pair of binoculars after he was being brought back.[35]

The defence resumes

After Jenkin had confirmed that Kemp did he not propose to call any of the other employees of Reiss & Co., two of whom had also visited him that morning, the case for the defence resumed. Leung Wo was recalled for cross-examination. Kemp asked him a series of questions about his movements on the days leading up to the murder and, with the help of a map, during the chase. When this failed to elicit much new information, the judge, Rees-Davies, took over. He asked Leung why he thought that he, and not one of the other three running men, had been seized. Leung replied that they were ahead of him and had already dispersed by the time the men who seized him appeared on the scene.

Rees-Davies — What did you think you were being held down for?

Leung Wo — I did not know why they did that.

Rees-Davies — Do you mean to suggest that if you were knocked down in the street as an innocent man, do you mean to say that you would not have called out?

Leung Wo — I could not speak until after I was taken away, until after I had drawn my breath.

Then, after further questioning along the same lines,

Rees-Davies — Do you know or have you any suspicion as to the two men whom you saw running away?

Leung Wo — I do not know them at all.

Rees-Davies — They are entirely unknown to you?

Leung Wo — Entirely unknown to me.

---

35. It was not uncommon at this time for jurors, particularly special jurors, to question witnesses, sometimes to the dismay of counsel. At the last murder case tried with a special jury, in 1915, defence counsel, Eldon Potter, had expressed surprise that a special jury had been empanelled, complaining they were not there 'to act as amateur detectives'. The special jury was at the request of counsel for the prosecution, Jenkin, who also arranged for the murder scene – a bed and a blood-stained mosquito net and matting – to be recreated in court. 'The place fairly reeked with blood,' complained Potter. A mother and her son in Tam Shui Hang village, near the frontier, were accused of murdering a woman the husband had brought home from Demerara. They were both acquitted. *HKDP*, 3 and 7 December 1915; *SCMP*, 3, 4, and 7 December 1915.

Rees-Davies — Does the same answer apply to the other seven or eight men you saw running away?

Leung Wo — I know none of them.

Rees-Davies — You haven't heard from any of your friends who these men were, either the two men or the seven or eight men?

Leung Wo — I do not know anything at all about them.[36]

Asked if he heard people shouting in Chinese 'Seize him! Stop him!' Leung said he heard nothing. Asked where he was running to, Leung replied, 'I was running for nothing.'

After a break for tiffin, Leung was brought back a third time at the request of the jury. The foreman, Herbert Bird, said that the jury wanted to know why, if Leung did not become a seaman until December, he had joined his guild in October. This failed to elicit anything specific, but Jenkin later established that, because business was bad, he had registered early in order to get work when the opportunity arose. Bird then asked whether, since the deceased and the accused had the same surname, they were of the same clan or family. Leung replied that he did not know where the deceased was from and had never seen him before (Leung is a very common Cantonese surname). At the jury's request, the revolver was handed to Leung a second time. Rees-Davies told him to open it. After struggling with it, Leung said he could not open it. Rees-Davies then tried and also failed to open it. He passed it to Bird, who had no difficulty opening the breach.

Jenkin called eight other witnesses for the defence. Four of them were men working near Statue Square when the murder occurred. Each of them, from different perspectives, gave evidence consistent with that given by Leung Wo.

Ng Kam-shiu, a mason on the scaffolding at the Prince's Pavilion, saw three men on the Praya and three at the corner of the garden. One of them, a tall and stout man, lifted the curtain of the hood of the rickshaw and flung his right arm upwards, at which point Ng heard a shot. All six men ran towards the statue, followed by a European and two men from the fire float. Another two men from the float held up the man who fell from the rickshaw. He did not see the accused until the firemen brought him back.

Li Kam, a mason working on the pillars near the statue, saw the accused hanging around the statue. He heard a noise like a firecracker and saw two men run from the Praya past the statue. Seven or eight men then came running from the same direction, and the accused ran with them. He saw the firemen and a European: he did not recognize him as Captain Morgan, though he said he could not tell Europeans apart. Of the two men running ahead, one was short and thin, the other was tall.

Li Shek-yeung, a foreman on the scaffolding on the bank extension, saw ten or twenty persons running through the square, and a European – or at least a man in European

36. Trial transcript, CO 129/475, 111–112.

clothes. Among a group of three at the head of the runners, two men, well ahead of the third, turned right on reaching Des Voeux Road. He saw the taller of the two throw something over the railing into the garden and then put his hat on. Li showed how the object was thrown using the revolver in court. He saw the third man cross the tramline on Des Voeux Road and run up Wardley Street. He later saw a 'little man' brought back in custody but could not recognize him because there were too many people at the time. The man who threw the object was taller and stouter than the accused.

Ngai Chuk-wan, a stonecutter on the bank extension, heard a commotion and saw two men run through Statue Square and turn right at Des Voeux Road. In the square, one of them briefly stopped running and waved his arms. Behind these two was a small man who ran across the tramline, followed by a European and two firemen.

Kemp failed to shake their evidence. His cross-examination of the third witness, Li Kam, descended into repartee. Kemp asked him if his sight was good.

> **Li Kam** — Whether my sight is good or not, I have told you what I have seen.
>
> **Kemp** — I am going to suggest that this whole story of yours is a fabrication.
>
> **Li Kam** — It is quite true; I saw what happened.
>
> *Then, after further questions about Li's eyesight,*
>
> **Li Kam** — I must have good sight before I can be a mason—(Laughter).
>
> **Kemp** — Were you working hard at your plastering?
>
> **Li Kam** — I looked at the prisoner because he was hanging round.
>
> *Li is then tested on his eyesight and on his idea of the passage of time, with reference to the clock on the opposite wall of the courtroom. Kemp is satisfied with the results.*
>
> **Rees-Davies** — Were you afraid he was going to shoot you?—(Laughter).
>
> **Li Kam** — No. I was wondering why he was looking at the pillars. I thought he was a man who had never seen such things before—(Laughter).
>
> **Jenkin** — Probably right, too—(More laughter).[37]

Frustrated by his lack of headway, Kemp declined to cross-examine the fourth of these witnesses, Ngai Chuk-wan. When the trial resumed on day four he announced that he did not intend to cross-examine any further the witnesses for the defence. There was, he said, a direct conflict between them and the witnesses for the prosecution, and therefore 'the witnesses for the defence must be telling falsehoods'.

Kemp had asked the defence witnesses how they had come to give evidence. His implication was that they had been suborned or intimidated. The masons Ng Kam-siu and Li Kam replied that Brutton had spoken to their master, who had taken them to Brutton's office. The foreman Li Shek-yeung said he went twice to Brutton's office and told Brutton

37. *HKWP*, 25 March 1922.

what he had seen. Pressed by Kemp on whether he had talked to his fellow-workmen about the matter, Ng, 'with some heat,' retorted, 'Of course I would not talk about it! Would you dare to talk about it, here and there, about someone being shot?'

To meet claims that the evidence was 'cooked', Jenkin called Ngai Piu, the contractor in charge of the bank extension, who had helped find two of the witnesses for the defence. Against objections from Kemp, and waiving the rule against hearsay evidence, Rees-Davies allowed Jenkin to examine Ngai on what the witnesses had said to him *before* they went to Brutton's office. Ngai said a clerk from Brutton's office had asked him if he knew anything about the murder. At first Ngai had refused to help, because 'regarding things in Hongkong it is better not to interfere'. He nevertheless asked Li Shek-yeung and Ngai Chuk-wan what they had seen, and they gave accounts similar to what they subsequently told the court. When the clerk paid him a second visit, Ngai Piu agreed to fetch the two men, who were eventually persuaded to go to see Brutton.

Jenkin also called the Chief Warder of Victoria Gaol, James West, and Brutton himself to give evidence about an identity parade held in the gaol a few days before the trial. Unusually, this had been carried out at the request of the defence. Its purpose was not to identify the culprit but to allow two of the defence witnesses to identify the 'little man' they had seen running behind the two other men. West explained that the parade, held in the presence of the Superintendent, John Franks, consisted of fourteen men on remand plus the accused, who, in line with standard practice, chose his place in the parade. Each witness in turn promptly identified the accused as the man in question before being taken into another room. Brutton testified that no one in his office had told Leung that the parade was going to take place, or had any contact with the witnesses immediately before the parade, except to call them in. When Jenkin asked Brutton if anything had been done to 'fake' the identity parade, Rees-Davies interjected to say this was 'quite unnecessary. I am quite sure a gentleman of Mr Brutton's standing would not.'[38]

Closing speeches

Jenkin began his closing speech with an expression of sympathy to the family of Leung Yuk-tong for what was 'a most cold-blooded and dastardly crime'. Referring again to the state of opinion outside the court, he appealed to jurors to steel themselves against 'the jocular cynicisms of your fellow clubmen should you find this man "not guilty"'.

> I know, as you know, that outside of this Court this man has been condemned, hanged, drawn and quartered hundreds of times by lay judges who have never been inside this

38. After the trial Brutton wrote to ask Kemp to confirm that his claim that the defence evidence was fabricated was not 'a direct imputation against me and against my office as the solicitor having the conduct of the defence'. Kemp readily did so. The letters were published in the press. *HKDP*, 1 April 1922.

> Court. They pick up scraps of the evidence from reading the newspapers and, though knowing absolutely nothing about it, they feel quite fitted to take the place of the Chief Justice and Jury and decide the verdict.[39]

'You are strong enough to take the right decision if you think he is not guilty,' he said.

Jenkin went over the weaknesses in the prosecution's case. The main witness, Captain Morgan, had 'failed signally to identify the man in any shape or form'. He had said the pillar was not there when it was. He had 'blundered hopelessly' over Harold Green's position. And it was inconceivable that he had failed to see the murderer throw the gun over the railings into the garden. He asked the jury whether they could convict on the strength of evidence that was 'so palpably fallacious and untrustworthy'. As to why the accused was running, Jenkin said that everybody else was running too, and that was 'only natural'. He had said nothing when brought down by Pereira because he was 'nearly strangled' and could hardly breathe. It was easy enough for the prosecution to say the defence evidence had been fabricated. But the jury required more proof than a mere assertion. 'The evidence of the witnesses for the defence was stamped with honesty by the identification parade last Saturday,' he said. The prosecution had asked why they had not come forward before. But then why did so few Europeans come forward?

> It is all very well for the Attorney General to sit down and say that he will not cross-examine the witnesses. With its minions, its detective department and so on, if the Crown, in the preparation of its case, had done as Mr Brutton had done, had gone to all of the offices which overlooked the *locus in quo* and had collected the evidence which possibly was available then they might have been able to say, 'here is the evidence of a number of Europeans of standing and it is in direct conflict with the evidence for the defence.'[40]

Kemp's response, in his concluding speech, was that it was equally open to the defence to go to the offices overlooking the square and call *European* witnesses to prove that a large number of men were running ahead of the prisoner. As for the witnesses for the defence, Kemp said that each of them came from a different section of the route of the pursuit, so that their evidence could not be tested one against the other. Each told a short, simple story, which was all the more difficult to break down in cross-examination. He hoped the Jury had noticed their demeanour, 'so very clear and distinct' in answer to Jenkin, said Kemp, 'but when I began, so stupid and evasive.' On the other hand, he asserted, although there were natural discrepancies due to differences of recollection, the witnesses for the prosecution were trustworthy: 'if the Jury believed that Captain Morgan did not lose sight of the prisoner they must find the prisoner guilty of murder.'

39. *HKWP*, 25 March 1922.
40. *HKWP*, 25 March 1922.

The summing up and verdict

Chief Justice Rees-Davies then summed up. It was purely a case of identity, he said. The only question for the jury was whether the prosecution had 'established in their minds, to the exclusion of all doubt, that the prisoner was the assassin'. Although the prosecution did not need to show motive, the suggestion was that the accused had been engaged to assassinate Leung Yuk-tong, who 'had taken some active part in the strike, for which the seamen sought revenge'. If the jury accepted the evidence of the defence they could return only one verdict. If they rejected it 'they must reject all of it, which would amount to a finding that there had been a conspiracy on the part of a number of Chinese witnesses to defeat the administration of justice'. He then made this observation:

> Gentlemen, I have had experience now for some years of Chinese witnesses and am perfectly justified in saying this to you that while most Chinamen come into the box to speak the truth and promote the administration of justice, I am bound to tell you that collusion of witnesses to tell a story having no regard to the truth of that story at all is not, I regret to say, uncommon. I have had to find, as a fact, that the most extraordinary details, carefully interwoven; one witness building the foundation, another adding the superstructure and a third carrying it a little further until the chain of evidence becomes so conclusive that the Court, in ordinary circumstances, would be convinced; I have had to find as a fact that such evidence has been entirely and absolutely unfounded and built up purely for the purpose.[41]

'In view of that observation,' he advised the jury, 'it is for you to weigh the evidence on both sides.' He then read over the evidence of the main witnesses for the prosecution, since it was taken some days before. Referring to Captain Morgan's 'correction of a slip he made' about Green's position, Rees-Davies remarked,

> It is a thing I constantly have to comment on in this Court, that intelligent European witnesses are always hazarding a guess instead of saying 'I don't know.' They say, 'Oh yes, I think it was so-and-so,' and later have to withdraw it. And then counsel, naturally, comment on it.[42]

With regard to the fireman Fung Chi, Rees-Davies said that, although he was called by the prosecution, his evidence largely corroborated the evidence of the defence: 'if his story was to be accepted it very largely broke down the case for the Crown so I questioned him.' As Rees-Davies read over the transcript of this part of the evidence, Jenkin interrupted to ask him to point out that Fung's evidence at trial was substantially the same as that he had given to the magistrate in committal proceedings.

41. *HKWP*, 25 March 1922.
42. *HKWP*, 25 March 1922.

Rees-Davies commented briefly on the evidence of the accused. He asked if his statement to the police ('I was passing the Hongkong and Shanghai Bank, I do not know what was the matter') was reasonable for someone who had been running away. 'A man with a clear conscience would desire to clear himself,' he said. He did not propose to read out the defence evidence since it was still fresh in the jury's memory. He then noticed he had overlooked the evidence of Larkins, the last-minute prosecution witness. He proceeded to read this, saying it corroborated Morgan's story. With the usual remarks about proof beyond reasonable doubt, he asked the jury to go and consider their verdict. After half an hour the jury returned with a question for the judge:

> **Herbert Bird (the foreman)** — We understood you to say that if we have no reasonable doubt that the man Captain Morgan saw leaving the rear of the rickshaw is the prisoner in the dock we can find him guilty.
>
> **Rees-Davies** — That is exactly what I did say.
>
> **Bird** — Irrespective of whether he saw him fire the shot, or not?
>
> **Rees-Davies** — Taking the whole of Captain Morgan's evidence, if you have no reason to doubt the truth of it, you should find him guilty.
>
> **Jenkin** — Irrespective of whether he fired the shot or not?[43]

Bird then briefly consulted the other jurors and said they were ready to give their verdict. They found the accused, Leung Wo, guilty of murder.

Jenkin immediately rose to his feet and moved in arrest of judgment so that the judge could reserve certain legal questions for the Full Court. There were two main grounds. One was wrongful admission of the evidence of Larkins after the close of the prosecution's case. 'But you agreed to it!' exclaimed Rees-Davies. Jenkin replied that he had been 'driven' into withdrawing his objection as a matter of strategy because the gist of the evidence had been overheard by the jury. Rees-Davies refused to reserve this question, saying it would possibly be a 'loophole for quashing the conviction'. The second ground was misdirection by Rees-Davies when asked by the jury if they could find the accused guilty regardless of whether Morgan saw him fire the shot. Kemp, who also thought Rees-Davies had phrased this badly, interjected that Morgan never said he saw the shot fired at all.[44] Stressing that he had directed the jury to consider Morgan's evidence 'as a whole', Rees-Davies refused

43. *HKWP*, 25 March 1922.

44. Kemp later described as 'regrettable' Rees-Davies's failure to add that, before they could find Leung guilty, the jury must be ready 'to find by way of inference that he did actually fire the shot'. He also remarked that, in refusing to reserve the point on Larkins's evidence because it would create a possible loophole for quashing the conviction, Rees-Davies seemed 'momentarily to have overlooked' a recent amendment to the Criminal Procedure Ordinance allowing the Full Court to order a new trial when ruling on a point reserved. He added that he would probably not have called Larkins had he had time to think it over. Kemp, Notes on the evidence, 19 and 28 April 1922, CO 129/475, 70–74; Ordinance No. 10 of 1921.

to reserve this question too, saying the remedy was a petition to the Privy Council. Jenkin asked if he would suspend judgment while he drew up a petition. Rees-Davies refused. He then proceeded to ask Leung Wo if he had anything to say why sentence should not be passed on him:

> **Leung Wo** — I have. I want to make my statement there. *Pointing to the witness-box.*
>
> **Rees-Davies** — No, you cannot do that. I can't give you that concession.
>
> **Leung Wo** — I have committed no offence. I was there looking at people plastering up pillars. I suddenly heard a bang as of the firing of crackers and then saw two men running past me like flying. Seven or eight men then ran. When they got to the Queen's Statue they separated. They ran past the Statue and I ran.
>
> **Rees-Davies** — You have told us all this before. Unless you have anything to say in addition to what you told us in the witness box, it will be a waste of time.
>
> **Leung Wo** — In that case I have nothing to say except to ask Your Lordship to act on reason. I don't know how to say anything else. I leave the matter in Your Lordship's hands and ask you to have mercy on me.[45]

Rees-Davies then pronounced sentence of death, telling Leung Wo that it was 'a dastardly crime and you took away the life of someone for a motive best known to yourself, but as far as we know, a man who had done no harm.' Leung had been 'calm but anxious-looking' throughout the trial. Now he broke down. 'I have done no wrong. I want to say something. I must say more before I die,' he said through sobs. He struggled with two Indian constables and a European sergeant as they removed him from the dock.

The petition to the Privy Council

The closing scenes of Leung Wo's trial would 'go towards making it one of the most memorable criminal cases in Hongkong's legal history,' remarked the *China Mail*. The newspapers were lavish in their use of superlatives at this time. But this trial surely marked a low point in Hong Kong's judicial history. It was held at a time of mounting disaffection between government and people, fuelled by the confrontations leading to Leung Yuk-tong's assassination and the killing of unarmed civilians on the Tai Po Road. When, halfway through the trial, Jenkin had spoken of the desire of 'sound-thinking men in the heat of the moment' to lynch Leung Wo, the *Mail* had departed from the convention of not commenting on trials in progress to warn that 'in Hongkong those heated moments have visibly been multiplying, and growing in duration'. It recalled 'a prominent business man declaiming publicly in Ice House Street during the strike that all the Guild officials should be led out on the Praya and shot'. It pointed to 'all sorts of sentiments showing that this community – even the

45. *SCMP*, 24 March 1922.

presumably "sound thinking" sections of it – is not so devoted to the principles of law and order as a civilized community ought to be.'[46]

Poor preparation by the prosecution and weakness on the part of the judge brought these sentiments to the surface in Leung's trial. The investigation had been 'slovenly', said the *Daily Press*. Much of the police force had been diverted to deal with the strike. Its Chinese members had faced conflicts of loyalty: twenty-three were dismissed or pensioned off and thirty-one others were demoted or otherwise disciplined in the aftermath of the strike. Even without the distraction of the strike, detection rates were low: for twenty-five known murders in 1921 only ten arrests had been made and two convictions secured. The *Daily Press* observed a pattern of incompetence in the force's detective work. This was illustrated in the Woping Theatre murder trial, and in the acquittal, after contradictory police evidence, of the only man tried for the Gresson Street murders of 1918, in which ten people were killed during a police raid on a house in Wan Chai.[47] The government's lawyers were also negligent, said the *Daily Press*. The late appearance of Larkins, of his own volition, showed how little effort had been made to obtain evidence from the many Europeans in offices near the scene of the murder: they, the *Daily Press* assumed, were not susceptible to intimidation.[48] Wakeman, the Crown Solicitor, responsible for preparing the evidence, had been preoccupied not only with the inquest into the Tai Po Road shootings but also with his retirement one week after the conclusion of the trial.

The Attorney General, Joseph Kemp, produced notes on the evidence in preparation for an appeal to the Privy Council. After observing that the three main prosecution witnesses – Morgan, Green, and Larkins – had testified 'with great care and fairness', he analysed the evidence of Leung Wo with the aim of buttressing the case against him. He claimed to see a contrast between Leung's actions and the stereotypical behaviour of 'The Chinese' in general. For one who had spent so little time in the city, Leung Wo 'displayed a remarkable knowledge of Hong Kong,' said Kemp.

> The Chinese are notoriously inaccurate in matters of topography and street names. In spite of this limited residence the prisoner spoke glibly of the Central District, Wanchai, the Central Market, the Western Market, Stanley Street, the Naval Yard, Connaught Road (usually though not always called by Chinese the Sea Front) and the Hongkong &

46. *CM*, 23 and 24 March 1922.
47. Five policemen, three gang members, and two bystanders. The evidence of the key prosecution witness, the head of Chinese detectives, Sun Tai, contradicted statements by him to another police officer and the evidence of another police witness. On being acquitted, the accused, Ng Ling, was arrested on another, unconnected murder charge. He was later discharged and, along with an uncooperative prosecution witness in the Gresson Street case, deported as an undesirable. *HKDP* 20–22 March 1918; *SCMP*, 20–22 and 26 March and 6, 12, and 18 April 1918; ExCo Minutes, 2 and 26 May 1918, CO 131/54, 275 and 284.
48. *HKDP*, 27 March 1922.

> Shanghai Bank. He arrived alone, found his way alone across the harbour to his boarding house, and set out alone 'for the Naval Yard' on the morning of the murder.[49]

Kemp said that Leung had slipped up in saying that, had he not been seized, he would have turned towards Central District, apparently forgetting his story that he was going to meet his friend at the Naval Yard, which lay in the opposite direction. He could give no reason for running, saying only that other people were running too, or that he 'was running for nothing'. 'The Chinese are notoriously averse to mixing themselves up in street rows and police court cases and other people's business,' Kemp remarked.[50]

Similar generalizations about Chinese behaviour had pervaded the summing up by the Chief Justice, Sir William Rees-Davies. After nearly twenty-five years of colonial service, Rees-Davies was nearing the end of his career. His long leave had not improved his declining health; there were rumours he would not return.[51] When he did return, a heavy judicial workload awaited him. He was also saddled with a commission on fusion of the legal profession. He was, moreover, 'busy every spare moment' chairing the executive committee for the Prince's visit: that task was made all the more distasteful because 'so many busybodies want to push themselves'.[52] His exhaustion showed in moments of confusion during Leung Wo's trial. His frustration with the ongoing Penang will case bolstered his belief that the Chinese witnesses in Leung's case were part of a conspiracy to defeat the ends of justice. The idea that one side or the other was engaged in 'a wholesale conspiracy' found its way in turn into his judgment on the Penang case seven months later.[53]

Judges often commented on the systematic perjury behind some civil cases tried at this time. But it was unusual for them to imply that the *whole* of the defence in a criminal trial was a conspiracy. In fact, it was rare for defence witnesses, other than the accused, to be called at all: they were called for only a small minority of the seventy-five defendants tried for murder in the ten years before Leung's case.[54] In the latest such case, a murder of a travelling trader, tried in August 1920, the defence had great difficulty in getting its witnesses to attend at all. The court rejected one because he knew nothing of the case and fined another for leaving before being called to testify. Counsel for the accused (Jenkin again) asked the judge to order three other witnesses to remain in court until the trial was over. The defence had tried but failed to get other witnesses, he said, adding that this 'was

49. Kemp, Notes on the evidence, 28 April 1922, CO 129/475, 67.
50. Kemp, Notes on the evidence, 19 and 28 April 1922, CO 129/475, 65–74.
51. *HKT*, 19 April 1921.
52. The commission, composed of lawyers and businessmen, does not appear to have produced a report but was unanimously opposed to fusion. Rees-Davies to Risley, 23 February 1922, CO 129/474, 310–312.
53. *HKDP*, 2 November 1922.
54. Witnesses for the defence, other than the accused, were called on behalf of ten of the seventy-five defendants tried for murder from July 1912 to March 1922; twenty-four of the defendants gave evidence. The reports of three cases are insufficient to determine whether defence witnesses were called.

common enough in Chinese cases'. Given colonial assumptions about the contradictory or exaggerated nature of much 'Chinese evidence', it often made tactical sense for the defence to avoid calling witnesses, but instead to attempt to expose flaws in the prosecution's case.[55] In addition, under procedural rules at this time, prosecuting counsel had a right of reply if the defence called witnesses other than the accused, giving the prosecution the last word before the judge's summing up.

When, therefore, prosecutor, judge, and jury in Leung Wo's case were confronted with clear, consistent, and unshakeable evidence from four Chinese witnesses for the defence, it seemed to them only natural that this was coordinated by some invisible hand. The efforts of the defence to show that this was not so carried little weight. The defects in the evidence of Captain Morgan, on the other hand, were excused by the judge as the tendency of European witnesses to 'hazard a guess'. These attitudes were deepened by the tensions and anxieties outside the courtroom. The strike and its messy conclusion had badly damaged the prestige of the British authorities and mercantile elite. Whether Leung Wo had really murdered Leung Yuk-tong seemed less important than the need to reassert power through what amounted to a judicial lynching. At best, justice was not seen to be done. At worst, an innocent man was condemned to death.

Since arriving in Hong Kong in September 1919, Governor Stubbs had confirmed fifteen death sentences and commuted none.[56] On 21 April 1922, on the unanimous advice of his Executive Council, he confirmed the death sentence on Leung Wo, subject to the outcome of the petition to the Privy Council. The Judicial Committee of the Privy Council was the final court of appeal from courts in the British Empire, outside the UK itself. The empire was now at its farthest extent, holding sway over a quarter of the world's population. The law lords on the Judicial Committee often stressed that it was not a general court of criminal appeal, and that leave to appeal would not be granted 'unless by a disregard of the forms of legal process, or by some violation of the principles of natural justice or

55. Successfully in the travelling traders case. Both victim and accused carried goods and remittances between Hong Kong and places in mainland China. The victim was stabbed after leaving a shop with $200 and was taken to hospital. The next day a magistrate took a dying deposition from him in the presence of the accused: this formed the main evidence against him. Jenkin argued that the deposition was inadmissible because the accused was not given enough notice to engage a solicitor, or told what the offence was. The judge, Gompertz, admitted the deposition but reserved these points for the Full Court, suspending judgment when the jury found the accused guilty. The Full Court (Gompertz and Wood) quashed the conviction. *HKDP*, 24–26 August and 4 September 1920; *R v Leung Tai* [1920] HKLR 62.

56. In his entire six-year term as governor he confirmed twenty-seven death sentences and commuted five (his predecessor, May, had confirmed nine and commuted eight). Among the twenty-seven persons hanged was the first woman executed in Hong Kong, Chan Pak, hanged with her lover, Wong Yuk, on 28 November 1923 for the murder of her husband: Patricia O'Sullivan, *Women, Crime and the Courts: Hong Kong 1841–1941* (Hong Kong: Blacksmith Books, 2021), 227–233. In three of the cases of commutation, one victim was a woman and two were children (one a girl killed by her adoptive mother); another involved the poisoning by a woman of her husband; in the fifth, an Indian guard was convicted of murdering a colleague in a fight.

otherwise, substantial and grave injustice has been done'.[57] In the words of the *Hongkong Weekly Press*, it was a 'rich man's court', its role being 'not to correct the injustice of local courts, but simply to decide disputed questions of law, which is a different thing'.[58] The Judicial Committee had decided many civil cases from Hong Kong, but had so far heard only one criminal appeal: the *Ibrahim* case of 1912–1914, which became an authority on confessions. The crime had occurred in the foreign settlement on Shameen Island in Canton, but the case was transferred out of convenience from the British Supreme Court in China to Hong Kong.[59]

A right to appeal to the Privy Council lay in all civil cases where the amount in dispute was of or above a certain value: $5,000 at this time.[60] In other civil cases leave to appeal had to be obtained either from the Full Court of the Supreme Court, if it held that the question was of great general or public importance, or by petition direct to the Privy Council for special leave to appeal. There was no right of appeal in criminal cases. Nor, despite some ambiguity in the rules, did a colonial court have any power to grant leave to appeal to the Privy Council in criminal cases.[61] The only course open to Leung Wo was therefore to petition the Privy Council direct for special leave to appeal. In early July news was telegraphed to Hong Kong that the Judicial Committee had declined leave to appeal. On 30 August, after the government had received confirmation by letter, Leung Wo was hanged in Victoria Gaol. He protested his innocence to the end and made no confession before he

57. *In re Abraham Mallory Dillett* (1887) 12 AC 459, cited in *Ibrahim v The King* [1914] UKPC 1.
58. *HKWP*, 12 March 1898.
59. This was Jenkin's first murder trial. Kemp prosecuted and Rees-Davies presided as judge. Ibrahim, an Afghan soldier in the 126th Baluchistan Infantry Regiment of the British Army, was accused of murdering an Indian officer. He was deemed a British subject under British extraterritorial jurisdiction in China. He had confessed to his commanding officer but pleaded not guilty at trial. The jury could not agree on a verdict, reportedly because some of the (mostly British) jurors were opposed to capital punishment. Ibrahim was found guilty in a retrial. On appeal, Jenkin challenged the conviction on the grounds that that the Hong Kong Supreme Court did not have jurisdiction, the 1911 Revolution had annulled the treaties on extraterritoriality, and Ibrahim was not a British subject. Ibrahim obtained leave to appeal to the Privy Council *in forma pauperis*: his counsel there, Albert Romer Macklin, argued further that Ibrahim's confession was inadmissible because he had made it to a senior officer while under armed guard. Accepting this point, the Judicial Committee ruled that no statement by the accused was admissible in evidence against him unless it was shown to have been voluntary 'in the sense that it has not been obtained from him either by fear of prejudice or hope of advantage exercised or held out by a person in authority'. But it also held that the jury had not been influenced by Ibrahim's confession and that the evidence against him was enough to convict. Ibrahim was hanged in Hong Kong on 17 July 1914. *SCMP*, 22–24 October, 19–26 November, and 10 and 17 December 1912; Reports by Bucknill, Attorney General, 27 November and 17 December 1912, CO 129/399, 154–157; Crown Agents to Colonial Office, 21 June 1913, CO 129/404, 355–360; *Ibrahim v The King* [1914] UKPC 1; *HKDP*, 17 July 1914; Clark, *Gunboat Justice*, II, 173–176.
60. Rules for Appeals to the Privy Council, 1909, and Judicial Committee Rules, 1908, *The Laws of Hongkong* (Rev. edition, Hong Kong: Noronha & Co., 1913), III, 262–291.
61. The absence of such a power was confirmed by the Judicial Committee in *Chung Chuck* v. *R.*, [1930] AC 244 (1929) and stressed by Colonial Office Circular 9337/47, 12 December 1947, CO 129/548/4, encl. 13.

was hanged. Shortly after the execution his elder brother applied for Leung's corpse so that the family could bury it. The government refused the application. Leung was buried in the Chinese Cemetery at Caroline Hill known as the Coffee Plantation, then the usual place for burying executed criminals.[62]

A permanent state of emergency: The 1925–1926 Strike-Boycott

The Prince's visit passed without incident. An exhausted Rees-Davies took to his sickbed after it was over. He continued as Chief Justice until his retirement in early 1924. 'Please don't object,' wrote Stubbs in a private note to the Colonial Office urging an enhanced pension. 'If you do he won't retire and although everybody loves the dear old thing everybody will agree that he isn't up to his work. Also he would probably die.'[63]

In parallel, the Foreign Office campaigned to have Stubbs removed from Hong Kong. His mishandling of the seamen's strike – in particular the shootings on the Tai Po Road – had worsened Anglo-Chinese relations, they said. James Jamieson, the Consul General in Canton, who had helped end the strike, produced a damning account of blunders by Hong Kong officials. Stubbs had no knowledge of 'the Chinese language or temperament,' he wrote. He had 'little else than office experience (he was a Colonial Office clerk) and no outlook beyond the needs of the colony,' echoed Sir Victor Wellesley, an assistant under-secretary in the Foreign Office. Others complained that his erratic schemes in support of successive governments in Canton clashed with Britain's wider interests in China: these now included cultivating Sun Yat-sen, whom he had once regarded as 'a menace to civilization.'[64] Staff in the Colonial Office agreed that 'tact or judgment' were not Stubbs's strong points but were unable to find another position for him.[65] He received a warning from the Secretary of State but remained Governor until 1925.[66]

---

62. So called after attempts to grow coffee there in the 1850s. *HKDP*, 10 July and 31 August 1922; *SCMP*, 4 September 1922.
63. Stubbs to A.E. Collins, 15 August 1923, CO 129/481, 129–130.
64. Jamieson to Alston, 11 and 13 March 1922, CO 129/477, 279–281 and 283–285; Jamieson, 'Relations Between Hong Kong & Canton', 28 September 1922, FO 371/8030, 243; Minute by Wellesley, 25 April 1924, and 'Incidents giving serious cause for criticism of the Governor of Hongkong', August 1924, FO 371/10266, 88 and 98–102; Memoranda on Stubbs (1923), CO 129/483, 212–221.
65. Officials considered swapping him with Sir Laurence Guillemard, Governor of the Straits Settlements and High Commissioner for the Federated Malay States (1920–1927) but had doubts about Stubbs's ability to handle the Malay sultans. Minutes by Grindle, 29 August and 20 September 1923, CO 129/483, 209–211.
66. Stubbs was then, consecutively, Governor of Jamaica, Cyprus, and Ceylon, where his predilection for emergency powers led to a constitutional crisis. In 1937, urged by planters, he used powers still in force from World War I to order the deportation of Mark Bracegirdle, an Australian communist working among plantation labourers. Mass rallies were held in support of Bracegirdle. The State Council passed a vote of censure against Stubbs. Bracegirdle was released on a writ of habeas corpus by the Supreme Court, which held that he could not be deported for exercising his right to free speech. Stubbs retired soon afterwards. Devonshire to Stubbs, 22

After the seamen's strike Stubbs was determined to be prepared for the next confrontation, which he saw as inevitable. This came in the form of the Canton–Hong Kong Strike-Boycott of 1925–1926, which was triggered by events in the treaty ports. On 30 May 1925 British police fired on anti-imperialist demonstrators in Shanghai, killing eleven and wounding many others. This sparked more protests. On 23 June, during a violent demonstration at Shameen, forces under British control fired into the crowd, killing fifty-two demonstrators. Organized by the Canton government – an uneasy alliance between the Kuomintang and the recently formed Chinese Communist Party – the Strike-Boycott was aimed at nothing less than driving the British out of Hong Kong. By July, some 250,000 workers, a third of Hong Kong's population, had left for Canton. Trade plummeted by 50 per cent in 1925. Property values fell by 60 per cent, share prices by 40 per cent. Hundreds of shops closed. There were runs on the smaller Chinese banks and a massive drain on currency. Agitators maintained the strike through intimidation and violence.

This time Stubbs had no reason to complain about apathy among the Chinese elites. Chinese organizations rallied to join the fight against Bolshevism. Individuals enrolled in the Special Police Reserve and other essential services. The Chinese representatives on the Legislative Council, Robert Kotewall and Shouson Chow, took over the coordination of anti-strike measures, organizing counterpropaganda through street lectures, posters, pamphlets, and a new (initially) pro-establishment newspaper, the *Kung Sheung Daily News*. They formed a secretive 'Labour Protection Bureau', headed by an ex-army general and staffed by men 'of a bold type'. The aim was to recruit workers to fill the place of strikers, protect those who stayed at their jobs, and 'intimidate the intimidators'.[67] Stubbs dabbled with schemes to finance anti-Bolshevik activities in Canton, including a contemplated coup d'état, with money raised privately in Hong Kong. These came to nothing. In late 1925 Stubbs was replaced by Sir Cecil Clementi, a government cadet and a sinologist with many years of experience in Hong Kong and Canton. An iron fist in a velvet glove, Clementi combined a more conciliatory approach with threats of military force. The Canton government brought the Strike-Boycott to an end in September 1926 after the new leader of the Kuomintang, Chiang Kai-shek, focused his efforts on reunifying China with the launch of the Northern Expedition.[68]

Stubbs's legacy was the Emergency Regulations Ordinance, enacted at the height of the seamen's strike. Drafted by Kemp, this was based, not on the recent UK Emergency Powers Act 1920, but on the Defence of the Realm Act 1914 and Imperial orders in

---

December 1923, CO 129/483, 197–198. *In re Mark Antony Lyster Bracegirdle* [1937] LKHC 8; K.M. de Silva, *A History of Sri Lanka* (Colombo: Vijitha Yapa Publications, 2005), 539–541.

67. Memorandum by Kotewall, CO 129/489, 430–464.

68. Chan Lau, *China, Britain and Hong Kong*, 176–219.

council proclaimed in World War I (in force in Hong Kong until July 1922).[69] The UK's own Emergency Powers Act required the government to proclaim a state of emergency before it could make emergency regulations, placed limits on their scope, and required parliamentary approval for them to continue beyond seven days. The Hong Kong ordinance contained no such safeguards. It empowered the Governor in Council to make regulations on any matter without declaring a state of emergency or obtaining approval from the Legislative Council. During the 1925–1926 Strike-Boycott, regulations were made to increase magistrates' powers, proscribe organizations inimical to the interests of the colony, censor Chinese newspapers, restrict withdrawals from Chinese banks, and extend police powers. Some of these regulations, notably the controls on the press and public assemblies, were retained after the strike and augmented over the years.[70] Along with the Peace Preservation Ordinance, deportation, and other controls, the emergency regulations equipped the government with the apparatus of a police state. Purges of communists, in cooperation with militarist regimes in Canton, enabled Clementi to maintain a degree of stability in Hong Kong for the rest of the 1920s.[71]

Rees-Davies's successor as Chief Justice was Sir Henry Gollan, who, among many other duties, served on an international commission into the May 30th Incident in Shanghai. In a report that bore echoes of the verdict on the Tai Po Road shootings, Gollan held that the order by a British police inspector to fire on demonstrators was necessary and justifiable.[72] On Gollan's retirement in 1930 Sir Joseph Kemp described him as 'the best Chief Justice we have ever had or are ever likely to have'.[73] Kemp was Gollan's successor. In 1932 he was to preside over the most celebrated murder trial in Hong Kong's pre-war history: the Village Road Murder, the subject of the next chapter.

---

69. Kemp, Report on Ordinance No. 5 of 1922, 8 March 1922, CO 129/474, 333–334; ExCo Minutes, 14 February 1922, CO 131/60, 285.
70. Max W.L. Wong, 'Social Control and Political Order – Decolonisation and the Use of Emergency Regulations in Hong Kong', *HKLJ*, Vol. 41 (2011–2012): 133–164.
71. Chan Lau Kit-ching, *From Nothing to Nothing: The Chinese Communist Movement and Hong Kong, 1921–1936* (Hong Kong: Hong Kong University Press, 1999), 176–189.
72. The other commissioners were Findley Johnson, from the Philippines Supreme Court, and Kitaro Suga, Chief Justice of the Hiroshima Appeals Court. Each produced a separate report. Suga largely agreed with Gollan. Johnson found the inspector was not to blame but criticized the British Commissioner of Police for not having taken charge of the situation. The Chinese government refused to take part in the inquiry, and no Chinese witnesses came forward. Macleay to Chamberlain, 2 January 1926, FO 371/11665, 184–196.
73. *HKDP*, 3 April 1930.

9

Money Versus Justice

The Village Road Murder, 1932

Cheng Kwok-yau (鄭國有) was the grandson of Chung Keng Quee, the Penang millionaire whose disputed estate had so agitated the Chief Justice, Sir William Rees-Davies in 1922.[1] The defendant in that case was Chung's widow, Lim Ah Chan, who ran the family's property empire from its headquarters, the Kwong Hoi Kee, on Queen's Road. She was one of the richest women in Hong Kong. In May 1928 Cheng Kwok-yau, then sixteen years old, attended a concert by the China Song and Dance Troupe from Shanghai. This group of young girls performed works by its manager, Li Jinhua, in a style blending Chinese folk songs with American jazz. The star was Li's daughter, the nineteen-year-old Lai Ming-fai, a film actress whose signature piece, 'Maomao yu', became famous as China's first modern pop song:

> The fine rain always falls,
> The light breeze always blows.
> Light breeze, fine rain, green willow.
> Oh, green willow!
> Darling, I don't want your gold,
> Darling, I don't want your silver.
> I only want your heart.
> Oh, your heart!

---

1. See Chapter 8.

The writer Lu Xun compared Lai's recording of this song to a cat being strangled. The Ministry of Education in Nanking later banned it as vapid and salacious.[2]

Cheng Kwok-yau became infatuated with Lai Ming-fai.[3] He treated her and the troupe to dinner. He wrote love letters to her when the troupe moved on to Singapore. He joined her there for several months, took her upcountry to his hometown of Ipoh, and proposed marriage. Her father, who was 'modern in his outlook', gave his consent and acquiesced in their sharing a room. But, because Cheng's own family opposed the match, he and Lai decided to delay marriage until he came into his inheritance at the age of twenty-one. Cheng followed Lai back to Shanghai and stayed for several months, lavishing presents on her. He returned to Hong Kong in April 1930, heavily in debt, having spent the whole of an $80,000 advance from his inheritance. Two months later Lai joined him.

They settled in a rented house at 50 Village Road in Happy Valley, a modern suburb next to the racecourse: the neighbourhood was second in desirability only to the Peak District, which was reserved for Europeans. Lai Ming-fai, her mother, her amah, and her friends Bessie and Annie Au all lived there under Cheng's 'protection'. Driving around in his Baby Austin, Cheng idled away his time with billiards at the South China Athletic Association; gambling at the Chinese Civil Servants Club; films in air-conditioned theatres; dinners at expensive restaurants; and drink, women, and opium at the nightclubs in Shek Tong Tsui. He attracted an entourage of hangers-on and paid for everything. At home, Cheng and Lai shared a bedroom but slept in separate beds, ostensibly to preserve her virginity for marriage, but really, she later said, because he had 'a disease'. One day Cheng took her to see a house in Stubbs Road he was planning to buy for their marital home. There they renewed their promises and made plans to marry in May or June 1932.

The fly in the ointment was George Fung Tak-him. Like Cheng, Fung was from a well-known family. His grandfather was the late Fung Wa-chuen, a director of the Tung Wah Hospital, and a justice of the peace. His father, Fung Shiu-wah, was comprador to a European trading firm. George Fung was a friend of Cheng. He had met Lai Ming-fai during her visit to Hong Kong in 1928 and had stayed with her and Cheng at her father's house in Shanghai in 1930. Older than Cheng by five years, he had married a woman named Ho in 1928, but their affection faded after he gave her a disease. They divorced in Shanghai in 1931. Fung returned to Hong Kong and started spending time with Lai, usually in the company of Bessie or Annie Au, but sometimes alone, especially during Cheng's absences in Macao and Canton. Lai knew Cheng was seeing other women – plenty of other women,

2. 毛毛雨, 1927. *KSDN*, 25 December 1929; Szu-wei Chen, 'The Rise and Generic Features of Shanghai Popular Songs in the 1930s and 1940s', *Popular Music* 24, no. 1 (2005): 123n2; Andrew F. Jones, *Yellow Music: Media Culture and Colonial Modernity in the Jazz Age* (Durham, North Carolina: Duke University Press, 2001), Chapter 3.

3. The main sources for this section are the reports of evidence given at committal proceedings in *SCMP*, *HKDP*, *WTYP*, and *KSDN*, 27 April 1932–9 July 1932. Much of this evidence was challenged by the defence at trial.

she later recalled. She fell in love with Fung. They planned to move to Shanghai as soon as he could find a job: he had no regular employment and lived precariously on money lent by his brother, and by Cheng and other friends.

Cheng soon became jealous of Lai's friendship with Fung. He warned her not to go out with him. The jealousy grew, and on Saturday 20 February 1932 they had a bitter quarrel. The next day, presuming Cheng to be on a trip to Canton, Lai went with Fung to a tea dance at the Repulse Bay Hotel. In fact, Cheng's purported trip to Canton was cover for a secret visit to Annie Au at a bungalow he was renting for her in Repulse Bay. At about 5:45 p.m. Lai received a message from her amah that Cheng had returned early. She immediately took a taxi back to Village Road. On the way, at a secluded spot on Wong Nai Chung Road, she encountered Cheng in his Austin. They got out of the cars and had another quarrel. He accused her of ingratitude and of seeing Fung without his consent. He took back the engagement ring and other jewellery. When they got back to the house he allegedly slapped and kicked her. She left to join Fung in a restaurant. Fung flew into a rage when he heard what had happened and wanted to confront Cheng. She persuaded him to find a place for her in Kowloon. The next morning she moved into the Nathan Hotel, where she shared a room with her mother. Fung took a room of his own. Lai later moved in with him. They agreed to get married in Canton on 3 April.

A few days after she had moved out, Lai met Cheng in the Grill Room of the Hongkong Hotel to hand over the rest of the jewellery he had given her. He refused to accept it and said he would take her back if she stopped going out with Fung. She asked if Cheng would let her and Fung live in peace. Cheng allegedly replied, 'No. I will spend all my money to prevent you two from living happily.' Left with no money of her own, Lai was reduced to borrowing from her amah, Lau So, until her father sent funds from Shanghai.

Two weeks after the breakup, Cheng met Edward Zimmern at a game of billiards and the two went to the races together. Zimmern was from a well-connected Eurasian family and knew Cheng's elder brother. He was the youngest son, born posthumously, of Andrew Zimmern (Shi Bing-kwong), chief clerk of the law firm Wilkinson & Grist. An elder brother, George She, was training for the Bar in England. The twenty-six-year-old Edward, however, was a drifter who had spent several years in Shanghai in one lowly job after another before returning penniless to Hong Kong. After dinner and drinks he asked Cheng for a job. Cheng took him on as his bodyguard for $40 a month. 'I have many enemies,' he said. 'You must follow me where I go. What I eat you eat.' Already sensing Zimmern was a blabbermouth, he told him to keep his eyes open and his mouth shut.

Zimmern had never heard of Lai Ming-fai but had known George Fung for several years. According to his testimony, late one night at the Chui Hang Club in Shek Tong Tsui, Cheng told him of his hatred of Fung, who had not only taken away his lover but also owed him money. Cheng wanted to teach him a lesson. One night, as they were leaving the club, Cheng, in tears, asked Zimmern to get him a knife so he could go to the Nathan Hotel and 'have it out with Fung'. When Zimmern asked how he knew they were in the Nathan Hotel, Cheng said he had two men shadowing them. Zimmern talked him out of going. But a few days later, on Sunday 20 March, at Cheng's request, he arranged a dinner in Kowloon and got 'a few boys' together. The plan was to go to Fung's hotel, 'give him a good hiding', and let Cheng slap his face. The dinner, with singsong girls and a good deal of alcohol, did not end until past 1 a.m. They went to the Nathan Hotel and found Fung's room. There was no answer to their knocks on the door. The plan fell apart, and Cheng blamed Zimmern. They retired to another room, ordered a jar of opium, and discussed what to do next. It was now nearly 3 a.m.

One of the 'boys' assembled by Zimmern that night was Sydney Christie, an old friend who had shared lodgings with him in Shanghai; they had overlapped by a year at the Diocesan Boys' School, Christie being younger by five or six years. Christie was also from a Eurasian family, albeit one less well placed than Zimmern's. His father had been a ship's captain. Both parents had died while he was young, and he had been brought up by an adopted uncle. He had taken various jobs during his time in Shanghai. He had also spent four months in prison there for stealing a girl's ring, although on another occasion he had been commended for helping arrest an armed robber. After returning to Hong Kong, he worked as a motor mechanic in Tsim Sha Tsui, sleeping at the garage. Cheng now allegedly turned to Christie for help. Sprawled on the hotel bed after a pipe of opium, he asked him how much money he would want to kill Fung: 'If I offer you $10,000 will you do it with a gun?' Christie suggested poison, winking at the startled Zimmern, who was lying next to Cheng. The discussion continued over opium until they left the hotel at 4:30 a.m. and took the Star Ferry back to Hong Kong Island. Cheng was doubtful about using poison, preferring a gun. He had a trusted driver who would drive Christie away after the shooting. 'Should anything happen to you I will have Mr Jenkin retained for you,' he promised. Christie insisted on poison and explained, over breakfast at the Prince's Café, how potassium cyanide would work. Chemistry had been his favourite subject at school.

The three took a room in the Tung Shan Hotel on Connaught Road West to discuss how Christie would go about poisoning Fung. Cheng said they should find out what sentence Christie would receive if caught: he was not yet twenty-one; perhaps he would be spared the death penalty. They drove to Central to find a lawyer, stopping at two chemists on the way to buy a syringe and cyanide, which they said was for photographic work. After parking in Statue Square, Zimmern and Cheng went to the solicitors Lo & Lo in Alexandra House and consulted Zimmern's cousin, M.W. Lo. Zimmern did most of the talking, but Cheng nervously put the question: 'I have a brother who is something of a maniac. He is under age, and in the event of his fighting and killing somebody would that be a capital offence?' Lo said the brother should see a doctor or take a holiday. Being under twenty-one would not save him from hanging, unless he was found insane or the sentence was commuted. He charged them $5 for this advice. They returned to the car, where Christie was waiting. Zimmern told him about Lo's advice. Cheng said he had nothing to fear: 'If you doubt my word, here is $10 for you and Zimmern to consult other lawyers.'

Christie then went with Zimmern to see Edgar Davidson of Hastings, Dennys and Bowley, on the corner of Ice House Street and Des Voeux Road. Zimmern asked whether, if a man killed his enemy in a fight while drunk, or hired a minor to do it, the killing would be manslaughter. After a brief discussion Davidson said, 'Pay my fee and leave my room.' Finally, Christie and Zimmern consulted C.Y. Kwan in his office on Des Voeux Road. They put to him the following hypothetical question: if A's girl has been taken away by B and A kills B would that be manslaughter? Kwan answered 'No'.

Zimmern and Christie were, in fact, hatching a plot of their own. They had no intention of harming Fung, they later testified. Their aim was simply to make money out of Cheng. They planned to forewarn Fung, take him into their confidence, and use him as a 'mock victim'. They would jab him with an empty syringe. Fung would pretend to collapse and would be taken away in full view of Cheng. Believing the poison had worked, he would hand over the promised $10,000, which would be shared between Zimmern, Christie, and Fung. Cheng would not dare go to the police if he found out. Christie had outlined the planned swindle to Zimmern while they were walking to Davidson's office. Ignorant of all this, a couple of days later Cheng tried the cyanide out on a chicken, killing it instantly. He threw the dead bird into a reservoir.

Zimmern did not think Cheng had much confidence in the poison plot. Cheng reminded him he had hired people to shadow Fung. Increasingly he spoke 'with double meaning'. Zimmern was, in consequence, now also doubtful about Christie's plot to fake the murder and swindle Cheng. He decided he wanted nothing to do with it. He told Cheng that there were no prospects in following him around cinemas and gambling clubs and that he intended to go to Canton. On Thursday 24 March he went with Christie to pack clothes at his home on Arbuthnot Road: he planned to leave for Canton the next day in the hope of getting a job through Admiral Chan Chak of the Guangdong Navy, whom he had met at a dinner in Shek Tong Tsui.[4] Zimmern and Christie returned to the Tung Shan Hotel in the afternoon to find Cheng in the room smoking opium. The rest of the day followed a familiar pattern: a film at the New World Theatre; snooker at the South China Athletic Association; dominoes at the Chinese Civil Servants' Club, where Cheng won $148; dinner at Jimmy's Kitchen; and dancing at the Pauline Dancing Academy. Christie left them to spend the evening with a girlfriend in Kowloon.

---

4. Chan Chak was to become an important figure in wartime Hong Kong. As head of a Temporary Joint Liaison Office of All Chinese Organizations in Hong Kong, in December 1941 he averted a Triad uprising by raising money to buy off the Triad leaders, and organized vigilantes to eliminate fifth columnists. His daring escape by boat on the day of the British surrender is recounted in Tim Luard, *Escape from Hong Kong: Admiral Chan Chak's Christmas Day Dash, 1941* (Hong Kong: Hong Kong University Press, 2012).

Throughout the evening Cheng was nervous and agitated. He did not like the film (*A Man's Man,* starring William Haynes) so they left early. He sent back the steak at Jimmy's Kitchen and was curt with the waiter. At about 9 p.m., after a telephone call at the Pauline Dancing Academy, he said he had to return to Village Road to get money to bet with at the Chui Hang Club, despite having in his pocket most of the $148 he had won at dominoes. Cheng drove the Austin with Zimmern sitting beside him, with a friend, Lau Mo-kwong, who had joined them in the afternoon, in the back. When they got to Happy Valley they saw a crowd of people in Shan Kwong Road, near the Yeung Wo Hospital. Cheng said it must be a motor accident and sped past the scene into Village Road, his hands shaking. He went into his house, leaving Zimmern and Lau in the car. When he emerged ten minutes later Zimmern suggested they drive back down Shan Kwong Road to observe two suspicious-looking men who had passed the car. Cheng exclaimed, 'Damn it! Do you want me to walk the road of death!' He reversed the car and drove them back to Central by another route, avoiding the crowd outside the hospital.

Instead of going straight to the Chui Hang Club, Cheng left the car at the family headquarters, the Kwong Hoi Kee, on Queen's Road Central. He sent Lau away, locked the garage door, took Zimmern inside the shop, and peeped through a shutter. By now he was pale and trembling. When Zimmern asked what the matter was, he said, 'Fung is dead.' Asked how he knew, Cheng replied that Lai Ming-fai had rung him up at the house and had sworn vengeance. Cheng grabbed Zimmern by the lapel and warned him to keep his mouth shut. They took a bus to Shek Tong Tsui, arriving at about 10:30 p.m. Cheng won $51 at dominoes. At 4:30 a.m. he told Zimmern to go to Canton, giving him $50 for himself and $10 to pass on to Christie. 'The trouble is that you drink and talk too much,' said Cheng. Zimmern found Christie at the hotel. They had breakfast, and Zimmern boarded the 8 a.m. steamer to Canton. Before doing so he bought a newspaper to see if what Cheng had told him was true.

The newspapers reported that, shortly after 8:30 p.m. the night before, George Fung, 'a popular member of the Chinese younger set', was shot in the back while walking arm-in-arm with Lai Ming-fai on Shan Kwong Road near the corner of Yick Yam Street. Having visited friends who lived nearby, they were on their way to a dinner dance at the King's Restaurant in Central, a smart new venue popular for its Filipino jazz ensemble, Martin's Rhythm Boys. The bullet pierced Fung's heart. Helped by Lai, he staggered to a nearby house and collapsed. Dr Ho Sai-chuen from the Yeung Wo Hospital was passing in his car at the time and had Fung moved to the hospital. Fung died within twenty minutes. Before losing consciousness he told Dr Ho that he did not see the man who shot him. The gunman, dressed in a long coat, had fled, but the police found the gun: they could offer no motive and were pursuing all possible inquiries.[5]

---

5. *SCMP* and *HKDP,* 25 March 1932.

That afternoon Cheng visited Central Police Station with his solicitor, George Hall Brutton, to offer assistance. Two days later, on Sunday 27 March, he met Christie, who asked him 'Did you kill George Fung?' Cheng replied that he did not. He then said he must get Zimmern's corroboration of his movements on the night of the 24th. He wrote these down in English on a piece of paper and asked Christie to memorize them, tear up the note, and go to Canton to find Zimmern. Christie and Zimmern returned on the 31st and were promptly arrested: police officers from Hong Kong had been watching them in Canton. Despite being Hong Kong-born British subjects, they were detained for several weeks under the Deportation Ordinance. This was an example, like the Ho Chi Minh case, then in its closing stages, of how that ordinance was open to abuse.[6]

On Monday 4 April Cheng was asked to attend again at the Central Police Station. He was charged with procuring the murder of George Fung. Brutton suggested bail of $20,000 or $30,000. The magistrate refused,[7] and Cheng was remanded in custody.

Committal Proceedings, 26 April–8 July 1932

Cheng Kwok-yau's relationship with Lai Ming-fai, his hatred towards George Fung, and his offer of $10,000 to have Fung killed were described in sordid detail in the committal proceedings. These took place in Central Magistracy on 25 afternoons spread over ten weeks. The hearings, the longest so far in Hong Kong, were a public sensation. Early on the first day, smartly dressed men and women packed the public seats in the small courtroom where Cheng had appeared on remand. Seeing the crowds outside, staff moved proceedings to the large courtroom, causing a 'wild scramble' for seats and indignation when Europeans were given priority. Although the hearing was to begin at 2:30 p.m., the court was filled by noon. Hundreds of others waited outside.

The proceedings were reported in such minute detail that one of the leading Chinese-language papers, the *Kung Sheung Daily News*, ran out of type and had to use triangles, circles, and other symbols to represent the leading figures. Combined with the blanked-out words and lines in the censored reports of Japanese aggressions in China, these gave

6. Under the Deportation Ordinance (as it stood in 1932) a Hong Kong-born person could be deported if he did not have a certificate of his British birth and a parent who was also a British subject. Zimmern and Christie were not in this category since they were Hong Kong-born British subjects, with fathers who were British subjects. Nor were they guilty of any of the offences (such as champerty and maintenance, and offences relating to public documents) for which a British subject could be deported. The only provision that might conceivably apply to them was section 4(1)(e), which enabled the Governor in Council to deport a British subject acting in a manner 'prejudicial to public safety, or to the defence, peace or security' of the King's dominions. Amendments in 1931 had increased the detention period prior to a decision on deportation from six days, renewable for periods of four days, to fourteen and seven days respectively.
7. A magistrate's power to grant bail in murder cases had in any case been abolished in Hong Kong in 1890.

the papers a strangely moth-eaten appearance.[8] The papers devoted much space to Lai Ming-fai's appearance and dress – a blue and white polka-dotted cheongsam on the first day, a black cheongsam on the second. A gossipy pamphlet, summarizing the news for readers in Shanghai and Beijing, revealed that her luggage at the Nathan Hotel included over forty pairs of shoes.[9] Lai insisted on giving evidence in Shanghainese, despite being fluent in Cantonese. Cheng, who spoke Cantonese and a little English, heard her evidence through two interpreters – one rendering Shanghainese into English, the other English into Cantonese. Brutton asked if she could be questioned in Cantonese. She refused, and the magistrate had no power to compel her to do so.[10]

The magistrate was Edward Wynne Jones, a cadet officer without legal training. Another cadet, Roger Lindsell, prosecuted. Lindsell had been called to the Bar in England in 1930 after studying law on leave and while a magistrate in Hong Kong. On his return he acted as Puisne Judge before being appointed Public Prosecutor in March 1932, with an office in Central Police Station. The post was created in 1927 to take the strain off the Attorney General. Its first incumbent was Henry Somerset Fitzroy, a barrister with previous practice in Hong Kong who had returned to private practice. Lawyers viewed 'with apprehension' the appointment as his successor of a cadet officer who had never been 'in active legal practice'.[11] The Cheng case was Lindsell's first murder prosecution.

The charge against Cheng was 'counselling, procuring and commanding a certain person unknown to commit a felony, to wit, to kill and murder George Fung'. Lindsell's opening speech – so detailed that Cheng's interpreter had difficulty keeping up – dwelt on the 'eternal triangle' between Cheng, Lai, and Fung, and the poison plot of Christie and Zimmern: the aim was to show that Cheng had both a motive and an intention to kill Fung. Direct evidence of the murder itself, however, was slender. Lai had seen a man follow her and Fung shortly before the murder; his hat was pulled down and she did not see his face. A

8. Under emergency regulations in force since 1925, editors of Chinese-language newspapers were required, prior to publication, to submit all news stories to the Secretariat for Chinese Affairs, where censors deleted text they deemed detrimental to Britain's foreign relations or to the colonial government generally. The censors were especially active at this time of Japan's aggression towards China: one of the leading newspapers, the *Kung Sheung Daily News*, was suppressed for two months in late 1931 for publishing an article on Manchuria that had been disallowed by the censors. Other newspapers were suppressed in 1932. ExCo Minutes, 19 November 1931, CO 131/84, 212; *HKGG*, 29 October 1931; *SCMP*, 31 October 1931; Michael Ng, *Political Censorship in British Hong Kong* (Cambridge: Cambridge University Press, 2022), Chapter 2.

9. Huang Jingliang, *The Story of the Tragic Death of Lai Ming-fai's Lover* (Hong Kong: Fuji hezuoshe, 1932) [黃景量，黎明暉愛侶慘死記（香港：福記合作社, 1932）], 70. Padded with biographical information and tittle-tattle, the account covers the proceedings only up to the seventh day.

10. Detailed reports are in *SCMP*, *HKDP*, *KSDN*, and *WTYP*, 27 and 30 April, 18, 20, 21, 27, 28, and 31 May, 1, 3, 7, 8, 10, 14, 21–24, and 28–30 June, and 1, 5, 7, and 9 July 1932. The *Kung Sheung* and *Wa Tsz Yat Po* used the same agency for their reports. The *South China Morning Post* had acquired the *Hongkong Telegraph* in 1916: their reports are practically identical, although the editorial comment is different.

11. *HKH*, 22 October 1931.

hawker had heard the shot and the footsteps of someone running behind his stall towards a nearby lane. As the charge indicated, the prosecution had no idea who had pulled the trigger or what his connection, if any, was with Cheng. Despite going to the police shortly after the murder, Cheng had told them nothing about the case.

The hearings dragged on. Lindsell called twenty-nine witnesses but failed to show any link between Cheng and the unknown gunman. There was, however, plenty to entertain the throngs of spectators. Zimmern, clean-cut in a smart jacket and flashy tie, testifying for the prosecution, gave an elaborate account of his three weeks as bodyguard to 'Mr Cheng'. Christie supplemented his account of the poison plot. Their stories were corroborated by many minor witnesses – the hotel room boys, the dispensary staff, the lawyers, and Cheng's other companions. Cross-examination by Cheng's solicitor, Brutton, failed to reveal any glaring discrepancies. It did, however, underline the inescapable fact that the plot had no direct link with the murder of Fung. By June the case was floundering. Busy with other cases, the magistrate was getting impatient. Spectators melted away. Then, on 23 June, the eighteenth day, after a series of fruitless exchanges with room boys about the etiquette of closing hotel room doors, Lindsell said he might wish to call evidence beyond that which he had outlined in his opening speech weeks earlier.

The police had made a breakthrough. Earlier that week a German businessman, Alwin Goeke, was being driven in his Studebaker when police stopped his car and arrested his chauffeur. Rumours spread that the arrest had something to do with the Village Road Murder; that three other persons had been arrested in Hong Kong, and one in Shanghai. The police took the chauffeur to Goeke's house in Pok Fu Lam, where they unscrewed the padlocked door of his quarters. In a basket hanging from the wall they found an automatic pistol and ammunition. The chauffeur, Chui Yung-sham, was charged with unlawful possession of arms and committed for trial. While in custody he made 'a very important statement' about the Village Road Murder.[12] That same week, police in Shanghai arrested the man they suspected of having shot George Fung.

On Monday 27 June, day nineteen of the committal hearings, the prosecution called witness number thirty-three, the chauffeur Chui Yung-sham. His evidence was so great a departure from the increasingly stale story of the poison plot that Lindsell presented a long supplement to his opening speech – one introducing a new cast of characters and making no mention of Zimmern, Christie, or the other members of Cheng's entourage. Lindsell deleted the words 'person unknown' in the charge against Cheng and inserted the name of the man arrested in Shanghai: Wong Nam-heung,[13] a Shanghainese who had worked in Hong Kong as a chauffeur for some years. After his arrest in Shanghai he was taken before

---

12. *SCMP*, 27 June 1932.

13. 黃楠香, 黃能香 or 黃能相, variously romanized in reports as Wang (or Wong) Neng-siang, Wang Nien-siang, and, in Cantonese, Wong Nam-sheung.

the First Special District Court, where the judge remanded the case to allow the Hong Kong police to produce evidence. The plan, said Lindsell, was to have Wong brought to Hong Kong for trial. However, there was no treaty allowing the extradition of Chinese nationals to Hong Kong, and the courts of the Nationalist government were vigilant in protecting their jurisdiction. Moreover, the new Chinese Criminal Code empowered these courts to try murders and other serious crimes committed by Chinese nationals outside the territory of the Republic of China.[14] The Shanghai court refused extradition and instructed the Hong Kong police representatives to bring their charge against Wong in Shanghai.[15]

Chui Yung-sham had fainted when the police found the gun in his quarters. It therefore came as a relief when, at Central Police Station, Chief Detective Inspector Reynolds informed him he would perhaps receive a pardon if he told the whole truth about the murder. Similar offers had been made to Zimmern and Christie, but no formal arrangements were made at this stage. Brutton complained that the offers amounted to inducements 'to give evidence in the way the Crown hoped it would be given'.

The thirty-eight-year-old Chui gave his account of the plot in a matter-of-fact manner. He knew Cheng's driver, Lau Hing, who, like Wong Nam-heung, was also from Shanghai. They had met at Lau's request on 23 February, two days after Lai's breakup with Cheng, in the Wan Chai flat of another Shanghainese, Tong Ching-kwai, a driver for the Hongkong Hotel. After more meetings in cafes and opium divans, Chui found the assassin, Wong Nam-heung, through a mutual acquaintance known as 'Blind Monk'. Using expenses paid out by Lau, Chui and Wong took a room in a hotel opposite the Nathan Hotel and watched Fung's movements. They rented a cubicle (a partitioned room) at 17 Man Chung Fong in Happy Valley, near Cheng's house, a short distance from the house of Chan Wing-yung at 14 Shan Kwong Road, where Fung and Lai were frequent visitors. Chui placed in the cubicle a gun – an old Spanish automatic he had bought some years earlier while serving in a warlord army; it was worn out and prone to jamming. On 18 March, Chui, Wong, and Tong lay in wait on Shan Kwong Road while Fung and Lai left No. 14 and got into a car. Wong was expected to shoot Fung at this point, but the gun jammed when he pulled the trigger. Unaware of what had happened, Fung and Lai got into the car and drove off.

According to Chui, it was the failure of this attempt that prompted Cheng to offer the $10,000 to Christie and Zimmern to kill Fung. But the 'quartette' of motor-drivers (as the press now called them) had not given up. Fearing Wong's nerve was failing, Chui found a second gunman, a Cantonese known only as Kwan, and replaced the old gun with a newer one, a German automatic. On the evening of 24 March they made a second attempt. As Fung and Lai emerged from 14 Shan Kwong Road, Wong and Kwan followed them on foot. Chui watched from a taxi parked further up Shan Kwong Road. He saw a flash and heard a

14. 中華民國刑法 [Criminal Code of the Republic of China] (1928), article 7.
15. *SCMP*, 24 and 26 June and 14 and 26 July 1932.

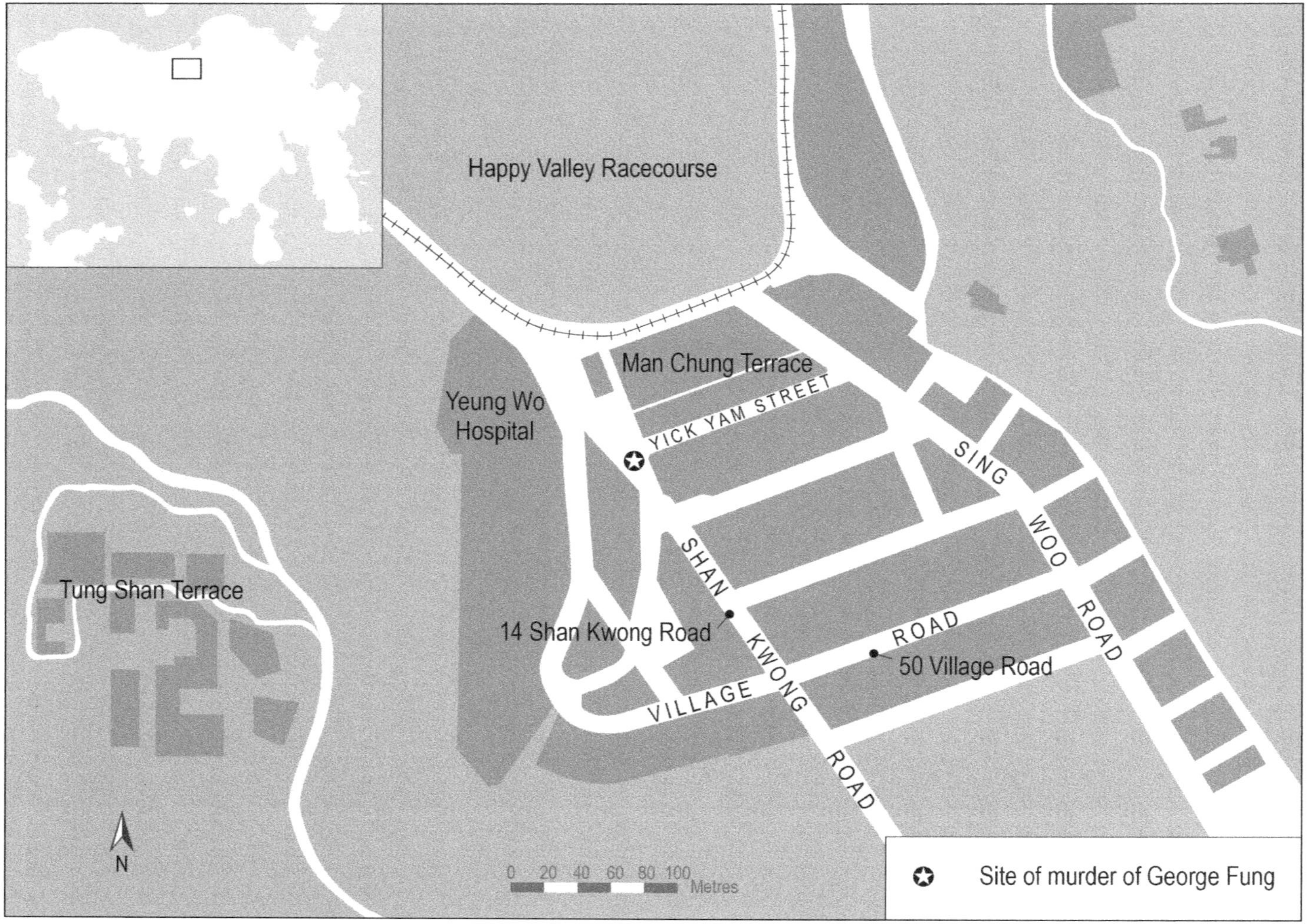

Map 6: The Village Road Murder, 1932

shot and a scream. He told the driver to drive him around the neighbourhood. Wong and Kwan walked briskly to No. 17 Man Chung Fong. Lau let them in through the back. Kwan left by the front door and boarded a tram. Chui stopped the taxi and picked up Wong and Tong. In the same taxi, he took Tong to his flat in Wan Chai and Wong to the Star Ferry. Chui returned to his quarters at Pok Fu Lam.

Two days after the murder, on 26 March, Chui went to Tong's flat to meet Lau Hing, Cheng's chauffeur. Lau handed him four $500 notes. After changing them for smaller notes, Chui paid $500 to Wong (or possibly $300, according to a note on the sums kept by Chui), $250 to Tong (as a loan), and $120 to Kwan. The $500 for Wong was because he was the one who had killed Fung, Chui told the court. After expenses, the remaining $1,000 or so went into Chui's pocket. His possession of such a large sum reached the ears of the police and led to his arrest, along with his wife and Tong.

The new evidence came as a complete surprise to Brutton. 'I can get no information at all from my client: he knows none of these men, never seen them,' he said. He received permission to postpone his cross-examination of Chui, so he could conduct 'the vast amount of investigations' Chui's evidence now 'entailed on the defence'. In the event, he cross-examined neither Chui nor any of the other new witnesses: Tong Ching-kwai, who lent his flat to the conspirators; the moneychanger who changed the $500 notes; the tailor who sublet the cubicle at Man Chung Fong; the driver of the taxi hired by Chui on the night of the murder; and others. They all corroborated Chui's account. Yet none of the evidence directly implicated Cheng himself. Brutton submitted there was no case to go before a jury. The magistrate, Wynne Jones, agreed that the evidence was scattered – 'a bit here and a bit there and a bit somewhere else' – but said he only had to be satisfied there was a connecting thread joining the evidence in such a way as to form a prima facie case. He had found such a thread and therefore proposed to commit Cheng for trial.

Asked under caution if he wished to make any statement, Cheng replied that his solicitor would speak on his behalf. Brutton reserved his defence. Wynne Jones then committed Cheng for trial in the Supreme Court.

Judges and the decline in conviction rates

The judge in Cheng's trial was Sir Joseph Kemp, formerly Attorney General, now Chief Justice. Kemp had joined the government as a cadet in 1898 and had spent his entire career in Hong Kong. During their earlier quarrels with Chief Justice Piggott (1905–1912) governors had promoted the idea of appointing legally trained cadets to the Supreme Court. Sir Matthew Nathan suggested that one judge should be a cadet and the other a former colonial attorney general. His successor, Sir Frederick Lugard, proposed a 'legal class' of cadets, trained as barristers and given priority in judicial positions. Wishing to appoint 'real lawyers', the Colonial Office dismissed the idea as 'impractical and absurd'.[16] But Nathan's dual system was followed, if only by default, up to the late 1930s.[17] The cadets were called to the Bar while on leave, some with exemptions from the full number of terms; they did not serve pupillage, or practise privately, a prerequisite for judicial office in England.[18] Kemp's term as Chief Justice (1930–1933) marked the apogee of this policy. By 1932 the whole judiciary – two judges and four magistrates – consisted of cadets. Kemp himself was a cadet *and* an ex-Attorney General. Neither he nor the Puisne Judge, John Wood, had worked outside Hong Kong or in private practice; nor had any of the magistrates.

The practice of appointing judges from the civil service had long since drawn criticism from the legal profession that the bench was being filled by 'book-made' lawyers with scant experience of advocacy.[19] The policy nevertheless helped absorb a surfeit of cadets at a time when legislators were calling for them to be replaced by professionals in some departments.[20] The mix of ex-attorneys general and legally qualified cadets produced judges who tended to see eye to eye with the executive on matters crucial to British interests. They were sometimes helpful to the prosecution in criminal trials where trade and British prestige were at stake, notably in the piracy trials of the 1920s,[21] and in Leung Wo's case (Chapter 8). There were occasional lapses. In 1931, for example, cadet judges were persuaded into ruling that piracy was not piracy if no goods were taken: the decision alarmed shipowners

16. Nathan to Lyttelton, 10 December 1904, CO 129/324, 442–444; Lugard to Harcourt, 20 April 1911, CO 129/376, 423–461. The system in British India went further: a large proportion of the judiciary, including in the higher courts, was composed of 'Civilians' – judges without formal legal training who were members of the Indian Civil Service: Abhinav Chandrachud, *An Independent, Colonial Judiciary: A History of the Bombay High Court During the British Raj, 1862–1947* (New Delhi: Oxford University Press, 2015), 222–231.
17. From 1939, when magistrates were placed under the general disciplinary control of the Chief Justice (rather than the executive government), the cadet magistrates were replaced with barristers from within Hong Kong or from the Colonial Legal Service. Among the first was Harold Sheldon KC (1940), one of the prosecutors in Cheng Kwok-yau's trial. 'Police Magistrates: Placing Under Chief Justice' (1939), CO 129/581/12; 'Legal Department Vacancies: Magistrates and Crown Counsel' (1939), CO 129/582/4.
18. Pupillage was mandatory for barristers to enter practice from 1959 in England and 1968 in Hong Kong.
19. May to Long, 8 February 1918, CO 129/447, 121–188; Munn, 'Margins of justice in colonial Hong Kong'.
20. *HKH*, 10 February 1930, 22 October 1931, and 6 October 1932.
21. The two biggest piracy cases of these years, both tried in 1927, were the *Sunning* and *Irene* piracies (eight and seven hanged respectively). In both cases problems of identification were complicated by the pirates' disguising themselves as passengers. The *Sunning* pirates were captured by the crew after a fight in which eleven pirates were killed. The *Irene* was sunk by a British submarine when it refused to obey an order to stop: the crew and most passengers were saved. Ruling that it was an 'act of state', Gollan dismissed a claim from its owners, the China Merchants Steam Navigation Co., for over half a million dollars in damages against the submarine's captain. *SCMP*, 19–28 January and 22–24 November 1927; 'China – Piracy: Legal Proceedings arising out of case of S.S. "Irene"' (1929), CO 129/515/1; *HKT*, 16–31 January and 1–9 February 1929.

and prompted a reference by the government to the Privy Council, which advised that judges should exercise 'a little common sense' when interpreting international law.[22]

Yet, whether they were cadets or ex-attorneys general, the judges of these years were certainly not 'prosecution-minded' when trying criminal cases in which the interests of the colony were not directly at risk. This was especially true of murders: the 1920s saw a steady decline in the conviction rate; by the end of the decade it had fallen from above 60 per cent to below 50 per cent. In 1931 only one of nine persons tried for murder was convicted: a Filipino found guilty but insane after killing a European on a British ship.[23] Declining conviction rates reflected a more stringent approach to evidence by judges, greater sympathy towards defendants in their summing up, and a readiness to direct juries to acquit where the evidence was so defective as to be a waste of the court's time. This was particularly apparent under Chief Justice Sir Henry Gollan 1924–1930. A protégé of Frederick Lugard in Africa, Gollan had served as Attorney General or Chief Justice in four colonies. By the time he arrived in Hong Kong he had a strong reputation as judge, debater, and law draftsman. His rigorous handling of trials set the tone for other judges.

Other factors also contributed to low conviction rates. Although still small, the legal community was gaining critical mass and a greater sense of professionalism. New generations were returning with fresh ideas from the universities and Inns of Court. Some had trained with the best lawyers in England and had observed high standards of advocacy and cross-examination in the Old Bailey. Many also had roots in Hong Kong and were familiar with its customs and languages. Among those active in criminal cases were Leo D'Almada e

22. Twelve men were tried for a piracy on the high seas off Pedro Blanco (near the location of the *Caesar* and *Carl* piracies: see Chapter 3). The men, in two junks, chased a cargo junk and fired shots, but were captured and handed over to the Royal Navy before they could board. The jury found them guilty, but J.R. Wood, Acting Chief Justice, referred legal points raised by Lo Hin-shing, counsel for the defence, to the Full Court. Lo's argument was that no one could be convicted of piracy where no *actual* robbery had taken place. His authority was the 1873 Privy Council decision in the *Kwok A-Sing* case, which had affirmed an old definition that 'piracy is only a sea term for robbery'. Moreover, neither case law nor statute law offered support for convicting a non-British national of piracy where no robbery was involved. On this reasoning, the Full Court (Wood and Lindsell) acquitted the men. The Law Officers in London were clear that the Supreme Court *did* have jurisdiction, and that a mere attempt to rob also constituted piracy. Since the acquittal could not be reversed, the Secretary of State sought an interpretation from the Privy Council on the validity of the Full Court's decision for future reference. The Judicial Committee's report, delivered by the Lord Chancellor, Viscount Sankey, pointed out the absurdity of supposing that armed men sailing the seas could, hypothetically, kill everyone on board a ship without committing piracy unless they stole something. *R v Chung Tam Kwong and 12 Others* (1931–32) 25 HKLR 31. *In the matter of a Reference under the Judicial Committee Act, 1833, in the matter of* Piracy jure gentium JCPC [1934] UKPC 54 (26 July 1934); 'Law of Piracy', CO 129/534/9 (1931), CO 129/541/1 (1932) and CO 129/543/4 (1933).
23. A returning student on the *Empress of Russia*, en route from California to Manila, shot two men, one of whom died. He refused to see the lawyer assigned to him and insisted on pleading guilty: Kemp directed that a plea of not guilty be entered. After the verdict of guilty but insane, Kemp ordered that he be detained pending the King's pleasure. *SCMP*, 7 May 1931.

Castro Jr, William Thomas Tam, and Lo Hin-shing. Learning from veterans such as Francis Jenkin and George Hall Brutton, they took care in preparing cases and addressing juries. For their part, juries were now more diverse, with a large sprinkling of Chinese, Portuguese, Eurasians, and other Asians. Some juries participated actively in trials and spoke up if they felt their time was being wasted by half-baked prosecutions.

The greatest single factor in the low conviction rates, however, was the poor quality of evidence. Many cases collapsed when counsel exposed confessions that had been induced or coerced, or obtained without caution. Blunders in identity parades, errors in handling exhibits, and contradictions in police testimony continued to stymie prosecutions. Steps were taken to improve the efficiency of the force during these years. A criminal investigation department was formed in 1922. Training improved. Powers of arrest and search were increased. Officers were incentivized with rewards and medals. The force grew by 50 per cent between 1922 and 1932 to over 2,000 men, supplemented by the District Watch, private guards, and the Police Reserve. Photography was now used at scenes of crime. Experts were able to distinguish human from other animal blood. Fingerprinting was introduced as early as 1904, shortly after Scotland Yard began using it to detect crime. Yet, in contrast to their use for detection by the Shanghai police, fingerprints in early twentieth-century Hong Kong were used mainly for identifying repeat offenders, deportees, and licensed hawkers.[24] After the strikes of the 1920s, and growing agitation against Japanese aggressions in China, the stress was on political policing and on the many new duties imposed on the police, from censoring films to licensing motorcars. The multinational force was as unwieldy as ever: Weihaiwei and Russian recruits were now added to the European, Cantonese, and Indian contingents.[25]

---

24. A work by a police interpreter Ng Ping-u, *The Art of Fingerprinting* [伍冰壺, 指紋法] (Hong Kong, 1919) stresses the uses of fingerprints in identifying recidivists but says little about their use in detecting crime. Interviewed in 1949, another fingerprint expert, Hugh Morgan, recalled the first use of fingerprints in a criminal trial in a case in 1937, in which a Chinese cabin-boy shot a British captain on board a Chinese customs cruiser in Hong Kong waters – a rare criminal case heard on appeal by the Privy Council, because of a dispute over jurisdiction (see page 34, note 133). In fact, fingerprints were used earlier, in detecting a couple of burglaries and a robbery in the late 1920s. They were also used in two murder cases in 1929 and 1930 to identify victims who had previously been convicted or deported. When asked by Francis Jenkin whether any search had been made for fingerprints in a murder case in 1930, in which three men were put on trial, the officer in charge of the preliminary investigation, Inspector Fallon, replied, 'I do not know anything about fingerprints and there were no vessels for us to take impressions with.' In this case, three men, identified by a police informer in an irregular identity parade, were accused of murdering a Buddhist priest. The only material witness was a thirteen-year-old servant girl, whom even the Chief Detective Inspector in charge of the investigation described as 'a wholly unreliable witness'. After Jenkin had concluded his opening speech for the defence, the jury asked the judge (Kemp) to stop the trial. They then returned a verdict of not guilty. *SCMP*, 14 February 1927, 9 September 1929, 6–8, 13, and 30 May and 27 July 1930, and 12 January 1949.
25. The Weihaiwei police were recruited from the British leased territory of Weihaiwai in Shandong. The Russians, émigrés from the Revolution and Civil War, were employed mainly as anti-piracy guards on ships.

If conviction rates were low for murders, the rate of known murder cases reaching the Supreme Court was even lower: it dipped to 23 per cent in 1932, when thirty murders reported to the police resulted in only seven persons brought to trial: five were convicted, an unusually high conviction rate. The Police Report for 1932 noted that a trial in May that year had produced the first murder convictions since 1929:[26] three men were convicted and hanged for the murder of a student on the hillside near the Peak before sending a $10,000 ransom demand to his family. Lasting ten days, the Victoria Gap Murder trial was Hong Kong's longest murder trial so far. The judge, John Wood, commended the new head of criminal investigation, A.N. Reynolds, and the student's uncle, Tsang Koon-ching, a solicitor's clerk, for their work in bringing the case to trial.[27]

In the 1929 case alluded to in the Police Report, Yim Yat-hong, a fifty-five-year-old unemployed sandalwood worker, attacked men with a chopper while they were sleeping in guild premises, killing one of them. He pleaded guilty and refused to change his plea, despite efforts to get him to do so by his barrister, William Thomas Tam, by his solicitor, Frank Hingsum Kwok, and by the judge, Sir Henry Gollan. The gaol's medical officer had found no sign of insanity, even though Yim had tried to gouge the eyes of a warder with a chopstick. Usually in a murder case the judge changed a guilty plea to not guilty in case the verdict was manslaughter or guilty but insane. Gollan could easily have done this. But the prosecutor, Henry Somerset Fitzroy, cited a recent case in England in which the Court of Criminal Appeal had declined to intervene when a judge had accepted a guilty plea. Gollan declared he felt bound by this. 'Visibly moved', he sentenced Yim to death. Yim interrupted twice, saying, 'Never mind, I don't mind dying.' He was hanged on 22 October 1929. A year later the law was changed to allow judges to reject guilty pleas in capital cases.[28] One of the accused in the Victoria Gap Murder was the first to benefit: Wood changed his guilty plea to not guilty. After a trial in which he was defended by Fitzroy (now in private practice), he was acquitted. He was later convicted of demanding money with menaces through the ransom note and sentenced to life imprisonment.[29]

26. The report does not take into account a piracy case in 1930 in which two men were convicted of murder and hanged. Nor does it mention six insanity cases in this period (one unfit to plead; five guilty but insane, including the Filipino case mentioned above). One of these was the murder of five staff of the Hung On Bank while they were asleep in the bank building by a former employee: he had been dismissed years earlier but had been invited to stay for a few nights. The insanity verdict, and a misunderstanding about Kemp's order for him to be detained 'until His Majesty's Pleasure is known', prompted the Bank to petition the Secretary for Chinese Affairs for the man to be tried again. The petition suggested he had a grievance about his dismissal; it asked why, if the culprit was insane, he had singled out the sons of the bank's owners as his victims while leaving other employees unharmed. *SCMP*, 16–18 and 23 July 1930; *HKDP*, 23 July 1930.
27. *SCMP*, 3–19 May and 24–27 May 1932.
28. The amendment drew on a similar provision in Ceylon. The English case was *R v Clarke* (1929) 21 Crim App Rep 81. *SCMP* and *CM*, 20 September 1929; *R v Yim Yat Hong* (1929–30) 24 HKLR 8(1); *HKH*, 2 October 1930; Ordinance No. 17 of 1930.
29. *SCMP*, 26–28 April and 19 May 1932.

R v Cheng Kwok-yau
Counselling, procuring, and commanding murder, 8–24 August 1932

Dressed in a suit and tie, Cheng Kwok-yau shook his head and pleaded not guilty when the interpreter, Ng Chak-wing, translated the charge. The charge now alleged that

> Cheng Kwok-yau, *alias* Cheng Wan, on divers dates between the 23rd day of February 1932 and the 24th day of March 1932 (both dates inclusive) in this Colony, through one Lau Hing, did counsel, procure and command Chui Yung-sham and Wong Nam-sheung to do and commit a certain felony, by them committed on the 24th day of March 1932, at Wongneichung in this colony, that is to say, to murder Fung Him, *alias* George Fung.

Cheng was tried in a special criminal session by a special jury, the first in a capital trial since the Praya Murder of 1922. The foreman was Geoffrey Archbutt JP, manager of the Union Insurance Society of Canton. The others were leading businessmen, three of them also justices of the peace.[30] This was *par excellence* a 'taipan jury', as special juries came to be described. The Attorney General, Chaloner Grenville Alabaster OBE, KC, appointed from the private Bar in succession to Kemp, attended court on the first day. His purpose was not to prosecute but to move for the admission of Hong Kong's first 'lady barrister', Mrs Lo Soon Kim Teo.[31] The prosecution was jointly conducted by Harold Sheldon, a barrister in private practice in Hong Kong since 1925, and the Public Prosecutor, Roger Lindsell.

Cheng was represented by three barristers: Eldon Potter KC, JP, Francis Jenkin CBE, KC, JP, and Richard Chuan Ho Lim BA. Born in Singapore, Lim had studied at the University of Hong Kong, Middle Temple, and the Geneva School for International Studies; he was admitted to practise in 1931. Potter, the oldest barrister in Hong Kong, had practised since 1907. He and Jenkin had been contemporaries at Gray's Inn and were close friends. Jenkin was now at the peak of his reputation, having represented Ho Chi Minh in 1931 and taken silk the same year. Potter and Jenkin were much in demand, appearing often on opposite sides and sometimes together; they had both successfully represented Lim Ah Chan, Cheng's grandmother, in the Penang Millionaire Will case; Brutton, who, under special legislation, had appeared as counsel for her opponent, was now the instructing solicitor in Cheng's case. Never before in Hong Kong had a defendant in a murder trial been represented by three counsel.

---

30. The six other jurors were David Biggar (American), manager, The Chase Bank; Johan Heinrich Jessen (Danish), partner, Jebsen & Co.; Philip Cassidy JP (British), partner, John D. Hutchison & Co.; Kan Tong-po (Chinese), chief manager of the Bank of East Asia; Kenneth Greig JP (British), manager, Tai Koo Dockyard & Engineering Co. Ltd; Marcus Johnson JP (British), partner, Mackinnon, Mackenzie & Co, and later, in 1936, a member of the Legislative Council.
31. In the event, Mrs Lo, who had practised with great success in the Straits Settlements, did not appear in any case in Hong Kong. *SCMP*, 9, 10, and 17 August 1932.

The trial made other records. Lasting ten full days and two half-days, it was Hong Kong's longest murder trial so far. 'Unprecedented crowds' gathered outside the Law Courts hoping to see the trial, some having waited since the early hours. Many were fashionably dressed Chinese women. When the doors opened shortly before 9 a.m. hundreds scrambled for seats. Others clustered around the entrances, where police struggled to stop them rushing into the courtroom. It was, said the *Hongkong Telegraph*, 'one of the most sensational murder cases in the history of the Colony'.

The new evidence had shifted the focus from the hare-brained poison plot of Christie and Zimmern to the conspiracy with the four chauffeurs. Yet the case against Cheng was still incomplete. Awaiting trial in Shanghai, the alleged gunman, Wong Nam-heung, was out of reach. Cheng's alleged agent in the murder, his chauffeur Lau Hing, had fled to the country near Shanghai, according to his wife, Lau So, who was also Lai Ming-fai's amah. Lau So too had vanished after testifying at the Magistracy. Chui's eleventh-hour revelations had made the poison plot a sideshow. Yet the prosecution gave it as much prominence as it had in committal proceedings. This was necessary, said Lindsell in his opening speech, to show Cheng's 'deliberate desire and intention to get George Fung put out of the way'. The poison plot was one of three classes of evidence: Lai would attest to motive and the actual murder; Zimmern and Christie would show active intention; Chui and others would show Cheng's complicity in the plot with Lau Hing.

The prosecution was therefore practically a repeat of the committal proceedings. Most of the same witnesses, called in roughly the same order, gave the same evidence in chief, taking up a similar amount of time. This time, however, they were subject to cross-examination, with the defence, as usual, seeking out discrepancies between their depositions and their evidence at trial. The newspapers, in lurid headlines, reported their evidence as if it was all new. Some advertised the hearings in advance with bold headlines. The reports in the main newspapers were almost verbatim, extending on some days to two or three pages.[32] Although interest sagged when minor witnesses appeared, spectators continued to attend in droves. They watched in rapt attention as Lai Ming-fai wept over a photograph of George Fung. They were 'breathless' when Zimmern gave his 'startling evidence'. They laughed at his flippant replies to Jenkin and at his account of how Cheng had thrown the poisoned chicken into a reservoir to prevent anyone from eating it. Only Cheng remained 'utterly without expression, preserving a stolid calm'.

There was 'a stir in the Court' when Jenkin began what the press described as his 'brilliant' and 'gruelling' cross-examination of Zimmern, in English. Gruelling it may have been, but there were no breakthroughs. Jenkin called Zimmern a rogue, a swindler,

32. The account here draws on *SCMP*, *HKDP*, and *CM*, 8–32 August and 1–16 September 1932; and Judge's Notes of the Trial and Full Court Hearing, CO 129/541/11.

a blackmailer. But Lindsell had already said as much in his depiction of Zimmern as 'the black sheep of a well-known Hongkong family' when explaining the tainted nature of his evidence. Zimmern, who had been unwell, was invited by Kemp to take a seat. His terse and evasive replies exasperated Jenkin. 'Don't try to tell me what questions to ask,' Jenkin barked. When Jenkin declared the poison plot to be 'purely imaginary', Zimmern offered to swear to it by cutting off a cock's head, an old Chinese method of making an oath. Jenkin put it to him that the plan to take a gang of 'boys' to beat up Fung after the boozy dinner in Kowloon was 'engineered by you and entirely at your suggestion'.

Zimmern — That is entirely false.

Jenkin — That you and Christie had worked the whole thing out in that room [at the Nathan Hotel]?

Zimmern — That is an allegation.

Jenkin — That you wanted to get Cheng involved in an assault on Fung?

Zimmern — No.

Jenkin — I put it to you that Cheng was at last persuaded into coming to this dinner, and into crossing to the Hotel, but only on the basis that nothing more was to happen than the slapping of Fung's face.

Zimmern — Not so.

Jenkin — Did you tell this to the learned Magistrate: 'Cheng said all he wanted us to do was to get hold of Fung so that he (Cheng) could slap Fung's face?'

Zimmern — Yes, that is so.

Jenkin — I put it to you that Cheng was reluctant to come to the dinner and was late and finally had to be telephoned?

Zimmern — He was playing snooker.

Jenkin — You were host at the dinner?

Zimmern — Yes, at Cheng's permission.

Jenkin — And you had your girl there?

Zimmern — Not my girl, a public girl.

Jenkin — Well, a girl?

Zimmern — I'm not a Solomon. How could I have eight girls (Laughter).[33]

Christie was equally unyielding, insisting that Cheng wanted Fung dead. When Jenkin declared his account of the discussions with Cheng to be false, Christie was adamant:

---

33. *CM*, 15 August 1932.

Christie — That is an allegation and I would like you to prove I am lying.

Jenkin — I think I have done it.

Christie — And I think you have not.[34]

Potter and Jenkin had tried to have Zimmern's and Christie's evidence excluded on the ground that it had no connection with a murder 'by different people at a different time and under an entirely different set of circumstances'. Sheldon replied that it showed motive, means and opportunity, as well as preparations by Cheng to murder Fung. Arguments over the admissibility of evidence took up a whole afternoon with the jury absent. Kemp adjourned the trial for a day to think it over. When the court resumed he allowed the evidence to be adduced but agreed to a request from Potter to reserve the question of its admissibility for the Full Court at the end of the trial.

Another difficulty arose with the conditional pardons offered to Zimmern and Christie. This came up after Zimmern had completed his two days of evidence. Sheldon then tendered the Attorney General's consent to a conditional pardon and asked the court to grant it. Kemp, however, ruled that section 104 of the Criminal Procedure Ordinance required such pardons to be granted *before* evidence was given. Potter objected to any conditional pardon, saying the practice was unprecedented. 'These men have been earning their pardons throughout – first in the Police Court and now here,' he complained. Kemp said he had never known section 104 to have been used before.[35] He refused the pardon for Zimmern, but granted one to Christie before he gave evidence.

Chui Yung-sham also received a conditional pardon before giving evidence. He was now serving a year's imprisonment after pleading guilty to illegal arms possession.[36] 'Phlegmatic, and without a trace of emotion in his face,' according to the *South China Morning Post*, he was at times 'insolent, but for the most part sullen' during his long cross-examination. Again, Jenkin began with invective. 'The prosecuting counsel, in opening his case, described you as a dangerous and worthless scoundrel,' he said to Chui through the interpreter.

34. *SCMP*, 17 August 1932.

35. Turning Queen's evidence had a long history in England and had been allowed in Hong Kong as early as 1847: see Chapter 3. The Letters Patent were amended in 1875 to affirm the Governor's power to grant a pardon to any accomplice giving information and evidence leading to the conviction of the principal offender. Section 104 of the Criminal Procedure Ordinance, No. 13 of 1899, codified this by empowering a court, with the consent of the Attorney General, to pardon any person accused or suspected of, or put on trial for, any indictable offence, on condition of his giving full and true evidence; the pardon could be withdrawn if evidence was withheld or falsely given. Although a few trials in the early twentieth century relied on accomplice evidence, this may indeed have been the first use of section 104. Section 104 was used often after World War II, especially in the big corruption and drug trafficking trials of the 1970s.

36. *SCMP*, 24, 27, and 28 July and 3 August 1932.

Chui — I don't agree, although that was the criticism of the Crown.

Jenkin — You are a gunman?

Chui — Yes.

Kemp — Gunman is an ambiguous term.

Jenkin — You are a man who will use a gun for an unlawful purpose.

Chui — No.

Jenkin — You are a self-confessed murderer?

Chui — By the word 'murderer' are you referring to this case, or generally?

Jenkin — You may be a murderer generally, as you say, but I am referring to this case.

Chui — You may refer to this case, but you cannot refer generally. What right have you to say that?

Jenkin — You are the type of man that would stick at nothing, who would not hesitate to do anything unlawful?

Chui — No.

Jenkin — You would perjure yourself to save your neck.

Chui — You may say so, but I do not.[37]

And so it continued, with Jenkin describing the story of the abortive shooting on 19 March as 'a tissue of lies', and the hiring of the second gunman, Kwan, as another lie, only to receive the same blunt denials. The *China Mail* described this a 'severe grilling'. But Jenkin was making no headway. Chui was clearly aware of the terms of his pardon.

Jenkin's aim was to protect Cheng by severing any link between his chauffeur, Lau Hing, and Chui's alleged plot. He pointed to contradictions in Chui's evidence about who was present at the shooting attempt on 19 March. First, he had said that Lau had not been there. Now he was saying that Lau was present, and that Tong Ching-kwai was not one of the group, or even part of the conspiracy. Jenkin accused Chui of changing his story to match what Tong had said at committal proceedings. But Chui said he had no idea what Tong had said; they had been kept apart and had never had a chance to discuss the case. Tong, detained on deportation warrants since his arrest, later confirmed this. In any case, said Chui, he did not mean the events on the 19th. More lies, said Jenkin, who then accused him of perjury over other details: the rental of the cubicle, the placing of the guns there, and events on the night of the murder. 'Your story as regards the whole of the matter, including Lau, is a concoction,' he said. 'It is all true,' replied Chui.

Sheldon began his re-examination of Chui by stating that the defence had repeatedly asserted that witnesses were giving false evidence. He did not know if the defence now denied that Fung was shot by Wong Nam-heung and asked that it indicate if that was so.

37. *SCMP*, 20 August 1932.

Potter erupted at this: he had 'never heard such a question put by a Crown Prosecutor in the whole of my life'. It was one of many tetchy moments between counsel. Earlier, Sheldon had asked that Potter stop repeating the words 'nonsense, nonsense' loudly under his breath while Zimmern was answering Jenkin's questions. Sheldon took Chui through the inconsistencies alleged by Jenkin, clarifying that when he said that Lau had not been present at the attempt on the 19th he meant he had not actually been on the street. He had been lounging in bed at Cheng's house on Village Road. Afterwards, he had sent his wife, Lau So, to summon Chui to explain what had gone wrong.

The last few days were taken up with police witnesses. As usual, Jenkin tried to depict the investigation as slipshod. This proved difficult. The police had been slow but thorough. They survived cross-examination unscathed, although some discovered that their hats, left in the corridor outside, had been stolen while they were in court.[38] After the prosecution closed its case, Potter made a submission of no case to answer in the absence of the jury. There was, he said, 'literally no evidence which could be left to the jury' to show that Cheng had procured Lau Hing to arrange the murder. They were therefore thrown back on Zimmern and Christie, who had also failed to bridge the gap. In any case, their evidence was intended to prove motive, not agency. Sheldon replied that the logic of this was that there could be no conviction in such a case if neither the accused nor the assassin gave evidence: there was always a gap. Kemp agreed there was a 'distinct gap' but held there was enough evidence for the case to go to the jury.

The defence called no witnesses. On the penultimate day of the trial, Sheldon gave the closing speech for the prosecution, saying the case had been 'immeasurably strengthened' during the trial. The defence had tried to show that Cheng's visit to Fung's hotel was all part of a subtle plot by Zimmern and Christie to get him involved in an assault on Fung; that Cheng's wish to slap Fung's face was evidence merely of 'jocular humour'; that 'this young man of wealth and importance, with many attractions for women', had already tired of Lai Ming-fai. Yet how, asked Sheldon, could this sit with his threat to spend all his money to prevent Lai and Fung living happily together?

> When he knew she had gone, his vanity and conceit were irreparably wounded. The girl he had supported for years had gone to live with a penniless man – had left him, the rich, eligible young man, for this man of no substance, George Fung. What was in his mind that night was no sense of humour. He had not only lost his girl. He had lost 'face'.

The only explanation, said Sheldon, was the story by Zimmern and Christie. The defence had claimed it was a pack of lies – that they had gone into the witness box 'to swear the prisoner's life away' after failing to swindle him out of $10,000, because Zimmern thought

38. Two topees and two felt hats, left on radiators, were taken. The thief, Pang Cheung, an 'office-boy' in a European firm, was caught when taking the fourth hat; pawn tickets for the other hats were found on him. The magistrate, Wynne Jones, took a lenient view and bound him over. *SCMP*, 22 August 1932.

Cheng had double-crossed him when he saw him go, with Brutton, to the police. Yet, despite the ingenuity of the defence, their evidence had 'not been shaken one iota'.

As for the chauffeurs' plot, Sheldon admitted it was 'a matter of regret' that Chui, the organizer, was not also in the dock. But sometimes the prosecution 'had to decide to let one man go free in order that justice might be dealt to another rather than that both should escape'. Chui's pardon was conditional on his telling the whole truth. Was it likely he would tell a false story, which, if shown to be false, would imperil his own neck? There were, as usual, minor discrepancies in evidence, but the corroboration between the abortive shooting on 19 March and Cheng's meeting with Zimmern the next day was 'extraordinary'. So was the evidence of Cheng's behaviour on the night of the murder. The defence's weaknesses had been revealed in cross-examination.

> All they had blandly said to each of the Crown witnesses was 'You are a liar', or 'that is another lie' or 'just a tissue of lies'. Yet they could not suggest one single solitary reason why these people and witnesses should have endeavoured to swear away this man's life.

Sheldon wondered if the jury had pictured Fung 'walking down the street, being shot down defencelessly and helplessly without a chance'. He knew they would not fail in their duty. 'In the name of the whole community in whose interest it was vitally important that all crimes of this nature should be punished, and by punishment, suppressed, he asked them to convict the prisoner.'

By not calling witnesses the defence had secured the all-important last word. Potter gave the closing speech. He seized on Sheldon's last remark. Never before, he thundered, had he heard a Crown counsel ask the jury to take into account the fact that a man was shot in cold blood. The case had been talked about everywhere. He did not suggest 'the presence of the opposite sex in court has necessarily increased that talking, but it has been talked about by us all'. The jury had to focus only on the evidence. The prosecution itself, said Potter, had described that of Zimmern and Christie as 'tainted', and had called Chui and his friends 'dangerous and worthless scoundrels'. He denounced the use of conditional pardons. He did not know who was behind that legislation.[39] But the result was a travesty. 'Here you have three men who are still struggling for their pardon.' They were trying their best to secure a conviction 'because in that lies their own safety'. Sheldon's claim – that he did not know what the defence was – was nonsense. 'The accused has to prove nothing.' The *South China Morning Post* observed the 'atmosphere of drama' at this point. 'The silence

39. The provision, in Ordinance, No. 13 of 1899 was lifted from the Indictable Offences (Procedure) Ordinance 1891 of British Guiana. Sir John Carrington, Chief Justice of Hong Kong 1896–1901, had drafted both ordinances, as well as a new Code of Civil Procedure and a new edition of the ordinances; in all, his law drafting in four colonies amounted to 7,877 pages. Although he received praise for this in Hong Kong, the Colonial Office complained that 'he was always taking long leave on the ground of consolidating statutes and spending it in the All Souls Library at Oxford'. Minute by Hugh Cox, Assistant Under-Secretary (Legal) with Carrington to the Under-Secretary of State, 22 April 1907, CO 129/345, 679–686.

hanging over the audience was broken only by the penetrating voice of defending counsel. His every gesture was followed by the crowded courtroom.'

Most of the rest of Potter's three-hour speech was devoted to discrepancies in evidence: Lai's original statement to the magistrate that, far from being consumed with jealousy, Cheng had grown 'colder and colder' towards her; the evidence from Lau Mo-kwong that Cheng was behaving normally on the evening of the murder; the absence of any 'shutter' at the Kwong Hoi Kee, despite Zimmern's testimony that Cheng had peeped through one when leaving his car there; and Chui's prevarications. He asked the jury to apply a test: 'If this man was a rational being could he have done this?' Could Lau Hing, Cheng's trusted chauffeur, have driven Lai around to carry on her affair with Fung without telling Cheng? Would Cheng, Zimmern, and Christie really have bought poison and consulted lawyers so openly if they intended to take part in a murder? Would Cheng have gone to smack Fung's face at the Nathan Hotel, knowing this would draw the attention of the police, when he had already made arrangements to have him murdered?

Kemp then summed up in an unusual way. Instead of reviewing the evidence in detail, he decided to deal with it on general lines. Counsel on both sides had analysed the evidence 'very fully and very powerfully,' he said. The jury had followed the trial 'with unusually competent judgment'. He went into the question of conditional pardons. He did not like them; they risked making the recipients 'a little complacent, a little anxious to help the prosecution'. But Chui, Christie, and Zimmern (who did not, in fact, receive a pardon) were intelligent enough to know that if they did not tell the truth the pardons would be withdrawn. If Chui was willing to tell any lie to earn his pardon, he could easily have invented some story implicating Cheng. Yet he did not implicate Cheng at all.

Kemp said that, in order to convict, the jury must first believe both branches of evidence: the Christie-Zimmern evidence about the $10,000 offer to kill Fung; and Chui's evidence that Cheng's chauffeur was the man who organized the murder. There was, he observed, 'a distinct gap between Chui and the accused'. And, while it was admitted that Cheng had lost Lai, whom he had supported for many years, and probably felt resentment against the man who had taken her away, this was 'a very different thing from murderous hate' and 'still far removed from active steps with a view to murder'. The jury, he suggested, might reasonably say they were satisfied or not satisfied with either or both branches. If they were satisfied with both branches, they must then take the further, final step of satisfying themselves beyond reasonable doubt that Lau was the agent of Cheng: that was 'the kernel of the whole trial'. Kemp urged the jury to disregard any point of fact on which he had expressed his own view too definitely.

The summing up took less than twenty-five minutes. There was much chattering in the crowded courtroom while the jurors retired. After forty minutes they returned. The court went silent. Cheng stood up as the clerk put the usual questions. A gasp went round the court when the foreman delivered the verdict of guilty. Potter jumped to his feet to ask Kemp to reserve the legal points that had arisen during the trial. Addressing Cheng, Kemp said he would postpone judgment until the Full Court had considered them. He then exempted the jurors from jury service for ten years – an exceptionally long period.

The Full Court heard arguments on the reserved points the following week. Counsel for the defence contended that the evidence of Zimmern and Christie was inadmissible in that it was an attempt to establish complicity in one crime by evidence of complicity in another. They argued that Kemp had been wrong in summing up in general terms. Where there was such a mass of evidence it was essential for the judge to carefully sift and explain it to the jury 'to prevent their being lulled into a miscarriage of justice'. The summing up, said Jenkin, contained not a single sentence of the slightest assistance to jurors on how they could bridge the gap between the evidence of Chui and that of Zimmern and Christie. They must have retired 'with blurred and confused minds'.[40]

Counsel on both sides argued their points during two days of hearings, citing over a hundred English cases. The judges, Kemp and Wood, gave their judgment two weeks later, on 12 September, in the presence of practically the whole legal profession. Wood reviewed the evidence and the law at length. He held that Kemp had been right in admitting the Zimmern-Christie evidence, and that the case had been properly left to the jury on sufficient evidence. Kemp concurred with Wood's judgment and the conviction was affirmed. At the end of these proceedings Richard Lim, the third barrister in Cheng's defence team, said they would be applying for special leave to appeal to the Privy Council. He asked if the court would state that the matter was a question of public and general importance and defer sentencing for three months. The court refused both requests.[41]

Cheng was brought back for sentencing the next day. 'Europeans and Chinese, men and women, in all walks and stations of life' – nearly 2,000 people – crammed the courtroom and corridors. Hundreds more waited outside. After being led into the dock, Cheng took a good look at the spectators, smiling all the time, and nodding when he noticed an acquaintance. He was in mourning clothes, unshaven, with a black tie, cream suit, and black armband: his grandmother, Lim Ah Chan, the family's hundred-year-old matriarch, had died shortly after the verdict. Cheng was still smiling when Kemp entered carrying a black cap. He remained calm as Kemp pronounced sentence of death and bowed when he had finished. Large crowds waited outside to see Cheng, handcuffed for the first time, taken back to Victoria Gaol in a prison van.[42]

40. *HKDP* and *SCMP*, 1 and 13 September.

41. Lim cited the procedure in the Ibrahim case in 1912 (see Chapter 8) where the Full Court had facilitated an appeal to the Privy Council by stating that the case was of great general and public importance, and the Chief Justice had arrested sentence until the Privy Council had heard the case. Kemp ruled that the Full Court was not a sentencing court, and he knew of no authority empowering him, as trial judge, to respite sentence. *CM*, 12 September 1932; *SCMP*, 17 December 1912.

42. *CM*, 14 September 1932; *HKDP*, *SCMP*, and *KSDN*, 15 September 1932.

A Henry II defence: The petition to the Privy Council

The Acting Governor, Thomas Southorn, respited Cheng Kwok-yau's execution for three months while the petition for leave to appeal went to the Privy Council; this was later extended by another month. The petition was handled by Richard Lim and Deacons the solicitors. Lim denied rumours that Potter and Jenkin had gone to argue the case in London; they had, in fact, gone on holiday. In alerting the Colonial Office, Southorn described the case as one of great importance. There was no 'political issue', as there had been with Leung Wo, the subject of the last such petition. But the crime had been carried out by a hired assassin in a form of vicarious murder that was always difficult to bring home to the instigator. The prosecution had also largely relied on accomplice evidence. The difficulties 'were increased by the great wealth at the disposal of the accused and his friends and the disappearance from the Colony of some of the persons concerned.'[43]

The petition broadly repeated the arguments put to the Full Court by Potter and Jenkin, laying stress on what it described as the failure by Kemp to properly direct the jury on law and facts: in particular, he had omitted to warn them that the evidence of accomplices should be corroborated by other witnesses. The barrister engaged to submit the petition to the Judicial Committee on 13 December was Sir William Jowitt KC, formerly Attorney General in Ramsay MacDonald's governments. The case, said Jowitt, reminded him of Thomas Beckett, Archbishop of Canterbury 1162–1170, whose assertions of the rights of the Church drove King Henry II to declare, 'Will no one rid me of this turbulent priest?' Four of Henry's knights, thinking to please him, rode to Canterbury and murdered Beckett. 'After that possibly they were promptly arrested and very possibly hanged,' said Jowitt.[44] 'I should have thought the jury would have acquitted Henry if he had been brought to trial,' said Lord Wright, a member of the committee. However, the committee dismissed Cheng's petition without calling on the Crown to respond.[45]

The save Cheng Kwok-yau campaign

Versions of the Henry II defence were put forward in petitions urging clemency for Cheng Kwok-yau. The first petition was a private affair. It was drafted by Wong Kwong-tin JP, a former Supreme Court interpreter, now Chairman of the Chinese General Chamber of Commerce, and promoted by Li Hoi-tung JP, a leading figure in the Tung Wah Hospital.

---

43. *KSDN*, 23 September 1932; ExCo Minutes, 29 September and 8 December 1932, CO 131/87, 189 and 236; Southorn to Cunliffe-Lister, 13 October 1932, CO 129/541/10, 41–42.
44. The King took no action against them, but the Pope ordered them to do penance as crusaders in the Holy Land: Frank Barlow, *Thomas Beckett* (Berkeley and Los Angeles: University of California Press, 1986), 257–258.
45. Petition of Cheng Kwok-yau, CO 129/541/10, 19–35; *News Chronicle*, 14 December 1932; *SCMP*, 16 December 1932 and 5 January 1933.

The signatories were restricted to the 'gentry and merchants of Hong Kong': Chinese bankers, businessmen, and justices of the peace, many of whom did not wish their names to be made public. The petition pleaded that Cheng's grandfather had done great service for the British in Malaya; that Cheng never intended to kill Fung but was led on by the hoodlums Zimmern and Christie; that Cheng and Lai Ming-fai, having become engaged and having lived together for months, were husband and wife in Chinese eyes; that Fung's affair with Lai had provoked this ignorant and impetuous youth; and that Chinese custom demanded severe punishment for seducing a man's wife. The petition was signed by about 230 leading citizens. It was translated into English and presented to the Secretary for Chinese Affairs by the legislator Tso Seen-wan OBE, JP in December 1932 shortly after news of the failure of the petition to the Privy Council.[46]

The petition for mercy also failed. On 12 January 1933 the Executive Council advised against clemency by a majority of seven to two. The Governor, Sir William Peel, accepted the advice and fixed the date of execution for 24 January, two days before Chinese New Year. Cheng began his tearful farewells to family and friends. He had been baptized a Catholic on Christmas Eve, taking the name Paul. A 'wonderful change' had come over him, reported D.M.D. Stephen, the editor of a Jesuit periodical. He was no longer 'the irresponsible youth of yesterday bent on pleasure and enjoyment'. Cheng now busied himself with sponsoring a new school in Sai Ying Pun. But he was also despondent. 'Money! Houses! Cars! A lovely wife! A beautiful mistress! Filial sons and good grandchildren!' he wrote to a friend. 'Everything is now just an empty prospect!'[47]

The letter appeared in the *Kung Sheung Daily News* as part of a new campaign for mercy. A second petition was drawn up for signature by people of all classes, Chinese and non-Chinese. Copies were left in clubs, theatres, restaurants, newspaper offices, and the Kwong Hoi Kee. The first petition, signed only by men of substance, had given the impression of 'Money v. Justice' and 'Influence v. Justice,' said the *South China Morning Post*; it had failed to reflect the true weight of public opinion. The new petition made eight points, some echoing the first – Cheng's youth, the seduction of his affianced wife, his sense of grievance, and the incitement by his associates. It added to these the 'great agony of mind' Cheng had suffered, his repentance, the element of doubt in the conviction, and a feeling that hanging him would 'serve no purpose that could not also be served by a long term of imprisonment'. This new campaign sparked editorials not only about Cheng's case but also about the legal system. If Hong Kong had a proper court of criminal appeal the case would have been thoroughly reviewed, said the *Telegraph*. It proposed that capital cases should

46. A rumour that Fung's father was one of the signatories was denied by Fung's brother. *WTYP*, 26 November 1932 and 13 January 1933; *KSDN*, 30 September and 13 October 1932, 12 January 1933; *SCMP*, 14 and 24 October, and 15 and 20 December 1932.
47. ExCo Minutes, 12 January 1933, CO 131/89, 19; letter from D.M.D. Stephen, Editor, *Messenger of the Sacred Heart for the Far East*, *SCMP*, 14 January 1933; *KSDN*, 5, 13, 14 and 18 January and 24 February 1933.

be tried by juries of twelve rather than seven, and that jury service be extended to women. Others pointed to the abolition of the death penalty in thirteen European countries and the recommendation of a recent parliamentary committee that it should be suspended as an experiment in England. The *Post* suggested the creation of a new degree of murder, one for which the death penalty was not mandatory.[48]

Although the *Daily Press* agreed there were grounds for mercy, it criticized the launch of the new campaign *after* the Governor had made his decision. It took its rivals to task for using the case as a pretext for attacking the legal system. A correspondent calling himself 'Figaro' asked if the editors of the *Telegraph* and *Post* realized 'that feeling is such amongst the poor Chinese classes that there would be possibilities of a riot if the law was interfered with and the Government intimidated in this case?' Where, asked A. Hanson in Canton, would the petitioners be when the next convicted murderer happened to be 'a poverty stricken and desperate foki[49] or coolie who has neither recanted his religion nor been provided with the means of postponing the course of the law?' Cheng's supporters had answers to such criticisms. 'Isn't he a product of our age?' asked D.M.D. Stephen in another letter to the *Post*. 'How far has West Point [Shek Tong Tsui] and all that it stood for contributed to the lad's downfall?' His letter was heavily censored when it appeared in Chinese translation in the next day's *Kung Sheung Daily*.[50] Far from helping him, the stories of vast sums spent on Cheng's defence, said the *Post*, had embarrassed him more seriously than 'the legendary poverty which requires that Justice be blind'.[51] Cheng had reportedly spent over $200,000 – half his private wealth – on lawyers' fees, and had run up large debts from his profligate spending. Creditors had delayed action, not knowing if he would be alive when he came of age in March 1933.[52]

The second petition reportedly garnered 17,000 signatures in a matter of days. A week after his confirmation of the death sentence, Peel reopened Cheng's case in the light of the petition, representations from ministers of religion and others, and a letter urging mercy from three members of the jury, including the foreman, Geoffrey Archbutt, and Kan Tong-po (the jury had made no such recommendation when giving its verdict). The case had caused Peel much anxiety. It was his first capital case in Hong Kong and probably his first anywhere: most of his career had been in Malaya, where the sultans retained the prerogative of mercy. The number of Executive Councillors now in favour of clemency

48. *HKT*, 13 January 1933; letter from C. Champkin, *HKT*, 16 January 1933; *SCMP*, 13, 14, and 18 January 1933; *KSDN*, 16–21 January 1933; *WTYP*, 17–20 January 1933.
49. 伙記: a shop assistant, waiter or other employee.
50. The censored part of the letter, represented by the usual blank spaces, called for the cabarets, dance halls, gambling clubs, and brothels at Shek Tong Tsui to be closed down, and for stricter censorship of films. *SCMP*, 17 January 1933; *KSDN*, 18 January 1933.
51. *HKDP*, 14, 17, and 19 January 1933; *SCMP* 13 January 1933.
52. *WTYP*, 14 January 1933; *SCMP*, 25 March 1933.

for Cheng had increased from two to four, but five were still opposed. Peel nevertheless decided to commute the death sentence to life imprisonment against the majority view. His reasons were increased support within the council, the plea for commutation by three jurors, and 'the very serious injury done to the prisoner by the murdered man'.[53]

Released from the condemned cell, Cheng was put to 'hard labour', learning how to typeset and making envelopes. He gained weight, read religious books, and looked to the day when he would leave prison and become a useful member of society, perhaps in fourteen years (the usual length of a life sentence, according to a legal expert), perhaps less with good behaviour and intercessions from priests. These comforts were short lived. Cheng fell into depression, mumbling constantly to himself, had a mental breakdown, and spent time in the gaol hospital. In 1934, after a fight with other prisoners, he was moved to the European section of the gaol, where he slept on a bed and ate a Western diet. When reporters asked why, they were told that it was because he was a British national, and that only one other Chinese prisoner enjoyed such treatment. A European prisoner in the next cell observed that Cheng was in a desperate plight, 'on the borderline of insanity'.[54]

Cheng's elder brother, Cheng Kwok-on, maintained press interest in the case through bulletins of prison visits by the family. Their mother, the second concubine of his late father, seized opportunities to obtain a full pardon. She petitioned the government on the silver jubilee of King George V in 1935; on the accession of his son, Edward VIII, in 1936; and again on the eve of the centenary of the British occupation of Hong Kong, in December 1940.[55] Cheng finally left prison in 1941. He was one of some 2,500 convicts released when Japanese forces invaded Hong Kong.[56] He lived a quiet bachelor life after his release. He died in 1963 at the age of fifty-one at the family residence at Tung Shan Terrace, Stubbs Road, a short distance from where George Fung was murdered.[57]

In 1934, after legal proceedings in courts in Shanghai, Cheng's hired gunman, Wong Nam-heung, was sentenced to life imprisonment by the Nantao District Court for the murder of George Fung: the Chinese Criminal Code gave judges the option of the death penalty or life imprisonment in murder cases.[58] Lai Ming-fai, who gave evidence against Wong, rejected offers to play herself in films about the murder. She did, however, appear in 'The Love Debt', a film purporting to tell her life story and depicting 'a most thrilling

53. *WTYP*, 20 January 1933; ExCo Minutes, 19 January 1933, CO 131/89, 23–24; Peel to Cunliffe-Lister, 3 February 1933, CO 129/541/10, 11–12.
54. *KSEN*, 19 January 1933; *KSDN*, 29 April and 2 August 1933, and 17, 18, and 27 March 1934; letter from '9908', *SCMP*, 1 May 1935.
55. *KSDN*, 11 April 1935; *SCMP*, 1 May 1935; *WTYP*, 10 February 1936 and 27 December 1940.
56. CO 129/582/11 'Disposal of Convicts in Event of War' (1939); John Luff, *The Hidden Years: Hong Kong 1941–1945* (Hong Kong: South China Morning Post), 156.
57. *SCMP*, *KSDN*, and *Ta Kung Pao*, 25 April 1963.
58. *SCMP*, 19 November 1934.

triangular love affair', which was briefly shown in Hong Kong in 1933.[59] In 1934 she married Lu Zhongyen, the son of a wealthy Shanghai financier.[60] She died in December 2003 at the age of ninety-four. Edward Zimmern, the other star witness in the case, was executed during the Japanese occupation, probably for espionage.[61]

The Cheng Kwok-yau case resonated over the years. It became a benchmark for its length and degree of 'sensation' and was recalled in the obituaries of the many lawyers connected with it,[62] including that of Cheng's counsel, Francis Jenkin. Since his wife's return to England in the late 1920s, Jenkin had become increasingly lonely. Loneliness turned to depression when his daughters also left home, two to pursue acting careers. He began to behave erratically. On the night of Sunday 1 March 1936 he swallowed nearly the whole contents of a bottle of sleeping pills: his servant found him unconscious and roused him with the help of a doctor. Three days later the servant found him lying dead in bed. Jenkin had shot himself in the head with a revolver he had brought home from his chambers.[63]

Parallel parables: Keung Tsz-pan

Eighteen months after the commutation of Cheng's death sentence another murder brought into focus the influence of public sentiment on the exercise of mercy. In 1934 Keung Tsz-pan, a young man resident in Hong Kong, went to pursue theological studies in Canton, leaving behind Keung Wai-lan,[64] a woman from his village in Guangdong to whom he was apparently married. During his absence she went to live with another man, Yim Chun. On his return, Keung tried to persuade her to leave Yim, but to no avail. On the night of 20 July, armed with a rope and a long knife, Keung climbed into their top-floor cubicle in Sham Shui Po and stabbed them both in the heart while they were asleep. He injured his foot while climbing down and was found in the street by a policeman.

Keung confessed to the killings but pleaded not guilty to murder. His counsel, Lo Hin-shing, argued that he had lost control on seeing the two lovers naked in bed. Under the

59. A review in the *South China Morning Post* praised the film, an early Cantonese talkie, as marking 'the opening of a new era in Chinese cinematographic art'. The film, however, appears not to have survived. *CM*, 6 September 1932; *SCMP*, 13 September 1932, and 19 and 22 April 1933; *KSEN*, 20 April 1933.

60. *KSEN* and *SCMP*, 19 April 1934.

61. Eric Peter Ho, *Tracing My Children's Lineage* (Hong Kong: Centre of Asian Studies, University of Hong Kong, 2010), 220.

62. Roger Lindsell, who died in retirement in South Africa in 1941; George Hall Brutton, in retirement in Somerset in 1947; Eldon Potter, in Hong Kong in 1951; and Harold Sheldon, in a road accident in Devon in 1951. *SCMP*, 23 November 1941, 16 September 1947, and 5 July and 26 August 1951.

63. Jenkin's eldest daughter was Wendy Barrie, who at the time of his death was already a famous film actress. His second daughter, Paddy Jenkin, was a stage actress. A third daughter, Hazel Mills Jenkin, whom Jenkin had adopted from the family of a military friend, left for England only two weeks before his death. *HKDP*, *SCMP*, *CM*, *KSDN*, and *WTYP*, 5 March 1936.

64. Keung Sau-lin in some reports.

'infidelity defence' developed in Victorian England, the killing under provocation of an adulterous wife or her lover, or both, could be reduced to manslaughter.[65] Qing law was even more lenient: if a man killed *both* his wife *and* her paramour immediately on discovering them in flagrante delicto he received no punishment.[66] Qing law no longer applied in China and had little influence on criminal law in Hong Kong, except for penal policy and in the laws against adultery by Chinese women. But the values it embodied still had force. It was also still common for rural communities to deal brutally with adultery by women. Keung had a burning grievance. Yet the knife and rope suggested the killings were premeditated. Moreover, according to evidence from her father, Keung Wai-lan was never married to him: it would have been contrary to custom for members of the same clan to marry each other; in any case, said the father, Keung was already married to a woman from another village. Keung was convicted of murder and sentenced to death.[67]

Shortly after Keung's trial a letter appeared in the *South China Morning Post* from 'Lazarus' entitled 'Parallel Parables'. The letter contrasted Cheng's case with Keung's: the 'rich young man' had been spared because he had influential friends; the 'poor young man had no friends of influence in the city to plead for him', and in due course was put to death. But Lazarus was wrong. Keung did have influential friends, in the Anglican Church. At his trial, the Reverend Lee Kau-yan, Vicar of St Mary's Church, Causeway Bay, had testified that Keung Tsz-pan and Keung Wai-lan had attended his former church, St Stephen's in Pokfulam Road; he had assumed they were married. After the trial Lee gave interviews to the press, mobilized the clergy, and launched a public petition to 'save Keung Tsz-pan'.[68] The petition argued that the Keungs *were* married to each other and had two children; that Keung had been provoked by his wife's adultery; and that Qing law and Chinese custom justified the killings in his mind. It did not question the verdict but submitted there were sufficient grounds to commute the sentence.[69]

Over 9,000 persons signed the petition at churches, theatres, and department stores. The three Chinese members of the Legislative Council signed a separate letter asking for clemency. However, by a majority of five to four, Executive Councillors advised that the law should take its course. For a second time, Peel went against this advice and commuted the death sentence to life imprisonment. His reasons were public support for commutation, the provocation and mental distress suffered by Keung, and the conclusion that, while

65. Kesselring, 'No Greater Provocation? Adultery and the Mitigation of Murder in English Law'.
66. Jones, *The Great Qing Code*, article 285.
67. Marriage of persons with the same surname was also an offence under the now-defunct Qing Code (article 107), punishable by flogging and dissolution of the marriage. *SCMP* and *HKDP*, 18–20 September 1934; Transcript of Chief Justice's notes of trial, 17–19 September, CO 129/550/1, 17–33.
68. *SCMP*, 22 and 25–28 September and 2–6 and 9 October 1934; *KSDN*, 23–30 September and 1, 6, 8, 9, and 12 October 1934; *Tien Kwong Po*, 22–30 September and 1–12 October 1934.
69. Petition on behalf of Keung Tsz-pan, October 1934, CO 129/550/2, 34–42.

Keung was not legally married to Keung Wai-lan, she had lived with him as a concubine and had borne him two children. Peel did not mention Chinese custom in his report, but staff in the Colonial Office were concerned that ideas 'repugnant to our conception of law and ethics' had formed a ground for clemency. It was only a short step from this to accepting that 'long established tribal custom' might exempt a person from the death penalty for murders during clan vendettas, wrote one official.[70] His superiors, however, rejected his suggestions to raise the matter with Peel.

The successful petitions on behalf of Cheng and Keung illustrate a growing sense of common cause among the different communities of Hong Kong. This found expression in initiatives to bridge cultural gaps in campaigns against poverty, child abuse, and other social evils. The next case to attract petitioning on a similar scale was the Nullah Murder, which was making its way through the courts as Lazarus wrote his letter to the *South China Morning Post*. A 'racial' murder of a European child allegedly committed by a desperate outsider, this was an even more starkly powerful 'parallel parable' than the Keung case. The case is discussed in the next chapter.

70. Minute by H.E. Bader, 30 November 1934, CO 129/550/2, 2–5.

10

'Race Fear'

The Nullah Murder, 1934

Ng Loi-yuen (吳來源) had not planned to disembark at Hong Kong. Hoping to find work in Singapore, he had borrowed $10 for a passage from his native place of Swatow (Shantou), the largest city in the Chiu Chow district of Guangdong. Swindlers cheated him out of $5. When, during the voyage, the crew discovered he had no ticket, they took another $3 and turned him off the ship at Hong Kong. Ng spent the night at the Swatow Drawn Work Company, a shop on Pedder Street selling lace and embroidery. He had worked there some years earlier but had been dismissed; his younger brother still worked there. Now, stranded and dejected, Ng was 'full of sorrow and very unhappy at being cheated'.[1]

The day of Ng's arrival in Hong Kong, Thursday 21 June 1934, was one of strong winds and heavy rain. At night the rain intensified. Boulders crashed down the hillsides. Landslips blocked roads. Queen's Road was turned into a river, and the racecourse at Happy Valley became a lake. The Botanical Gardens in Central registered almost ten inches, the Wong Nai Chung Reservoir over eleven. It was the heaviest rainfall in eight years. Water rationing was lifted. The island's nullahs – the man-made channels draining water into the sea – were swollen from the downpour.[2]

The next day Ng Loi-yuen had breakfast with the staff of the Swatow shop.[3] He then wandered the streets and spent what was left of his money on alcohol. Shortly after 3 p.m. he arrived at a bridge over the Albany Nullah, the channel next to the Lower Peak Tramway Station. Five children from the nearby army quarters – three boys and two girls

1. Petition on behalf of Ng Loi-yuen, *KSDN*, 21 October 1934; Evidence of Wong Shu-kat, 7 September 1934, *R v Ng Loi-yuen*, Judge's notes, CO 129/550/7, 109.
2. *SCMP*, 22, 23 and 25 June 1934.
3. The narrative here draws mainly on the Minute of Committal Proceedings, CO 129/550/7, 150–192.

aged between five and eight – were playing on the bridge, throwing stones into the torrent nine feet below. Allegedly, Ng grabbed the children and threw them one by one into the nullah before jumping in himself. Alternatively, some or all of the children jumped, or fell, or slipped into the nullah just as Ng threw himself off the bridge.

Few saw what happened on the bridge, but the area along the nullah was busy with workmen and soldiers of the Welsh Borderers, the regiment then stationed in Hong Kong. Two chair-bearers, waiting near the bridge, heard screams. They rescued the youngest girl, Fay Bromley, who was kneeling on a step beneath the bridge, up to her waist in water. Hau Luk, a fitter at the Peak Tramway, helped the youngest boy, Tony Flood, who had scrambled to the bank. The other three children were carried by the water down the nullah, which passed under two more bridges before entering a tunnel under Queen's Road and the Naval Yard. From there it debouched into the harbour near the bathing pool of the Victoria Recreation Club. The water in the nullah was barely two feet deep, but the gradient was steep, the current was strong, and the bottom was paved with worn granite slabs. A third child, Norman Stone, was lifted out by Yung Sou, one of several men repairing a pipe next to the nullah. The two other children, the eight-year-old twins Mary and Michael Pine, were washed towards the tunnel, along with Ng Loi-yuen.

While this was happening, Hou Wing-hong, a coffee-bar assistant at the NAAFI[4] canteen, was enjoying a cigarette break. He heard screams and saw people shouting on the bridge leading to Flagstaff House, the residence of the General Officer Commanding. Hou ran down and saw Mary struggling in the nullah. He jumped in and threw his arms around her but was swept off his feet by the current. At that moment, Sidney Bowles, an army accountant, was walking along Murray Path next to the nullah. He jumped in but was also swept down the nullah. Lying crossways, he attempted to block the current with his body. But Hou and Mary were washed over his legs, and Michael went over him with a bump. Bowles then felt the bump of a fourth person passing over him. At the tunnel mouth Hou managed to scramble to his feet, still holding Mary. He carried her to the side. As he did so, he saw two other people being washed into the tunnel. Mary called out 'my brother!' Hou ran in after the other two, leaving her outside the tunnel. But it was too dark. He returned to see Bowles lift Mary up and hand her to a soldier.

Two other soldiers, Philip Simmons and Thomas McCarthy, then entered the tunnel to look for Michael Pine. The tunnel – about 400 yards long – was dark except for three places where gratings let in light. About 250 yards in, the soldiers ran into Ng Loi-yuen, who was standing against the wall, his face visible in the light from one of the gratings. Simmons asked him what he was doing. When he received no reply, he took Ng by the shoulders and called McCarthy over. Ng struggled and bit Simmons's hand. Two other soldiers, one with an electric torch, helped subdue him. When he continued to resist, they turned him over

4. The Navy, Army and Air Force Institutes, an organization running shops and canteens for service personnel.

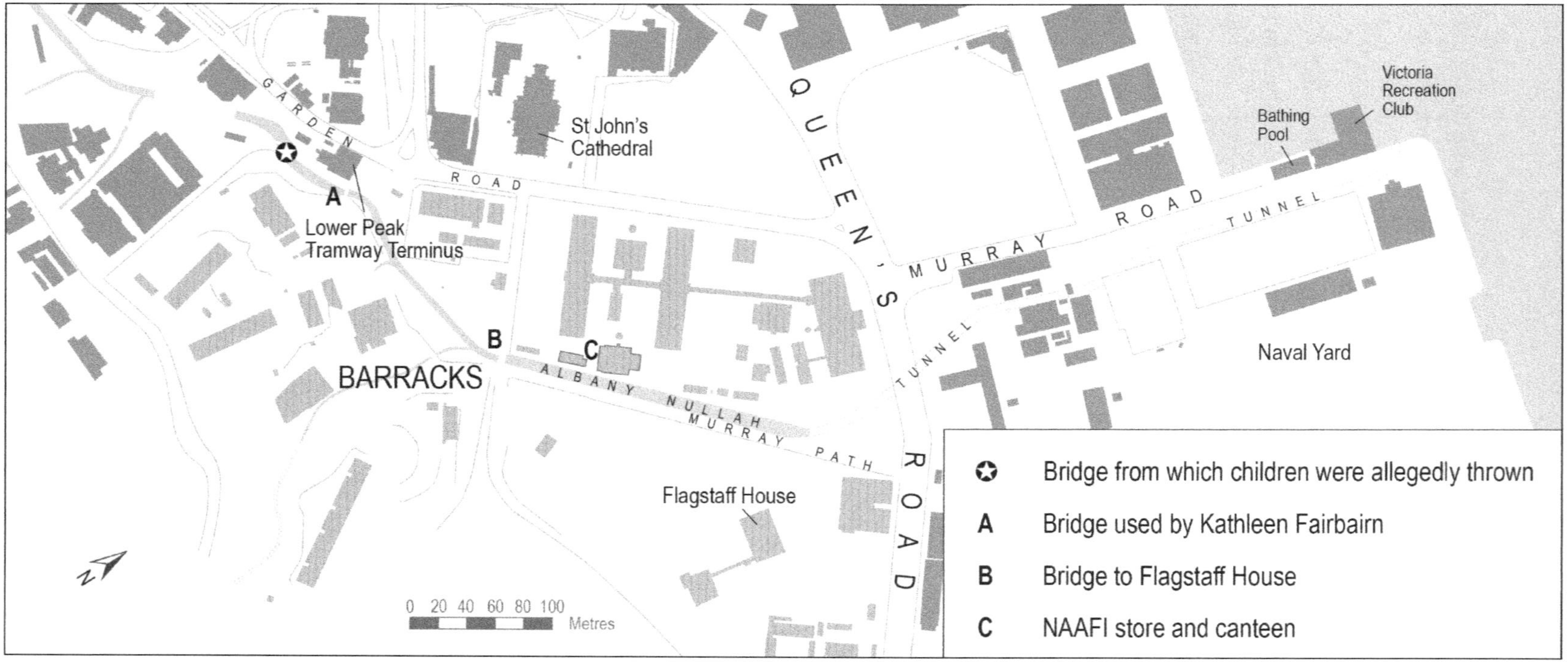

Map 7: The Nullah Murder, 1934

and carried him out 'frog fashion', face downwards. After more struggles, Ng went limp and was hauled out of the nullah with a rope. Soldiers applied artificial respiration and Ng was put into an ambulance, barely conscious and trembling with shock, his right thighbone fractured by the fall from the bridge.

Michael Pine was swept down the tunnel into the sea. Edward Sellars, a sentry on the bridge leading to Flagstaff house, saw him pass under the bridge with a man holding onto him. He and another soldier, William O'Kelly, raced down Murray Path to Queen's Road. They commandeered a rickshaw to take them to the mouth of the nullah. O'Kelly ran through the Victoria Recreation Club and down the slip to the harbour. He saw Michael about fifty yards out, jumped in, and brought him ashore. Michael was unconscious, with a deep gash at the back of his head. He died three hours later in the Civil Hospital without regaining consciousness. The cause of death was a fractured skull.

On the way to the Civil Hospital, Ng Loi-yuen asked the ambulance attendant for wine and was given a glass of water. In the detention ward, dazed and smelling of alcohol, he repeated over and over that he had been drinking. The doctors took a urine sample. On the evening of 6 July, while Ng was still in hospital, two other prisoners escaped by prizing open iron bars on a lavatory window. Ng was found in his bed, but with the plaster cast on his leg soaked off: he had apparently tried to join them.[5] Among his possessions, left in a basket at the shop on Pedder Street, police found three letters written in Chinese. The longest, signed by Ng and dated 10 December 1933, called on students to observe the *Three Principles of the People*, the manifesto of Sun Yat-sen. It urged them to die for their country: 'only those who are as determined as I can be righteous and heroic men'. Another letter, unsigned and undated, declared, 'He who dares to kill the Europeans will be a great hero. Please be a righteous and brave man who will be a hero.'[6]

On 9 July 1934 Ng was formally charged with the murder of Michael Pine. In response, he said, 'I was drunk. I was unconscious. I had a wound too.' Committal hearings began on 1 August before the magistrate Eric Hamilton.[7] The prosecutor was the Assistant Attorney General, John Fraser MC, a cadet officer who, after training while on leave, had been called

5. Yeung Wai, charged with loitering in a hotel, was recaptured in the grounds of the hospital and later sentenced to three months for loitering and an additional four months for escaping; Lau Sing, facing a charge of returning from banishment, appears to have made a clean getaway. *SCMP*, 7 and 11 July 1934.
6. Exhibits 7A, 7B, and 7C, with the Report of Committal Proceedings, CO 129/550/7, 186–189.
7. A government cadet, poet, newspaper columnist, and radio cricket commentator. In 1919 he began a libel action against the *Daily Press* and *China Mail* after they published a pseudonymous letter (by the solicitor Francis Bowley) implying that the dire state of crime on the outlying islands was due to his 'poetical and laissez faire' attitude as assistant district officer. The matter was settled with published apologies, each side paying its own costs. Despite having been assured of support by the former Governor, Sir Francis May, the government declined to reimburse Hamilton for his solicitor's fees, which amounted to $2,000 (a sum in excess of his annual salary). The fees apparently went unpaid. Severn to Milner, 12 April and 18 August 1919, CO 129/454, 158–226 and CO 129/455, 208–219; note of 22 March 1920, CO 129/460, 290.

to the Bar by Middle Temple in 1931. Thirty-three witnesses gave evidence over five afternoons. Friends of Ng in Hong Kong raised money for lawyers. His counsel was Richard Lim, instructed by J.M. Hall (Sin Man-lim), a member of a prominent Eurasian family and a solicitor since 1917.[8] Lim called no witnesses. When asked if he had anything to say, Ng replied, 'I have no money therefore I commit suicide. I have nothing more to say.' Hamilton then committed him for trial.

R v *Ng Loi-yuen*
Murder, 20–22 August 1934

The judge at Ng's trial was the new Chief Justice, Alasdair Duncan Atholl MacGregor, a Scotsman educated at Edinburgh and Oxford Universities and called to the Bar by Lincoln's Inn in 1908. MacGregor practised law in London: in 1911 he was part of the defence team in the Clapham Common Murder trial, in which Steinie Morrison, a Russian Jewish immigrant, was convicted of murdering another Russian Jew on evidence so doubtful it prompted a judicial inquiry.[9] He then embarked on a colonial career as administrator, magistrate, and Crown counsel. His most recent position was Attorney General of Kenya 1929–1933. In that colony, except for capital crimes, Europeans and Africans were tried in separate courts, some imposing sentences which, in MacGregor's words, were 'so severe as to be almost savage.'[10] In 1930 he prosecuted in the Kijabe Murder trial, in which an African man was acquitted of murdering the missionary Hulda Stumpf.[11] MacGregor's appointment as Chief Justice of Hong Kong in 1934 was his first senior judicial position. He had earlier declined an offer of the Hong Kong attorney generalship on the elevation of Sir Joseph Kemp to the bench in 1930. The position went instead to the barrister C.G. Alabaster, a candidate preferred by Governor Sir Cecil Clementi for his local knowledge.[12]

MacGregor arrived in Hong Kong in February 1933. He tried three murders prior to the Nullah Murder, all of which took place in the New Territories. Following a pattern of

---

8. Hall was the son of Sin Tak-fan (Stephen Hall, 1856–1924), a solicitor's clerk and interpreter, substantial property owner, and leading figure in the Chinese community. Petition on behalf of Ng Loi-yuen, *KSDN*, 21 October 1934; *SCMP*, 17 May 1977.
9. Morrison's death sentence was commuted to life imprisonment. *SCMP*, 5 December 1933; H. Fletcher Moulton, ed., *Trial of Steinie Morrison* (Notable British Trials Series: London: William Hodge & Co., 1922).
10. Quoted in Brett Shadle, 'White settlers and the law in early colonial Kenya', *Journal of East African Studies*, Vol. 4, No. 3 (2010): 510–524, note 44.
11. David M. Anderson, 'Women Missionaries and Colonial Silences in Kenya's Female "Circumcision" Controversy, 1906–1930', *English Historical Review*, Vol. 83, No. 565 (December 2018): 1512–1545; *SCMP*, 5 December 1933.
12. Although the salary was slightly higher in Hong Kong, it was, observed an official in the Colonial Office, 'absurd' to suppose that it was a promotion to go from Attorney General of Kenya to Attorney General 'of a little place like Hong Kong.' Minute by Calder, 5 December 1930, CO 129/523/3, 16.

these years, two resulted in the discharge of the accused, and one in a verdict of manslaughter. In one case, a man allegedly pushed his cousin off a boat near Cheung Chau after a quarrel over her marriage plans. Her body was not found. The eyewitness evidence was unsatisfactory. When the jury failed to agree on a verdict, Macgregor remanded him to the next sessions. The Attorney General, however, entered a *nolle prosequi*, and he went free.[13] In another case, a man and a woman were tried for battering the woman's husband to death in a temple in near Yuen Long. The prosecution was unable to show whether the man or the woman had carried out the killing. There was no evidence of common purpose. MacGregor therefore directed the jury to acquit them.[14] In the third case, a cowherd at Castle Peak killed his colleague, a fourteen-year-old boy, after a quarrel over a girlfriend. He withdrew a confession made to the police, told the magistrate he had no recollection of the incident, and testified at trial that he had been intoxicated after taking some 'English medicine' that smelled of alcohol. The jury convicted him of manslaughter and MacGregor sentenced him to seven years' imprisonment.[15]

John Fraser had prosecuted all three cases. He was now also prosecutor in Ng Loi Yuen's trial.[16] Richard Lim was Ng's counsel. Since appearing in Cheng Kwok-yau's trial in 1932, Lim had been defence counsel in five murder trials, including two of the New Territories cases.[17] The jury at Ng's trial consisted of three Portuguese, a German, a Chinese, and two British. All were from the class of assistants, accountants, clerks, and engineers who formed most of the common jurors' list.[18]

The prosecution called the thirty-three witnesses who had appeared at committal proceedings. Most were participants or observers in the rescue of the children and Ng Loi-yuen: MacGregor commended one of them, the canteen assistant Hou Wing-hong, for his 'very great promptitude and very great pluck' in saving Mary Pine. But only two witnesses had actually seen Ng – or someone resembling him – throw children from the bridge. One was the eight-year-old Mary Pine herself. At committal proceedings the magistrate was satisfied she knew the difference between truth and falsehood but doubted if she understood an oath: she had therefore made an unsworn statement. Since then, said Fraser, she had been instructed on the meaning of an oath and now understood it. MacGregor allowed

13. *SCMP*, 21 and 23 March 1934; *HKDP*, 21 March 1934.
14. *SCMP*, 1 August 1934.
15. *SCMP*, 18 May and 18 September 1934.
16. The main sources for the trial are *SCMP* and *HKDP*, 21–23 August 1934; and *CM*, 20–22 August 1934.
17. The Cheung Chau case and the Temple case. He withdrew from the latter after MacGregor refused to allow the man and the woman to be tried separately. *SCMP*, *HKDP*, 24 and 26 July 1934.
18. Ernest Wilfrid Blackmore (foreman), civil engineer, Blackmore & Blackburn Ltd (British-Australian); Charles Marcelino Correa, accountant, Swan Culbertson & Fritz (Portuguese); Lawrence Wong, clerk, States Steamship Co. (Chinese); Fernando Jose Remedios, assistant, Union Insurance Co. (Portuguese); Otto Hetchel, merchant, F. Feld & Co. (German); Henrique Alberto Alves, assistant, John D. Hutchison & Co. (Portuguese); Hugh Craig Meeke, assistant, Bank Line Ltd (British).

her to take the oath against objections from Lim. She then identified Ng as the man who had thrown her and her brother into the nullah. Ng had held her in the nullah and had hit her, she testified. She described what he was wearing – a white coat, black trousers and a straw hat – and how she had picked him out at an identity parade. Cross-examined by Lim, she said that a long time ago, before the day of the murder, she and other children had gone down into the nullah without telling her mother. She also detailed the order in which the children had been thrown in: first Tony Flood, then Norman Stone, Michael Pine, Fay Bromley, and finally herself.

The other eyewitness was Kathleen Fairburn, the wife of the sworn measurer,[19] a resident of MacDonnell Road, just up the hill from the Lower Peak Tramway Station. She said she suddenly heard screams when walking from her home through the barracks and across a footbridge over the nullah. She looked up at another footbridge some twenty yards upstream and saw a Chinese man with a girl and a boy. The man wore a white jacket, dark trousers, and a straw hat. She saw him throw the boy over the far side of the bridge, and then the girl, before climbing over the railings and jumping in himself. He had his back to her all the time. She ran up the path to the other bridge and saw a girl and a boy being rescued by the chair-bearers and a soldier. At an identity parade she picked out the accused by his thin physique, long and shaggy hair, high cheek bones, and 'sunken-in cheeks'.

There were gaps between Fairburn's evidence at trial and what she had previously said: in her deposition before the magistrate she had said that, as the man climbed over the railings, he turned very slightly towards her and she had a glimpse of the side of his face. In an interview with the *South China Morning Post* shortly after the incident she had said, 'I think the man was an old beggar who usually sits near the tramway. He is the only Chinese I have ever seen wearing one of those old sailor's hats. I could not be certain as I only saw his back.'[20] The interview was not in evidence. But her deposition was. Lim read back to her the passage in which she claimed to have glimpsed Ng's face: she confirmed this was so. He quizzed her on the colour of the girl's dress, which she could not remember, and on other parts of her deposition, which was then read out in full.

The witnesses for the prosecution finished their evidence in the afternoon of the second day of the trial. Fraser put in English translations of the anti-European letters. Lim then made a submission of no case to answer in the absence of the jury. The only evidence against Ng Loi-yuen was from Mary Pine, said Lim. Kathleen Fairburn had seen two children thrown from the bridge, but the victim named in the indictment, Michael Pine, was not one of them. The case was based purely on suspicion, Lim argued. He cited a recent case in England in which the Court of Criminal Appeal had quashed a murder conviction based on suspicion and circumstantial evidence: the case, *R v Wallace*, was the first capital

19. A person employed by shipping companies to certify correct measurements of cargo.
20. *SCMP*, 23 June 1934.

conviction to be overturned by that court on the ground that the verdict was not supported by the evidence.[21] MacGregor ruled against Lim and, when the jury returned, called on him to open the defence. Lim replied that he did not intend to put Ng in the witness box or to call any evidence beyond the statements made by Ng to the police and the magistrate, one to the effect that he was drunk and unconscious from his injury, the other that he had no money and was contemplating suicide.

Fraser then gave his closing speech. The 'clear and unfaltering evidence' of Kathleen Fairburn, he said, was supported by Mary Pine and by other witnesses who had rescued the children. Ng smelt of alcohol after the incident and claimed he was drunk. But the urine sample taken on his admission to hospital showed he was only slightly intoxicated. The letters among his possessions suggested a motive to kill Europeans, said Fraser. In his statement to the magistrate he had also said that he intended to kill himself.

In his closing speech, Lim said there were two questions for the jury: 'Was Michael Pine thrown into the water? If so, was he thrown by the accused?' Michael was not one of the two children whom Kathleen Fairburn had seen thrown from the bridge, said Lim. It was probable, he suggested, that some or all of the children were playing by the water's edge, and that one got caught by the current and dragged the others in. Ng may have either fallen off the bridge or jumped in under the influence of drink, although Lim added that drunkenness was not part of the defence. It was possible that Ng threw the two smallest children from the bridge while Michael, Mary, and Norman were playing below. But even a sober man could not throw as many as five children into the nullah without some resistance. Why did they not run away? Two witnesses, housewives from the military quarters, on seeing the children in the nullah, had even assumed that Ng was trying to rescue them. Ng's statements had mentioned suicide, not murder. Only one of the letters found in his possessions – the vaguest and least incriminating – bore his signature. The others spoke of killing Europeans, not children. It was possible he did not even know their contents. Lim could imagine someone who really believed the letters taking an adult with him, but not children. 'Children are far too sacred.'

To Lim's embarrassment, MacGregor then asked Ng if he would confirm the instructions he had given to Lim to call no witnesses, or if he wished to give evidence on oath or make a statement from the dock. This confused Ng, who started to say he was completely drunk at the time of the incident. When the interpreter put the question again, Ng confirmed that Lim had acted on instructions. MacGregor adjourned the trial, saying his summing up would be a long one, and he would give it the next day.

---

21. Wallace was a middle-aged insurance agent accused of murdering his wife. So controversial was the verdict of murder against him that the Church of England organized intercessory prayers at Liverpool Cathedral, praying for the appeal judges to be 'guided in true justice'. *R v Wallace* (1931) 23 Cr App R 32; Hargrave Lee Adam, *Murder Most Mysterious* (London: Sampson Low, Marston & Co., 1932), 252–253.

The summing up lasted over two hours. MacGregor began by referring to the 'dramatic and emotional interest' that the case had inevitably aroused, and the 'many stories and rumours' the jurors were likely to have heard. He instructed them to return a verdict only in accordance with the evidence. They were to put out of their minds any idea of a 'racial conflict' in the case, and, still more, any 'emotionalism' from the fact that the victim was a little boy. He reminded them that the accused was not charged with inflicting injury on any child but Michael Pine. The evidence of Kathleen Fairburn, he said, was that two children had been thrown in. Other evidence showed that two children had been picked up near the bridge. But it did not necessarily follow they were the same two children. He noted that Ng had struggled hard when brought out of the nullah and had tried to join the prisoners who escaped from the hospital. The jury should not draw unfair inferences from this: it was reasonable to think that if Ng had woken up to find himself detained on a serious charge he would try to get away if he could.

The story was a strange one, said MacGregor. 'It would not have appeared possible for one person, no matter how diabolical his intentions, to throw five children one after the other into the nullah.' An ordinary child, seeing its companions seized in this way, would probably have run away. This was the submission of the defence, which had suggested the children were down at the water's edge when they were swept away. Yet it was also improbable that the children were all swept away at the same time, and even more improbable that, just at that moment, the accused jumped from the bridge. The letters showed Ng was 'a man of strange ideas'. If they were to be believed, he thought it was a 'glorious thing to kill a man'. He was rankled at having been cheated in Swatow, and, without work or money, was determined to commit suicide. The prosecution had asked the jury to put all these factors together and say, 'What more glorious consolation was his than to commit suicide in that nullah and take with him these children!' The defence, however, had said they could not attach much importance to the letters, that they may even have been put in Ng's basket by someone else. No one had been called to say that Ng had preached, practised, or discussed 'such dreadful views'.

MacGregor noted that a defence of drunkenness might reduce murder to manslaughter. The onus was on the defence, which would have to prove that the accused had been so much under the influence of alcohol as to have been incapable of forming an intent to murder. The defence had not offered such evidence. The medical witnesses had testified that, from the results of his urine test, Ng could only have been moderately drunk: 'He would not have been, say, drunk enough to walk in front of a tram car.' MacGregor left the jury with three options: not guilty, if the death was accidental or not caused by the accused; guilty of murder, if they were satisfied that he threw Michael Pine off the bridge and that in the nullah Michael had sustained the fractured skull that killed him; or guilty of manslaughter, if, having found he threw Michael in, they concluded he was too drunk to be capable of forming the intention to kill him.

The jury retired at 12:20 p.m. At 1 p.m. MacGregor asked if there was any likelihood of a verdict in the next few minutes. When the foreman, Ernest Blackmore, said no, MacGregor asked the Registrar to order in tiffin for the jurors and adjourned until 2:15 p.m. At 3:15 p.m. the foreman announced they found it impossible to agree on a verdict and saw no possibility of agreeing if given more time. MacGregor concluded there was nothing more to be done. He was prepared to retry the case the following week. 'It was two months since the occurrence and human memory was not always infallible and the sooner the trial could take place the better.' He then exempted the jurors from further jury service for two years, 'in view of the lengthy trial'. The trial had lasted three days.

Juries and capital punishment

Four of the twenty murder trials since 1931, including Ng Loi-yuen's, had ended in hung juries. In Hong Kong such outcomes were mainly confined to capital cases, where unanimous verdicts were required. Among the other cases was the Tsang Foo Villas Murders, in which six members of a Japanese household were killed during riots in 1931 triggered by Japan's invasion of Manchuria. Five persons, including a fourteen-year-old boy, were tried for the murders. The police evidence against them was confused. The jury acquitted four and could not reach a verdict on the fifth, who was not retried.[22] Since discussions in the jury room were secret, the reasons can only be guessed at. The *nolle prosequis* in that case and in the Cheung Chau Murder, and the acquittal of a defendant, Wong Cheung, who was retried in another case, appear to have been mainly due to weak prosecution evidence. It is also possible that the varied nationalities making up three of the hung juries, including the jury in Ng's trial, made it difficult to reach an agreement.[23]

Rumours spread that the jurors in Ng Loi-yuen's trial had failed to agree because one or more of them was opposed in principle to capital punishment. The rumours were strong enough to prompt special measures. On the day after Ng's trial, another murder trial began. This was the 'Balcony Murder', in which a man was accused of pushing a woman to her death from a house in Sham Shui Po. Before the jurors were sworn, the judge, Chief Justice MacGregor, said it had been represented to him that some of them might have conscientious objections to the death penalty. If so, he asked them to speak up to avoid being 'in a position to have to weigh your duty on the one hand and your conscientious feelings on the other'. The jurors were four Westerners and three Chinese. None spoke up. They returned

22. The jury consisted of three Chinese, three British, and a Portuguese. *SCMP*, 19–24 November 1931.
23. The jurors in the Tsang Foo Villas trial were three Chinese, two British, a Portuguese, and an American; in Wong Cheung's first trial the jurors were three Portuguese, two Chinese, and two British. Wong was accused, with his father (who had absconded), of murdering a lodger in their flat. *SCMP*, 24–30 June and 7–11 July 1931.

a verdict of manslaughter. MacGregor sentenced the accused to ten years' imprisonment, saying it was a borderline case, close to murder.[24]

From then on, MacGregor secured 'death-qualified' juries by asking the same question at the start of every capital trial. Other Hong Kong judges did so up to the 1950s. In a trial in 1954 the whole jury stood up when the judge put the question.[25] In a case in 1959 no fewer than twenty-two jurors voiced objections to the death penalty.[26] The practice was apparently not followed in other colonies, although conscientious objections, and the reluctance of Buddhist jurors to convict capitally, were among arguments behind a legislative council motion calling for abolition in Ceylon in 1928.[27] No juror raised a conscientious objection in Hong Kong in the 1930s. But capital punishment had by now attracted public debate, spurred by a worldwide trend towards abolition. By the early 1930s the death penalty was abolished or in abeyance in fourteen European countries, eight US states, and much of South America. In the parts of China controlled by the Kuomintang, and even among some warlord provinces, the death penalty as a *judicial* punishment was increasingly rare.[28] In Australia, Queensland had abolished the death penalty in 1922 and executions were now rare in other states. In Britain, a select committee, appointed during a Labour administration, had recommended in 1930 that the death penalty be suspended for an experimental period of five years. The Labour government

---

24. There were contradictions among the prosecution witnesses. A decision by a policeman to take the accused back to the scene of the crime, where he was seen by two of the prosecution witnesses, also vitiated the subsequent identity parade. *SCMP* and *HKDP*, 24, 25, and 28 August 1934.
25. Thinking they may have misunderstood, the judge put the question again. One juror said he had no religious scruples but did not like to serve on the jury. Two others said they had conscientious objections and were excused. The rest were sworn with two new jurors. The jury acquitted the defendant, a reporter accused of murdering his wife: *SCMP*, 4 and 10 November 1954. The securing of 'death-qualified' juries, by quizzing jurors on their views on the death penalty, has become a key stage in capital trials in some parts of the US.
26. Seven jurors raised objections and were replaced. The trial was aborted when a juror was seen speaking with a witness. During balloting of a jury for the retrial, fourteen jurors raised objections and were replaced. As the usher was about to administer the oath, one of the replacements rose to voice his objection. The judge, A.D. Scholes, told him that, as a juror, he was concerned only with the verdict, not with any sentence that might be passed. When the juror persisted, Scholes exempted him but also ordered him to remain in court throughout the trial. Four inmates of the Cape Collinson Boys' Training Centre were accused of murdering a warder. One was found guilty and, after proof that he was over eighteen, sentenced to death and hanged. *SCMP*, 1 April–20 May 1959.
27. House of Commons, *Report from the Select Committee on Capital Punishment* (London: His Majesty's Stationery Office, 1931), lxviii. Occasionally in England jurors were excused after raising conscientious objections themselves.
28. Frank Dikötter, *Crime, Punishment and the Prison in Modern China* (Hong Kong: Hong Kong University Press, 2002), 178–181; David T. Johnson and Franklin E. Zimring, *The Next Frontier: National Development, Political Change, and the Death Penalty in Asia* (Oxford: Oxford University Press, 2009), 247–253.

fell in 1931. The new Conservative-dominated National government declined to adopt the recommendation.[29]

The UK select committee heard arguments for abolition from the Archbishop of York, William Temple, and other clergymen. Its report, written by the chairman, James Barr, a Presbyterian minister and Labour Member of Parliament, stressed that abolition was consistent with Christian faith. The Hong Kong press reported on the select committee and on initiatives elsewhere to abolish the death penalty – and on its restoration in Fascist Italy and Nazi Germany. In a debate at the University of Hong Kong in October 1933, students rejected the motion 'that capital punishment should be abolished' by a majority of fifty to twenty-two. But in his New Year message in 1934 the Bishop of Victoria, Ronald Hall, urged 'euthanasia of the Death Sentence'. Hong Kong, he said, was an ideal 'Imperial Laboratory' for a measure that could 'prove invaluable to places less ably governed'.

> We are small enough and compact enough to make experiments which will be of service not only to Britain but to China. The proportion of educated people in the European community must be almost unique in the world. The proportion in the Chinese community, in spite of the large number of labourers and artizans, is very considerable.[30]

Hall elaborated these ideas in a letter published in English- and Chinese-language newspapers on 1 and 2 August 1934, just as committal hearings in the Nullah Murder case began. He proposed that every death sentence should be commuted for an experimental period of twenty years. He advanced familiar arguments about the failure of the death penalty as a deterrent and its origins in a retributive view of punishment – a view 'no longer considered tenable by any outstanding Christian thinker'. In a reference to the campaign to save Cheng Kwok-yau, he made a further point. Capital punishment meant not only 'treating a person impersonally' but also 'destroying that person'. Yet, once a murderer became 'known intimately as a person' to the community, 'the demand for commutation of sentence becomes acute'. For this reason, wrote Hall, 'it would be virtually impossible for the death sentence to be carried out on any European. We would know so much about his temptations, about his difficulties, about the reasons that led him to act that we would insist that the full vigour of the law was stayed in his case.'[31]

The government did not pursue Hall's proposal. On the contrary, it was now contemplating measures to tackle the persistently low rate of murder convictions. In February 1934 the Governor in Council considered a proposal to exclude Portuguese from juries in

29. House of Commons, *Report from the Select Committee on Capital Punishment*, lxvii–lxix, lxxvii–lxxx, and c; Harry Potter, *Hanging in Judgment: Religion and the Death Penalty in England from the Bloody Code to Abolition* (London: SCM Press, 1993), Chapter 11.
30. *St John's Review*, Vol. VI, No. 1 (January 1934): 4–5.
31. *HKT*, 1 August 1934; *HKDP*, *SCMP*, and *KSDN*, 2 August 1934. For Cheng Kwok-yau see Chapter 9.

murder trials but decided to take no action.[32] Portugal had abolished capital punishment in 1867. In this age of nationalism some of Hong Kong's Portuguese community were now identifying more deliberately with Portugal and its culture.[33] There is, however, no clear evidence that they espoused abolitionism, or, if they did, that it led to the low conviction rates in murder trials: 33 per cent in 1933, 20 per cent in 1934, 18 per cent in 1935. The proposal may have been prompted by a case tried two months earlier, in which a jury with a Portuguese majority acquitted a man of the murder of an elderly boatwoman. That verdict, however, was probably due, not to conscientious objections, but again to the usual weaknesses in the prosecution's case. The main evidence was from an alleged accomplice. After defence witnesses had testified to an alibi, the foreman announced that the jury had decided to acquit and did not wish to hear closing speeches. The judge, John Wood, said, 'I will record your verdict, Gentlemen, and my sympathies are with you.'[34]

Bishop Hall's proposals, the hung jury in Ng Loi-yuen's trial, and MacGregor's attempts to weed out jurors with conscientious objections prompted a series of editorials. The *South China Morning Post* and *Hongkong Daily Press* were sympathetic towards the idea of a twenty-year moratorium on hangings. The *Post* again suggested juries of twelve and allowing defendants the right of peremptory challenge to jurors. Quoting the views of a judge in England, the *China Mail* floated the idea of a second degree of murder, for which the death penalty was not mandatory: this was the practice in many European countries and in some parts of the British Empire. The *Mail* also highlighted the benefits of involving the public, as jurors, in 'a mixed population full of racial and religious prejudices', so they would come to learn 'how carefully cases are tried'. The *Telegraph* and the *Daily Press* welcomed the Chief Justice's measure as a practical way of preventing personal principles from obstructing the workings of justice. The *Daily Press* also criticized the practice of allowing

32. ExCo Minutes, 21 February 1934, CO 131/91, 38. Coincidentally, in a trial the next month, a man charged with wounding his wife with intent to cause grievous bodily harm objected to Portuguese sitting on the jury on the ground that the main witness against him, his ex-concubine, had 'several sweethearts who are Portuguese'. The judge, Lindsell, overruled him. The trial continued with Portuguese making up three of the seven jurors. The accused, undefended, was convicted of wounding but acquitted on the charge of intent. The case prompted the *South China Morning Post* to call for defendants to be given legal aid and for a right of peremptory challenge of jurors to be extended to the defence. *SCMP*, 20 and 21 March 1934.
33. See Vivian Kong, *Multiracial Britishness: Global Networks in Hong Kong, 1910–45* (Cambridge: Cambridge University Press, 2024), Chapter 4; and Catherine S. Chan, *The Macanese Diaspora in British Hong Kong: A Century of Transimperial Drifting* (Amsterdam: Amsterdam University Press, 2021), Chapter 5.
34. *SCMP* and *HKDP*, 19 and 20 December 1933. Portuguese are recorded as having sat as jurors on at least four of the six murder trials in 1933, two of which resulted in murder convictions. Jurors' names are not recorded for the two other trials, both of which arose out of the same murder and resulted in acquittals, one on the direction of the judge, the other after the judge said it would be dangerous to rely on the evidence of one of the main prosecution witnesses, a police informer: *SCMP* and *HKDP*, 2 and 3 February 1933.

jurors to mix with others during adjournments in murder trials. It urged greater efforts to ensure jurors knew enough English to follow speeches by counsel and the summing up.[35]

Some of these ideas were responses to an option taken by the Acting Attorney General, Roger Lindsell, for Ng's retrial: the use of a special, or 'Taipan', jury. Lindsell explained to the press that in difficult cases the judge or the Attorney General could order a special jury;[36] and that, though special juries were now rare in criminal cases, they had been used in Cheng Kwok-yau's trial and in the trial of Carvalho Yeo, a clerk convicted in 1928 of defrauding the government.[37] Lindsell added that the special jury list consisted 'almost entirely of heads and assistant heads of firms', who were of 'any nationality, as opposed to the Common Jury, which is, roughly speaking, drawn from English-speaking people not in those positions'.[38] If this was an attempt to persuade the public that Ng would be retried by a more ethnically diverse jury it was misleading. About 70 per cent of the seventy-one special jurors were British; 11 per cent were Chinese; another 11 per cent were Portuguese. Of the 2,700 common jurors, 30 per cent were Chinese and 16 per cent Portuguese; the rest were from all parts of the world, with a large number, but not an absolute majority, from Britain and its dominions. Even so, the special jury balloted for Ng's retrial was a diverse one: it consisted of two Chinese, three British, a Hong Kong-born Irishman, and a Hong Kong-born member of a prominent Jewish family; but no Portuguese.

R v Ng Loi-yuen
Murder retrial, 5–7 September 1934

The special jurors empanelled for Ng Loi-yuen's retrial were

William Thomas (foreman), acting manager, Chartered Bank.

Edward Cock MBE, JP, chief manager, Hong Kong and Whampoa Dock Co. Ltd.

Felix Ellis, stockbroker, Ellis and Edgar.

John Fleming, chartered accountant, Lowe, Bingham and Matthews.

William Goggin, manager, Bank Line Ltd (a shipping company).

Sum Pak-ming JP, Sum Pak Ming & Co (a shipping agent).

35. The *Daily Press's* gossip columnist had recently mentioned a case in which a Japanese juror had sat through a manslaughter trial only to tell the other jurors in broken English that he had not understood what had been said. *SCMP*, 3 and 27 August 1934; *CM*, 14 August 1934; *HKDP*, 4 and 30 August 1934.

36. The Attorney General could simply order a special jury by giving notice. A judge could order a special jury on application by the accused, but if he did so the accused was required to deposit with the Registrar a sum sufficient to cover the remuneration of special jurors at a rate of $25 each per day, should the judge order remuneration to be paid. Jury Ordinance, No. 6 of 1887 (1924 edition), s. 16 and 28.

37. See Munn, 'Carvalho Yeo and the 1928 Hong Kong Treasury Swindle'.

38. *SCMP* and *CM*, 25 August 1934.

Wong Tak-kwong, manager, Fung Tang Imports & Exports, formerly Supreme Court Translator, 1910–1915.

The judge, Chief Justice MacGregor, asked if any among them felt that, 'this being a capital trial which may result therefore in the death sentence being passed (whether that sentence is ever carried out or not), you have such conscientious objection to that sentence that your services on the jury will bring your conscience into direct conflict with your duty on the jury.' No one spoke up and the jurors were duly sworn.[39]

As in Ng Loi-yuen's first trial, John Fraser prosecuted and Richard Lim defended. Lim was instructed in this trial, not by J.M. Hall, but by Theodore Kemble of Wilkinson & Grist, a solicitor of two years' standing in Hong Kong: the money raised by Ng's friends had run out and Kemble and Lim were now assigned at public expense.[40] The prosecution called most of the witnesses who had appeared in the first trial and two new witnesses. Doris Pine, the mother of the twins Michael and Mary, testified that, on 22 June, on returning from shopping, she saw her husband at the Lower Peak Tramway Station. After he told her what had happened, she rushed home to find Mary being put to bed by the amah. She found bumps on the back of Mary's head and spine, and bruises and cuts on her arms and legs. She also found two 'very peculiar marks' on her neck: the skin was not broken, but there were 'circular impressions' just above the collar bone.

The other new witness was Eric Davies, eight-and-a-half years old, who gave evidence on oath after satisfying the judge that he understood its meaning and knew that if he told lies, 'I may be punished and put in prison.' The jury complained they could not hear him, so he gave evidence from the usher's box instead of the witness stand. Eric lived with his parents in the army quarters. He had been with the other children on 22 June, 'all bunched together' on the bridge, throwing stones into the nullah. After a while he left the others to go home for a drink. As he walked up the path he heard a scream. He ran back and saw Fay Bromley in the water and Tony Flood down on the side of the nullah. He did not see anyone else. Kathleen Fairburn then testified. Lim again tested her evidence against her deposition. 'I am telling just the same story as I told before the Magistrate and at the former trial,' she said when re-examined by Fraser.

Doris Pine, Eric Davies, and Kathleen Fairbairn testified on the morning of the second day of the trial after judge, jury, interpreter, lawyers, and defendant had made a visit to the site of the incident. After an adjournment for tiffin, Fraser announced that the next witness, Mary Pine, had fallen ill and was in hospital with a fever. The trial went on with other witnesses. The next day Fraser reported that Mary had measles and could not be discharged for another ten days. Because her deposition before the magistrate had not been

39. The main sources for this trial are the Judge's notes and transcript of his summing up, CO 129/550/7, 94–137; *HKDP*, *SCMP*, and *KSDN*, 6–8 September 1934.

40. *KSDN*, 30 October 1934.

taken on oath it could not be put it in as evidence.[41] Nor was there any way of adducing her evidence at the first trial. Proceedings resumed with other witnesses. Fraser then requested an adjournment until Mary had recovered. MacGregor refused. Jurors had other matters to attend to, he said; it was 'a very serious matter' to allow such a case to stand over for so long. This put Fraser in a position of some embarrassment since he had already outlined Mary's evidence in his opening speech.

Lim then made a submission of no case to answer on the basis that none of the evidence connected the accused with the alleged murder. MacGregor sent the jury out and heard and then rejected Lim's arguments. Asked if he wished to give evidence, Ng chose to make an unsworn statement from the dock. 'I am not used to taking intoxicating liquor,' he said. 'On that day I had plenty of liquor and I do not know what happened to me afterwards.' The defence called no witnesses. Fraser's closing speech largely repeated his speech in the first trial, except that he now had to deal with the absence of evidence from Mary Pine. The case was simple, he said; her inability to give evidence did not change 'one tittle' the case for the Crown. In the afternoon Lim gave his closing speech, this time also advancing a defence of drunkenness: the medical evidence was that Ng's pulse was extremely high on admission to hospital; the effect of being in the cold water in the nullah would have been to sober him up; the urine sample, taken from Ng some hours after the incident, was 'valueless', he said. If the jury concluded he was incapable of forming any intention of killing the children, then the verdict must be manslaughter.

MacGregor's summing up was slightly more against the accused than in the first trial. He told the jury to ignore what the prosecution had said about Mary Pine's evidence and to treat with care the evidence from her mother about the marks on her neck: there was nothing to indicate the accused had inflicted them. The evidence was circumstantial and finely balanced, he said. It was clear that Michael Pine had died from an injury to his head in the nullah, but no one had seen the accused throw him in. Eric Davies had heard a scream while walking home from the bridge. Kathleen Fairburn had seen a man throw two children from the bridge. She had picked him out at an identity parade conducted with scrupulous fairness.[42] The evidence of many other witnesses showed that Ng was the only man with the children in the nullah. He had stated that he intended to commit suicide. Letters among his possessions suggested a motive to kill Europeans. The defence, on the other hand, had argued that the letters may have been planted; that the three eldest children had gone down to play by the nullah and the other two had fallen in. Why did

41. Shortly afterwards, drawing on the UK's Children Act 1908, the Evidence Ordinance was amended to allow unsworn evidence of a child who understood the duty of speaking the truth, including written statements, provided that no one was liable to be convicted on such evidence alone. Ordinance No. 33 of 1934.

42. The police had been trying to improve identity parades with reference to a recent Royal Commission, cited in this trial. *Report of the Royal Commission on Police Powers and Procedure* (London: His Majesty's Stationery Office, 1929).

the children not run away? Perhaps they were engrossed in their stone-throwing. Perhaps some were standing on the rails. If the defence's explanation was to be believed, it was a remarkable coincidence that the children on the bridge and those down by the nullah all fell in at the same time, just as the accused himself jumped.

The jury retired at 4:45 p.m. and returned at 6 p.m. for further guidance on jury unanimity and on what bearing the degree of intoxication had on any verdict. After clarifications by MacGregor, the jury retired again and returned at 6:30 p.m. with a verdict of guilty of murder and a strong recommendation to mercy. This was interpreted to Ng. When asked if he had anything to say before sentence was passed, he said

> I too fell into the nullah and was injured. My legs were swollen. I do not know what happened to me. I have a grandmother in Swatow who is over eighty years old and a father over sixty. I have a wife in the country and a son who is barely two years old. All of them depend on me for a living. If I am put to death they will die of starvation. I deny having committed murder. I had drunk so much wine I did not know what was happening. I beg your Lordship to recommend me for mercy and spare me the death penalty. I swear I will drink no more.[43]

MacGregor pronounced sentence of death. To the jury he expressed, 'the thanks of the community for the patience and attention with which they had sat through a long and admittedly trying case.' He exempted them from jury service for two years.

Two weeks later Ng Loi-yuen's lawyers, Richard Lim and Theodore Kemble, informed the press they intended to appeal against the conviction to Hong Kong's Court of Criminal Appeal, which had been established eighteen months earlier, in March 1933.[44]

Judicial reform and the Court of Criminal Appeal

In the early 1930s the Hong Kong government made three important judicial reforms: the conferral on the Supreme Court of powers to grant divorces; the creation of juvenile courts; and the formation of a Court of Criminal Appeal. These reforms were largely welcomed by the colonial community as being long overdue. Judges in England had been hearing divorce petitions since 1858. Chief Justice Piggott had argued for similar facilities in Hong Kong in 1910.[45] Juvenile courts had existed in England for a quarter of a century. In 1930 the Legislative Council unanimously passed a resolution moved by Robert Kotewall calling

43. *KSDN*, 8 September 1934 (author's translation).

44. *SCMP* and *HKDP*, 21 September 1934.

45. The measure was, however, opposed by the Legislative Councillor representing Portuguese residents, J.P. Braga, because it was class legislation, applicable only to Christian marriages and their civil equivalents, and thus denied to the great majority of the population. *SCMP*, 19 March 1910; Royal Commission on Divorce and Matrimonial Causes, *Minutes of Evidence* (London: His Majesty's Stationery Office), Vol. 1, 337–347; *HKH*, 27 October 1934.

for separate courts and training institutions for offenders under the age of sixteen.[46] The conviction of a barrister of perjury in 1929, and his subsequent vindication by his Inn of Court, prompted newspaper editorials and Legislative Council questions about a court of criminal appeal.[47] The reform, however, was not a local initiative but a measure ordered by the Secretary of State. Hong Kong's Court of Criminal Appeal owed its origins to an alleged injustice against a white man, not in Hong Kong, but in a remote colonial outpost in Africa.

In November 1928 Benjamin Knowles, a colonial medical officer, was convicted of murdering his wife and sentenced to death by the Chief Commissioner's Court of Ashanti, a territory annexed in 1902 to the Gold Coast Colony. He was tried by a magistrate acting as judge and sitting without a jury. He was unrepresented because lawyers were not permitted to appear in the Ashanti courts. After the Governor commuted his death sentence to life imprisonment, Knowles appealed to the Privy Council. His lawyers argued that it was unlawful for a judge to try a capital case without a jury. The Judicial Committee gave no opinion on this but quashed the conviction on the ground that the judge had misdirected himself in omitting the possibility of manslaughter. Knowles's case became a cause célèbre.[48] It prompted a circular from the Secretary of State in 1930 instructing colonies to submit proposals for independent courts of criminal appeal, if they did not already have them, along the lines of the Court of Criminal Appeal established in England in 1907. Courts of criminal appeal, it said, would lessen the possibility of miscarriages of justice,

46. Earlier in the year, Kotewall had highlighted the large number of boys being caned on the orders of the courts. This was brought to the attention of the Secretary of State, Lord Passfield, who instructed Peel to take action on a model ordinance produced for the Colonial Office Conference in 1930. Peel appointed a committee chaired by Lindsell (then a magistrate), with Kotewall and the solicitor Lo Man-kam as members. Its report formed the basis for reforms in Hong Kong. These included separate juvenile courts, a probation system, and industrial schools. Report on the Measures Required for the Institution of Juvenile Courts in Hong Kong, *Hong Kong Sessional Papers*, 3/1931; *HKH*, 19 June and 2 October 1930 and 28 January 1932; CO 129/527/13, 'Juvenile offenders' (1930); Ordinance No. 1 of 1932.

47. Robert Instone Brewer was convicted of making false statutory reports relating to the liquidation of the Instone Banking Corporation, which he had founded in 1927. The Acting Chief Justice, John Wood, sentenced him to four months' imprisonment with hard labour. Lawyers in Hong Kong believed the trial had been prejudiced by Wood's refusal to allow the charges against Brewer to be tried together rather than separately. A report prepared for the Colonial Office by the Solicitor General of the Straits Settlements concluded that Wood had also misdirected the jury on several points. The Acting Attorney General, C.G. Alabaster, referred the case to the Benchers of Brewer's Inn of Court, Middle Temple, who decided they could find no justification for his conviction. Brewer had already served his sentence. After petitioning the Governor, he received a free pardon and £1,000 in compensation. CO 129/535/4 and 5, 'N.I. Brewer' (1931); *SCMP*, 17 November 1930; *HKH*, 4 December 1930; *HKDP*, 5 December 1930.

48. Albert Lieck, ed., *Trial of Benjamin Knowles* (London: William Hodge & Co., 1933).

improve the standard of justice in the lower courts, and relieve governors of some of the burden of exercising the prerogative of mercy.[49]

No such court existed in Hong Kong. Since 1873, the Full Court of the Supreme Court could hear appeals on facts as well as law in civil cases, but in criminal cases it could decide only questions of law referred to it by the trial judge. At first, the Full Court consisted of the Chief Justice and the Puisne Judge, the only two judges in Hong Kong, one of whom had tried the case under appeal. If they disagreed the Chief Justice had a casting vote. Appeals were therefore, in essence, appeals to the Chief Justice, including appeals against his own decisions. In his quarrels with Chief Justice Piggott over reform of the court, Governor Lugard described this as a 'farce'. The anomaly was partly resolved in 1912 by the addition of a third judge of the Full Court: the senior judge of the British Supreme Court for China in Shanghai, who would visit twice a year to sit with the two Hong Kong judges on civil appeals. But the old arrangement where two judges decided questions of law referred to the Full Court by a trial judge was maintained. The reforms therefore had little, if any, impact on criminal justice.[50]

The Hong Kong government responded to the 1930 circular by proposing that a Full Court of two or three judges should hear appeals from criminal trials on questions of fact as well as law, and against sentences. Appellants would obtain either leave to appeal from the Full Court or a certificate from the trial judge that the case was a fit one for appeal. An appellant in a capital case, or one involving a question of law, would be assigned a solicitor and counsel at the discretion of the Chief Justice. The Full Court would be empowered to confirm the original judgment and sentence, or quash the conviction, or vary the sentence, or order a new trial – a power included at the request of the judges, Kemp and Wood, and one not available in England until 1964.[51] The option of allowing only two judges to hear criminal appeals took into account the difficulty of obtaining the services of the Shanghai judge at short notice. The judges had asked for the option for the trial judge to be a member of a Full Court of two judges hearing a criminal appeal, since the colony had only two judges, and, in their view, temporary appointments of barristers were undesirable. This was overruled by the Colonial Office on the grounds that an appeal from a trial by the Chief Justice would be unlikely to succeed and an appeal from the Puisne Judge would, in effect,

49. Circular by the Secretary of State, Lord Passfield, 22 May 1930, CO 323/1061/14, encl. (3). I am grateful to Christopher Corns for sharing with me this and other sources on this topic.

50. The Shanghai judge was added pending the addition of a permanent third judge. A permanent third judge was not added until after World War II, although temporary judges were appointed in the 1930s. Supreme Court Ordinance, No. 12 of 1873; Criminal Procedure Ordinance, No. 9 of 1899 s. 78; Full Court Ordinance, No. 27 of 1912; Christopher Corns, *Criminal Appeals in Hong Kong* (Hong Kong: Sweet & Maxwell, 2019), Chapter 2.

51. Legislation in 1921 had already empowered the Full Court to order a new trial on deciding a question of law reserved by the trial judge. In introducing the legislation, Kemp, then Attorney General, noted expressions of regret by appeal judges in England that the 1907 legislation had not given them such powers. *HKH*, 23 June 1921; Ordinance No. 10 of 1921; *HKDP*, 4 September 1920.

be an appeal to the Chief Justice alone. Instead, the legislation on criminal appeals enacted in 1933 prohibited the trial judge from sitting on an appeal where the Full Court consisted of only two judges. The Governor also retained a power introduced in 1912 to make temporary appointments to the Full Court of barristers of seven or more years' standing if permanent judges were unavailable.[52] For Ng Loi-yuen's appeal it was necessary to make use of these powers.

Ng Loi-yuen v R
Hong Kong's first murder appeal, 8–17 October 1934

Some newspapers reported that Ng Loi-yuen's appeal was the first criminal appeal under the new system. Although it was the first murder case, the first appeal had in fact taken place in April 1933, three weeks after the creation of the Court of Criminal Appeal. That appeal was heard by three judges: Acting Chief Justice John Wood (the trial judge); the Acting Puisne Judge, Roger Lindsell; and Philip Jacks, an additional puisne judge appointed temporarily to hear the appeal. They quashed the conviction of Joseph Besa for obtaining money by false pretences by means of a bounced cheque, after concluding there were discrepancies in the prosecution evidence.[53]

Forming a Full Court for Ng's appeal posed difficulties. On 20 September 1934, during the Supreme Court's long vacation, Chief Justice MacGregor and his wife went on a month-long trip to northern China. Before leaving, he made proposals to the Governor, Sir William Peel, on the composition of the court. Two experienced barristers, Eldon Potter KC and Francis Jenkin KC, were in Hong Kong at this time. But Peel appointed two of the only three officials with the required seven years' standing as barristers: Philip Jacks and James Hayden.[54] Jacks was about to retire after nearly thirty years of service in Hong Kong, mainly as Land Officer. Qualified initially as a solicitor, he had been called to the Bar by Inner Temple in 1922 and had acted at various times as a judge.[55] Hayden, also a former solicitor, had been called to the Irish Bar in 1926 and had served as a magistrate in Uganda

52. Ordinances Nos. 5 and 8 of 1933; Criminal Appeal Rules 1933, *HKGG*, 12 May 1933; CO 323/1157/6 and 323/1197/9 'Criminal Appeal: Formation of Courts of, in Colonies: Eastern' (1931 and 1932). *HKH*, 16 March 1933.
53. Besa, from Manila, was immediately rearrested on leaving the court pursuant to an extradition request by the US government in the Philippines. A habeas corpus action on Besa's behalf failed to obtain his release and he was extradited in June. *SCMP*, 13 and 27 April, 4 and 16 May, and 7 June 1933.
54. C.G. Alabaster, the Attorney General, was on leave. Roger Lindsell, acting in his place, had only recently been called to the Bar. The third official with sufficient standing was the Assistant Land Officer, Frederick Eaves, who had been called to the Bar in 1923.
55. Notably, in the trial of Carvalho Yeo in 1928. For his biography see Rohan Price, *Going Native: The Passions of Philip Jacks* (Victoria: Australian Scholarly Publishing Ltd, 2016).

before becoming Official Receiver in Hong Kong in April 1934. He returned to Africa in 1937 as a judge of the Supreme Court of Kenya.[56]

Richard Lim, for Ng Loi-yuen, and John Fraser, for the Crown, argued the case before Jacks (president) and Hayden over four days in early October.[57] Ng was not in court. The appeal was on several grounds: **first**, that the judge had wrongfully refused to withdraw the case from the jury after the defence's submission of no case to answer; **secondly**, that he should have ordered a new trial when the prosecution failed to produce Mary Pine as a witness; **thirdly**, that the verdict was against the weight of the evidence; **fourthly**, that, without Mary's evidence, the evidence of Kathleen Fairburn was wrongfully admitted because it was evidence of *similar facts* that were not admissible until a prima facie case had been established for the offence with which Ng was charged, the murder of Michael Pine; **fifthly** that there had been a miscarriage of justice in that the prosecution's outlining of Mary's evidence in its opening had seriously prejudiced the defence; and, **sixthly**, that the judge had misdirected the jury by failing to state clearly the defence's argument that some of the children not seen by Fairburn had gone down to the nullah, and by laying too much stress on the marks found on Mary's neck.

The court had MacGregor's typed-up notes of evidence and a transcript of his summing up, but no record of the speeches of counsel. This gave rise to disagreements over what exactly Fraser had said when outlining Mary Pine's prospective evidence in his opening speech. Lim claimed that Fraser had said that Mary would testify that Ng had thrown all five children into the nullah – a claim denied by Fraser. Lim argued that, despite warnings to the jury to ignore it, the judge's summing up had been influenced by the references to Mary's ungiven evidence. In any case, said Lim, once the prosecution had outlined it the mischief had been done. No amount of warning by the judge could have undone it; the warnings had, on the contrary, drawn more attention to it. The judge had also prejudiced the jury by describing the marks on Mary's neck as 'circumstantial evidence of considerable importance' which the jury should fit 'into the whole of this great jigsaw of pieces', even though there was no evidence of how they had been inflicted.

Lim cited numerous judgments from the Court of Criminal Appeal in England: by the second day of the hearing over seventy volumes of law reports and textbooks had been laid out in court. Among the cases were *R v Wallace* (1931) and *R v Smith* (1915), the 'Brides in the Bath' murders, in which the court held that similar fact evidence was admissible only if a prima facie case had been established for the offence with which the accused was charged.[58] The question, said Lim, was not whether Ng was guilty or not, but whether

56. *HKDP*, 26 February 1937.

57. The main sources for the appeal are the judges' notes and judgment, CO 129/550/7, 13–80; and *HKDP* and *SCMP*, 9, 10, 12, 13, and 18 October 1934.

58. In the Brides in the Bath case, George Smith was convicted of the murder of Bessie Mundy, whom he had bigamously married, by drowning her in a bath. The prosecution produced evidence of similar, subsequent murders

he had had a fair trial, and whether the jury might have given a different verdict if they had not heard the prosecution's disclosures about Mary's evidence.

Lim took a day and a half to argue his case. Fraser took two half-days to respond on behalf of the Crown. He argued that the verdict was not against the weight of the evidence: the prosecution had proved that Ng was on the bridge when the incident occurred, and that he was the only person, other than the children, in the nullah immediately after the incident. As for the argument that the judge should have ordered a new trial when Mary Pine failed to appear, Fraser said it was for the defence, not the prosecution, to apply for this, and the defence did not do so. The prosecution, he said, had asked for an adjournment until Mary was ready to give evidence, but the judge had refused because it would have disadvantaged the accused by strengthening the prosecution's case. Lim interjected that this was never mentioned at trial: the reason was that the jury would forget the evidence after so long an adjournment.

Dealing with the point that Fairburn's evidence should not have been admitted without the evidence of Mary Pine, Fraser said that throwing the five children from the bridge was not five separate but similar acts, but acts constituting a single transaction contemporaneous with the offence charged: *R v Smith* therefore did not apply; even if it did, a prima facie case had been made without Fairburn's evidence. The judge had given ample warning that Michael Pine was not one of the two children she had seen thrown by Ng. It was, however, possible that he *was* one of them: here, Lim interjected that she had never said that, and it was clear that Michael was not one of the two children.

On the last two grounds of appeal, Fraser said that most, if not all, of his statements about Mary Pine's evidence in his opening address had been corroborated by other witnesses. Judge and counsel had given adequate warnings to the jury to disregard that part of his opening speech. Fraser cited eight English appeal cases to support this point. He then cited over a dozen more on the question of misdirection by the judge in summarizing the defence's case. The authorities, he said, showed that it was open to the defence to interrupt the summing up to correct misstatements, and that a failure to deal with evidence – even important evidence – did not amount to misdirection. As for the marks on Mary's neck, the judge had stressed there was no direct evidence to connect them with the accused, and it was for the jury to fit them into the whole picture. Fraser added that it was extremely unlikely from the position and nature of the marks that they were caused by an inanimate

---

by Smith to show 'system' as proof of guilt. On appeal, Smith's counsel, Sir Edward Marshall Hall, argued that the evidence was inadmissible because no prima facie case had been made out. The court held that a prima facie case *had* been made and that the trial judge had properly directed the jury on what use they could make of the evidence. It dismissed the appeal, but, in confirming that evidence of similar acts became admissible once a prima facie case had been made, the judgment set a precedent for the use of system to show intention in other murder trials. *R v Smith* (1916) 11 Cr. App. R. 229; Eric R. Watson, ed., *Trial of George Joseph Smith* (London: William Hodge & Co., 1922).

object: Hayden here interjected to suggest they might have been caused when she was being rescued. Fraser concluded by remarking that if it really was supposed that the jury had understood none of the warnings by the judge, this would be imputing to them 'such a low mentality' that their verdict would be of no account. 'My Lords,' he reminded the court, 'there was a special jury in this case!'

Through their various interjections the judges had made it clear where their sympathies lay. Their unanimous judgment, read out by Jacks on 17 October, agreed with Fraser on every point. In such a long summing up it was 'easy to pick out a word here or a phrase there for criticism,' they said. But 'the manner in which the case was left to the Jury was eminently fair in every respect'. The Chief Justice, as trial judge, had properly exercised his discretion in admitting evidence. His summing up had left no doubt in the minds of the jury what the actual defence was. The verdict was a rational one based on the evidence. There was no miscarriage of justice. They dismissed the appeal, stressing, however, that they did not wish that their decision 'should in any way affect the strong recommendation for mercy made by the Jury at the conclusion of the trial'.

The campaign to save Ng Loi-yuen

While awaiting the outcome of his appeal, Ng Loi-yuen was, in accordance with the new appeals system, treated as a prisoner awaiting trial. Once his appeal was dismissed he was returned to the condemned cell. A petition was then launched in an effort to persuade the Governor to commute his death sentence. The promoters were the Chiu Chow Native Place Association and the Anglican Church. The prospects for success seemed strong. A week before the dismissal of Ng's appeal, the petition for Keung Tsz-pan, advanced by an Anglican priest, had resulted in a commutation of his death sentence.[59] Now, in the light of Bishop Hall's views on the 'depersonalizing' effects of the death penalty, the petition for Ng sought to humanize him in the eyes of the public. It described how Ng, a twenty-eight-year-old[60] assistant in a chemist's shop in Swatow, had lost his job and hoped to find work in Singapore; how, cheated of the money he had borrowed, he was stranded in Hong Kong. It referred only briefly to the incident at the nullah, repeating Ng's claim that he had no recollection of it: the drink, and distress at his predicament, had made him lose his mind, it said. His eighty-eight-year-old grandmother had fainted when she heard of his sentence. She was now so grief-stricken she no longer wished to live. His wife and infant son had no one else to support them. The petition accepted the verdict as just. But it also pointed out

59. See Chapter 9.

60. Some other reports, for example, in the *South China Morning Post* and *Wah Kiu Yat Po*, give his age as thirty-eight.

that the jury's strong recommendation to mercy showed that they, too, felt deep sympathy for Ng.[61]

Copies of the petition were placed in churches, newspaper offices, shops, and banks. The *Kung Sheung Daily News* and its associated papers gave it prominence and traced its progress, interviewing the promoters and Ng's lawyers and younger brother. These papers had already devoted much space to Ng's case. Even before the appeal, the *Kung Sheung Daily News* published a two-part editorial on the importance of mercy, embellished with quotations from Shakespeare, Lombroso, and the *Rites of Zhou*. The editorial criticized MacGregor's question to jurors about conscientious objections as tantamount to a direction to *convict* the accused; it also discussed the points of doubt concerning Ng's guilt.[62] Other papers were less interested: the English-language press barely mentioned the petition, and, although many Westerners signed it, some were reportedly opposed. The petition garnered 24,352 signatures – many more than the 9,000 for Keung Tsz-pan, and the 17,000 for Cheng Kwok-yau. On 6 November, two days before the Governor in Council met to consider Ng's sentence, the petition was submitted to the Secretary for Chinese affairs by Lam Chi-sat, chairman of the Chiu Chow association; the Reverend Lee Kau-yan of the Anglican Church; and Father Emilio Teruzzi, Catholic chaplain to Victoria Gaol.[63]

On 8 November Governor Peel and his Executive Council considered Ng's case with the aid of the notes of the retrial, translations of the anti-European letters found among Ng's possessions, and a report from MacGregor: this included the strong recommendation to mercy by the jury. Although they had given no reason, MacGregor suggested jurors may have felt that Ng had undergone the strain of two trials, or that drink had disordered his judgement. He added that, without this recommendation, he could not offer anything on Ng's behalf. The council advised against commutation by a majority of six to two. Peel ordered that the law should take its course.[64]

This was Peel's second and last confirmation of a death sentence. In the first case, Fan Hing was convicted in July 1933 of murdering his elderly landlady for her money and jewellery: the jury made no recommendation for mercy and the Executive Council was unanimously against commutation. During Peel's term (9 May 1930–17 May 1935) his deputy, Thomas Southorn, had confirmed three other death sentences, and Peel had commuted three, including those on Cheng Kwok-yau and Keung Tsz-pan.[65] Because Peel

61. *KSDN*, 21 October 1934.
62. *KSDN*, 22 and 23 September 1934.
63. *KSDN*, 3 and 7 November 1934.
64. ExCo Minutes, 8 November 1934, CO 131/91, 230–231; MacGregor to Peel, 12 September 1934, CO 129/550/7, 88–93.
65. A total of forty-seven persons were tried for murder during Peel's term but only fourteen were convicted of murder, and only eight of these convictions resulted in death sentences: the other six were detained at His Majesty's pleasure having been found guilty but insane, or, in one case, guilty but under the age of sixteen.

had to explain why he went against the majority advice of his council, his reasons for commuting their death sentences were clear. In Ng's case, the minutes record only the decision and the fact that the advice was by a majority of six to two. The reasons why Peel and his council ignored the jury's recommendation and the petition for mercy can thus only be guessed at. Perhaps it was because the victim was a child. Perhaps they were influenced by the possible motive in Ng's letters – a political element absent from the Cheng and Keung cases. Perhaps, in the spirit of the Secretary of State's circular, they felt that the failure of Ng's appeal had relieved them of the burden of the exercise of mercy.

Some observers thought they knew the reason. People were saying that Ng would have been spared if the victim had been Chinese, the *Kung Sheung Evening News* declared. The case was the talk of the town, it said. If Ng really was an evil murderer who deserved death, people would be cursing and spitting on him, yet, on the contrary, they were doing their utmost to save his life. They could not fathom why the government had ignored such a strong expression of public opinion. When they compared Ng's treatment with the mercy shown to Cheng Kwok-yau, they could only conclude that the law existed to serve the rich. Ng's life was hanging by a thread, said the editorial; the integrity of the law also hung on this thread. If the government wished to avoid treating human lives like ants' it should handle the case according to the wishes of the people of Hong Kong.[66]

Bishop Hall also believed he knew the reason. On Sunday 21 October, at the end of the Supreme Court's long vacation, soon after the failure of Ng's appeal, he held a 'Judicial Service' at St John's Cathedral, attended by judges, magistrates, and lawyers. This was one of a series of services for different professions – businessmen, seafarers, hospital workers – reflecting Hall's belief in practical Christianity. The cathedral magazine likened it to services at the opening of the assizes in English towns and cities.[67] Hall used this opportunity to expatiate on the 'impersonal' nature of justice. Judges, he said, were like anaesthetists.

> The anaesthetist, by removing consciousness, converts a person into an impersonal organism. In the judicial profession you are continually compelled to apply local anaesthetics to the body corporate of society. You treat this person or that person as less than personal, for the sake of the health of the rest of society.

This was not to belittle the law: 'You have to be just before you are generous, but justice is not in itself generosity. Justice is net practice and not cricket.' It had to be impersonal, 'hence the bandage on the statue,' said Hall, referring to the goddess Justice on court buildings. Yet British justice drew from Christianity a respect for personality shown in its preference for case law over codes or general principles. That was why the bandage covered only one

66. *KSEN*, 17 November 1934. The *KSDN* editorials of 22 and 23 September made similar comparisons between Ng's and Cheng's cases.

67. *St John's Review*, November 1934, 394. See Moira M.W. Chan-Yeung, *The Practical Prophet: Bishop Ronald O. Hall of Hong Kong and His Legacies* (Hong Kong: Hong Kong University Press, 2015).

eye.[68] Hall's metaphors were not entirely satisfactory: justice was more than net practice; the blindfold on the statue of Justice on the pediment of Hong Kong's Law Courts covered both eyes. He did not mention Ng Loi-yuen. But his message was clear: justice had been done in Ng's case; the Governor must now show generosity.

When Governor Peel declined to commute Ng's sentence, Bishop Hall wrote a confidential letter to Sir Philip Cunliffe-Lister, Secretary of State for the Colonies. He did not criticize Peel, who, he said, had 'won universal affection and esteem by his keen sense of personal values and of justice in every matter of this kind'. Nor did he question the outcome of the trial, though he drew attention to the strong recommendation to mercy by a special jury 'composed of some of the Colony's most respected citizens'. His concern was whether the members of Peel's Executive Council had 'a sufficiently wide experience to take a broad enough view in a case of this difficulty'. He feared there was 'a possibility that the unconscious influence of race fear may have prejudiced the decision in a case which, by its peculiar circumstances, demanded generosity as well as justice'. For this reason, it was 'essential that the matter be reviewed at home'.[69]

H.E. Bader, the official in the Colonial Office who had proposed asking Peel for an explanation of his commutation in Keung Tzs-pan's case, now advised that Peel should be asked to submit a report on Ng's case and to postpone execution until the Secretary of State had reviewed it. Once again, the legal advisers in the Colonial Office opposed any intervention. Cunliffe-Lister remarked that he had repeatedly told the House of Commons that the prerogative of mercy was vested in governors personally, and that it would be 'most improper' for him to intervene. Peel was told to inform Hall of this and to ask him to make his representations to Peel himself.[70]

While the campaign for clemency was in progress, Ng's lawyers, Richard Lim and Theodore Kemble, drew up a petition to the Privy Council seeking special leave to appeal *in forma pauperis*: this would excuse him from paying the usual fees and lodging security. Lim and Kemble gave their services gratis. Funds for printing the required numbers of copies and paying the Privy Council agents (the solicitors registered to act in such cases) were raised by the Chiu Chow Native Place Association.[71] Peel formally respited Ng's

68. *SCMP*, 22 October 1934.

69. The Executive Council was indeed inexperienced. Of the six official members, two were acting (D.W. Tratman as Colonial Secretary and Lindsell as Attorney General) and one (N.L. Smith, Secretary for Chinese Affairs) had been appointed two weeks earlier. The other three official members had served for periods ranging from ten months to three years. The three unofficial members (H.E. Pollock, Sir Shouson Chow, and Sir William Shenton) had longer experience but were on leave. C.G.S. Mackie, a businessman, acted for Pollock, and Robert Kotewall, the only non-European, acted for Chow. Both had previously briefly acted as Executive Councillors. Hall to Secretary of State, 22 November 1934, CO 129/550/6, 32–34.

70. Minutes by Bader, 10 December 1934, H.G. Bushe, 11 December 1934, and Cunliffe-Lister, 14 December; Secretary of State to Peel, 18 December 1934, CO 129/550/6, 2–7 and 14.

71. *KSEN*, 8 February 1935; *KSDN*, 20 February 1935.

sentence until 17 February 1935, pending the outcome: the government was forced to deny rumours in the Chinese press that he was to be hanged without waiting for the Privy Council's response. The Judicial Committee considered the petition on 19 February 1935 and advised that it be dismissed: this was approved by the King in Council two days later.[72] Although the decision was quickly telegraphed to the Governor, the news was not made public in Hong Kong until the last week of March, when the government also announced that Ng's execution would take place on Friday 29 March.

A last, unusual intervention took place two days before the execution. When warders asked him if he wished to make a final statement, Ng replied that he wanted to see Chief Justice MacGregor. An official was urgently despatched to the Supreme Court, to present a note with the request to MacGregor, while he was in the middle of hearing another problematic murder trial.[73] MacGregor agreed to see Ng on condition that his lawyers, Richard Lim and Theodore Kemble, were also present. They assembled in MacGregor's chambers on 27 March with the interpreter Ng Chak-wing in attendance. MacGregor took down Ng Loi-yuen's statement but told him he had said nothing new to justify a recommendation to mercy. He forwarded the record to the Governor, who declined to put it before the Executive Council when it met the next day.[74]

Ng Loi-yuen was hanged in Victoria Gaol at 5:30 a.m. on Friday 29 March 1935. It was Hong Kong's first execution since August 1933.[75] In the afternoon, after the usual inquest, his body was buried in the Coffee Plantation at So Kon Po in the presence of his younger brother, Loi-yim. Ng's last wish was that Loi-yim should take care of his son.[76]

European victims, Chinese murderers

Two days after the hanging, an editorial in the *Kung Sheung Daily News* asked why Ng was hanged, despite petitions by the community, when Keung Tsz-pan, a confessed murderer, had escaped death. Luck played a part, it said. 'But there is always a reason. Let us think what it is.' The next few sentences, however, were deleted by the censors.[77]

72. *SCMP*, 19 November 1934; CO 129/551/13: 'Ng Loi Yuen (Death Sentence): Appeal to Privy Council' (1935).
73. Three men were tried for murdering another man during a robbery at Castle Peak. After the jury had retired, the Portuguese foreman returned to request clarification on the difference between murder and manslaughter and for it to be explained to a Chinese juror by an interpreter. MacGregor refused. The jury convicted one of the men of manslaughter and acquitted the other two. Counsel made a formal protest against the inclusion of a juror who did not understand English. MacGregor merely advised the juror to apply to be taken off the jury list if he was uncomfortable about his knowledge of English. *SCMP*, 26–28 March 1935.
74. *KSDN*, 30 March 1935.
75. The only other death sentence confirmed by Peel, on Fan Hing.
76. *KSDN*, 30 March 1935; *Wah Kiu Yat Po*, 29 March 1935.
77. *KSDN*, 31 March 1935.

Perhaps the reason was self-evident anyway. Most likely it was the one given by the *Kung Sheung Evening News* on 17 November, which the censors, notoriously inconsistent,[78] had allowed to stand: the victims were European; they were, moreover, European *children*, which the colonial community naturally considered to be among its most vulnerable members.[79] In fact, Europeans young and old saw themselves as a vulnerable, exposed minority in a violent and politically charged environment. Michael Pine was an army child. Ng Loi-yuen had anti-European letters in his possession. Yet, regardless of any overt political motives, violence by Chinese against Europeans tended to be treated as a direct challenge to colonial order and authority. Police investigations were therefore more painstaking than in purely Chinese cases, often extending far beyond Hong Kong's borders. Official rewards for information on suspects were more generous. The usual amount where the victim was Chinese was $250, if a reward was offered, rising to $500 in some cases if the victim was a woman. If the victim was European, the reward might range from $500 to $1,000, or more. Large amounts, regardless of nationality, were also offered in cases where victims were policemen, or watchmen, or wealthy businessmen.[80] As the Shau Kei Wan murder of 1869 illustrated, the higher the reward, the greater the temptation to fabricate evidence.[81]

Murders of Europeans by Chinese were rare. Excluding piracies and murders at sea, the last case tried before the Nullah Murder to fall broadly within this category, and the first since the Gaol Murders of 1919, was the murder of Mrs R. Mackay in August 1927. Born in China, Mrs Mackay was the daughter of a Chinese mother and a Scottish father. Her husband was the timekeeper at the Taikoo Dockyard. She was set upon by two men on a footpath near Chai Wan while returning home with her young nephew after visiting a friend. The reward was raised from $250 to $500, and then to $1,000. Two men were convicted and hanged purely on circumstantial evidence.[82] The next case after Ng's struck at the highest levels of society. In May 1938 Sybil Challinor, wife of the local head of Imperial Chemical Industries, was stabbed to death in her bed in a frenzied attack by her 'cookboy'

78. They acted like 'tin gods', deleting passages according to the state of their livers, said the solicitor Lo Man-kam when defending another newspaper, the *Hong Kong Shun Po*, whose editors and printers were charged with publishing two anti-Japanese articles without submitting them for censorship. They were sentenced to fines and imprisonment, the latter suspended for twenty-four hours to give them the opportunity to publish an apology. Instead of doing so, they promptly closed down the newspaper and absconded. *HKDP*, 2, 8, 12, 13, 15, 21, and 22 June and 4 July 1928; Ng, *Political Censorship in British Hong Kong*, 28–42.
79. See David M. Pomfret, *Youth and Empire: Trans-Colonial Childhoods in British and French Asia* (Stanford, California: Stanford University Press, 2015), Chapter 4.
80. Some rewards offered by private parties were higher. Among the highest was that offered by the family of Lee Hysan, one of Hong Kong's wealthiest men, who was assassinated in May 1928. The reward of $10,000 was raised to $20,000 after two days. The assassin was never found. *SCMP*, 3 and 5 May 1928.
81. See Chapter 4.
82. *SCMP*, 27–30 September and 1 October 1927.

in their house on the Peak. The Challinors were about to return to England. The cookboy, thirty-year-old Lam Chun, had been given notice but was denied a reference letter because of unsatisfactory work. Lam believed another servant was spreading rumours he had leprosy. Despite opinions from medical experts, supported by other witnesses, that he had a mental age of fourteen, suffered from 'epileptic equivalent', and was prone to 'maniacal outbursts', a special jury convicted him of murder. The Executive Council unanimously advised against mercy and Lam was hanged.[83]

No public petitions were raised on behalf of Lam Chun. The last of the mass petitions was in 1937 for Chiu Yuk-fai, a twenty-four-year-old draughtsman in the Public Works Department. Chiu was convicted of the murder of Cheung Yuk-ching, a shopkeeper's concubine with whom he had become intimate. He had tried to retrieve from her fake documents he had concocted in a bizarre plan to help her recover debts owed to her, which was really a trick to get her to pay for a pleasure trip to Macao. Angered by the deception, she had demanded money for the documents, threatening to make trouble with Chiu's father, a respectable merchant. Chiu sought help from To Wai-man, an ex-soldier and ex-convict. Promising to pay Cheung the money, Chiu lured her to an empty flat in Tsim Sha Tsui owned by his father, where To was supposed to stupefy her with smoke from a drugged cigarette and then grab the documents. But, instead of blowing smoke in her face, To threw a cloth over her head and strangled her. In a panic, they burned the body with charcoal inside the flat. Neighbours saw smoke and called the fire brigade. To Wai-man fled. Chiu was arrested, tried, convicted, and sentenced to death.[84]

This sordid case was the last great sensation of the interwar years. Four papers were fined for publishing accounts prejudicial to the trial. Chief Justice MacGregor said he had never come across worse contempts.[85] Hundreds of spectators attended the trial, some of them so rowdy that MacGregor issued a warning that the court was 'not a place of public entertainment'. Chiu testified he had no idea that To Wai-man would kill Cheung Yuk-ching. Doubts about his guilt became the subject of a public petition promoted by his family and signed by over 2,000. In a separate petition, the trial jury regretted not having recommended mercy and now asked for clemency because they believed the murder was not premeditated. The Officer Administering the Government, Norman Lockhart Smith, confirmed the death sentence on the advice of the majority of the Executive Council. The council reconsidered the case two weeks later after a further petition and again confirmed

83. *HKDP*, *SCMP*, and *KSDN*, 12–14 July 1938; ExCo Minutes, 3 August 1938, CO 131/98, 168; *SCMP*, 18 August 1938.

84. *SCMP* and *HKDP*, 28–30 April and 1 May 1937.

85. H.C. Macnamara, counsel for one of them, said that the editor had assumed that, since the article had been passed by the government censors, it was not objectionable. That was no defence, he acknowledged, but it was 'some illustration of the value or otherwise of the censorship'. *SCMP*, 23 April 1937.

the sentence. Chiu was hanged on 11 June 1937. In a rare concession, his family was allowed to take away his body for burial.[86]

The following month Japan launched a full-scale invasion of China. The hostilities rapidly moved closer to Hong Kong, and in October 1938 Japanese forces captured the city of Canton. Hundreds of thousands of people sought sanctuary in Hong Kong, swelling the population from about a million in 1937 to 1.8 or even 2 million by June 1940.[87] Civil society now applied its energies to 'national salvation' beyond Hong Kong and supporting the growing numbers of refugees within.[88] The government was confronted with the dual challenge of dealing with the crime and other social effects of this massive influx, while also preparing the city for what a few years earlier had been almost unthinkable: a Japanese attack on Hong Kong itself.

86. *SCMP*, 14, 19, and 24 May and 12 June 1937; *Tien Kwong Morning News*, 9 May 1937; *KSDN*, 9, 15, 17–19, and 24 May 1937; ExCo Minutes, 26 May and 8 June 1937.

87. Report of the Excess Population Committee, CO 129/587/15, encl. 1.

88. See Lu Yan, 'Together with the Homeland: Civic Activism for National Salvation in British Hong Kong', *Modern China* Vol. 40, No. 6 (November 2014): 639–674.

11

The Death Penalty in Decline

Capital Crime and Justice, 1946–1966

At 3:40 a.m. on 3 March 1966 a fire broke out at the Hung Kee Bookstore on the ground floor of 34 Luen Shing Street, Fanling, a market town in the New Territories. The fire gutted the bookshop and smoke spread to the house next door. Nine people were killed, most of them by asphyxiation: three women, a man, and five children, two of whom were brothers employed in the shop who were sleeping in the cockloft above. So shocking was the tragedy that the Governor, Sir David Trench, and Princess Margaret, then visiting Hong Kong, sent condolences to the victims' families.[1] An inquiry into the fire by a magistrate found reasonable cause to suspect that the bookshop's owner, the thirty-seven-year-old Tsui Pui-hung, had deliberately started it.[2]

Tsui was committed for trial on two charges of murdering his employees Lau Chi-ming (fifteen) and Lau Wai-ming (fourteen), and one of arson. Evidence showed he had taken out two large insurance policies for the shop, bought four gallons of kerosene the day before the fire, and been seen entering the shop shortly before the fire broke out. He knew that the Lau brothers were sleeping on the premises, said the prosecuting Crown counsel, Geoffrey Grimmet. After a nine-day trial, the jury of six men and one woman found Tsui not guilty of murder but guilty of manslaughter and arson. The verdicts were made possible by a recent change in the law abolishing the old common law rule of felony murder (or constructive malice), whereby a death caused in the commission of a felony, whether intended or not, was deemed to be murder.[3] The jury rejected Tsui's claim that he did not start the fire but apparently accepted his protestations that he would never wish to kill his two

1. *SCMP*, 3 and 4 March and 21 May 1966.
2. *SCMP*, 10, 21, and 27 May 1966.
3. Homicide Ordinance, No. 16 of 1963 s. 2.

young employees: that would have been like 'chopping off my two arms', he had said. The judge, John Williams, endorsed the verdict. The financial losses suffered by Tsui were great, he said; perhaps the public did not comprehend the dangers of fire, he observed. Williams sentenced Tsui to eight years' imprisonment for each of the manslaughters and four for arson, the sentences to run concurrently. For a deliberate crime resulting in the deaths of nine people Tsui would serve a mere eight years – less with good behaviour.[4]

Tsui was one of thirty men in eighteen murder cases tried by the Supreme Court in 1966. Five were found not guilty. Nineteen were convicted of manslaughter and received sentences ranging from eighteen months to life.[5] Five of these had changed their pleas from not guilty to guilty of manslaughter, which were accepted by the judge and the prosecution. Some of the cases resulted from disputes over money. Others originated in petty quarrels, arising, for example, when a factory worker killed a co-worker who had knocked clothing off his table (two years' imprisonment),[6] or when a farmer killed his wife for not feeding the pigs (eighteen months).[7] Six of the thirty defendants were convicted of murder. Three of these, Pakistani watchmen who had killed a man in a fight, had their convictions reduced to manslaughter on appeal.[8] Of the other three, one, being under eighteen, was detained during Her Majesty's pleasure. One, who stabbed a fifteen-year-old girl to death in a quarrel with her family, had his sentence commuted to twelve years' imprisonment. The third, Wong Kai-kei, who had killed a watchman during a robbery, was the last person to be hanged in Hong Kong. He was only the second person to be hanged in over four years.

The decline in hangings in the early 1960s took place during a time of peace. Crime rates were declining. The courts were taking a lenient view of the many pathetic cases that came before them, the result of poverty, overcrowding, and desperation. This was in marked contrast to the decade of turbulence following World War II and civil war in China, when a rapid influx of population brought with it a renewal of gangsterism and politically motivated crime. The courts responded with severe and exemplary punishment. Judges routinely added flogging to sentences for violent crimes. New capital offences were created. By the late 1950s the number of hangings exceeded by a large margin the total in England,

4. *SCMP*, 7, 8, 18, 19, 21, 22, 24, and 25 June and 3–6, 9, 10, 13, 16, and 17 August 1966; *Ta Kung Pao*, *KSDN*, and *Wah Kiu Yat Po*, 17 August 1966.
5. The two sentenced to life imprisonment were found guilty of manslaughter by reason of diminished responsibility under a new provision introduced in the Homicide Ordinance 1963. One had chopped his wife to death. The other had beaten a factory co-worker to death with a hammer. Both were diagnosed as suffering from paranoid schizophrenia and were told they would be released if they recovered. One had his sentence changed on appeal to committal to a mental hospital. *SCMP*, 18 and 19 January, 11–13 and 25 August, and 26 November 1966.
6. *SCMP*, 13–15 December 1966.
7. He had killed her in 1959 and buried her body under the pigsty. He pleaded guilty to manslaughter, claiming she had attacked him with a chopper first. *SCMP*, 16 and 17 August 1966.
8. *SCMP*, 29–31 December 1965 and 4–8 and 11–14 January, 23–25 February, and 1, 3, and 11 March 1966.

where reforms leading to the abolition of the death penalty were now in progress.[9] This chapter explores attitudes to capital punishment in the twenty years following the end of World War II against the background of transformations in the nature of capital crime and changing sensibilities among jurors, judges, and the ruling elite.

The aftermath of war and revolution

From 25 December 1941 to 1 September 1945 Hong Kong was a captured territory of the Japanese Empire. The new regime attempted to erase all traces of British rule as it harnessed Hong Kong's resources to the war effort. Thousands of people were executed by order of the Japanese authorities, many after torture by the Kempeitai (the military police). A million people – over half the population – were forcibly deported to China. Many of them perished at sea or were left to die in remote bays and islands. Those remaining in Hong Kong suffered disease and starvation as food supplies ran short. After forty-four months of Japanese occupation, the city was like 'a patient nearly drained of the lifeblood', a 'sick and seedy shadow' of its former self.[10]

The war cast a longer shadow over Hong Kong's courts. As early as 1931, Japan's invasion of Manchuria prompted attacks on Hong Kong's Japanese population. Eight anti-Japanese rioters were killed by police and six Japanese were killed by rioters: four men and a fourteen-year-old boy were tried for their murder and acquitted.[11] After liberation, 165 Japanese servicemen were tried by British and Australian military tribunals in Hong Kong in 1946–1948 for war crimes during the occupation: twenty-five were executed in Stanley Prison and their bodies buried at sea.[12] Another Japanese officer, an interpreter of British nationality, was convicted of treason by the Supreme Court and hanged.[13] Four Hong Kong civilians were also convicted of treason, one by a court under the British Military Administration, the others by the Supreme Court in 1946–1947: three were

9. The number of hangings in the five-year period 1956–1960 was twenty-four in Hong Kong and fifteen in England and Wales.
10. Eduardo Gosano, quoted in Vicky Lee, *Being Eurasian: Memories Across Racial Divides* (Hong Kong: Hong Kong University Press, 2004), 70; MacDougall to Gater, 5 December 1945, CO 129/594/6, 13.
11. See Chapter 10. Governor's statement, *HKH*, 1 October 1931.
12. Suzannah Linton, *Hong Kong's War Crimes Trials* (Oxford: Oxford University Press, 2013); Dean Aszkiewelovicz, *The Australian Pursuit of Japanese War Criminals* (Hong Kong: Hong Kong University Press, 2017), Chapter 4.
13. Inouye Kanao, an interpreter at the Sham Shui Po Prisoner of War Camp, was convicted by a war crimes court for assaulting prisoners of war and being concerned in the ill-treatment and deaths of civilians under torture. After conviction he appealed on the ground that, being Canadian born, he was a British subject and outside the court's jurisdiction. He was then tried and convicted of high treason by the Supreme Court, where he denied he was a British subject. Trial of Inouye Kanao, 1946, TNA WO 235/927; *CM*, 23 April 1947; *Inouye Kanao v R* (1946–1947) 31 HKLR 66.

executed.[14] After the defeat of Japan, civil war between Nationalists and Communists resumed in China, leading to the founding of the People's Republic of China in 1949. Wartime grudges persisted long after the end of hostilities. In March 1950, for example, a man confessed to murdering a woman in a village near Yuen Long: she had betrayed his comrades in the Red Army guerrillas to Japanese soldiers, he alleged.[15] A murder in 1958 resulted from a quarrel between a former Nationalist soldier and a businessman, now a factory owner in Hong Kong, over the proceeds of a smuggling operation in Shanghai during the civil war.[16]

Reflecting broader changes in colonial policy, the British Military Administration (1 September 1945–1 May 1946) announced a new approach to government centring on better social services, a greater share in government for local people, and equality before the law.[17] 'In a democracy, as opposed to an autocracy, there is no privileged class in the eyes of the law,' said its head, Rear-Admiral Cecil Harcourt, on the opening of the courts in September 1945.[18] In 1946 the returning civil Governor, Sir Mark Young, repealed discriminatory laws[19] and drew up proposals for municipal government on a broad franchise. The new '1946 outlook' was nowhere more apparent than in the interim courts established by the British Military Administration. The General Military Court, the equivalent of the Supreme Court, operated without juries and included military officers on the bench. But its presiding judge, Leo D'Almada e Castro, was a Hong Kong-born barrister, a member of the pre-war Legislative Council, and the leading representative of the Portuguese community. The chief prosecutor was another Hong Kong Portuguese, the solicitor Marcus da Silva. One of the last cases tried by this court was that of George Wong, a collaborator of the Japanese, who was convicted of high treason in April 1946. The trial, said D'Almada when passing sentence of death, signalled 'the return of justice to this colony'.[20]

This sudden localization (or lusitanization) of the courts was short-lived. It was made necessary by the deaths in combat or internment of most of the pre-war magistrates and

14. George Wong, convicted by the General Military Court on 18 April 1946, and So Leung and Tsui Kwok-ching, convicted by the Supreme Court on 27 June and 19 July 1946 respectively. The death sentence on the fourth, Lai Kit, was commuted to life imprisonment, reduced in 1953 to eighteen years.
15. He was convicted of murder and hanged on 25 April. *SCMP*, 4 March 1950.
16. The accused, claiming to have served as a colonel in the Kuomintang Army, was convicted and hanged after an unsuccessful appeal. *SCMP*, 29 and 30 April and 1–3, 6–7 May, and 10 June 1958.
17. 'The British Military Administration in Hong Kong', 3, in CO 129/595/9; Philip Snow, *The Fall of Hong Kong: Britain, China and the Japanese Occupation* (New Haven, Connecticut: Yale University Press, 2003), 199; Tsang, *A Modern History of Hong Kong*, 138–141; Gavin Ure, *Governors, Politics and the Colonial Office* (Hong Kong: Hong Kong University Press, 2012), 75–77.
18. *SCMP*, 24 September 1945.
19. Ordinances Nos. 10 and 11 of 1946, repealing Nos. 18 of 1918 and 14 of 1919, which required the Governor's consent for residence on the Peak and part of Cheung Chau Island, in practice restricting the districts to Europeans.
20. The trial is reported in *SCMP*, 2–19 April 1946.

judges: the Chief Justice, Sir Atholl MacGregor, died on the voyage back to England a few weeks after liberation, having ceremonially but abortively re-opened the Supreme Court on 3 September 1945, shortly after his release from internment.[21] With the restoration of civil government in May 1946, British judges were again installed in the Supreme Court. E.H. Williams, a legally qualified cadet officer who had acted as judge before the war, acted as Chief Justice and presided over the remaining treason trials until the arrival in July of a permanent appointee, Sir Henry Blackall.[22]

At the opening of the Supreme Court's criminal sessions on 18 October 1946 Blackall declared that life and property were 'more insecure in this great city of Hongkong at present than in the most backward parts of Africa.'[23] Twenty-four of the thirty-seven cases in that month's sessions alone involved the use of firearms. Most were armed robberies by criminal gangs. Some raided dwelling-houses or held up public buses. They were, remarked Blackall, like the highwaymen of eighteenth-century England. Citizens who slayed robbers in defence of their lives and property would be entitled to acquittal on the ground of justifiable homicide, he said. Armed robbers should expect sentences of life imprisonment. It might be necessary 'to ask the Government to consider the introduction of the death penalty for certain of these offences,' he added.[24]

Within weeks of liberation people had begun returning to Hong Kong at the rate of about 100,000 a month.[25] By 1946 the population was 1.8 million. It rose to over 3.1 million in 1961 and to 3.8 million in 1966. As people escaped the civil war 1946–1949, the Communist Revolution 1949, and the Great Leap Forward 1958–1962, Hong Kong became a city of immigrants. When United Nations embargoes during the Korean War 1950–1953 stifled its entrepôt trade and forced it to industrialize, Hong Kong also became a city of factory workers. The rapid influx of population imposed huge pressures

---

21. Among the other pre-war judges, Paul Cressall, the permanent Puisne Judge who had replaced Roger Lindsell in 1941, died in internment. John Fraser, a former prosecutor and temporary judge, was beheaded by the Japanese authorities on Stanley Beach in October 1943, along with thirty-one other men and one woman sentenced to death for having illegal radio sets, passing messages to British agents and other offences. During their trials they were not told what the charges were, or provided with interpretation, or allowed to put questions. *SCMP*, 3 and 4 September, 24 October 1945, and 7 November 1945; *The Times*, 17 November 1945; Snow, *The Fall of Hong Kong*, 186.
22. As a sergeant in the Chinese Machine Gun Company of the Hong Kong Volunteers, Williams had been a prisoner of war during the occupation.
23. Born and educated in Ireland, and called to the Irish Bar in 1912, Blackall fought in World War I before serving as Crown counsel in Kenya (1919–1923) and Nigeria (1923–1932), Attorney General of Cyprus (1932–1936) and the Gold Coast (1936–1943), and Chief Justice of Trinidad and Tobago and President of the West Indian Court of Appeal (1943–1946). After serving as Chief Justice of Hong Kong (1946–1948), he was President of the West African Court of Appeal until his retirement in 1951. His obituary in *The Times*, 7 November 1981, described him as 'one of the most brilliant members of the Colonial Legal Service.'
24. *SCMP*, 19 October 1946.
25. *The British Military Administration Hong Kong*, April 1946, CO 129/595/9, 12.

on resources, police, and the courts. Along with the law-abiding majority, it brought gangsters, casual criminals, and agents of the defeated Kuomintang government. The border with mainland China was closed in 1950. This reduced cross-border crime and inhibited the ability of criminals to abscond. At the same time, deportation of time-expired convicts and other 'dangerous characters', used extensively in the late 1940s and early 1950s, effectively ended in 1955 when the Chinese authorities refused to take any more deportees. As a result, said the Governor, Sir Alexander Grantham, 'we were saddled with thousands of the worst criminal elements', and with more gangsters per square mile than any other city.[26]

The pressures came to a head with the Double-Tenth riots on 10 October 1956, the anniversary of the outbreak of the 1911 Revolution. The removal by officials of Nationalist flags from the walls of a resettlement estate triggered several days of rioting in Kowloon and Tsuen Wan. The violence was promoted by members of the 14K Triad Society, a wing of the Kuomintang which had degenerated into a criminal network. Governor Grantham blamed the riots on opportunist gangsters. But he also pointed to the desperate living conditions in the resettlement estates, erected urgently in the 1950s to house the hundreds of thousands of migrants from mainland China.

> The people themselves for the most part live at a bare subsistence level; they own little or no personal property; the great majority have no real stake in the Colony. Employment is difficult and in some cases indifferently paid. They are people who have fled from their homeland and it is not surprising if their fate has engendered a sense of frustration and bitterness.[27]

The 1956 riots were the bloodiest civil disturbances in post-war Hong Kong, resulting (according to official reports) in the loss of sixty lives, forty-four of them from police fire.[28] Over 6,000 people were arrested and 3,000 were convicted of riot- and curfew-related offences.[29] Four men were hanged for the murder of the wife of the Swiss Vice-Consul when the taxi she was travelling in with her husband was set on fire by rioters at the junction of Castle Peak Road and Tai Po Road.[30] Another man was convicted of murder during a mob attack on the premises of a left-wing union in Tsuen Wan: thirty-one people were beaten and paraded through the streets; five of them later died. The conviction was reduced to

---

26. Munn, 'Our Best Trump Card', 39–40; Alexander Grantham, *Via Ports: From Hong Kong to Hong Kong* (Hong Kong: Hong Kong University Press, 1965), 192; Notes of a Meeting with the Secretary of State, 4 June 1950, CO 537/5240, encl. 10.
27. Grantham to Secretary of State for the Colonies, 23 December 1956, in *Report on The Riots in Kowloon and Tsuen Wan, October 10th to 12th, 1956* (1956), i.
28. Grantham to Secretary of State, 23 December 1956, in *Report on The Riots in Kowloon and Tsuen Wan*, iv.
29. *Report on The Riots in Kowloon and Tsuen Wan*, 54.
30. *Tse Sang and Others v The Crown* [1957] HKLR 132; *SCMP*, 11–22 January, 26–28 February, 2 and 3 March, and 12, 20, and 24 July 1957.

manslaughter on appeal, with a sentence of life imprisonment, on the ground that the trial judge had erroneously withdrawn from the jury the option of a manslaughter verdict.[31]

Patterns of capital crime and capital justice

For the twenty years from May 1946 to the last hanging in November 1966, the annual police reports record over 550 homicides. Most, where detected, were prosecuted as murders.[32] Although the number of homicides fluctuated from year to year, from a low of thirteen in the fiscal year 1956/57 to a high of forty-nine in 1965/66, the quinquennial figures were broadly constant.[33] They show a marked decline in proportion to the increasing population.[34] The detection rate improved markedly, from 35 per cent in 1946–1951 to 84 per cent in 1961–1966. This was attributable to the closing of the border in 1950, better detection methods, and greater co-operation between public and police.

From May 1946 up to the last capital trial resulting in execution in September 1966 the Supreme Court tried 230 cases of murder involving 320 defendants: 138 (43 per cent) were convicted of murder,[35] and another 100 (31 per cent) of manslaughter.[36] In addition, the Supreme Court tried and convicted four men for treason in 1946–1947. It tried six men in 1951–1954 under an emergency regulation extending capital punishment to explosives and arms offences, five of whom were convicted and two hanged. And it tried three men in the only trial for piracy with violence of these years, in 1946: two were convicted and sentenced to death; their sentences were commuted to life imprisonment.

Improved detection rates led to an increase in the number of persons tried for murder: as many as forty in 1965 and thirty in 1966 – over twice the average of the years 1946–1964. Yet, as detection rates and prosecutions increased, conviction rates for murder declined:

---

31. *Chan Hon v The Crown* [1957] HKLR 241; *SCMP*, 27–30 March, 2–4 April, 24 May, and 1 and 25 June 1957.
32. The General Military Court tried only one murder, in March 1946. The twenty-seven-year-old Lam Tim-cheung was convicted of murdering his adoptive mother at Kam Shan Village, Tai Po. She had 'bought' him at the age of six and he had worked for her in her paddy fields. But she had chased him away after the Japanese invasion for being a 'bad son' and he had lived as a beggar ever since. When, after the war, she refused to lend him money for a friend who had lost money in gambling, he shot her with a gun lent to him by that friend. Lam was executed on 1 April 1946 in the first hanging in Stanley Prison since liberation. *SCMP*, 12 February, 3 March, and 4 April 1946.
33. 120 in 1946–1951; 153 in 1951–1956; 139 in 1956–1961; 146 in 1961–1966. The police, court, and other official reports were now generally by fiscal year, from 1 April to 31 March.
34. The annual homicide rate per 100,000 population ranged from 1.7 (1950/51) to 0.6 (1961/62). The average annual rates by quinquennium declined from 1.2 (1946–1951) to 0.8 (1961–1966).
35. In addition, twelve were found guilty but insane; two others were found unfit to plead.
36. Estimates based on annual police reports and newspaper reports of trials, supplemented, for trials leading to convictions, by a notebook of capitally convicted prisoners 1956–1971: HKPRO HKRS519-1. Court statistics up to 1964/65 give only the totals of criminal cases tried in the Supreme Court, without breaking them down by offences.

from 75 per cent in 1946 to 10 per cent in 1966 (quinquennially, from 65 per cent in 1946–1950 to 23 per cent in 1962–1966). In parallel, a growing proportion of homicides tried as murders resulted in manslaughter verdicts: sixty-three of the 101 persons tried for murder in 1962–1966 were convicted of manslaughter, compared with twenty-one convicted of murder. Most manslaughter convictions resulted from verdicts by juries. In some other cases judge and prosecution accepted a plea of manslaughter at, or shortly after, the commencement of trial. In a few cases the Court of Criminal Appeal reduced murder convictions to manslaughter. In contrast, only eight of the sixty-four persons tried for murder in 1946–1950 were convicted of manslaughter, compared with forty-two convicted of murder. Partly in consequence of the declining number of murder convictions, and the growing tendency of governors to commute capital sentences, the number of hangings also declined, from thirty-six in 1946–1950[37] to six in 1962–1966. No hangings took place in 1963 or 1964. One person was hanged in 1965 and one in 1966. Despite the rise in murder prosecutions in the mid-1960s, the use of capital punishment was in steep decline some years before its discontinuance after 1966.

The explanations for the fall in murder convictions lie in the changing nature of capital crime; a general decline in serious crime from the late 1950s to the mid-1960s; higher detection rates; and a lenient approach by the courts towards the growing proportion of homicides resulting from private quarrels rather than robberies or political acts. Reports of serious crime fell by half, from a peak of 775 per 100,000 population in 1955/56 to a low of 391 in 1963/64.[38] The rate of reported serious crime then began to rise. By the early 1970s it had returned to the level of the mid-1950s. By 1975 it was nearly double that level, at 1,341 per 100,000. People's willingness to report crime was influenced by other factors than the actual crime rate. Fears of reprisals, distrust of the authorities, and police corruption may have depressed reported crime rates in the 1950s and 1960s. Conversely, the Fight Violent Crime campaigns in the 1970s and the creation of the Independent Commission Against Corruption in 1974 encouraged greater reporting.[39] Nevertheless,

37. This includes four hanged for treason. Another twenty-five war criminals were hanged in Hong Kong during these years.

38. Commissioner of Police, *Annual Reports*, 1946–1966. Figures are for the years ending 31 March. Pre-1956 figures were adjusted in the 1955/56 Report to reflect changes in reporting crime. Previous annual statistics continued to be adjusted in subsequent years: the figures here are based on the latest available adjusted statistics. Although the change in in 1956 was designed to follow practice in the UK, the criminal statistics for England and Wales report on the number of offenders committing indictable offences rather than the incidence of serious crime. While these are broadly comparable, they are not identical. It is, however, clear that, while reported serious crime in Hong Kong declined, the number of offenders per 100,000 in England and Wales rose from 611 in 1956 to 976 in 1964. Home Office, *Criminal Statistics: England and Wales, 1964* (HMSO, 1965, Comnd 2815), Appendix II.

39. Harold Traver, 'Crime and Socio-Economic Change in Hong Kong', *Southeast Asian Journal of Social Science*, Vol. 8, Nos. 1–2 (1980): 103–127; Carol Jones and Jon Vagg, *Criminal Justice in Hong Kong* (London: Routledge, 2007), 323–324 and Chapter 15.

despite concerns about Triads, juvenile offenders, and drug trafficking, there was a sense, at least in official narratives, that crime was not only under control in the 1960s but was also declining in proportion to the rising population. Hong Kong, remarked one official in 1971, had enjoyed 'a prolonged post-war period of relative honesty and safety'.[40]

By far the greatest factor in the decline in murder convictions was the changing nature of homicides. Post-war annual police reports up to 1961 record a variety of motives behind murders: sudden quarrels or family disputes; fights; revenge (including political murders); gain (mainly robberies); escape from custody; love affairs and jealousy; suicide pacts; illegal operations (abortions); insanity; and 'unknown'. The 1946/47 report classifies the motives behind the twenty-six known cases of murder that year into fourteen for gain, ten for revenge, one of homicidal insanity, and one unknown.[41] The 1960/61 report (the last to analyse motives) classifies the twenty-six murders that year into fourteen from love affairs, eight from sudden quarrels or disputes, one during a robbery, and one with a political background.[42] A broad survey of murder trials between 1946 and 1966 shows a similar shift: a decline in murders arising from robberies and political conflicts, and a rise in those resulting from quarrels and what were loosely described as 'love affairs': these ranged from murders of adulterous wives or their lovers to half-consummated suicide pacts, which were treated as murder up to 1963. The weapons commonly used in homicides also changed, from firearms and bombs in the early post-war years to knives, choppers, and other items of daily use. Many of the victims – well over half in some years[43] – were women and children.

The nature of capital offences thus shifted from killings of strangers in robberies or political conflicts to killings of colleagues, acquaintances or family members; from threats to order and dangers to the wider public to isolated fights and 'apparently trivial domestic disputes which burst into blind violence'.[44] The former attracted harsh punishment and special measures. The latter, where not premeditated or especially brutal, elicited a degree of sympathy from the courts and often resulted in manslaughter verdicts or acquittals. 'Hardship and overcrowding were frequently the underlying cause,' observed the Commissioner of Police in 1954.[45] 'It was not surprising that living in such conditions

---

40. A.T. Clark to Secretary for Home Affairs, 22 December 1971, HKPRO HKRS260-1-22, encl. 25: Clark, a barrister and administrative officer, had arrived in Hong Kong in 1960 and had not witnessed the violence of the early post-war years.
41. Commissioner of Police, *Annual Report 1946–1947*, 21.
42. Commissioner of Police, *Annual Report 1960–1961*, 20.
43. The victims were women or children in eleven out of the fourteen cases tried in 1952; nine of the sixteen cases in 1954 (in one of which there were three female victims); seven of the eleven cases in 1955; seven of the thirteen cases in 1959; seven of the eight cases in 1960; and six of the nine cases in 1964.
44. Commissioner of Police, *Annual Departmental Report 1953–1954*, 31.
45. Commissioner of Police, *Annual Departmental Report 1953–1954*, 31. See Lu Yan, *Crossed Paths: Labor Activism & Colonial Governance in Hong Kong, 1938–1958* (Ithaca, New York: Cornell University Press, 2019), 281–282 and 325–328.

caused a certain amount of friction from time to time,' said prosecuting counsel W.A. Blair-Kerr later that year, when describing a fatal fight on the hottest night of the year in a bed-space flat in Sham Shui Po inhabited by over forty people. The cause was the opening of a verandah door, which brought in fresh air for some but blocked the light from the sole electric bulb for others. A quarrel between two women escalated into a fight between their husbands. One woman was fatally stabbed in the abdomen while trying to protect her husband against a cobbler's knife wielded by the accused. The accused, the forty-seven-year-old shoemaker Yau Tak, was acquitted. The judge, James Reynolds, 'entirely agreed' with the verdict. At his prompting, the prosecution withdrew a further charge of wounding the victim's husband with intent to murder so that the accused could be released from custody.[46]

Temporary extensions of capital punishment 1945–1956

The crime of which Yau Tak was acquitted contrasted with the organized violent crime that plagued Hong Kong in the aftermath of the Japanese occupation. In response to this violence, the authorities enacted temporary legislation to extend the scope of capital punishment to include crimes other than murder. Most of this legislation went unused, but an emergency regulation prescribing capital punishment for non-fatal crimes involving arms or explosives, in force from 1950 to 1956, resulted in the prosecution of six men: four were convicted, two of whom were hanged.

Offences against the armed forces 1945–1946

On 13 September 1945 the British Military Administration proclaimed that various offences against the armed forces were 'punishable with death or with imprisonment or fine or both'. The offences ranged from armed resistance to wilfully misleading the forces in the execution of duty. Several persons, including some servicemen, were convicted of pilfering and other non-capital offences under the proclamation. No one was convicted capitally. The proclamation was repealed upon the restoration of civil government in May 1946.[47]

The Suppression of Robbery Ordinance 1947–1948

In March 1947, giving effect to Chief Justice Blackall's warning the previous October, the Legislative Council passed in one sitting the Suppression of Robbery Ordinance 1947.

46. *SCMP*, 23–26 November 1954.

47. Proclamation No. 7, 13 September 1945, *Hong Kong (British Military Administration) Gazette*, 12 October 1945; Leo D'Almada e Castro, Quarterly Report, Judicial Section, November 1945, CO 129/595/9, 198.

The ordinance removed the requirement to prove common intention in an armed robbery resulting in death: now every participant was liable to the death penalty unless he could prove he was not aware that one or more of the others had an offensive weapon.[48] This was a response to the 'prevalence of the wanton shooting and wounding by Chinese robbers', much of it 'unnecessary to the robbery'.[49] In force from 16 April 1947, the ordinance was to expire after a year unless extended by resolution of the Legislative Council. Over 300 cases of armed robbery were reported to the police in 1947 (less than half the number in the previous year). Seven of them were fatal. None was tried under this ordinance, although the police pointed to two cases where it might be applicable.[50] The Governor, Sir Mark Young, also cited 'a particularly revolting and brutal murder and robbery' of a European as justification for extending it.[51] However, the Secretary of State, who had not been consulted in advance, believed the legislation to be open to objection in 'the light of modern attitudes towards capital punishment'. He was also concerned that 'the Chinese may make political capital out of the existence of this measure, especially if a Chinese should be sentenced to death under it and executed'.[52] In view of this, the government did not seek an extension, and the ordinance expired, unimplemented, in April 1948.

---

48. Ordinance No. 13 of 1947; *HKH*, 13 March 1947.
49. Memo by Detective Chief Inspector A.H. Elston, 27 December 1947, HKPRO HKRS163-1-227, encl. (21).
50. The first was the attempted robbery of a man carrying his four-year-old son on Canton Road on the night of 12 October 1947, in which one of the three robbers fatally stabbed the son. The second was the robbery of a pair of rubber shoes from a stonebreaker on Tai Po Road on the night of 25 December 1947: when he resisted one of the three robbers shot him in the stomach. Neither case appears to have gone to court. Memo by A.H. Elston, 27 December 1947, HKPRO HKRS163-1-227, encl. (21).
51. While hiking in the Kowloon Hills on 11 February, Lytton Bevis Wood and Ronald Ross, directors of the trading firm Deacon & Co., were attacked by four men. One fired a revolver at Ross's head, but it failed to go off. They then beat up Wood and Ross, took their watches and money, tied them up, and threw Wood into a stream and Ross into some undergrowth. Wood drowned. Ross feigned death and survived. Three men were tried for Wood's murder by a special jury of European and Chinese businessmen. All three alleged they had been beaten by police into signing confessions: in a hearing in the absence of the jury, the judge, Ernest Williams, ruled their confessions admissible. The jury convicted two, Lau Hoi and Ho Cheuk-kui, but were unable to reach a verdict on the third, Li Chung-chun, who had not been identified by Ross and had an alibi. Li was not retried. After the failure of their appeals, based mainly on wrongful admission of the confessions, Lau and Ho were hanged on 7 September 1948. The case prompted an amendment to the Criminal Procedure Ordinance restating the rule in English law that a decision by a judge to hear evidence in the absence of the jury on the admissibility of a statement by the accused did not prevent the jury from considering the same evidence for the purpose of deciding what weight should be given to the statement: the judgment by the Court of Appeal had negated this rule. *SCMP*, 25–29 May and 22–23 July 1948; *Lau Hoi and Ho Cheuk Kui v R* (1948) 32 HKLR 49; Ordinance No. 45 of 1949.
52. Secretary of State to Governor, 16 December 1947 and 17 March 1948, HKPRO HKRS163-1-227, encls. 16 and 22.

Emergency regulations 1950–1956

The Secretary of State also had reservations about plans to extend capital punishment through the Emergency Regulations Ordinance 1922. Used extensively in the 1950s and 1960s for a variety of purposes, this ordinance empowered the Governor in Council to make regulations in the public interest on any matter without reference to the Legislative Council whenever he considered an emergency or public danger to exist. In December 1949, following the Communist victory in the civil war in China, the Governor in Council enacted a code of some 130 emergency regulations in anticipation of civil unrest, terrorism by Kuomintang agents, and increased crime. With some exceptions, regulations in this code were not brought into force until the disturbances of 1967.[53] At the same time, the government drafted, but did not enact, two further sets of emergency regulations: one was designed to simplify court proceedings and empower magistrates to try any except capital offences; the other applied the mandatory death penalty to over thirty offences that would otherwise attract life imprisonment.[54] In 1950 the government requested the Supreme Court judges to revive the practice, then in abeyance, of sentencing armed robbers and other violent offenders to whipping with the cat-o'-nine-tails. The judges readily acceded.[55]

Officials in the Colonial Office were concerned that the resumption of flogging, shortly after it had been abolished as a judicial punishment in England, was a form of 'legalized violence' that demeaned the recipients.[56] They were also critical of the proposed wholesale extension of the death penalty in the draft Emergency (Capital Punishment) Regulations through opaque references to existing ordinances, though they did not oppose their promulgation in the event of an extreme emergency.[57] These regulations were never brought into force. However, the Secretary of State consented to the use of emergency regulations to make certain offences punishable by death, subject to approval by the Legislative Council. An amendment to the Emergency Regulations Ordinance in 1949 required the council's

53. Emergency (Principal) Regulations 1949, *HKGG*, Supplement No. 2, 28 December 1949.

54. The proposed capital offences included setting fire to ships, buildings, and property; poisoning or wounding with intent to murder; carrying arms or ammunition; and felonies committed in the course of assisting an enemy (meaning any person or group of persons declared by the Governor in Council to be an enemy or manifesting a seditious intention within the meaning of the Sedition Ordinance 1938, or seeking 'in any way to promote internal disorder'). Draft Emergency (Administration of Justice) Regulations and Emergency (Capital Punishment) Regulations 1949 and memorandum by J.B. Griffin, Attorney General, 24 June 1949, CO 537/5240.

55. ExCo Minutes, 23 May 1950, CO 131/123, 115.

56. The term 'legalized violence' was used by the Colonial Office's Social Welfare Advisor, W.H. Chinn, in a meeting between Colonial Office officials with Governor Grantham in London on 28 June 1950. A related concern discussed at the meeting was the large number of juvenile offenders, mostly illegal hawkers, sentenced to caning at this time (4,531 in 1948 and 4,367 in 1949), which was the subject of a question in the House of Commons only two weeks before the meeting. CO 537/5240, encl. 9; *HC Deb 15 June 1950 vol 476 c44W*.

57. Minute by J.J. Paskin, 29 June 1950, CO 537/5240.

consent to any regulation carrying the death penalty.[58] This was followed in October 1950 by a resolution by the council approving the mandatory death penalty for any person convicted of carrying or possessing bombs, grenades, or other explosives, or using arms, ammunition, or explosives without lawful authority, whether or not death or injury resulted. The new provision was inserted in the Emergency (Principal) Regulations 1949 as 'Regulation 116-A'.[59] Acting Chief Justice Williams described it as a measure 'welcomed by all law-abiding members of the community'.[60]

In moving the resolution, the Attorney General, John Griffin, said that robberies with arms and explosives had become 'endemic' in Hong Kong and 'a state of war and unrest' persisted in Far Eastern countries. He was referring not only to China but also to the 'Malayan Emergency' of 1948–1960, a communist-led insurgency against British rule. Similar measures had been adopted in Malaya and Singapore. In arguing for their deterrent value in Hong Kong, however, Governor Grantham stressed that the bomb outrages and shootings in Hong Kong were not the work of organized political groups; they were instead carried out by common criminals, opportunists, and 'professional thugs, sent out by the Nationalists to operate against China'.[61] Explosives had been used by Kuomintang agents to sabotage aeroplanes at Kai Tak Airport in April 1950 in a dispute over their ownership between the new People's Republic of China and the Kuomintang government in Taiwan.[62] Since 1946, anonymous bomb threats with demands for money, at the rate of about 150 a year, had been sent to hotels, restaurants, and theatres. Some had political motives, others were practical jokes, but most were attempts at extortion or revenge.[63] A few threats were carried out. In 1947 a small girl was killed and twenty-six people injured by a bomb set off at the Ko Shing Theatre: the culprit, a former anti-Japanese saboteur, was convicted of murder and hanged.[64] In another incident, in August 1950, a three-year-old girl and a

58. Ordinance No. 40 of 1949.

59. The measure drew on an emergency regulation enacted in Malaya in 1948. An earlier regulation of December 1949 had already increased the maximum penalty for carrying arms or explosives from ten years to life imprisonment. Note by Griffin, 20 May 1950, HKRS260-1-22, encl. (49); *HKH*, 11 October 1950.

60. *CM*, 18 January 1951.

61. Notes of the Meeting with the Governor of Hong Kong, 28 June 1950 and Notes of a Meeting in the Secretary of State's Room, 4 June 1950, CO 537/5240, encls. 9 and 10.

62. *SCMP*, 3–6 April 1950. See Victor S. Kaufman, 'The United States, Britain and the CAT Controversy', *Journal of Contemporary History*, Vol. 40, No. 1 (2005): 95–113.

63. Commissioner of Police, *Annual Reports*, 1946–1947, 23, and 1950–1951, 24 and 30.

64. Tse Kwok-wah, a travelling trader, was arrested by police in Canton and brought to Hong Kong. He was also implicated in two other explosions and in demands for money with menaces from a teahouse and a hotel. The letters to these establishments purported to come from the 'Chinese Overseas Youth Movement'. The special jury trying Tse was discharged when one of the jurors said he had knowledge of the case. In a retrial another special jury found him guilty after retiring for five minutes. When Chief Justice Blackall passed sentence of death, Tse raised a clenched fist and shouted, 'Long live the Communists!' Evidence was given at his retrial that

fifteen-year-old boy were killed when a bomb went off in their home.[65] Earlier that year wire mesh had been installed on the ground-floor windows of the Supreme Court Building as a precaution against bombs.[66] Of equal concern was the use of firearms in murders, robberies, and other offences as weapons flooded into the city in the aftermath of war: 447 such cases occurred in 1950 alone.[67] Among the victims, forty police officers were killed on duty between September 1946 and March 1951, most by gunfire, some in shoot-outs with gangsters.[68]

The first prosecutions under Regulation 116-A took place in 1951. In March, Siu Ming, a former policeman, was convicted of using an automatic pistol in a robbery. After an unsuccessful appeal on the ground of mistaken identity, he was hanged on 11 May.[69] The second case, in January 1952, produced a constitutional challenge. To Lam-sin and Chan Sang robbed a bank at gunpoint of over $300,000. They were charged with robbery. To was further indicted under Regulation 116-A after police found grenades in his room. His counsel, Brook Bernacchi, moved to quash the indictment on the ground that the regulation and the Emergency Regulations Ordinance were *ultra vires* because there was no emergency: the regulation, said Bernacchi, was 'nothing more than an act by the Governor to legalise State murder'. The Full Court, however, held that the Legislative Council had full powers to delegate the enactment of emergency regulations. In any case, it had decided in 1949 that a regulation imposing the death penalty could only be made with its approval. On Bernacchi's advice, To then refused to plead; he also objected that not all the jurors were Chinese.[70] The judge, Trevor Gould, entered a 'not guilty' plea and dismissed his objection. But, after a three-day trial, the jury could not agree on a verdict. A retrial was ordered, but the prosecution withdrew the capital charge. To and Chan had already pleaded guilty to the robbery: they received sentences of eleven and fourteen years' hard labour respectively, and twelve strokes of the cane.[71]

Three further cases were tried under Regulation 116-A. In June 1953 Hui Kwong, one of a band of robbers tried for attempted murder in a gunfight with police in Kowloon City,

---

he had been trained in the use of explosives for sabotage against the Japanese. *SCMP*, 29 and 31 July and 1 and 6–8 August 1947.

65. A man with a grudge against the girl's father, who had refused to lend him money, allegedly placed a smoking parcel containing dynamite on their dining table while the family were eating lunch. The parcel then exploded. He was tried for murder but, for reasons that are unclear, found not guilty. *SCMP*, 27–30 November 1950.
66. *SCMP*, 9 May 1950.
67. In the year ending 31 March 1950 police seized 300 revolvers and pistols, 142 rifles, 133 machine guns, 24 shotguns, 3,278 swords, bayonets and knives, and 32,108 rounds of ammunition. *SCMP*, 28 April 1956.
68. Commissioner of Police, *Annual Report*, 1950–1951, 9.
69. Siu Ming, Death Sentence Passed on, HKRS41-1-6744; *SCMP*, 7–9 March, 7 April, and 12 May 1951.
70. One juror was allowed to step down because of conscientious objections to the death penalty.
71. *In the Matter of S.81 of the Criminal Procedure Ordinance, Cap. 221, and in the Matter of R v To Lam Sin alias Lam Chai alias To Tsat alias To Tsan Lam* (1952) 36 HKLR 1; *SCMP*, 17–19, 22–25, and 31 January 1952.

was additionally charged under the regulation with using firearms. Hui pleaded guilty and appealed for mercy, claiming he was drunk. He was hanged on 21 July.[72] Another case in 1953 resulted in an acquittal.[73] In the last case, in April 1954, Au Keng and Wong Wai-hung were sentenced to death for an attack on a fishing junk near Aberdeen, in which a man was shot in the leg. Their counsel, Vincent D'Alton and Samuel Gittins, successfully appealed on the grounds that the judge's directions to the jury on questions of law were insufficient, the police statement by Au had not been voluntary, and the only witness to pick out Au and Wong at an identity parade had seen the police taking them away in handcuffs the day before. Au and Wong pleaded guilty to possession of arms and ammunition and received sentences of imprisonment and caning.[74]

Concerned about Regulation 116-A, the Secretary of State had asked for six-monthly reports on its use. In May 1954 he requested a full report if the Governor wished to retain it.[75] By now, the death penalty had become a political issue in the UK. A Royal Commission on Capital Punishment, appointed in 1949 to review the use of the death penalty in the UK, had produced its report in 1953 after a series of controversial capital cases.[76] Motions carried in the House of Commons urging the abolition of capital punishment in 1948, and again in 1956, were defeated by the Lords. Prosecutions under Regulation 116-A were suspended in anticipation of the 1956 debate. Grantham acknowledged that strong arguments would be required for retaining 'a regulation providing death for an offence where no death

72. The judge, Courtenay Reece, opted not to change the plea to not guilty. An appeal to the Governor by the solicitor P.C. Woo and the barrister Brook Bernacchi for commutation went unheeded. *SCMP*, 1, 3, and 22 July 1953.
73. Ho Tei shot a policeman and a soldier during a chase after a robbery in Wan Chai. He was acquitted on the capital charge but pleaded guilty to robbery and possession of a revolver and was sentenced to seven years' hard labour. *SCMP*, 23 and 24 July and 7 August 1953.
74. *Au Keng and Wong Wai Hung v The Crown* (1954) 38 HKLR 142; *SCMP*, 6–9 April, 21 and 22 May, and 14 and 20 July 1954.
75. Secretary of State to Governor, 22 September 1950, HKPRO HKRS260-1-22, encl. 49; Max W.L. Wong, 'Social Control and Political Order – Decolonisation and the Use of Emergency Regulations in Hong Kong', *Hong Kong Law Journal*, Vol. 41 (2011–2012): 145–147.
76. Two cases caused particular unease among politicians and the general public. (1) The execution of Timothy Evans in 1950 for the murder of his wife and infant daughter in the house where they lodged in Notting Hill, London. Three years after his execution, John Christie, his downstairs neighbour and the main witness against him, confessed to the murder of Mrs Evans and to the murder of other women whose remains were found in the house. After a long campaign and a series of inquiries, Evans was posthumously pardoned in 1966. (2) The execution of nineteen-year-old Derek Bentley in January 1953 for the murder of a police constable during an attempted burglary. Bentley, who was unarmed, had allegedly called out to his accomplice, the sixteen-year-old Christopher Craig, 'Let him have it, Chris', after a policeman had told him to hand over his gun. Craig, being under eighteen, was detained at Her Majesty's pleasure. Bentley was posthumously pardoned in 1993. Block and Hostettler, *Hanging in the Balance*, Chapter 12.

is caused'.[77] In April 1956 he revoked the regulation following a decline in arms-related crime.[78]

Reductions in the scope of capital punishment, 1952–1966

The campaigns to abolish capital punishment in the UK resulted, first, in the Homicide Act 1957, which greatly reduced the scope of capital punishment, and, finally, in the suspension of capital punishment for murder in Great Britain in 1965, and its permanent abolition in 1969. Hong Kong adopted only part of the 1957 Homicide Act, in 1963. It did not abolish capital punishment until 1993, although all death sentences from 1967 onwards were commuted. In practice, through commutations and the tendency of the courts to reduce murder to manslaughter, capital punishment had declined rapidly even before 1967. The Hong Kong government also rejected calls at this time to extend the death penalty to drug manufacturers and traffickers.[79]

Raising the minimum age for capital punishment, 1952

In November 1952 the minimum age at which a person could be sentenced to death was raised from sixteen to eighteen, being the age at the time of the offence. This was a response to a request from the Secretary of State for colonies to bring their laws into line with reforms in the UK in 1933 and 1948.[80] Those over eighteen convicted of murder were to be detained at Her Majesty's pleasure at a place directed by the Governor: in practice this was indefinite detention, with periodic reviews, in a young prisoners' section in Stanley Prison. From 1953 to 1966, five youths aged between sixteen and eighteen were convicted of murder and sentenced in this way. Several others and a few under sixteen were charged with murder but convicted of manslaughter: the usual sentence was committal to a training centre for between nine months and three years, with the exact term decided by the Commissioner of Prisons on the basis of progress made.[81]

---

77. Grantham to Secretary of State, 6 April 1956, CO 1030/6, 62.
78. *HKGG* (Supplement No. 2), 27 April 1956, 123–124; *SCMP*, 28 April 1956.
79. This followed the advice of the Narcotics Advisory Committee. *SCMP*, 14 October 1964.
80. In 1933 the UK raised the minimum age to eighteen at the date of sentence. This was amended in in 1948 to specify that the age was the age at the time of the offence. Colonial Office Circular 837/52, 22 August 1952, HKPRO HKRS1-1-7338, encl. 1; Ordinance No. 29 of 1952; Children and Young Persons Act 1933 s. 53 amended by the Criminal Justice Act 1948 s. 16.
81. Training centres, modelled on Borstals in England, were established in Hong Kong in 1953 for offenders between the ages of fourteen and eighteen (raised to twenty-one in 1954). The minimum age was lower than the sixteen years for Borstals, reflecting a long-established official view that 'the Chinese juvenile matures earlier than his European counterpart'. Ordinances No. 5 of 1953 and 52 of 1954; *HKH*, 11 February 1953.

The UK Homicide Act 1957 and the Hong Kong Homicide Ordinance 1963

The UK Royal Commission on Capital Punishment 1949–1953 did not recommend abolition of capital punishment: since its mandate was to consider whether it should be limited or modified, it did not categorically address this point. Its recommendations focused instead on mitigating the rigidity of the law of murder in its provision of 'a single punishment for a crime widely varying in culpability'.[82] These recommendations were partly implemented by the Homicide Act 1957, which was an attempt at a compromise between retention and abolition of the death penalty – a half-way measure that satisfied no one. It was nevertheless the most important reform of the law on capital punishment in nearly a hundred years.

The Homicide Act 1957 was divided into two main parts. **Part I, section 1** abolished the common law rule of 'constructive malice' or 'felony murder', whereby a killing during some other offence constituted murder, whether or not it was intentional: such a killing now required the same malice aforethought as did any other murder, either express, in an intent to kill, or implied, in an intent to cause grievous bodily harm. **Section 2** introduced the defence of 'diminished responsibility'. This was defined as 'such abnormality of mind' as to substantially impair the mental responsibility of the accused for his acts. It went further than the narrower defence of insanity (which continued to be available); if proven by the defence, it reduced murder to manslaughter. **Section 3** extended the defence of provocation to 'things said' and left it to the jury to decide if provocation, by words or deeds, was enough to make a reasonable man lose his self-control, thereby reducing the offence to manslaughter: previously, 'mere words' could not amount to provocation. **Section 4** reduced from murder to manslaughter a killing by a survivor of a suicide pact, where it was proved he or she was acting in pursuance of such a pact.

The provisions in Part I of the act were largely uncontroversial. Those in **Part II** did not follow the Royal Commission's recommendations and were more problematic. **Section 5** defined five categories of capital murder: murder (1) committed in the course or furtherance of theft, (2) caused by shooting or explosion, (3) committed in the course of resisting arrest or escape or rescue from legal custody, (4) of a police officer in the execution of his duty, or (5) of a prison officer by a prisoner. This section further provided that, if two or more persons were found guilty of murder in any one of these categories, only the one who actually did the killing was guilty of capital murder. **Section 6** also prescribed the death

---

82. Its main recommendation was to give juries discretion to decide whether extenuating circumstances justified reducing the death penalty to a lesser sentence. It also recommended raising the minimum age at which a person could be hanged from eighteen to twenty-one; abolishing the doctrine of constructive malice (felony murder, or death during the commission of a felony); and modifying the defence of insanity. Royal Commission on Capital Punishment 1949–1953, *Report* (Cmd 8932, HMSO, 1953), Chapter 14; Block and Hostettler, *Hanging in the Balance*, 151–152.

penalty for anyone convicted of murder who had previously been convicted of murder on a different occasion. **Section** 7 abolished the death penalty for all other forms of murder, which, under **section 9**, now became punishable by imprisonment for life. Among other provisions in the act, **section 10** of **Part III** simplified the form of sentence of death to be pronounced by the judge to the effect that the convicted person was to 'suffer death in the manner authorised by law'.

Part II of the act was subjected to much criticism. Its division of murder into two degrees was an idea rejected by the Royal Commission: it had instead recommended giving discretion to juries to decide whether extenuating circumstances justified a lesser penalty than death. The division created anomalies. For example, murder in the course of theft was a capital offence, while the murder of a kidnap victim or of a woman after a rape to prevent identification of the culprit was not. Murder by shooting or explosion was capital, but a carefully planned murder by poison, a knife, or any other means was not. Critics described the act as 'badly drafted, irrational and muddled', and 'riddled with anomalies and inconsistencies'. But they welcomed it as 'removing capital punishment from nearly all killings of passion and depression' – the forms of homicide most prevalent in Britain at this time, and in Hong Kong.[83] Upon the suspension of the death penalty in Britain in 1965 the distinction between capital and non-capital punishment in any case became immaterial, and the whole of Part II was repealed.[84]

Hong Kong's version of the Homicide Act was the Homicide Ordinance enacted in 1963. The ordinance excluded the whole of the problematic Part II and adopted only Part I and the new form of sentence of death in section 10. Although the changes were proposed after consultations between the Legal Department, the Judiciary, and the Medical and Health Department, the government gave no explanation for excluding Part II.[85] Most likely, officials were aware of the many criticisms of Part II in Britain and wished to retain the death penalty in Hong Kong as a deterrent for all forms of murder, even though it was now rarely used. In any case, the exclusion made no practical difference. The two men hanged in Hong Kong between the enactment of the Homicide Ordinance in May 1963 and the discontinuance of capital punishment after 1966 were both convicted of murders that fell squarely within the definition of capital murders in Part II of the UK Act: one had murdered his victims by explosion, the other in furtherance of theft.

83. Block and Hostettler, *Hanging in the Balance*, Chapter 15; Graham Hughes, 'The English Homicide Act of 1957: The Capital Punishment Issue, and Various Reforms in the Law of Murder and Manslaughter', *Journal of Criminal Law and Criminology*, Vol. 49, No. 6 (March–April 1959): 521–532; J. Ll. J. Edwards, 'The Homicide Act 1957: A Critique', *British Journal of Delinquency*, Vol. 8, No. 1 (July 1957): 49–61; Glanville Williams, 'The Working of the Homicide Act', *Howard Journal*, Vol. 10, No. 4 (July 1961): 298–317.

84. Murder (Abolition of Death Penalty) Act 1965 s. 3(2) and schedule.

85. Ordinance No. 13 of 1963; *HKH*, 10 April and 8 May 1963; *SCMP*, 11 April 1963. The bill passed without debate. No discussion of the Homicide Act is recorded in the reports of the Law Reform Committee, appointed in the years 1956–1964 to examine the applicability of recent UK legislation to Hong Kong.

In practice, Hong Kong had also anticipated, or even exceeded, some of the provisions in Part I of the UK Act before they were introduced in the territory. The courts were already taking a sympathetic approach towards survivors of suicide pacts. In a case in 1952, Chan Kiu-heung and his girlfriend, Li Sui-lan, both nineteen years old, drank Lysol (a disinfectant) in a boarding house in Kowloon. Sensing a strong smell, a room boy found them unconscious. Li died but Chan survived. The two were from neighbouring villages attending the same school in Sai Kung. Chan's elders had told him he must finish school before they could marry. The jury – three women and four men – convicted him of murder with a strong recommendation to mercy. The Chief Justice, Sir Gerard Howe, sentenced him to death. Adding his support to the recommendation to mercy, Howe remarked that it was a 'pathetic story', illustrating 'the depths of despair and the complete loss of hope to which young people are only too prone'. At Howe's suggestion, the Governor in Council, Sir Alexander Grantham, commuted the death sentence to two years' probation. The prosecuting counsel in Chan's case was Patrick Yu.[86]

Two further cases in the 1950s suggested that it was now impossible to convict in suicide pact cases. In 1955, two workers in the same factory had abusive husbands who were drug addicts and were demanding that their wives go into prostitution to pay for their addiction. The women locked themselves in a hotel room in Kowloon and took heroin, leaving farewell letters to their sons explaining why they had done this. A room boy heard their groans, broke into the room, and called an ambulance. The survivor, twenty-five-year-old Kong Mei-lin, was charged with murder and acquitted after an impassioned speech by her counsel, Patrick Yu (now in private practice). Yu later revealed that the prosecution had privately told him it intended to advise the Governor to grant Kong a pardon if she was convicted. In his memoirs, Yu described the acquittal 'as a complete vindication of the jury system'.[87] In the other case, in 1957, Ho Sam-mui, a thirty-three-year-old concubine, and her lover, Yuen Kam-wah, a twenty-four-year-old waiter, drank Lysol in a hotel room in Wan Chai, leaving four letters to relatives suggesting a suicide pact. They were discovered unconscious by room boys and taken to hospital. Yuen died but Ho survived. At her trial she denied any knowledge of the suicide notes, claiming Yuen had asked her to meet him in the hotel so they could elope. After seeing him drink the Lysol, she had decided to do the same. In his closing address, Ho's counsel, Henry Hu, attacked Hong Kong's outdated

---

86. Patrick Yu was serving as the first Chinese Crown counsel in the Legal Department at this time. He resigned later in the year because of the discriminatory treatment of Chinese employees. *SCMP*, 30 April and 12 June 1952; *KSDN*, 30 April 1952; ExCo Minutes, 27 May 1952, CO 131/147, 148; 'Chan Kiu Heung' (1952), HKPRO HKRS41-1-7334.

87. The prosecution entered a *nolle prosequi* on a further charge of attempted suicide (a common law offence until 1967). The case is recollected, largely from memory, by Patrick Yu in *A Seventh Child and the Law* (Hong Kong: Hong Kong University Press, 1998), Chapter 1; *SCMP*, 9 and 10 November and 29 December 1955.

system of concubinage and described her as a 'victim of a legal injustice', telling the jury that 'if you convict her it will be a further injustice to her'.[88]

The courts also adopted the enlargement of the scope of provocation in the UK Homicide Act even before similar provisions were enacted in Hong Kong. In an appeal decided in January 1962, nearly eighteen months before the passing of the Homicide Ordinance, the Full Court held that words alone *could* amount to provocation sufficient to reduce murder to manslaughter. This example of 'judge-made law', described by one commentator as 'a judicial attempt to force the pace of law reform', was rare in colonial Hong Kong.[89] The case was also unusual in that the murder took place in a wealthy family following a family dispute over the will of a prominent businessman, Ma Tsui-chiu JP, who had died in 1959. In a departure from custom, Ma's will had named his wife, his concubine, his younger son, and a grandson as executors and trustees, passing over the elder son, Ma Wai-fun. The grandson was also made managing director of Ma Tsui-chiu's company. Ma Wai-fun suffered from tuberculosis and, according to his counsel, was schizophrenic. His resentment at his exclusion festered when the executors took no action to liquidate and distribute his father's assets. One evening in August 1961, after his younger brother ignored his request to discuss the matter, Ma lost his temper, picked up a knife, and stabbed his younger brother to death. He was tried in November that year, convicted of murder, and hanged in June 1962 after an unsuccessful appeal in Hong Kong and a rejected petition to the Privy Council.

Among several grounds of appeal, Ma's counsel, Desmond O'Reilly Mayne, argued that the trial judge, Richard Mills-Owens, had wrongfully withheld from the jury the option of manslaughter and had misdirected them on provocation by confining himself to the 'critical time' of the killing itself, without considering the events leading up to it. This argument was echoed in the reasons given by the Governor, Sir Robert Black, for commuting the death sentence against the majority advice of his council in a contemporaneous case.[90] The Full Court held that the judge was correct in withdrawing manslaughter from

88. *Ta Kung Pao* and *SCMP*, 3–6 and 9 July 1957.

89. *Ma Wai Fun (No. 2) v The Queen* [1962] HKLR 61; R.W. Cannon, 'Judge-Made Law in the Colonies', *International and Comparative Law Quarterly*, Vol. 13 (January 1964): 284–288; Peter Wesley-Smith, *The Sources of Hong Kong Law* (Hong Kong: Hong Kong University Press, 1994, repr. 1996), 112.

90. In September 1961 Lee Chun-chuen, 'a Hoklo man of limited intellect' was convicted of the murder of his father-in-law, Tsang Kan-kong. The two came to Hong Kong in the mid-1950s and opened a confectionary shop together. They fell out when Lee discovered that Tsang had written to Lee's wife in China telling her that Lee was dead and she should remarry. On receiving this false news, Lee's mother tried to commit suicide. His wife later remarried. Lee wrote letters to relatives about his intention to revenge himself on his father-in-law. According to his statement to the police, he lay in wait for Tsang and beat him to death with a hammer before jumping in the sea in an attempt to kill himself. Later in court, however, Lee claimed that Tsang had attacked him first. The jury's recommendation to mercy was not endorsed by the judge, Blair-Kerr. Lee's appeals against conviction, partly on the ground of insufficient direction on the law of provocation by the trial judge, were rejected by the Full Court and the Privy Council. Six of the eleven members of the Executive Council advised

the jury. However, in a judgment delivered by W.A. Blair-Kerr, the court held that it would be 'unsafe' to accept the old common law rule, now extinct in England, that 'words alone cannot amount to provocation in law'. The modification to common law by *Ma Wai-fun* was soon to be embodied in the Homicide Ordinance 1963.

In the same judgment, Blair-Kerr endorsed another 'important point' raised by O'Reilly Mayne: that in Hong Kong the term 'reasonable man', the standard against which a jury was asked to assess whether there had been provocation, should not mean 'reasonable Englishman'. 'What constitutes provocation to the average Briton may leave the average Chinese unmoved, and vice versa.' When applying the English law of provocation to Hong Kong, he ruled,

> juries ought to be told that the reasonable man, with respect to the particular accused person on trial, is an ordinary Hong Kong resident of the same race and way of life as the accused. It may be that we are imposing a more onerous burden on Hong Kong jurymen than the burden which rests on jurymen in England, because it may be that a jury of Britons in Hong Kong will have to make appropriate adjustments in their approach to a trial of a Chinese or a Filipino or a Japanese, and a Chinese jury may similarly have to make adjustments in their approach to the trial of a Briton, and so on.[91]

Such an approach, suggested Blair-Kerr, was in any case already 'implicit in the common sense displayed by the average Hong Kong jury'.

Blair-Kerr's reflections on the nature of jury trials in Hong Kong are revealing. They were a recognition, from his experience as prosecutor and judge in many murder trials, of the pains now taken by juries to do justice in the tragic cases that came before them. As a description of the composition of juries, however, they were misleading. There was now almost no such thing as a 'jury of Britons' or a 'Chinese jury'. For many years now juries had consisted of mixed nationalities. Moreover, Blair-Kerr's use of the old-fashioned term 'jurymen' belied the fact that nearly all juries, including the one that had tried Ma Wai-fun, now included women as well as men.[92] In some other capital cases at this time juries had a majority of women.

---

the Governor, Sir Robert Black, to let the law take its course. Black, who agonized over this case, commuted the sentence to fifteen years' imprisonment, observing that Lee had 'brooded over the enormity of the injury' done to him. 'Although the law has to take into account the suddenness as well as the gravity of the provocation, other considerations enter into deciding whether or not to exercise the prerogative of mercy.' Black added that among the other factors were Chinese opinion, which regarded Tsang's acts as very provocative; the recommendation to mercy by the jury; and the fact that two of the three Chinese members of his council had recommended mercy. *Lee Chun-chuen v The Queen* [1961] HKLR 709 and [1962] UKPC 24; ExCo Minutes, 28 August 1962, extract in HKPRO HKRS41-1-9245, encl. 84; private information.

91. *Ma Wai Fun (No. 2) v The Queen* [1962] HKLR 61.
92. From the 1950s, newspaper reports of trials ceased to give the names of jurors but usually indicated how many were women and how many men.

The advent of women jurors

At the time of Ma Wai-fun's trial, in August 1961, the jury list consisted of 14,988 common jurors and 342 special jurors. This was over twice the number of jurors in 1951, and over four times the number in 1941. Chinese names now formed the largest single category, accounting for approximately 46 per cent all names in 1961 and 50 per cent in 1963 (compared with about 40 per cent in 1951 and 43 per cent in 1941). The non-Cantonese romanizations suggest the lists included large numbers of middle-class Chinese from Shanghai and other northern cities, in addition to the steadily growing number of Cantonese jurors. The rest of the 1961 list (in rough order of numbers) consisted of British, Portuguese, Eurasian, European and American, South Asian, and other Asian names.

From 1956, jury lists ceased to be published annually in the *Government Gazette* and were incorporated in the biennial Registers of Electors for the Urban Council. In 1960 the task of compiling the jury list was transferred from the Registrar of the Supreme Court to the Commissioner of Registration, who was also responsible for compiling the Register of Electors and issuing identity cards: these had become compulsory for all persons over twelve years of age in 1949.[93] The change helped increase the size of the jury list, particularly the Chinese component. The greatest reform, however, came in 1947 with the inclusion of women in the list, over a quarter of a century after a similar measure in the UK in 1919. In contrast to many other judicial reforms, this resulted not from an instruction by the Secretary of State, but from a campaign within Hong Kong. One newspaper described it as 'the first blow in the local feminist movement'.[94] Unlike the UK reform, it produced an immediate and substantial enlargement of the jury list.

At a public meeting held at the Hong Kong YWCA on 19 March 1947, women from various communities unanimously requested the 'privilege and obligation' of serving on juries. Chief Justice Blackall and government officials welcomed the idea, not least because it was an opportunity 'to spread the burden of jury service which weighs more heavily in the Colonies than in England'.[95] Amendments to the Jury Ordinance followed.[96] The Supreme Court issued notices requiring eligible women to apply. Blackall gave a lecture at the (all-male) Rotary Club and a radio talk welcoming 'the advent of the fair sex' and urging women to come forward. He predicted that the proportion of women jurors

93. The requirement in 1960 for the Registrar to issue jury service notices to *every* applicant for an identity card who appeared eligible risked overloading the jury list with unqualified persons, since many did not take up the option to apply for exemption on the ground that they were unable to understand English. In 1962 greater flexibility was given to the Commissioner to not issue jury service notices to apparently unqualified persons. Ordinances Nos. 39 of 1960, 28 of 1962, and 64 of 1984; *HKH*, 24 August 1960 and 25 July 1962.

94. *SCMP*, 14 March 1947.

95. G.M. Hazlerigg and Nancy Kwok to Colonial Secretary, 21 March 1947 and Blackall to Griffin, Attorney General, 23 May 1947, HKPRO HKRS41-1-2890.

96. Ordinance No. 37 of 1947; *HKH*, 17 July 1947; *SCMP*, 17 and 21 October 1947.

would far exceed that in England because Hong Kong had no property qualifications.[97] By December, 1,873 women had registered. Most were Europeans, but many Portuguese, Eurasians, and South Asians, as well as a hundred or so Chinese women, also enlisted. The 1,873 names were added to a list of some 3,000 male jurors, boosting it by over 60 per cent. Over the next decade the numbers continued to increase.[98]

Isolated letters appeared in the newspapers insisting that the proper place for women was in the home.[99] As in England, a judge, on his own initiative or at the request of the prosecution or defence, had powers to order an all-male or an all-female jury, and, upon application by a female juror, to exempt her from serving because of the nature of the evidence. In contrast to the attempts in England and other jurisdictions earlier in the century to keep women off juries, these powers appear to have been used sparingly.[100] In a trial in June 1948 the prosecutor, Alfred Lonsdale, raised objections when no fewer than six women's names were drawn in succession. The judge asked the sixth woman to stand down, but the next two names were also women. Only on the third attempt was a man's name drawn.[101] Generally, however, the reform was welcomed. In the first trial with women jurors, four women sat with three men in a murder case in January 1948, in which the skeleton of the victim was produced in court. The women jurors took a special interest in proceedings, each carefully examining the exhibit, reported the *Kung Sheung Daily News*. 'Those who thought that the sight of a human skeleton would unnerve the women jurors were doomed to disappointment,' observed the *China Mail*. By the middle of the year lawyers were agreed that 'the women of Hong Kong have more than justified their right to serve on juries'. One barrister told the *Mail* that 'since women jurors were empanelled, the standard of intelligence of Hong Kong juries has been raised considerably'.[102]

There was perhaps something more than male condescension in these remarks. The public meeting on 19 March marked the establishment of the Hong Kong Council of Women, an influential organization led by well-connected members of the Chinese and

97. *SCMP*, 24 September 1947. Property qualifications were finally abolished in England in 1972.

98. In contrast, the addition of women to the jury list in Hong Kong's nearest comparator, Singapore, was muted. This came in 1950 at the initiative of a lawyer-legislator, John Laycock. Only thirty women were added to the 6,700-strong jury list that year, and eighty-nine the following year. *Singapore Free Press*, 2 February 1950 and 12 September 1951.

99. A letter from a Charles Wong arguing that women's intellects were inferior to men's and that, being 'soft-hearted', they were liable to make the wrong decisions, prompted responses from 'W. Eva', 'Miss Revolutionist', and 'A Chinese Woman' challenging his arguments and criticizing his grammatical mistakes *SCMP*, 2 and 4 July 1948.

100. See Kevin Crosby, 'Keeping Women Off the jury in 1920s England and Wales', *Legal Studies* (2017): 695–717; and Andrew L-T. Choo and Jill Hunter, 'Gender Discrimination and Juries in the 20th Century: Judging Women Judging Men', *International Journal of Evidence & Proof*, Vol. 22, No. 3 (2018): 192–217.

101. *SCMP*, 1 June 1948.

102. *CM*, 6 January and 14 May 1948; *KSDN*, 6 January 1948.

British elites. The Governor's wife, Lady Grantham, was its honorary president.[103] The council took an interest in issues such as legal aid, juvenile offenders, the training of probation officers, and reform of traditional marriage laws.[104] It also fielded women in elections, including the first (unsuccessful) female candidate in an election to the Legislative Council, in 1948.[105] How far women changed the dynamics in the jury room is impossible to say. Many clearly took up the duty with enthusiasm. It is also possible that, in the culture of those times, male jurors were better behaved and more conscientious in their duties when women were present. Certainly, juries from this time generally took longer to consider their verdicts. The inclusion of migrant professionals from other Chinese cities and the growth in the 1950s and 1960s of a permanent middle class may also have encouraged this. Concerns about comprehension of English among Chinese-speaking jurors continued to be raised from time to time. Nevertheless, as Patrick Yu remarks, the advantage enjoyed by a bilingual juror 'in being able to put a proper interpretation on crucial intonations or inflections of Chinese-speaking witnesses could hardly be over-emphasized'.[106]

This was not, however, trial by one's peers. The English-language qualification and the disproportionate numbers of non-Chinese jurors continued to produce juries that were unrepresentative of the people who came before the courts. It was a system in which an educated, ethnically diverse bourgeoisie tried working-class people, many of whom were new immigrants struggling to adapt to Hong Kong. The prevalence of crime in the resettlement estates and squatter villages of Kowloon, in contrast to the predominantly Hong Kong Island addresses on the jury lists, reinforces an impression that residents of the wealthier parts of the territory were trying defendants from the poorer districts – the haves judging the have-nots. Possibly out of a sense of *noblesse oblige*, most juries worked conscientiously to deliver justice at a time when doubts about the efficacy and morality of capital punishment were gaining ground.

---

103. The convenors of the March meeting were Nancy Kwok, daughter of the surgeon Li Shu-fan, and G.M. Hazlerigg, wife of the Governor's advisor on political reform.
104. Hong Kong Council of Women, *Annual Reports* 1947–1958.
105. The government had, for the first time, appointed twenty-four women justices of the peace in December 1947. At this time, justices of the peace (160 in all) elected one of their number to serve on the Legislative Council. When a temporary vacancy occurred in 1948, the Council of Women put forward the solicitor Rosa Loseby as a candidate. She lost to the businessman Norman Marsh by a large margin. The Council of Women also petitioned the Governor, with encouragement from the visiting Minister of State, Lord Listowel, to appoint a woman to the Legislative Council. This eventually materialized in 1965 in the appointment of Ellen Li, one of the first women justices of the peace and a prominent member of the Council of Women. *SCMP*, 7 and 8 May 1948; HKRS41-1-2890 'Jury Service' (1947); Hong Kong Council of Women, *Annual Report* 1947–1948, 7.
106. Yu, *A Seventh Child and the Law*, 154.

The death penalty in decline

For five years in the second half of the 1950s, and again in 1962, the number of hangings in Hong Kong exceeded or equalled that in England and Wales. This was in part a reflection of the dramatic decline in hangings in the UK after the creation of non-capital murders by Homicide Act 1957. Although in Hong Kong all murders continued to be capital murders, the city saw its own dramatic decline in executions in the early 1960s. The number of persons tried for murder between 1950 and 1965 was broadly constant at an average of about seventeen a year. But conviction rates for murder declined from 65 per cent in 1951 to 30 per cent in 1965, and 22 per cent in 1966, as more murder prosecutions resulted in manslaughter convictions. Partly because of this, and because governors and their deputies were less willing to confirm capital sentences, the number of executions declined from forty-two in the period 1950–1955, to twenty-three in 1956–1960, and eleven in 1961–1966, despite an 85 per cent increase in population in those fifteen years. The figures reflect the atmosphere of peace that had descended on Hong Kong from the later 1950s, and a shift in the general nature of murders from armed robberies to private quarrels. They also suggest a growing aversion towards the death penalty among Hong Kong's elite, both as a deterrent to crime and as a just punishment.

The debates on abolition of the death penalty in the UK, and similar debates in other countries, were widely reported in Hong Kong. Officials and judges studied the report of the Royal Commission 1949–1953 with great interest but searched hard for a 'conclusive argument' for capital punishment as a deterrent. The reason why no such argument could be found, said C.J. Norman, the Commissioner of Prisons, was that 'it did not exist'.[107] Earlier, as Superintendent of Stanley Prison, Norman had attended twenty-four hangings: the experience had convinced him that 'we have no right to take life judicially, nor to call on others to carry out such a sentence'.[108] In 1956 a *South China Morning Post* editorial welcoming the defeat by the House of Lords of a proposal for abolition in the UK sparked a series of letters. The first, by Brook Bernacchi, a barrister, Urban Councillor, and founder of the Reform Club of Hong Kong, set out the moral and practical arguments against capital punishment. This was followed by other letters, some agreeing with him, others in support of retention.[109] Three years later, Bernacchi welcomed as 'momentous news' the conscientious objections to the death penalty by fourteen jurors balloted successively in the trial of four youths for the murder of a warder at Cape Collinson Training Centre. It was ridiculous, he added, that, after the 1957 Homicide Act, Hong Kong did not now even have the

107. Norman to Colonial Secretary, 11 January 1955, HKPRO HKRS125-3115.
108. The twenty-four hangings included those of Japanese war criminals. C.J. Norman, Note on Capital Punishment, 1975, CJ Norman Papers: I am indebted to Kirsty Norman for sharing this with me.
109. *SCMP*, 12, 13, 17, 18, and 21 July 1956.

same law as existed in England. This prompted another spate of letters for and against the death penalty, as did the hanging later that year of one of the Cape Collinson youths.[110]

In his 1959 letter Bernacchi had urged 'the people of Hong Kong to speak with one voice against capital punishment'.[111] But the people did not rally to the call. The newspaper debates were a minority pursuit, confined to the English-speaking elite and focused mainly on high principles and events in the UK, and a belief that the UK and France were now the only two countries in Western Europe where the death penalty was still in use. Towards the end of 1964, however, a murder conviction in Hong Kong, the first in a year, gave rise to a more broad-based debate. This had a special significance because it took place when Parliament was about to pass the bill to suspend capital punishment in Great Britain.

On 30 September 1964 Lai Chun-hing, a nineteen-year-old unemployed plumber's apprentice, was convicted of the murder of his wife. From one angle, this was one of a class of murders, common in Hong Kong, where a man killed a woman out of jealousy: proprietorial attitudes among males towards their female partners were behind at least a dozen murders of women or their lovers tried in the 1950s and early 1960s. Lai had married Mok Yuk-yee in early 1963. They took a room in the Lei Cheng Uk Resettlement Estate, next door to Lai's mother. Lai not only demanded money from Mok but pawned her possessions. After the birth of their daughter, Mok got a job as a nightclub hostess. She was seen by Lai's friends with other men. This led to violent arguments. In early 1964, after Lai had beaten her in the street, Mok gave her baby to the care of an aunt and went to live with her mother. She continued to see Lai, but the marriage was strained. On 9 July, Lai, his mother, and Mok had lunch together in an attempt at reconciliation. This went badly wrong. Later that day, Mok was found chopped to death, naked, on the bed in Lai's room. After fleeing by taxi to the New Territories, Lai gave himself up a few days later.[112]

The evidence against Lai was clear. After a three-day trial, the jury of five men and two women found him guilty of murder. Then the case became complicated. The judge, A. D. Scholes, deferred sentence so that that Lai's exact age could be ascertained. Two days later a radiologist testified from X-rays that Lai could have been a few months below or above eighteen at the time of the murder. A birth certificate produced by the prosecution showed that he was born in January 1944, making him over eighteen at the time of the murder, but Lai's counsel, Ronald Arculli, argued that it could not be relied on. Scholes ordered Lai to stand in front of him so he could examine him. After doing so, he retired for half an hour before returning to say that, from the doctor's evidence and Lai's appearance, he had

110. *SCMP*, 16, 17, 19, and 26 April and 14, 16, 19, 26, 28, and 30 May and 18, 23, 25, September 1959.

111. *SCMP*, 16 April 1959.

112. *SCMP*, 19 August, 26 and 30 September, and 1 October 1964; *KSDN*, 30 September, and 1 October 1964; 'Lai Chun Hing' (1964), HKPRO HKRS146-13-27.

concluded that Lai was not under eighteen at the time of the murder. Scholes then put on the black cap and sentenced Lai to death.[113]

After the Full Court rejected an appeal from Lai, the case sparked public debate and letters to the press. Some called for Lai to be spared the death penalty. Others, describing him as a delinquent (a 'fei-tsai', 飛仔), pointed to the growing incidence of violent crime and demanded that the law take its course.[114] Several petitions were sent to the Governor, Sir David Trench, pleading that Lai was immature and uneducated, that his daughter would be deprived of a father as well as a mother, that the murder was not premeditated but had been triggered by his desire for respectability for himself and his wife. 'Ironically, it was because of his care for his wife and not hatred that caused the whole tragedy,' said a petition from the Hongkong and Kowloon Tenants' Association. The Urban Councillor Elsie Elliott, a champion of the poor, echoed these points in a letter to the Governor, begging him to 'give this young man another chance in life' whatever his real age. Neighbours interviewed by staff of the Home Affairs Department, now a standard part of post-trial proceedings, were also sympathetic: the consensus was that he was 'a victim of environment, and that in a place like this Resettlement Estate, one could hardly expect to be able to breed good sons or daughters'.[115] At a press conference organized by the Hong Kong and Kowloon Tenants' Association, Lai's mother claimed responsibility for her son's death sentence, having lied about his age when making a statutory declaration to help him apply for a job in England: she had used documents for her deceased elder son, whose name was also romanized as 'Chun-hing'; in fact, her younger son was born in October 1946, making him under eighteen at the time of the murder.[116]

On 5 December, three days before the Executive Council was due to consider Lai's case, sixteen prominent residents petitioned the Governor for mercy. Among them were five unofficial Legislative Councillors, two retired unofficial members of the Executive Council, a member of the Urban Council, three practising barristers, a prominent solicitor, the Dean of St John's Cathedral, and a leading member of the Council of Women.[117] There

113. *SCMP* and *KSDN*, 3 October 1964.

114. *KSEN*, 22 November 1964; *Wah Kiu Yat Po*, 28 November 1964; *KSDN*, 5 December 1964; *SCMP*, 24 November and 7 December 1964.

115. Lei Cheng Uk Estate was the site of the outbreak of the 1956 riots, when staff of the estate removed Nationalist flags from the walls of one of the housing blocks on 10 October 1956, the Republican National Day. Report by Paul K.C. Tsui, November 1964, HKPRO HKRS146-13-27, encl. 34(12).

116. *SCMP*, 17 and 27 November and 7 December 1964.

117. Dhun Ruttonjee, Sidney Gordon, Woo Pak-chuen, G.R. Ross, and K.A. Watson (Legislative Councillors); Leo D'Almada QC and Sir Sik-nin Chau (former Executive Councillors); Brook Bernacchi QC, Oswald Cheung, and Gerald de Basto (barristers); F.D. Hammond (solicitor and Chairman of the Legal Aid Committee); A.de O. Sales (appointed Urban Councillor); Violet Chan (Treasurer, Hong Kong Council of Women); Kenneth K.C. Wong and J.L. Marden (businessmen); and the Very Reverend John Foster (Dean of St John's Cathedral). Petition to the Governor, 5 December 1964, HKPRO HKRS146-13-27, encl. 40; *SCMP*, 6 December 1964.

was, said the petition, considerable doubt whether Lai was over eighteen when the offence was committed. The Labour government, the petition observed, planned to abolish the death penalty in Great Britain (the abolition bill had received its first reading only the day before) and it was now accepted no more hangings would take place there: although Hong Kong had its own legislature, 'it is, we believe, accepted in matters of this sort the Colony follows the example of the United Kingdom.' Yet Hong Kong had not, in fact, followed the UK when, nineteen months earlier, the Legislative Council (among whose members were two signatories to the petition) passed the Homicide Ordinance, omitting the distinctions between capital and non-capital murders in the UK Homicide Act 1957: if it had included those distinctions, Lai would not have been facing the death penalty.

At the meeting of the Executive Council on 8 December 1964 Governor Trench, on the advice of members, commuted Lai Chun-hing's death sentence to eighteen years' imprisonment. Lai's case was an illustration of Bishop Hall's dictum twenty years earlier that, once a murderer became 'known intimately as a person' to the community, 'the demand for commutation' became acute.[118] The case also suggested that support for the death penalty was now in rapid decline.

The last five hangings

No one was hanged in Hong Kong in 1964, or in 1963 or 1965. Only three persons, in one case, were hanged in 1962, and two – including the last person hanged – in 1966. These were all premeditated murders which elicited no sympathy from juries, governors, or the general public.

The Three Wolves: Lee Wai, Ngai Ping-kin, and Ma Tsan, 1962

The three hangings in 1962 resulted from one of the most sensational murder cases in Hong Kong's history, the subject of films and true crime books.[119] Lee Wai, Ngai Ping-kin, and Ma Tsan were tried for the murder of the businessman Wong Ying-kau, whom they had kidnapped in June 1959 and then killed. A month after the killing, Wong's father, the banker Wong Sik-pun, received a note, with his son's severed ear, demanding $500,000. The murder came to light in 1961 when the gang also kidnapped Wong Sik-pun and boasted to him of having beaten his son to death after he had refused to co-operate. Calling themselves the 'Wild Wolf Gang', the men wore masks painted with wolves' faces in their dealings with Wong Sik-pun. They released him after two weeks in return for a $500,000

118. See Chapter 9.
119. For example, 'Kidnap' (天網) (1974) directed by Cheng Kang; 'Sentenced to Hang' (三狼奇案) (1989), directed by Taylor Wong; 陳非, 三狼案：二十年目擊奇案精選 [Chen Fei, *The Three Wolves Murder Case*] (Hong Kong: Literary Bookstore, 1978).

ransom. Later in 1961, police arrested several men, one of whom led them to the remains of Wong Ying-kau buried in a hillside on the south side of Hong Kong Island. After a seventeen-day trial before the Acting Chief Justice, Ivo Rigby, and a special jury, Lee, Ngai and Ma were convicted of murder and sentenced to death. They appealed unsuccessfully, partly on the ground that press reports (for which various newspaper editors were convicted of contempt) had prejudiced the jury. The Privy Council rejected their petition for leave to appeal. They were executed on 28 November 1962.[120]

Lau Pui, 1965–1966

Death sentences for murder were passed on nine men in 1965. All were commuted except the one imposed on Lau Pui on 29 December. On 21 September 1965 an explosion took place in a hut in Kowloon Tsai (a village and squatter settlement then being redeveloped), killing three men and injuring twenty other people. The hut was an illicit gambling den whose manager had refused Lau's request for a job the day before. Lau and another man, Kung Fat, both unemployed heroin addicts with Triad connections, were tried by a jury of two women and five men (reduced to four when one fell ill on the second day). Kung Fat (fifty), a former fireworks maker, had allegedly made the bomb from potassium chlorate and metal fragments. Lau Pui (thirty-five) had carried it into the hut and set it off. Both made confessions but claimed they had been forced by police to sign them without knowing their contents: Lau Pui said that police had given him heroin before asking him to sign. After a trial lasting eight days, the jury found them guilty of murder. The Governor in Council, Sir David Trench, commuted Kung's death sentence to twenty years' imprisonment but confirmed the death sentence on Lau, who was hanged on 15 April 1966.[121]

Wong Kai-kei, 1966

The last person to be hanged in Hong Kong was Wong Kai-kei (黃啓基), a twenty-six-year-old shop assistant employed by the Chung Kin Chinese Products Emporium, a department store in Sham Shui Po. Well educated and from a comfortable background, Wong was born and raised in Saigon (now Ho Chi Minh City), where he worked for a while in the family's watch shop. Shortly after being conscripted for military training he fled to Cambodia. He

120. *Lee Wai and others v The Queen* [1962] HKLR 351; *SCMP*, 20 February–15 March, 7 July, 10 October, and 25 and 29 November 1962.

121. Lau and Kung unsuccessfully sought leave to appeal on grounds, in Lau's case, that the judge had wrongfully admitted evidence about his Triad activities, and in Kung's case (relying on a sixteenth-century precedent), that the bomb he had confessed to making was not the one that killed the persons in the case. *SCMP*, 30 September, 13 October, 2–12 November, and 11, 14, 15, 21–26, and 30 December 1965 and 11 and 12 February and 3 March 1966.

arrived in Hong Kong in 1963 on a Cambodian passport and found a job at the department store on a monthly salary of $120, later raised to $270. He was happy in his job, had good prospects, and was treated well by his employer and colleagues, who knew him as 'Vietnam boy' (安南仔, or 'Annam boy').[122]

At about 11:30 p.m. on 2 July 1966 Wong left the flat on Nathan Road which he shared with students. He took with him a metal pipe wrapped in newspaper and a paper bag containing cotton gloves he had bought at the department store earlier that day. He rang the doorbell of the manager's flat on the second floor and was let in by the manager's seventy-two-year-old mother, Sit Kwai-ying. He told her he had left his wristwatch in the store and wanted to get it back. She let him pass through the flat and down an inner staircase into the store. On the mezzanine floor he encountered the store's watchman, the fifty-year-old Chan Fat-sang, and hit him on the head with the metal pipe. When Chan tried to run away, Wong hacked him to death with a chopper grabbed from a display case. Wong then went back up the stairs to the flat and attacked Madam Sit with the chopper, striking her several times on the head, face, and wrist until she was unconscious. In the manager's office in the flat he found two cash boxes, took them down to the ground floor of the store, and smashed them open with a hammer from another display case, taking $4,473 in cash. He then let himself out of the front door of the store with the watchman's keys.

The manager of the store, Lau Tak-sing, returned home at about 1 a.m. and found the flat locked. Seeing through a window his mother lying in a pool of blood and, failing to rouse the watchman, he called the police and fire brigade. His mother, now conscious, said it was 'Vietnam boy' who had attacked her. The police searched Wong's flat and found blood-stained clothes and the money from the store. In a statement under caution, Wong admitted the robbery and the attacks on Chan and Sit, saying he needed $5,000 to obtain an identity card and had no friends who would give him such a large amount. He had no intention of murdering anyone, he said. Yet there were no marks on his body to suggest he had defended himself in a struggle. In the opinion of the pathologist, some of Chan's wounds were inflicted while he was already unconscious.

At his trial for the murder of Chan Fat-sang in September 1966, Wong claimed he had found Madam Sit lying in a pool of blood when he went to get his wristwatch. She had told him that someone had struck her. Not knowing the procedures, he had not telephoned the police. Being 'scared and confused', he had run away. The money found in his flat was from his mother in Vietnam, he now claimed. The police had dictated the confession to him and had beat him when he hesitated to write it down. This was a common claim by defendants at this time. In some cases it was substantiated. But, after holding a 'voir dire',[123] the judge,

122. The account here is drawn mainly from ExCo Memorandum XCR(66)254, HKPRO HKRS41-2-654, and *SCMP* and *KSDN*, 1, 2, 6, 7, and 9 September 1966.

123. A trial within a trial in which the judge, in the absence of the jury, determined whether a confession was admissible – then a feature in many criminal trials in Hong Kong.

Brendan Jennings,[124] admitted Wong's statement, reminding the jury in his summing up that they too must be satisfied that it was voluntary. The other evidence, including that from Madam Sit, pointed strongly to Wong's guilt. At noon on the last day of the eight-day trial the jury of four women and three men retired. They returned at 2:15 p.m. with a verdict of guilty of murder. They made no recommendation to mercy. Neither did Jennings, who described the murder as a brutal one, designed to remove all traces of Wong's connection with the robbery. He sentenced Wong to death. Following the practice at this time, in his report to the Governor he recommended a sentence of twenty years' imprisonment should the Governor decide to commute the death sentence.

Neither Jennings's report nor any of the other reports submitted to the Governor in Council showed much sympathy for Wong. In a failed appeal and a petition for mercy, Wong continued to insist that he was falsely accused and forced into writing a confession under threats of being beaten to death. His sister-in-law, visiting Hong Kong to see relatives (not, she was at pains to point out, to see Wong), was surprised by his air of indifference towards the death of Chan Fat-sang. His probation officer described him as 'a man of double standard of morality' who 'lives part of his time in a world of fantasy and make-believe', the result, he conjectured, of a 'faulty upbringing'. His girlfriend, a dance hostess who visited him several times in prison, was the only person to whom he made a confession, after she had 'lectured' him about his 'repeated and fantastic lies' and his 'stubbornness in maintaining a story of innocence': 'I did not know why I did such a thing,' he said to her in tears. The case aroused no public feeling, reported Paul Tsui, the Chief Assistant Secretary for Chinese Affairs. None of the hundreds of community leaders in contact with liaison staff from his department had made even a passing comment on it. 'By and large people seem indifferent to the outcome of the case.'

On 1 November 1966, on the advice of the Executive Council, the Governor, Sir David Trench, ordered that the law should take its course. Wong Kai-kei was hanged in Stanley Prison on 16 November 1966.[125]

The last hangings took place towards the end of a decade of penal reform in Hong Kong. In 1956, probation, previously available only to persons under the age of twenty-one, was extended to all adults in suitable cases.[126] Partly as a result of this, a greater use of bind overs and warnings to first offenders, and a general decline in crime, the number of

124. Jennings, a District Judge since 1959, had acted as Puisne Judge at various times since 1963 and was shortly to retire. He was called to the Irish Bar in 1937 and to the London Bar by Middle Temple in 1951. Before transferring to Hong Kong as a magistrate in 1958 he had worked with a firm of lawyers in Rangoon, served in the Burma Rifles during World War II, and then worked as a Crown counsel in Singapore and in various judicial and government legal positions in Penang and Malaya. *SCMP*, 16 December 1966.

125. ExCo Minutes, 1 November 1966, HKPRO HKRS425-3-41, 285; *SCMP*, 17 November 1966.

126. On its introduction in 1933, probation was restricted to offenders under sixteen. It was extended to the sixteen to twenty-one age group in 1947. Ordinances Nos. 11 of 1947 and 57 of 1956.

persons sentenced to imprisonment in the fiscal year 1966/67 was less than 70 per cent of the number a decade earlier, despite a 50 per cent increase in population.[127] Reforms promoted by C.J. Norman, Commissioner of Prisons 1953–1968, had turned Hong Kong's prison system into a model for other jurisdictions: these included professionalization of staff, the introduction of open prisons, and an emphasis on rehabilitation.[128] Corporal punishment, though still authorized by law, had not been used as a prison punishment since 1952, and was now, at least for the time being, rarely imposed by the courts on adults: a committee reporting in 1966 recommended its total abolition.[129] In 1967 an amendment to the Criminal Procedure Ordinance prohibited courts from sentencing offenders aged between sixteen and twenty-one to imprisonment unless they were satisfied there was no other appropriate punishment.[130]

The tide, however, was now turning. In 1965, a committee on violent juvenile crime (which had recommended the 1967 amendment) observed a marked increase in crimes of violence by persons under the age of twenty-five and growing concerns in the community about the 'hooligan' problem.[131] In April 1966 the Star Ferry Riots, the worst public disturbances since 1956, caused the death of one person and losses from looting and destruction of property estimated at $20 million. A commission of inquiry chaired by the Chief Justice, Sir Michael Hogan, found widespread evidence of discontent with poor housing and inadequate education, and a sense among young people of 'not belonging'. Rates of violent crime quadrupled between the late 1950s and 1970 and quadrupled again by the mid-1970s. Politicians, editorialists, and members of the public now demanded the resumption of capital punishment.

127. In the year 1956/57, when the population was 2.53 million, 20,470 persons were sentenced to imprisonment. In 1966/67, when the population was 3.75 million, 14,209 persons were so sentenced – a decline from 807 persons per 100,000 population to 375. Commissioner of Prisons, *Annual Reports* 1956/57 and 1966/67.

128. The eminent Scottish psychiatrist, Sir David Henderson, described Stanley Prison after his visit in 1956 as 'almost an ideal organization characterized by a spirit of enterprise, of personal touch and an humanitarian outlook which one does not often meet'. Commissioner of Prisons, *Annual Report 1956/1957*, 15.

129. The recommendation was not implemented. *Report of the Committee to Examine the Law and Practice Relating to Corporal Punishment in Hong Kong* (Hong Kong: Government Printer, 1966).

130. The change, based on provisions in the English Criminal Justice Act 1967, followed recommendations by a working party on young offenders in 1965. A similar provision in the Juvenile Offenders Ordinance 1932 already applied to offenders under sixteen. Ordinance No. 66 of 1967.

131. *Report of the Working Part to Advise on the Adequacy of the Law in Relation to Crimes of Violence Committed by Young Persons* (Hong Kong: Government Printer, 1965), 4 and 7.

12

'A Thing of the Past'

The Road to Abolition, 1966–1993

In a radio talk in 1968, John Rear, a lecturer in law at the University of Hong Kong, spoke of 'an apparent ambivalence in the Chinese attitude towards crime and punishment'.

> From conversation and from correspondence to the newspapers you might think that there was a general approval of severity in punishment; yet when they get into the jury box our citizens appear to change from hawks into doves. It is a commonplace amongst the legal profession here that juries do not like convicting for murder and in the large majority of cases refuse to do so.[1]

Out of thirty murder trials in the fiscal year 1966/67, observed Rear, twenty-two persons were convicted. But the verdict in nineteen cases was not murder but manslaughter.[2] Even a terrorist, tried in February 1968 for the murder of two men and an eight-year-old girl in November 1967, was convicted only of manslaughter, yet the bomb was clearly intended to be lethal.[3] The bomb came in a year marked, first, by anti-government protests and riots, a spillover from the Cultural Revolution in China, then by terrorism. Seventeen people were killed by explosions or incendiary attacks. Another thirty-four died from shootings

---

1. 'Some Aspects of Criminal Justice', a talk on Radio Hong Kong on 13 April 1968, in John Rear, *This Is the Law: A Series of Broadcasts* (Hong Kong: Radio Hong Kong, 1969), 71–76.
2. The fiscal year in Hong Kong is 1 April–31 March.
3. The bomb went off in a parcel in Mong Kok. Lo Shui-yan, a thirty-seven-year-old factory worker, whom police had seen standing over the parcel, was tried for murder. The prosecution asked for a 'murder or nothing' verdict, saying the bomb was powerful enough to drive shrapnel through a passing van some eighty feet away. But the jury convicted him of manslaughter. Lo refused legal aid, claiming in a statement from the dock that he had been framed. The judge, Timothy Creedon, sentenced him to twelve years' imprisonment. *SCMP*, 20–23 February and 1 March 1968.

or other causes.[4] In the only other murder trial resulting from the 1967 disturbances, three policemen, falsely accused of beating to death a man charged with possessing inflammatory posters, were convicted of manslaughter but exonerated on appeal.[5]

Hong Kong juries, said Rear, were rendering the distinction between murder and manslaughter meaningless by finding defendants guilty of manslaughter when the only reasonable interpretation of the evidence was that they intended either to kill or to seriously harm their victims. Many judges now tended to 'sum up for manslaughter' where they felt that the jury would acquit if the issue was put to them as 'a straight alternative between murder or acquittal'. Yet, because of the secrecy of jury deliberations, it was impossible to ascertain the real reasons for verdicts that were often 'quite incomprehensible'.

> To what extent do juries decide strictly on the basis of the evidence? How much, if at all, are they affected by newspaper reports of the earlier committal proceedings? Do they in fact ignore, as the judge asked them to do, evidence which is put forward but ruled inadmissible by the judge? How much do they feel hampered by the lack of a written transcript of the trial to which they can refer? To what extent are they influenced by counsel's final addresses or, even, by the skill and bearing of counsel themselves? To what extent do they allow themselves to be influenced by the expression of the judge's own personal views on the evidence?

Rear nevertheless attempted an explanation. One possibility was that 'the average man in Hong Kong is in favour of harsh punishment as long as it is meted out by authority and he does not have to share in the responsibility for it'. But the more likely reason, he suggested, was that the abolition of the death penalty was 'in accord with the wishes of Hong Kong people'. Hong Kong, he observed, was now 'out of step' with Great Britain, where capital punishment had been suspended since 1965. He had even heard it suggested that the retention of the death penalty in Hong Kong was 'a form of racial discrimination, an indication that Government do not regard the Chinese as fit or mature enough for a less severe law'. Did the government think that because there was no public agitation on the point there was no demand for a change?

---

4. 'Hong Kong Disturbances 1967', FCO 40/154, encl. 12, Appendix 6; *Gary Ka-wai Cheung, Hong Kong's Watershed: The 1967 Riots* (Hong Kong: Hong Kong University Press, 2009).
5. The victim, Lee On, had been charged with possessing inflammatory posters under emergency regulations. He died of a ruptured kidney shortly after appearing before a magistrate at the North Kowloon Magistracy. Three police officers on duty at the magistracy were tried for his murder and convicted of manslaughter. The judge, Sir Ivo Rigby, sentenced them to prison terms ranging from six to eight years. Their convictions were quashed on appeal. In a judgment critical of Rigby's handling of the case, the Chief Justice, Sir Michael Hogan, described the evidence as 'so weak and incomplete that in our view a jury properly directed could not have convicted the accused upon it'. He added that, if the guilt was removed from the three accused it could only be replaced by 'a pall of suspicion spreading over a wider section of the police force'. *SCMP*, 24 October–7 November 1967 and 9 January–3 February 1968; *Cheung Kam Yin and Others v The Queen* [1968] HKCA 64; Yu, *A Seventh Child and the Law*, Part 2, Chapter 6.

Other observers offered further reasons. Echoing Rear's analysis, people interviewed by the Home Affairs Department a few years later said that jurors did not want to bear the psychological burden of being responsible for another's death. They were also afraid of reprisals from accomplices. Some preferred to err on the side of leniency, especially if their English was poor. The Commissioner of Police, in contrast to Rear, believed that the non-implementation of the death penalty made juries reluctant to return murder verdicts. Concerned about the number of manslaughter verdicts, the Chief Justice acknowledged that it was natural for juries to 'shrink from returning a verdict of guilty of murder, which we all know is a capital offence'.[6]

What Hong Kong people really thought about the death penalty soon became a burning issue. As violent crime increased in the 1970s, the 'apparent ambivalence' that Rear detected in attitudes was superseded by strong public support for capital punishment. Community leaders, claiming to know the will of the people, demanded the restoration of capital punishment for murderers. The 'racial discrimination' which, according to Rear, prevented abolition of the death penalty in Hong Kong, was turned on its head by politicians who now contended that, in refusing to allow hangings to take place, the government in London was ignoring cultural differences between East and West. This concluding chapter explores how these controversies played out in the debates leading to the de facto repeal of the death penalty in 1975 and its final abolition in 1993.

The death penalty in suspense

Neither John Rear nor anyone else could have known that the hanging of Wong Kai-kei in November 1966 was to be Hong Kong's last execution.[7] For the next seven years manslaughter verdicts in murder trials continued to exceed murder convictions by a factor of three to one. Of the forty-five persons sentenced to death in the seven years from April 1966, twelve had their convictions quashed or reduced to manslaughter on appeal. Except for Wong Kai-kei, the other thirty-four had their death sentences reduced to prison terms ranging from ten years to life.[8] Whereas for most earlier cases they were unrecorded, the

6. Singapore, where juries were showing an even greater reluctance to convict capitally, dealt with the matter more decisively. Instead of abolishing the death penalty, in December 1969 Lee Kuan Yew's government abolished juries, replacing them with two judges in murder trials. Juries had already been restricted to capital trials since 1960. Secretariat for Home Affairs, 'Public Attitudes to Crime and Punishment', April 1972, and Sutcliffe to Roberts, 12 February 1972, HKPRO HKRS260-1-22, encls. 53 and 34; *SCMP*, 12 May 1972; Andrew Phang Boon Leong, 'Jury Trial in Singapore and Malaysia: The Unmaking of a Legal Institution', *Malaya Law Review*, Vol. 25 (1983): 50–86.
7. For Wong Kai-kei's case see Chapter 11.
8. Out of 409 persons committed for trial for murder in the seven years up to March 1973, 68 were convicted of murder and 205 of manslaughter; 99 were either acquitted or had the prosecutions withdrawn; another 37 were still awaiting trial. Of the 68 convicted of murder, 23 were sentenced to detention at Her Majesty's

reasons for commutation in most of these cases were set out in a note by the Attorney General, Denys Roberts, in 1973. They included lack of premeditation; questions about the accused's sanity; the influence of alcohol; doubts about the verdict; the lapse of time between sentence and review by the Executive Council; recommendations to mercy by the judge; and, in the growing number of murders in gang fights, the youth of the accused, provocations in earlier fights, and uncertainty about who struck the fatal blow.[9]

The Secretary of State periodically asked governments of the UK's remaining dependent territories to review their policies on capital punishment: in 1965, when the death penalty in Great Britain (but not Northern Ireland) was suspended for five years; in 1970, after abolition was made permanent; and again in April 1973. Seven replied that their legislatures, which were elected, were opposed to abolition. One, the New Hebrides, an Anglo-French condominium, said that the French government, which had not yet abolished the death penalty, would oppose such a measure.[10] The government of Hong Kong, the only territory without an elected legislature, replied that the Executive Council had advised against abolition. In 1970 the Governor, Sir David Trench, added that it might be necessary to implement the death penalty 'if there were to be a conviction for murder in the case of a violent crime'.[11]

'Where Hong Kong is concerned, so far as the faint pulse of public thinking can be felt there seems little objection to capital punishment,' remarked the *South China Morning Post* on the hanging in April 1966 of Lau Pui for murdering three people with a homemade bomb. Lau's execution, the first since 1962, showed that Hong Kong would not 'even by tacit consent' conform with practice in the UK. Capital punishment, the *Post* concluded, was not 'a burning issue in the Colony where reformers tend to concern themselves with pockets rather than ethics'.[12] Those, like John Rear, who *were* concerned with ethics, were a small minority. But they continued to press their case in speeches and letters to the press.

During the 1967 disturbances the Executive and Legislative Councillor Kan Yuet-keung[13] called for the death penalty to be mandatory for bomb offences, whether fatal or not. The call was prompted by the deaths of two children in a bomb explosion and the murder of the radio host Lam Bun and his cousin by a petrol bomb tossed into his car: Lam had satirized the protests in his show *Can't Stop Striking*. The culprits were never brought

pleasure because they were under eighteen or found insane. Registrar, Supreme Court, *Annual Departmental Reports*, 1966–1973, supplemented by Statistics from Commissioner of Prisons, in Penlington to O'Keeffe, 21 November 1975, FCO 40/650, encl. 57.

9. Hong Kong: Convictions for Murder 1966–1973, FCO 40/551, encl. 46. This account was prepared by Roberts partly from his notes at Executive Council meetings and partly from memory.
10. The other territories were the Bahamas, Bermuda, Belize, the British Virgin Islands, the Cayman Islands, Montserrat, and the Turks and Caicos Islands. Minute by P.H. Grattan, 15 May 1973, FCO 40/447, encl. 107A.
11. Minute by K.M. Wilford, 3 December 1970, FCO 40/299, encl. 21.
12. *SCMP*, 16 April 1966. See Chapter 11 for Lau Pui's case.
13. A banker and solicitor, son of Kan Tong-po, a founder of the Bank of East Asia.

to justice. Outraged by the bombings, the Chinese-language press joined Kan's call. Kan's office received a parcel bomb.[14] Officials drafted proposals along the lines of Emergency Regulation 116-A, in force in the early 1950s, and discussed them with Lord Shepherd, the Labour minister responsible for Hong Kong, during his visit in October 1967. Shepherd publicly declared his opposition to the idea.[15] Instead, the government, through emergency regulations, temporarily expanded the sentencing powers of the lower courts to provide swift, deterrent justice without trial by jury.[16]

On his return to London, Shepherd was congratulated in Parliament for making it clear there was 'no consideration of a return to the death penalty in the present crisis'.[17] This, along with his statement in Hong Kong, appears to have been taken as an indication that the British government would allow no more hangings to take place.[18] It was reinforced by private comments made later by Trench to the Legislative Councillor Woo Pak-chuen that he had to reprieve all convicted murderers because the Labour government, in office until 1970, would never permit an execution.[19] Yet this was neither the official position nor the message put out to the public. A background note prepared by the Foreign and Commonwealth Office (FCO) in September 1967 stated that capital punishment, though rarely carried out, had been retained in Hong Kong 'partly because the Chinese have a particular horror of certain rare crimes (e.g. patricide) and partly because they regard the

14. *HKH*, 23 August 1967; Cheung, *Hong Kong's Watershed*, 89–91 and 119–120.
15. Ministers were, however, prepared to allow the death penalty for attempted murder by explosives if conditions deteriorated further. Brief No. 1, October 1967, FCO 40/139; Hong Kong to Commonwealth Office, 29 August 1967, FCO 40/49, encl. 427; Hogan to Gass, 21 September 1967, ExCo Memorandum XCC (67)86, Annex C; FCO 40/118 'Hong Kong: Legal Affairs: Bomb Offences: Proposed Introduction of Death Penalty' (1967).
16. Emergency regulations issued in August and October 1967 (cancelled in May 1968) respectively removed the District Court's limit of five years' imprisonment for explosives and arms offences and increased the limit to ten years for all emergency offences and explosives offences under other laws. A separate emergency regulation (No. 118 of the Emergency (Principal) Regulations 1949), brought into force in 1950 but unused since then, empowered courts to sentence persons to up to ten years' imprisonment for consorting with persons in possession of arms or explosives. This extended to magistrates' courts because the qualification 'on conviction on indictment' had been inadvertently left out. On 29 July 1967, under this regulation, the magistrate Paul Corfe sentenced twenty-one persons to six years' imprisonment. Two days later the government amended the regulation by inserting the missing words. *HKGG* Legal Supplement No. 2, 1 August, 1 September and 27 October 1967; *SCMP* 30 July 1967.
17. *SCMP*, 18 October 1967; HL Deb 09 November 1967 vol 286 cc558–84.
18. A note for the Executive Council in 1989 stated that in 1967 'the Minister of State responsible for Hong Kong, Lord Shepherd, made it clear in Question Time that the Government would disapprove of any future hangings. The Governor of Hong Kong accepted this as an instruction and henceforth all death sentences were commuted.' XCRI(89)1, 10 January 1989, FCO 40/2728, encl. 2.
19. Record of meeting between Anthony Royle MP and Woo Pak-chuen, 14 September 1973, FCO 40/449, encl. 197. Royle, Shepherd's successor as Minister of State in Edward Heath's Conservative government, replied that he had never heard of this. He explained that capital punishment was not a party-political issue in the UK but a matter of conscience. Royle, along with many other Conservative Members of Parliament, including Edward Heath, was an abolitionist.

death penalty as the token of the Government's power and intention to maintain law and order'.[20] In July 1968, when Trench commuted the first death sentences since Shepherd's visit, officials reassured the public that there were no plans to abolish capital punishment.[21]

The official reassurances were partly a response to calls for abolition by the Chairman of the Bar Association, Gerald de Basto, shortly before the commutations were announced. The death penalty was uncivilized, he said. It had no deterrent effect because most murders were not premeditated.[22] The speech prompted reports in the Chinese-language press that many barristers and some religious leaders shared de Basto's view, but that legislators, such as Woo Pak-chuen and Ellen Li, believed that now was not the time to dispense with the death penalty. The death penalty could not prevent crime, said the *Kung Sheung Evening News*, but did its abolition mean that people would no longer commit crime? For countries that had already abolished capital punishment the answer was a definite 'no'. Although Hong Kong had now returned to normal after the disturbances, abolition would encourage leftists with murder in their hearts to become even more fearless, said the editorial. If the kind of inhuman murderers who had killed Lam Bun and children with bombs were spared the death penalty, what kind of security could society expect?[23]

'The young thug of today' and the rise in violent crime

As commutation of death sentences became the general rule, the awkward contradiction between policy and practice persisted. While crime rates were low the debate on capital punishment was sporadic and subdued. Public opinion, as far as it could be gauged, supported retention of the death penalty. Yet, for as long as murders mostly resulted from private quarrels, people did not complain if it was not used. However, as violent crime increased, demands for the resumption of hangings became more insistent. Violent crime quadrupled between the late 1950s and 1970 and quadrupled again by the mid-1970s. Reported homicides rose from 27 in 1965/66 to 85 in 1970/71 and 118 in 1972/73. Increasingly, said the Commissioner of Police, 'quasi-triad' gangs of young men were preying on vulnerable people, using 'extreme and unnecessary violence, leading to serious woundings, and on many occasions homicide'.[24] Some committed crime 'for the sheer thrill and bravado of it', said the Chief Justice, Sir Ivo Rigby. Thefts and robberies by youths were no longer

20. Background Note, FCO 40/118, encl. 4.
21. *KSEN*, 7 and July 1968; *SCMP*, 10 July 1968; replies to enquiries from *Hong Kong Standard*, 4 July 1968 and *Seng Weng Evening News*, 18 July 1968, HKPRO HKRS70-2-180.
22. These views did not prevent de Basto from presiding, as a temporary Commissioner of the Supreme Court, over a murder trial in 1973 and sentencing one of the accused to death. *SCMP*, 10 January 1973.
23. *KSDN*, 7 and 13 July 1968; *KSEN*, 8 and 9 July 1968; *Wah Kiu Yat Po*, 8 and 10 July 1968.
24. Commissioner of Police, *Annual Report 1972–1973*, 17.

the result of poverty, he said in 1972, but 'because these same young persons see so much money and affluence around them that they want a share in the luxuries'.[25]

In 1970 Governor Trench drew the FCO's attention to the growth in robberies, gang fights, sexual offences, and homicides. The crimes had no political motives, he wrote. And Hong Kong's crime rate was much lower, and the detection rate much higher, than in comparable cities. But people were 'both unused to violent crime in Hong Kong and aware of how bad it can get amongst their own people when it gets out of control'. The problem was worsened by overcrowding, secret societies, 'and the apparent lack of impact of current correctional methods on the attitudes of the young thug of today'. Those who used violence were 'all too often indifferent to the more lenient and enlightened forms of correction which we have increasingly introduced here'. The courts, he noted, were also criticized for taking an 'unduly lenient view' towards youth crime. They had little choice. Legislation enacted in 1967 prohibited them from sentencing persons under twenty-one to imprisonment unless no other punishment was appropriate.[26] Trench proposed modifying this restriction and implementing measures advocated by Chief Justice Rigby: greater use of corporal punishment, and the introduction of detention centres to deliver a 'short, sharp shock' and produce in young offenders 'a very real sense of relief at being released and a determination not to see the inside of such a place again'.[27]

Restrictions on imprisonment for young offenders were removed for a wide range of crimes by an amendment proposed in early 1971 by the Legislative Councillor Kan Yuet-keung.[28] With the support of legislators and encouragement of Rigby, the courts revived corporal punishment, which was extended to a wider variety of offences by adults.[29] Detention centres for young offenders, modelled on institutions in England, were established in 1972 under Trench's successor, Sir Murray MacLehose.[30] MacLehose introduced a mandatory minimum sentence of six months' imprisonment for anyone over fourteen

25. Sir Ivo Rigby, speeches at the Opening of the Assizes, 22 January 1970 and at the Rotary Club of Kowloon, 11 May 1972, *SCMP*, 23 January 1970 and 12 May 1972.
26. Trench to Monson, 6 August 1970, FCO 40/299, encl. 1.
27. *SCMP*, 23 January 1970.
28. These included rape, manslaughter, affray, and other violent offences, and various dangerous drugs offences. *HKH*, 24 February 1971; Ordinance No. 5 of 1971 s. 10A.
29. Legislation in early 1970 removed impediments to corporal punishment resulting from a series of Supreme Court judgments. Rigby issued a practice note in June that year stating that he and other Supreme Court judges had no objection to courts imposing caning in crimes involving substantial violence or sexual assaults on girls under sixteen. In 1971 it became possible for a court to add caning to a sentence of probation for an adult offender. Assault with intent to rob, aggravated burglary, affray, and possession of an offensive weapon were added to the offences for which adult offenders could be caned. Certain drug offences were included in 1974, and in 1975 escape from prison was added. Ordinances Nos. 19 and 20 of 1971, 42 of 1974; LN 96 of 1975.
30. Courts could sentence first offenders aged between fourteen and twenty-one to a term in a detention centre of between one and six months, to be determined in each case by the Commissioner of Prisons: Ordinance No. 12 of 1972.

convicted of possession of an offensive weapon in a public place. The maximum sentence a magistrate could impose for this offence was increased from two to three years. Police were given extra powers of stop and search in such cases.[31] In June 1973 caning also became available as a punishment for this offence.[32] To address complaints that the courts were too lenient, MacLehose enacted legislation allowing the Attorney General to apply to the Full Court for reviews of sentences he considered excessive or inadequate.[33]

Among Hong Kong's many problems there was none he had discussed more widely since his arrival in late 1971 than the problem of growing crime, said MacLehose in his first policy address, in October 1972.[34] In May 1973 he mobilized the public in support of a city-wide 'Fight Violent Crime Campaign'. The aim, he said, was 'to make honest men feel safe again and criminals feel isolated, afraid and marked'.[35] A publicity blitz, starting in mid-May, was followed by a month-long 'action phase' from mid-June. The police were reinforced with part-time auxiliary police officers. They swept neighbourhoods, stopping and searching tens of thousands of people. Police whistles were distributed to the public through neighbourhood fight-crime committees. Mobile reporting centres were set up and people were urged to report crime by dialling 999 or raising a 'hue and cry'. Faced with a backlog of cases, the Judiciary undertook to try offenders more quickly with the aid of temporary additional judges, appointed as 'Commissioners of the Supreme Court' under legislation enacted in 1970.[36] Under pressure from both politicians and the police, Chief Justice Rigby produced statistics to show a 'hardening of the attitude of the Judiciary' through more severe sentences.[37] To encourage this trend, MacLehose enacted legislation to increase the maximum sentencing powers of the District Court from five to seven years' imprisonment with the aim of providing quicker justice without juries.[38]

MacLehose's fight-crime measures received strong support from political leaders, the press, and kaifong (or neighbourhood) associations but encountered opposition from lawyers. The Bar Association, increasingly critical of government policy, had formed a committee of lawyers and academics in 1972 to study crime and punishment. Among its members were staff of the recently established Department of Law at the University of

31. Formerly, a police officer could only stop and search a person if he was acting suspiciously or was suspected of having committed, or of being about to commit, an offence. Now they could stop and search anyone. Ordinance No. 75 of 1972.
32. Ordinance No. 45 of 1973.
33. The provision was initially temporary but was made permanent in 1979. A similar provision already existed in New Zealand, Australia, Canada, and Singapore, and was introduced in England in 1988. *HKH*, 26 April and 10 May 1978; Ordinances Nos. 18 of 1972 and 20 of 1979.
34. *HKH*, 18 October 1972.
35. *SCMP*, 31 May 1973.
36. Ordinance No. 9 of 1970.
37. Rigby to Roberts, 30 October 1972, HKPRO HKRS 260-1-22, encl. 80.
38. Ordinance No. 43 of 1973.

Hong Kong. One of these was John Rear, who drafted the committee's report and wrote articles for the newspapers and the new *Hong Kong Law Journal*, of which he was editor.[39] The committee accepted that violent crime was increasing but it had little faith in the solutions offered by the government. Corporal punishment, it said, was a form of 'communal revenge' inconsistent with British standards of humanity and justice. Long prison terms worked least well with the very people on whom they were to be inflicted – young and first offenders – because they led to association with criminals, loss of work, and erosion of family ties. Mandatory custodial sentences were nothing less than 'a declaration by the Government of lack of confidence in the courts'. Many lawyers were dismayed by the Fight Violent Crime Campaign and the expansion of the District Court's jurisdiction. 'We are supposed in Hong Kong to have a scrupulously fair judicial system which is the envy of most countries in the Far East,' said the barrister Henry Litton QC. 'And yet the Government, along with the rock-and-roll jingles and the fanfares and the trumpets, is quite prepared to undermine one of the foundations of the common law system of criminal justice – namely trial by jury.'[40]

On 10 April 1973 MacLehose decided not to commute the death sentence imposed on Tsoi Kwok-cheong, a young man convicted of murder six months earlier. No date was fixed for the hanging but, according to standard practice, it would take place within three or four weeks, coinciding with the launch of the Fight Violent Crime Campaign. Although MacLehose denied any connection, the decision to hang Tsoi came to dominate the campaign. For supporters of Maclehose's tough measures a hanging was exactly what Hong Kong needed. To critics it was a cynical and macabre sacrifice to popular opinion. The controversy deepened a rift between political leaders in Hong Kong and the British government at a time when Parliament was again debating the death penalty: on 11 April, the day after MacLehose's decision, the House of Commons rejected a motion to restore the death penalty for certain forms of murder; in mid-May it was due to debate a bill to abolish capital punishment in Northern Ireland.

Tsoi Kwok-cheong

Tsoi Kwok-cheong (蔡國昌) was, in his own words, 'an ignorant and illiterate Chinese male who had never received any education'. He was born in 1944 to a farming family in Zhongshan, a district north of Macao. After the death of his father he went to Macao in 1961 and worked as a labourer in various shops. In June 1966 he was 'smuggled' into Hong Kong. He found work in a metalwork shop in Kowloon. After twelve months the owner

39. The Chairman was Gerald de Basto QC. The lawyer members were Miles Jackson-Lipkin, Robert Wei, Martin Lee, Francis Eddis, and Kemal Bokhary. The academics were Rear, Bernard Downey, Frank H.H. King, Margaret Kinsey, and Erik Kvan. Hong Kong Bar Association, *Annual Statement*, 1972–73, 49–55 and *Fighting Crime*.
40. Address to the Lion's Club, June 1973, in Hong Kong Bar Association, *Annual Statement*, 1973–74, 19–23.

suspected him of stealing and sacked him. Tsoi then found casual work in food stalls and at an illegal gambling den on Cheung Chau, one of the outlying islands. According to a friend, he was 'greedy', in a 'poor relationship' with his co-workers, and dissatisfied with the $30 per day he earned at the gambling den. A heavy gambler himself, he lost nearly $1,000 in a single session at a den he frequented in Yuen Long, where a friend of his father lived. He mixed with 'bad characters', fell into debt, and had quarrels with other gamblers.[41] In 1968 he was bound over for stealing a bicycle and a chicken. In February 1971 he stole a sacred relic from the Pak Tai Temple on Cheung Chau: a Song dynasty sword which fishermen had dredged up over a century before and placed there as a symbol of good fortune. Tsoi confessed to the theft when questioned by police about a burglary of $6,000 from a department store in Kwun Tong. He admitted the burglary offence too and was sentenced to sixteen months' imprisonment.[42] After his release in December 1971 he resumed his gambling habit.

On the evening of Wednesday 26 January 1972 Tsoi attended a wedding party at a restaurant near Yuen Long. Expecting a fight, he took with him three paint scrapers, which he had purchased that day. A fight duly broke out at a gambling table in a back room, during which a drunken Tsoi stabbed someone with one of the scrapers. When a police car arrived, Tsoi and two of his friends, Chiu Hoi-kwok and Tsang Wai-keung, left the restaurant and walked towards Yuen Long to find a taxi, taking a long rest on the way to sober up. At Hung Mo Kiu, a bridge across the Kam Tin River, they heard the clatter of a mahjong game from a nearby shop. Having lost all their money at gambling, they decided to rob the occupants. It was now about 2 a.m. Tsoi handed two of the paint scrapers to Chiu and Tsang. The three then masked their faces with handkerchiefs and entered the shop. They found three men and a woman, Kwok Sheung-chong, the owner, sitting at the mahjong table. They turned off the light and demanded money. Two of the men handed over $170. Unknown to the robbers, Madam Kwok's husband and children were upstairs in a cockloft. Knowing that one of her sons was still awake studying she called to him in the Chiu Chow dialect, which Tsoi and his friends did not understand. The son roused his father and elder brother and they descended from the cockloft to confront the robbers. In the ensuing commotion, bottles were thrown around the darkened room. The robbers fled, chased by the occupants

41. Tsoi Kwok-cheong, statement, 18 May 1972, and petition to Governor, 4 January 1973, Antecedent history of Tsoi Kwok-cheong, and Tin Ching-lung (probation officer), Social Enquiry: Memorandum for Executive Council: Death Sentence Passed on Tsoi Kwok-cheong, 18 January 1973, HKPRO HKRS41-2-1044, encl. 19.

42. The theft was widely publicized. When Tsoi heard about the seriousness of its loss on the radio he dared not take the sword home with him but instead buried it on the hillside near the Fanling Golf Club. The sword was returned to the temple shortly after Tsoi's conviction. *SCMP*, 17 February and 22 and 25 March 1971 and 18 April 1973.

of the shop. Before making his escape, Tsoi fought with the eldest son, Ng Sung-por, and stabbed him in the heart with his paint scraper.[43]

Ng Sung-por died in hospital. In May the police arrested Tsoi, Chiu, and Tsang for another robbery, in Wan Chai. They denied that robbery but admitted the one at Hung Mo Kiu. At first Tsoi thought he had only injured Ng. When charged with his murder he said he would plead guilty to manslaughter. On 2 November 1972, after an eight-day trial, in which he claimed his confession was extracted by force, Tsoi was convicted of murder and robbery by a jury of two women and five men – three Chinese, three Westerners, and an Indian. The judge sentenced him to death. Chiu, also charged with murder, was convicted of manslaughter and robbery and received a prison sentence of ten years. Charged only with robbery, Tsang was convicted and sentenced to six and a half years. Their appeal was dismissed on 21 December 1972.[44] The deceased Ng Sung-por (twenty-one) had been employed by the Yuen Long District Office: his colleagues there collected over $6,000 for his family. He was also, significantly, an auxiliary police constable. The Legislative Council granted compensation of $17,000 to his family under a rarely used provision dating from 1949: in moving the motion, the Acting Attorney General, Graham Sneath, praised Ng for recognizing 'a duty to assist in resistance to crime'.[45]

The trial judge in Tsoi's case was Michael Morley-John, a District Court judge and former government lawyer appointed as a Commissioner of the Supreme Court in 1970.[46] When sentencing Tsoi's accomplices, Chiu and Tsang, he called for a ban on 'needle-sharp' triangular paint scrapers.[47] Along with sharpened triangular files, these were now frequently used as weapons in robberies, which rose by over 50 per cent in 1972/73 over the previous year; in contrast, detection rates plunged from 69 per cent to 29 per cent.[48] In his report on Tsoi's trial to the Governor, Morley-John remarked that this type of robbery had reached 'alarming proportions'. Tsoi was clearly the leader of the enterprise, he wrote, and stayed and fought after the other two had run away. 'Your Excellency may well consider that an example should be made,' he suggested.[49]

43. Morley-John, report to the Governor, 7 November 1972 and Tsoi Kwok-cheong, statement, 18 May 1972, HKPRO HKRS41-2-1044, encl. 19; *Wah Kiu Yat Po* and *KSDN*, 27 January 1972.

44. *Tsang Wai Keung, Chiu Hoi Kwok and Tsoi Kwok Cheong v The Queen*: Judgment by Rigby CJ and Briggs and McMullin JJ, HKPRO HKRS41-2-1044, encl. 19.

45. In May 1973, as part of the Fight Violent Crime Campaign, more comprehensive schemes were announced for compensation to victims, or their dependants, injured or killed in crimes of violence or by police officers. *HKH*, 13 December 1972 and 23 May 1973; Ordinance No. 37 of 1947, incorporated into No. 31 of 1966 s. 95.

46. He became a permanent Supreme Court judge in 1973.

47. *SCMP*, 4 November 1972.

48. In 1972/73, 8,176 robberies were recorded, only 22 of which were with firearms, compared with 5,374 in 1971/72 and 17 with firearms. The 1967 disturbances had prompted a general disarming through police action and a two-week arms and ammunition amnesty. Commissioner of Police, *Annual Report 1972–1973*, Appendix 11.

49. Morley-John, report to the Governor, 7 November 1972, HKPRO HKRS41-2-1044, encl. 19.

The Executive Council considered Tsoi's case on 10 April 1973, four weeks after the Full Court issued its judgment on his failed appeal. The minutes baldly state that 'having considered the advice tendered the Governor ordered: that the law should take its course'. A separate note by the Attorney General records that there were 'no mitigating factors'.[50] Hearing of the decision, the father of Ng Sung-por said that if the government could not find a hangman he would do the job himself. A temple official on Cheung Chau said that Tsoi's fate was the result of a deadly curse on the sacred sword. Reporting the decision the next day, the *South China Morning Post* noted that there were nine other men in Stanley Prison whose death sentences remained to be considered by the Executive Council. It also said that, 'by coincidence', the House of Commons was that very day due to debate a private member's bill to reintroduce capital punishment for murders by firearms or explosives, or of police or prison officers.[51]

Avoiding a row in Parliament: Tsoi's petition to the Queen

MacLehose was 'distressed' by the coincidence between his decision to let Tsoi Kwok-cheong hang and the debate on capital punishment in the House of Commons the following day. 'If only you had warned me I could so easily have postponed the decision,' he replied to an FCO telex reminding him of the debate, and asking when his decision would be made public.[52] The enquiry came too late. A press release had been issued and the newspapers had already reported it.

On 11 April 1973 the House of Commons rejected the motion to reintroduce the death penalty. A month later, on 14 May, it was due to debate a bill to abolish the death penalty in Northern Ireland. The bill was expected to be passed, and eventually did so. Allowing an execution in Hong Kong at this time risked a motion of censure against the British government. This in turn might force the resignation of Edward Heath's Conservative government because votes on capital punishment were free votes according to the consciences of individual Members of Parliament.[53]

As editors and politicians digested the news that Tsoi would be hanged, another coincidence came to dominate the controversy now gathering momentum in Hong Kong. Supporters and opponents alike linked the decision to the Fight Violent Crime Campaign. 'We could hardly support the forthcoming anti-crime campaign if murderers were allowed

50. MacLehose to Sir Duncan Watson, 28 March 1973, FCO 40/445, encl. 4D; ExCo Minutes, 10 April 1973; Hong Kong: Convictions for Murder 1966–1973, FCO 40/551, encl. 46.
51. *SCMP*, 11 and 18 April 1973.
52. MacLehose to Watson, 10 April 1973, Douglas-Home to MacLehose, 10 April 1973, and MacLehose to Wilford, 11 April 1973, FCO 40/445, encls. 10, 11, and 12.
53. Hong Kong and Indian Ocean Department, Talking Points, 5 June 1973, FCO 40/447, encl. 119; *SCMP*, 30 May 1973.

to escape the death penalty,' declared the *Ming Pao*. Both it and the *Kung Sheung Daily News*, in an editorial linking the campaign with the resumption of the death penalty, noted the overwhelming support for the decision among kaifong and other community groups.[54] A petition to the Secretary of State, initiated by the Anglican and Catholic bishops and signed by over seventy lawyers, academics, and other residents, found the coincidence between the Governor's decision and the 'much heralded' anti-crime campaign 'very disturbing'. The petition, published in the *South China Morning Post* on 27 April, observed that it was 'an incontrovertible fact' that the public had been led to believe that the death penalty was 'a thing of the past in Hongkong'. If a change of policy was contemplated, the Governor should have reminded the public that it was still in force.[55]

A reminder of sorts had, in fact, already been issued. In February 1973, in response to a question in the Legislative Council, the Colonial Secretary gave an assurance that efficient arrangements could be made to carry out an execution should it be necessary.[56] Even before that announcement, MacLehose had prepared the ground with ministers in London. The death penalty could never be 'a response to public clamour', he had written on a list of options prepared by the Attorney General, Roberts, for a meeting with Anthony Royle, the Minister of State, in November 1972. But 'something extra is required to shock young criminals and back up the deterrent effect of the police presence. We can think of nothing else that would have a similar effect'.[57] In March 1973 he commuted two death sentences against the majority advice of the Executive Council.[58] He then informed the FCO that 'we are fast approaching a time when I shall feel obliged to let the law take its course'. He undertook to send to the FCO the papers on 'all borderline cases' before they went to the Executive Council so that the Secretary of State could be briefed: 'I of course detest the prospect but believe my duty to be clear.' In March he forwarded the papers

54. *Ming Pao*, 13 April 1973; *KSDN*, 20 April 1973.

55. Although most of the signatories were declared opponents of the death penalty, some were not. One, the barrister Miles Jackson Lipkin, wrote a further letter to the press a few days later clarifying both that he supported the restoration of capital punishment and that the original letter was 'neither for nor against hanging' but was concerned with 'deeper and graver issues vitally affecting the authority and dignity of H.M. Government' – the lack of certainty in punishment. Another signatory, the barrister Henry Litton, while serving temporarily as a Commissioner of the Supreme Court in 1972, had sentenced two young men to death. *SCMP*, 26 February 1972 and 27 April and 2 May 1973.

56. The question was from Peter Williams, the representative of the General Chamber of Commerce. It is possible that the government planted the question – a common practice at the time. *HKH*, 14 February 1973.

57. 'Problem of Crime in Hong Kong', and MacLehose to Roberts, 5 and 8 November 1972, HKRS 260-1-22.

58. On Li Wai-leung (twenty-one) and Hassan Solueman (nineteen). The murder arose from a fight in which a group of young men attacked another man after he had trodden on the foot of one of the attackers in a nightclub. The attackers went away and returned with knives, with which they fatally stabbed the man. MacLehose's reasons for commutation were the age of the accused, the fact that most of the stab wounds were not aimed at vital organs, and the recommendation of a reprieve by the trial judge. Hong Kong: Convictions for Murder 1966–1973, FCO 40/551, encl. 46.

on Tsoi Kwok-cheong, warning that it was 'a particularly bad case in which mitigating circumstances will be hard to find'. Reading them, Anthony Rushford, one of the FCO's legal advisors, wondered if the case really was much worse than others that had been commuted. The Secretary of State, Sir Alec Douglas-Home, nevertheless reassured MacLehose: 'The constitutional position is clear. I will continue to support you in your personal exercise of this heavy responsibility.'[59]

But the constitutional position was not clear, and ministerial support for MacLehose began to waver as fears grew of a 'row in parliament'. Up to the 1940s, secretaries of state had generally refused to intervene in death sentences confirmed by governors, holding to the principle that the royal prerogative of mercy was delegated to governors alone.[60] In a circular issued in 1947, in the aftermath of a controversial case from the Gold Coast, the Secretary of State, Arthur Creech Jones, confirmed this principle but added that if some exceptional case indicating a miscarriage of justice was brought to the attention of the Secretary of State he would not 'shut his eyes to it'. The delegation of the prerogative of mercy to colonial governors did not 'entirely empty' the King of his own prerogative, he said, even though it was unlikely a minister would ever have to advise the King to intervene. The 'Creech Jones formula', as it became known, was confirmed by an FCO circular in 1971.[61]

Officials in the FCO could find no evidence of a miscarriage of justice in Tsoi's case. They were initially inclined not to recommend any intervention by the Queen. They nevertheless asked to be assured that Tsoi was aware that he could petition the Queen and that he would not be executed until adequate time had been allowed for a petition to be considered.[62] The Attorney General, Denys Roberts, duly arranged for a notice to be read out to the illiterate Tsoi advising him of this right. He also sent a copy to Tsoi's solicitor, William Lore, who replied that, since legal aid did not cover proceedings overseas, he 'did not foresee' any assignment of lawyers to assist in such a petition. 'Personally,' he added, 'I feel that the punishment fits the crime in this case.' He also believed that defence counsel

---

59. MacLehose to Watson, 8 and 28 March 1973, Note by Rushton on minute by Stuart, 29 March 1973, and Douglas-Home to MacLehose, 6 April 1973, FCO 40/445, encls. 1, 4D, 5, and 9.
60. This reflected a principle encapsulated by the Permanent Under-Secretary for the Colonies, Sir George Fiddes, in relation to another case from the Gold Coast, that the prerogative must be exercised solely on the Governor's responsibility. The principle was cited by Colonial Office officials in the case of Ng Loi-yuen in 1934: see Chapter 10. Fiddes expanded on this in his book on the Colonial Office, giving three reasons: (1) a governor and his executive council, assisted by the trial judge, were best able to take into account all the surrounding circumstances; (2) the delay in bringing in the Colonial Office 'would be the practical abolition of the death penalty'; and (3) it would give 'a very odious advantage to the rich' who were able to employ lawyers to put their case to the Colonial Office. George Fiddes, *The Dominions and Colonial Offices* (London: G.P. Putnam's Sons Ltd, 1926).
61. Circulars 9337/47, 12 December 1947 and HXC 14/501/3, 13 May 1971, FCO 40/445, encl. 13.
62. Douglas-Home to MacLehose, 10 April 1973 and Minute by A.C. Stuart, 13 April 1973, FCO 40/445, encls. 11 and 13; minute by A.D. Watts, 18 April 1973, FCO 40/446, encl. 16.

at the trial shared these feelings.[63] But, whatever his own views on the case, Tsoi's counsel, Francis Eddis, undertook to help him prepare a petition, aided by his pupil, Ronnie Wong, a former lecturer in law at the University of Hong Kong.[64]

In his petition to the Queen, Tsoi confessed to killing Ng Sung-por but said he had acted in self-defence and had never planned to kill anyone: the paint scrapers were merely intended to frighten. When the Ngs descended from the cockloft into the darkened room, 'brandishing some kind of weapon', he and his two friends had tried to escape but he had run straight into the three men. 'It was a pure accident that your humble petitioner and not one of his two friends found himself up against the justifiably angry three men who had come down from the cockloft.' He had only struck Ng once, giving him time to run away. He had not mentioned any of this at trial because he thought it would be better to deny everything. He acknowledged his previous crimes – committed, he claimed, to pay for medicine for his mother in China. But he had never used violence in those cases. He pointed to the custom in Hong Kong for the Governor to grant clemency in all murder convictions in the past six years: he was sure that many of those murders displayed 'considerably greater intentional viciousness'. He had hoped to petition the Privy Council, but, having no resources or friends to take up the matter, had not taken steps in time. He asked the Queen to 'transform the sentence of death into a sentence of imprisonment'.[65]

The FCO received Tsoi's petition to the Queen on 20 April 1973. At first, officials planned to recommend that it be rejected. The case had no mitigating circumstances, they concluded. With rising crime and 'the very different situation in the Asian colony of Hong Kong', the 'predominantly Chinese population expects the law to be enforced'.[66] However, the Minister of State, Anthony Royle, an abolitionist, disagreed. He concluded that Tsoi's crime was no worse than those in which clemency had been granted in the past. He also feared 'a major Parliamentary political storm' at a time when the Commons were about to vote for the abolition of capital punishment in Northern Ireland. The Secretary of State, Sir Alec Douglas-Home, who was not an abolitionist, briefed the Prime Minister, Edward Heath, who was.[67]

---

63. Born in British Columbia, William Lore was the first Chinese Canadian to serve in the Royal Canadian Navy. He was part of Admiral Harcourt's fleet which landed in Hong Kong on 30 August 1945. After the war he obtained a BA in Jurisprudence from Oxford University and set up practice as a solicitor in Hong Kong. Roberts to Lore, 11 April 1973 and Lore to Roberts, 11 April 1973, HKPRO HKRS 41-2-1044, encls. 24 and 26; Chinese Canadian Military Museum website, entry for William K.L. Lore.
64. Eddis was a member of the Bar Association's special committee on crime and punishment. Roberts assured him that a suitable fee would be paid for his services. Roberts to Eddis 13 April 1973 and Eddis to Roberts, 17 April 1973, HKPRO HKRS 41-2-1044, encls. 30 and 31.
65. Petition of Tsoi Kwok-cheong, 17 April 1973, HKPRO HKRS 41-2-1044, encl. 31(2) and 32.
66. A.C. Stuart to Wilford and Royle, 24 April 1973, FCO 40/446, encl. 21.
67. Royle to Douglas-Home and Douglas-Home to Heath, 24 April 1973, FCO 40/446, encls. 22 and 24.

As interest in Tsoi's case grew among Members of Parliament, doubts about the wisdom of rejecting his petition set in. At a ship-launching ceremony in Newcastle, the Chief Justice of Hong Kong, Sir Ivo Rigby, told Royle he did not think the Governor would face any serious embarrassment if he was overruled. Douglas-Home asked MacLehose if the death penalty could be held to have 'fallen into desuetude'. MacLehose replied that the Executive Council had thrice rejected proposals to abolish it. Both his predecessor, Trench, and his Attorney General, Roberts, had told him it was coincidence, not policy, that no hanging had taken place since 1966; Roberts nevertheless detected a recent hardening of opinion in the council, which may have affected its view of mitigating circumstances. Moreover, '99 per cent of the population' not only believed the death penalty remained in force but had 'progressively and vociferously expressed concern at the failure to apply it'. Wishing, however, to be helpful, MacLehose immediately followed this with a second telex stating that, if the choice was between causing 'great local indignation' by granting Tsoi's petition and 'a prolonged publicised and bitter running battle in the UK in which Hong Kong was the subject of damaging controversy', then an act of clemency would be preferable. 'Hong Kong can never afford to be, or to appear to be, at loggerheads with the houses of parliament or the bulk of public opinion in the UK, or *a fortiori* with HMG,' he wrote.[68]

Royle agreed that a political row in England caused by a hanging in Hong Kong would damage the city's image. This image was already tarnished by perceptions that it was an unreconstructed 'industrial colony', where (in the words of an FCO official) power lay in the hands of 'a few rich men' and the masses lived in 'appalling conditions of urban squalor'.[69] A 'racial' question of a new kind now also emerged. 'If Tsoi is hanged,' asked Royle, 'what would be the position in say three months' time if a similar case involving a European arose?'[70]

---

68. Douglas-Home to MacLehose, 3 May 1973, and MacLehose to Douglas-Home, 4 and 5 May 1973, FCO 40/446, encls. 47, 50, and 51.
69. Minute by E.O. Laird, 21 September 1970, FCO/264, encl. 5. These perceptions were magnified by the Godber scandal, a series of articles in *The Times* in January 1974 about the poor quality of justice in Hong Kong, and the publication later that year of the scathing polemic *Hong Kong: A Case to Answer*, which depicted Hong Kong as resembling a banana republic.
70. Two cases of homicide by Europeans had only recently been concluded: (1) In November 1972 the conviction of Graham Edwards for murder was reduced to manslaughter by the Privy Council; the Supreme Court then sentenced him to fifteen years' imprisonment. Edwards was an Australian who had travelled to Hong Kong in pursuit of Dr Ronald Coombe (with whose wife he was having an affair) intending to blackmail him over indecent photographs he had found in Coombe's house. When Edwards appeared at Coombe's twelfth-floor room in the Hong Kong Hotel, Coombe took out a knife. In the ensuing fight Edwards grabbed the knife and stabbed Coombe twenty-seven times. He then left by the window and escaped over the roof in what the Full Court described as an 'athletic feat' requiring 'nerves of steel'. He was convicted of murder. His appeal was rejected by the Full Court. However, the Judicial Committee held there was evidence of provocation. (2) In December 1972 the Governor commuted to twenty years' imprisonment the death sentence on an Irish soldier, William Wilson, for murdering a taxi driver in a drunken frenzy. Royle to Douglas-Home, 7 May 1973, FCO

FCO officials now looked for ways to avoid a hanging. They asked MacLehose to arrange a psychiatric examination of Tsoi. They pondered whether the trial judge's advice that an example should be made had led to an act of policy rather than a decision on the merits of the case.[71] They asked if the matter could be referred to the Privy Council. The advice from the Privy Council was that a special reference, though theoretically possible, was inappropriate because it had been used only rarely in major constitutional or legal issues, which did not arise in this case.[72] On 8 May, Douglas-Home informed MacLehose (quoting his own words back at him) that an execution would surely lead to 'a prolonged publicised and bitter running battle in which Hong Kong was the subject of damaging controversy'. Taking this to mean that a reprieve would follow, MacLehose urged that it to be done as soon as possible: the case had 'dragged on dangerously and somewhat inhumanely long already'. Douglas-Home then informed the Prime Minister of predictions of 'one hell of a Parliamentary row' if an execution took place in Hong Kong, and of the possibility that a motion of censure by the opposition would be carried 'with the support of our convinced abolitionists'. If the political reasons were overwhelming, he concluded, 'I would have (against my reading of the actual case) to advise clemency.'[73]

On 14 May 1973, on the advice of her Secretary of State, Alec Douglas-Home, Queen Elizabeth II granted a pardon to Tsoi Kwok-cheong conditional that he be imprisoned for life.[74]

A row in Hong Kong

The Queen's commutation of Tsoi's death sentence may have averted a political crisis in the UK. But it caused resentment in Hong Kong. Leading Chinese-language newspapers had so far been subdued in their coverage of the decision to let Tsoi hang. Apart from linking it to the Fight Violent Crime Campaign, they had largely confined their commentary to speculation about why Tsoi was singled out (because his victim was an auxiliary policeman?) and when he would be hanged (in mid-May?). Some had attacked the petition

---

40/446, encl. 54; *Graham Edwards v The Queen* [1971] HKCA 10; *Graham Edwards v The Queen*, Privy Council Appeal No. 6 of 1972; *SCMP*, 26–28 July, 24 November, and 6 December 1972.

71. Minute by A.C. Stuart, 7 May 1973, and Douglas-Home to MacLehose, 8 May 1973, FCO 40/446, encls. 57 and 61.
72. Tsoi had already exhausted the fourteen-day time limit, from the date of final judgment in Hong Kong, for petitioning the Privy Council for an appeal. Minute by A.D. Watts, 8 May 1973, FCO 40/446, encl. 59.
73. The details of these (and some later exchanges) are not entirely clear because some documents in the FCO files are withheld or redacted and because discussions were by telephone or between MacLehose and the FCO official, A.C. Stuart, during Stuart's visit to Hong Kong. Douglas-Home to MacLehose, 8 May 1973, MacLehose to Douglas-Home, 10 May 1973, and Douglas-Home to Heath, 10 May 1973, FCO 40/446, encls. 61, 63, and 67.
74. Instrument of pardon, 14 May 1973, HKPRO HKRS41-2-1044, encl. 42.

from the bishops and lawyers. The *Ming Pao* suggested that most of the signatories were opposed to the old Chinese dictum that 'killers must die' (殺人者死) because they were wealthy foreigners who lived on the Peak and had no experience of violent crime. The real victims were poor and middle-class Chinese.[75] Newspapers had also reported comments by a visiting Member of Parliament, John Tilney, that Hong Kong need not abolish the death penalty.[76] In contrast, the leading English-language paper, the *South China Morning Post*, received a stream of letters mostly critical of MacLehose's decision, some dramatically so.[77] A law lecturer, Roberto Ribeiro, gave a graphic description of how hangings were carried out. His colleague John Rear, suggested that the Governor should ask his Executive Councillors to carry out Tsoi's execution: 'let us bring the gallows to Statue Square and you can do the job at midday, in public, where the example can be seen for what it is – and at the same time you can prove your sincerity and your appetite for the task.' Not everyone saw the irony in this suggestion.[78]

The news of the commutation turned this commentary on its head. In an editorial on 16 May the *Morning Post* regretted that it had been announced just after the Fight Violent Crime Campaign had 'moved into first gear' but said it would have been 'reprehensible in the extreme to have used a man's life as a virtual campaign gimmick'.[79] The Chinese-language press erupted in anger. The decision showed an utter lack of understanding of the dire state of law and order in Hong Kong and the desire of its citizens for severe punishment, said the *Kung Sheung Daily News* and the *Wah Kiu Yat Po*; the *Wah Kiu* had earlier announced the launch of a signature campaign calling for enforcement of the death penalty. The *Ming Pao* ran four editorials on four successive days attacking the decision as a blow to the fight-crime campaign. It announced a survey of public opinion to show the British government how Chinese people really felt about the death penalty. The FCO seemed to think that the demands of seventy-odd barristers and church leaders represented public opinion in Hong Kong, it said.[80] Some weeks later, the *Sing Tao* concluded that Chinese lives and property were 'not worth a fly's head' when the prestige of the mother country was at stake.[81]

75. *Ming Pao*, 3 May 1973.
76. *Wah Kiu Yat Po*, 19, 22, and 30 April 1973; *KSDN*, 20, 25, 28, and 30 April and 1, 11, and 14 May 1973; *Ming Pao*, 1 and 3 May 1973; *KSEN*, 1 May 1973.
77. On 5 May the paper announced that the subject would be closed the following day. *SCMP*, 19, 21, 26, and 27 April and 1, 2, 3, 5, and 6 May.
78. *The Star*, an English-language tabloid, interviewed six random people in Statue Square: three agreed with Rear's 'suggestion'; the other three said he should be hanged privately. *SCMP*, 30 April and 6 May 1973; *The Star*, 3 May 1973.
79. *SCMP*, 16 May 1973.
80. *Wah Kiu Yat Po*, 13 and 17 May 1973; *Ming Pao*, 16–19 May 1973.
81. *Sing Tao Jih Pao*, 21 June 1973.

With some exceptions, politicians and community organizations also denounced the commutation. Senior police officers saw it as a blow to the morale of the force. Kaifong leaders threatened to withdraw support for the Fight Violent Crime Campaign. On 21 May members of 120 civic bodies attended a rally where they voted unanimously to launch a million-signature campaign to retain capital punishment.[82] MacLehose's briefing to the Executive Council on the commutation was received with 'cold anger and frustration in a way I have not hitherto experienced, and I was obliged to keep a strong grip to prevent the proceedings getting out of hand'. Kan Yuet-keung (now Sir Y.K. Kan) threatened to resign. Capital punishment had been abolished nowhere else in the Far East, he told the Minister of State a few months later; a repetition of 'HMG's actions in the Tsoi case' would be 'totally unacceptable'.[83] MacLehose himself was embarrassed by being publicly overruled on an issue so important to public opinion. 'A lesser man than Governor MacLehose would have resigned on the spot,' recalled Andrew Stuart, the head of the Hong Kong and Indian Ocean Department of the FCO.[84]

In fact, MacLehose did discuss resignation, not in reaction to the decision on Tsoi but in case the royal prerogative was again used to overrule him. 'Local indignation would be very great,' he advised the FCO. 'Further, the spectacle of the Governor in Council being overruled is thoroughly bad for this government's authority and a repetition should not be risked.' There would be wholesale resignations from the councils because people like Kan would not serve if they were to be overruled 'on the theory that since Hong Kong is a colony it must do as it is told,' he wrote. 'My own position would be shaken. The shock to police morale would be considerable. Murders would continue, and each one could be an excuse for a further outcry along the lines "But for the British my son would not have died."'[85] In September 1973 he told visiting Members of Parliament that if he was 'again overridden as last time, he would have to offer his resignation because his authority and credibility in the Colony would be destroyed'.[86] No one blamed MacLehose for his predicament. He was in no doubt that he had the support of the people. Tsoi's reprieve, he declared in his policy address in October, was 'against the express advice of the Governor in Council and the wishes of the overwhelming majority of the population'.[87]

In that address MacLehose observed that the year had been 'shot through with important and sometimes dramatic events'. One of these had occurred only three weeks after

82. *KSDN*, 17 May 1973; *Oriental Daily News*, 18 May 1973.
83. MacLehose to Secretary of State, 16 May 1973, FCO 40/446, 86(c); FCO to MacLehose, 16 January 1974, FCO 40/551, encl. 13.
84. Andrew Stuart, *Of Cargoes, Colonies and Kings: Diplomatic and Administrative Service from Africa to the Pacific* (London: Bloomsbury Publishing, 2004), 104.
85. MacLehose to Secretary of State, 1 June and 19 July 1973, FCO 40/448, encls. 115 and 149.
86. Walter Clegg MP to Douglas-Home, 2 October 1973, FCO 40/413, encl. 149.
87. *HKH*, 17 October 1973.

Tsoi's reprieve. On 8 June 1973 Peter Godber, a senior Hong Kong police officer under investigation for corruption, evaded immigration controls at Kai Tak Airport and escaped to England. His offence – being in control of unexplained assets disproportionate to his official emoluments – did not exist in the UK. Under the 'double criminality rule', extradition to Hong Kong was thus impossible. As the scale of his venality became known, students launched a 'Bring Back Godber' campaign and inveighed against 'corrupt British colonialism'. Already incensed by the refusal to allow hangings, politicians in Hong Kong now questioned a colonial relationship that allowed a corrupt police officer to escape justice by seeking sanctuary in the mother country. Godber and the death penalty were always taken together, reported visiting Members of Parliament on their discussions in Hong Kong.[88] The two issues reflected 'strange weaknesses in our link with Britain', remarked the legislator Joyce Symons in the debate on MacLehose's address. The death penalty, said an FCO official a few months later, was 'the main current irritant in Anglo-Hong Kong relations'.[89]

Godber was eventually extradited to Hong Kong in January 1975 on a new charge of accepting a bribe, which was a crime in both the UK and Hong Kong. He was convicted on the evidence of other corrupt police officers and sentenced to four years' imprisonment. The Godber episode prompted MacLehose to establish the Independent Commission Against Corruption (ICAC) in 1974. With strong public support, the ICAC took determined action to root out corruption in the police and other organizations. The other main irritant in Anglo-Hong Kong relations – the question of capital punishment – was also dealt with in 1975, albeit less decisively.

Avoiding another potential Tsoi situation

In July 1973 ministers considered the implications of Tsoi's case for Britain's other dependent territories. They agreed that, in those with elected legislatures, abolition or retention of the death penalty should be left to local decision. The Creech Jones formula still applied. Ministers would only intervene if there were clear signs of a miscarriage of justice. The exception was Hong Kong, the only territory with no elected legislature. With its population of 4 million, five times that of all the other territories combined, it had the highest incidence of homicides – now, in the early 1970s, about a hundred per annum, four times that in the early 1960s.[90]

Ministers discussed various options for Hong Kong: putting the case for retaining the death penalty in Hong Kong to a free vote in the House of Commons; or a free vote of the members of the Executive and Legislative Councils, backed by some opinion sampling, 'as

88. Walter Clegg MP to Douglas-Home, 2 October 1973, FCO 40/413, encl. 149.

89. *HKH*, 31 October 1973; Watson to Goronwy-Roberts, 11 June 1974, FCO 40/552, encl. 86.

90. Cabinet Defence and Oversea Policy Committee: 'The Death Penalty in Dependent Territories', and Stuart to Watson, 20 July 1973, FCO 40/448, encls. 146 and 151.

being the nearest thing to an expression of representative opinion available in Hong Kong'; or even 'some sort of referendum in Hong Kong'. Each option was problematic. Members of Parliament were unlikely to vote to retain the death penalty for Hong Kong when they had voted against it for the UK. Nor would they be impressed by a vote by unofficial councillors in Hong Kong, since they were all appointed and were 'mostly wealthy businessmen'. A referendum had 'dangerous' implications for the UK, where public opinion also still strongly supported the death penalty.[91] The Prime Minister, Edward Heath, had in any case ruled it out, fearing it could lead to a 'major conflict with HMG and Parliament' and 'loud demands for a referendum on capital punishment here'.[92]

Small-scale street polls in Hong Kong at this time showed that a majority supported the use of the death penalty.[93] The largest of the signature campaigns, launched in 1975 by the Civic Association's Anti-Crime Commission, gained over 270,000 signatures in support of capital punishment.[94] Such initiatives had no difficulty in securing support in the abstract. Yet public attitudes in specific cases showed an ambivalence similar to that found among juries. Executive Council papers on death sentences included reports from the Home Affairs Department on community views in the neighbourhoods where victim and prisoner lived. Most contained a standard formula that the consensus was that death sentences should be carried out as a deterrent to violent crimes, but that the case in question had aroused 'no special interest'. Occasionally, there was sympathy for the prisoner. For example, the case of Leung Wing-sang (twenty), condemned to death in January 1974 for his part in a fatal gang raid on an apartment house run by a rival gang, prompted a petition for mercy from people in the resettlement estate where his family lived on the grounds that he had fallen into bad company and was the sole support of his ailing parents. Later inquiries revealed more to Leung's case than had at first appeared: he had been 'sacrificed' in a deal done between leaders of his gang and the police to spare others from prosecution.[95]

91. An opinion poll cited in the 1964 Commons debate found that eighty per cent of the public opposed abolition. Later surveys showed that support for the restoration of capital punishment did not fall below fifty per cent until 2014. After the murder of children in Southport in 2024, support for restoration rose to fifty-five per cent: *The Times*, 29 January 2025.

92. Cabinet Defence and Oversea Policy Committee: The Death Penalty in Dependent Territories, FCO 40/448, encl. 146; Bridges to Royle, 11 May 1973, FCO 40/446, encl. 69.

93. See, for example, *Sunday Post Herald*, 29 April 1973; and *The Star*, 3 May 1973. In contrast, in a street poll by the *South China Morning Post* three years earlier, shortly after the death penalty was permanently abolished in Great Britain, forty-three out of sixty-one people thought it should be abolished in Hong Kong: *SCMP*, 10 January 1970.

94. *SCMP*, 10 May 1975.

95. During the trial of two European police officers for corruption in 1975, it was alleged that a station sergeant had conspired with the leaders of Leung's gang to give him up in return for leaving the rest of the gang alone. Told that he would only be tried for wounding with intent to do grievous bodily harm, and promised a sum of $10,000 for his mother, Leung co-operated. He confessed to having chopped the victim, an apartment-house manager, who had then jumped to his death from a fifth-floor window. The Governor appointed a commission

No such sympathy had arisen in the case of Tsoi Kwok-cheong: even his few friends and distant relatives in Hong Kong had nothing positive to say about him.

In the light of Tsoi's reprieve the decision by ministers was to leave things as they were but also to draw up a contingency plan in preparation for 'another potential "TSOI" situation'. Such a situation was expected to arise as soon as October 1973.[96] This approach had the support of MacLehose, who was adamant that the death penalty should be retained on the understanding it would be enforced 'very sparingly and only in cases in which no mitigating circumstances exist, the decision on the latter to rest with the Governor in Council'. Abolition by the UK government would appear 'capricious and arbitrary'. It would convey 'an implication of Western superiority in humanity, which is as offensive as I know it is unintended', he insisted in an emotionally charged telex.[97] Unilateral abolition by the UK nevertheless featured as an option in a contingency plan discussed during a visit to London by MacLehose and endorsed by ministers.

Under the contingency plan, in future capital cases the Governor would warn the Secretary of State whether or not, if so advised by the Executive Council, he intended to allow the law to take its course. He would forward all papers on the case. If he planned to reprieve, he would stand by the decision, if necessary rejecting the council's formal advice that the accused should be executed. If he planned to confirm the death sentence, he would, within five weeks, receive notification from the Secretary of State <u>either</u> of his support for the execution <u>or</u> of his decision to abolish the death penalty in Hong Kong by a UK order in council before the execution could take place: the Governor would have three weeks to explain the decision to the Executive Council and seek its support. The entire process would take about eight weeks.[98]

The contingency plan formally maintained the constitutional position that the Governor in Council decided whether to let the law take its course. But, under further procedures agreed between the FCO and MacLehose, the consultation would start even earlier. The Governor would, in each problematic case, send the trial transcript, the appeal judgment (if any), the probation officer's report, and other papers to the FCO as early as

---

of inquiry, held by the judge Yang Ti-liang. It concluded that a deal had indeed been done but that, even if the jury had known about it, it was unlikely that their verdict would have been different: Leung had been sacrificed but not framed. The Governor in Council considered, but decided against, pardoning Leung. As a result of the inquiry, five other gang members were convicted of the murder in 1977. ExCo Memorandum: Death Sentence on Leung Wang alias Leung Wing-sang, 23 July 1974, XCR(74)132; *Report of the Commission of Inquiry into the Leung Wing-sang Case* (1976).

96. Minute by P.M. Kelly, 17 August 1973, FCO 40/448, encl. 168.
97. 'What has stirred up the Governor', minuted Douglas-Home on this outburst. 'Was he not told of the gov. committee's decision the other day?' In the confusion of crossed communications, MacLehose was still under the impression that the British government was planning to abolish the death penalty in Hong Kong. MacLehose to Secretary of State, 19 July 1973, FCO 40/448, encls. 49 and 50.
98. Norman-Walker to Secretary of State, 29 August 1973, FCO 40/448, encl. 178.

possible. The FCO would in turn forward them to the Home Office, whose experts would look for reasons for a reprieve. The Governor would then deploy these reasons at the Executive Council, first off the record, then at an official meeting. These additional procedures were intended to avoid triggering the contingency plan, which would probably break down anyway: ministers were unlikely to support an execution; they were even less likely to do so after Heath's Conservative government gave way to a minority Labour government in February 1974.[99] Equally, the Executive Council was unlikely to acquiesce in abolition by the UK government. By drawing UK officials further into the exercise of mercy, the procedures severely limited the Governor's freedom of action. The aim was to ensure that no death sentence would be carried out even in the worst cases.

Several 'worst cases' were on the horizon in 1973. The first was that of Lam Po, who had been twice sentenced to death for murder. He was first convicted in July 1971 for his part in an arson attack on the shop of a business partner to whom he owed money, in which eleven people were killed.[100] The Officer Administering the Government, Sir Hugh Norman-Walker, commuted his death sentence to thirty years' imprisonment, against a thirteen-to-one vote by the Executive Council for the law to take its course.[101] In 1973, in Stanley Prison, after repeated bullying by other inmates, Lam had stabbed a fellow prisoner to death. At trial, despite pleading not guilty, he refused legal aid and asked the judge to measure his neck so he could be hanged. When the judge passed sentence of death Lam bowed and said, 'thank you, this is what I want.' Legal aid officers persuaded him to appeal, but he insisted his sentence was fair. The Full Court dismissed the appeal.[102]

Officials in the FCO and Home Office scrutinized the papers on Lam's case and found reasons to support commutation. He was not represented at trial. His statement that he had killed in revenge, on which the prosecution had relied, had been made without caution to two prison officers – persons in authority. One of them did not understand Cantonese, in which case his account of Lam's actual words may have been hearsay. Lam may have refused to cross-examine witnesses because he did not understand procedures. He may have demanded to be hanged because, if acquitted, he would still have had to live with his fellow prisoners and warders for the rest of his first sentence. None of this had been mentioned by the trial judge in his summing up. MacLehose deployed these points in an informal discussion with the Executive Council, which then, on 11 December, formally

---

99. Minute by Stuart, 25 January 1974, FCO 40/551, encl. 17; Note for Executive Council: Death Sentence on Lam Po, XCSI(73)2, 16 November 1973, FCO 40/649, encl. 7.

100. *SCMP*, 13 January, 3–5 and 10, 17, and 22 June, 30 November and 1 December 1971 and 22 February 1972; *Lam Po alias Lam Po Tai and others v The Queen* [1972] HKCA 102.

101. Sir Hugh Norman-Walker, Colonial Secretary 1969–1973, declared himself on his retirement to be an opponent of capital punishment. *SCMP*, 30 September 1973.

102. *KSDN*, 3, 5, 8–12, 16, and 22–23 June and 22 July 1971 and 16 August 1973; *SCMP*, 16 August and 29 September 1973; ExCo Memorandum: Death Sentence on Lam Po, 23 July 1974, XCR(73)274, HKPRO HKRS41-2-991.

advised commutation.[103] The commutation avoided the prospect of triggering the contingency plan during a planned visit to Hong Kong by the Prime Minister.[104]

Three other difficult cases followed in quick succession, with similar results. MacLehose described the first as 'alarmingly similar to Tsoi's'. Leung Ping-fat, convicted of the murder of a coffin-shop employee during a robbery, was reprieved mainly on the ground that the trial judge had withdrawn from the jury the defences of provocation and self-defence.[105] Chan Hon-tong, convicted of the murder of a young amah in a 'particularly difficult' case, was reprieved because of a 'scintilla of doubt' about the circumstantial evidence against him.[106] In the third case, neither MacLehose nor officials in London could find any mitigating circumstances for Liu Chu, who was convicted of murdering a watchman who had chased him after he had mugged a woman at knifepoint. But MacLehose reprieved him anyway because he believed the new Labour government was unlikely 'to countenance any execution in any circumstances'.[107] This belief was confirmed by the new Secretary of State, James Callaghan, in a meeting with MacLehose in June 1974.[108]

As with Tsoi Kwok-cheong, extraneous political considerations played a part in these deliberations. In Leung Ping-fat's case, FCO officials were worried about the possibility of 'an unfortunate coincidence' with an execution likely to take place at the same time in another dependent territory, Belize.[109] Edward Youde, a future Governor of Hong Kong,

103. MacLehose to Secretary of State, 3 October and 7 and 11 December 1973, FCO 40/449, encls. 203 and 239 and FCO 40/450, encl. 246; Stuart to Rushford, 6 September 1973, and Stuart to Brennan, Home Office, 22 October 1973, FCO 40/449, encls. 206 and 209; Douglas-Home to MacLehose, 4 October 1973, FCO 40/449, encl. 204B.

104. The visit, planned for January 1974, did not take place. Briefing note on the death penalty, FCO 40/415, encl. 104A; MacLehose to Stuart, 22 November 1973, FCO 449, encl. 231A.

105. Douglas-Home to MacLehose, 26 November 1973, and MacLehose to Secretary of State, 7 December 1973, FCO 40/449, encls. 225 and 240; Douglas-Home to MacLehose, 13 December 1973, and MacLehose to Secretary of State, 15 and 19 December 1973, FCO 40/450, encls. 248, 249, and 254.

106. P.M. Kelly to Stuart, FCO 40/450, encl. 258; C.H. Prior, Home Office, to Stuart, 3 January 1973, Douglas-Home to MacLehose, 3 January 1974, and MacLehose to Secretary of State, 5 March 1974, FCO 40/551, encls. 4, 5, and 43.

107. P.M. Kelly to Stuart, 3 January 1974, Stuart to Rushford, 7 January 1974, Stuart to C.H. Prior, Home Office, 7 January 1973, MacLehose to Secretary of State, 14 January 1973, C.H. Prior to Stuart, 17 January 1974, Stuart to MacLehose, 18 January 1974, Secretary of State to MacLehose, 4 February 1974, Stuart to MacLehose, 12 February 1974, MacLehose to Secretary of State, 18 February 1974, Rushford to Kelly, 19 February 1974, minute by R.B. Crowson, 20 February 1974, and MacLehose to Watson, 5 March 1974, FCO 40/551, encls. 3, 6, 7, 10, 11, 12, 26, 29, 30, 34, 36, and 45.

108. Record of Conversation between the FCO Secretary and the Governor of Hong Kong, 24 June 1974, FCO 40/552, encl. 90.

109. The Governor of Belize (a self-governing territory), on the unanimous advice of his advisory council, had refused to commute a death sentence imposed on a man for the murder of a policeman. The execution took place in March 1974 with no publicity in the UK. Douglas-Home to MacLehose, 13 December 1973, FCO 40/450, encl. 248; Champion to Watson, 22 March 1974, and Callaghan to MacLehose, 5 April 1974, FCO 40/552, encls. 57 and 70.

was concerned that some Executive Councillors wished to see exemplary executions as a deterrent to murders in the course of robberies regardless of the merits of each case.[110] Consideration of Liu Chu's case was postponed for several weeks because of elections in the UK in February 1974: it would be unfortunate, FCO officials and MacLehose agreed, if the first issue in Hong Kong for the new government was the death penalty.[111] In Hong Kong, the Executive Council was beginning to baulk at the system of advance consultation with the FCO. In May 1974 MacLehose had 'a very rough ride' with Liu Chu's case. In July, when another death sentence came up, Sir Y.K. Kan and other members said that it was misleading for ministers to continue to tell Parliament that the prerogative of mercy was delegated to the Governor 'when the harsh fact was that the Governor would not be supported by HMG if he were to decide that the law should take its course'.[112] Interest in the death penalty among politicians and in the press continued, sparked by criticisms of commutations and promises by visiting Members of Parliament that they would raise the matter in London. In June 1974 a petition to the Queen from kaifong leaders requested a royal decree instructing the Hong Kong government to reimpose the death penalty for murders committed in robberies.[113]

Further problematic cases followed in 1974 and 1975. Some were shocking. All placed yet more strain on the fragile system agreed between MacLehose and London, and on his relations with the Executive Council: a fatal stabbing of a woman in a robbery;[114] murders in gang fights;[115] the first woman convicted of murder since the war;[116] a parricide in which the son hired a gang to do the killing.[117] The 'crunch case' came in May 1975, when the Executive Council reviewed the death sentences imposed on seven men for a murder during an armed robbery in 1974 at a branch of the Chartered Bank in Kowloon. The men had injured several of the bank staff with blows from their revolvers, and had left with $462,000, taking a female member of staff as hostage. During their escape they shot bystanders and a police sergeant, who died from a bullet in his head. There were no mitigating circumstances. It was 'the worst case I have known', remarked MacLehose.

---

110. Minute by Youde, 19 December 1973, FCO 40/450, encl. 255.
111. Douglas-Home to MacLehose, 12 February 1974, MacLehose to Watson, 5 March 1974, and Watson to MacLehose (draft), FCO 40/551, encls. 29, 45, and 50.
112. MacLehose to Stuart, 19 August 1974, FCO 40/553, encl. 113.
113. MacLehose to Watson, 14 May 1974, FCO 40/552, encl. 79; Petition from the Hong Kong & Kowloon Joint Kai-fong Research Council, 20 July 1974, FCO 40/553, encl. 106.
114. ExCo Memorandum: Death Sentence on Lau Ming-chiu, 10 December 1974, XCR(74)203.
115. ExCo Memoranda: Death Sentence on Leung Wang alias Leung Wing-sang, 23 July 1974, XCR(74)132 and Death Sentence on Lai For-pui, 24 September 1974 XCR(74)163; Death Sentence on Tse Yung-tim and Lam Kwok-wah, 26 March 1974, XCR(74)61; Death Sentence on Cheng wing-fei, 25 June 1974, XCR(74)115.
116. Wan Mui-mui, convicted along with three men of beating to death a man who had attempted to defraud their call-girl establishment. ExCo Memorandum: Death Sentence on Chau Cheuk-yin, Lai Fai, Wan Mui-mui, and Liu Sim-shun, 23 April 1974, XCR(74)79.
117. ExCo Memorandum: Death Sentence on Kwan Yip-chuen, 11 March 1975, XCR(75)49.

Yet he was confident he could get it through the Executive Council. Two months earlier, after he had persuaded them to unanimously advise commutation in the parricide case, members had asked for a 'full discussion of the whole issue'. During that discussion MacLehose had agreed that members should feel free to abstain from giving advice in cases in which they would otherwise have advised execution. Ministers had warmly congratulated him on this 'compromise'.[118] However, when on 27 May the council considered the Chartered Bank robbery-murder, all eight unofficial members and one official member abstained. They made it clear they would have advised that the law should take its course but preferred to abstain because advice to commute would have been incompatible with their oaths of office. MacLehose commuted all seven death sentences, to outrage among police officers and the general public.[119]

De facto abolition, 1975

MacLehose and other officials had hoped that the death penalty issue would go away when crime rates declined. But rates of violent crime continued to be high, peaking at 419 per 100,000 population in 1974/75, nearly four times the rate in 1969/70 and ten times that of 1964/65. Homicide rates were between two and three per 100,000 in the early 1970s, well over double those of the 1960s.[120] In 1974/75, reported homicides reached a record 122, compared with 103 in 1973/74 and 118 in 1972/73. The detection rate for homicides averaged 65 per cent in the early 1970s. For robbery, the other crime that most worried politicians and the public, the detection rate declined from 64 per cent in 1970/71 to 17 per cent in 1974/75, with slightly higher rates for the smaller number of robberies with firearms (67 per cent in 1970/71, declining to 24 per cent in 1974/75). Deterrence by fear of detection was the most potent weapon against crime, MacLehose said in 1972, and

118. Members had also proposed that the Queen should 'regularize the local position by suspending (not abolishing) the death penalty in Hong Kong by an Order in Council', an idea which MacLehose advised against on the grounds that it would be misunderstood by the public; would be tantamount to abolishing the death penalty for ever, which members did not want; and would reignite local feelings of frustration and damage Hong Kong–UK relations. MacLehose to Duncan, 25 March 1975, ExCo Minutes, 18 March 1975, and Records of meetings between Callaghan and Goronwy-Roberts and MacLehose, 9 and 11 April 1975, FCO 40/649, encls. 8, 9, 12, and 14.

119. MacLehose to Secretary of State, 27 May 1975, and ExCo Minutes, 27 May 1975, FCO 40/649, encls. 15 and 26.

120. Commissioner of Police, *Annual Reports*, 1961–1975, summarized in Harold Traver, 'Crime Trends', Table 2.1, in *Crime and Justice in Hong Kong*, ed. Harold Traver and Jon Vagg (Hong Kong: Oxford University Press, 1991), 13.

again in 1973.[121] But the police were overwhelmed. Large-scale prosecutions for corruption were also undermining their detective capacity. The campaign for capital punishment intensified.

The campaign came to a head in the debate on the Governor's policy address in October 1975. The debate was opened by the senior unofficial legislator, the businessman Chung Sze-yuen. Chung was also a member of the Executive Council, one of the nine members who had abstained from advising on the Chartered Bank robbery-murder. He referred to the rising crime rate. Along with the state of the economy, this was the issue most on people's minds. The Chinese newspapers, the kaifong associations, and the man in the street were all saying 'we are not putting sufficient emphasis on the fear of punishment as an effective deterrent to violent crime'.

> We often hear the following comments. The terms of imprisonment with certain exceptions are generally too lenient. There is almost a complete absence of corporal punishment. The material standard of living in the prisons is even better than the normal standards of living of many prison inmates if they were on the outside. The most frustrated remark, however, is: 'Why can't our local Government be allowed to carry out the death penalty?'

It might be that the death penalty was no deterrent in the West, said Chung. But 99 per cent of local people believed it to be the most effective punishment among Chinese. Hong Kong had autonomy in trade policy, he said. 'The British Government in Whitehall should respect the view of our people and give our Government complete autonomy in carrying out the death penalty.' Other legislators echoed this call. One of them, Joyce Symons, headmistress of the Diocesan Girls' School, suggested that the death penalty be restored for a trial period of three years.[122]

The debate took place on a day when a man was sentenced to death after having set fire to a flat during a robbery, killing a woman and her baby.[123] It prompted some twenty editorials in the Chinese-language press demanding the resumption of capital punishment. The *Kung Sheung Daily News* suggested using Hong Kong's military contribution to the UK, another vexed issue, as a bargaining weapon. Leaders of sixty-four kaifong associations announced plans for another petition.[124]

MacLehose decided it was now time for a public statement of policy. Helped by Sir Denys Roberts, now Colonial Secretary, he put to the FCO a draft response to legislators. The draft described in stark terms the position faced by the Hong Kong government. It listed three choices: (1) continue to commute every death sentence in the hope that

---

121. *HKH*, 18 October 1972 and 17 October 1973.
122. *HKH*, 22 and 23 October 1975.
123. *SCMP* and *KSDN*, 23 October 1975.
124. Hong Kong press review, 22 October to 29 October 1975, FCO 40/650; *KSDN*, 23 October 1975; *Hong Kong Standard*, 27 October 1975.

circumstances in the UK would in time change so that Hong Kong would be allowed to carry out hangings; (2) abolish the death penalty by legislation either in Hong Kong or in the UK; (3) leave the death penalty on the statute books but commute all death sentences to life imprisonment. Option (1) was unlikely to materialize. Option (2) could only be achieved with the support of the Legislative Council, or by a request from the Governor for legislation by the UK, which he would only do if he had the support of his councils. The Governor was therefore left only with option (3). This, he acknowledged, would not be 'a substantial advance on present practice'.[125]

Officials in the FCO accepted that MacLehose's room for manoeuvre was now exhausted and that some form of response was necessary. They discussed other options, such as reapplying the Creech Jones formula to Hong Kong, or 'putting the ball into Parliament's court' by forming a select committee. In the end, after a series of exchanges with MacLehose, they settled on a pared-down statement focusing only on option (3). 'It would be advisable to avoid exposing quite so much ground and giving possible hostages for the future,' they told MacLehose. A much-reduced text was agreed with MacLehose on 5 November, to be read out by Roberts during the replies by officials in the policy debate the following day.[126]

The Governor, said Roberts, fully recognized 'the fierceness of conviction with which so many residents of Hong Kong hold the view that, unless the death penalty is carried out in appropriate cases, the flood of crime and violence will not be turned back'. He had reflected to the Secretary of State in the strongest terms 'the wish of Hong Kong' for a restoration of the death penalty. But the issue did not end there. Prisoners sentenced to death had the right to petition the Queen for clemency. The Queen acted on the advice of the Secretary of State, who had to take into account the likely reaction of Parliament, which did not support the death penalty. The Governor had therefore decided on a change of practice that would go some way towards meeting the feelings of the community. In future, whenever the Governor commuted the death penalty, he would impose life imprisonment, unless 'in exceptional circumstances' he felt able to accept advice from the Executive Council that a lesser sentence should be imposed. Life imprisonment, Roberts told the press afterwards, 'will mean precisely what it says and the prisoner will not be released for the term of his natural existence'.[127]

Fortunately for condemned prisoners with mitigating circumstances this did not mean quite what it implied. Seven of the nineteen capital commutations in the year after Roberts's statement were to fixed prison terms, one as short as ten years. Life sentences

125. MacLehose to Secretary of State and Watson, 1 November 1975, FCO 40/650, encls. 37 and 38.
126. Minute by D.F. Milton, 3 November 1975, and telex exchanges between MacLehose and FCO, 4–6 November 1975, FCO 40/650, encls. 40–48.
127. *HKH*, 6 November 1975; *SCMP*, 7 November 1975.

were also subject to periodic review.[128] The *Hong Kong Law Journal* described the statement as 'a rather dubious pre-determination of the Governor's discretion to reprieve under the Royal Instructions', which was 'not likely to enhance general respect for the law'. It doubted whether allowing death sentences to be carried out would anyway have led to anything more than 'slight embarrassment' for the minister concerned. It also wondered if Stanley Prison could house so many life-sentence prisoners.[129] But the Chinese-language press welcomed the statement. The *Oriental Daily* said that life imprisonment would have the same deterrent effect as capital punishment. It was more horrible than capital punishment, said the *Tin Fung Yat Po*, a communist paper. The *Ming Pao* concluded that it was a giant step forward. Only the *Kung Sheung Daily News* was opposed. What right did Parliament have to interfere in the will of the people of Hong Kong, it asked. How could Hong Kong people tolerate such stubborn, old-fashioned imperialism?[130]

Formal abolition, 1993

The 'life means life' announcement in 1975 did not satisfy everyone. Opinion surveys in the 1980s revealed strong but declining support for retaining the death penalty, and less support for carrying it out.[131] Proponents of capital punishment continued to raise their views with British politicians. Judges complained of the 'pantomime' of having to pass sentence of death: 'It doesn't add to the dignity of the proceedings if everyone knows it will not happen,' said Sir Denys Roberts, now Chief Justice, in 1982.[132] In the 1983 policy

128. The proportion of commutations of death sentences to life imprisonment in 1976–1987 was 71 per cent, compared with 25 per cent in 1966–1975. These figures were produced for a review of the practice of commutations of death sentences, after some Executive Councillors expressed concern about whether the policy stated by Roberts was being consistently applied. Under prison rules, life sentences were subject to review after four years, and thereafter every two years, by the Board of Review – Long Term Prison Sentences. The board was established in 1959. It was chaired by the Attorney General until 1988 and thereafter by a judge. Note for Executive Council: Commutation of Death Sentences and Subsequent Remission, XCCI(87)59, FCO 40/2376, encl. 37; Prison Rule 69A, LN 5 of 1967.
129. Editorial by H.L. (Henry Litton), *HKLJ*, Vol. 6, No. 1 (1976): 2–4.
130. The *Wah Kiu Yat Po* also published a letter from kaifong leaders criticizing the statement. Weekly summary of editorial comment in the Chinese-language newspapers, 5–11 November 1975, FCO 40/650, encl. 58; *KSDN* and *Wah Kiu Yat Po*, 8 November 1975.
131. In a survey of 1,312 people commissioned by the *South China Morning Post* in 1986, 68 per cent of respondents believed that murderers should be executed, while only 12 per cent believed they should not (the same level of support as in a contemporaneous survey in Canada). In a crime victimization survey of 50,956 people in 1989, about half of respondents believed the death penalty should not be abolished but only 28 per cent thought that persons sentenced to death should be executed. Younger respondents tended to be less supportive of the death penalty. *SCMP*, 15 December 1986; *Crime and Its Victims in Hong Kong 1989: A Report on the Crime Victimization Survey Conducted in January 1990 by the Census & Statistics Department, Hong Kong Government*, 15–16 and Table 64.
132. Sir Alan Huggins, Justice of Appeal made similar remarks: *SCMP*, 10 August 1981 and 3 September 1982.

debate, the legislator Lydia Dunn, who was also an Executive Councillor, called for abolition. It was 'a mockery' for judges to go through the ritual of pronouncing the death sentence 'when everyone knows that it will not be carried out,' she said. The Attorney General, Michael Thomas, after declaring his opposition to capital punishment, agreed, but said that 'given the feelings of the ordinary people of Hong Kong and of Parliament' there was no prospect either of abolishing it or implementing it.[133]

Homicide rates had declined since their peak in the early 1970s. Violent crime generally continued to rise, peaking in the early 1980s and again in the late 1980s. But crime rates were low by world standards. Hong Kong gained a reputation as a 'safe city', sustained by a large and increasingly professional police force, strict gun laws, and a peaceful and law-abiding population.[134] This reputation came under strain when, in the late 1980s, armed robberies of banks and jewellery shops increased. A few led to large-scale shootouts between police and robbers in the busiest parts of the city. In 1990–1992 a dozen such fights took place, prompting renewed concerns among politicians and the public, particularly about cross-border robberies by gangs moving easily between Hong Kong and mainland China.[135] Opinion surveys now showed a rise in support for capital punishment.[136] The concerns culminated in a motion in the Legislative Council in June 1991 calling for the government to implement the death penalty.

Hong Kong had undergone dramatic change in the fifteen years since Sir Denys Roberts's statement on capital punishment in 1975. The city had evolved from an 'industrial colony' into a flourishing centre of international trade and finance. In 1984, under the Joint Declaration by the People's Republic of China and the UK, British rule was to end in 1997. Hong Kong would become a Special Administrative Region of China with a high degree of autonomy. Its legal system, freedoms, and way of life would be preserved under a Basic Law of the People's Republic. China and the UK set out to ensure a smooth transition towards a government composed of local people. The first step was taken in 1985, when twenty-four of the Legislative Council's fifty-seven members were elected: twelve by a district-based electoral college and twelve by functional constituencies made up of businesses and the

---

133. Parliament had again recently rejected a motion to restore capital punishment. *HKH*, 26 October and 10 November 1983.

134. Roderic Broadhurst, King Wa Lee, and Ching Yee Chan, 'Crime trends', in *Understanding Criminal Justice in Hong Kong*, ed. Wing Hong Chui and T. Wing Lo (Cullompton: Willan Publishing, 2008).

135. This section relies extensively on Jon Vagg, 'Robbery, Death and Irony: How an Armed Robbery Wave in Hong Kong Led to the Abolition of the Death Penalty', *The Howard Journal*, Vol. 36, No. 4 (November 1997): 393–405; and David T. Johnson and Franklin E. Zimring, *The Next Frontier: National Development, Political Change, and the Death Penalty in Asia* (Oxford: Oxford University Press, 2009), Appendix B.

136. A survey commissioned by the *South China Morning Post* in October 1990 found 71 per cent support for the death penalty; a survey of 1,011 people in Kwun Tong commissioned by the Legislative Councillor Poon Chi-fai in June 1991, shortly before the motion debate, found 84 per cent support. *SCMP*, 5 November 1990 and 26 June 1991.

professions, the latter increased to fourteen in 1988. When the motion on capital punishment came up in 1991, the council consisted of twenty-six unofficial members elected on a limited franchise, twenty appointed unofficial members, and eleven official members. The council reflected a spectrum of political views, conservative and progressive.

Now nearing the end of its term, the 1988–1991 council sat during a period of anxiety about the future, heightened by the suppression of student protests in Beijing on 4 June 1989. The 1980s also saw an increase both in offences punishable capitally in mainland China and in the number of executions.[137] Partly to address people's anxieties, the council passed the Hong Kong Bill of Rights Ordinance on 5 June 1991, embodying in local law most of the provisions of the International Covenant on Civil and Political Rights (ICCPR): the UK had extended the covenant to Hong Kong in 1976. Combined with amendments to the Letters Patent, the ordinance effectively gave the Bill of Rights a higher status than other Hong Kong laws. It also empowered the courts to strike down laws that were inconsistent with it.[138] The ordinance prompted reviews of existing legislation, the repeal of many reverse-onus offences, the abolition of judicial flogging, and the decriminalization of homosexual acts between consenting adult males. Although it restricted the use of the death penalty, the Bill of Rights did not explicitly prohibit it: the UK had not adopted a protocol added to the ICCPR in 1989 requiring its abolition. Nevertheless, the pervasive influence of the Bill of Rights was apparent in the debate on the death penalty. Participants in an international conference on human rights held in Hong Kong only the week before had signed a letter calling for abolition: this was read out during the debate.

The motion was moved by Kingsley Sit Ho-yin, a representative of the South Kowloon electoral college constituency and a member of the Liberal Democratic Federation, a party composed mainly of conservative businesspeople and professionals. The motion was that 'in view of the increasing concern caused by the present law and order situation, this Council urges the Government to resume immediately the carrying out of the death penalty'. Introducing the motion, Sit noted that 243 death sentences imposed on convicted murderers since 1966 had been commuted to imprisonment. He asked whether this was

137. Timothy Brook, 'Capital Punishment and State Sovereignty in China', *Sungkyun Journal of East Asian Studies*, Vol. 11, No. 2 (2011): 107–121; Michelle Miao, 'Capital Punishment in China: A Populist Instrument of Social Governance', *Theoretical Criminology*, Vol. 17, No. 2 (2013): 233–250.

138. Ordinance No. 59 of 1991: s. 3 provided that all pre-existing legislation that did not admit of a construction inconsistent with the ordinance was, to the extent of the inconsistency, repealed; s. 4 required all subsequent legislation to be construed so as to be consistent with the ICCPR. An amendment to article 7 of the Letters Patent prohibited the making of any law that restricted rights and freedoms in a way that was inconsistent with the ICCPR: *HKGG*, Legal Supplement No. 2, 7 June 1991. The Letters Patent ceased to have effect in 1997 and s. 3 and 4 of the ordinance were not adopted as laws of the Hong Kong SAR. However, Article 39 of the Basic Law states that the ICCPR as applied to Hong Kong shall remain in force and be implemented through the laws of the Hong Kong SAR, and that any restrictions on the rights and freedoms of residents shall not contravene these provisions.

fair to the victims. He doubted if any of the 243 had been wrongly convicted: even to raise such a question showed a lack of confidence in the courts. Public opinion supported carrying out the death penalty, he said. The government should take account of the wishes of the people and 'not just follow the viewpoints of the British Government'. This would 'sound an alarm to murderers who kill with *mens rea* and who pay little regard to the safety of other people by firing guns in public places'.[139]

In what the *South China Morning Post* described as 'a distasteful charade', Sit had prepared the ground by distributing pictures of armed robbers with nooses around their neck.[140] But the debate did not go as planned. When it came to his turn to speak, Martin Lee QC, chairman of the United Democrats of Hong Kong and the representative of the legal functional constituency, proposed an amendment aimed at capsizing Sit's motion:

> That, in view of [~~the increasing concern caused by the present law and order situation, this Council urges the Government to resume immediately the carrying out of the death penalty~~] both the need to deter and prevent crime and the importance of Hong Kong maintaining the highest standards of a modern, humane community, this Council urges the Government to strengthen the capability of the police force to fight crime and calls for legislative measures to be introduced into this Council which would abolish the death penalty and replace it with life imprisonment.[141]

In moving the amendment, Lee recalled a case in 1968 in which he had defended a man on a charge of murdering an elderly woman while robbing her of her jewellery. He gave this man the pseudonym 'Cheung Sam'. Cheung received a death sentence, which was commuted to twenty years. During his years in prison, reduced by a third for good behaviour, Cheung studied to matriculation level. On his release, he found a job, raised a family, and became a productive member of society. 'Many people would have thought that Cheung Sam deserved to be hanged twenty-four years ago; and yet he was not. But on any view, our community is not worse off because of that.' Study after study had demonstrated that the death penalty had no deterrent effect, said Lee. Its only value was political. 'It is a simple convenient answer to a very difficult problem, and its beguiling simplicity makes it an answer that is sure to find favour with an electorate anywhere in the world.' But, he added, this did not mean that legislators should follow public opinion polls.

Addressing the practical aspects of capital punishment, Lee referred to the many cases elsewhere in the common law world in which people convicted of murder had later been found to be innocent. He observed that juries in Hong Kong had been extremely reluctant to return murder verdicts which they knew might result in hanging. This showed that, whereas people were 'more than prepared' to support Sit's motion when approached in

139. *HKH*, 26 June 1991.

140. *SCMP*, 25 and 26 June 1991.

141. *HKH*, 26 June 1991: the crossed-out text here indicates the words deleted from the original motion. The rest of the text consists of additional working by Lee.

the streets, 'once they are called upon to serve as jurors inside a courtroom, they are not prepared to put their convictions into action'. The real answer to violent crime, Lee suggested, lay in strengthening the police. He cited a recent interpretation by the European Court of Human Rights that article 6(6) of the ICCPR (article 2 of the Hong Kong Bill of Rights), restricting the use of capital punishment, also imposed a duty to take steps towards abolition. He read out a statement from the Bar Committee in support of abolition and said he had heard that almost all High Court judges supported abolition. He also cited reports in the pro-communist press that the Chinese government favoured the resumption of the death penalty in Hong Kong. 'Under such circumstances, can we truly be confident that after 1997 the death penalty will not apply to crimes other than murder?'

A total of twenty-nine unofficial members spoke in the debate. They made references to the Chinese classics, Buddhist scriptures, the Bible, the works of Lenin and Mao Zedong, and experience of capital punishment in Hong Kong and around the world. Seven spoke in support of Sit's motion, and fourteen for Lee's amendment; the rest supported neither the motion nor the amendment, mostly because, although they endorsed the sentiments behind the motion, there was no realistic prospect of a change in practice. Speaking on behalf of the government, the Secretary for Security, Alistair Asprey, said that, if the majority of the council voted for abolition of the death penalty, the administration would consider bringing forward legislation to achieve it.

The council endorsed Martin Lee's amendment by a majority of twenty-four to twelve, with five abstentions; eight of the votes in favour were from official members, who were allowed a free vote. After a final speech by Kingsley Sit, the council then agreed to the motion as amended by Lee. What had been inconceivable a decade or so earlier had now come to pass: a partly elected, broadly representative Legislative Council had voted for the abolition of the death penalty.

The government moved slowly. The motion came as 'something of a surprise' to officials. Anticipating 'some awkward motions' on other subjects, they were also anxious that 'nothing should be said to imply a LegCo vote is necessarily binding on the Hong Kong Government': this was apparently necessary because the newly constituted Legislative Council in October 1991 was even more unpredictable than its predecessor; it was elected on a broader franchise, with additional functional constituencies, eighteen seats elected by universal suffrage, and only three official members.[142] Public opinion, though less strident than in the 1970s, still supported the death penalty. Armed robberies continued to plague the city. Officials were also concerned about the possible reaction of the Chinese government, though in the end it did not present obstacles. In any case, the legislation was complex, requiring amendments to eleven different ordinances, as well as decisions on what punishments should apply to treason and piracy with violence.

142. Minute by K.A.M. Saunders, 9 July 1991, FCO 40/3285, encl. 41.

The Executive Council considered options in March 1992.[143] In November the government introduced a bill to replace capital punishment with mandatory life imprisonment for murder, treason, and piracy with violence. The bill was scrutinized by a Legislative Council committee, which concluded that treason and piracy should attract a discretionary life sentence because they were offences 'of a category entirely different from murder'. With amendments on these lines, the bill was passed by the Legislative Council on 21 April 1993 and enacted by the Governor, Christopher Patten, on 22 April 1993 – nearly 150 years after Hong Kong's first hanging.[144] For a few years, the law was more progressive than that of the UK, which, until 1998, retained the death penalty for treason and piracy with violence.

On 14 May 1993, the judge Edward Bewley pronounced Hong Kong's first life sentence for murder, on a man convicted of the rape and murder of a teenage dance hostess. Death sentences on forty-one other prisoners were commuted to life imprisonment.[145] In 1993, eighty-six homicides were reported to the police, and ninety-six in 1994. The number fell to seventy-three in 1995, and then to an average of seventy per annum in 1996–2000, forty-four in 2001–2010, and thirty-three in 2011–2020, the lowest rates since World War II. These trends illustrate what has become a truism everywhere: that the death penalty has no relevance as a deterrent to crime. Low murder rates, high detection rates, and a general aversion to violence of any kind have put an end to calls for capital punishment. The death penalty has ceased to be an issue in Hong Kong. It is now a thing of the past.

143. Memorandum for ExCo: Abolition of Capital Punishment, 17 March 1992, XCC(92)47, FCO 40/3616, encl. 14.

144. Ordinance No. 24 of 1993.

145. Commissioner of Correctional Services, *Annual Review 1993*, 14.

Acknowledgements

Many friends and colleagues have made the writing of this book enjoyable and productive by sharing research, discussing ideas, commenting on draft extracts, and giving advice and encouragement. Among these are Amelia Alsop, Neil Andrews, David Bellis, Robert Bickers, Timothy Brook, John Brennan, John Carroll, Chen Xinyu, Kelvin Chan, Anita Chung, David Clayton, Christopher Corns, Peter Cunich, Stephen Davies, David Hall, David Hodson, Jenny Huangfu Day, Vaudine England, the late Christopher Homfray, Lucy Humbert, Peter Jordan, Douglas Kerr, the late Ralph Kiggell, Vivian Kong, Kwong Chi-man, Ivan Lee, Cathy Lilburne, Lim Tay Her, Alastair McClure, John Massey, Fionnuala McHugh, Simon Miles, Michael Ng, Kirsty Norman, Patricia O'Sullivan, Christopher Roberts, Jeremy Salkeld, Kim Salkeld, Mitra Sharafi, Elizabeth Sinn, Marco Wan, and John D. Wong.

I am especially grateful to the following friends, teachers, and experts: to the Hon. Andrew Li Kwok-nang for first suggesting that I write a book of this kind; to John Davison, Clive Grossman, Graham Hutchings, Victor Joffe, and Robin McLeish for their intensive reading of the manuscript; to Garfield Lam, Head of Archives and Special Collections, The University of Hong Kong Libraries, for recommending and making available sources, particularly during the years of COVID when access was restricted; to Bernard Hui and staff of the Hong Kong Public Records Office for their assistance over many years; to the late Nanna Man for helping me understand the Chinese sources and for saving me from many mistakes; to Ada Au-Yeung for drawing the maps; to Jason Beerman for his careful editing of the text and for his helpful advice; to the three anonymous readers of the manuscript; and to the Publishers and staff at Hong Kong University Press, in particular,

Peter Daniell for commissioning this work and for his advice in the early stages of the project, and Michael Duckworth and Kenneth Yung for bringing the book to fruition.

As always, my partner Nick Lee Guan Ling has given me constant support throughout this challenging project by advising on aspects of Chinese culture, organizing visits to crime scenes, and patiently putting up with endless discussions on Hong Kong's legal history.

This book is dedicated to the memory of my father, Patrick Munn. As a detective for most of his career in the Lincolnshire Police he investigated many murders and other serious crimes. For a few years in the 1970s he was also police prosecutor in the Horncastle Magistrates' Court: watching him at work from the public gallery during school holidays first sparked my interest in criminal justice. Although he did not live to see this book in print, his advice in its early stages – and in all my endeavours – was a great help and encouragement. I will always be grateful to him and my mother, Lucy, for nurturing my early interest in history and making it possible for me to pursue it at university and beyond.

Christopher Munn
Hong Kong
March 2025

A Note on Sources

The research for this book has relied on official sources, newspapers, law reports, and scholarly books and articles. The main sources consulted are listed below. The date ranges reflect the periods for which the sources were consulted. The list is not exhaustive: full citations for works not included are given on first appearance in the footnotes.

Archival sources

The National Archives, Kew, London, United Kingdom

CO 129: Hong Kong, Original Correspondence 1841–1951
CO 131: Sessional Papers 1844–1966 (including Executive Council minutes)
CO 133: Hong Kong, Miscellanea (including *Blue Books* of Statistics, etc.)
FCO 40: Registered Files, Hong Kong and other territories 1965–1992

Hong Kong Public Records Office

HKRS41: Files Relating to the General Administration of the Colonial/Government Secretariat 1870–1979 (including policy on criminal justice and capital cases)
HKRS101: Correspondence Relating to the Magistrate's Court, Police, and Prisons 1885–1890
HKRS425: Executive Council Minutes and Papers 1966–1979

Published sources

Annual Reports of the Judiciary, Police, and Prisons/Correctional Services 1946–1992
China Mail 1845–1970

Friend of China 1845–1858
Hong Kong Government Gazette 1853–1992 (including statistics, departmental reports, and ordinances as enacted)
Hong Kong Hansard (Legislative Council Proceedings) 1890–1993
Hong Kong Sessional Papers 1886–1937
Hong Kong Law Reports 1905–1962
Hongkong Daily Press 1866–1941
Hongkong Telegraph 1881–1934
Hongkong Weekly Press 1898–1922
Kung Sheung Daily News (香港工商日報) 1929–1975
Kung Sheung Evening News (香港工商晚報) 1933–1973
Overland China Mail 1863–1905
South China Morning Post 1903–1993
Wa Tsz Yat Po (香港華字日報) 1903–1936

Official records of proceedings and verbatim transcripts, some based on judges' notes of evidence, are available for the main trials in Chapters 5, 8, 9, and 10. Additionally, and for the chapters for which official records are unavailable or only partly available, I have relied on newspaper reports of proceedings. Some of these, particularly in the early twentieth century, are so detailed as to be almost verbatim. Different reports examined in the three or four main English-language papers and (for the early twentieth century) two leading Chinese-language papers, allow comparisons between sources and fill in some of the gaps left out of judges' notes: these include the atmosphere and physical aspects of the courtroom and participants, the arguments of counsel, and the directions by the judge.

In addition, confidential official correspondence, including reports by the trial judges and the views of governors and their councils, provide further perspective in some of the more controversial cases. These are supplemented by commentaries and correspondence in the newspapers on verdicts and proceedings. Jury Lists, available for most years, provide information on the employment and addresses of jurors, much of which can be supplemented by biographical information in newspapers or on the internet. For the period after World War II, Executive Council submissions, many with detailed background information, survive for many persons sentenced to death.

The statistical sources are more problematic. From the late 1840s to 1940, the courts provided annual statistics in some detail. From 1946 to the mid-1960s the statistics are far less detailed and, in contrast to those for the earlier years, do not break down crimes, verdicts, and sentences for the Supreme Court: for these years it has been necessary to extrapolate statistics from other, uneven sources, such as the annual police reports and newspapers. Executive Council minutes record confirmations and commutations of death sentences for most years. Annual *Blue Book* reports on gaols and prisoners from the 1890s to 1939 record the number of hangings. There are, however, discrepancies among sources and errors within particular sources. Usually they are minor, but it has not been possible to reconcile all of them. In addition, the absence of full statistics and of extant Executive Council minutes for 1940 and 1941 means that the fate of some persons condemned to death in those years cannot be conclusively ascertained.

For these reasons the statistical information in this book should be read with caution.

A Note on Currencies, Prices, and Values

Various currencies circulated in early Hong Kong: silver Mexican, Spanish, US, and (from 1895) British trade dollars; Chinese silver taels and copper cash; the pound sterling; Indian rupees; and Japanese yen. The silver-based Hong Kong dollar was created in 1862. Fluctuations in the exchange rate between the Hong Kong dollar and the pound sterling in the early twentieth century prompted the government to peg the Hong Kong dollar to the pound under a currency board system in 1935 at the rate of 16 dollars to the pound. This was maintained until 1972, when the Hong Kong dollar was pegged to the US dollar at HK$5.65 to US$1.00 (revised to HK$5.085 in 1974). From 1974 to 1983 the Hong Kong dollar was allowed to float against other currencies. In 1983 it was again linked to the US dollar under a currency board system at HK$7.80 to US$1.00.

The prices and values in the table below refer to years in or around which the key trials in this book took place. They are drawn from official sources – mainly the annual *Hong Kong Blue Books* up to 1941, and, for the years after World War II, reports by the Labour Department, Census and Statistics Department and other departments, and Government Secretariat staff lists. The table is intended as a rough guide to the value and purchasing power of the sums of money mentioned in this book.

Year	Rice $/lb	Pork $/lb	Sugar $/lb	Unskilled labourer: $/day	Chief Justice: monthly pay	Magistrate (highest paid): monthly pay	$ to £ rate
1857	0.04	0.16	0.06	0.20	£250 ($1,200)	£83 ($400)	4.8
1878	0.04	0.18	0.11	0.17	$1,000	$317	5.4
1904	0.05	0.23	0.07	0.42	$1,125	$572	10.9
1919	0.15	0.27	0.27	0.45	£167 ($893)	£76 ($406)	5.4
1933	0.09	0.41	0.20	0.65	£217 ($3,142)	£117 ($1,696)	14.5
1959	0.36	3.16	0.24	4.00	$4,650	$2,900	16.0
1966	0.51	2.46	0.41	7.00	$10,500	$5,000	16.0
1973	1.01	4.65	1.11	18.00	$17,000	$7,200	14.1

Index

About the Author

Christopher Munn served as an administrative officer in the Hong Kong government and in various positions in the Hong Kong Monetary Authority. His publications include *Anglo-China: Chinese People and British Rule in Hong Kong, 1841–1880* and (with May Holdsworth) *Crime, Justice and Punishment in Colonial Hong Kong*.

www.ingramcontent.com/pod-product-compliance
Ingram Content Group UK Ltd.
Pitfield, Milton Keynes, MK11 3LW, UK
UKHW051043120926
8556IPUK00031B/873

9 789888 876884